Principles and Practice of Structural Equation Modeling

Methodology in the Social Sciences
David A. Kenny, Founding Editor
Todd D. Little, Series Editor

This series provides applied researchers and students with analysis and research design books that emphasize the use of methods to answer research questions. Rather than emphasizing statistical theory, each volume in the series illustrates when a technique should (and should not) be used and how the output from available software programs should (and should not) be interpreted. Common pitfalls as well as areas of further development are clearly articulated.

Recent Volumes

CONFIRMATORY FACTOR ANALYSIS FOR APPLIED RESEARCH
  Timothy A. Brown

DYADIC DATA ANALYSIS
  David A. Kenny, Deborah A. Kashy, and William L. Cook

MISSING DATA: A GENTLE INTRODUCTION
  Patrick E. McKnight, Katherine M. McKnight, Souraya Sidani, and Aurelio José Figueredo

MULTILEVEL ANALYSIS FOR APPLIED RESEARCH: IT'S JUST REGRESSION!
  Robert Bickel

THE THEORY AND PRACTICE OF ITEM RESPONSE THEORY
  R. J. de Ayala

THEORY CONSTRUCTION AND MODEL-BUILDING SKILLS: A PRACTICAL GUIDE
FOR SOCIAL SCIENTISTS
  James Jaccard and Jacob Jacoby

DIAGNOSTIC MEASUREMENT: THEORY, METHODS, AND APPLICATIONS
  André A. Rupp, Jonathan Templin, and Robert A. Henson

APPLIED MISSING DATA ANALYSIS
  Craig K. Enders

ADVANCES IN CONFIGURAL FREQUENCY ANALYSIS
  Alexander A. von Eye, Patrick Mair, and Eun-Young Mun

PRINCIPLES AND PRACTICE OF STRUCTURAL EQUATION MODELING, Third Edition
  Rex B. Kline

Principles and Practice of Structural Equation Modeling

THIRD EDITION

Rex B. Kline

Series Editor's Note by Todd D. Little

THE GUILFORD PRESS
New York   London

© 2011 The Guilford Press
A Division of Guilford Publications, Inc.
72 Spring Street, New York, NY 10012
www.guilford.com

Printed in the United States of America

This book is printed on acid-free paper.

Last digit is print number: 9   8   7   6   5   4   3   2   1

Library of Congress Cataloging-in-Publication Data

Kline, Rex B.
  Principles and practice of structural equation modeling / Rex B. Kline. —
3rd ed.
     p. cm. — (Methodology in the social sciences)
  Includes bibliographical references and index.
    ISBN 978-1-60623-877-6 (hardcover) — ISBN 978-1-60623-876-9 (pbk.)
  1. Structural equation modeling. 2. Social sciences—Statistical methods—
Data processing. I. Title.
  QA278.K585 2011
  519.5′3—dc22

                                                                2010020226

For my family—Joanna, Julia Anne, and Luke Christopher

Great knowledge sees all in one.
Small knowledge breaks down into the many.

—CHUANG TZU, fourth or third century BCE, China
(in Merton, 1965, p. 40)

Series Editor's Note

It is a pleasure to write an introductory note for a book that is so popular you can simply refer to it as "the Kline book" and everyone will know what you mean. Rex Kline is a quantitative expert with that rare ability to provide clear and accessible guidance on how to best use structural equation modeling (SEM) to answer critical research questions. It takes a very special author to overcome students' fears and engage them in the principles and practice of SEM. In each edition of his book Kline has done just this, and with each edition it gets better and better! The literature on SEM is always evolving and being refined. To keep up with this literature is a challenge even to the quantitative expert. Thankfully, we have Rex Kline to rely on.

If you are a fan of the earlier editions, I think you will find the improvements to the third edition both welcome and enlightening. For example, based on the helpful feedback of readers like you, Kline has reorganized Part II to model the phases and steps one follows in a typical analysis, from initial model specification, to identification considerations, to parameter estimation, to evaluating hypotheses, and, finally, to model respecification. Pedagogically, he has also added useful exercises with answers and informative topic boxes that cover key concepts, core techniques, and specialized issues in the world of SEM. He also elegantly addresses "troublesome" examples, which leads to discussions of how to handle known problems that arise in SEM analyses.

If you have not looked at "the Kline book," or not in a while, I encourage you to take a look at this third edition. Kline provides an accurate and authoritative "translation" of the technical world of SEM for students and applied researchers alike. It is the Rosetta stone for understanding SEM and for showing substantive researchers how to use SEM in the conduct of their science. It strikes a tidy balance between the technical and the practical aspects of SEM so that you will be able to both clarify and expand your knowledge of the vast possibilities of SEM. It serves as a conduit for substantive researchers to stay connected to the ever-changing field of SEM.

Since the first edition, the book's success is the consensus viewpoint of critical reviewers and researchers—who lean heavily on it. The second edition was a complete and thorough update to the best practice in the field and saw pedagogic changes that elevated the second edition to a bonafide bestseller in the social and behavioral sciences. And the third edition is nothing short of remarkable in terms of its authoritative summary of an ever-advancing field. The chapter dedicated to the use of different software packages (Chapter 4) is expanded. Coverage of assessing the identification status of measurement models with correlated errors and complex indicators is updated in Chapter 6. Chapter 7 gives expanded coverage of estimation, including more specific information for analyzing models with categorical outcome variables. Chapter 12 expands coverage of estimating interactive effects and multilevel SEMs. And the list goes on! You can see by the praise of the many reviewers of this latest edition that Rex Kline has managed to take "the Kline book" to another level of clarity and coverage.

TODD D. LITTLE
University of Kansas
Lawrence, Kansas

Preface and Acknowledgments

It's not often in life that you get three chances at something. Thus, it was a privilege for me to write the third edition of this book. This edition builds on the strengths of the second by presenting structural equation modeling (SEM) in a clear, accessible way for readers without extensive quantitative backgrounds. Many new examples of the application of SEM to actual research problems are included in this edition, but, like the second edition, these examples come from a wide range of disciplines, including education, psychometrics, business, and psychology. I selected some of these examples because there were technical problems in the analysis, such as when output from a computer program contains error messages. These "troublesome" examples give a context for discussing how to handle various problems that can crop up in SEM analyses. That is, not all applications of SEM described in this book are picture perfect, but neither are actual research problems.

There are many changes in this edition from the second edition, all intended to enhance the pedagogical presentation of SEM and cover recent developments in the field, especially concerning how structural equation models—and the corresponding research hypotheses—should be tested. These changes are as follows:

1. Part II of the third edition, about core SEM techniques, is now organized according to phases of the analysis, starting with model specification, going on to consideration of its identification status, next to estimation, and then to the testing of hypotheses and model respecification (Chapters 5–8). In contrast, the second edition covered this material on a more technique-by-technique basis. I think that the new organization corresponds more closely to how researchers usually proceed with an SEM analysis. It should also give students a better view of the "big picture" concerning major issues that apply in most applications of SEM.

2. There are now exercises with suggested answers for all chapters that introduce prerequisite statistical and measurement concepts (Part I) and also for all chapters in Part II about core techniques. These exercises give students additional opportunities for

learning about SEM by responding to questions that test their concept knowledge. Some exercises also involve the analysis of structural equation models with actual data sets (i.e., learning by doing). All of these features also support self-study of SEM; that is, they should help readers who wish to learn about SEM but are not participating in a formal course or seminar.

3. Website support for this edition is even stronger than that of the second edition. For example, readers can freely download for every detailed example in Part II all syntax, data, and output files for each of three widely used SEM computer tools: EQS, LISREL, and Mplus. This allows readers to reproduce the analysis on their own computer using the corresponding computer tool. Even if the reader uses a different computer tool for SEM, all of these files can be opened with a standard text editor, such as Windows Notepad. That is, the reader does not need to have EQS, LISREL, or Mplus installed on his or her computer in order to view the contents of these files. And for readers who already use one of three computer tools for SEM (e.g., LISREL), it can be educational to view the results of the same analysis generated by a different computer tool (e.g., Mplus). Other resources for readers may be found on the book's website (described in Chapter 1), the address of which is presented on page 3.

4. The chapter on hypothesis testing in SEM (Chapter 8) reflects some of the most recent thinking in this area that is described by several different authors in a special issue on SEM in the journal *Personality and Individual Differences* (Vernon & Eysenck, 2007). Briefly, there is a general consensus that (a) standard practices for evaluating models in SEM have been lax and, consequently, (b) researchers need to take a more rigorous, skeptical, and disciplined approach to hypothesis testing. How to do so is a major theme of Chapter 8 and indeed of the whole book.

5. There is more coverage in this edition of two advanced topics in SEM: the estimation of interactive effects of observed or latent variables and multilevel analysis (Chapter 12). Many developments have taken place recently in each of these areas, and more and more researchers are estimating models in which these types of effects are represented. Accordingly, the chapter on how to fool yourself with SEM (Chapter 13) is now expanded to include the failure to consider these types of effects, among other more prosaic ways to become irrational with SEM.

6. Several chapters feature topic boxes about concepts, techniques, or specialized issues in the conduct of SEM. These boxes offer relatively short summaries of topics that complement or elaborate on the presentation in the main text. More advanced topics are covered in chapter appendices, which allows readers of various skill levels to get more out of the book.

C. Deborah Laughton, Publisher, Methodology and Statistics, at The Guilford Press, has a special knack for giving me exactly the type of feedback I need at precisely the right moment in the writing process. She collected reviews of the second edition and drafts for the third edition from a variety of scholars with differing backgrounds and levels of experience, from those just learning about SEM to renowned professors whose work is very widely known in their respective fields. C. Deborah sent these reviews to me without identifying their authors, and the content of the reviews was extremely helpful in the planning and writing of this edition. C. Deborah, thanks again for all your work and support. The names of the reviewers were revealed to me only after the writing was done, and their original comments were not associated with their names. A big thanks to all the persons listed next (in alphabetical order) who put in a lot of time and effort to communicate their thoughts about the book in various stages of its writing; their comments and suggestions were invaluable:

- Alan C. Acock, Department of Human Development, Oregon State University
- Noel A. Card, John and Doris Norton School of Family and Consumer Sciences, Division of Family Studies and Human Development, University of Arizona
- David F. Gillespie, Department of Social Work, Washington University in St. Louis
- Debbie Hahs-Vaughn, College of Education, Department of Educational Research, Technology, and Leadership, University of Central Florida
- Lance Holbert, Department of Communications, Ohio State University
- Jacob Marszalek, School of Education, Research and Psychology, University of Missouri–Kansas City
- Richard A. Posthuma, College of Business Administration, University of Texas at El Paso
- James Schreiber, School of Education, Department of Foundations and Leadership, Duquesne University
- Greg Welch, School of Education, Department of Psychology and Research in Education, University of Kansas
- Craig Wells, School of Education, Department of Educational Policy, Research, and Administration, University of Massachusetts at Amherst
- Duan Zhang, Morgridge College of Education, Quantitative Research Methods, University of Denver

It was a pleasure to work with the Methodology in the Social Sciences Series Editor at Guilford, Todd D. Little, in putting together the final version of this book. His comments were very helpful, and it was a pleasure to meet Todd when he visited Concordia University in Montréal in November 2009. Betty Pessagno served as the copyeditor for the original manuscript, and her work and suggested changes improved the clarity of the presentation. I also appreciate the efforts of the Guilford production editor, William Meyer, in preparing the final version of this book. I asked Lesley Hayduk of the Department of Sociology at the University of Alberta to review a draft of Chapter 8 about hypothesis testing in SEM. Les has long advocated for a more rigorous approach to testing in SEM, and the rest of the field is catching up to this viewpoint. I was hoping that Les's comments would give the final version of Chapter 8 more backbone, and I was not disappointed. Thanks, Les, for saying the kinds of things I needed to hear about this crucial topic.

The most recent versions of computer tools for SEM were generously provided for me by Multivariate Software (EQS), Muthén and Muthén (Mplus), and Scientific Software International (LISREL). In particular, I wish to thank Linda Muthén and Peter Bentler for their comments on earlier drafts of descriptions of, respectively, Mplus and EQS. And once again, my heartfelt thanks to my wife, Joanna, and children, Julia and Luke, for all their love and support while writing this book.

REX B. KLINE
Montréal
rex.kline@concordia.ca

Contents

PART II. CORE TECHNIQUES

Part I

Concepts and Tools

1

Introduction

The book is intended to serve as a guide to the principles, assumptions, strengths, limitations, and application of structural equation modeling (SEM) for researchers and students who do not have extensive quantitative backgrounds. Accordingly, the presentation is conceptually rather than mathematically oriented, the use of formulas and symbols is kept to a minimum, and many examples are offered of the application of SEM to research problems in various disciplines, including psychology, education, health sciences, marketing, and management. When you finish reading this book, I hope that you will have acquired the skills to begin to use SEM in your own research in an informed, disciplined way. The following adage attributed to poet Eugene F. Ware is pertinent here: All glory comes from daring to begin. Let's do just that.

THE BOOK'S WEBSITE

This book has a website on the Internet; the address is *www.guilford.com/kline*
    From the site, you can freely access or download the following resources:

- Computer files for every example of SEM analyses in Chapters 7–12 for three widely used SEM computer tools—EQS, LISREL, and Mplus.
- Links to related web pages, including sites with more information about computer data analysis in SEM.
- A supplemental reading about the estimation of curvilinear effects of observed and latent variables in SEM.

    The purpose of the website for this book is to support a learning-by-doing approach to SEM. Specifically, the availability of both data summaries and syntax files means that you can reproduce the analyses for most of the examples in this book using the corresponding SEM computer tool. Even without access to a particular program, such as EQS, you can still download and open on your own computer the EQS output file for a particular analysis and review the results. This is because all of the computer files on this book's website are plain-text (ASCII) files that require nothing more than a basic text editor, such as Notepad in Microsoft Windows, to view their contents. Even if you are using an SEM computer tool other than EQS, LISREL, or Mplus, it is still worthwhile to review the computer files on the site. This is because (1) common principles about programming apply across different SEM computer tools, and (2) it can be helpful to view the same analysis from somewhat different perspectives. Some of the exercises for this book involve extensions of the original analyses for these examples, so there are plenty of opportunities for practice with real data sets. Suggested answers for all exercises are presented at the end of the book.

PEDAGOGICAL APPROACH

You may be reading this book while participating in a course or workshop on SEM. This context offers the potential advantages of the structure and support available in a classroom setting, but formal coursework is not the only way to learn about SEM. Another is self-study, a method through which many researchers learn about what is, for them, a new statistical technique. (This is how I first learned about SEM, not in classes.) I assume that most readers are relative newcomers to SEM or that they already have some knowledge of the area, but wish to hone their skills. Consequently, I will speak to you (through my author's voice) as one researcher to another, not as a statistician to the quantitatively untutored. For example, the instructional language of statisticians is matrix algebra, which can convey a lot of information in a relatively small amount of space, but you must already be familiar with linear algebra to decode the message. There are other, more advanced works about SEM that emphasize matrix representations (Bollen, 1989; Kaplan, 2009; Mulaik, 2009), and these works can be consulted by those interested in such presentations (i.e., when you are ready). Instead, fundamental concepts about SEM are presented here using the language of researchers: words and figures, not matrix algebra. I will not shelter you from some of the more technical aspects of SEM, but I aim to cover requisite concepts in an accessible way that supports continued learning.

You may be relieved to know that you are not at a disadvantage if at present you have no experience using an SEM computer tool. This is because the presentation in this book is not based on the symbolism or syntax associated with a particular software package. A number of books are linked to specific SEM computer tools, including

- Byrne (2006, 2009, 2010) for, respectively, EQS, Amos, and Mplus.
- Blunch (2008) for Amos.
- Diamantopoulos and Siguaw (2000), Hayduk (1996), and Kelloway (1998) for LISREL.
- Mueller (1996) for both LISREL and EQS.

Software-centric books can be invaluable for users of a particular computer tool, but perhaps less so for others. Instead, essential principles of SEM that users of *any* computer tool must understand are emphasized here. In this way, this book is more like a guide to writing style and composition than a handbook about how to use a particular word processor. Besides, becoming proficient with a particular software package is just a matter of practice. But without strong concept knowledge, the output one gets from a computer tool for statistical analyses—including SEM—may be meaningless or, even worse, misleading.

As with other statistical techniques, there is no gold standard for notation in SEM. Although the symbol set associated with the original syntax of LISREL is probably the most widely used in advanced works about SEM, it features a profusion of subscripted lowercase Greek letters (e.g., ϕ_{23}, Λ_{31}) for individual model parameters, uppercase Greek letters for parameter matrices (e.g., Φ, Λ_x), and two-letter acronyms for parameter matrices (e.g., TE for theta–epsilon) or matrix forms (e.g., DI for diagonal) that can be confusing to follow unless you have memorized the entire system. Instead, this book uses a minimum number of alphabetic characters to represent various aspects of SEM such as observed versus latent variables.

Learning to use a new set of statistical techniques is like making a journey through a strange land. Such a journey requires a substantial commitment of time, patience, and a willingness to tolerate the frustration of initial uncertainty and inevitable trial and error. But this is one journey you do not have to make alone. Think of this book as a travel atlas or even as someone to counsel you about language and customs, what to see and what to avoid, and what lies just over the horizon. I hope that the combination of a conceptually based approach, numerous examples, and the occasional bit of practical advice presented in this book will help to make this statistical journey a little easier, maybe even enjoyable. (Imagine that!)

GETTING READY TO LEARN ABOUT SEM

Listed next are suggestions about the best way to prepare yourself for learning about SEM. I offer these suggestions in the spirit of giving you a healthy perspective at the beginning of this journey, one that empowers your sense of being a researcher.

Know Your Area

Strong familiarity with the theoretical and empirical literature in your research area is the single most important thing you need for SEM. This is because everything, from the specification of your initial model to modification of that model in subsequent reanalyses to interpretation of the results, must be guided by your domain knowledge. So you need first and foremost to be a *researcher*, not a statistician or computer geek. This is true for most kinds of statistical analysis, in that the value of the product (numerical results) depends on the quality of the ideas (your hypotheses) on which the analysis is based.

Otherwise, that familiar expression about computer analysis, "garbage in, garbage out," applies.

Know Your Measures

Kühnel (2001) reminds us that learning about SEM has the by-product that newcomers must deal with fundamental issues of measurement. Specifically, the analysis of measures with strong psychometric characteristics, such as good score reliability and validity, is essential in SEM. For example, it is impossible to analyze a structural equation model with latent variables that represent hypothetical constructs without thinking about how to measure those constructs. When you have just a single measure of a construct, then it is especially critical for this single indicator to have good psychometric properties. Likewise, the analysis of measures with deficient psychometric characteristics could bias the results. Unfortunately, measurement theory is too often neglected nowadays in undergraduate and graduate degree programs in psychology (Frederich, Buday, & Kerr, 2000) and related areas, but SEM requires strong knowledge in this area. Some crucial measurement-related concepts are considered in Chapter 3.

Review Fundamental Statistical Concepts and Techniques

Before learning about SEM, you should have a good understanding of (1) principles of multiple correlation/regression,[1] (2) the correct interpretation of results from statistical tests, and (3) data screening techniques. These topics are reviewed in the next two chapters, but it may help to know now why they are so important. Some kinds of statistical results in SEM are interpreted exactly as regression coefficients in multiple regression (MR). Values of these coefficients are corrected for the presence of correlated predictors in SEM just as they are in MR. The potential for bias due to the omission of a predictor that is correlated with others in the equation is basically the same in SEM and MR. The technique of MR plays an important role in data screening. There are many statistical tests in SEM, and their correct interpretation is essential. So with strong knowledge of these topics, you are better prepared to learn about SEM.

Use the Best Research Computer in the World

Which is the human brain; specifically—*yours*. At the end of the analysis in SEM—or any type of statistical analysis—it is you as the researcher who must evaluate the degree of support for the hypotheses, explain any unexpected findings, relate the results to those of previous studies, and reflect on implications of the findings for future research. These are all matters of judgment. A statistician or computer geek could help you to select appropriate statistical tools, but not with the rest without your domain knowledge. As

---

[1]The simpler term *multiple regression* is used from this point.

aptly put by Pedhazur and Schmelkin (1991), "no amount of technical proficiency will do you any good, if you do not think" (p. 2).

Get a Computer Tool for SEM

Obviously, you need a computer tool to conduct the analysis. In SEM, many choices of computer tools are now available. Some of these include EQS, LISREL, and Mplus, but there are still more, including Amos, CALIS/TCALIS of SAS/STAT, Mx, RAMONA of SYSTAT, and SEPATH of STATISTICA. There are freely available student versions of Amos, LISREL, and Mplus, and student versions are great for honing basic skills. However, student versions are typically limited in terms of the number of variables that can be analyzed, so they are not generally suitable for more complex analyses. However, Mx can analyze a wide range of structural equation models, and it is freely available over the Internet. All the SEM computer tools just mentioned, and others, are described in Chapter 4. The website for this book (p. 3) has links to home pages for SEM computer tools.

Join the Community

An electronic mail network called SEMNET operates over the Internet and is dedicated to SEM.[2] It serves as an open forum for discussion and debate about the whole range of issues associated with SEM. It also provides a place to ask questions about analyses or about more general issues, including philosophical ones (e.g., the nature of causality). Members of SEMNET come from different disciplines, and they range from newcomers to seasoned veterans. Many works of the latter are cited in this book. (I subscribe to SEMNET, too.) Sometimes the discussion gets, ah, lively (sparks can fly), but this is the nature of scientific discourse. Whether you participate as a "lurker" (someone who mainly reads posts) or as an active poster, SEMNET offers opportunities to learn something new. There is even a theme song for SEM, the hilarious *Ballad of the Casual Modeler* (Rogosa, 1988). I think that you might enjoy listening to it, too.[3]

CHARACTERISTICS OF SEM

The term **structural equation modeling** (SEM) does not designate a single statistical technique but instead refers to a family of related procedures. Other terms such as **covariance structure analysis**, **covariance structure modeling**, or **analysis of covariance structures** are also used in the literature to classify these techniques together under a single label. These terms are essentially interchangeable, but only the first will be used

---

[2]*www2.gsu.edu/~mkteer/semnet.html*

[3]*www.stanford.edu/class/ed260/ballad.mp3*

throughout this book. Another term that you may have heard is **causal modeling**, which is a somewhat dated expression first associated with the SEM technique of path analysis. For reasons elaborated later, the results of an SEM analysis cannot generally be taken as evidence for causation. Wilkinson and the Task Force on Statistical Inference (1999) were even more blunt when they noted that use of SEM computer tools "rarely yields any results that have any interpretation as causal effects" (p. 600). Some newcomers to SEM have unrealistic expectations in this regard. They may see SEM as a kind of magical technique that allows one to discern causal relations in the absence of experimental or even quasi-experimental designs. Unfortunately, no statistical technique, SEM or otherwise, can somehow "prove" causality in nonexperimental designs. The correct and realistic interpretation of results from SEM analyses is emphasized throughout this book. Summarized next are the characteristics of most applications of SEM.

A Priori Does Not Mean Exclusively Confirmatory

Computer tools for SEM require you to provide a lot of information about things such as which variables are assumed to affect other variables and the directionalities of these effects. These a priori specifications reflect your hypotheses, and in total they make up the model to be analyzed. In this sense, SEM can be viewed as confirmatory. That is, your model is a given at the start of the analysis, and one of the main questions to be answered is whether it is supported by the data. But as often happens, the data may be inconsistent with your model, which means that you must either abandon your model or modify the hypotheses on which it is based. In a **strictly confirmatory** application, the researcher has a single model that is accepted or rejected based on its correspondence to the data (Jöreskog, 1993), and that's it. However, on few occasions will the scope of model testing be so narrow.

A second, somewhat less restrictive context concerns the testing of **alternative models**, and it refers to situations in which more than one a priori model is available (Jöreskog, 1993). This context requires sufficient theoretical or empirical bases to specify more than one model; the particular model with acceptable correspondence to the data may be retained, but the rest will be rejected.

A third context, that of **model generation**, is probably the most common and occurs when an initial model does not fit the data and is subsequently modified by the researcher. The altered model is then tested again with the same data (Jöreskog, 1993). The goal of this process is to "discover" a model with three properties: It makes theoretical sense, it is reasonably parsimonious, and its correspondence to the data is acceptably close.

Explicit Distinction between Observed and Latent Variables

There are two broad classes of variables in SEM, observed and latent. The observed class represents your data—that is, variables for which you have collected scores and entered in a data file. Another term for observed variables is **manifest variables**. Observed variables can be categorical, ordinal, or continuous, but all latent variables in SEM are continuous. There are other statistical techniques for analyzing models with categorical latent variables, but SEM deals with continuous latent variables only.

Latent variables in SEM generally correspond to **hypothetical constructs** or **factors**, which are explanatory variables presumed to reflect a continuum that is not directly observable. An example is the construct of *intelligence*. There is no single, definitive measure of intelligence. Instead, researchers use different types of observed variables, such as tasks of verbal reasoning or memory capacity, to assess various facets of intelligence. Latent variables in SEM can represent a wide range of phenomena. For example, constructs about attributes of people (e.g., intelligence, neuroticism), higher-level units of analysis (e.g., groups, geographic regions), or measures, such as method effects (e.g., self-report, observational), can all be represented as latent variables in SEM.

An observed variable used as an indirect measure of a construct is referred to as an **indicator**. The explicit distinction between factors and indicators in SEM allows one to test a wide variety of hypotheses about measurement. Suppose that a researcher believes that variables X_1, X_2, and X_3 tap some common domain that is distinct from the one assessed by X_4 and X_5. In SEM, it is relatively easy to specify a model where X_1–X_3 are the indicators of one factor and X_4–X_6 are indicators of a different factor. If the fit of the model just described to the data is poor, then this measurement hypothesis would be rejected. The ability to analyze both observed and latent variables distinguishes SEM from some more standard statistical techniques, such as the analysis of variance (ANOVA) and MR, which analyze observed variables only.

Another class of variables in SEM corresponds to residual or error terms, which can be associated with either observed variables or factors specified as outcome (dependent) variables. In the case of indicators, a residual term represents variance unexplained by the factor that the corresponding indicator is supposed to measure. Part of this unexplained variance is due to random measurement error, or score unreliability.[4] The explicit representation of measurement error is a special characteristic of SEM. This is not to say that SEM can compensate for gross psychometric flaws—no technique can— but this property lends a more realistic quality to an analysis. Some more standard statistical techniques make unrealistic assumptions in this area. For example, it is assumed in MR that all predictor variables are measured without error. In diagrams of structural equation variables, residual terms may be represented using the same symbols as for substantive latent variables. This is because error variance must be estimated, given the whole model and the data; thus in this sense error variance is not directly observable in the raw data. Also, residual terms are explicitly represented in the syntax or diagrams of some SEM computer tools as latent variables. Even if they are not, error variance is estimated in basically all SEM analyses, and estimates about the degree of residual variance often have interpretive import.

As already mentioned, it is possible in SEM to analyze substantive latent variables

---

[4]The other part of unexplained variance is systematic (i.e., reliable) but unrelated to the underlying construct. Another term for this part of residual variance is *specific variance*.

or observed variables (or any combination of the two) as outcome variables. For such variables, each will typically have an error term that represents variance unexplained by their predictors. It is also possible to specify either observed or latent variables (or any combination of the two) as predictors in structural equation models. This capability permits great flexibility in the types of hypotheses that can be tested in SEM. I should say now that models in SEM do not necessarily have to have substantive latent variables at all. (Most structural equation models have error terms represented as latent variables, however.) That is, the evaluation of models that concern effects only among observed variables is certainly possible in SEM. This describes the technique of path analysis, a member of the SEM family.

Covariances Always, but Means Can Be Analyzed, Too

The basic statistic of SEM is the covariance, which is defined for two continuous observed variables X and Y as follows:

$$cov_{XY} = r_{XY} \ SD_X \ SD_Y \tag{1.1}$$

where r_{XY} is the Pearson correlation and SD_X and SD_Y are their standard deviations. A covariance represents the strength of the association between X and Y and their variabilities, albeit with a single number. Because the covariance is an unstandardized statistic, its value has no upper or lower bound. For example, covariances of, say, –1,003.26 or 13.58 are possible. In any event, cov_{XY} conveys more information than r_{XY}, which says something about association in a standardized metric only.

To say that the covariance is the basic statistic of SEM means that the analysis has two main goals: (1) to understand patterns of covariances among a set of observed variables and (2) to explain as much of their variance as possible with the researcher's model. The part of a structural equation model that represents hypotheses about variances and covariances is the **covariance structure**. The next several chapters outline the rationale of analyzing covariance structures, but essentially all models in SEM have a covariance structure.

Some researchers, especially those who use ANOVA as their main analytical tool, have the impression that SEM is concerned *solely* with covariances. However, this view is too narrow because means can also be analyzed in SEM, too. But what really distinguishes the analysis of means in SEM is that means of latent variables can be estimated. In contrast, ANOVA is concerned with means of observed variables only. It is also possible in SEM to analyze effects traditionally associated with ANOVA, including between-group and within-group (e.g., repeated measures) mean contrasts. For example, in SEM one can estimate the magnitude of group mean differences on latent variables, something that is not really feasible in ANOVA.

When means are analyzed along with covariances in SEM, the model has both a covariance structure and a **mean structure**, and the mean structure often represents the estimation of factor means. Means are not analyzed in most SEM analyses—that is, a mean structure is not required—but the option to do so provides additional flexibility. For example, sometimes we are interested in estimating factors by analyzing covariances among the observed variables, but also want to test whether means on these latent variables are equal across different groups, such as boys versus girls. In this case, both covariances and means would be analyzed in SEM. At other times, however, we are not interested in means on the latent variables. Instead, we are concerned only with factor covariances, and focus solely on what are the latent variables or factors, based on analysis of the covariances among the observed variables. In the second case just mentioned, we may only want to know how many factors underlie the scores on the observed variables. But in the first case, we may be interested in both questions—that is, how many factor underlie the indicators, and whether boys and girls have different means on each of these factors.[5]

SEM Can Be Applied to Experimental Data, Too

Another too narrow view of SEM is that it is appropriate only for data from nonexperimental designs. The heavy emphasis on covariances in the SEM literature may be at the root of this perception, but the discussion to this point should suggest that this belief is without foundation. For example, between-group comparisons in SEM could involve experimental conditions to which cases are randomly assigned. In this context, the application of SEM could be used to estimate group differences on latent variables that are hypothesized to correspond to the observed outcome measures in a particular way. Techniques in SEM can also be used in studies that have a mix of experimental and nonexperimental features, as would occur if cases with various physical disorders were randomly assigned to receive particular kinds of medications.

SEM Requires Large Samples

Attempts have been made to adapt SEM techniques to accommodate smaller sample sizes (e.g., Nevitt & Hancock, 2004), but it is still generally true that SEM is a large-sample technique. Implications of this property are considered throughout the book, but I can say now that some kinds of statistical estimates in SEM, such as standard errors, may not be accurate when the sample size is not large. The likelihood of technical problems in the analysis is greater, too.

Because sample size is such an important issue, let us now consider the bottom-line question: What is a "large enough" sample size in SEM? It is difficult to give a single answer because several factors affect sample size requirements. For example, the analysis of a complex model generally requires more cases than that of a simpler model. This is because more complex models have more **parameters** than simpler models. More precise definitions of parameters are given later in this volume, but for now you can

---

[5]Bruce Thompson, personal communication, April 22, 2008.

view them as hypothesized effects that require statistical estimates based on your data. Models with more parameters require more estimates, so larger samples are necessary in order for the results to be reasonably stable. The type of estimation algorithm used in the analysis affects sample size requirements, too. There is more than one type of estimation method in SEM, and some types need very large samples because of assumptions they make (or do not make) about the data. Another factor involves the distributional characteristics of the data. In general, smaller sample sizes are needed when the distributions of continuous outcome variables are all normal in shape and their associations with one another are all linear.

A useful rule of thumb concerning the relation between sample size and model complexity that also has some empirical support was referred to by Jackson (2003) as the **N:q rule**. This rule is applicable when the estimation method used is **maximum likelihood** (ML), which is by far the method used most often in SEM. Indeed, ML is the default method in most SEM computer tools. Properties of ML estimation are described in Chapter 7, but it is no exaggeration to describe this method as the motor of SEM. (You are the driver.) In ML estimation, Jackson (2003) suggested that researchers think about minimum sample size in terms of the ratio of cases (N) to the number of model parameters that require statistical estimates (q). An ideal sample size-to-parameters ratio would be 20:1. For example, if a total of $q = 10$ model parameters require statistical estimates, then an ideal minimum sample size would be 20×10, or $N = 200$. Less ideal would be an $N:q$ ratio of 10:1, which for the example just given for $q = 10$ would be a minimal sample size of 10×10, or $N = 100$. As the $N:q$ ratio decreases below 10:1 (e.g., $N = 50$, $q = 10$ for a 5:1 ratio), so does the trustworthiness of the results.

It also helps to think about recommended sample size in more absolute terms. A "typical" sample size in studies where SEM is used is about 200 cases. This number corresponds to the approximate median sample size in surveys of published articles in which SEM results are reported. These include an earlier review by Breckler (1990) of 72 articles in personality and social psychology journals and a more recent review by Shah and Goldstein (2006) of 93 articles in management science journals. However, a sample size of 200 cases may be too small when analyzing a complex model, using an estimation method other than ML, or distributions are severely non-normal. With < 100 cases, almost any type of SEM may be untenable unless a very simple model is evaluated. Such simple models may be so bare-bones as to be uninteresting. Barrett (2007) suggested that reviewers of journal submissions routinely reject for publication any SEM analysis where $N < 200$ unless the population studied is restricted in size. This recommendation is not standard practice, but it highlights the fact that analyzing small samples in SEM is problematic. One of these problems is low statistical power. I will show you in Chapter 8 how to estimate power in SEM.

Less Emphasis on Statistical Tests

A great many effects can be tested for statistical significance in SEM, ranging from things such as the variance of a single variable up to entire models evaluated across multiple samples. There are four reasons, however, why the results of statistical tests may be less relevant than other types of techniques, including ANOVA and MR. First, SEM allows the evaluation of entire models, which brings a higher-level perspective to the analysis. Statistical tests of individual effects represented in models may be of interest, but at some point you must make a decision about the whole model: Should it be rejected?— modified?—if so, how? Thus, there is a sense in SEM that the view of the entire landscape (the whole model) has precedence over that of specific details (individual effects).

The second reason statistical tests play a smaller role in SEM concerns the general requirement for large sample sizes discussed earlier. With most statistical tests, it is possible to have results that are "highly significant" (e.g., $p < .0001$) but trivial in absolute magnitude when the sample size is large. By the same token, virtually all effects that are not nil will be statistically significant in a sufficiently large sample. In fact, if the sample size is large, then a statistically significant result just basically confirms a large sample (Thompson, 1992), which is a tautology, or a needless repetition of the same sense in different words.

The third reason is that statistical significance (i.e., p values) for effects of latent variables is *estimated* by the computer, but this estimate could change if, say, a different estimation algorithm is used or sometimes even across different computer tools for the same analysis and data. Differences in estimated p values across different software packages are usually not great, but small differences in p can affect hypothesis testing (e.g., $p = .053$ vs. $p = .047$ for the same effect when testing at the .05 level).

The fourth reason is not specific to SEM, but concerns most kinds of statistical analyses in the behavioral sciences: We should in general be more concerned with estimating the sizes or magnitudes of effects (i.e., effect sizes) than with the outcome of statistical tests (e.g., Kline, 2004). Also, SEM gives better estimates of effect size than traditional techniques for observed variables, including MR and ANOVA. Suggestions for the conduct of statistical significance testing in SEM will be discussed at various points throughout the book.

SEM and the General Linear Model

You may know that ANOVA is just a special (restricted) case of MR. The two techniques are based on the same underlying mathematical model that belongs to a larger family known as the **general linear model** (GLM). The multivariate techniques of MANOVA (i.e., multivariate ANOVA) and canonical correlation, among others, are also part of the GLM. The whole of the GLM can be seen as just a restricted case of SEM (Fan, 1997). So learning about SEM really means extending your repertoire of data analysis skills to the next level, one that offers even more flexibility than the GLM.

WIDESPREAD ENTHUSIASM, BUT WITH A CAUTIONARY TALE

It cannot be denied that SEM is increasingly "popular" among researchers in many different disciplines. This has become evident by the growing numbers of computer tools for SEM, formal courses at the graduate level, continuing-education workshops, and articles in research journals where the authors describe the results of SEM analyses. It is also difficult to look through an issue of a research journal in psychology, education, or other areas and not find at least one article that concerns SEM. Interest in SEM has also expanded to other disciplines, including wildlife management (Grace, 2006, 2008), communication sciences (Holbert & Stephenson, 2002), medical research (DiLalla, 2008), administrative pharmacy (Schreiber, 2008), and pediatric psychology (Nelson, Aylward, & Steele, 2008), to name a few.

It is not hard to understand this growing interest in SEM. As described by David Kenny in the Series Editor's Note in the previous edition of this book, researchers love SEM because it addresses the questions they want answered and it "thinks" about research the way researchers do. The brief description given earlier of the kinds of hypotheses that can be tested in SEM only hints at its flexibility. However, there is evidence that many—if not most—published reports of the application of SEM have at least one flaw so serious that it compromises the scientific value of the article. MacCallum and Austin (2000) reviewed about 500 applications of SEM in 16 different psychology research journals, and they found problems with the reporting in many of these reports. For example, in about 50% of the articles, the reporting of parameter estimates was incomplete (e.g., unstandardized estimates were omitted); in about 25% the type of data matrix analyzed (e.g., a correlation vs. a covariance matrix) was not described; and in about 10% the model specified or the indicators of factors were not clearly specified. Shah and Goldstein (2006) reviewed 93 articles published in four management science journals. In a majority of articles, Shah and Goldstein (2006) found that it was difficult to determine the model actually tested or the complete set of observed variables. Along the same lines, they found in 31 out of 143 analyses that the model described in the text did not match the statistical results reported in text or tables, and the method of estimation was not mentioned in about half of the articles.

Both sets of authors of the review studies just described found similar kinds of problems in their respective sets of articles. For example, MacCallum and Austin (2000) found that about 20% of studies used samples of fewer than 100 cases. Shah and Goldstein (2006) found that the $N{:}q$ ratio was < 10:1 in about 70% of studies and < 5:1 in about 30%. The author of the typical article in these sets of reviewed studies did not consider alternative models that might account for the same pattern of observed covariances just as well as the author's preferred model. Such alternative models are known as **equivalent models**. Ignoring equivalent models is a form of **confirmation bias** whereby researchers test a single model, give an overly positive evaluation of that model, and fail to consider other explanations of the data (Shah & Goldstein, 2006). The potential for confirmation bias is further strengthened by the relative lack of replication. Specifically, most SEM studies are "one-shot" studies that do not involve cross-validation or a split-sample approach. The need for large samples in SEM undoubtedly hinders the ability of researchers to replicate their analyses. But whether results reported in most SEM studies would be found across independent samples is typically unknown.

The problems just described—and others covered later—are serious, and they indicate that our collective enthusiasm about SEM has outstripped our good judgment about its proper use. Accordingly, a major goal of this book is to teach you how to avoid common mistakes in the use of SEM and thereby guide you toward more sound, correct practices in all phases of the analysis. I want *you* to use SEM intelligently and get as much out of its application as possible.

FAMILY HISTORY AND A REMINDER ABOUT CONTEXT

Because SEM is a collection of related techniques, it does not have a single source. Part of its origins date to the early years of the 20th century with the development of what we now call exploratory factor analysis, usually credited to Charles Spearman (1904). A few years later, the biogeneticist Sewell Wright (e.g., 1918) developed the basics of path analysis. Wright demonstrated how observed covariances could be related to the parameters of a model that represents both direct and indirect causal effects among a set of variables. In doing so, he also showed how these effects could be estimated from sample data. Wright also invented path diagrams, which are graphical representations of direct and indirect effects that we still use to this day. In hindsight, Wright's innovations are remarkable. The technique of path analysis was subsequently introduced to the behavioral sciences by various authors, including Blalock (1961) and O. Duncan (1966), among others (see the annotated bibliography by Wolfle, 2003).

The measurement (factor analysis) and structural (path analysis) approaches were integrated in the early 1970s in the work of basically three authors: K. Jöreskog, J. Keesling, and D. Wiley, into a framework that Bentler (1980) called the **JWK model**. One of the first widely available computer programs able to analyze models based on the JWK framework—now called SEM—was LISREL, developed by K. Jöreskog and D. Sörbom in the 1970s and subsequently updated by them several times.

The 1980s and 1990s witnessed the development of more computer programs and a rapid expansion of the use of SEM techniques in many different areas of the behavioral sciences. There have been many recent developments, too, many of which represent the extension of models about continuous latent variables to other kinds of analyses. For example, there are now many works in the SEM literature about the estimation of growth and change over time on latent variables (i.e., latent growth curve modeling; e.g., Duncan, Duncan, Strycker, Li, & Alpert, 1999) and also about the estimation of curvilinear and interactive effects of latent variables (e.g., Schumaker & Marcoulides, 1998). Work by Muthén (1984) concerning estimation methods for non-normal data, such as when the indicators are dichotomous or ordered-categorical (ordinal) variables, further extended the range of application of SEM. Another major recent development concerns the convergence of SEM and techniques for multilevel analysis, which are applied in data sets where scores (cases) are grouped into higher-order units, such as siblings within families (Muthén, 1994). Within each level, the scores may not be independent, and multilevel techniques take this dependency into account. Recent versions of some SEM computer tools, including EQS, LISREL, and Mplus, feature built-in syntax for multilevel analyses.

The origin of the term *causal modeling* dates to Wright's pioneering work, but here is a critical point: Wright invented path analysis in order to estimate the magnitudes of effects when the basic causal pathways were *already known* (e.g., genetics). That is, given a true causal model, the technique of path analysis could be applied to estimate it for observed variables. However, this is *not* how we generally use path analysis or related SEM techniques for analyzing latent variables today. In the behavioral sciences, we *rarely* know the true causal model. Instead, we usually *hypothesize* a causal model, and then we test that model using sample data. This context of use is vastly different from that of Wright's. Specifically, when the true causal model is unknown but our hypothesized model fits the data, about all we can say is that our model is consistent with the data, but we cannot claim that our model is proven. In this way, SEM can be seen as a **discomfirmatory technique**, one that can help us to reject false models (those with poor fit to the data), but it basically *never* confirms your particular model when the true model is unknown. Bollen (1989) put it this way (emphasis in original):

> If a model is consistent with reality, then the data should be consistent with the model. But, if the data are consistent with the model, this does not imply that the model corresponds to reality. (p. 68)

EXTENDED LATENT VARIABLE FAMILIES

Latent variables in structural equation models are assumed to be continuous. There are other statistical techniques for analyzing models with categorical latent variables. The levels of a categorical latent variable are **classes**, and they represent a mixture of subpopulations where membership is not known but is inferred from the data. Thus, a goal of the analysis is to identify the nature and number of latent classes. The technique of **latent class analysis** is a type of factor analysis but for categorical indicators and latent variables. A special kind of latent class factor model that represents the shift from one of two different states, such as from nonmastery to mastery of a skill, is a **latent transition model**. There are also analogs of techniques, such as MR, for the analysis of categorical latent variables. In **latent class regression**, a criterion is predicted by estimated class membership and other variables that covary with class membership. In contrast to standard regression techniques for continuous variables, the predictors in latent class regression can be a mix of continuous, categorical, or **count variables**,[6] and the criterion can be a continuous, categorical, or repeated-measures variable. It is also not assumed in latent class regression that the same prediction equation holds for all cases.

Until recently, SEM was generally viewed as a relatively distinct family of techniques from those just mentioned for analyzing categorical latent variables. However, this view is changing because of recent attempts to express all latent variable models within a

---

[6]A count variable is the number of times an event happens over a particular period of time such as the number of automobile accidents over the past 5 years. Distributions of such variables are often positively skewed.

common mathematical framework (Bartholomew, 2002). For example, Muthén (2001) described the analysis of **mixture models** with latent variables that may be continuous or categorical. When both are present in the same model, the analysis is basically SEM conducted across different inferred subpopulations. The Mplus computer program is especially adept at analyzing a variety of latent variable models. This is because it can analyze all basic kinds of SEM models and mixture models, too. Both kinds of analyses just mentioned can also be combined with a multilevel analysis in Mplus. Computer tools like Mplus blur the distinction between SEM and techniques such as latent class analysis, latent regression analysis, multilevel analysis, and mixture models analysis. So SEM itself is a member of an extended family of techniques for latent variable modeling. See Skrondal and Rabe-Hesketh (2004) for more information.

PLAN OF THE BOOK

The topic of SEM is very broad, and not every aspect of it can be covered comprehensively in a single volume. With this reality in mind, I will now describe the topics covered in this book. Part I introduces concepts essential to understanding the rationale of SEM. The main goal of Chapters 2 and 3 is to review basic statistical principles and techniques that form the foundation for learning about SEM. These topics include MR, the correct interpretation of statistical tests, and bootstrapping (Chapter 2), and the screening and preparation of data for SEM (Chapter 3). Computer tools for SEM are described in Chapter 4.

Part II consists of six chapters devoted to core SEM techniques. Most SEM analyses described in the research literature involve these core techniques. Chapter 5 concerns the specification of path analysis (PA) models, confirmatory factor analysis (CFA) measurement models, and models with characteristics of both PA and CFA models, or structural regression (SR) models. Chapter 6 is about identification of these models, or whether it is theoretically possible for the computer to derive a unique estimate of each and every model parameter. Estimation methods in SEM are considered in Chapter 7, especially the default method of ML. How to analyze path models is also demonstrated in this chapter. The critical question of how to evaluate the fit of a model to your data is dealt with in Chapter 8. Hypothesis testing strategies, the evaluation of alternative models, and what to report about model fit are also outlined in this chapter. The last two chapters of Part II are about core kinds of latent variable models in SEM: Chapter 9 deals with the technique of CFA, and Chapter 10 extends these ideas to the evaluation of SR models, the most general of basic structural equation models. The analysis of models across multiple samples is also considered in Chapter 9.

Part III gives you an overview of some more advanced topics and suggestions for avoiding mistakes. Chapter 11 deals with the analysis of means in SEM, including latent growth models and the estimation of group mean differences on latent variables. Chapter 12 introduces the estimation of interactive effects of latent variables and multilevel analysis in SEM. These presentations are not as detailed, but it is beyond the scope of this book to cover these topics in greater depth. Instead the goal is to make you aware of possibilities for these more advanced analyses and to provide references for further study. Chapter 13 is written as a kind of "how-not-to" manual that summarizes ways that researchers can mislead themselves with SEM. Read this chapter as a cautionary tale about common mistakes to avoid.

SUMMARY

Essential characteristics of SEM were considered in this chapter, including its a priori nature, the potential to explicitly differentiate between observed and latent variables, and the capability to analyze covariances as well as means. The SEM family is a flexible set of techniques, applicable to both experimental and nonexperimental data. It is no wonder that more and more researchers across different disciplines are applying SEM in their own studies. However, in too many studies there are some serious problems with the way that SEM is used or with how the analysis is described and the results are reported. How to avoid getting into trouble with SEM will be a major theme in later chapters. In the meantime, the ideas introduced in this chapter set the stage for reviewing fundamental statistical principles that underlie SEM in the next chapter.

2

Fundamental Concepts

You should bring to a journey of learning about SEM prerequisite knowledge about some fundamental statistical concepts. One is the technique of multiple regression (MR). Although MR analyzes observed variables only, many of the principles that underlie it generalize directly to SEM. Next, the correct interpretation of statistical tests in general is considered, as are some special issues about their use in SEM. The basic logic of bootstrapping, a computer-based resampling procedure with increasing application in SEM, is also discussed. Some advice: *Even if you think that you already know some of these topics, you should nevertheless read this whole chapter carefully.* This is because many readers tell me that they learned something new after hearing about the issues outlined next.

MULTIPLE REGRESSION

I assume that you are already familiar with bivariate correlation and regression. You can find reviews of these topics in just about any introductory statistics book.[1] The logic of MR is considered next for the case of two continuous predictors, X_1 and X_2, and a continuous criterion Y, but the same ideas apply when there are ≥ 3 predictors. Pearson correlations among the predictors and the criterion are represented with the symbols r_{Y1}, r_{Y2}, and r_{12}. These coefficients are known as **zero-order correlations** because they do not control for intercorrelation. For example, r_{Y1} does not control for the possibility that $r_{Y2} \neq 0$ (X_2 also covaries with Y) or that $r_{12} \neq 0$ (the predictors are correlated). Features of MR especially relevant to SEM are emphasized next.

---

[1]See G. Garson's online *StatNotes* for a review: *http://faculty.chass.ncsu.edu/garson/PA765/statnote.htm*

Ordinary Least Squares Estimation

With two predictors, the form of the unstandardized regression equation is

$$\hat{Y} = B_1 X_1 + B_2 X_2 + A \tag{2.1}$$

where $\hat{Y}$ is a predicted score. The term $\hat{Y}$ is a **composite**, or a weighted linear combination of the two predictors, X_1 and X_2. Equation 2.1 has both a covariance structure and a mean structure. The covariance structure corresponds to the unstandardized regression coefficients B_1 and B_2, and the mean structure to the intercept (constant) A. The values of B_1, B_2, and A are estimated with the method of **ordinary least squares** (OLS) so that the **least squares criterion** is satisfied. The latter means the sum of the squared residuals, or $\Sigma (Y - \hat{Y})^2$, is as small as possible in a particular sample. The method of OLS estimation is a **partial-information method** or a **limited-information method** because it analyzes the equation for only one criterion at a time.

Residuals in OLS estimation are uncorrelated with each of the predictors. That is,

$$r_{(Y-\hat{Y})1} = r_{(Y-\hat{Y})2} = 0 \tag{2.2}$$

where the residuals are represented in each subscript by the term $(Y - \hat{Y})$ and the predictors X_1 and X_2 by, respectively, the terms 1 and 2. The equality represented in Equation 2.2 is required in order for the computer to derive a unique set of regression weights that satisfies the least squares criterion. Conceptually, assuming the independence of residuals and predictors permits estimation of the relative predictor power of the latter (e.g., B_1 for X_1), with omitted (unmeasured) predictors held constant. Bollen (1989) refers to this assumption as **pseudoisolation** of the measured from the unmeasured predictors. Other implications of this assumption are considered later.

The overall multiple correlation between the predictors and the criterion, $R_{Y\cdot12}$, is actually just the Pearson correlation between the observed and predicted scores, or

$$R_{Y\cdot12} = r_{Y\hat{Y}} \tag{2.3}$$

Unlike Pearson correlations, though, the range of multiple correlations is 0–1.0. The value of $R^2_{Y\cdot12}$ indicates the proportion of explained variance. For example, if $R_{Y\cdot12} = .40$, then $R^2_{Y\cdot12} = .16$, so we can say that X_1 and X_2 together explain 16% of the total variance in Y. The values of B_1, B_2, and A in Equation 2.1 in a particular sample are those that maximize predictive power. Consequently, OLS estimation **capitalizes on chance**, which implies that (1) $R^2_{Y\cdot12}$ tends to overestimate the population proportion of explained variance ρ^2, and (2) it is possible that similar values of B_1, B_2, and A may not be found in a replication sample.

There are many corrections that downward adjust R^2 values as a function of sample size and the number of predictors (Yin & Fan, 2001). Perhaps the most common correction is Wherry's (1931) equation

$$\hat{R}^2 = 1 - (1 - R^2)\left(\frac{N-1}{N-k-1}\right) \tag{2.4}$$

where $\hat{R}^2$ is the adjusted estimate of ρ^2 and k is the number of predictors. The statistic $\hat{R}^2$ is a **shrinkage-corrected R^2**. In small samples, the value of $\hat{R}^2$ can be quite a bit less than that of R^2. The value of the former can even be negative; in this case, $\hat{R}^2$ is interpreted as though its value were zero. As the sample size increases for a constant number of predictors, values of $\hat{R}^2$ and R^2 are increasingly similar, and in very large samples they are essentially equal. That is, it is unnecessary to correct for positive bias in very large samples.

Regression Weights

The **unstandardized regression coefficients** B_1 and B_2 in Equation 2.1 indicate the expected raw score difference in Y, given a difference of a single point in one predictor while we are controlling for the other. For example, if $B_1 = 5.40$ and $B_2 = 3.65$, then the expected difference on Y is 5.40 points given a difference on X_1 of 1 point, with X_2 held constant. Likewise, a 1-point difference on X_2 predicts a 3.65-point difference on Y while controlling for X_1. Because unstandardized coefficients reflect the scales of their respective predictors, values of Bs from predictors with different raw score metrics are not directly comparable. Thus, one cannot conclude for this example that the relative predictive power of X_1 is greater than that of X_2 because $B_1 > B_2$. The **intercept** A is a constant that equals the value of $\hat{Y}$ when the scores on both predictors are zero ($X_1 = X_2 = 0$). It can be expressed as a function of the unstandardized coefficients and the means of all variables as follows:

$$A = M_Y - B_1 M_1 - B_2 M_2 \tag{2.5}$$

In contrast, means have no bearing on the values of the regression coefficients B_1 and B_2.

The regression equation for standardized variables is

$$\hat{z}_Y = b_1 z_1 + b_2 z_2 \tag{2.6}$$

where z_1 and z_2 are, respectively, standardized scores (normal deviates[2]) on X_1 and X_2, and b_1 and b_2 are, respectively, the **standardized regression coefficients**. The latter are also called **beta weights** because each standardized coefficient estimates a population parameter designated by the symbol β. Beta weights indicate the expected difference on the criterion in standard deviation units, controlling for all other predictors. Also, their values can be directly compared across predictors. For example, if $b_1 = .40$, it means that the difference in Y is expected to be .40 standard deviations large, given a difference

---

[2] $z_1 = (X_1 - M_1)/SD_1$, $z_2 = (X_2 - M_2)/SD_2$.

on X_1 of one full standard deviation controlling for X_2. The term b_2 has the analogous meaning except that X_1 is held constant. If $b_1 = .40$ and $b_2 = .80$, then we could say that the relative predictive power of X_2 is exactly twice that of X_1 in standard deviation units because the ratio b_2/b_1 equals $.80/.40$, or 2.0.

Because beta weights are adjusted for intercorrelations among the predictors (and with the criterion, too), their absolute values are usually lower than those of the corresponding bivariate correlations (e.g., $b_1 = .40$, $r_{Y1} = .60$). This is not always true, though. Absolute values of b weights can exceed those of the corresponding correlation (e.g., $b_1 = .80$, $r_{Y1} = .60$). It is also possible for absolute values of b weights to exceed 1.0 or even for the signs of a beta weight and the corresponding correlation to be in opposite directions (e.g., $b_1 = -.40$, $r_{Y1} = .20$). When any of these cases occur, a suppression effect is indicated. Suppression is dealt with later.

For two predictors, the formulas for their beta weights are

$$b_1 = \frac{r_{Y1} - r_{Y2}\, r_{12}}{1 - r_{12}^2} \quad \text{and} \quad b_2 = \frac{r_{Y2} - r_{Y1}\, r_{12}}{1 - r_{12}^2} \tag{2.7}$$

The numerators in Equation 2.7 reflect one aspect of holding the other predictor constant.[3] In the formula for b_1, for example, the product of both bivariate correlations that involve the other predictor, X_2, is literally subtracted out of the bivariate correlation for X_1. The denominators in Equation 2.7 adjust the total standardized variance by removing the proportion shared by the two predictors. When there are ≥ 3 predictors, the formulas for the beta weights are more complicated but follow the same principles. The relation between unstandardized and standardized regression weights is expressed next:

$$B_1 = b_1 \left(\frac{SD_Y}{SD_1} \right) \quad \text{and} \quad B_2 = b_2 \left(\frac{SD_Y}{SD_2} \right) \tag{2.8}$$

The statistic $R_{Y\cdot12}^2$ can also be expressed as a function of the beta weights and the bivariate correlations of the predictors with the criterion. With two predictors,

$$R_{Y\cdot12}^2 = b_1\, r_{Y1} + b_2\, r_{Y2} \tag{2.9}$$

The role of beta weights as corrections for the other predictor is apparent in this equation. Specifically, if $r_{12} = 0$ (the predictors are independent), then $b_1 = r_{Y1}$ and $b_2 = r_{Y2}$ (Equation 2.7), which means that $R_{Y\cdot12}^2$ is just the sum of r_{Y1}^2 and r_{Y2}^2. However, if $r_{12} \neq 0$ (the predictors covary), then b_1 and b_2 do not equal the corresponding bivariate correlations and $R_{Y\cdot12}^2$ is not the simple sum of r_{Y1}^2 and r_{Y2}^2 (it is less).

As mentioned, beta weights can be directly compared across different predictors within the same sample. However, it is *not* generally correct to directly compare beta

---

[3]In a bivariate regression analysis with a single predictor X, the standardized regression coefficient is r_{XY}, the Pearson correlation with the criterion Y.

weights for the same predictors but across different samples, especially if those samples have different variances. This is because beta weights are standardized based on the variability in a particular sample (e.g., Equation 2.8 but solved for each of b_1 and b_2). If the within-group variances are not the same, then the basis of that standardization is not constant.[4] It is usually better to compare *unstandardized* regression coefficients across different samples. The same point holds in SEM analyses: It is the unstandardized solution that we directly compare across groups.

Presented in Table 2.1 is a small data set with scores on X_1, X_2, and Y. Assume that scores on these variables are from, respectively, a test of working memory, phonics skill, and reading achievement. Exercise 1 for this chapter will ask you to calculate and interpret the results for these data summarized next:

$$R_{Y \cdot 12} = .801, \quad R^2_{Y \cdot 12} = .641$$
$$B_1 = .242, \quad B_2 = .193, \quad A = 10.771$$
$$b_1 = .320, \quad b_2 = .599$$

An alternative to using a commercial computer program for the chapter exercises is a freely available calculating webpage for MR.[5] See the website for this book (p. 3) for links to other online calculating pages.

Assumptions

The statistical assumptions of MR are stringent, probably more so than many researchers realize. They are summarized next:

1. Regression weights reflect linear relations only. If there are also curvilinear relations, then values of regression weights will underestimate predictive power.

2. Statistical tests in MR assume that the residuals are normally distributed and have uniform variances across all levels of the predictors. The latter characteristic is **homoscedasticity**, and its opposite, **heteroscedasticity**, can be caused by outliers, severe non-normality in the observed scores, or more measurement error at some levels of the criterion or predictors. In the next chapter I will show you how to screen your data for heteroscedasticity.

3. It is assumed that the scores on the predictors are perfectly reliable (no measurement error). This assumption is necessary because there is no direct way in MR to represent less-than-perfect score reliability for the predictors. Consequences of minor

---

[4]Here is another example: Suppose that the same multiple-choice exam is administered in each of two different classes. For each class, scores are reported as the proportion correct, but relative to the highest score in each group, not the total number of items. Although the proportions in each class are standardized and have the same range (0–1.0), they are not directly comparable across the classes if the highest scores in each group are unequal.

[5]*http://home.ubalt.edu/ntsbarsh/Business-stat/otherapplets/MultRgression.htm*

TABLE 2.1. Example Data Set for Multiple Regression

Case	X_1	X_2	Y
A	3	65	24
B	8	50	20
C	10	40	22
D	15	70	32
E	19	75	27

violations of this requirement may not be critical, but more serious ones can result in bias. This bias can affect not only the regression weights of predictors measured with error but also those of other predictors. However, it is difficult to anticipate the direction of this **error propagation**. Depending on sample intercorrelations, some regression weights may be biased upward (too large), but others may be biased in the other direction. There is no requirement that the criterion should be measured without error, but the use of a psychometrically inadequate measure of it can reduce the value of R^2. When the predictors are measured without error but the criterion is measured with error, beta weights tend to be too small, but not the unstandardized regression weights. If the predictors are measured with error, too, then these effects for the criterion could be amplified, diminished, or canceled out, but it is best not to hope for the latter. See Liu (1988) for more information.

4. It is assumed that omitted predictors are uncorrelated with measured predictors, or those in the equation. This requirement is a consequence of the fact that the residuals are uncorrelated with the predictors in OLS estimation. This is a strong assumption, one that is probably violated in most applications of MR (and SEM, too). This assumption also concerns the issue of specification error, which is considered next.

Specification Error

Specification error refers to the problem of omitted predictors that account for some unique proportion of total criterion variance but are not included in the analysis. A related term is **left-out-variable error** or, more lightheartedly, the "heartbreak of L.O.V.E." The idea of specification error in SEM is even broader than in MR, but the omission of relevant predictors is a concern in SEM, too. Suppose that $r_{Y1} = .40$ and $r_{Y2} = .60$ for, respectively, predictors X_1 and X_2. A researcher measures only X_1 and uses it as the sole predictor of Y. The standardized regression coefficient for the *included predictor* in this bivariate analysis is $r_{Y1} = .40$. If the researcher had the foresight to also measure X_2, the *omitted predictor*, and enter it along with X_1 as a predictor in an MR analysis, the beta weight for X_1 in this analysis may not equal .40. If not, then r_{Y1} as a standardized regression coefficient with X_1 as the sole predictor does not reflect the true predictive power of X_1 compared with b_1 derived with both predictors in the equation. However, the difference between r_{Y1} and b_1 varies with r_{12}, the correlation between the included and omitted predictors. Specifically, if the included and omitted predictors are unrelated

$(r_{12} = 0)$, there is no difference $(r_{Y1} = b_1)$ because there is no correction for correlated predictors. But as the absolute value of their correlation increases $(r_{12} \neq 0)$, the amount of the difference between r_{Y1} and b_1 due to the omission of X_2 becomes greater.

Presented in Table 2.2 are the results of three pairs of regression analyses. In all pairs, X_2 is considered the omitted predictor.[6] One member of each pair of analyses is a bivariate regression with X_1 as the sole predictor, and the other member is an MR with both X_1 and X_2 in the equation. Constant across all three sets of analyses are the bivariate correlations between the predictors and the criterion $(r_{Y1} = .40, r_{Y2} = .60)$. The only thing that varies across the three sets is the value of r_{12}, the correlation between the predictors. Reported for each analysis in Table 2.2 are the standardized regression weights $(r_{Y1}$ for the bivariate regression; b_1 and b_2 for the MR) and also the overall multiple correlation $(R_{Y.12})$ for the regression of Y on both X_1 and X_2. For each case in the table, compare in the same row the value of r_{Y1} in boldface with that of b_1, also in boldface. The difference between these values (if any) indicates the amount by which the bivariate standardized regression coefficient for X_1 does not accurately reflect its predictive power relative to when X_2 is also in the equation.

Note in Table 2.2 that when the omitted predictor X_2 is uncorrelated with the included predictor X_1 (case 1, $r_{12} = 0$), the standardized regression weight for X_1 is the same regardless of whether or not X_2 is in the equation $(r_{Y1} = b_1 = .40)$. However, when $r_{12} = .30$ (case 2), the value of b_1 is lower than that of r_{Y1}, respectively, .24 versus .40. This happens because b_1 controls for the correlation between X_1 and X_2, whereas r_{Y1} does not. Thus, r_{Y1} *overestimates* the association between X_1 and Y relative to b_1. In case 3 in the table, the correlation between the included and omitted predictors is even higher $(r_{12} = .60)$, which for these data results in an even greater discrepancy between r_{Y1} and b_1 (respectively, .40 vs. .06).

Omitting a predictor correlated with others in the equation does not always result in overestimation of the predictive power of an included predictor. For example, if X_1 is the included predictor and X_2 is the omitted predictor, it is also possible for the absolute value of r_{Y1} to be *less* than that of b_1 (i.e., r_{Y1} *underestimates* the relation indicated by b_1)

TABLE 2.2. Examples of the Omitted Variable Problem

| | | Predictor(s) | | |
| | | Both X_1 and X_2 | | |
Case	X_1 only	X_1	X_2	$R_{Y.12}$
1. $r_{12} = 0$	**.40**	**.40**	.60	.72
2. $r_{12} = .30$	**.40**	**.24**	.53	.64
3. $r_{12} = .60$	**.40**	**.06**	.56	.60

Note. Numerical values for X_1 and X_2 are standardized regression coefficients. For all cases, X_2 is considered the omitted variable; $r_{Y1} = .40$ and $r_{Y2} = .60$.

---

[6]The same principles hold if X_1 is the omitted predictor and X_2 is the included predictor.

or even for r_{Y1} and b_1 to have different signs. Both cases indicate suppression. However, overestimation due to omission of a predictor probably occurs more often than underestimation (suppression). Also, the pattern of bias may be more complicated when there are several included and omitted variables (e.g., overestimation for some included predictors; underestimation for others).

Predictors are typically excluded because they are not measured. Thus, it is difficult to know by how much and in what direction regression coefficients may be biased relative to what their values would be if all relevant predictors were included. However, it is unrealistic to expect the researcher to know and be able to measure all relevant predictors. In this way, all regression equations are probably misspecified to some degree. If omitted predictors are uncorrelated with included predictors, the consequences of specification error may be slight. Otherwise, the consequences may be more serious. Careful review of theory and research is the main way to avoid a serious specification error by decreasing the potential number of left-out variables.

Suppression

Perhaps the most general definition is that **suppression** occurs when either the absolute value of a predictor's beta weight is greater than its bivariate (zero-order) correlation with the criterion or the two have different signs. So defined, suppression implies that the estimated relation between a predictor and a criterion while controlling for the other predictors is a "surprise," given the bivariate correlations. Suppose that X_1 is amount of psychotherapy, X_2 is degree of depression, and Y is number of prior suicide attempts. The bivariate correlations in a hypothetical sample are

$$r_{Y1} = .19, \quad r_{Y2} = .49, \quad \text{and } r_{12} = .70$$

Based on these results, it may seem that psychotherapy is harmful because of its positive association with suicide attempts ($r_{Y1} = .19$). When both predictors (depression, psychotherapy) are entered as predictors in the same regression equation, however, the results are

$$b_1 = -.30, \quad b_2 = .70, \quad \text{and } R_{Y \cdot 12} = .54$$

The beta weight for psychotherapy (−.30) has the opposite sign of its bivariate correlation with the criterion (.19), and the beta weight for depression (.70) exceeds its bivariate correlation (.49).

The "surprising" results just described are due to controlling for other predictors. Here, people who are more depressed are also more likely to be in psychotherapy ($r_{12} = .70$). Depressed people are more likely to try to harm themselves ($r_{Y2} = .49$). Corrections for these associations in MR reveal that the relation of psychotherapy to suicide attempts is actually negative once depression is controlled. It is also true that the relation of depression to suicide attempts is even stronger once psychotherapy is controlled. Omit either psychotherapy or depression from the analysis—a specification error—and the bivariate regression results with the remaining predictor are misleading. This example concerns **negative suppression**, where the predictors have positive correlations with the criterion and each other, but one receives a negative beta weight in the analysis.

A second type of suppression is **classical suppression**, where one predictor is uncorrelated with the criterion but receives a nonzero beta weight controlling for another predictor. For example, given the following correlations in a hypothetical sample,

$$r_{Y1} = 0, \quad r_{Y2} = .60, \quad \text{and } r_{12} = .50$$

the results of an MR analysis are

$$b_1 = -.40, \quad b_2 = .80, \quad R_{Y\cdot12} = .69$$

This example of classical suppression (i.e., $r_{Y1} = 0$, $b_1 = -.40$) demonstrates that bivariate correlations of zero can mask true predictive relations once other variables are controlled. There is also **reciprocal suppression**, which can occur when two predictors correlate positively with the criterion but negatively with each other. See Shieh (2006) for more information about suppression.

Death to Stepwise Regression, Think for Yourself

There are two basic ways to enter predictors into the equation: One is to enter all predictors at once, or **simultaneous entry**. The other is to enter predictors over a series of steps, or **sequential entry**. Entry order can be determined according to one of two different standards, theoretical (rational) or empirical (statistical). The rational standard corresponds to **hierarchical regression**, where *you* tell the computer a fixed order of entry for the predictors. For example, sometimes demographic variables are entered at the first step, and then entered at the second step is a psychological variable of interest. This order not only controls for the demographic variables but also permits evaluation of the predictive power of the psychological variable, over and beyond that of simple demographic variables.

An example of the statistical standard is **stepwise regression**, where the *computer* selects predictors for entry based on statistical significance (e.g., which predictor, if entered into the equation, would have the most statistically significant regression weight?). After they are selected, predictors at a later step can also be removed from the equation according to statistical test outcomes (e.g., if a predictor's regression weight is no longer statistically significant). The stepwise process stops when there could be no statistically significant increase in R^2 by adding more predictors. There are variations on stepwise regression—for example, some methods select predictors but do not later remove them (**forward inclusion**), and others begin with all predictors in the equation and then automatically remove them (**backward elimination**)—but all such methods are directed by the computer, not you.

Stepwise regression and related methods pose many problems, so many that such methods are now basically forbidden in some research areas (e.g., Thompson, 1995), and for good reason, too. One problem is extreme capitalization on chance. Another is that not all regression computer programs print correct values of statistical tests in stepwise regression; that is, the computer's choices may actually be wrong. Both of these problems imply that whatever final set of predictors happen to be selected by the computer in empirically driven procedures is unlikely to replicate. Worst of all, such methods give the illusion that the researcher does not have to think about the problem. Sribney (1998) offers this advice: "Personally, I would no more let an automatic routine select my model than I would let some best-fit procedure pack my suitcase" (Ronan Conroy's Comments section, para. 8).

In SEM, there are methods for modifying structural equation models with poor fit to the data that are analogous to empirically based methods in MR. These methods in SEM indicate the particular effects that would result in the greatest improvement in fit if those effects were added to the model. Some SEM computer tools, such as LISREL, offer an **automatic modification** (AM) option that mechanically adds effects according to statistical criteria. Such purely exploratory options greatly capitalize on chance; they also give the illusion that you need not think about the problem. I do not recommend the use of AM-type options. Instead, the modification of your model should be guided mainly by your hypotheses, just as its specification in the first place should be so guided. There is a role in SEM for more limited empirically based methods, but they should be used in a way that respects your hypotheses. These issues are elaborated in Chapter 8, on hypothesis testing in SEM.

PARTIAL CORRELATION AND PART CORRELATION

The technique of **partial correlation** concerns the phenomenon of **spuriousness**: if the observed relation between two variables is due to ≥ 1 common cause(s), their association is spurious. To illustrate this concept, consider these zero-order correlations between vocabulary breadth (Y), shoe size (X_1), and age (X_2) in a hypothetical sample of children not all the same age:

$$r_{Y1} = .50, \quad r_{Y2} = .60, \quad \text{and } r_{12} = .80$$

Although the correlation between shoe size and vocabulary breadth is fairly substantial (.50), it is hardly surprising because both are caused by a third variable, age (i.e., maturation).

The partial correlation $r_{Y1\cdot2}$ removes the influence of a third variable X_2 from both X_1 and Y. The formula is

$$r_{Y1\cdot2} = \frac{r_{Y1} - r_{Y2}\, r_{12}}{\sqrt{(1 - r_{Y2}^2)(1 - r_{12}^2)}} \tag{2.10}$$

The denominator in Equation 2.10 adjusts the total standardized variance of both Y and X_1 for their overlap with X_2. Applied to the hypothetical correlations just listed, the partial correlation between shoe size and vocabulary breadth controlling for age is $r_{Y1\cdot2}$ = .04. (An exercise will ask you to calculate this partial correlation.) Because the association between X_1 and Y essentially disappears when X_2 is controlled, their observed relation r_{Y1} = .50 may be a spurious one. The technique of SEM readily allows the representation of presumed spurious associations due to common causes.

Equation 2.10 for partial correlation can be extended to control for two or more external variables. For example, the higher-order partial correlation $r_{Y1\cdot23}$ estimates the association between X_1 and Y controlling for both X_2 and X_3. There is a related coefficient called **part correlation** or **semipartial correlation** that partials external variables out of either of two variables, but not both. The formula for the part correlation $r_{Y(1\cdot2)}$ for which the association between X_1 and X_2 is controlled but not the association between Y and X_2 is presented next:

$$r_{Y(1\cdot2)} = \frac{r_{Y1} - r_{Y2}\, r_{12}}{\sqrt{1 - r_{12}^2}} \tag{2.11}$$

Note that the denominator in Equation 2.11 adjusts the total standardized variance only for the overlap of X_1 with X_2. Given the same bivariate correlations among these three variables reported earlier, the part correlation between vocabulary breadth (Y) and shoe size (X_1) controlling only the latter for age (X_2) is $r_{Y(1\cdot2)}$ = .03. This result (.03) is somewhat smaller than the partial correlation for these data, or $r_{Y1\cdot2}$ = .04. In general, $r_{Y1\cdot2}$ is larger in absolute value than $r_{Y(1\cdot2)}$. An exception is when r_{12} = 0; in this case, $r_{Y1\cdot2}$ = $r_{Y(1\cdot2)}$.

Relations among the squares of the various correlations just described can be nicely illustrated with a Venn-type diagram like the one in Figure 2.1. The circles represent the total standardized variances of the criterion Y and the predictors X_1 and X_2. The regions in the figure labeled a–d make up the total standardized variance of Y, so

$$a + b + c + d = 1.0$$

Areas a and c in the figure represent the portions of Y uniquely predicted by, respectively, X_1 and X_2, but area b represents the simultaneous overlap (redundancy) of the predictors with Y. Area d represents the proportion of unexplained variance. The squared zero-order correlations of the predictors with the criterion and the overall squared multiple correlation can be expressed as sums of the areas a, b, c, or d in Figure 2.1, as follows:

$$r_{Y1}^2 = a + b \quad \text{and} \quad r_{Y2}^2 = b + c$$
$$R_{Y\cdot12}^2 = a + b + c = 1.0 - d$$

The squared part correlations correspond directly to the unique areas a and c in Figure 2.1. Each of these areas also equals the *increase* in the total proportion of explained variance that occurs by adding a second predictor to the equation. That is,

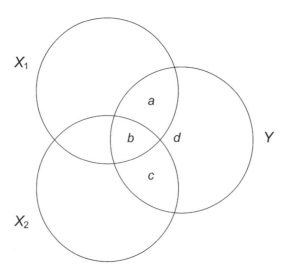

FIGURE 2.1. Venn diagram for the standardized variances of Y, X_1, and X_2.

$$r^2_{Y(1\cdot2)} = a = R^2_{Y\cdot12} - r^2_{Y2} \tag{2.12}$$

$$r^2_{Y(2\cdot1)} = c = R^2_{Y\cdot12} - r^2_{Y1}$$

In contrast, the squared partial correlations correspond to areas a, c, and d in Figure 2.1, and each estimates the proportion of variance in the criterion explained by one predictor but not the other. The formulas are

$$r^2_{Y1\cdot2} = \frac{a}{a+d} = \frac{R^2_{Y\cdot12} - r^2_{Y2}}{1 - r^2_{Y2}} \tag{2.13}$$

$$r^2_{Y2\cdot1} = \frac{c}{c+d} = \frac{R^2_{Y\cdot12} - r^2_{Y1}}{1 - r^2_{Y1}}$$

Note that the numerator of each expression in Equation 2.13 is a squared part correlation. The denominators in Equation 2.13 correct the total standardized variance of the criterion for its overlap with the other predictor. These denominators are generally < 1.0, which explains why squared partial correlations are generally larger than squared part correlations. Suppose that $R^2_{Y\cdot12} = .40$ and $r^2_{Y2} = .25$. These results follow:

$$r^2_{Y(1\cdot2)} = .40 - .25 = .15$$

$$r^2_{Y1\cdot2} = .15/(1 - .25) = .20$$

In words, predictor X_1 uniquely explains .15, or 15% of the total variance of Y (squared part correlation). Of the variance in Y not already explained by X_2, predictor X_1 accounts for .20, or 20% of the remaining variance (squared partial correlation). See G. Garson (2009) for an online review of partial correlation and part correlation.[7]

When predictors are correlated—which is just about always—beta weights, partial correlations, and part correlations are alternative ways to describe in standardized terms the relative explanatory power of each predictor controlling for the rest. None is more "correct" than the other because each gives a different perspective on the same data. However, remember that unstandardized regression coefficients (B) are preferred when comparing results for the same predictors across different samples.

OTHER BIVARIATE CORRELATIONS

When all observed variables are continuous, it is Pearson correlations that are usually analyzed in SEM as part of analyzing covariances. (Recall that cov_{XY} is the product of r_{XY} and the standard deviations of each variable; Equation 1.1.) However, noncontinuous variables can be analyzed in SEM, too, so you need to know something about other kinds of bivariate correlations. There are other forms of the Pearson correlation for observed variables that are either categorical or ordinal. For example:

1. The **point-biserial correlation** (r_{pb}) is a special case of r that estimates the association between a dichotomous variable and a continuous one (e.g., gender, weight).
2. The **phi coefficient** ($\hat{\phi}$) is a special case for two dichotomous variables (e.g., treatment-control, relapsed-not relapsed).
3. **Spearman's rank order correlation** or **Spearman's rho** is for two ranked variables.

It is also possible in SEM to analyze non-Pearson correlations that assume the underlying data (i.e., on a latent variable) are continuous and normally distributed instead of discrete. For example:

1. The **biserial correlation** is for a continuous variable and a dichotomy (e.g., agree-disagree), and it estimates what the Pearson r would be if both variables were continuous and normally distributed.
2. The **polyserial correlation** is the generalization of the biserial correlation that does basically the same thing for a continuous variable and a categorical variable with three or more levels.
3. The **tetrachoric correlation** for two dichotomous variables estimates what r would be if both variables were continuous and normally distributed.

---

[7]*http://faculty.chass.ncsu.edu/garson/PA765/partialr.htm*

4. The **polychoric correlation** is the generalization of the tetrachoric correlation that estimates *r* but for categorical variables with two or more levels.

Computing polyserial or polychoric correlations is complicated (Nunnally & Bernstein, 1994) and requires specialized software such as PRELIS, which is the part of LISREL for manipulating, generating, and transforming data. The PRELIS program can be used to estimate polyserial or polychoric correlations, depending on the types of variables in the data set. It can also estimate results for **censored variables**, which have large proportions of their scores at minimum or maximum values. Consider the variable "price paid for a new car in the last year." In a hypothetical sample, only 10% bought a new car year in the last year, so the scores for rest (90%) are zero. This variable is censored because not everyone buys a new car every year. Instead of deleting the 90% of the cases who did not purchase a new car, PRELIS would attempt to estimate results for this variable in the whole sample assuming that the underlying distribution is normal. Options for analyzing non-Pearson correlations in SEM are considered in Chapter 7.

LOGISTIC REGRESSION

Sometimes outcome variables are dichotomous or binary variables. Examples include graduated–did not graduate and survived–died. Some options to analyze dichotomous outcomes in SEM are based on the logic of **logistic regression** (LR). This technique is generally used instead of MR when the criterion is dichotomous. Just as in MR, the predictors in LR can be either continuous or categorical. However, the regression equation in LR is a logistic function that approximates a nonlinear relation between the dichotomous outcome and a linear combination of the predictors. An example of a logistic function for a hypothetical sample is illustrated in Figure 2.2. The closed circles in the figure represent along the *Y*-axis whether cases with the same illness either improved ($Y = 1.0$) or did not improve ($Y = 0$). Along the *X*-axis, the closed circles in the figure represent scores on a composite variable made up of various indexes of healthy behavior (exercise, preventative care, etc.). The logistic function fitted to the data in Figure 2.2 is S-shaped, or **sigmoidal** in form. This function generates predicted probabilities of improvement, given scores on the healthy behavior composite.

The estimation method in logistic regression is not OLS. Instead, it is usually ML estimation but is applied after transforming the binary outcome into a **logit variable**, which is typically the natural logarithm—base *e*, or approximately 2.71828—of the **odds** of the target outcome. The latter tell us how much more likely it is that a case is a member of the target group instead of a member of the other group (Wright, 1995), and it equals the probability of the target outcome divided by the probability of the other outcome. An example follows.

Suppose that 60% of the cases improved over a particular time, but the rest, or 40%, did not. Assuming that improvement is the target outcome, the odds of improvement are calculated here as .60/.40, or 1.5. That is, the odds are 3:2 in favor of improvement.

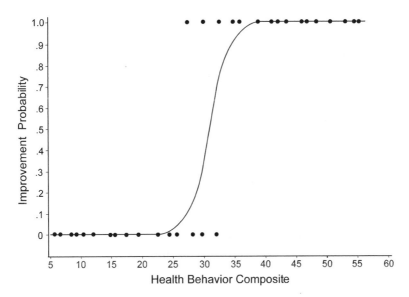

FIGURE 2.2. Example of a logistic function where closed circles represent actual data values and the curve represents predicted probabilities.

Regression coefficients for each predictor in LR can be converted into an **odds ratio**, which estimates the difference in the odds of the target outcome for a one-point difference in the predictor, controlling for all other predictors. For example, if the estimated odds ratio for amount of exercise were 5.60, then the odds of improvement are 5.6 times greater for each one-point increase on the exercise variable, holding constant other predictors. Values of odds ratios less than 1.0 would indicate for this example a relative reduction in the odds of improvement given higher scores on that predictor, and odds ratios that equal 1.0 would indicate no difference in improvement odds for any value of the predictor. See Peng, Lee, and Ingersoll (2002) for more information about LR.

STATISTICAL TESTS

Characteristics of statistical tests especially relevant for SEM are emphasized next.

Standard Errors

Perhaps the most basic form of a statistical test is the **critical ratio**, which is the ratio of a sample statistic over its **standard error**. The standard error is the standard deviation of a **sampling distribution**, which is a probability distribution of a statistic based on all possible random samples, each based on the same number of cases. A standard error estimates **sampling error**, the difference between sample statistics and the corresponding population parameter. Given constant variability among population cases, standard error varies inversely with sample size. This means that distributions of statistics from larger samples are generally narrower (less variable) than distributions of the same statistic from smaller samples.

There are textbook formulas for the standard errors of statistics with simple distributions. By "simple" I mean that (1) the statistic estimates a single parameter and (2) the shape of the distribution is not a function of that parameter. For example, the textbook formula for estimating the standard error of the mean is

$$SE_M = \frac{SD}{\sqrt{N}} \qquad (2.14)$$

It is more difficult to estimate standard errors for statistics that do not have simple distributions. There are approximate methods amenable to hand calculation for some statistics, such as sample proportions, where distribution shape and variability depend on the value of the population proportion. Such methods generate **asymptotic standard errors** that assume a large sample. However, if your sample is not large, such estimated standard errors may not be accurate. But some other statistics, such as the multiple correlation R, have distributions so complex that there may be no approximate standard error formula for hand calculation. Estimation of standard error in such cases may require specialized software (Kline, 2004, chap. 4). In SEM, standard errors for effects of latent variables are estimated by the computer, but these estimates are just that. This means that their values could change if, say, a different estimation method is used. So do not overinterpret results of statistical tests for latent variables.

Power and Types of Null Hypotheses

In large samples under the assumption of normality, a critical ratio is interpreted as a z-statistic in a normal curve with a mean of zero and a standard deviation that equals the standard error. A rule of thumb for large samples is that if the absolute value of this z-statistic exceeds 2.00, the null hypothesis (H_0) that the corresponding parameter is zero is rejected at the .05 level of statistical significance ($p < .05$) for a two-tailed test (H_1). The precise value of z for the .05 level is 1.96 and for the .01 level it is 2.58. Within small samples, critical ratios approximate a t-distribution instead of a z-distribution, which necessitates the use of special tables to determine critical values of t for the .05 or .01 levels. Within large samples, t and z for the same sample statistic are essentially equal.

The failure to reject some null hypothesis is a meaningful outcome only if (1) the power of the test is adequate and (2) the null hypothesis is at least plausible to some degree. Briefly, **power** is the probability of rejecting the null hypothesis when there is a real effect in the population (H_1 is true, H_0 is not). Power varies directly with the magnitude of the real population effect and your sample size. Other factors that affect power include:

1. The level of statistical significance (e.g., .05 vs. .01) and the directionality of H_1 (i.e., one- or two-tailed tests).

2. Whether the samples are independent or dependent (i.e., a between- or within-subject design).

3. The particular test statistic used.

4. The reliability of the scores.

The following combination generally leads to the greatest power: a large sample, the .05 level of statistical significance, a one-tailed (directional) H_1, a within-subject design, a parametric test statistic (e.g., t) rather than a nonparametric statistic (e.g., Mann–Whitney U), and scores that are very reliable. The power of a study should be estimated when the study is planned but *before* the data are collected (Wilkinson & the Task Force on Statistical Inference, 1999). Ideally, power should be as high as possible, such as > .85. If power is only about .50, then the odds of rejecting a false null hypothesis are no greater than guessing the outcome of a coin toss. In fact, tossing a coin instead of conducting the study would be just as likely to give the correct decision and would save time and money, too (Schmidt & Hunter, 1997). How to estimate power in SEM is described in a later chapter, but the typical power of certain kinds of statistical tests in SEM are often relatively low even in large samples.

The type of null hypothesis tested most often in the behavioral sciences is a **nil hypothesis**, which says that the value of a population parameter or the difference between two parameters is zero. A nil hypothesis for the t-test of a mean contrast is

$$H_0: \mu_1 - \mu_2 = 0$$

(i.e., $H_0: \mu_1 = \mu_2$), which predicts that two population means are exactly equal. However, it is unlikely that the value of *any* population parameter (or difference between two parameters) is exactly zero, especially if zero implies the complete absence of an effect or association. It is also possible to specify a **non-nil hypothesis** for the t-test, such as

$$H_0: \mu_1 - \mu_2 = 5.00$$

but this is rarely done in practice. As the name suggests, a non-nil hypothesis is a statement that a population difference or effect is not zero.

It is more difficult to specify and test non-nil hypotheses for other types of statistical tests, such as the F-test when comparing ≥ 3 means. This is because computer programs almost always assume a nil hypothesis. Nil hypotheses may be appropriate when it is unknown whether effects exist at all, such as in new research areas where studies are mostly exploratory. Such hypotheses are less suitable in established research areas when it is already known that an effect is probably not zero. Perhaps most statistical results reported in literature are associated with nil hypotheses that are implausible. An example of an implausible nil hypothesis in the environmental sciences is the assumption of equal survival probabilities for juvenile and adult members of a species (Anderson, Burnham, & Thompson, 2000). When a nil hypothesis is implausible, then (1) it is a "straw man" argument (a fallacy) that is easily rejected and (2) estimated probabilities of data (p) under that unlikely hypothesis are too low.

It is important not to misinterpret the outcome of a statistical test in any type of data analysis. See Topic Box 2.1 for a review of the "Big Five" misinterpretations of statistical significance.

Statistical Tests in SEM

Here is a critical point about statistical tests in SEM: In ML estimation (and in some other methods, too), *standard errors are generally calculated for the unstandardized solution only.* You can see this fact when you look through the output of an SEM computer tool and find no standard errors printed for standardized estimates. This means that

---

TOPIC BOX 2.1

The "Big Five" Misinterpretations of Statistical Significance*

There is ample evidence that many of us do not know the correct interpretation of outcomes of statistical tests, or p values. For example, at the end of a standard statistics course, most students know how to calculate statistical tests, but they do not typically understand what the results mean (Haller & Krauss, 2002). About 80% of psychology professors endorse at least one incorrect interpretation of statistical tests (Oakes, 1986). It is easy to find similar misinterpretations in books and articles (Cohen, 1994), so it seems that psychology students get their false beliefs from teachers and also from what students read. However, the situation is no better in other behavioral science disciplines (e.g., Hubbard & Armstrong, 2006).

Most misunderstandings about statistical tests involve overinterpretation, or the tendency to see too much meaning in statistical significance. Specifically, we tend to believe that statistical tests tell us what we want to know, but this is wishful thinking. Elsewhere I described statistical tests as a kind of collective Rorschach inkblot test for the behavioral sciences in that what we see in them has more to do with fantasy than with what is really there (Kline, 2004). Such wishful thinking is so pervasive that one could argue that much of our practice of hypothesis testing based on statistical tests is myth.

In order to better understand misinterpretations of p values, let us first deal with their correct meaning. Here it helps to adopt a **frequentist perspective** where probability is seen as the likelihood of an outcome over repeatable events under constant conditions except for chance (sampling error). From this view, a probability does not apply directly to a single, discrete event. Instead, probabil-

*Part of this presentation is based on Kline (2009, chap. 5).

ity is based on the expected relative frequency over a large number of trials, or in the long run. Also, there is no probability associated with whether or not a particular guess is correct in a frequentist perspective. The following mental exercises illustrate this point:

1. A die is thrown, and the outcome is a 2. What is the probability that this particular result is due to chance? The correct answer is *not* $p = 1/6$, or .17. This is because the probability .17 applies only in the long run to repeated throws of the die. In this case, we expect that .17 of the outcomes will be a 2. The probability that any particular outcome of the roll of a die is the result of chance is actually $p = 1.00$.

2. One person thinks of a number from 1 to 10. A second person guesses that number by saying, 6. What is the probability that the second person guessed right? The correct answer is *not* $p = 1/10$, or .10. This is because the particular guess of 6 is either correct or incorrect, so no probability (other than 0 for "wrong" or 1.00 for "right") is associated with it. The probability .10 applies only in the long run after many repetitions of this game. That is, the second person should be correct about 10% of the time over all trials.

Let us now review the correct interpretation of statistical significance. You should know that the abbreviation p actually stands for the conditional relative-frequency probability:

$$p \left(\begin{array}{c} \text{Result or} \\ \text{more extreme} \end{array} \middle| \begin{array}{c} H_0 \text{ true, random sampling,} \\ \text{other assumptions} \end{array} \right)$$

which is the likelihood of a sample result or one even more extreme (a range of results) assuming that the null hypothesis is true, the sampling method is random sampling, and all other assumptions for the corresponding test statistic, such as the normality requirement of the t-test, are tenable. Two correct interpretations for the specific case $p < .05$ are given next. Other correct definitions are probably just variations of the ones that follow:

1. Assuming that H_0 is true (i.e., every result happens by chance) and the study is repeated many times by drawing random samples from the same population, less than 5% of these results will be even more inconsistent with H_0 than the particular result observed in the researcher's sample.

2. Less than 5% of test statistics from random samples are further away from the mean of the sampling distribution under H_0 than the one for the observed result. That is, the odds are less than 1 to 19 of getting a result from a random sample even more extreme than the observed one.

Described next are what I refer to as the "Big Five" false beliefs about p values.

Three of the beliefs concern misinterpretation of p, but two concern misinterpretations of their complements, or $1 - p$. Approximate base rates for some of these beliefs, reported by Oakes (1986) and Haller and Krauss (2002) in samples of psychology students and professors, are reported beginning in the next paragraph. What I believe is the biggest of the Big Five is the **odds-against-chance fallacy**, or the false belief that p indicates the probability that a result happened by chance (e.g., if $p < .05$, then the likelihood that the result is due to chance is $< 5\%$). Remember that p is estimated for a range of results, not for any particular result. Also, p is calculated assuming that H_0 is true, so the probability that chance explains any individual result is already taken to be 1.0. Thus, it is illogical to view p as somehow measuring the probability of chance. I am not aware of an estimate of the base rate of the odds-against-chance fallacy, but I think that it is nearly universal in the behavioral sciences. It would be terrific if some statistical technique could estimate the probability that a particular result is due to chance, but there is no such thing.

The **local Type I error fallacy** for the case $p < .05$ is expressed as follows: I just rejected H_0 at the .05 level. Therefore, the likelihood that this particular (local) decision is wrong (a Type I error) is $< 5\%$ (70% approximate base rate among psychology students and professors). This belief is false because any particular decision to reject H_0 is either correct or incorrect, so no probability (other than 0 or 1.00; i.e., right or wrong) is associated with it. It is only with sufficient replication that we could determine whether or not the decision to reject H_0 in a particular study was correct. The **inverse probability fallacy** goes like this: Given $p < .05$; therefore, the likelihood that the null hypothesis is true is $< 5\%$ (30% approximate base rate). This error stems from forgetting that p values are probabilities of data under H_0, not the other way around. It would be nice to know the probability that either the null hypothesis or alternative hypothesis were true, but there is no statistical technique that can do so based on a single result.

Two of the Big Five concern $1 - p$. One is the **replicability fallacy**, which for the case of $p < .05$ says that the probability of finding the same result in a replication sample exceeds .95 (40% approximate base rate). If this fallacy were true, knowing the probability of replication would be useful. Unfortunately, a p value is just the probability of the data in a particular sample under a specific null hypothesis. In general, replication is a matter of experimental design and whether some effect actually exists in the population. It is thus an empirical question and one that cannot be directly addressed by statistical tests in a particular study. Here I should mention Killeen's (2005) p_{rep} statistic, which is a mathematical transformation of $1 - p$ (i.e., generally, $p_{rep} \neq 1 - p$) that *estimates* the average probability of getting a result of the same sign (direction) in a hypothetical replication, assuming random sampling. Killeen suggested that p_{rep} may be less subject to misinterpretation than p values, but not everyone agrees (e.g., Cumming, 2005). It is better to actually conduct replication studies than rely on statistical prediction.

The last of the Big Five, the **validity fallacy**, refers to the false belief that the probability that H_1 is true is greater than .95, given $p < .05$ (50% approximate base rate). The complement of p, or $1 - p$, is also a probability, but it is just the probability of getting a result even *less* extreme under H_0 than the one actually found. Again, p refers to the probability of the data, not to that of any particular hypothesis, H_0 or H_1. See Kline (2004, chap. 3) or Kline (2009, chap. 5) for descriptions of additional false beliefs about statistical significance.

It is pertinent to consider one last myth about statistical tests, and it is the view that the .05 and .01 levels of statistical significance, or α, are somehow universal or objective "golden rules" that apply across all studies and research areas. It is true that these levels of α are the conventional standards used today. They are generally attributed to Carl Fisher, but he did *not* advocate that these values be applied across all studies (e.g., Fisher, 1956). There are ways in decision theory to empirically determine the optimal level of α given estimate of the costs of various types of decision errors (Type I vs. Type II error), but these methods are almost never used in the behavioral sciences. Instead, most of us automatically use $\alpha = .05$ or $\alpha = .01$ without acknowledging that these particular levels are arbitrary. Even worse, some of us may embrace the **sanctification fallacy**, which refers to dichotomous thinking about p values that are actually continuous. If $\alpha = .05$, for example, then a result where $p = .049$ versus one where $p = .051$ is practically identical in terms of statistical outcomes. However, we usually make a big deal about the first (it's significant!) but ignore the second. (Or worse, we interpret it as a "trend" as though it was really "trying" to be significant, but fell just short.) This type of black-and-white thinking is out of proportion to continuous changes in p values. There are other areas in SEM where we commit the sanctification fallacy, and these will be considered in Chapter 8. This thought from the astronomer Carl Sagan (1996) is apropos: "When we are self-indulgent and uncritical, when we confuse hopes and facts, we slide into pseudoscience and superstition" (p. 27). Let there be no superstition between us concerning statistical significance going forward from this point.

results of statistical tests are available only for unstandardized estimates. Researchers often assume that results of statistical tests of unstandardized estimates apply to the corresponding standardized estimates. For samples that are large and representative, this assumption may not be problematic. You should realize, however, that the level of statistical significance for an unstandardized estimate does not automatically apply to its standardized counterpart. This is true in part because standardized estimates have their own standard errors, and the ratio of a standardized statistic over its standard error may not correspond to the same p value as the ratio of that statistic's unstandardized counterpart over its standard error. This is why you should (1) always report the unstandardized estimates with their standard errors and (2) not associate results of statistical tests for unstandardized estimates with the corresponding standardized estimates. An example follows.

Suppose in ML estimation that the values of an unstandardized estimate, its standard error, and the standardized estimate are, respectively, 4.20, 2.00, and .60. In a large sample, the unstandardized estimate would be statistically significant at the .05 level because $z = 4.20/2.00$, or 2.10, which exceeds the critical value (1.96) at $p < .05$. Whether the standardized estimate of .60 is also statistically significant at $p < .05$ is unknown because it has no standard error. Consequently, it would be inappropriate to report the standardized estimate by itself as

$$\times\ .60*$$

where the asterisk designates $p < .05$. It is better to report both the unstandardized and standardized estimates and also the standard error of the former, like this

$$\checkmark\ 4.20*\ (2.10)\ .60$$

where the standard error is given in parentheses and the asterisk is associated with the unstandardized estimate (4.20), not the unstandardized one (.60). Special methods in SEM for estimating correct standard errors for the standardized solution are described in Chapter 7.

Central and Noncentral Test Distributions

Conventional tests of statistical significance are based on central test distributions. A **central test distribution** assumes that the null hypothesis is true, and tables of critical values for distributions such as t, F, and χ^2 found in many introductory statistics textbooks are based on central test distributions. In a **noncentral test distribution**, however, the null hypothesis is *not* assumed to be true. Some perspective is in order. Families of central test distributions of t, F, and χ^2 are special cases of noncentral distributions of each test statistic just mentioned. Compared to central distributions, noncentral distributions have an extra parameter called the **noncentrality parameter**, which is often represented in the quantitative literature by the symbol Δ for the t statistic and by λ for the F and χ^2 statistics. This extra parameter indicates the degree of departure from the null hypothesis. An example follows.

Central t-distributions are described by a single parameter, the degrees of freedom df, but noncentral t-distributions are described by both df and Δ. Presented in Figure 2.3

are two t-distributions each where $df = 10$. For the central t-distribution in the left part of the figure, $\Delta = 0$. However, $\Delta = 4.17$ for the noncentral t-distribution in the right side of the figure. Note that the latter distribution in Figure 2.3 is positively skewed. The same thing happens but in the opposite direction for negative values of Δ for t-distributions. In a two-sample design, the positive skew in the noncentral t-distribution would arise due to sampling of positive mean differences because $\mu_1 - \mu_2 > 0$ (i.e., H_0: $\mu_1 - \mu_2 = 0$ is false).

Noncentral test distributions play an important role in certain types of statistical analyses. Computer programs that estimate power as a function of study characteristics and the expected population effect size analyze noncentral test distributions. This is because the concept of power assumes that the null hypothesis is false, and in a power analysis it is false to the degree indicated by the hypothesized effect size. A nonzero effect size generally corresponds to a value of the noncentrality parameter that is also not zero. Another application is the estimation of confidence intervals based on sample statistics that measure effect size, such as standardized mean differences (d) for mean contrasts or R^2 in regression analyses. Effect size estimation also assumes that the null hypothesis—especially when it is a nil hypothesis—is false. See Kline (2004) for more information about confidence intervals for effect sizes.

In SEM, some measures of model fit are based on noncentral test distributions, especially noncentral χ^2-distributions. These statistics indicate the degree of **approxi-**

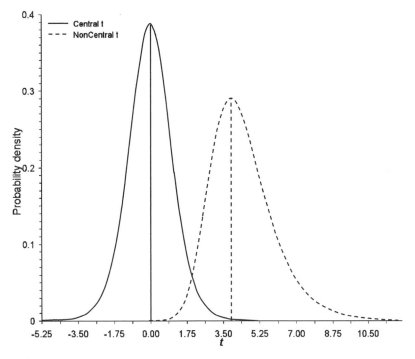

FIGURE 2.3. Distributions of central t and noncentral t for 10 degrees of freedom and where the noncentrality parameter equals 4.17 for noncentral t.

mate fit of your model to the data. That is, these fit indexes allow for an "acceptable" amount of departure from **exact fit** or **perfect fit** between model and data. What is considered "acceptable" departure from perfection is related to the estimated value of the noncentrality parameter for the χ^2 statistic that the computer calculates for your model. Other fit statistics in SEM measure the degree of departure from perfect fit, and these indexes are generally described by central χ^2-distributions. Assessment of model fit against these two standards, exact versus approximation, is covered in Chapter 8.

BOOTSTRAPPING

Bootstrapping is a computer-based method of resampling developed by B. Efron (e.g., 1979). There are two general kinds of bootstrapping. In **nonparametric bootstrapping**, your sample (i.e., data file) is treated as a pseudopopulation. Cases from the original data set are randomly selected with replacement to generate other data sets, usually with the same number of cases as the original. Because of sampling with replacement, (1) the same case can appear in more than one generated data set and (2) the composition of cases will vary slightly across the generated samples. When repeated many times (e.g., 1,000), bootstrapping simulates the drawing of numerous random samples from a population. Standard errors are estimated in this method as the standard deviation in the empirical sampling distribution of the same statistic across all generated samples. Nonparametric bootstrapping generally assumes only that the sample distribution has the same shape as that of the population distribution. In contrast, the distributional assumptions of many standard statistical tests, such as the t-test for means, are more demanding (e.g., normal and equally variable population distributions). A raw data file is necessary for nonparametric bootstrapping. This is not true in **parametric bootstrapping**, where the computer randomly samples from a theoretical probability density function specified by the researcher. This is a kind of Monte Carlo method that is used in computer simulation studies of the properties of particular estimators, including those of many used in SEM that measure model fit.

It is important to realize that bootstrapping is not a magical technique that can somehow compensate for small or unrepresentative samples, severely non-normal distributions, or the absence of actual replication samples. In fact, bootstrapping can potentially magnify the effects of unusual features in a small data set (Rodgers, 1999). More and more SEM computer programs, including Amos, EQS, LISREL, and Mplus, feature optional bootstrap methods. Some of these methods can be used to estimate the standard errors of a particular model parameter estimate or a fit statistic; bootstrapping can be used to calculate confidence intervals for these statistics, too. Bootstrapping methods are also applied in SEM to estimate standard errors for non-normal or categorical data and when there are missing data.

An example of the use of nonparametric bootstrapping to empirically estimate the standard error of a Pearson correlation follows. Presented in Table 2.3 is a small data set for two continuous variables where $N = 20$ and the observed correlation is $r_{XY} = .3566$.

TABLE 2.3. Example Data Set for Nonparametric Bootstrapping

Case	X	Y	Case	X	Y
A	12	16	K	16	37
B	12	46	L	13	51
C	21	66	M	18	32
D	16	70	N	12	53
E	18	27	O	22	52
F	16	27	P	12	34
G	16	44	Q	22	54
H	14	69	R	12	5
I	16	22	S	14	38
J	18	61	T	14	38

I used the nonparametric bootstrap procedure of SimStat for Windows (Version 2.5.5; Provalis Research, 1995–2004[8]) to resample from the data set in Table 2.3 in order to generate a total of 1,000 bootstrapped samples each with 20 cases. Presented in Figure 2.4 is the empirical sampling distribution of r_{XY} across the 1,000 bootstrapped samples. SimStat reported that the mean of this distribution is .3482 and the standard deviation is .1861. The former result (.3482) is close to the observed correlation (.3566), and the latter (.1861) is actually the bootstrapped estimate of the standard error of the observed correlation. The 95% bootstrapped confidence interval calculated by SimStat based on the distribution in the figure is –.0402 to .6490, and the bias-adjusted confidence interval is –.0402 to .6358.[9] One could use the method of nonparametric bootstrapping to estimate standard errors or confidence intervals for multiple correlations, too.

SUMMARY

Reviewed in this chapter were fundamental statistical concepts that underlie many aspects of SEM. One of these is the idea of statistical control—the partialing out of variables from other variables, a standard feature of most models in SEM. A related idea is that of spuriousness, which happens when an observed association between two variables disappears when controlling for common causes. The phenomenon of suppression is also related to statistical control. Suppression occurs in some cases when the sign of the adjusted relation between two variables differs from that of their bivariate correlation. One lesson of suppression is that values of observed correlations can mask true relations between variables once intercorrelations with other variables are controlled. Another is the importance of including all relevant predictors in the analysis. This is because the omission of predictors that are correlated with those included in the model is a specification error that may bias the results. Special issues concerning statistical

---

[8]You can download a free 30-day trial version of the full version of SimStat from *www.provalisresearch.com*

[9]In nonparametric bootstrapping, bias correction controls for lack of dependence due to possible selection of the same case ≥ 2 times in the same generated sample.

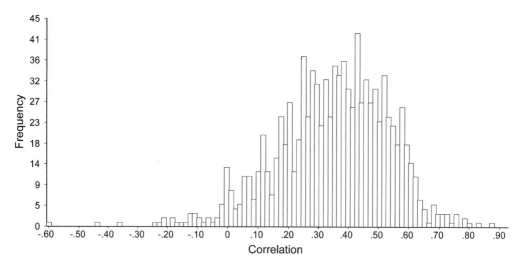

FIGURE 2.4. Empirical sampling distribution for the Pearson correlation r_{XY} in 1,000 bootstrapped samples for the data in Table 2.3.

tests were also considered, including the need to avoid common misinterpretations of statistical significance. Results of statistical tests in SEM generally apply to unstandardized estimates only, not to the corresponding standardized estimates. Also reviewed in this chapter was the basic logic of bootstrapping, a resampling technique that can be applied to estimate standard errors for statistics with complex distributions.

RECOMMENDED READINGS

The book by Cohen, Cohen, West, and Aiken (2003) is considered by many as a kind of "bible" of the multiple regression technique. The suggested chapters in Kline (2004) concern the correct interpretation of statistical tests and related statistics, such as standard errors (chaps. 1–3), and an introduction to bootstrapping (chap. 9). A more comprehensive review of bootstrap methods for estimation, regression, forecasting, and simulation is available in Chernick (2008).

Chernick, M. R. (2008). *Bootstrap methods: A guide for practitioners and researchers* (2nd ed.). Hoboken, NJ: Wiley.

Cohen, J., Cohen, P., West, S. G., & Aiken, L. S. (2003). *Applied multiple regression/correlation analysis for the behavioral sciences* (3rd ed.). Mahwah, NJ: Erlbaum.

Kline, R. B. (2004). *Beyond significance testing: Reforming data analysis methods in behavioral research.* Washington, DC: American Psychological Association.

EXERCISES

1. For the data in Table 2.1, calculate $R_{Y\cdot12}$, the unstandardized regression equation, and the standardized regression weights. Interpret the results assuming X_1, X_2, and Y are, respectively, measures of working memory, phonics skill, and reading achievement.

2. Calculate scores on $\hat{Y}$ and $Y - \hat{Y}$ for the data in Table 2.1. Show that $R_{Y\cdot12} = r_{Y\hat{Y}}$. Also show that the equality expressed in Equation 2.2 is true.

3. Calculate scores on $\hat{z}_Y$ and $z_Y - \hat{z}_Y$ for the data in Table 2.1. Show that the residuals in standardized form are uncorrelated with each predictor in standardized form.

4. Calculate a shrinkage-corrected $R^2_{Y\cdot12}$ for the data in Table 2.1. Interpret the results.

5. Calculate $R_{Y\cdot12}$, b_1, and b_2, given $r_{Y1} = .40$, $r_{Y2} = .50$, and $r_{12} = -.30$. Describe the results.

6. Use Equation 2.10 to calculate the partial correlation between X and Y controlling for W, given these Pearson correlations: $r_{XY} = .50$, $r_{XW} = .80$, and $r_{YW} = .60$.

7. Suppose that the 95% confidence interval for the difference between two means in a particular sample is 75.25–84.60. Explain what is wrong with this statement: "There is a 95% chance that the interval 75.25–84.60 contains the population mean difference $\mu_1 - \mu_2$."

8. Find three incorrect definitions of statistical significance on the Internet. *Hint:* In Google, type "define: statistical significance." Explain what is wrong with each.

3

Data Preparation

The main topics of this chapter—data preparation and screening—are critical for two reasons. First, the most widely used estimation methods in SEM make specific distributional assumptions about the data. These assumptions must be taken seriously because violation of them could result in bias. Second, data-related problems can make SEM computer programs fail to yield a logical solution. A researcher who has not properly prepared and screened the data could mistakenly believe that the model is at fault. Also reviewed are concepts from measurement theory about score reliability and validity. It is not possible to cover all aspects of data screening and psychometrics in a single chapter, but more advanced works are cited throughout, and these should be consulted for more information. This adage attributed to Abraham Lincoln sets the tone for this chapter: If I had eight hours to chop down a tree, I'd spend six sharpening my axe.

FORMS OF INPUT DATA

Most primary researchers—those who conduct original studies—input raw data files for a **primary analysis** with SEM computer programs. These same researchers may be surprised to learn that the raw data themselves are not necessary for many—and perhaps most—types of SEM. This is also true, however, for many other statistical techniques. For example, presented in the top part of Table 3.1 is syntax that instructs SPSS to conduct a one-way analysis of variance (ANOVA) using only summary statistics that include group means, standard deviations, and sizes. In the bottom part of the table is SPSS syntax for conducting a multiple regression analysis with summary statistics that include the sample correlation matrix, means, and standard deviations. The "Matrix Data" commands in both sets of syntax define the summary statistics.

The capability to analyze summary statistics provides the basis for a **secondary analysis** where data collected by others are reanalyzed but where the raw data are

TABLE 3.1. Examples in SPSS Syntax of Statistical Analyses Conducted with Summary Statistics

<u>Analysis of variance</u>

```
comment one-way anova with summary statistics.
matrix data variables=GROUP rowtype_ DV/factors=GROUP.
begin data
1 n 50
2 n 55
3 n 65
1 mean 66.25
2 mean 60.25
3 mean 69.30
1 sd 23.50
2 sd 23.25
3 sd 22.95
end data.
oneway DV by GROUP/statistics=descriptives/matrix=in(*).
```

<u>Multiple regression</u>

```
comment mr with summary statistics.
matrix data variables=v1 to v4/contents=mean sd n corr
  /format=lower nodiagonal.
begin data
10.25 8.50 9.15 5.40
3.45 4.50 7.35 5.30
100 100 100 100
.35
.40 .30
.30 .35 .50
end data.
regression matrix=in(*)/variables=v1 to v4/dependent=v4/enter.
```

unavailable. The technique of meta-analysis is a type of secondary analysis in which summary statistics from a set of primary studies are analyzed altogether. Many journal articles about the results of SEM contain enough information, such as correlations and standard deviations, to create a matrix summary of the data, which can then be submitted to a computer program for analysis. Thus, readers of these works can, with no access to the raw data, replicate the original analyses or estimate alternative models not considered in the original work. You can replicate analyses described in this book using the data matrix summaries that accompany each example (see p. 3). This is a great way to learn because you can make mistakes using someone's data before analyzing your own.

Basically all SEM computer tools accept either a raw data file or a matrix summary of the data. If a raw data file is submitted, the program will create its own matrix, which is then analyzed. You should consider the following issues when choosing between a raw data file and a matrix summary as program input:

1. Some special kinds of analyses require raw data files. One is when non-normal data are analyzed with an estimation method that assumes normality—this includes the default method of maximum likelihood (ML)—but test statistics are calculated that correct for non-normality. You should know that default ML estimation does *not* handle incomplete raw data files. However, there are special forms of ML estimation available in some SEM computer tools—including Amos, EQS, LISREL, and Mplus—for analyzing incomplete data sets. For analyses that do not involve any of these applications—and many do not—either the raw data or a matrix summary of them can be analyzed.

2. Matrix input offers a potential economy over raw data files. Suppose that 1,000 cases are measured on 10 variables. The raw data file may be 1,000 lines (or more) in length, but a matrix summary for the same data might be only 10 lines long.

3. Sometimes one might "make up" a data matrix using theory or results from a meta-analysis, so there are no raw data, only a matrix summary. A made-up data matrix can be submitted to an SEM computer tool for analysis. This is also a way to diagnose certain technical problems that can crop up in SEM. This point is elaborated in later chapters.

If means are not analyzed, there are two basic types of summaries of raw data—correlation matrices with standard deviations and covariance matrices. For example, presented in the top part of Table 3.2 are the correlation matrix with standard deviations (left) and the covariance matrix (right) for the raw data in Table 2.1 on three variables. (Whenever possible, four-decimal accuracy is recommended for matrix input. Precision at this level helps to minimize rounding error in computer analysis.) Both of these matrices in Table 3.2 are in **lower diagonal form** where only the unique values of correlations or covariances are reported in the lower-left-hand side of the matrix. Most SEM computer programs accept lower diagonal matrices as an alternative to full ones,

TABLE 3.2. Matrix Summaries of the Data in Table 2.1

Variables			Variables		
X_1	X_2	Y	X_1	X_2	Y
Summaries without means					
Correlations, standard deviations			Covariances		
1.0000			38.5000		
.4699	1.0000		42.5000	212.5000	
.6013	.7496	1.0000	17.5000	51.2500	22.0000
6.2048	14.5773	4.6904			
Summaries with means					
Correlations, standard deviations, means			Covariances, means		
1.0000			38.5000		
.4699	1.0000		42.5000	212.5000	
.6013	.7496	1.0000	17.5000	51.2500	22.0000
6.2048	14.5773	4.6904	11.0000	60.0000	25.0000
11.0000	60.0000	25.0000			

with (redundant) entries above and below the diagonal, and can "assemble" a covariance matrix given the correlations and standard deviations.

It may be problematic to submit for analysis just a correlation matrix without standard deviations or specify that all standard deviations equal 1.0, which standardizes everything.[1] This is because the default method of ML estimation (and most other methods, too) assumes that the variables are unstandardized. This means that if a correlation matrix without standard deviations is analyzed, the results may not be correct. This point is elaborated in Chapter 7 about estimation, but potential problems include the derivation of incorrect standard errors for standardized estimates if special methods for standardized variables are not used. Some SEM computer programs give warning messages or terminate the run if the researcher requests the analysis of a correlation matrix only with standard ML estimation. Thus, it is generally safer to analyze a covariance matrix or a correlation matrix with standard deviations. Accordingly, covariances are analyzed for almost all of the examples presented in this book. When a correlation matrix only is analyzed, I use a special method described in Chapter 7 for standardized variables. The issues just discussed about the pitfalls of analyzing correlation matrices without standard deviations explain why you must clearly state in written reports the specific kind of data matrix analyzed and the estimation method used to do so.

Matrix summaries of raw data must consist of the covariances *and* means whenever means are analyzed in SEM. Presented in the lower part of Table 3.2 are matrix summaries of the data in Table 2.1 that include the correlations, standard deviations, and means (left) and the covariances and means (right). Both of these matrices convey the same information. Even if your analysis does not concern means, you should nevertheless report the means of all variables. You may not be interested in analyzing the means, but someone else may be. Always report sufficient summary statistics (including the means) so that others can reproduce your results in a secondary analysis (McDonald & Ho, 2002).

POSITIVE DEFINITENESS

The data matrix that you submit for analysis to an SEM computer tool should have the property that it is **positive definite** (PD), which is required for most estimation methods. A matrix that lacks this characteristic is **nonpositive definite** (NPD), and attempts to analyze such a data matrix will probably fail. A PD data matrix has the properties summarized next (Wothke, 1993):

1. The matrix is **nonsingular**, or invertible. In most kinds of multivariate analyses (SEM included), the computer needs to derive the inverse of the data matrix as part of linear algebra operations. A matrix that is not invertible is **singular**.

---

[1]By the same token, it would also be problematic to convert raw scores to z scores and then submit for analysis the data file of standardized scores.

2. All eigenvalues of PD matrices are positive (> 0). An **eigenvalue** is the variance of an **eigenvector**, which is a linear combination of the observed variables where all the weights are not zero. An eigenvalue is the unstandardized proportion of variance explained by the corresponding eigenvector, and the variance of that composite (its eigenvalue) cannot logically be less than zero. The total number of pairs of eigenvalues and eigenvectors for a data matrix equals the number of observed variables. For example, if a covariance matrix is based on 10 variables, then there are a total of 10 eigenvalue-eigenvector pairs.

3. A related property is that the **determinant** of a PD matrix is greater than zero. If the determinant is zero, then the matrix is singular. A determinant equals the serial product (the first times the second times the third, and so on) of the eigenvalues, so if a determinant is negative, then some odd number of the eigenvalues (1 or 3 or 5, etc.) must be negative. A negative determinant indicates an NPD matrix.

4. In a PD data matrix, none of the correlations or covariances are **out of bounds**. An out-of-bounds matrix element is one that would be mathematically impossible to derive if all entries were calculated using data from the same cases. This property is explained next.

The value of the Pearson correlation between two variables X and Y is limited by the correlations between these variables and a third variable W. Specifically, the value of r_{XY} must fall within the following range:

$$(r_{XW} \times r_{YW}) \pm \sqrt{(1 - r_{XW}^2)(1 - r_{YW}^2)} \qquad (3.1)$$

For example, if $r_{XW} = .60$ and $r_{YW} = .40$, then the value of r_{XY} must be within the range $.24 \pm .73$ (i.e., $-.49-.97$). Any other value for r_{XY} would be out of bounds. Another way to view Equation 3.1 is that it specifies a **triangle inequality** for values of correlations among three variables measured in the same sample.[2]

In a PD data matrix, the maximum absolute value of cov_{XY}, the covariance between X and Y, must respect the upper limit defined next:

$$\max \left| cov_{XY} \right| \leq \sqrt{s_X^2 \, s_Y^2} \qquad (3.2)$$

where s_X^2 and s_Y^2 are, respectively, the sample variances of X and Y. In words, the maximum absolute value for the covariance between any two variables is less than or equal to the square root of the product of their variances. Otherwise, the value of cov_{XY} is out of bounds. For example, given

$$cov_{XY} = 13.00, \quad s_X^2 = 12.00, \quad \text{and } s_Y^2 = 10.00$$

---

[2]In a geometric triangle, the length of a given side must be less than the sum of the lengths of the other two sides but greater than the difference between the lengths of the two sides.

then the covariance between X and Y would be out of bounds because

$$13.00 > (12.00 \times 10.00)^{1/2} = 10.95$$

which violates Equation 3.2. The value of r_{XY} for this example is also out of bounds because it equals 1.19. An exercise will ask you to verify this fact.

An NPD data matrix has at least one eigenvalue ≤ 0. Many computer programs for multivariate statistical analyses, including those for SEM, print eigenvalues in the output, so this sign of trouble is apparent. An eigenvalue of zero indicates that the matrix is singular. A negative eigenvalue could indicate a few different problems. One is the presence of an out-of-bounds entry in the data matrix (i.e., Equations 3.1–3.2 do not hold). Another is perfect collinearity either between a pair of variables (e.g., $r_{XY} = 1.00$) or between a variable and at least two others (e.g., $R_{Y \cdot XW} = 1.00$). It can also happen that near-perfect collinearity (e.g., $r_{XY} = .95$) manifested as positive but near-zero eigenvalues can cause matrix inversion operations to fail. It is easy to spot bivariate collinearity by inspecting the correlation matrix. A way to detect multivariate collinearity among three or more variables is described later in this chapter. See Topic Box 3.1 for more information about causes of nonpositive definiteness in the data matrix and possible solutions.

DATA SCREENING

Before analyzing in SEM either a raw data file or a matrix summary, the original data file should be screened for the problems considered next. Some of these potential problems are causes of NPD data matrices, but others concern distributional assumptions for continuous outcomes.

Collinearity

Extreme collinearity can occur because what appear to be separate variables actually measure the same thing. Suppose that X measures accuracy and Y measures speed. If $r_{XY} = .95$, for example, then variables X and Y are redundant despite their different labels (speed is accuracy and vice versa). Either one or the other could be included in the same analysis, but not both. Researchers can inadvertently cause extreme collinearity when composite variables and their constituent variables are analyzed together. Suppose that a questionnaire has 10 items and the total score is summed across the items. Although the bivariate correlations between the total score and each of the individual items may not be high, the multiple correlation between the total score and the items must equal 1.00, which is collinearity in its most extreme form.

Some methods and statistics to detect collinearity among three or more variables are summarized next. Most of these are available in regression diagnostics procedures of programs for general statistical analyses, such as SPSS and SAS/STAT:

TOPIC BOX 3.1

Causes of Nonpositive Definiteness and Solutions

Many points summarized here are from Wothke (1993).* Some causes of nonpositive definite (NPD) data matrices are listed next. Most can be detected through careful data screening:

1. Extreme bivariate or multivariate collinearity among the observed variables.
2. The presence of outliers, especially those that force values of correlations to be extremely high.
3. Pairwise deletion of cases with missing data.
4. Making a typing mistake when transcribing a data matrix from one source, such as a table in a journal article, to another, such as a command file for computer analysis, can also result in an NPD matrix. For example, if the value of a covariance in the original matrix is 15.00, then mistakenly typing 150.00 in the transcribed matrix could generate an NPD covariance matrix with elements that violate Equation 3.2. It is so easy to make a typing mistake during manual entry of a data matrix that errors are almost guaranteed, especially when the number of variables exceeds 10 or so. Follow this simple but effective advice from Wilkinson and the Task Force on Statistical Inference (1999) whenever you transcribe a data matrix: *look at the data*, that is, carefully compare, entry by entry, the original data matrix with your transcribed matrix before you attempt to analyze it with the computer.
5. Plain old sampling error can generate NPD data matrices, especially if the number of cases is relatively small or the sample is unrepresentative. The former condition can be addressed by increasing the sample size; the unrepresentativeness may be the result of using a sampling method that selects atypical cases.
6. Sometimes matrices of *estimated* Pearson correlations, such as polyserial or polychoric correlations derived for noncontinuous observed variables (Chapter 2), are NPD. This may be especially true if polyserial or polychoric correlations are estimated in a pairwise manner instead of simultaneously estimating the whole correlation matrix. Pairwise calculation of non-Pearson correlations is an older method that required less computer memory, but this goal is less relevant given today's personal computers with relatively large memory capacities. Modern computer tools, such as the PRELIS program of LISREL, can simultaneously estimate the whole correlation matrix.

*See also E. Rigdon's webpage on nonpositive definite matrices in SEM at *www2.gsu. edu/~mkteer/npdmatri.html*

Here is a tip about diagnosing whether a data matrix is positive definite before submitting it for analysis to an SEM computer program: Copy the full matrix (with redundant entries above and below the diagonal) into a text (ASCII) file, such as Microsoft Windows Notepad. Next, point your Internet browser to a free, online matrix calculator and then copy the data matrix into the proper window on the calculating webpage.* Finally, select options on the webpage to derive the determinant and eigenvalues of the data matrix. Look for outcomes that indicate nonpositive definiteness, such as near-zero, zero, or negative eigenvalues.

Some SEM computer programs, such as LISREL, offer options for making a **ridge adjustment** to an NPD data matrix. The ridge technique iteratively multiplies the diagonal entries of the matrix by a constant > 1.0 until negative eigenvalues disappear (the matrix becomes positive definite). For covariance matrices, ridge adjustments increase the values of the variances until they are large enough to exceed any out-of-bounds covariance entry in the off-diagonal part of the matrix (Equation 3.2 will be satisfied). This technique "fixes up" a data matrix so that necessary algebraic operations can be performed (Wothke, 1993). However, the resulting parameter estimates, standard errors, and model fit statistics will be biased after applying a ridge correction. For this reason, I do not recommend that you use a ridge technique to analyze an NPD data matrix unless you are very familiar with linear algebra (i.e., you know what you are doing and why). Instead, you should try to solve the problem of nonpositive definiteness through data screening or increasing the sample size.

There are other contexts where you may encounter NPD matrices in SEM, but these generally concern (1) matrices of parameter estimates for your model or (2) matrices of covariances or correlations predicted from your model that could be compared with those observed in your sample. A problem in the analysis is indicated if any of these matrices is NPD. We will deal with these contexts in later chapters.

*www.bluebit.gr/matrix-calculator/

1. Calculate a **squared multiple correlation** (R_{smc}^2) between each variable and all the rest. That is, run several multiple regressions, each with a different variable as the criterion and the rest as predictors. The observation that $R_{smc}^2 > .90$ for a particular variable analyzed as the criterion suggests extreme multivariate collinearity.

2. A related statistic is **tolerance**, which equals $1 - R_{smc}^2$ and indicates the proportion of total standardized variance that is unique (not explained by all the other variables). Tolerance values < .10 may indicate extreme multivariate collinearity.

3. Another is the **variance inflation factor** (VIF). It equals $1/(1 - R_{smc}^2)$, the ratio

of the total standardized variance over unique variance (tolerance). If the first is more than 10 times greater than the second, or VIF > 10.0, the variable in question may be redundant.

There are two basic ways to deal with extreme collinearity: eliminate variables or combine redundant ones into a composite. For example, if X and Y are highly correlated, one could be dropped or their scores could be summed (or averaged) to form a single new variable, but note that the total score (or average) must replace both X and Y in the analysis. Extreme collinearity can also happen between latent variables when their estimated correlation is so high that it is clear they are not distinct. This issue is considered in Chapter 9.

Outliers

Outliers are scores that are different from the rest. A case can have a **univariate outlier** if it is extreme on a single variable. There is no single definition of "extreme," but a common rule is that scores more than three standard deviations beyond the mean may be outliers. Univariate outliers are easy to find by inspecting frequency distributions of z scores (e.g., $| z | > 3.00$ indicates an outlier). A **multivariate outlier** has extreme scores on two or more variables, or its pattern of scores is atypical. For example, a case may have scores between two and three standard deviations above the mean on all variables. Although no individual score may be considered extreme, the case could be a multivariate outlier if this pattern is unusual in the sample.

The detection of multivariate outliers without extreme individual scores is more difficult, but there are a few options:

1. Some computer programs for SEM, such as EQS and Amos, identify cases that contribute the most to multivariate non-normality as measured by Mardia's (1970) index, and such cases may be multivariate outliers. In order for cases to be screened by the computer, a raw data file must be analyzed.

2. Another method is based on the **Mahalanobis distance** (D) statistic, which indicates the distance in standard deviation units between a set of scores (**vector**) for an individual case and the sample means for all variables (**centroid**), correcting for intercorrelations. Within large samples with normal distributions, D^2 is distributed as a central chi-square (χ^2) statistic with degrees of freedom equal to the number of variables. A value of D^2 with a low p value in the appropriate central χ^2-distribution may lead to rejection of the null hypothesis that the case comes from the same population as the rest. A conservative level of statistical significance is usually recommended for this test (e.g., $p < .001$). Some computer programs for general statistical analyses, including SPSS and SAS/STAT, can print D (or D^2) for individual cases; Amos also prints Mahalanobis distances. See Filzmoser (2005) for more information about detecting multivariate outliers.

Let us assume that an outlier is not due to a data entry error (e.g., 99 was entered instead of 9) or the failure to specify a missing data code (e.g., –9) in the data editor of a statistics computer tool; that is, the outlier is a valid score. One possibility is that the case does not belong to the population from which you intended to sample. Suppose that a senior graduate student audits a lower-level undergraduate class in which a questionnaire is distributed. The auditing student is from a different population, and his or her questionnaire responses may be extreme compared with those of classmates. If it is determined that a case with outlier scores is not from the same population as the rest, then it is best to remove that case from the sample. Otherwise, there are ways to reduce the influence of extreme scores if they are retained. One option is to convert extreme scores to a value that equals the next most extreme score that is within three standard deviations of the mean. Another is to apply a mathematical transformation to a variable with outliers. Transformations are discussed later in this chapter.

Missing Data

The topic of how to analyze data sets with missing observations is complicated. Entire books and special sections of journals (Allison, 2001; Little & Rubin, 2002; McKnight, McKnight, Sidani, & Figueredo, 2007; West, 2001) are devoted to it. This is fortunate because it is not possible here to give a comprehensive account of the topic. The goal instead is to acquaint you with basic analysis options, explain the relevance of these options to SEM, and provide references for further study.

Ideally, researchers would always work with complete data sets, ones with no missing values. Otherwise, prevention is the best approach. For example, questionnaire items that are clear and unambiguous may prevent missing responses, and completed forms should be reviewed for missing responses before research participants leave the laboratory. In the real world, missing values occur in many (if not most) data sets, despite the best efforts at prevention. Missing data occur for many reasons, including hardware failure, software bugs, missed appointments, and case attrition. A few missing values, such as less than 5% on a single variable, in a large sample may be of little concern. This is especially true if the reason for data loss is **ignorable**, which means accidental or not systematic. Selection among methods to deal with the missing observations in this case is pretty much arbitrary in that the method used does not tend to make much difference. A systematic data loss pattern, on the other hand, means that incomplete cases differ from cases with complete records for some reason, rather than randomly. Thus, results based only on the cases with complete records may not generalize to whole population. This situation is more difficult because the use of different methods for handling missing data could yield different results, perhaps all biased.

Most methods that deal with missing observations assume that the data loss pattern is ignorable. There are two general kinds of ignorable patterns, **missing at random** (MAR) and **missing completely at random** (MCAR). If the missing observations on some variable X differ from the observed scores on that variable only by chance, the data loss pattern is MAR. If, in addition to the property just mentioned, the presence versus absence of data on X is unrelated to any other variable in the data set, the data loss pattern is MCAR. Note that MCAR is just a stronger assumption about the randomness of data loss than MAR, but it may be doubtful whether the assumption of MCAR holds in real data sets.

It is not easy in practice to determine whether the data loss pattern is systematic or ignorable, especially when each variable is measured only once. This is because there is no single test that provides definitive evidence of either MAR or MCAR. Instead, researchers typically examine various features of their data for indications of systematic data loss. For example, a multivariate statistical test by R. Little concerns whether the MCAR assumption is tenable, given the data (Little & Rubin, 2002). Plausibility of the MAR assumption can be examined through a series of comparisons with the t-test of cases with missing observations on some variable with cases who have complete records on other variables. The finding of appreciable differences in these comparisons may help to identify the nature of the data loss mechanism. A related tactic involves the creation of a dummy-coded variable that indicates whether a score is missing or present and then examining cross-tabulations with other categorical variables, such as gender or treatment condition. Some computer programs for general statistical analyses have special procedures for analyzing missing data patterns. An example is the Missing Values procedure of SPSS, which can conduct all these diagnostic tests. The PRELIS module of LISREL also has extensive capabilities for analyzing missing data patterns.

There is no magic statistical "fix" that will remedy systematic data loss. About the best that can be done is to attempt to understand the nature of the underlying data loss pattern and then accordingly qualify your interpretation of the results. If the selection of one option for dealing with missing data instead of another makes a difference in the results and it is unclear which option is best, then you should report both sets of findings. This makes it plain that your results depend on how missing observations were handled. This approach is a kind of **sensitivity analysis** in which data are reanalyzed under different assumptions—here, using alternative missing data techniques—and the results are compared with the original findings. Always explain in written summaries the extent of missing observations in your sample and the steps you took to deal with them in the analysis (Burton & Altman, 2004). Too many researchers neglect to inform their readers about this critical information (e.g., Roth, 1994).

The methods for dealing with missing observations described here fall into four categories (Vriens & Melton, 2002):

1. **Available case methods** that analyze only the data available through deletion of incomplete cases. Techniques include listwise deletion and pairwise deletion.

2. **Single-imputation methods** that replace each missing score with a single calculated score. Techniques in this category include mean substitution and regression-based substitution.

3. **Model-based imputation** methods that take greater advantage of the structure in the data compared with single imputation methods, and they can generate more than

one estimated score for each missing observation, that is, **multiple imputation**. An example includes the expectation–maximization algorithm.

4.   A special form of full-information ML estimation for incomplete data sets that is applied to raw data files only and does not delete cases or impute missing observations.

Available case methods and single imputation are "classical" techniques that are available in various kinds of statistical analyses. These classical techniques are generally easy to understand, but they "are ad hoc procedures that attempt to make the best of a bad situation in ways that are seemingly plausible but have no theoretical rationale" (Arbuckle, 1996, p. 243). This is because classical techniques take little advantage of the information in the data. They also typically assume that the data loss pattern is MCAR, which is unrealistic. Classical techniques tend to yield biased estimates under the less strict assumption of MAR, and even more so when the data loss pattern is systematic. In contrast, techniques such as model-based imputation are more complicated, but they use more information in the data and generally assume a data loss pattern that is MAR, not MCAR. When the data loss pattern is not random, these more sophisticated techniques will also yield biased estimates, but perhaps less so compared with classical techniques (Arbuckle, 1996; Peters & Enders, 2002; Wiggins & Sacker, 2002).

Available Case Methods

There are two basic kinds of available case methods: listwise and pairwise deletion. In **listwise deletion**, cases with missing scores on any variable are excluded from all analyses. The effective sample size with listwise deletion includes only cases with complete records, and this number can be much smaller than the original sample if missing observations are scattered across many records. It is no surprise that standard errors estimated after applying listwise deletion are usually larger than those based on the entire data set. In regression analyses, listwise deletion of incomplete cases generates reasonably accurate estimates when the missing data mechanism depends on the predictors, but not on the criterion (Little & Rubin, 2002).

An advantage of listwise deletion is that all analyses are conducted with the same number of cases. This is not so with **pairwise deletion**, in which cases are excluded only if they have missing data on variables involved in a particular analysis. Suppose that $N = 300$ for an incomplete data set. If 280 cases have no missing scores on variables X and Y, then the effective sample size for cov_{XY} is this number. If fewer or more cases have valid scores on X and W, however, the effective sample size for cov_{XW} will not be 280. It can happen with pairwise deletion that no two terms in a covariance matrix are based on the same subset of cases. It is this property of the method that can give rise to out-of-bounds covariances or correlations. Accordingly, pairwise deletion is not generally recommended for use in SEM unless the number of missing observations is small. Presented in Table 3.3 is a small data set with scores on X, Y, and W but with missing observations on all three variables. The covariance matrix generated by pairwise deletion for these data is NPD. An exercise will ask you to verify this fact.

TABLE 3.3. Example of an Incomplete Data Set

Case	X	Y	W
A	42	8	13
B	34	10	12
C	22	12	—
D	—	14	8
E	24	16	7
F	16	—	10
G	30	—	10

Single-Imputation Methods

The most basic method is **mean substitution**, which involves replacing a missing score with the overall sample mean. A variation is **group-mean substitution**, in which a missing score in a particular group (e.g., men) is replaced by the group mean. The variation may be preferred when group membership is a predictor in the analysis or when a structural equation model is analyzed over groups. Both methods are simple, but they can distort the distribution of the data by reducing variability. Suppose in a data set where $N = 75$ that 15 cases have missing values on some variable. Substituting the mean of the 60 valid cases will result in the mean for the whole sample and the mean for the $N = 60$ cases after substitution, both being equal. However, the variance for the $N = 60$ scores before substitution will be greater than the variance for the $N = 75$ scores after substitution. Mean substitution also tends to make distributions more peaked at the mean, too, which further distorts the underlying distribution of the data (Vriens & Melton, 2002).

A somewhat more sophisticated single-imputation technique is **regression-based imputation**, in which each missing score is replaced by a predicted score using multiple regression based on nonmissing scores on other variables. Suppose that there are five trials in a learning task and each trial yields a continuous score. As a result of equipment failure, the score for Trial 4 for some cases is not recorded. In this method, specify Trials 1–3 and 5 as predictors of Trial 4 (the criterion) in a regression analysis based on scores from all complete cases. From this analysis, record the values of the four unstandardized regression coefficients (B_1–B_3, B_5) and the intercept (A). An imputed score for Trial 4 is the predicted score ($\hat{Y}_4$), given scores on the other four trials (designated with X in the following equation), the regression coefficients, and the intercept, as follows:

$$\hat{Y}_4 = B_1 X_1 + B_2 X_2 + B_3 X_3 + B_5 X_5 + A$$

Regression-based substitution uses more information than mean substitution. It is best to generate predicted scores based on data from the whole sample, not from just one group. This is because regression techniques can be affected by range restriction, which can happen when scores from a particular group are less variable compared with scores for the whole sample.

A more sophisticated single-imputation method is **pattern matching**. In this method, the computer replaces a missing observation with a score from a case with the most similar profile of scores across other variables. The PRELIS program of LIS-REL can use pattern matching to impute missing observations. Another is **random hot-deck imputation**. This technique separates complete from incomplete records, sorts both sets of records so that cases with similar profiles on background variables are grouped together, randomly interleaves the incomplete cases among the complete ones, and replaces missing scores with those on the same variable from the nearest complete record. This nearest record is not guaranteed to have the most similar pattern of scores. All single-imputation methods tend to underestimate error variance, especially if the proportion of missing observations is relatively high (Vriens & Melton, 2002).

Model-Based Imputation Methods

These methods can generally replace a missing score with ≥ 1 imputed (estimated) values from a predictive distribution that explicitly models the underlying data loss mechanism. In nontechnical terms, a model for both the complete data and the incomplete data is defined under these methods. The computer then estimates means and variances in the whole sample that satisfy a statistical criterion. One model-based method is the **expectation–maximization** (EM) **algorithm**, which has two steps. In the E (expectation) step, missing observations are imputed by predicted scores in a series of regressions in which each incomplete variable is regressed on the remaining variables for a particular case. In the M (maximization) step, the whole imputed data set is submitted for ML estimation. These two steps are repeated until a stable solution is reached across the M steps. Among SEM computer tools, EM-type algorithms are available in EQS and LISREL; it is also available in the Missing Values procedure of SPSS. Two SAS/STAT procedures, MI and MIANALYZE, impute multiple values for missing observation, but they are based on a different method. See Peng, Harwell, Liou, and Ehman (2007) for more information.

Special Form of ML Estimation for Incomplete Data

This special method is available in some SEM computer tools, including Amos, Mx, LIS-REL, and Mplus, and it does not delete cases or impute missing observations. Instead, it partitions the cases in a raw data file into subsets, each with the same pattern of missing observations. Relevant statistical information, including means and variances, is extracted from each subset, so all cases are retained in the analysis. This means that parameter estimates and their standard errors are calculated directly from the available data without deletion or imputation of missing values. Arbuckle (1996), Enders and Bandalos (2001), and Peters and Enders (2002) found in computer simulation studies that special ML-based methods for incomplete data generally outperformed classical methods. See Horton and Kleinman (2007) for information about other missing data techniques.

Multivariate Normality

Estimation in SEM with ML—either the default form that does not handle missing observations or the special form that does—assumes **multivariate normality** or **multinormality** of continuous outcome variables. This means that:

1. All the individual univariate distributions are normal.
2. The joint distribution of any pair of the variables is bivariate normal; that is, each variable is normally distributed for each value of every other variable.
3. All bivariate scatterplots are linear, and the distribution of residuals is homoscedastic.

Because it is often impractical to examine all joint frequency distributions, it can be difficult to assess all aspects of multivariate normality. There are statistical tests intended to detect violation of multivariate normality, including Mardia's (1985) test and the Cox–Small test (Cox & Small, 1978), among others. However, all such tests are limited by the fact that slight departures from normality could be statistically significant in a large sample. Fortunately, many instances of multivariate nonnormality are detectable through inspection of univariate distributions.

Univariate Normality

Skew and kurtosis are two ways that a distribution can be non-normal, and they can occur either separately or together in a single variable. Skew implies that the shape of a unimodal distribution is asymmetrical about its mean. **Positive skew** indicates that most of the scores are below the mean, and **negative skew** indicates just the opposite. Presented in the top part of Figure 3.1 are examples of distributions with either positive skew or negative skew compared with a normal curve. For a unimodal, symmetrical distribution, **positive kurtosis** indicates heavier tails and a higher peak and **negative kurtosis** indicates just the opposite, both relative to a normal distribution with the same variance. A distribution with positive kurtosis is described as **leptokurtic**, and a distribution with negative kurtosis is described as **platykurtic**. Presented in the bottom part of Figure 3.1 are examples of distributions with either positive kurtosis or negative kurtosis compared with a normal curve. Note that skewed distributions are generally leptokurtic. This means that remedies for skew, such as transformations, may also fix a kurtosis problem. Blest (2003) describes a kurtosis measure that adjusts for skewness.

Extreme skew is easy to spot by inspecting graphical frequency distributions or histograms. Two other types of visual displays helpful for detecting skew are **stem-and-leaf plots** and **box plots** (**box-and-whisker plots**). For example, presented in the left part of Figure 3.2 is a stem-and-leaf plot for $N = 64$ scores. The lowest and highest scores are, respectively, 10 and 27. The latter is an outlier that is > 5 standard deviations above the mean ($M = 12.73$, $SD = 2.51$). In the stem-and-leaf plot, the numbers to the left side of the vertical line ("stems") represent the "tens" digit of each score, and each number to

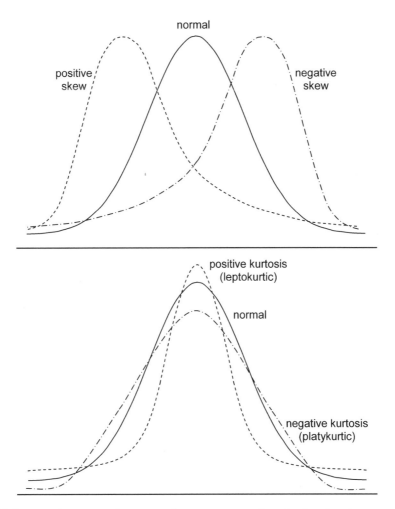

FIGURE 3.1. Distributions with positive skew or negative skew (top) and with positive kurtosis or negative kurtosis (bottom) relative to a normal curve.

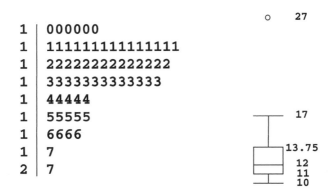

FIGURE 3.2. A stem-and-leaf plot (left) and a box plot (right) for the same distribution ($N = 64$).

the right ("leaf") represents the "ones" digit. The shape of the stem-and-leaf plot in the figure indicates positive skew.

Presented in the right side of Figure 3.2 is a box plot for the same scores. The bottom and top borders of the rectangle in a box plot correspond to, respectively, the 25th percentile (1st quartile) and the 75th percentile (3rd quartile). The line inside the rectangle of a box plot represents the median (2nd quartile). The "whiskers" are the vertical lines that connect the first and third quartiles with, respectively, the lowest and highest scores that are not extreme, or outliers. The length of the whiskers shows how far nonextreme scores spread away from the median. Skew is indicated in a box plot if the median line does not fall within the center of the rectangle or if the "whiskers" have unequal lengths. In the box plot of Figure 3.2, the 25th and 75th percentiles are, respectively, 11 and 13.75; the median is 12; and the lowest and highest scores that are not extreme are, respectively, 10 and 17. The high score of 27 is extreme and thus is represented in the box plot as a single open circle above the upper "whisker." The box plot in the figure indicates positive skew because there is a greater spread of scores above the median.

Kurtosis is harder to spot by eye when inspecting frequency distributions, stem-and-leaf plots, or box plots, especially in distributions that are more or less symmetrical. Departures from normality due to skew or kurtosis may be apparent in **normal probability plots**, in which data are plotted against a theoretical normal distribution in such a way that the points should form an approximate straight line. Otherwise, the distribution is non-normal, but it is hard to discern the degree of non-normality due to skew or kurtosis apparent in normal probability plots. An example of a normal probability plot is presented later.

Fortunately, there are more precise measures of skew and kurtosis. Perhaps the best known standardized measures of these characteristics that permit comparison of different distributions to the normal curve are the **skew index** (SI) and **kurtosis index** (KI), which are calculated as follows:

$$\text{SI} = \frac{S^3}{(S^2)^{3/2}} \quad \text{and} \quad \text{KI} = \frac{S^4}{(S^2)^2} - 3.0 \tag{3.3}$$

where S^2, S^3, and S^4 are, respectively, the second through fourth **moments about the mean**:

$$S^2 = \frac{\Sigma(X-M)^2}{N}, \ S^3 = \frac{\Sigma(X-M)^3}{N}, \text{ and } S^4 = \frac{\Sigma(X-M)^4}{N} \tag{3.4}$$

The sign of SI indicates the direction of the skew, positive or negative, and a value of zero indicates a symmetrical distribution. The value of KI in a normal distribution equals zero, and its sign indicates the type of kurtosis, positive or negative.[3]

---

[3]Some computer programs calculate the kurtosis index as KI = $S^4/(S^2)^2$. In this case, a value of 3.0 indicates a normal distribution, a value greater than 3.0 indicates positive kurtosis, and a value less than 3.0 indicates negative kurtosis.

The ratio of the value of either SI or KI over its standard error is interpreted in large samples as a *z*-test of the null hypothesis that there is no population skew or kurtosis, respectively. These tests may not be helpful in large samples because even slight departures from normality could be statistically significant. An alternative is to interpret the absolute values of SI or KI, but there are few clear-cut standards for doing so. Some guidelines can be offered, however, based on computer simulation studies of estimation methods used by SEM computer programs (e.g., Curran, West, & Finch, 1997). Variables with absolute values of SI > 3.0 are described as "extremely" skewed by some authors of these studies. There is less consensus about the KI, however—absolute values from about 8.0 to over 20.0 of this index are described as indicating "extreme" kurtosis. A conservative rule of thumb, then, seems to be that absolute values of KI > 10.0 suggest a problem, and absolute values of KI > 20.0 indicate a more serious one. For the data in Figure 3.2, SI = 3.10 and KI = 15.73. By the rules of thumb just mentioned, these data are severely non-normal. Before analyzing non-normal data with a normal theory method, such as ML, corrective action should be taken.

Transformations

One way to deal with univariate normality—and thereby address multivariate normality—is through **transformations**, meaning that the original scores are converted with a mathematical operation to new ones that may be more normally distributed. The effect of applying a transformation is to compress one part of a distribution more than another, thereby changing its shape but not the rank order of the scores. This describes a **monotonic transformation**. Transformations for three types of non-normal distributions and practical suggestions for using them are offered next. Recall that transformations for skew may also help for kurtosis:

1. *Positive skew.* Before applying these transformations, you should add a constant to the scores so that the lowest value is 1.00. A basic transformation is the square root function, or $X^{1/2}$. It works by compressing the differences between scores in the upper end of the distributions more than the differences between lower scores. Logarithmic transformations are another option. A logarithm is the power (exponent) to which a base number must be raised in order to get the original number, such as $10^2 = 100$, so the logarithm of 100 in base 10 is 2.0. In general, distributions with extremely high scores may require a transformation with a higher base, such as $\log_{10} X$, but a lower base may suffice for less extreme cases, such as the natural log base $e \cong 2.71828$ for the natural log transformation, or ln X. However, using a base that is too high for the degree of skew could result in loss of resolution. This is because gaps between higher scores could be made so small that useful information is lost. For even more extreme skew, the inverse function $1/X$ is an option. As noted by Osborne (2002), the inverse transformation makes small numbers very large and large numbers very small. Because the function $1/X$ reverses the order of the scores, it is recommended that you first reflect or reverse the original scores before taking their inverse. Scores are reflected by multiplying them by –1.0. Next, you

should add a constant to the reflected scores so that the minimum score is at least 1.0 before taking the inverse.

2. *Negative skew.* All the transformations just mentioned also work for negative skew when they are applied as follows: First, reflect the scores, and then add a constant so that the lowest score equals 1.0. Next, apply the transformation, and then reflect the scores again to restore the original ordering (Osborne, 2002).

3. *Other types of non-normality.* Odd-root functions, such as $X^{1/3}$, and sine functions tend to bring in outliers from both tails of the distribution toward the mean. Odd-powered polynomial transformations, such as X^3, may help for negative kurtosis.

There are many other kinds of transformations, and this is one of their potential problems: It can be difficult to find one that works with a particular set of scores. A class of power transformations known as **Box–Cox transformations** (Box & Cox, 1964) may require less trial and error. The most basic form of the Box–Cox transformation is defined only for positive data values, but you can always add a constant to the scores so that there are no negative values. The basic Box–Cox transformation is

$$X^{(\lambda)} = \begin{cases} \dfrac{X^\lambda - 1}{\lambda}, & \text{if } \lambda \neq 0; \\[2mm] \log X, & \text{if } \lambda = 0. \end{cases} \tag{3.5}$$

where the exponent λ is a constant selected to normalize a set of scores. There are computer algorithms for finding an optimal value of λ, one that both normalizes the scores and results in the maximum correlation between the original and transformed scores. It is relatively easy to find on the Internet macros for implementing the Box–Cox transformation in SAS/STAT (e.g., Friendly, 2006). There are many variations on the basic Box–Cox transformation, some for more specialized situations (Yeo & Johnson, 2000). Box–Cox transformations are also applied in regression analyses to deal with heteroscedasticity, which is considered momentarily.

Other potential drawbacks of transformations are briefly considered. Some distributions can be so severely non-normal that basically no transformation will work. Another problem is that the scale of the original variable is lost when scores are transformed. If that scale is meaningful, such as postoperative survival time, then its loss could be a sacrifice. Results of statistical analyses of transformed scores do not directly apply to the original scores.

An example of using transformations to normalize the scores in Figure 3.2 where SI = 3.10 and KI = 15.73 is presented next. I added a constant (–9.0) to these scores so that the lowest score is 1.0 before applying the transformation $X^{1/2}$. For the square-root-transformed scores, SI = 1.24 and KI = 4.13. Even greater reduction in nonnormality for these data is afforded by the transformation ln X, for which SI = –.04 and KI = .46 after its application.

Linearity and Homoscedasticity

Linear relations and homoscedasticity (uniform distributions) among residuals are aspects of multivariate normality. The presence of bivariate curvilinear relations is easy to detect by looking at scatterplots. It is possible in SEM to estimate curvilinear relations—and interaction effects, too—using the same basic method as in multiple regression. Chapter 12 deals with this topic.

Heteroscedasticity (nonuniform distributions) among residuals may be caused by non-normality in X or Y, more random error at some levels of X or Y than at others, or outliers. For example, presented in Figure 3.3 is a scatterplot for $N = 18$ scores. One case has an extreme score (40) on Y that is more than three standard deviations above the mean. For these data, $r_{XY} = -.074$, and the linear regression line is nearly horizontal. However, these results are affected by the outlier. When the outlier case is removed, then $r_{XY} = -.772$ for $N = 17$, and the new regression line better fits the remaining data (see Figure 3.3).

Presented in the top part of Figure 3.4 is the normal probability plot for the standardized regression residuals (converted to z scores) for the data in Figure 3.3 with the outlier included. The plotted points of the expected versus observed cumulative probabilities for the residuals clearly do not fall along a diagonal line. Presented in the middle part of Figure 3.4 is the histogram of the standardized residuals for the same data with a superimposed normal curve. Both kinds of displays just described indicate that the residuals for the data in Figure 3.3 are not normally distributed when the outlier is included. At the bottom of Figure 3.4 is a scatterplot of the standardized residuals against the standardized predicted scores ($\hat{z}_Y$) for the same data. The residuals are not evenly distributed around zero throughout the entire length of this scatterplot. See Belsley, Kuh, and Welsch (2004) for more information about regression diagnostics.

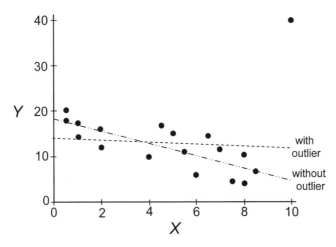

FIGURE 3.3. Scatterplot with outlier ($N = 18$) and the linear regression lines with and without ($N = 17$) the outlier.

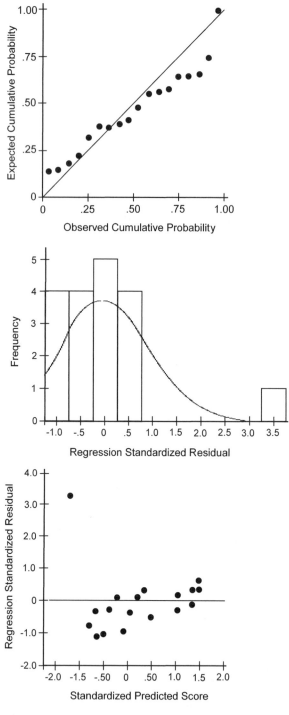

FIGURE 3.4. Plots for regression diagnostics: A normal probability plot of the standardized residuals (top), a histogram of the standardized residuals (middle), and a scatterplot of the standardized residuals and predicted scores (bottom) for the data in Figure 3.3 with the outlier included ($N = 18$).

Transformations can be helpful in remedying heteroscedasticity due to non-normality but may not be very useful when the cause is differential score reliability. Some heteroscedastic relations are expected, especially for developmental variables. For instance, age is related to height, but variation in height increases from childhood to adulthood. One way to take direct account of expected heterogeneity is to analyze a latent growth model, in which it is no special problem to estimate different variances across occasions of a repeated measures variable. The analysis of latent growth models in SEM is discussed in Chapter 11.

Relative Variances

Covariance matrices in which the ratio of the largest to the smallest variance is greater than, say, 10.0, are **ill scaled**. Analysis of an ill-scaled covariance matrix in SEM can cause problems. Most estimation methods in SEM are **iterative**, which means that initial estimates are derived by the computer and then modified through subsequent cycles of calculation. The goal of iterative estimation is to derive better estimates at each stage, ones that improve the overall fit of the model to the data. When improvements from step to step become small, iterative estimation stops because the solution is stable. However, if the estimates do not converge to stable values, then the process may fail. One cause is variances of observed variables that are very different in magnitude, such as $s_X^2 = 12.00$ and $s_Y^2 = .12$. When the computer adjusts the estimates from one step to the next in an iterative process for an ill-scaled matrix, the sizes of these changes may be huge for variables with small variances but trivial for others with large variances. Consequently, the entire set of estimates may head toward worse rather than better fit.

To prevent this problem, variables with extremely high or low variances can be rescaled by multiplying their scores by a constant, which changes the variance by a factor that equals the squared constant. For example:

$$s_X^2 = 12.00; \quad \text{so } s_{X \times .10}^2 = .10^2 \times 12.00 = .12$$

Likewise:

$$s_Y^2 = .12; \quad \text{so } s_{Y \times 10}^2 = 10^2 \times .12 = 12.00$$

Rescaling a variable in this way changes its mean and variance but not its correlation with other variables. This is because multiplying a variable by a constant is just a linear transformation that does not affect relative differences among the scores. An example with real data follows.

Roth, Wiebe, Fillingim, and Shay (1989) administered measures of exercise, hardiness, fitness, stress, and illness in a sample of university students. Reported in Table 3.4 is a matrix summary of these data (correlations and variances). The largest variance and smallest variances in this matrix (see the table) differ by a factor of more than 27,000, so the covariance matrix is ill scaled. I have seen some SEM computer programs fail to

TABLE 3.4. Example of an Ill-Scaled Data Matrix

Variable	1	2	3	4	5
1. Exercise	—				
2. Hardiness	–.03	—			
3. Fitness	.39	.07	—		
4. Stress	–.05	–.23	–.13	—	
5. Illness	–.08	–.16	–.29	.34	—
Original s^2	4,422.25	14.44	338.56	44.89	390,375.04
Constant	1.00	10.00	2.00	10.00	.10
Rescaled s^2	4,422.25	1,440.00	1,354.24	4,489.00	3,903.75
Rescaled SD	66.50	37.95	36.80	67.00	62.48

Note. These data (correlations and variances) are from Roth et al. (1989); $N = 373$. Note that low scores on the hardiness measure used by these authors indicate greater hardiness. In order to avoid confusion due to negative correlations, the signs of the correlations that involve the hardiness measure were reversed before they were recorded in this table.

analyze this matrix due to this characteristic. To correct this problem, I multiplied the original variables by the constants listed in Table 3.4 (e.g., 10.0 for hardiness) in order to make their variances more homogeneous. Among the rescaled variables, the largest variance is 4,489.00 for stress, and the smallest variance is 1,354.24 for fitness, about a 4:1 ratio. The rescaled matrix is not ill scaled.

SELECTING GOOD MEASURES AND REPORTING ABOUT THEM

It is just as critical in SEM as in other types of statistical analyses to (1) select measures with strong psychometric characteristics and (2) report these characteristics in written summaries. This is because the product of measures, or scores, is what you analyze. If the scores do not have good psychometric properties, then your results can be meaningless. Unfortunately, the quality of instruction about measurement has declined over the last 30 years or so. For example, about one-third of psychology PhD programs in North America offer no formal training in measurement, and measurement courses have disappeared from many undergraduate psychology programs (Aiken, West, Sechrest, & Reno, 1990; Frederich, Buday, & Kerr, 2000). This state of affairs puts both students and established researchers in a difficult spot: They are expected to select measures for their research, but they may lack the skills needed in order to critically evaluate those measures.

It also seems that lax education about measurement has begotten widespread poor reporting practices in our research literature. For example, Vacha-Haase, Ness, Nilsson, and Reetz (1999) found no mention of score reliability in one-third of the articles published from 1990 to 1997 in three different counseling or psychology journals. Only about one-third reported reliability coefficients for the scores actually analyzed in the study, and the rest described score reliability information from previous studies or sources, such as test manuals. The latter practice is **reliability induction**. Too many authors who invoke reliability induction (inferring from particular coefficients calculated in other samples to a different population) fail to explicitly compare characteristics of their sample with those from cited studies.

Thompson and Vacha-Haase (2000) speculated that another cause of poor reporting practices is the apparently widespread but false belief that it is *tests* that are reliable or unreliable, not *scores* in a particular sample. That is, if researchers believe that reliability, once established, is an immutable property of the test, then they may put little effort into estimating score reliability in their own samples. They may also adopt a "black box" view of reliability that assumes that reliability can be established by others, such as a select few academics who conduct measurement research. This false belief also implies that it is wasteful to devote significant resources to teaching about measurement.

Fortunately, there are some bright spots in this otherwise bleak picture. If you have already taken a measurement course, then you are at some advantage in learning about SEM. Otherwise, you are encouraged to recognize that this gap in your background is a potential handicap. Formal coursework is not the only way to learn more about measurement. Just like learning about SEM, more informal ways to learn measurement theory include participation in seminars or workshops and self study. For self-study I recommend Thorndike and Thorndike-Christ (2010) as a good undergraduate-level book and Nunnally and Bernstein (1994) as a strong graduate-level book that covers both classical test theory and more modern approaches.

Score Reliability

Score reliability, the degree to which scores in a particular sample are free from random measurement error, is estimated as one minus the proportion of total observed variance due to random error. These estimates are reliability coefficients, and a reliability for the scores of variable X is often designated with the symbol r_{XX}. Because r_{XX} is a proportion of variance, its theoretical range is 0–1.00. For example, if $r_{XX} = .80$, then it is estimated that $1 - .80 = .20$, or 20% of total observed score variance is due to random error. As r_{XX} approaches zero, the scores are more and more like random numbers, and random numbers measure nothing. It can happen that an empirical reliability coefficient is less than zero. A negative reliability coefficient is usually interpreted as though its value were zero, but such a result ($r_{XX} < 0$) indicates a serious problem with the scores.

The type of reliability coefficient reported most often in the literature is **coefficient alpha** also called **Cronbach's alpha**. This statistic measures **internal consistency reliability**, the degree to which responses are consistent across the items within a measure. If internal consistency is low, then the content of the items may be so heterogeneous that the total score is not the best possible unit of analysis for the measure. A conceptual equation is

$$\alpha_C = \frac{n\,\overline{r}_{ij}}{1 + (n-1)\,\overline{r}_{ij}} \qquad (3.6)$$

where n is the number of *items* (not cases) and $\overline{r}_{ij}$ is the average Pearson correlation between all pairs of items. For example, given $n = 20$ items with a mean interitem correlation of .30, then

$$\alpha_C = 20\,(.30)/[1 + (20 - 1)\,.30] = .90$$

Internal consistency reliability is greater as there are more items, or the mean interitem correlation is increasingly positive. In manifest variable analyses where there is no direct representation of latent variables, it is generally best to analyze measures that are internally consistent. This is also generally good advice for latent variable methods, including SEM, but see Little, Lindenberger, and Nesselroade (1999, p. 207) for more information about some exceptions to this general rule.

Estimation of other kinds of score reliability may require multiple measurement occasions, test forms, or examiners. For example, **test–retest reliability** involves the readministration of a measure to the same group on a second occasion. If the two sets of scores are highly correlated, then random error due to temporal factors may be minimal. **Alternate- (parallel-) forms reliability** involves the evaluation of the stability of scores across different versions of the same test. **Interrater reliability** is relevant for subjectively scored measures: if independent examiners do not consistently agree in their scoring, then examiner-specific factors may contribute unduly to observed score variability.

In manifest variable analyses, there is no gold standard as to how high coefficients should be in order to consider score reliability as "good," but here are some guidelines: Generally, reliability coefficients around .90 are considered "excellent," values around .80 are "very good," and values around .70 are "adequate." If $r_{XX} < .50$, most of the observed score variance is due to random error, an unacceptable amount of imprecision in most research. Note that somewhat lower levels of score reliability can be tolerated in latent variable methods compared with observed variable methods, if the sample size is sufficiently large (e.g., Little et al., 1999). Whenever possible—and it usually is, especially for internal consistency reliability—report score reliability coefficients in your own samples. You should also cite values of reliability coefficients reported in other published sources (reliability induction), but note that published coefficients may not generalize to your particular sample. So tell your readers whether or not they do based on similarities between your sample and samples described in published sources.

Low score reliability has many detrimental effects in manifest variable analyses. Poor reliability reduces the power of statistical tests; it also generally attenuates effect sizes below their true (population) values. Unreliability in the scores of two different variables, X or Y, attenuates their observed correlation. This formula from classical measurement theory shows the exact relation:

$$\max \left| \hat{r}_{XY} \right| = \sqrt{r_{XX}\, r_{YY}} \tag{3.7}$$

where $\max \left| \hat{r}_{XY} \right|$ is the theoretical (estimated) maximum absolute value of the correlation. That is, the absolute correlation between X and Y can equal 1.00 only if scores on both variables are perfectly reliable. Suppose that r_{XX} = .10 and r_{YY} = .90. Given this information, the theoretical maximum absolute value of r_{XY} can be no higher than (.10 × .90)$^{1/2}$, or .30. A variation of Equation 3.7 is the **correction for attenuation**:

$$\hat{r}_{XY} = \frac{r_{XY}}{\sqrt{r_{XX}\,r_{YY}}} \qquad (3.8)$$

where $\hat{r}_{XY}$ is the *estimated* validity coefficient if scores on both measures were perfectly reliable and r_{XY} is the observed (sample) validity coefficient. In general, $\hat{r}_{XY}$ is greater in absolute value than r_{XY}. For example, given r_{XY} = .30, r_{XX} = .90, and r_{YY} = .40, then $\hat{r}_{XY}$ = .50. That is, we expect that the "true" correlation between X and Y would be .50, if scores on both measures were perfectly reliable. Because disattenuated correlations are only estimates, it can happen that their absolute values exceed 1.00. Disattenuating observed correlations is one way to take measurement error into account. A better way to do so is to use SEM where constructs are specified as latent variables, each measured by multiple indicators (i.e., analyze a measurement model). In fact, SEM is much more accurate at estimating correlations between factors or between indicators and factors than manifest variable methods (e.g., Little et al., 1999). Indeed, this property of SEM provides a major motivation for its use over observed variable methods.

Score Validity

Score validity concerns the soundness of the inferences based on the scores, and information about score validity conveys to the researcher whether applying a test is capable of achieving certain aims. All forms of score validity are subsumed under the broader concept of **construct validity**, which concerns whether scores measure the hypothetical construct the researcher believes they do. Hypothetical constructs are not directly observable (they are latent) and thus can be measured only indirectly through observed scores, or indicators. Messick (1995) expanded the concept of construct validity to include the relevance, utility, value implications, and social consequences of test use and interpretation. An example of the social consequences of testing includes the accurate and fair assessment of scholastic skills among minority children.

There is no single, definitive test of construct validity, nor is it established in a single study. Instead, measurement-related research usually concerns a particular facet of construct validity. Also, the relative importance of these facets usually depends on the context (setting, values, etc.), content (which trait is assessed), and goals of measurement. For example, the facet of **criterion-related validity** concerns whether the scores (X) relate to an external criterion (Y) against which the scores can be evaluated. Specifically, are sample values of r_{XY} large enough to support the claim that a test explains an appreciable amount of the variability on the criterion? Whether an admissions test for university predicts eventual grade point average is a question of criterion-related validity.

Convergent validity and discriminant validity involve the evaluation of measures against each other instead of against an external standard. A set of variables presumed to measure the *same* construct shows **convergent validity** if their intercorrelations are at least moderate in magnitude. In contrast, a set of variables presumed to measure *different* constructs shows **discriminant validity** if their intercorrelations are not too high. If $r_{XY} = .90$, for instance, then we can hardly say that variables X and Y measure distinct constructs. The SEM technique of confirmatory factor analysis (CFA) is one statistical tool (among others) for testing hypotheses about convergent and discriminant validity (Chapter 9).

Another facet of score validity is **content validity**, which concerns whether test items are representative of the domains they are supposed to measure. Content validity is often a critical concern for achievement tests, especially tests that are supposed to measure skills specific to a particular grade level, such as Grade 3 mathematics. It is important for other kinds of tests, too, such as symptom rating scales and attitude scales. For example, the items of a depression rating scale should represent the symptoms domains that make up clinical depression, including vegetative symptoms (e.g., poor sleep) and negative self-evaluation. Expert opinion is the basis for establishing content validity, not statistical analysis.

As in other kinds of statistical methods in the behavioral sciences, SEM requires the analysis of measures with good evidence for score validity. Because score reliability is generally required for score validity—but does not guarantee it—this requirement includes good score reliability, too (but see Little et al., 1999, for discussion of some exceptions to this general rule in SEM). Otherwise, the accuracy of the interpretation of the results is doubtful. That is, using SEM does not somehow free researchers from having to think about measurement.

SUMMARY

The most widely used estimation methods in SEM require screening the data for multivariate normality. It is also critical to select appropriate methods for handling missing data. These methods generally assume that the data loss pattern is random. The pairwise deletion of incomplete cases may be problematic because it can lead to covariance matrices that are not positive definite, and a positive definite data matrix is generally required in SEM. Computer tools for SEM typically accept either raw data files or matrix summaries of the data. Because most estimation methods in SEM assume the analysis of unstandardized variables, a covariance matrix is preferred over a correlation matrix without standard deviations when a matrix summary is the input and means are not analyzed. In written reports of the analysis you should provide information about the psychometric characteristics of your scores, such as their reliability, in your own samples. The analysis of measures with poor score reliability or validity can jeopardize the integrity of the results. Computer tools for SEM are described in the next chapter.

RECOMMENDED READINGS

Allison (2003) gives clear descriptions of missing data techniques for SEM, including the special ML method for incomplete raw data files. Little, Lindenberger, and Nesselroade (1999) describe a conceptual and statistical framework for understanding the relation between indicator selection, indicator psychometric characteristics, and construct measurement. Peng, Harwell, Liou, and Ehman (2007) describe modern techniques for analyzing incomplete data and characteristics of software tools in this area. Wothke (1993) offers many helpful suggestions for diagnosing nonpositive definiteness in data matrices and other instances of this problem in SEM. You can find a concise summary of score reliability and related topics in Thompson (2003).

Allison, P. D. (2003). Missing data techniques for structural equation modeling. *Journal of Abnormal Psychology, 112*, 545–557.

Little, T. D., Lindenberger, U., & Nesselroade, J. R. (1999). On selecting indicators for multivariate measurement and modeling with latent variables: When "good" indicators are bad and "bad" indicators are good. *Psychological Methods, 4*, 192–211.

Peng, C.-Y. J., Harwell, M., Liou, S.-M., & Ehman, L. H. (2007). Advances in missing data methods and implications for educational research. In S. S. Sawilowsky (Ed.), *Real data analysis* (pp. 31–78). Charlotte, NC: IAP.

Thompson, B. (Ed.). (2003). *Score reliability.* Thousand Oaks, CA: Sage.

Wothke, W. (1993). Nonpositive definite matrices in structural equation modeling. In K. A. Bollen & J. S. Long (Eds.), *Testing structural equation models* (pp. 256–293). Newbury Park, CA: Sage.

EXERCISES

1. Calculate the correlation matrix given the covariance matrix in lower diagonal form for variables X, W, and Y (in this order) presented next:

   ```
   42.25
   31.72        148.84
   63.05         82.84        376.36
   ```

2. Presented next are scores for 10 cases reported as (X, Y, W) and where a missing observation is coded as −9. Enter these scores into a data file with the appropriate missing data specification. Calculate the bivariate correlations using listwise deletion, pairwise deletion, and mean substitution. Describe the results:

   ```
   (-9,15,-9),    (12,23,48),  (13,25,38),  (-9,18,38),
   (15,20,39),    (13,15,35),  (17,-9,36),  (18,24,47),
   (19,21,42),    (17,-9,-9)
   ```

3. Given $cov_{XY} = 13.00$, $s_X^2 = 12.00$, and $s_Y^2 = 10.00$, show that the corresponding correlation is out of bounds.

4. Calculate the covariance matrix for the incomplete data in Table 3.3 using pairwise deletion. Show that this matrix is nonpositive definite. Also show that the corresponding correlation matrix contains an out-of-bounds value.

5. Use a computer tool for statistics to construct the normal probability plot for the data in Figure 3.2.

6. Remove the outlier (the score of 27) from the distribution in Figure 3.2 and recalculate the skew index and the kurtosis index for $N = 63$.

7. Why is it necessary to add a constant to the scores so that the lowest score equals 1.0 before applying a square root transformation or a logarithmic transformation?

8. Apply the square root transformation to the scores in Figure 3.2, but apply it to the original scores, not to the rescaled scores where a constant is added so that the lowest score equals 1.0. Then calculate the skew index and the kurtosis index. Compare these results to those reported in the text for the data in Figure 3.2 but rescaled where the lowest score is 1.0.

9. Presented next are scores on five dichotomously scored items (0 = wrong, 1 = correct) for eight cases (A–H). Use a computer tool for general statistical analyses to calculate internal consistency reliability using Equation 3.6 for these scores. If your computer tool has a reliability analysis procedure, then use it to verify your calculations:

```
A: 1, 1, 0, 1, 1        B: 0, 0, 0, 0, 0
C: 1, 1, 1, 1, 0        D: 1, 1, 1, 0, 1
E: 1, 0, 1, 1, 1        F: 0, 1, 1, 1 ,1
G: 1, 1, 1, 1, 1        H: 1, 1, 0, 1, 1
```

4

Computer Tools

Described in this chapter are major software tools. These include eight programs or procedures specifically intended for SEM: Amos, CALIS/TCALIS of SAS/STAT, EQS, LISREL, Mplus, Mx, RAMONA of SYSTAT, and SEPATH of STATISTICA. Two other programs originally created for other kinds of statistical analyses but with SEM capabilities are R and MATLAB, which are also described. Ways of interacting with SEM computer tools are outlined, and pros and con of different methods are considered. A major theme of this chapter is that the relative ease of use of modern computer tools should not lull you into thinking that SEM is easy or requires minimal conceptual understanding. In this sense, this adage by the Canadian scholar Marshall McLuhan is appropriate: We shape our tools and afterwards our tools shape us. I hope that computer tool use sharpens, rather than dulls, your ability to think critically about SEM.

EASE OF USE, NOT SUSPENSION OF JUDGMENT

Computer programs are critical tools for the conduct of SEM. About 30 years ago, LISREL was essentially the only widely available SEM program. At that time, LISREL and related programs were rather difficult to use because they (1) required users to generate a lot of rather arcane code for each analysis and (2) were generally available only on mainframe computers with stark command-line user interfaces. The abundance of relatively inexpensive yet powerful personal computers has dramatically changed this situation. Specifically, statistical software for personal computers with a graphical user interface (GUI) is easier to use than their character-based predecessors. "User friendliness" in contemporary SEM computer tools—and others for general statistical analyses—is a near-revolution compared with older programs.

For example, consider a feature of the most recent versions of Amos, EQS, LISREL, and the graphical version of Mx for personal computers. Users of any of these packages can still choose to write code in each application's native syntax. As an alternative, they can use a graphical editor to draw the model on the screen with geometric symbols such as boxes, circles, and arrows. The program then translates the figure into lines of code, which are then used to generate the output. Thus, (1) the user need not know very much (if anything) about how to write code in order to run a sophisticated statistical analysis, and (2) the importance of highly technical programming skills for conducting SEM is likely to diminish even further. For researchers who understand the fundamental concepts of SEM, this development can only be a boon—anything that reduces the drudgery and gets one to the results quicker is a benefit.

There are some potential drawbacks to "push-button modeling." For example, no- or low-effort programming could encourage the use of SEM in uninformed or careless ways. Thus, it is more important than ever to be familiar with the conceptual and statistical bases of SEM. Computer programs, however easy to use, should be only the tools of your knowledge and not its master. Steiger (2001) makes the related point that the emphasis on ease of use of computer tools can give beginners the false impression that SEM itself is easy. Indeed, some computer tools for SEM have been advertised with the tagline "SEM made easy!" This message may give the false impression that all one has to do is draw the model on the screen and let the computer take care of the rest. *Nothing could be further from the truth!* The reality is that things can and do go wrong in SEM. Specifically, beginners often quickly discover that analyses fail because of technical problems, including a terminated program run with cryptic error messages or uninterpretable output (Steiger, 2001). These things happen because actual research problems can be technical, and the availability of user-friendly computer tools does not change

"Hold down control and shift and press escape."

No, you won't need computer gurus to learn how to use modern SEM computer tools. Copyright 2009 by Clive Goddard. Reprinted with permission from CartoonStock Ltd. (*www.cartoonstock. com*)

this fact. This is why there is so much emphasis in this book on conceptual knowledge instead of teaching you how to use a particular computer tool: *In order to deal with problems in the analysis, you must understand what went wrong and why.*

HUMAN–COMPUTER INTERACTION

There are basically three ways to interact with SEM computer tools:

1. Batch mode processing is the method for users who already know a program's syntax. Lines of code that describe the model, data, and analysis are entered directly into an editor window that may be saved as an ASCII (text) file. Program code entered by the user is then executed with a "run" command. Virtually all SEM computer tools support this mode.

2. One method that does not require knowledge of program syntax uses "wizards," which are a series of templates (dialog boxes) that build the model and analysis as the user clicks with the mouse cursor on GUI elements such as text fields or check boxes. Once the wizard has all the information, it automatically writes the program code, which can then be run.

3. Another method that requires no programming is based on a drawing editor, which is a GUI that allows the user to specify the model by drawing it on the screen. The model is drawn using a set of more-or-less standard graphical symbols for model diagrams, including squares or rectangles for observed variables and circles or ellipses for latent variables (Chapter 5). When the diagram is finished, the analysis is run within the program's GUI. Although drawing editors are popular with beginners, you should note that there are times when using a drawing editor is actually a hindrance—see Topic Box 4.1 for more information.

CORE SEM PROGRAMS AND BOOK WEBSITE RESOURCES

There are a total of eight computer programs specifically constructed for SEM, each of which is used by many researchers today. Listed alphabetically, they are:

Amos	Mplus
CALIS/TCALIS procedures (SAS/STAT)	Mx
EQS	RAMONA procedure (SYSTAT)
LISREL	SEPATH procedure (STATISTICA)

There are free student versions of Amos, LISREL, and Mplus that place a limit on the size of the model or the number of variables that can be analyzed, but they are good learning tools. One of these programs, Mx, is a full-featured computer tool for model fitting that is available at no cost because it is not a commercial product. Other software programs

TOPIC BOX 4.1

Graphical Isn't Always Better

There are some possible drawbacks to controlling an SEM analysis by drawing the model on the computer screen:

1. It can be tedious to specify a complex model—one with lots of variables and paths—in a drawing editor. This is because the screen tends to fill up quickly with numerous graphical elements. The resulting visual clutter can make it difficult to keep track of what you are doing.

2. Conducting a multiple-group analysis where a model is simultaneously fitted to data from two or more independent samples can be difficult to carry out in a drawing editor. This is because it may be necessary to look through several different screens or windows in order to get all the information about model specification and data for each group.

3. Standard graphical symbols for model diagrams in SEM do not "translate" well for doing a multilevel analysis. The issue is considered in Chapter 12, but it would be hard to use a drawing editor to conduct a multilevel SEM analysis.

4. It seems that it would be easy to produce a publication-quality model diagram in a drawing editor, but this is not exactly true. Drawing editors in SEM programs offer limited options for "tweaking" the appearance of the diagram (e.g., changing line widths) compared with full-fledged drawing programs, such as Microsoft Visio.* To tell the truth, it takes a lot of time and fussing to make a publication-quality diagram in *any* drawing editor. But once you make a few examples, you can reuse graphical elements, such as those for error terms, in future diagrams.

As many researchers become more experienced using SEM computer tools, they tend to stop using a drawing editor to specify their models. For example, they may discover that it can be easier to specify a complicated model through a wizard that presents a series of templates. Other researchers eventually learn the syntax of their SEM computer tool and start working in batch mode. There are advantages to doing so. For example, it is often possible to work faster in batch mode than by using a drawing editor. All of the syntax for a complex model plus a matrix summary of the data may fit within a single screen of a text editor. The text file in which syntax is saved also serves as an archive that records the "his-

*I'll share a trade secret with you: All model diagrams in this book were created using nothing more than Microsoft Word AutoShapes. Maybe I'm biased, but I think these diagrams are not too bad. Sometimes you can do a lot with a simple but flexible tool. In this case, you do not need a professional-grade drawing program to make publication-quality model diagrams.

tory" of the analysis (model, data, output options, etc.). Syntax for modern SEM computer programs is not all that difficult to learn, no more so than, say, learning syntax for SPSS or SAS/STAT. Yes, there is tedium in working with syntax because every single line must be correct, but the same is true about working in a drawing editor: every single graphical element must be correct, or the analysis might fail. So don't fear the prospect of learning syntax and working in batch mode for your SEM analyses. Indeed, doing so is probably in your future, too.

can analyze structural equation models, but they are not used as often as the eight listed here. Some of these other computer tools are described later in this chapter.

The eight core SEM computer tools can analyze all of the structural equation models described in Part II of this book. Most of these programs can also analyze means or models across multiple samples, and EQS, LISREL, and Mplus each have special syntax for multilevel analyses (Chapter 12). The descriptions that follow emphasize the major features of each program. Specific capabilities of computer tools can change quickly as new versions are released, so refer to the websites listed here for the most current information.

The website for this book (see p. 3) has resources to help you learn how to work in the syntax of EQS, LISREL, or Mplus, three of the most widely used computer tools. For each detailed example in Chapters 7–10, you can download all computer files (syntax, data, output) for analyzing that example in EQS, LISREL, and Mplus. This will allow to you to run the input files in the corresponding computer tool. All syntax files are annotated with comments that help to explain model specification in a particular analysis. In addition, you can compare the contents of each syntax file with the corresponding model diagram in this book as a learning aid. Computer files can also be downloaded for research examples in Chapters 11–12.

Amos

Version 18.0 of Amos[1] (Analysis of Moment Structures) (Arbuckle, 1995–2009) is a Microsoft Windows program sold by SPSS, Inc., as either a stand-alone application (it does not need the SPSS environment to run) or as an optional part of SPSS. The version number of Amos reflects the current version number of SPSS, now known as PASW Statistics. The Amos program is made up of two modules, Amos Graphics and Amos Basic. Amos Graphics provides a GUI through which the user can specify the model by drawing it on the screen and control other aspects of the analysis. A set of graphical wizards is available that can automatically draw an entire latent growth model, among other

[1]*www.spss.com/AMOS/*

tasks. A special utility for testing alternative models is available through the Specification Search toolbar. In this utility, the user can designate particular paths in the model as optional, and Specification Search will analyze models with all possible subsets of the designated paths. Values of fit statistics for all tested models appear in a summary table, and the corresponding model diagram can be viewed by clicking with the mouse cursor in the table.

Amos Basic works in batch mode. Its syntax is flexible in that it does not use a fixed set of keywords for variable names. Instead, the user supplies labels for all variables. The Amos Basic editor is also a language interpreter for Microsoft Visual Basic. This means that users can write scripts in Visual Basic that modify the functionality of Amos Graphics, such as calculating a model fit statistic that is not otherwise reported in default program output.

Special features of Amos include the capability to generate bootstrapped estimates of standard errors and confidence intervals for all parameter estimates. Both nonparametric and parametric bootstrapping are available. Amos has a special maximum likelihood (ML) method for raw data files, in which some observations are missing at random and special estimation methods for censored data and ordered-categorical (ordinal) outcome variables. It has extensive capabilities for Bayesian estimation of model parameters, but their correct use requires knowledge of Bayesian statistics (Kline, 2004, chap. 9). Amos can also analyze mixture models with latent categorical factors that represent class membership. A free student version is available. It is identical to Amos 5.0 except that the student version is limited to eight observed variables and 54 model parameters.[2] There are also training videos available for the Amos student version.[3]

CALIS and TCALIS

The CALIS (Covariance Analysis and Linear Structural Equations) procedure is part of SAS/STAT 9.2,[4] a comprehensive package for general statistical analyses that runs under Microsoft Windows and operating systems for workstation computers, including Linux, OpenVMS, AIX, and Solaris. It analyzes a wide variety of structural equation models and also estimates parameters in analyses such as MR or multivariate linear regression. The TCALIS procedure is a new ("experimental") procedure in SAS/STAT 9.2. It allows greater flexibility than CALIS in testing structural equation models across multiple samples and in analyzing models with both a covariance structure and a mean structure. Because TCALIS is more capable than CALIS, the latter is not described further.

The TCALIS procedure runs only in batch mode; that is, the user must type commands in an editor window that describe the data and model and then run the program

---

[2]*www.amosdevelopment.com/download/*

[3]*www.amosdevelopment.com/video/index.htm*

[4]*www.sas.com/technologies/analytics/statistics/stat/index.html*

in the SAS environment. Models can be specified in TCALIS using one of *seven* different representational notations. These include LISREL-type matrix-based syntax, EQS-type equations-based syntax, and a notational system based on an approach to causal modeling known as the **reticular action model** (RAM) (McArdle & McDonald, 1984). The RAM approach includes a matrix-based system for specifying structural equation models and a set of graphical symbols for model diagrams. The RAM symbolism for model diagrams is used in this book and is introduced in the next chapter. Special features of TCALIS include the possibility of selecting from among eight different methods for calculating start values, or initial estimates of model parameters. Other options control the estimation process, such as the particular statistical search method used to find optimal parameter estimates. Output from an analysis in TCALIS can be automatically saved for input into the next run of the program for the same model and data. This capability is handy for checking whether or not a complex model is identified (Chapter 9).

EQS

Version 6.1 of EQS[5] (Equations) (Bentler, 2006) is a Microsoft Windows program that can be used for all stages of the analysis from data entry and screening to exploratory statistical analyses to SEM. There are also versions of EQS for UNIX or LINUX environments. The EQS data editor has many of the capabilities of a general statistical package, including conditional case selection, variable transformation, and merging of separate data files. Exploratory statistical analyses that can be conducted in EQS include ANOVA, covariate analysis, and factor analysis. There are also options for analyzing missing data patterns and model-based imputation of missing observations with the EM algorithm (Chapter 3).

The user can interact with EQS in three different ways: through batch mode; through wizards that collect information about the model and data and automatically write EQS programming syntax; or through a drawing editor. The last two ways do not require knowledge of EQS syntax. The drawing editor in EQS is its Diagrammer, which offers graphical tools for drawing the model on the screen. Tools available in the Diagrammer can automatically draw an entire path, factor, or latent growth curve model after the user completes a few templates about the variables, direct effects, measurement occasions, or residual terms. Both the Diagrammer and template-based wizards automatically write EQS syntax into a background window, which is then run by the user.

The syntax of EQS is based on the **Bentler–Weeks representational system**, in which the parameters of any covariance structure are regression coefficients for effects on dependent variables and the variances and covariances of independent variables. In the Bentler–Weeks model, dependent variables have error terms, but not the independent variables. All types of models in EQS are thus set up in a consistent way. Special strengths of EQS include the availability of several different estimation methods for non-

[5]*www.mvsoft.com/*

normal data, model-based bootstrapping, and the ability to correctly analyze a correlation matrix without standard deviations. The latest version features built-in syntax and special estimation methods for multilevel analyses. A future version of EQS will include capabilities for mixture modeling, latent class modeling, and analysis of item response theory measurement models.

LISREL

Version 8.8 of LISREL[6] (Linear Structural Relationships) for Microsoft Windows (Jöreskog & Sörbom, 2006) is an integrated suite of programs for all stages of the analysis, from data entry and management to exploratory data analyses to the evaluation of a wide range of structural equation models. Included with LISREL is PRELIS, which prepares raw data files and matrix summaries for analysis in LISREL or other computer programs. Many multivariate data screening and summarization options are available in PRELIS, including model-based imputation of missing data. The PRELIS program can also generate bootstrapped estimates, conduct simulation studies with variables specified to have particular distributional characteristics, and calculate polychoric and polyserial correlations.

The LISREL program offers an interactive mode that consists of a series of wizards that prompt the user for information about the model and data and then automatically write command syntax in a separate window. Interactive LISREL also allows the user to specify the model by drawing it onscreen through the Path Diagram functionality. Users already familiar with one of two different LISREL command syntaxes can as an alternative directly enter code into the LISREL editor and then run it by clicking with the mouse cursor on an icon. If the command "Path Diagram" is placed at the end of the editor file, LISREL will also automatically draw the model diagram that corresponds to the syntax file. This unique feature provides a way for the user to verify whether the model specified in syntax and estimated by LISREL is actually the one that he or she intended to analyze.

The original (classic) LISREL syntax is based on matrix algebra. This command syntax is not easy to use until after one has memorized the whole system. An advantage of the classic syntax is efficiency: one can often specify a complex model in relatively few lines of code. The other LISREL programming language is SIMPLIS ("simple LISREL"), which is not based on matrix algebra, nor does it require familiarity with the classic syntax. Programming in SIMPLIS requires little more than naming the observed and latent variables (but not error terms) and specifying paths with equation-type statements. Residual terms are automatically specified when SIMPLIS is used, which is convenient. Features of the latest version of LISREL include the capability to conduct exploratory factor analyses of ordinal variables in PRELIS and the addition of syntax commands in LISREL's classic, matrix-based programming language for multilevel analyses. (The

---

[6]*www.ssicentral.com/*

latter is not available in SIMPLIS.) The full commercial version of LISREL can be down-loaded for a free 15-day trial. There are also free student versions of LISREL available for the Microsoft Windows, Apple Macintosh OS 9 and X, and LINUX operating systems. The student versions are restricted to a total of 15 observed variables for both SEM analyses and multilevel analyses.[7]

Mplus

Version 6.0 of Mplus[8] (Muthén & Muthén, 1998–2010) runs under Microsoft Windows and is divided into a program for SEM, Mplus Basic, and three add-on modules for ana-lyzing additional kinds of latent variable models. Mplus Base analyzes all core types of structural equation models plus discrete- and continuous-time survival models. A spe-cial strength of Mplus is that it can analyze outcome variables that are any combination of continuous, dichotomous, ordinal, or count variables. For example, it automatically calculates odds ratios for dichotomous outcomes (Chapter 2). Also available in Mplus Base is an ML method for incomplete raw data files, special syntax for handling complex survey data (e.g., with stratification), and Monte Carlo methods for generating simulated random samples. Versions 5.1 and later feature the capability for **exploratory structural equation modeling** (ESEM) (Asparouhov & Muthén, 2009), which combines features of SEM and exploratory factor analysis. The logic of ESEM is introduced in the next chap-ter. Version 6.0 includes capabilities for Bayesian estimation (Asparouhov & Muthén, 2010).

The Mplus Base user interacts with the program in one of two different ways, in batch mode by writing programs in the Mplus language that specify the model and data or through a language generator (wizard) that prepares files for batch analysis. Through the Mplus language generator, the user completes templates about analysis details, such as where the data file is to be found and variable names. The user's responses are then automatically converted to Mplus language statements that are written to an editor win-dow, but the user must write the syntax that specifies the model. There is no model dia-gram input or output in Mplus Basic. However, it has a template-based module for gener-ating data graphics, including histograms, scatterplots, and item characteristic curves.

The Multilevel Add-On to Mplus Basic is for the multilevel analyses. It estimates multilevel versions of models for regression analysis, factor analysis, SEM, and time survival analysis. The Mixture Model Add-On analyzes mixture models with categori-cal latent variables. Mplus Base together with this add-on can analyze "classical" struc-tural equation models with continuous latent variables, latent structure models with categorical latent variables, and models with both continuous and categorical latent variables. The third optional module is the Combination Add-On, which contains all the features of the other two add-ons. It also supports the analysis of multilevel models with

---

[7]*www.ssicentral.com/lisrel/student.html*

[8]*www.statmodel.com/*

latent classes, such as a two-level mixture confirmatory factor analysis model or a two-level regression mixture analysis. There is a free demonstration (student) version that contains all the capabilities of the full version of Mplus except that is limited to eight observed variables and two between variables in a two-level analysis.[9]

Mx

Version 1.66b of Mx[10] (Matrix) (Neale, Boker, Xie, & Maes, 2003) is a matrix algebra processor and a numerical optimizer that can analyze structural equation models and other kinds of multivariate statistical models. It is freely available over the Internet and runs under several different operating systems, including Microsoft Windows, Apple Macintosh OSX, LINUX, and AIX. A new, open-source version of Mx, called OpenMx, is being developed for the R programming environment. A GUI for Mx is available for personal computers with Microsoft Windows. The installation of Mx with its GUI is referred to as Mx Graph. There are two different ways to specify a model in Mx Graph. The first is to write a script in the Mx programming language that describes the data and model and then run it in batch mode. The syntax of Mx is based on the McArdle–McDonald RAM matrix formulation, which represents structural equation models with three different matrices: **S** (symmetric) for covariances, **A** (asymmetric) for effects of one variable on another, and **F** (filter) for specifying the observed variables. See Loehlin (2004, pp. 44–46) for examples.

The second way to specify a model in Mx Graph is to use its drawing editor. This method does not require knowledge of the Mx programming language. After defining an external data file, the user can click on a list of variables, and these variables are then automatically displayed in the drawing editor. Model diagrams in Mx Graph use the McArdle–McDonald RAM symbolism. Mx Graph automatically writes the Mx syntax for the analysis that corresponds to the user's model diagram and then executes it. Special features of Mx Graph for SEM include the ability to calculate confidence intervals and statistical power for individual parameter estimates and analyze special types of latent variable models for genetics data. It also has nonparametric bootstrapping capabilities. Examples of Mx scripts for continuous or categorical variables of the kind analyzed in genetics research can be freely downloaded.[11]

RAMONA

M. Browne's RAMONA,[12] Reticular Action Model or Near Approximation, is the module for SEM in SYSTAT 13 (Systat Software, Inc., 2009), a comprehensive program for

---

[9]*www.statmodel.com/demo.shtml*

[10]*www.vcu.edu/mx/*

[11]*www.vcu.edu/mx/examples.html*

[12]*www.systat.com/*

general statistical analysis for Microsoft Windows. The user interacts with RAMONA in the general SYSTAT environment by submitting a batch file with commands that describe the model and data or by typing these commands at a prompt for interactive sessions. An alternative method is to use a wizard with graphical dialogs for naming observed and latent variables and specifying the type of data to be analyzed, but syntax that specifies the model must be typed directly in a text window by the user. Syntax for RAMONA is straightforward and involves only two parameter matrices, one for direct effects and the other for covariances between independent variables. Special features of RAMONA include the ability to correctly fit a model to a correlation matrix only. There is also a "Restart" command that automatically takes parameter estimates from a prior analysis as initial estimates in a new analysis. The RAMONA module cannot analyze a structural equation model across multiple samples, and there is no direct way to analyze means. There is a free student version of SYSTAT called MYSTAT, but it does not include RAMONA. The full version of SYSTAT can be downloaded for a free 30-day trial.[13]

SEPATH

J. Steiger's SEPATH[14] (Structural Equation Modeling and Path Analysis) is the SEM module in STATISTICA 9 Advanced (StatSoft Inc., 2009), an integrated program for general statistical analyses, data mining, and quality control. Structural equation models are specified in SEPATH with the PATH1 programming language that mimics the appearance of a model diagram based on McArdle–McDonald RAM symbolism. There are three ways to enter PATH1 code in SEPATH. First, users who already know the PATH1 language can enter syntax directly into a dialog box. The two other methods do not require PATH1 knowledge. One is a graphical path construction tool in which the user clicks with the mouse cursor on variable names or buttons that represent different types of paths for direct effects or covariances. The other method is a graphical wizard for specifying models with substantive latent variables, such as confirmatory factor analysis models. Both methods automatically write PATH1 syntax in a separate window.

The special strengths of SEPATH include the capabilities to correctly analyze a correlation matrix without standard deviations and generate simulated random samples in Monte Carlo studies. This program offers many options to precisely control parameter estimation, but their effective use requires technical knowledge of nonlinear optimization procedures. There is also a power analysis module in STATISTICA 9 Advanced (also by J. Steiger) that estimates the power of statistical tests of model fit in SEM (Chapter 8). The full version of STATISTICA can be downloaded for a free 30-day trial.[15]

OTHER COMPUTER TOOLS

Two other options for SEM are described next: R and MATLAB.

R

The R programming language and environment is an implementation of S, developed at Bell Labs as a computing environment for statistics, data mining, and graphics. The S-PLUS program by TIBCO Software, Inc., is a commercial version of S, but R is a free, cooperatively developed, and open-source version that can be downloaded over the Internet.[16] It runs on Unix, Microsoft Windows, and Apple Macintosh families of operating systems. A basic R installation has about the same statistical capabilities as some commercial programs, such as SPSS, but there are now over 1,700 add-on modules, or packages, that further extend R's analytical repertoire. For example, the package sem by J. Fox (2006) is designed specifically for structural equation modeling. Other packages for R support SEM analyses, including boot for bootstrapping and polychor for calculating polyserial and polychoric correlations.

The user interacts with R in one of two different ways. One is through a command prompt that accepts R programming language and numerical (data) input. Another is batch mode in which commands are entered in an editor before the entire file is executed (run). Researchers with no programming experience whatsoever may find the R user interface austere, but others should be able to work in a command-driven environment with little problem. The sem package uses the McArdle–McDonald RAM notational system to specify structural equation models. The model-fitting capabilities of sem are limited at present compared with those of commercial SEM tools. For example, sem cannot simultaneously estimate a model across multiple groups, but its capabilities may be extended in the future.

MATLAB

Version 7.10 of MATLAB[17] (Matrix Laboratory) (The MathWorks, Inc., 2010) is a commercial computing environment and programming language for data analysis. It has extensive capabilities for data manipulation and visualization, and there are many built-in functionalities for linear algebra, curve fitting, and optimization and numerical integration, among others. There are also optional add-ons that support more specialized kinds of analyses, including those for multivariate statistical techniques. Widely known in engineering and the natural sciences, MATLAB is increasingly being used by behavioral science researchers, too.

Similar to R, the main user interface for MATLAB is command-driven; that is, users

---

[16]*www.r-project.org/*

[17]*www.mathworks.com/*

enter MATLAB statements at a command prompt. However, this interface is supported by a GUI for the whole MATLAB environment. For example, users can drag a previous command from a command history window to the command prompt and then execute it. Many statistical and graphical functions are available by clicking with the mouse cursor on program icons. The user can also program MATLAB to conduct a specific type of analysis in batch mode processing. There are now some MATLAB routines for SEM. For example, Steele (2009) describes MATLAB code for SEM analyses in functional Magnetic Resonance Imaging (fMRI) studies; this code can be freely downloaded.[18] Goldstein, Bonnet, and Rocher (2007) describe a MATLAB routine for multilevel SEM analyses of comparative data on educational performance across different counties. At present, there are relatively few SEM-specific routines for MATLAB, but I expect this situation will change. A student version of MATLAB available at a reduced cost, and the full version can be downloaded for a free 15-day trial.[19]

SUMMARY

Many contemporary SEM computer tools are no more difficult to use than other computer programs for general statistical analyses. Ideally, this situation should allow you to be more concerned with the logic and rationale of the analysis than with the mechanics of carrying it out. The capability to specify a structural equation model by drawing it on the screen helps beginners to be productive right away. However, with experience you may find that specifying models in syntax and working in batch mode are actually faster and more efficient methods, and thus easier. Problems can be expected in the analysis of complex models, and no amount of user friendliness in the interface of a computer tool can negate this fact. When (not if) things in the analysis go wrong, you need, first, to have a good conceptual understanding of the nature of the problem and, second, basic computer skills in order to correct the problem. You should also not let ease of computer tool use lead you to carry out unnecessary analyses or select analytical methods that you do not really understand. The fundamental concepts and tools discussed in Part I of this book set the stage for the overview of core SEM techniques in Part II.

RECOMMENDED READINGS

Nachtigall, Kroehne, Funke, and Steyer (2003) describe an "SEM first-aid kit," or a discussion of typical problems—including those that concern computer programs—that beginners often encounter and possible solutions. Steiger (2001) reminds us that the availability of graphical user interfaces in SEM computer tools should not be seen as a shortcut to understanding the conceptual and statistical bases of the analysis.

---

[18]*www.dundee.ac.uk/medschool/staff/douglas_steele/structural_equation_modelling*

[19]*www.mathworks.com/downloads/web_downloads/trials*

Nachtigall, C., Kroehne, U., Funke, F., & Steyer, R. (2003). (Why) Should we use SEM? Pros and cons of structural equation modeling. *Methods of Psychological Research Online*, 8(2), 1–22. Retrieved March 24, 2009, from *aodgps.de/fachgruppen/methoden/mpr-online/issue20/art1/mpr127_11.pdf*

Steiger, J. H. (2001). Driving fast in reverse: The relationship between software development, theory, and education in structural equation modeling. *Journal of the American Statistical Association, 96,* 331–338.

Part II

Core Techniques

Specification

The specification of path analysis (PA) models, confirmatory factor analysis (CFA) measurement models, and structural regression (SR) models is the topic of this chapter. Outlined first are the basic steps of SEM and graphical symbols used in model diagrams. Some straightforward rules are suggested for counting the number of observations (which is not the sample size) in the analysis and the number of model parameters. Both of these quantities are needed for checking model identification (next chapter). Actual research examples dealt with in more detail in later chapters are also introduced. The main goal of this presentation is to give you a better sense of the kinds of hypotheses that can be tested with core structural equation models.

STEPS OF SEM

Six basic steps are followed in most analyses, and two additional optional steps, in a perfect world, would be carried out in every analysis. Review of these steps will help you to understand (1) the relation of specification, the main topic of this chapter, to later steps of SEM and (2) the utmost importance of specification.

Basic Steps

The basic steps are listed next and then discussed afterward, and a flowchart of these steps is presented in Figure 5.1. These steps are actually iterative because problems at a later step may require a return to an earlier step. (Later chapters elaborate specific issues at each step beyond specification for particular SEM techniques.)

1. Specify the model.
2. Evaluate model identification (if not identified, go back to step 1).

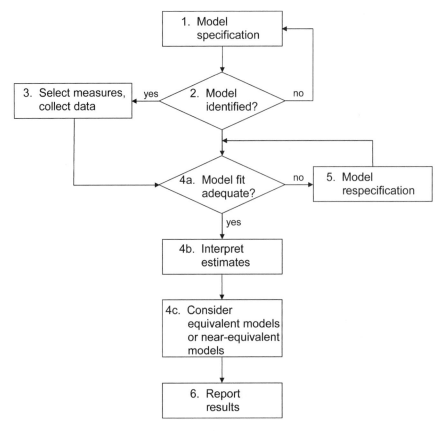

FIGURE 5.1. Flowchart of the basic steps of SEM.

3. Select the measures (operationalize the constructs) and collect, prepare, and screen the data.
4. Estimate the model:
   a. Evaluate model fit (if poor, skip to step 5).
   b. Interpret parameter estimates.
   c. Consider equivalent or near-equivalent models (skip to step 6).
5. Respecify the model (return to step 4).
6. Report the results.

Specification

The representation of your hypotheses in the form of a structural equation model is **specification**. Many researchers begin the process of specification by drawing a model diagram using a set of more or less standard graphical symbols (defined later), but the model can alternatively be described by a series of equations. These equations define the model's parameters, which correspond to presumed relations among observed or latent variables that the computer eventually estimates with sample data. *Specification is the most important step.* This is because results from later steps assume that the model is basically correct. I also suggest that you make a list of possible changes to the initial model that would be justified according to theory or empirical results. This is because it is often necessary to respecify models (step 5), and respecification should respect the same principles as specification.

Identification

If life were fair, the researcher could proceed directly from specification to collection of the data to estimation. Unfortunately, the analysis of a structural equation model is not always so straightforward. The problem that potentially complicates the analysis is that of **identification**. A model is identified if it is *theoretically* possible for the computer to derive a unique estimate of every model parameter. Otherwise, the model is not identified. The word "theoretically" emphasizes identification as a property of the model and not of the data. For example, if a model is not identified, then it remains so regardless of the sample size ($N = 100$, $1,000$, etc.). Therefore, models that are not identified should be respecified (return to step 1); otherwise, attempts to analyze them may be fruitless. Different types of structural equation models must meet the specific requirements for identification that are described in Chapter 6.

Measure Selection and Data Collection

The various activities for this step—select good measures, collect the data, and screen them—were discussed in Chapter 3.

Estimation

This step involves using an SEM computer tool to conduct the analysis. Several things take place at this step: (1) Evaluate model fit, which means determine how well the model explains the data. Perhaps more often than not, researchers' initial models do not fit the data very well. When (not if) this happens to you, skip the rest of this step and go to the next, respecification, and then reanalyze the respecified model using the same data. Assuming satisfactory model fit, then (2) interpret the parameter estimates. In written summaries, too many researchers fail to interpret the parameter estimates for specific effects. Perhaps concern for overall model fit is so great that relatively little attention is paid to whether estimates of its parameters are meaningful (Kaplan, 2009). Next, (3) consider equivalent or near-equivalent models. Recall that an equivalent model explains the data just as well as the researcher's preferred model but does so with a different configuration of hypothesized relations among the same variables (Chapter 1). For a given model, there may be many—and in some cases infinitely many—equivalent versions. Thus, the researcher needs to explain why his or her preferred model should not be rejected in favor of statistically equivalent ones. Too many authors of SEM studies fail to even acknowledge the existence of equivalent models (MacCallum & Austin, 2000). There may also be near-equivalent models that fit the same data just about as well as the researcher's preferred model, but not exactly so. Near-equivalent models are often just as critical a validity threat as equivalent models, if not even more so.

Respecification

A researcher usually arrives at this step because the fit of his or her initial model is poor. In the context of model generation, now is the time to refer to that list of theoretically justifiable possible changes I suggested you make when you specified the initial model. We will deal with respecification in more detail in Chapter 8, but a bottom line of that discussion is that a model's respecification should be guided more by rational considerations than purely statistical ones. Any respecified model must be identified; otherwise, you will be "stuck" at this step until you have an estimable model.

Reporting the Results

The final step is to accurately and completely describe the analysis in written reports. The fact that too many published articles that concern SEM are seriously flawed in this regard was previously discussed. These blatant shortcomings are surprising considering that there are published guidelines for reporting results of SEM (e.g., Boomsma, 2000; McDonald & Ho, 2002; Schreiber, Nora, Stage, Barlow, & King, 2006). An integrated set of suggestions for reporting the results of SEM analyses is presented in Chapter 10.

Optional Steps

Two optional steps in SEM could be added to the basic ones just described:

7. Replicate the results.
8. Apply the results.

Replication

Structural equation models are seldom estimated across independent samples either by the same researchers who collected the original data (internal replication) or by other researchers who did not (external replication). The need for large samples in SEM complicates replication. Nevertheless, it is critical to eventually replicate a structural equation model if it is ever to represent anything beyond a mere statistical exercise.

Application

Kaplan (2009) notes that despite about 40 years of application of SEM in the behavioral sciences, rarely are results from SEM analyses used for policy or clinically relevant prediction studies. Neglecting to properly carry out the basic steps (1–6) may be part of the problem.

The ultimate goal of SEM—or any other type of model-fitting technique—is to attain what I refer to as **statistical beauty**, which means that the final retained model (if any):

1. Has a clear theoretical rationale (i.e., it makes sense).
2. Differentiates between what is known and what is unknown—that is, what is the model's range of convenience, or limits to its generality?
3. Sets conditions for posing new questions.

That most applications of SEM fall short of these goals should be taken as a positive incentive for all of us to do better. These issues are elaborated in Chapter 8 about hypothesis testing in SEM.

MODEL DIAGRAM SYMBOLS

Model diagrams are represented in this book by using symbols from the McArdle–McDonald reticular action model (RAM). The RAM symbolism explicitly represents every model parameter. This property has pedagogical value for learning about SEM. It also helps you to avoid mistakes when you are translating a diagram to the syntax of a particular SEM computer tool. Part of RAM symbolism is universal in SEM. This includes the representation in diagrams of

1. Observed variables with squares or rectangles (e.g., □, ▭).
2. Latent variables with circles or ellipses (e.g., ○, ⬯).
3. Hypothesized directional effects of one variable on another, or **direct effects**, with a line with a single arrowhead (e.g., →).
4. Covariances (in the unstandardized solution) or correlations (in the standardized one) between independent variables—referred to in SEM as **exogenous variables**—with a curved line with two arrowheads (⤣).

The symbol described in (4) also designates an **unanalyzed association** between two exogenous variables. Although such associations are estimated by the computer, they are unanalyzed in the sense that no prediction is put forward about *why* the two exogenous variables covary (e.g., does one cause the other?—do they have a common cause?). In RAM symbolism (this next symbol is not universal), two-headed curved arrows that exit and reenter the same variable (↺) represent the variance of an exogenous variable. Because the causes of exogenous variables are not represented in model diagrams, the exogenous variables are considered free to both vary and covary. The symbols ⤣ and ↺ , respectively, reflect these assumptions. Specifically, the symbol

⌣ will connect every pair of observed exogenous variables, and the symbol ↻ will connect every observed or latent exogenous variable to itself in RAM symbolism.

This is not so for dependent (outcome, criterion) variables in model diagrams, which are referred to as **endogenous variables**. Unlike exogenous variables, the presumed causes of endogenous variables are explicitly represented in the model. Accordingly, endogenous variables are not free to vary or covary. This means in model diagrams that the symbol for an unanalyzed association, or ⌣, does not directly connect two different endogenous variables, and the symbol for a variance ↻ will not originate from and end with any endogenous variable. Instead, the model as a whole represents the researcher's account about *why* endogenous variables covary with each other and also with the exogenous variables. During the analysis, this "explanation" based on the model is compared with the sample covariances (the data). If the two sets of covariances, predicted and observed, are similar, the model is said to fit the data; otherwise, the "explanation" is rejected.

Model parameters in RAM symbolism are represented with only three symbols: →, ⌣, and ↻. The following rule for defining parameters in words parallels these symbols and is consistent with the Bentler–Weeks representational system for SEM that underlies the EQS computer program:

Parameters of structural equation models when means are not analyzed include (1) direct effects on endogenous variables from other variables, either exogenous or endogenous; and (2) the variances and covariances of exogenous variables.   (Rule 5.1)

That's it. The simple rule just stated applies to all of the core SEM models described in this chapter when means are not analyzed (i.e., the model has a covariance structure only, not also a mean structure). An advantage of RAM symbolism is that you can quickly determine the number of model parameters simply by counting the number of →, ⌣, and ↻ symbols in its diagram. Several examples and exercises in counting parameters are presented later.

As mentioned in the previous chapter on SEM computer tools, model diagrams in Amos and Mx Graph are based on RAM symbolism. In other programs, such as LISREL and Mplus, error terms are represented by a line with a single arrowhead that points to the corresponding endogenous variables. This representation is more compact, but do not forget that error terms have parameters (variances) that are typically estimated in the analysis. This is one advantage of RAM symbolism: what you see is what you get concerning model parameters that require statistical estimates.

SPECIFICATION CONCEPTS

Considered next are key issues in model specification.

What to Include

The following is a basic specification issue: given a phenomenon of interest—health status, unemployment, and so on—what variables affect it? Because the literature for newer research areas can be limited, so decisions about what to include in the model must sometimes be guided more by the researcher's experience than by published reports. Consulting with experts in the field about plausible specifications may also help. In more established areas, sometimes there is too *much* information. That is, so many potential causal variables may be mentioned in the literature that it is virtually impossible to include them all. To cope, the researcher must again rely on his or her judgment about the most crucial variables.

The specification error of omitting causal variables that covary with others in the model has the same general consequences in SEM as in multiple regression (MR) (Chapter 2). However, it is unrealistic to expect all causal variables to be measured. Given that most structural equation models may be misspecified in this regard, the best way to minimize potential bias is preventive: make an omitted variable an included one through careful review of extant theory and research.

How to Measure the Hypothetical Construct

The selection of measures is a recurrent problem in research, and this is no less true in SEM (Chapter 3). Score reliability is especially important in the SEM technique of PA, which is characterized by **single-indicator measurement**. This means that there is only one observed measure of each construct. Therefore, it is critical that each measure have good psychometric characteristics. It is also assumed in PA that the exogenous variables are measured without error ($r_{XX} = 1.00$). The potential consequences of measurement error in PA are basically the same as those in MR (Chapter 2). Recall that disattenuating correlations for measurement error is one way to take score reliability into account (Equation 3.7), but this is not a standard part of PA. However, a method to do so for single-indicator measurement is described in Chapter 10.

Another approach is **multiple-indicator measurement**, in which more than one observed variable is used to measure the same construct. Suppose that a researcher is interested in measuring reading skill among Grade 4 children. In a single-indicator approach, the researcher would be forced to select a sole measure of reading skill, such as a word recognition task. However, a single task would reflect just one facet of reading, and some of its score variance may be specific to that task, not to general reading ability per se. In a multiple-indicator approach, additional measures can be selected and administered. In this example, a second measure could be a comprehension task, and a third measure could involve word attack skills. Use of the three tasks together may reflect more aspects of reading, and the reliability of factor measurement tends to be higher with multiple indicators.

Each measure in a multiple-indicator approach is represented in the model as a separate indicator of the same underlying factor. This representation assumes convergent validity. Specifically, scores from multiple indicators presumed to measure a common construct should be positively correlated. Otherwise, the measurement model for these indicators may be rejected. The technique of CFA and the analysis of SR models both feature multiple-indicator measurement. The analysis of an SR model in particular can be seen as a type of latent-variable PA that accommodates multiple-indicator measurement.

Directionality

The specification of directionalities of presumed causal effects, or **effect priority**, is an important part of SEM. In the technique of PA, specifications about directionality concern observed variables only. In path diagrams, direct effects represented by the symbol → (i.e., paths) correspond to the researcher's hypotheses about effect priority. For example, if X and Y are two observed variables, the specification $X \rightarrow Y$ implies that X is causally prior to Y (X affects Y). This specification does not rule out other causes of Y. If other variables are believed to also affect Y, then the corresponding direct effects (e.g., $W \rightarrow Y$) can be added to the model, too.

Five general conditions must be met before one can reasonably infer a cause–effect relation (e.g., Mulaik, 2009; Pearl, 2000):

1. *Temporal precedence.* The presumed cause (e.g., X) must occur before the presumed effect (e.g., Y).[1]
2. *Association.* There is an observed covariation; that is, variation in the presumed cause must be related to that in the presumed effect.
3. *Isolation.* There are no other plausible explanations (e.g., extraneous variables) of the covariation between the presumed cause and the presumed effect.
4. *Correct effect priority.* The direction of the causal relation is correctly specified. That is, X indeed causes Y ($X \rightarrow Y$) instead of the reverse ($Y \rightarrow X$) or X and Y cause each other in a reciprocal manner ($X \rightleftarrows Y$).
5. *Known distributional form.* When dealing with **probabilistic causality** instead of **deterministic causality**, the forms of the distributions of the parameters are specified. Deterministic causality assumes that given a change in the causal variable, the same consequence is observed in all cases for the affected variable. It is probabilistic causality that is modeled in SEM, and it allows for changes to occur in affected variables at some probability < 1.0.[2] Estimation of these probabilities (effects) with sample data are typically based on specific distributional

---

[1] See Rosenberg (1998) for a discussion of Immanuel Kant's arguments about the possibility of simultaneous causation.

[2] Kenny (1979) suggested that probabilistic causality models are compatible with the view that some portion of unexplained variance is fundamentally unknowable because it reflects, for lack of a better term, free will—the ability of people to act on occasion outside of external influences on them.

assumptions. If these assumptions are not reasonable, then the estimates may be incorrect.

The second and third conditions just listed require that the association between X and Y is not spurious when controlling for common causes or when other causes of Y are included in the model (e.g., W). Temporal precedence is established in experimental or quasi-experimental designs when treatment begins (and perhaps ends, too) before outcome is measured. In nonexperimental designs, the hypothesis that X causes Y would be bolstered if X is measured before Y; that is, the design is longitudinal. But the expected value of the covariance between X and Y in a longitudinal design could still be relatively large even if Y causes X and the effect (X) is measured before the cause (Y) (Bollen, 1989, pp. 61–65). This could happen because X would have been affected by Y before either variable was actually measured in a longitudinal study. This phenomenon explains the fourth requirement for correct specification of directionality: Even if X actually causes Y, the magnitude of their association may be low if the interval between their measurements is either too short (effects take time to materialize) or too long (temporary effects have dissipated). The fifth requirement explains the importance of distributional assumptions: Estimates of causal effects may be biased if assumptions about their distributional forms, such as normality, across random samples are not tenable.

The assessment of variables at different times provides a measurement framework consistent with the specification of directional effects. But longitudinal designs pose potential difficulties, such as case attrition and extra resource demands. This is probably why most SEM studies feature concurrent rather than longitudinal measurement. If all variables are measured simultaneously, however, it is not possible to demonstrate temporal precedence. Therefore, the researcher needs a clear, substantive rationale for specifying that X causes Y instead of the reverse (or that X and Y mutually influence each other) when all variables are measured at once. This process relies heavily on the researcher to rule out alternative explanations of the association between X and Y and also to measure other presumed causes of Y. Both require strong knowledge about the phenomena under study. If the researcher cannot give a cogent account of directionality specifications, then causal inferences in nonexperimental designs are unwarranted. This is why many researchers are skeptical about inferring causation in nonexperimental designs. An example follows.

Lynam, Moffit, and Stouthamer–Loeber (1993) hypothesized that poor verbal ability is a cause of delinquency, but both variables were measured simultaneously in their sample. This hypothesis raises some questions: Why this particular direction of causation? Is it not also plausible that certain behaviors associated with delinquency, such as truancy, could impair verbal ability? What about other causes of delinquency? Some arguments offered by Lynam et al. are summarized next: Their participants were relatively young (about 12 years), which may preclude delinquent careers long enough to affect verbal ability. They cited the results of prospective studies which indicated that low verbal ability precedes antisocial acts. Lynam et al. measured other presumed causes of delinquency, including social class and motivation, and controlled for these variables in the analysis. The particular arguments given by Lynam et al. are not above criticism (e.g., Block, 1995), but they exemplify the types of arguments that researchers should provide to justify directionality specifications. Unfortunately, too few authors of nonexperimental studies give such detailed explanations.

Given a single SEM study in which hypotheses about effect priority are tested, it would be almost impossible to believe that all of the logical and statistical requirements had been satisfied for interpreting the results as indicating causality. This is why the interpretation that direct effects in structural equation models correspond to true causal relations is typically without basis. It is only with the accumulation of the following types of evidence that the results of SEM analyses *may* indicate causality (Mulaik, 2000): (1) replication of the model across independent samples; (2) elimination of plausible equivalent or near-equivalent models; (3) corroborating evidence from empirical studies of variables in the model that are manipulable; and (4) the accurate prediction of the effects of interventions.

Although as students we are told time and again that *correlation does not imply causation*, too many researchers seem to forget this essential truth. For example, Robinson, Levin, Thomas, Pituch, and Vaughn (2007) reviewed about 275 articles published in five different journals in the area of teaching and learning. They found that (1) the proportion of studies based on experimental or quasi-experimental designs declined from about 45% in 1994 to 33% in 2004. Nevertheless, (2) the proportion of nonexperimental studies containing claims for causality increased from 34% in 1994 to 43% in 2004. It seems that researchers in the teaching-and-learning area—and, to be fair, in other areas, too—may have become less cautious than they should be concerning the inference of causation from correlation. Robinson et al. (2007) noted that more researchers in the teaching-and-learning area were using SEM in 2004 compared with 1994. Perhaps the increased use of SEM explains the apparent increased willingness to infer causation in nonexperimental designs, but the technique does not justify it.

There are basically three options in SEM if a researcher is uncertain about directionality: (1) specify a structural equation model but without directionality specifications between key variables; (2) specify and test alternative models, each with different causal directionalities; or (3) include reciprocal effects in the model as a way to cover both possibilities. The first option just mentioned concerns exogenous variables, which are basically always assumed to covary (e.g., $X_1 \curvearrowright X_2$), but there is no specification about direct effects between exogenous variables. The specification of unanalyzed associations between exogenous variables in SEM is consistent with the absence of hypotheses of direct or indirect effects between such variables. A problem with the second option is that it can happen in SEM that different models, such as model 1 with $Y_1 \rightarrow Y_2$ and model 2 with $Y_2 \rightarrow Y_1$, may fit the same data equally well (they are equivalent), or nearly so. When this occurs, there is no statistical basis for choosing one model over another. The third option concerns the specification of reciprocal effects (e.g., $Y_1 \rightleftarrows Y_2$), but the specification of such effects is *not* a simple matter. This point is elaborated on later, but the inclusion of even one reciprocal effect in a model can make it more difficult to analyze. So there are potential costs to the inclusion of reciprocal effects as a hedge against uncertainty about directionality. If you are fundamentally uncertain about directionality, then you may not be ready to use SEM. In this case, conduct a **minimally sufficient analysis**, or use the simplest technique that will get the job done (Wilkinson & the Task Force on Statistical Inference, 1999). Simpler methods include regression techniques, such as canonical correlation when there are multiple predictor and outcome variables. A canonical correlation analysis requires no directionality assumptions among the variables in either set, predictor or outcome. There is no "embarrassment" in using a simpler statistical technique over a more complicated one, especially if the simpler technique is sufficient to test your hypotheses *and* if your comprehension of the more complex method is not strong. In general, it is better to resist the temptation to use the "latest and greatest" (i.e., more complicated) statistical technique when a simpler method will accomplish the task.

Model Complexity

There is another limit that must be respected in specification. It concerns the total number of parameters that can be estimated, or model complexity. This total is limited by the number of **observations** available for the analysis. In this context, the number of observations is *not* the sample size. Instead, it is literally the number of entries in the sample covariance matrix in lower diagonal form.[3] The number of observations can be calculated with a simple rule:

If v is the number of observed variables, then the number of obser-   (Rule 5.2)
vations equals $v(v + 1)/2$ when means are not analyzed.

Suppose that $v = 4$ observed variables are represented in a model. The number of observations is $4(5)/2$, or 10. This count (10) equals the total number of variances (4) and unique covariances (below the diagonal, or 6) in the data matrix. With $v = 4$, the greatest number of parameters that could be estimated by the computer is 10. Fewer parameters can be estimated in a more parsimonious model, but not > 10. The number of observations has nothing to do with sample size. If four variables are measured for 100 or 1,000 cases, the number of observations is still 10. Adding cases does not increase the number of observations; only adding *variables* can do so.

The difference between the number of observations and the number of its parameters is the **model degrees of freedom**, or

$$df_M = p - q \qquad (5.1)$$

where p is the number of observations (Rule 5.2) and q is the number of estimated

---

[3]Confusingly, LISREL uses the term *number of observations* in dialog boxes to refer to sample size, not the number of variances and unique covariances.

parameters (Rule 5.1). The requirement that there be at least as many observations as parameters can be expressed as the requirement that $df_M \geq 0$.

A model with more estimated parameters than observations ($df_M < 0$) is not amenable to empirical analysis. This is because such a model is not identified. If you tried to estimate a model with negative degrees of freedom, an SEM computer tool would likely terminate its run with error messages. Most models with zero degrees of freedom ($df_M = 0$) perfectly fit the data. But models that are just as complex as the data are not interesting because they test no particular hypothesis. Models with positive degrees of freedom generally do not have perfect fit. This is because $df_M > 0$ allows for the *possibility* of model–data discrepancies. Raykov and Marcoulides (2000) describe each degree of freedom as a dimension along which the model can *potentially* be rejected. Thus, retained models with greater degrees of freedom have withstood a greater potential for rejection. The idea underlies the **parsimony principle**: given two models with similar fit to the same data, the simpler model is preferred, assuming that the model is theoretically plausible.

Parameter Status

Each model parameter can be free, fixed, or constrained depending on its specification. A **free parameter** is to be estimated by the computer with the data. In contrast, a **fixed parameter** is specified to equal a constant. The computer "accepts" this constant as the estimate regardless of the data. For example, the hypothesis that X has no direct effect on Y corresponds to the specification that the coefficient for the path $X \rightarrow Y$ is fixed to zero. It is common in SEM to test hypotheses by specifying that a previously fixed-to-zero parameter becomes a free parameter, or vice versa. Results of such analyses may indicate whether to respecify a model by making it more complex (an effect is added—a fixed parameter becomes a free parameter) or more parsimonious (an effect is dropped—a free parameter becomes a fixed parameter).

A **constrained parameter** is estimated by the computer within some restriction, but it is not fixed to equal a constant. The restriction typically concerns the *relative* values of other constrained parameters. An **equality constraint** means that the estimates of two or more parameters are forced to be equal. Suppose that an equality constraint is imposed on the two direct effects that make up a feedback loop (e.g., $Y_1 \rightleftarrows Y_2$). This constraint simplifies the analysis because only one coefficient is needed rather than two. In a multiple-sample SEM analysis, a **cross-group equality constraint** forces the computer to derive equal estimates of that parameter across all groups. The specification corresponds to the null hypothesis that the parameter is equal in all populations from which the samples were drawn. How to analyze a structural equation model across multiple samples is explained in Chapter 9.

Other kinds of constraints are not seen as often. A **proportionality constraint** forces one parameter estimate to be some proportion of the other. For instance, the coefficient for one direct effect in a reciprocal relation may be forced to be three times the value of the other coefficient. An **inequality constraint** forces the value of a parameter estimate to be either less than or greater than the value of a specified constant. The specification that the value of an unstandardized coefficient must be > 5.00 is an example of an inequality constraint. The imposition of proportionality or inequality constraints generally requires knowledge about the relative magnitudes of effects, but such knowledge is rare in the behavioral sciences. A **nonlinear constraint** imposes a nonlinear relation between two parameter estimates. For example, the value of one estimate may be forced to equal the square of another. Nonlinear constraints are used in some methods to estimate curvilinear or interactive effects of latent variables, a topic covered in Chapter 12.

PATH ANALYSIS MODELS

Although PA is the oldest member of the SEM family, it is not obsolete. About 25% of roughly 500 articles reviewed by MacCallum and Austin (2000) concerned path models, so PA is still widely used. There are also times when there is just a single observed measure of each construct, and PA is a single-indicator technique. Finally, *if you master the fundamentals of PA, you will be better able to understand and critique a wider variety of structural equation models.* So read this section carefully even if you are more interested in latent variable methods in SEM.

Elemental Models

Presented in Figure 5.2 are the diagrams in RAM symbolism of three path models. Essentially, all more complex models can be constructed from these elemental models. A **path model** is a structural model for observed variables, and a **structural model** represents hypotheses about effect priority. The path model of Figure 5.2(a) represents the hypothesis that *X* is a cause of *Y*. By convention, causally prior variables are represented in the left part of the diagram, and their effects are represented in the right part. The line in the figure with the single arrowhead (→) that points from *X* to *Y* represents the corresponding direct effect. Statistical estimates of direct effects are **path coefficients**, which are interpreted just as regression coefficients in MR.

Variable *X* in Figure 5.2(a) is exogenous because its causes are not represented in the model. Accordingly, the symbol ↶↷ represents the fact that *X* is free to vary. In contrast, variable *Y* in Figure 5.2(a) is endogenous and thus is not free to vary. Each endogenous variable has a **disturbance**, which for the model of Figure 5.2(a) is an error (residual) term, designated as *D*, that represents unexplained variance in *Y*. It is the presence of disturbances in structural models that signal the assumption of probabilistic causality. Because disturbances can be considered latent variables in their own right, they are represented with circles in RAM symbolism. Theoretically, a disturbance can be seen as a "proxy" or composite variable that represents all unmeasured causes of the corresponding endogenous variable. Because the nature and number of these omitted causes is unknown as far as the model is concerned, disturbances can be viewed as

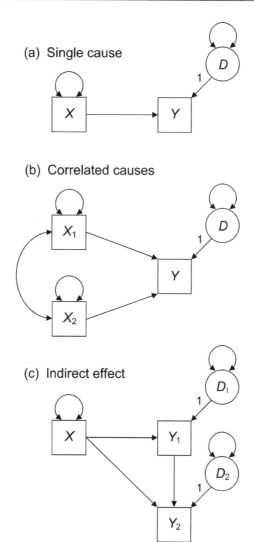

FIGURE 5.2. Elemental path models.

unmeasured (latent) exogenous variables. Accordingly, the symbol for the variance of an exogenous variable (⟨⟩) appears next to the disturbance in Figure 5.2(a).

Measurement error in the endogenous variable Y is manifested in its disturbance, so disturbances typically reflect both omitted causes and score unreliability. If scores on Y are unreliable, then its disturbance will be relatively large, which would be confounded with omitted causes. The path that points from the disturbance to the endogenous variable in Figure 5.2(a), or $D \rightarrow Y$, represents the direct effect of all unmeasured causes on Y. The numeral (1) that appears in the figure next to this path is a **scaling constant** that represents the assignment of a scale to the disturbance. This is necessary because disturbances are latent, and latent variables need scales before the computer can estimate anything about them. A scaling constant for a disturbance is also called an **unstandardized residual path coefficient**. The concept behind this specification for scaling a disturbance is explained in the next chapter, but it is required for identification. In contrast, exogenous variables do not have disturbances (e.g., X in Figure 5.2(a)). Therefore, it is generally assumed in PA that scores on exogenous variables are perfectly reliable. This assumption is just as unrealistic in PA as it is in MR.

Path coefficients are calculated holding all omitted causes constant (pseudoisolation; Chapter 2), which requires the assumption that all unmeasured causes represented by the disturbance are uncorrelated with measured causes of the corresponding endogenous variable. In Figure 5.2(a), it is assumed that D and X are uncorrelated. This is a strong assumption, one that is directly analogous to the assumption of uncorrelated residuals and predictors in MR.

The path model of Figure 5.2(b) represents the hypothesis of correlated causes. In this case, it is hypothesized that (1) both X_1 and X_2 are causes of Y, and (2) these exogenous variables covary. However, the model gives no account about *why* X_1 and X_2 covary. Accordingly, the curved line with two arrowheads that represents an unanalyzed association (↶↷) connects the squares for the two measured exogenous variables in Figure 5.2(b). Together, the symbols ↔ and ↶↷ in the figure represent the assumptions that X_1 and X_2 are free to, respectively, vary and covary, but for reasons that are unknown, at least according to the model. Measured exogenous variables are basically always assumed to covary, so the symbol ↶↷ routinely connects every pair of such variables in structural models.

Path coefficients for the two direct effects in Figure 5.2(b), $X_1 \rightarrow Y$ and $X_2 \rightarrow Y$, are each estimated controlling for the covariation between X_1 and X_2, just as in MR. This model assumes that all unmeasured causes of Y are uncorrelated with both X_1 and X_2. A natural question is: If measured exogenous variables can have unanalyzed associations, can a disturbance have an unanalyzed association with a measured exogenous variable, such as X_1 ↶↷ D? Such an association would imply the presence of an omitted cause that is correlated with X_1. This seems plausible, but, no, it is not generally possible to estimate covariances between and measured and unmeasured exogenous variables. (See Kenny, 1979, pp. 93–94 for conditions required to do so.) The only realistic way to cope with the restrictive assumption of uncorrelated measured and unmeasured causes is through careful specification.

Observe in the path model of Figure 5.2(c) that there are two direct effects on the endogenous variable Y_2 from other observed variables, one from the exogenous variable X and another from the other endogenous variable, Y_1. The latter specification gives Y_1 a dual role as, in the language of regression, both a predictor and a criterion. This dual role is described in PA as an **indirect effect** or a **mediator effect**.[4] Indirect effects involve one or more **intervening variables**, or **mediator variables**, presumed to "transmit"

---

[4]Note that the separate concept of a "moderator effect" refers to an interaction effect. Likewise, a "moderator variable" is one variable involved in interaction effect with another variable. Chapter 12 deals with the estimation of interaction effects in SEM.

some of the causal effects of prior variables onto subsequent variables. For the model of Figure 5.2(c), variable X is specified to affect Y_2 both directly and indirectly first by affecting Y_1, and then Y_1 in turn is presumed to have an effect on Y_2. The entire indirect effect just described corresponds to the three-variable chain $X \rightarrow Y_1 \rightarrow Y_2$.

Here is a concrete example: Roth, Wiebe, Fillingim, and Shay (1989) specified a path model of factors presumed to affect illness. Part of their model featured the indirect effect

$$\text{Exercise} \rightarrow \text{Fitness} \rightarrow \text{Illness}$$

The fitness variable is the mediator, one that, according to the model, is affected by exercise (more exercise, better fitness). In turn, fitness affects illness (better fitness, less illness). Just as direct effects are estimated in SEM, so too are indirect effects. The estimation of indirect effects is so straightforward in SEM that such effects are routinely included in structural models, assuming such specifications are theoretically justifiable.

Finally, the model of Figure 5.2(c) assumes that (1) the omitted causes of both Y_1 and Y_2 are uncorrelated with X and (2) the omitted causes of Y_1 are unrelated to those of Y_2, and vice versa. That is, the disturbances are independent, which is apparent in the figure by the *absence* of the symbol for an unanalyzed association ($\curvearrowright$) between D_1 and D_2. This specification also represents the hypothesis that the observed covariation between that pair of endogenous variables, Y_1 and Y_2, can be entirely explained by other measured variables in the model.

Types of Structural Models

There are two kinds of structural models. **Recursive models** are the most straightforward and have two basic features: their disturbances are uncorrelated, and all causal effects are unidirectional. **Nonrecursive models** have feedback loops or may have correlated disturbances. Consider the path models in Figure 5.3. The model of Figure 5.3(a) is recursive because its disturbances are independent and no observed variable is represented as both a cause and effect of another variable, directly or indirectly. For example, X_1, X_2, and Y_1 are specified as direct or indirect causes of Y_2, but Y_2 has no effect back onto one of its presumed causes. All of the models in Figure 5.2 are recursive, too. In contrast, the model of Figure 5.3(b) has a **direct feedback loop** in which Y_1 and Y_2 are specified as both causes and effects of each other ($Y_1 \rightleftarrows Y_2$). Each of these two variables is measured only once and also simultaneously. That is, direct feedback loops are estimated with data from a cross-sectional design, not a longitudinal design. **Indirect feedback loops** involve three or more variables, such as

$$Y_1 \rightarrow Y_2 \rightarrow Y_3 \rightarrow Y_1$$

Any model with an indirect feedback loop is automatically nonrecursive, too.

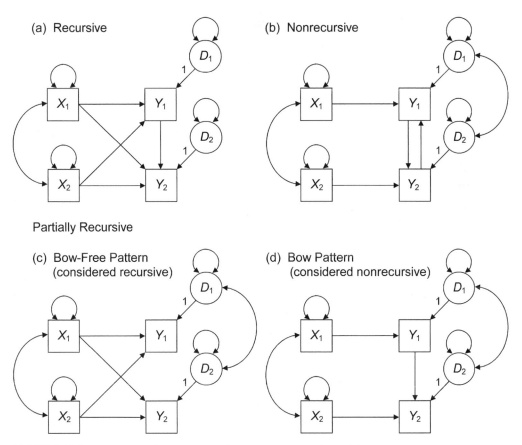

FIGURE 5.3. Examples of recursive and nonrecursive path models.

The model of Figure 5.3(b) also has a **disturbance covariance** (for unstandardized variables) or a **disturbance correlation** (for standardized variables). The term *disturbance correlation* is used from this point on regardless of whether or not the variables are standardized. A disturbance correlation, such as $D_1 \curvearrowright D_2$, reflects the assumption that the corresponding endogenous variables (Y_1, Y_2) share at least one common omitted cause. Unlike unanalyzed associations between measured exogenous variables (e.g., $X_1 \curvearrowright X_2$), the inclusion of disturbance correlations in the model is not routine. Why this is true is explained momentarily.

There is another type of path model, one that has unidirectional effects and correlated disturbances; two examples of this type are presented in Figures 5.3(c) and 5.3(d). Unfortunately, the classification of such models is not consistent. Some authors call these models nonrecursive, whereas others use the term **partially recursive**. But more important than the label for these models is the distinction made in the figure: Partially recursive models with a **bow-free pattern** of disturbance correlations can be treated in the analysis just like recursive models. A bow-free pattern means that correlated disturbances are restricted to pairs of endogenous variables *without* direct effects between them (see Figure 5.3(c)). In contrast, partially recursive models with a **bow pattern** of disturbance correlations must be treated in the analysis as nonrecursive models. A bow pattern means that a disturbance correlation occurs *with* a direct effect between that pair of endogenous variables (see Figure 5.3(d)) (Brito & Pearl, 2003). All ensuing references to recursive and nonrecursive models include, respectively, partially recursive models without and with direct effects among the endogenous variables.

Implications of the distinction between recursive and nonrecursive structural models are considered next. The assumptions of recursive models that all causal effects are unidirectional and that the disturbances are independent simplify the statistical demands for their analysis. For example, in the past MR was used to estimate path coefficients and disturbance variances in recursive path models. Today we use SEM computer tools to estimate recursive path models and all other kinds of models, too. The occurrence of a technical problem in the analysis is less likely for recursive models. It is also true that recursive structural models are identified, given that the necessary requirements for identification are satisfied (Chapter 6). The same assumptions of recursive models that ease the analytical burden are also restrictive. For example, causal effects that are not unidirectional, such as in a feedback loop, or disturbances that are correlated in a bow pattern cannot be represented in a recursive model.

The kinds of effects just mentioned can be represented in nonrecursive models, but such models require additional assumptions. Kaplan, Harik, and Hotchkiss (2001) remind us that data from a cross-sectional design give only a "snapshot" of an ongoing dynamic process. Therefore, the estimation of reciprocal effects in a feedback loop with cross-sectional data requires the assumption of **equilibrium**. This means that any changes in the system underlying a presumed feedback relation have already manifested their effects and that the system is in a steady state. That is, the values of the estimates of the direct effects that make up the feedback loop do not depend on the particular time point of data collection. Heise (1975) described equilibrium this way: it means that a dynamic system has completed its cycles of response to a set of inputs and that the inputs do not vary over time. That is, the causal process has basically dampened out and is not just beginning (Kenny, 1979). It is important to realize that there is generally no statistical way to directly evaluate whether the equilibrium assumption is tenable when the data are cross-sectional; that is, it must be argued substantively. Kaplan et al. (2001) note that rarely is this assumption explicitly acknowledged in the literature on applications of SEM where feedback effects are estimated with cross-sectional data. This is unfortunate because the results of computer simulation studies by Kaplan et al. (2001) indicate that violation of the equilibrium assumption can lead to severely biased estimates of the direct effects in feedback loops. Another assumption in the estimation of reciprocal effects in feedback loops with cross-sectional data is that of **stationarity**, the requirement that the causal structure does not change over time. Both assumptions just described, that of equilibrium and stationarity, are very demanding (i.e., probably unrealistic).

A feedback loop between Y_1 and Y_2 is represented in Figure 5.4(a) without disturbances or other variables. Another way to estimate reciprocal effects requires a longitudinal design where Y_1 and Y_2 are each measured at ≥ 2 different points in time. For example, the symbols Y_{11} and Y_{21} in the **panel model** shown in Figure 5.4(b) without disturbances or other variables represent, respectively, Y_1 and Y_2 at the first measurement occasion. Likewise, the symbols Y_{12} and Y_{22} represent the same two variables at the second measurement. Presumed reciprocal causation is represented in Figure 5.4(b) by the **cross-lag direct effects** between Y_1 and Y_2 measured at different times, such as $Y_{11} \to Y_{22}$ and $Y_{21} \to Y_{12}$. A panel model may be recursive or nonrecursive depending on its pattern of disturbance correlations.

Panel models for longitudinal data offer potential advantages over models with feedback loops for cross-sectional data. One is the explicit representation of a finite causal lag that corresponds to the measurement occasions. In this sense, the measurement occasions in a design where all variables are concurrently measured are *always* incorrect, if we assume that causal effects require a finite amount of time. However, the analysis of a panel model is no panacea for estimating reciprocal causality. For example, it can be difficult to specify measurement occasions that match actual causal lags. Panel designs are *not* generally useful for resolving effect priority between reciprocally related variables—for example, does Y_1 cause Y_2 or vice versa?—unless some restrictive assumptions are met, including that of stationarity. Maruyama (1998) reminds us that the requirement that there are no omitted causes correlated with those in the model is even more critical for panel models because of repeated sampling over time. The complexity of panel models can increase rapidly as more variables are added to the model (Cole & Maxwell, 2003). See Frees (2004) for more information about the analysis of panel data in longitudinal designs.

For many researchers, the estimation of reciprocal causation between variables measured simultaneously is the only viable alternative to a longitudinal design. Given all the restrictive assumptions for estimating such effects in a cross-sectional design, however, it is critical not to be too cavalier in the specification of feedback loops. One example is when different directionalities are each supported by two different theories (e.g., $Y_1 \to Y_2$ according to theory 1, $Y_2 \to Y_1$ according to theory 2). As mentioned, it can happen that two models with different directionality specifications among the same variables can fit the same data equally well. An even clearer example is when you haven't really thought through the directionality question. In this case, the specification of $Y_1 \rightleftarrows Y_2$ may be a smokescreen that covers up the basic uncertainty.

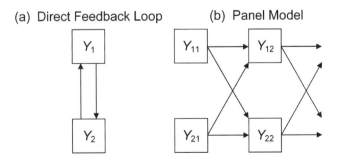

FIGURE 5.4. Reciprocal causal effects between Y_1 and Y_2 represented with (a) a direct feedback loop based on a cross-sectional design and (b) a cross-lag effect based on a longitudinal design (panel model) shown without disturbances or other variables.

Recall that the presence of a disturbance correlation reflects the assumption that the corresponding endogenous variables share at least one common unmeasured cause. The disturbances of variables involved in feedback loops are often specified as correlated. This specification often makes sense because if variables are presumed to mutually cause each other, then it seems plausible to expect that they may have shared omitted causes. In fact, the presence of disturbance correlations in particular patterns in nonrecursive models helps to determine their identification status (Chapter 6). In recursive models, disturbance correlations can be specified only between endogenous variables with no direct effect between them (e.g., Figure 5.3(c)). The addition of each disturbance correlation to the model "costs" one degree of freedom and thus makes the model more complicated. If there are substantive reasons for specifying disturbance correlations, then it is probably better to estimate the model with these terms than without them. This is because the constraint that a disturbance correlation is zero when there are common causes tends to redistribute this association toward the exogenous end of the model, which can result in biased estimates of direct effects. In general, disturbances should be specified as correlated if there are theoretical bases for doing so; otherwise, be wary of making the model overly complex by adding parameters without a clear reason.

Another complication of nonrecursive models is that of identification. There are some straightforward ways that a researcher can determine whether some, but not all, types of nonrecursive models are identified. These procedures are described in Chapter 6, but it is worthwhile to make this point now: adding exogenous variables is one way to remedy an identification problem of a nonrecursive model. However, this typically can only be done *before* the data are collected. *Thus it is critical to evaluate whether a nonrecursive model is identified right after it is specified and before the study is conducted.*

Before we continue, let's apply the rules for counting observations, parameters, and degrees of freedom to the recursive model in Figure 5.3(a). Because there are $v = 4$ observed variables in this model, the number of observations is $4(5)/2 = 10$ (Rule 5.2). It is assumed that the constants (1) in the figure, such as that for the path $D_1 \rightarrow Y_1$, are fixed parameters that scale the disturbances. Applying Rule 5.1 for counting free parameters gives us the results that are summarized in Table 5.1. Because the number of observations and free parameters for this model are equal (10), the model degrees of freedom are zero ($df_M = 0$). Exercise 3 for this chapter asks you to count the number of parameters and df_M for the other path models in Figure 5.3.

PA Research Example

Presented in Figure 5.5 is a recursive path model of presumed causes and effects of positive teacher–pupil interactions analyzed in a sample of 109 high school teachers and 946 students by Sava (2002).[5] This model reflects the hypothesis that both the level of

---

[5] I renamed some of the variables in Figure 5.5 in order to clarify the meaning of low versus high scores in the Sava (2002) data set.

TABLE 5.1. Number and Types of Free Parameters for the Recursive Path Model of Figure 5.3(a)

Model	Direct effects on endogenous variables		Endogenous variables		Total
			Variances (⌣)	Covariances	
Figure 5.3(a)	$X_1 \to Y_1$ $X_1 \to Y_2$ $Y_1 \to Y_2$	$X_2 \to Y_1$ $X_2 \to Y_2$	X_1, X_2 D_1, D_2	$X_1 \smile X_2$	10

school support for teachers (e.g., resource availability) and a coercive view of student discipline that emphasizes a custodial approach to education affect teacher burnout. All three variables just mentioned are expected to affect the level of positive teacher–pupil interactions. In turn, better student–teacher interactions should lead to better school experience and general somatic status (e.g., less worry about school) on the part of students. Note in Figure 5.5 the absence of direct effects from school support, coercive control, and burnout to the two endogenous variables in the far right side of the model, school experience and somatic status. Instead, the model depicts the hypothesis of "pure" mediation through positive teacher–pupil interactions.

The article by Sava (2002) is a model in that it offers a clear account of specification and a detailed description of all measures, including internal consistency score reliabilities. Sava (2002) reported the data matrices analyzed (covariance, correlation) and used an appropriate method to analyze a correlation matrix without standard deviations. This author also reported all parameter estimates, both unstandardized and stan-

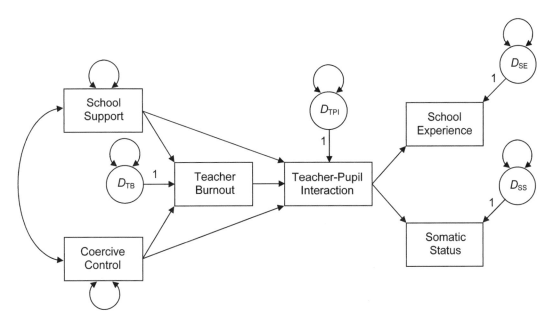

FIGURE 5.5. A path model of causes and effects of positive teacher–pupil interactions.

dardized, with the appropriate standard errors. However, Sava (2002) did not consider equivalent path models. Detailed analysis of the path model in Figure 5.5 is discussed in Chapter 7.

CFA MODELS

Issues in the specification of CFA models are considered next.

Standard CFA Models

The technique of CFA analyzes a priori measurement models in which both the number of factors and their correspondence with the indicators are explicitly specified. Presented in Figure 5.6 is an example of a **standard CFA model**—the type most often tested in the literature—with two factors and six indicators. This model represents the hypothesis that (1) indicators X_1–X_3 measure factor A, (2) X_4–X_6 measure factor B, and (3) the factors covary. Each indicator has a measurement error term, such as E_1 for indicator X_1. Standard CFA models have the following characteristics:

1. Each indicator is a continuous variable represented as having two causes—a single factor that the indicator is supposed to measure and all other unique sources of influence (omitted causes) represented by the error term.
2. The measurement errors are independent of each other and of the factors.
3. All associations between the factors are unanalyzed (the factors are assumed to covary).

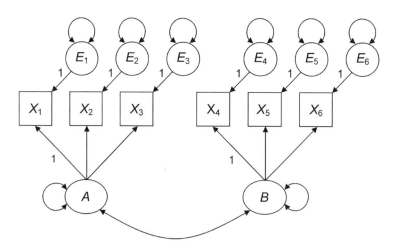

FIGURE 5.6. A standard confirmatory factor analysis model.

The lines with single arrowheads that point from a factor to an indicator, such as $A \rightarrow X_1$ in Figure 5.6, represent the presumed causal effect of the factor on the observed scores. Statistical estimates of these direct effects are called **factor loadings** or **pattern coefficients**, and they are generally interpreted as regression coefficients that may be in unstandardized or standardized form. Indicators assumed to be caused by underlying factors are referred to as **effect indicators** or **reflective indicators**. In this sense, indicators in standard CFA models are endogenous, and the factors are exogenous variables that are free to vary and covary. This also describes **reflective measurement**. The numeral (1) that appears in the figure next to the paths from the factors to one of their indicators (e.g., $B \rightarrow X_4$) are scaling constants that assign a metric to each factor, which allows the computer to estimate factor variances and covariances. The logic behind this specification and another option to scale factors is discussed in the next chapter, but scaling the factors is required for identification.

Each measurement error term in Figure 5.6 represents **unique variance**, a factor-analytic term for indicator variance not explained by the factors. Like disturbances in path models, measurement errors are proxy variables for all sources of residual variation that are not explained by the model. That is, they are unmeasured exogenous variables, so the symbol ↶ ↷ appears next to each of the error terms in the figure. The measurement errors in Figure 5.6 are specified as independent, which is apparent by the absence of the symbol for an unanalyzed association (↶↷) that connects pairs of measurement error terms. This specification assumes that all omitted causes of each indicator are unrelated to those for all other indicators in the model. It is also assumed that the measurement errors are independent of the factors.

Two types of unique variance are represented by measurement errors: random error (score unreliability) and all sources of systematic variance not due to the factors. Examples of the latter type include systematic effects due to a particular measurement method or the particular stimuli that make up a task. When it is said that SEM takes account of measurement error, it is the error terms in measurement models to which this statement refers. The paths in the figure that point to the indicators from the measurement errors represent the direct effect of all unmeasured sources of unique variance on the indicators. The constants (1) that appear in the figure next to paths from measurement errors to indicators (e.g., $E_1 \rightarrow X_1$) represent the assignment of a scale to each term.

The representation in standard CFA models that each indicator has two causes, such as

$$A \rightarrow X_1 \leftarrow E_1$$

in Figure 5.6, is consistent with the view in classical measurement theory that observed scores (X) are comprised of two components: a true score (T) that reflects the construct of interest and a random error component (E) that is normally distributed with a mean of zero across all cases, or

$$X = T + E \qquad\qquad (5.2)$$

The rationale that underlies the specification of reflective measurement in a standard CFA model comes from the **domain sampling model** (Nunnally & Bernstein, 1994, chap. 6). In this view of measurement, effect indicators X_1–X_3 in Figure 5.6 should as a set be internally consistent. This means that their intercorrelations should be positive and at least moderately high in magnitude (e.g., > .50). The same should also hold for indicators X_4–X_6 in the figure. Also, correlations among indicators of the same factor should be greater than cross-factor correlations. The patterns of indicator intercorrelations just described correspond to, respectively, convergent validity and discriminant validity in construct measurement. The domain sampling model also assumes that equally reliable effect indicators of the same construct are interchangeable (Bollen & Lenox, 1991). This means that the indicators can be substituted for each other without appreciably affecting construct measurement.

Sometimes the items of a particular indicator are negatively worded compared with other indicators of the same factor. Consequently, scores on that indicator will be negatively correlated with those from the other indicators, which is problematic from a domain sampling perspective. Suppose that a life satisfaction factor has three indicators. High scores on two indicators indicate greater contentment, but the third indicator is scaled to reflect degree of unhappiness, which implies negative correlations with scores from the other two indicators. In this case, the researcher could use **reverse scoring** or **reverse coding**, which reflects or reverses the scores on the negatively worded indicated indicator. One way to reflect the scores is to multiply them by –1.0 and then add a constant to the reflected scores so that the minimum score is at least 1.0 (Chapter 3). In this example, high scores on the unhappiness indicator are reflected to become low happiness scores, and vice versa. Now intercorrelations among all three indicators of the life satisfaction factor in this example should be positive.

It makes no sense to specify a factor with effect indicators that do not measure something in common. For example, suppose that the variables gender, ethnicity, and education are specified as effect indicators of a factor named "background" or some similar term. There are two problems here. First, gender and ethnicity are unrelated in representative samples, so one could not claim that these variables somehow measure a common domain.[6] Second, none of these indicators, such as a person's gender, is in any way "caused" by the some underlying "background" factor.

A common question about CFA concerns a minimum number of indicators per factor. In general, the absolute minimum for CFA models with two or more factors is two indicators per factor, which is required for identification. However, CFA models—and SR models, too—with factors that have only two indicators are more prone to problems in the analysis, especially in small samples. Also, it may be difficult to estimate measure-

---

[6]L. Wothke, personal communication, November 25, 2003.

ment error correlation for factors with only two indicators, which can result in a specification error. Kenny's (1979) rule of thumb about the number of indicators is apropos: "Two *might* be fine, three is better, four is best, and anything more is gravy" (p. 143; emphasis in original.)

Dimensionality of Measurement

The specifications that (1) each indicator loads on a single factor and (2) the error terms are independent describe **unidimensional measurement**. The first specification just mentioned describes **restricted factor models**. If any indicator loads on ≥ 2 factors or if its error term is assumed to covary with that of another indicator, then **multidimensional measurement** is specified. For example, adding the direct effect $B \rightarrow X_1$ to the model of Figure 5.6 would specify multidimensional measurement. There is controversy about allowing indicators to load on multiple factors. On the one hand, some indicators may actually measure more than one domain. An engineering aptitude test with text and diagrams, for instance, may measure both verbal and visual-spatial reasoning. On the other hand, unidimensional models offer more precise tests of the convergent and discriminant validity. For example, if every indicator in Figure 5.6 were allowed to load on both factors, an exploratory factor analysis (EFA) model that allows correlated factors (an oblique rotation) would be specified. It is **unrestricted factor models** that are estimated in EFA. (Other differences between CFA and EFA are outlined below.)

The specification of correlated measurement errors is a second way to represent multidimensional measurement. An error correlation reflects the assumption that the two corresponding indicators share something in common that is not explicitly represented in the model. Because error correlations are unanalyzed associations between latent exogenous variables (e.g., $E_1 \curvearrowright E_2$), what this "something" may be is unknown as far as the model is concerned. Error term correlations may be specified as a way to test hypotheses about shared sources of variability over and beyond the factors. For example, the specification of error correlations for repeated measures variables represents the hypothesis of **autocorrelated errors**. The same specification can also reflect the hypothesis of a common method effect. In contrast, the absence of a measurement error correlation between a pair of indicators reflects the assumption that their observed correlation can be explained by their underlying factors. This refers to the **local independence assumption** that the indicators are independent, given the (correctly specified) latent variable model.[7]

The specification of multidimensional measurement makes a CFA model more complex compared with a standard (unidimensional) model. There are also implications for identification. Briefly, straightforward ways can be used to determine whether a standard CFA model is identified, but this may not be true for nonstandard models

---

[7]W. Wothke, personal communication, November 24, 2003.

(Chapter 6). It is important to evaluate whether nonstandard CFA models are identified when they are specified and before the data are collected. This is because one way to respecify a nonidentified CFA model is to add indicators, which increases the number of observations available to estimate effects.

Other Characteristics of CFA

The results of a CFA include estimates of factor variances and covariances, loadings of the indicators on their respective factors, and the amount of measurement error for each indicator. If the researcher's model is reasonably correct, then one should see the following pattern of results: (1) all indicators specified to measure a common factor have relatively high standardized factor loadings on that factor (e.g., > .70); and (2) estimated correlations between the factors are not excessively high (e.g., < .90 in absolute value). The first result indicates convergent validity; the second, discriminant validity. For example, if the estimated correlation between factors A and B in Figure 5.6 is .95, then the six indicators can hardly be said to measure two distinct constructs. If the results of a CFA do not support the researcher's a priori hypotheses, the measurement model can be respecified in the context of model generation (Chapter 1).

Hierarchical confirmatory factor analysis models depict at least one construct as a second-order factor that is not directly measured by any indicator. This exogenous second-order factor is also presumed to have direct effects on the first-order factors, which have indicators. These first-order factors are endogenous and thus do not have unanalyzed associations with each other. Instead, their common direct cause, the second-order factor, is presumed to explain the covariances among the first-order factors. Hierarchical models of intelligence, in which a general ability factor (g) is presumed to underlie more specific ability factors (verbal, visual-spatial, etc.), are examples of theoretical models that have been tested with hierarchical CFA. This special type of CFA model is discussed in Chapter 9.

Contrast with EFA

A standard statistical technique for evaluating measurement models is EFA. Originally developed by psychologists to test theories of intelligence, EFA is not generally considered a member of the SEM family. The term *EFA* refers to a class of procedures that include centroid, principal components, and principal (common) factor analysis methods that differ in their statistical criteria used to derive factors. This technique does not require a priori hypotheses about factor–indicator correspondence or even the number of factors. For example, all indicators are allowed to load on every factor; that is, EFA tests unrestricted factor models. There are ways to conduct EFA in a more confirmatory mode, such as instructing the computer to extract a certain number of factors based on theory. But the point is that EFA does not require specific hypotheses in order to apply it.

Another difference between CFA and EFA is that unrestricted factor models are not generally identified. That is, there is no single, unique set of parameter estimates for a given EFA model. This is because an EFA solution can be rotated an infinite number of ways. Among rotation options in EFA—varimax, quartimin, and promax to name just a few—researchers try to select one that clarifies factor interpretation. A parsimonious explanation in EFA corresponds to a solution that exhibits **simple structure** where each factor explains as much variance as possible in nonoverlapping sets of indicators (Kaplan, 2009). There is no need for rotation in CFA because factor models estimated in this technique are identified. Factors are allowed to covary in CFA, but the specification of correlated factors is not required in EFA (it is optional).

Cause Indicators and Formative Measurement

The assumption that indicators are caused by underlying factors is not always appropriate. Some indicators are viewed as **cause indicators** or **formative indicators** that affect a factor instead of the reverse. Consider this example by Bollen and Lennox (1991): The variables income, education, and occupation are used to measure socioeconomic status (SES). In a standard CFA model, these variables would be specified as effect indicators that are caused by an underlying SES factor (and by measurement errors). But we usually think of SES as the *outcome* of these variables (and others), not vice versa. For example, a change in any one of these indicators, such as a salary increase, may affect SES. From the perspective of **formative measurement**, SES is a *composite* that is caused by its indicators. Chapter 10 deals with formative measurement models.

CFA Research Example

Presented in Figure 5.7 is a standard CFA measurement model for the Mental Processing scale of the first edition Kaufman Assessment Battery for Children (KABC-I) (Kaufman & Kaufman, 1983), an individually administered cognitive ability test for children 2½ to 12½ years old. The test's authors claimed that the eight subtests represented in the figure measure two factors, sequential processing and simultaneous processing. The three tasks believed to reflect sequential processing all require the correct recall of auditory stimuli (Word Order, Number Recall) or visual stimuli (Hand Movements) in a particular order. The other five tasks represented in the figure are supposed to measure more holistic, less order-dependent reasoning, or simultaneous processing. Each of these tasks requires that the child grasp a "gestalt" but with somewhat different formats and stimuli.

The results of several CFA analyses of the KABC-I conducted in the 1980–1990s generally supported the two-factor model presented in Figure 5.7 (e.g., Cameron et al., 1997). However, other results have indicated that some subtests, such as Hand Movements, may measure both factors and that some of the measurement errors may covary (e.g., Keith, 1985). Detailed analysis of the model in Figure 5.7 with data for 10-year-olds from the KABC-I's normative sample is described in Chapter 9.

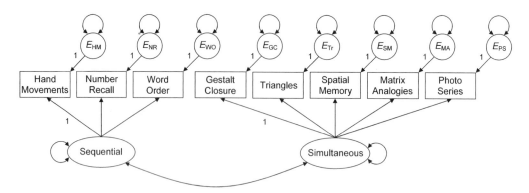

FIGURE 5.7. A confirmatory factor analysis model of the first-edition Kaufman Assessment Battery for Children.

STRUCTURAL REGRESSION MODELS

The most general kind of core structural equation model is an SR model, also called a full LISREL model. This term reflects the fact that LISREL was one of the first computer programs to analyze SR models, but any contemporary SEM computer tool can do so now. An SR model is the synthesis of a structural model and a measurement model. As in PA, the specification of an SR model allows tests of hypotheses about direct and indirect causal effects. Unlike path models, though, these effects can involve latent variables because an SR model also incorporates a measurement component that represents observed variables as indicators of underlying factors, just as in CFA. The capability to test hypotheses about both structural and measurement relations within a single model affords much flexibility.

Presented in Figure 5.8(a) is a structural model with observed variables—a path model—that features single-indicator measurement. The observed exogenous variable of this model, X_1, is assumed to be measured without error, an assumption usually violated in practice. This assumption is not required for the endogenous variables of this model, but measurement error in Y_1 or Y_3 is manifested in their disturbances. The model of Figure 5.8(b) is an SR model with both structural and measurement components. Its measurement model has the same three observed variables represented in the path model, X_1, Y_1, and Y_3. Unlike the path model, each of these three indicators in the SR model is specified as one of a pair for an underlying factor.[8] Consequently, (1) all the observed variables in Figure 5.8(b) have measurement error terms, and (2) effects for the endogenous latent variables, such as direct effects (e.g., $A \rightarrow B$) and disturbance variances (for D_B and D_C) are all estimated controlling for measurement error in the observed variables.

---

[8]I saved space in Figure 5.8 by showing only two indicators per factor, but remember that it is generally better to have at least three indicators per factor.

This SR model of Figure 5.8(b) also has a structural component that depicts the same basic pattern of direct and indirect causal effects as the path model but among latent variables ($A \rightarrow B \rightarrow C$) instead of observed variables. The structural model of Figure 5.8(b) is recursive, but it is also generally possible to specify an SR model with a nonrecursive structural model. Each latent endogenous variable in the structural model of Figure 5.8(b) has a disturbance (D_B, D_C). Unlike path models, the disturbances of SR models reflect only omitted causes and not also measurement error. For the same reason, path coefficients of the direct effects $A \rightarrow B$ and $B \rightarrow C$ in Figure 5.8(b) are corrected for measurement error, but those for the paths $X_1 \rightarrow Y_1$ and $Y_1 \rightarrow Y_3$ in Figure 5.8(a) are not.

The model of Figure 5.8(b) could be described as a **fully latent SR model** because every variable in its structural model is latent. Although this characteristic is desirable because it implies multiple-indicator measurement, it is also possible to represent in SR models an observed variable that is a single indicator of a construct. This reflects the reality that sometimes there is just a single measure of a some construct of interest. Such models could be called **partially latent SR models** because at least one variable in their structural model is a single indicator. However, unless measurement error of a single indicator is taken into account, partially latent SR models have the same limitations as path models outlined earlier. A way to address this problem for single indicators is described in Chapter 10.

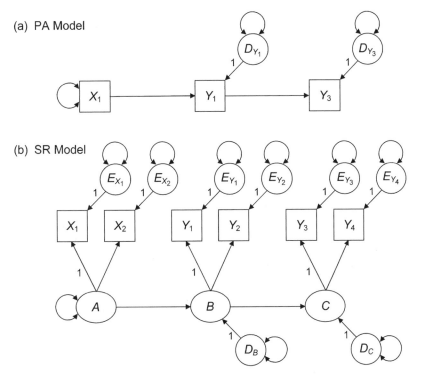

FIGURE 5.8. Examples of a path analysis model (a) and a structural regression model (b).

SR Model Research Example

Within a sample of 263 full-time university employees, Houghton and Jinkerson (2007) administered multiple measures of four constructs, including constructive (opportunity-oriented) thinking, dysfunctional (obstacle-oriented) thinking, subjective well-being (sense of psychological wellness), and job satisfaction. Based on their review of theory and empirical results in this area, Houghton and Jinkerson (2007) specified the four-factor fully latent SR model presented in Figure 5.9. The structural part of this model represents the hypotheses that (1) dysfunctional thinking and subjective well-being each have direct effects on job satisfaction; (2) constructive thinking has a direct effect on dysfunctional thinking; (3) the effect of constructive thinking on subjective well-being is mediated by dysfunctional thinking; and (4) the effects of constructive thinking on job satisfaction are mediated by the other two factors.

The measurement part of the SR model in Figure 5.9 features three indicators per factor. Briefly, indicators of (1) constructive thinking include measures of belief evaluation, positive self-talk, and positive visual imagery; (2) dysfunctional thinking includes two scales regarding worry about performance evaluations and a third scale about need for approval; (3) subjective well-being include ratings about general happiness and two positive mood rating scales; and (4) job satisfaction include three scales that reflect one's work experience as positively engaging.

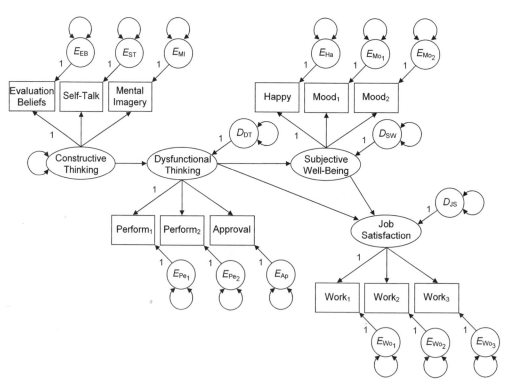

FIGURE 5.9. A structural regression model of factors of job satisfaction.

The article by Houghton and Jinkerson (2007) is exemplary in that the authors describe the theoretical rationale for each and every direct effect among the four factors in the structural model, provide detailed descriptions of all indicators including internal consistency score reliabilities, report the correlations and standard deviations for the covariance data matrix they analyzed, and test alternative models. However, Houghton and Jinkerson (2007) did not report unstandardized parameter estimates, nor did they consider equivalent versions of their final model. The detailed analysis of this SR model is described in Chapter 10.

EXPLORATORY SEM

Recall that Mplus has capabilities for exploratory structural equation modeling (ESEM) (Chapter 4). In ESEM, some parts of the measurement model are unrestricted instead of restricted. That is, the analysis incorporates features of both EFA and SEM. This type of analysis may be suitable when the researcher has weaker hypotheses about multiple-indicator measurement of some constructs than is ordinarily represented in CFA or SR models. Consider the ESEM model presented in Figure 5.10, which is also described in the Mplus 6 manual (Muthén & Muthén, 1998–2010, p. 90). The measurement model for factors A and B in the figure is an unrestricted EFA model where the indicators are allowed to load on every factor. In Mplus, the factor solution for this part of the model will be rotated according to the method specified by the user. Factors A and B are scaled by fixing their variances to 1.0, which standardizes them. In contrast, the measurement model for factors C and F in the figure is restricted where each indicator loads on a single factor. There is a structural model in Figure 5.10, too, and it features direct or indirect effects from the exogenous factors A and B onto the endogenous factors C and F. See Asparouhov and Muthén (2009) for more information about ESEM.

SUMMARY

Considered in this chapter were the specification of core SEM models and the types of research questions that can be addressed in their analysis. Path analysis allows researchers to specify and test structural models that reflect a priori assumptions about spurious associations and direct or indirect effects among observed variables. Measurement models that represent hypotheses about relations between indicators and factors can be evaluated with the technique of confirmatory factor analysis. Structural regression models with both a structural component and a measurement component can also be analyzed. Rules that apply to all the kinds of models just mentioned for counting the number of observations and the number of model parameters were also considered. The counting rules just mentioned are also relevant for checking whether a structural equation model is identified, which is the topic of the next chapter.

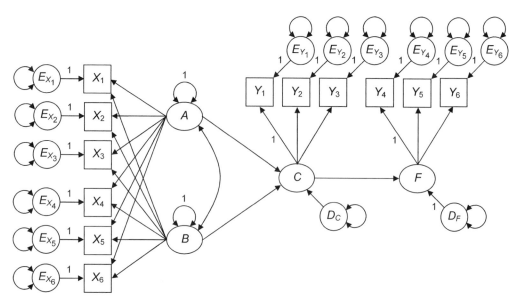

FIGURE 5.10. An exploratory structural equation model.

RECOMMENDED READINGS

MacCallum and Austin (2000) and Shah and Goldstein (2006) describe various types of shortcomings in articles published in psychology, education, and business journals in which results of SEM analyses are reported. Holbert and Stephenson (2002) survey the use of SEM in communication and note some of the same problems. All three articles should provide you with a good sense of common specification pitfalls to avoid.

Holbert, R. L., & Stephenson, M. T. (2002). Structural equation modeling in the communication sciences, 1995–2000. *Human Communication Research, 28,* 531–551.

MacCallum, R. C., & Austin, J. T. (2000). Applications of structural equation modeling in psychological research. *Annual Review of Psychology, 51,* 201–236.

Shah, R., & Goldstein, S. M. (2006). Use of structural equation modeling in operations management research: Looking back and forward. *Journal of Operations Management, 24,* 148–169.

EXERCISES

1. What is the "explanation" of Figure 5.3a about why scores on Y_1 and Y_2 are correlated?

2. Does the CFA model of Figure 5.6 have a structural component?

3. Count the number of free parameters for the path models of Figures 5.3(b)–5.3(d).

4. Calculate the model degrees of freedom for (a) Figure 5.5, (b) Figure 5.7, and (c) Figure 5.9.

5. How are covariates represented in structural models?

6. Respond to this question: "I am uncertain about the direction of causality between Y_1 and Y_2. In SEM, why can't I just specify two different models, one with $Y_1 \rightarrow Y_2$ and the other with $Y_2 \rightarrow Y_1$, fit both models to the same data, and then pick the model with the best fit?"

7. What is the difference between a measurement error (E) and a disturbance (D)?

8. Specify a path model where the effects of a substantive exogenous variable X_1 on the outcome variable Y_2 are entirely mediated through variable Y_1. Also represent in the model the covariate X_2 (e.g., level of education in years).

9. What is the role of sample size in SEM?

6

Identification

The topic of this chapter corresponds to the second step of SEM: the evaluation of identification, or whether it is theoretically possible for the computer to derive a unique set of model parameter estimates. This chapter shows you how to evaluate the identification status of core types of structural equation models analyzed within single samples when means are not also estimated. A set of identification rules or heuristics is introduced. These rules describe sufficient requirements for identifying certain types of core structural equation models, and they are relatively straightforward to apply. There may be no heuristics for more complex models, but suggestions are offered about how to deal with the identification problem for such models. Some of the topics discussed next require careful and patient study. However, many examples are offered, and exercises for this chapter give you additional opportunities for practice. A Chinese proverb states that learning is a treasure that will follow you everywhere. After mastering the concepts in this chapter, you will be better prepared to apply SEM in your own studies.

GENERAL REQUIREMENTS

There are two general requirements for identifying any structural equation model. Expressed more formally, these requirements are necessary but insufficient for identification; they are:

1. The model degrees of freedom must be at least zero ($df_M \geq 0$).
2. Every latent variable (including the residual terms) must be assigned a scale (metric).

Minimum Degrees of Freedom

Some authors describe the requirement for $df_M \geq 0$ as the **counting rule** (Kaplan, 2009). Models that violate the counting rule are not identified. Specifically, they are **underidentified** or **underdetermined**. As an example of how a deficit of observations leads to nonidentification, consider the following equation:

$$a + b = 6 \tag{6.1}$$

Look at this expression as a model, the 6 as an observation, and a and b as parameters. Because Equation 6.1 has more parameters (2) than observations (1), it is impossible to find unique estimates for its parameters. In fact, there are an infinite number of solutions, including ($a = 4$, $b = 2$), ($a = 8$, $b = -2$), and so on, all of which satisfy Equation 6.1. A similar thing happens when a computer tries to derive a unique set of estimates for the parameters of an underidentified structural equation model: it is impossible to do so, and the attempt fails.

This next example shows that having equal numbers of observations and parameters does not guarantee identification. Consider the following set of formulas:

$$a + b = 6 \tag{6.2}$$
$$3a + 3b = 18$$

Although this model has two observations (6, 18) and two parameters (a, b), it does not have a unique solution. Actually, an infinite number of solutions satisfy Equation 6.2, such as ($a = 4$, $b = 2$), ($a = 8$, $b = -2$), and so on. This happens due to an inherent characteristic of the model: the second formula in Equation 6.2 ($3a + 3b = 18$) is not unique. Instead, it is simply three times the first formula ($a + b = 6$), which means that it cannot narrow the range of solutions that satisfy the first formula. These two formulas can also be described as linearly dependent.

Now consider the following set of formulas with two observations and two parameters where the second formula is not linearly dependent on the first:

$$a + b = 6 \tag{6.3}$$
$$2a + b = 10$$

This two-observation, two-parameter model has a unique solution ($a = 4$, $b = 2$); therefore, it is **just-identified** or **just-determined**. Note something else about Equation 6.3: given estimates of its parameters, it can perfectly reproduce the observations (6, 10). Recall that most structural equation models with zero degrees of freedom ($df_M = 0$) that are also identified can perfectly reproduce the data (sample covariances), but such models test no particular hypothesis.

A statistical model can also have fewer parameters than observations. Consider the following set of formulas with three observations and two parameters:

$$a + b = 6 \qquad\qquad (6.4)$$
$$2a + b = 10$$
$$3a + b = 12$$

Try as you might, you will be unable to find values of a and b that satisfy all three formulas. For example, the solution ($a = 4$, $b = 2$) works only for the first two formulas in Equation 6.4, and the solution ($a = 2$, $b = 6$) works only for the last two formulas. At first, the absence of a solution seems paradoxical, but there is a way to solve this problem: Impose a statistical criterion that leads to unique estimates for an **overidentified** or **overdetermined** model with more observations than parameters. An example of such a criterion for Equation 6.4 is presented next:

> Find values of a and b that are positive and yield total scores such that the sum of the squared differences between the observations (6, 10, 12) and these totals is as small as possible.

Applying the criterion just stated to the estimation of a and b in Equation 6.4 yields a solution that not only gives the smallest squared difference (.67) but that is also unique. (Using only one decimal place, we obtain $a = 3.0$ and $b = 3.3$.) Note that this solution does not perfectly reproduce the observations (6, 10, 12) in Equation 6.4. Specifically, the three total scores obtained from Equation 6.4 given the solution ($a = 3.0$, $b = 3.3$) are (6.3, 9.3, 12.3). The fact that an overidentified model may not perfectly reproduce the data has an important role in model testing, one that is explored in later chapters.

Note that the terms *just-identified* and *overidentified* do not automatically apply to a structural equation model unless it meets both of the two necessary requirements for identification mentioned at the beginning of this section *and* additional, sufficient requirements for that particular type of model described later. That is:

1. A **just-identified structural equation model** is identified and has the same number of free parameters as observations ($df_M = 0$).
2. An **overidentified structural equation model** is identified and has fewer free parameters than observations ($df_M > 0$).

A structural equation model can be underidentified in two ways. The first case occurs when there are more free parameters than observations ($df_M < 0$). The second case happens when some model parameters are underidentified because there is not enough available information to estimate them but others are identified. In the second case, the whole model is considered nonidentified, even though its degrees of freedom could be greater than or equal to zero ($df_M \geq 0$). A general definition by Kenny (2004) that covers both cases just described is:

3. An **underidentified structural equation model** is one for which it is not possible to uniquely estimate all of its parameters.

Scaling Latent Variables

Recall that error (residual) terms in SEM can be represented in model diagrams as latent variables. Accordingly, each error term requires a scale just as every substantive latent variable (i.e., factor) must be scaled, too. Options for scaling each type of variable are considered next.

Error Terms

Scales are usually assigned to disturbances (D) in structural models or measurement errors (E) in measurement models through a **unit loading identification** (ULI) constraint. This means that the path coefficient for the direct effect of a disturbance or measurement error—the unstandardized residual path coefficient—is fixed to equal the constant 1.0. In model diagrams, this specification is represented by the numeral 1 that appears next to the direct effect of a disturbance or a measurement error on the corresponding endogenous variable. For example, the specification

$$D_{Y_1} \rightarrow Y_1 = 1.0$$

in the path analysis (PA) model of Figure 5.8(a) represents the assignment of a scale to the disturbance of endogenous variable Y_1. This specification has the consequence of assigning to D_{Y_1} a scale that is related to that of the unexplained variance of Y_1. Likewise, the specification

$$E_{X_1} \rightarrow X_1 = 1.0$$

in the CFA model of Figure 5.8(c) assigns to the error term E_{X_1} a scale related to variance in the indicator X_1 that is unexplained by the factor this indicator is supposed to reflect (A). Once the scale of a disturbance or measurement error is set by imposing a ULI constraint, the computer needs only to estimate its variance. If residual terms are specified as correlated (e.g., Figure 5.3(b)), then the residual covariance can be estimated, too, assuming that the model with the correlated residuals is actually identified.

The specification of *any* positive scaling constant, such as 2.1 or 17.3, would identify the variance of a residual term, but it is much more common for this constant to equal 1.0. A benefit of specifying that scaling constants are 1.0 is that for observed endogenous variables, the sum of the unstandardized residual variance and the explained variance will equal the unstandardized sample (total) variance of that endogenous variable. Also, most SEM computer programs make it easier to specify a ULI constraint for disturbances or measurement errors, or they do so by default.

Factors

Two traditional methods for scaling factors are described next. A more recent method by Little, Slegers, and Card (2006) is described later in this section. The first method is to use the same method as for error terms, that is, by imposing ULI constraints. For a factor this means to fix the unstandardized coefficient (loading) for the direct effect on any one of its indicators to equal 1.0. Again, specification of any other positive scaling constant would do, but 1.0 is the default in most SEM computer tools. In model diagrams, this specification is represented by the numeral 1 that appears next to the direct effect of a factor on one of its indicators. The indicator with the ULI constraint is known as the **reference variable** or **marker variable**. This specification assigns to a factor a scale related to that of the explained (common, shared) variance of the reference variable. For example, the specification

$$A \rightarrow X_1 = 1.0$$

in the CFA model of Figure 6.1(a) makes X_1 the reference variable and assigns a scale to factor A based on the common variance of X_1. Assuming that scores on each multiple indicator of the same factor are equally reliable, the choice of which indicator is to be the reference variable is generally arbitrary. One reason is that the overall fit of the model to the data is usually unaffected by the selection of reference variables. Another is consistent with the domain sampling model, wherein effect (reflective) indicators of the same factor are viewed as interchangeable (Chapter 5). However, if indicator scores are not equally reliable, then it makes sense to select the indicator with the most reliable scores as the reference variable. After all factors are scaled by imposing a ULI constraint on the loading of the reference variable for each factor, the computer must then only estimate factor variances and covariances.

The second basic option to scale a factor is to fix its variance to a constant. Specification of any positive constant would do, but it is much more common to impose a **unit variance identification** (UVI) constraint. This fixes the factor variance to 1.0 and also standardizes the factor. When a factor is scaled through a UVI constraint, all factor loadings are free parameters. A UVI constraint is represented in model diagrams in this book with the numeral 1 next to the symbol for the variance of an exogenous variable ($\curvearrowright$). For example, the variance of factor A is fixed to 1.0 in the CFA model of Figure 6.1(b). This specification not only assigns a scale to A, but it also implies that the loadings of all three of its indicators can be freely estimated with sample data. With the factors standardized, the computer must then only estimate the factor correlation. Note that scaling factors either through ULI or UVI constraints reduces the total number of free parameters by one for each factor.

Both methods of scaling factors in CFA (i.e., impose ULI or UVI constraints) generally result in the same overall fit of the model, but not always. A special problem known as constraint interaction occurs when the choice between either method affects overall model fit. This phenomenon is described in Chapter 9, but most of the time constraint interaction is not a problem. The choice between these two methods, then, is usually based on the relative merits of analyzing factors in standardized versus unstandardized form. When a CFA model is analyzed in a single sample, either method is probably acceptable. Fixing the variance of a factor to 1.0 to standardize it has the advantage of

(a) Unstandardized Factors

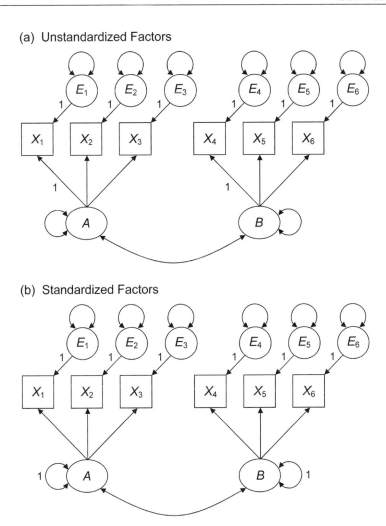

(b) Standardized Factors

FIGURE 6.1. Standard confirmatory factor analysis measurement models with unstandardized factors (a) and standardized factors (b).

simplicity. A shortcoming of this method, however, is that it is usually applicable only to exogenous factors. This is because although basically all SEM computer tools allow the imposition of constraints on any model parameter, the variances of endogenous variables are not considered model parameters. Only some programs, such as LISREL, SEPATH, and RAMONA, allow the *predicted* variances of endogenous factors to be constrained to 1.0. This is not an issue for CFA models, wherein all factors are exogenous, but it can be for structural regression (SR) models, wherein some factors are endogenous.

There are times when standardizing factors is *not* appropriate. These include (1) the analysis of a structural equation model across independent samples that differ in their variabilities and (2) longitudinal measurement of variables that show increasing (or decreasing) variabilities over time. In both cases, important information may be lost when factors are standardized. How to appropriately scale factors in a multiple-sample CFA analysis is considered in Chapter 9.

Exogenous factors in SR models can be scaled by imposing either a ULI constraint where the loading of one indicator per factor is fixed to 1.0 (the factor is unstandardized) or a UVI constraint where the factor variance is fixed to 1.0 (the factor is standardized). As mentioned, though, most SEM computer programs allow only the first method just mentioned for scaling endogenous factors. This implies that endogenous factors are unstandardized in most analyses. When an SR model is analyzed within a single sample, the choice between scaling an exogenous factor with either ULI or UVI constraints combined with the use of ULI constraints only to scale endogenous factors usually makes no difference. An exception is when some factors have only two indicators and there is constraint interaction, which for SR models is considered in Chapter 10.

Little, Slegers, and Card (2006) describe a third method for scaling factors in models where (1) all indicators of each factor have the same scale (i.e., range of scores) and (2) most indicators are specified to measure (load on) a single factor. This method does *not* require the selection of a reference variable, such as when ULI constraints are imposed, nor does it standardize factors, such as when UVI constraints are imposed. Instead, this third method for scaling factors relies on the capability of modern SEM computer tools to impose constraints on a set of two or more model parameters, in this case the unstandardized factor loadings of all the indicators for the same factor. Specifically, the researcher scales factors in the Little–Sleger–Card (LSC) method by instructing the computer to constrain the average (mean) loading of a set of indicators on their common factor to equal 1.0 in the unstandardized solution. So scaled, the variance of the factor will be estimated as the average explained variance across all the indicators in their original metric, weighted by the degree to which each indicator contributes to factor measurement. Thus, factors are not standardized in this method, nor does the explained variance of any arbitrarily selected indicator (i.e., that of the reference variance when imposing a ULI constraint) determine factor variance. The LSC method results in the same overall fit of the entire model to the data as observed when imposing either ULI or UVI constraints to scale factors. Also, the LSC method is appropriate for the analysis of a model in a single group, across multiple groups, or across multiple occasions (i.e., repeated measures)—see Little, Slegers, and Card (2006) for more information.

UNIQUE ESTIMATES

This is the penultimate aspect of identification: It must be possible to express each and every model parameter as a unique function of elements of the population covariance matrix such that the statistical criterion to be minimized in the analysis is also satisfied. Because we typically estimate the population covariance matrix with the sample covariance matrix, this facet of identification can be described by saying that there is a unique set of parameter estimates, given the data and the statistical criterion to be minimized.

Determining whether the parameters can be expressed as unique functions of the sample data is *not* an empirical question. Instead, it is a mathematical or theoretical question that can be evaluated by resolving equations that represent the parameters in terms of symbols that correspond to elements of the sample covariance matrix. This exercise takes the form of a formal mathematical proof, so no actual numerical values are needed for elements of the sample covariance matrix, just symbolic representations of them. *This means that model identification can—and should—be evaluated before the data are collected.* You may have seen formal mathematical proofs for ordinary least squares (OLS) estimation in multiple regression (MR). These proofs involve showing that standard formulas for regression coefficients and intercepts (e.g., Equations 2.5, 2.7, 2.8) are, in fact, those that satisfy the least squares criterion. A typical proof involves working with second derivatives for the function to be minimized. Dunn (2005) describes a less conventional proof for OLS estimation based on the Cauchy–Schwartz inequality, which is related to the triangle inequality in geometry as well as to limits on the bounds of correlation and covariance statistics in positive-definite data matrices (Chapter 3).

The derivation of a formal proof for a simple regression analysis would be a fairly daunting task for those without a strong mathematics background, and models analyzed in SEM are often more complicated than simple regression models. Also, the default estimation method in SEM, maximum likelihood (ML), is more complex than OLS estimation, which implies that the statistical criterion minimized in ML estimation is more complicated, too. Unfortunately, SEM computer tools are of little help in determining whether or not a particular structural equation model is identified. Some of these programs perform rudimentary checks for identification, such as applying the counting rule, but these checks generally concern necessary conditions, not sufficient ones.

It may surprise you to learn that SEM computer tools are rather helpless in this regard, but there is a simple explanation: Computers are very good at *numerical* processing. However, it is harder to get them to process symbols, and it is *symbolic* processing that is needed for determining whether a particular model is identified. Computer languages for symbolic processing, such as LISP (list processing), form the basis of some applications of computers in the areas of artificial intelligence and expert systems. But contemporary SEM computer tools lack any real capability for symbolic processing of the kind needed to prove model identification for a wide range of models.

Fortunately, one does not need to be a mathematician in order to deal with the identification problem in SEM. This is because a series of less formal rules, or **identification heuristics**, can be applied by ordinary mortals (the rest of us) to determine whether certain types of models are identified. These heuristics cover many, but not all, kinds of core structural equation models considered in this part of the book. They are described next for PA models, CFA models, and fully latent SR models. This discussion assumes that the two necessary requirements for identification ($df_M \geq 0$; latent variables scaled) are satisfied. Recall that CFA models assume reflective measurement where indicators are specified as caused by the factors (Chapter 5). Formative measurement models in which underlying observed or latent composites are specified as caused by their indicators have special identification requirements that are considered in Chapter 10.

It is frustrating that computers are of little help in dealing with identification in SEM, but you can apply heuristics to verify the identification status of many types of models. Copyright 2004 by Betsy Streeter. Reprinted with permission from CartoonStock Ltd. (*www.cartoonstock.com*).

RULE FOR RECURSIVE STRUCTURAL MODELS

Because of their particular characteristics, recursive path models are always identified (e.g., Bollen, 1989, pp. 95–98). This property is even more general: Recursive structural models are identified, whether the structural model consists of observed variables only (path models) or factors only (the structural part of a fully latent SR model). Note that whether the measurement component of an SR model with a recursive structural model is also identified is a separate question, one that is dealt with later in this chapter. The facts just reviewed underlie the following sufficient condition for identification:

Recursive structural models are identified.	(Rule 6.1)

RULES FOR NONRECURSIVE STRUCTURAL MODELS

The material covered in this section is more difficult, and so readers interested in recursive structural models only can skip it (i.e., go the section on CFA). However, you can specify and test an even wider range of hypotheses about direct and indirect effects (e.g., feedback loops) if you know something about nonrecursive structural models, so the effort is worthwhile.

The case concerning identification for nonrecursive structural models—whether among observed variables (path models) or factors (SR models)—is more complicated. This is because, unlike recursive models, nonrecursive models are not always identified. Although algebraic means can be used to determine whether the parameters of a nonrecursive model can be expressed as unique functions of its observations (e.g., Berry, 1984, pp. 27–35), these techniques are practical only for very simple models. Fortunately, there are alternatives that involve determining whether a nonrecursive model meets certain requirements for identification that can be checked by hand (i.e., heuristics). Some of these requirements are only necessary for identification, which means that satisfying them does not guarantee identification. If a nonrecursive model satisfies a sufficient condition, however, then it is identified. These requirements are described next for nonrecursive path models, but the same principles apply to SR models with nonrecursive structural components.

The nature and number of conditions for identification that a nonrecursive model must satisfy depend on its pattern of disturbance correlations. Specifically, the necessary order condition and the sufficient rank condition apply to models with unanalyzed associations between all pairs of disturbances either for the whole model or within blocks of endogenous variables that are recursively related to each other. Consider the two nonrecursive path models in Figure 6.2. For both models, $df_{\mathrm{M}} \geq 0$ and all latent variables are scaled, but these facts are not sufficient to identify either model. The model of Figure 6.2(a) has an indirect feedback loop that involves Y_1–Y_3 and all possible disturbance correlations (3). The model of Figure 6.2(b) has two direct feedback loops and a pattern of disturbance correlations described by some authors as **block recursive**. One can partition the endogenous variables of this model into two blocks, one with Y_1 and Y_2 and the other made up of Y_3 and Y_4. Each block contains all possible disturbance correlations ($D_1 \overset{\curvearrowleft}{\frown} D_2$ for the first block, $D_3 \overset{\curvearrowleft}{\frown} D_4$ for the second), but the disturbances across the blocks are independent (e.g., D_1 is uncorrelated with D_3). Also, the pattern of direct effects within each block is nonrecursive (e.g., $Y_1 \rightleftarrows Y_2$), but effects between the blocks are unidirectional (recursive). Thus, the two blocks of endogenous variables in the model of Figure 6.2(b) are recursively related to each other even though the whole model is nonrecursive.

Order Condition

The **order condition** is a counting rule applied to each endogenous variable in a non-recursive model that either has all possible disturbance correlations or that is block recursive. If the order condition is not satisfied, the equation for that endogenous variable is underidentified. One evaluates the order condition by tallying the number of variables in the structural model (except disturbances) that have direct effects on each endogenous variable versus the number that do not; let's call the latter *excluded variables*. The order condition can be stated as follows:

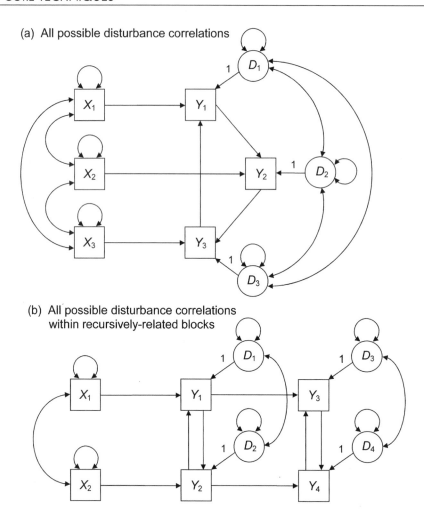

(a) All possible disturbance correlations

(b) All possible disturbance correlations within recursively-related blocks

FIGURE 6.2. Two examples of nonrecursive path models with feedback loops.

The order condition requires that the number of excluded variables for   (Rule 6.2)
each endogenous variable equals or exceeds the total number of
endogenous variables minus 1.

For nonrecursive models with correlations between all pairs of disturbances, the total number of endogenous variables equals that for the whole model. For example, the model of Figure 6.2(a) has all possible disturbance correlations, so the total number of endogenous variables equals 3. This means that a minimum of $3 - 1 = 2$ variables must be excluded from the equation of each endogenous variable, which is true here: There are three variables excluded from the equation of every endogenous variable (e.g., X_2, X_3, and Y_2 for Y_1), which exceeds the minimum number (2). Thus, the model of Figure 6.2(a) meets the order condition.

For nonrecursive models that are block recursive, however, the total number of endogenous variables is counted separately for each block when the order condition is evaluated. For example, there are two recursively related blocks of endogenous variables in the model of Figure 6.2(b). Each block has two variables, so the total number of endogenous variables for each block is 2. To satisfy the order condition, at least 2 – 1 = 1 variables must be excluded from the equation of each endogenous variable in both blocks, which is true here. Specifically, one variable is excluded from each equation for Y_1 and Y_2 in the first block (e.g., X_2 for Y_1), and three variables are excluded from each equation for Y_3 and Y_4 in the second block (e.g., X_1, X_2, and Y_2 for Y_3). Because the number of excluded variables for each endogenous variable in every block exceeds the minimum number, the order condition is satisfied for this model.

Rank Condition

Because the order condition is only necessary, we still do not know whether the nonrecursive models in Figure 6.2 are identified. Evaluation of the sufficient **rank condition**, however, will provide the answer. The rank condition is usually described in the SEM literature in matrix terms (e.g., Bollen, 1989, pp. 98–103), which is fine for those familiar with linear algebra but otherwise not. Berry (1984) devised an algorithm for checking the rank condition that does not require extensive knowledge of matrix operations, a simpler version of which is described in Appendix 6.A. A nontechnical description of the rank condition is given next.

For nonrecursive models with all possible disturbance correlations, the rank condition can be viewed as a requirement that each variable in a feedback loop has a unique pattern of direct effects on it from variables outside the loop. Such a pattern of direct effects provides a "statistical anchor" so that the parameters of variables involved in feedback loops can be estimated distinctly from one another. Look again at Figure 6.2(a). Each of the three endogenous variables of this model has a unique pattern of direct effects on it from variables external to their indirect feedback loop; that is:

$$X_1 \rightarrow Y_1, \quad X_2 \rightarrow Y_2, \quad \text{and } X_3 \rightarrow Y_3$$

This analogy does not hold for those models considered in this book to be nonrecursive that do not have feedback loops, such as partially recursive models with correlated disturbances in a bow pattern (e.g., Figure 5.3(d)). Therefore, a more formal means of evaluating the rank condition is needed; see Appendix 6.A. The identification rule for the rank condition for nonrecursive models that either have all possible disturbance correlations or that are block recursive is stated next:

Nonrecursive models that satisfy the rank condition are identified.   (Rule 6.3)

Rigdon (1995) describes a graphical technique for evaluating identification status that breaks the model down into a series of two-equation nonrecursive blocks, such as for a direct feedback loop. This graphical technique could complement or in some cases replace evaluation of the order condition and the rank condition using the methods described here. Eusebi (2008) describes a graphical counterpart of the rank condition, but it requires knowledge of undirected, directed, and directed acyclic graphs from graphical models theory.

Respecification of Nonidentified Nonrecursive Models

Now let's consider a nonrecursive model that is not identified and some options for its respecification. Presented in Figure 6.3 is a nonrecursive path model with all possible disturbance correlations based on an example by Berry (1984). In this model, let Y_1 and Y_2 represent, respectively, violence on the part of protesters and police. The direct feedback loop in this model reflects the hypothesis that as protesters become more violent, so do the police, and vice versa. The two measured exogenous variables, X_1 and X_2, represent, respectively, the seriousness of the civil disobedience committed by the protesters and the availability of police riot gear (clubs, tear gas, etc.). Immediately after its specification but before the data are collected, the researcher evaluates its identification status. Two problems are discovered: the model has more parameters (11) than observations (10), and the order condition is violated because there are no excluded variables for Y_2. Because this model fails the order condition, it will also fail the rank condition. An exercise will ask you to verify that $df_M = -1$ for the model of Figure 6.3 and also that it fails both the order condition and the rank condition.

What can be done about this identification problem? Because the data are not yet collected, one possibility is to add exogenous variables to the model such that (1) the number of additional observations afforded by adding variables is greater than the number of free parameters they bring to the model; (2) the number of excluded variables for Y_1 and Y_2 are each at least 1; and (3) the respecified model also meets the rank condition. Suppose that it is decided that a new exogenous variable, X_3, would be protesters' level of

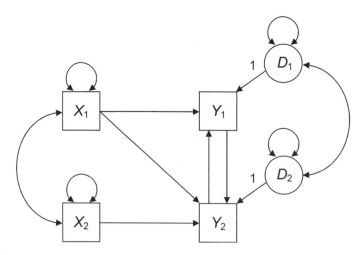

FIGURE 6.3. A nonrecursive model that is not identified.

commitment to nonviolence. The addition of the path $X_3 \rightarrow Y_1$ (Y_1 is protester violence) and unanalyzed associations between X_3 and the other two exogenous variables would accomplish the goals just listed. Thus, the model respecified in this way is identified. An exercise will ask you to verify this fact.

Equality and Proportionality Constraints

The imposition of an equality or a proportionality constraint on the direct effects of a feedback loop is one way to reduce the number of free parameters without dropping paths. For example, the specification that both direct effects of the reciprocal relation $Y_1 \rightleftarrows Y_2$ are equal means that only one path coefficient is needed rather than two. A possible drawback of imposing equality constraints on feedback loops is that they preclude the detection of unequal mutual influence. For example, Wagner, Torgeson, and Rashotte (1994) found in longitudinal studies that the effect of children's phonological processing abilities on their reading skills is about three times the magnitude of the effect in the opposite direction. If equality constraints were blindly imposed when bidirectional effects differ in magnitude, then not only may the model poorly fit the data but the researcher may miss an important finding. In contrast, a proportionality constraint allows for unequal mutual influence but on an a priori basis. For instance, it may be specified that the path $Y_1 \rightarrow Y_2$ must be three times the value of that for the path $Y_2 \rightarrow Y_1$. Like equality constraints, proportionality constraints reduce the number of free parameters, one for each pair of direct effects. However, the imposition of proportionality constraints generally requires knowledge about relative effect magnitudes.

"None-of-the-Above" Nonrecursive Models

If a nonrecursive structural model has either no disturbance correlations or less than all possible disturbance correlations such that the model is not block recursive, the order and rank conditions are generally too conservative. That is, such "none-of-the-above" nonrecursive models that fail either condition may nevertheless be identified. Unfortunately, there may be no sufficient condition that can be readily evaluated by hand to determine whether a none-of-the-above nonrecursive model is actually identified. Thus, the identification status of such models may be ambiguous. How to deal with structural equation models where identification status is unknown is discussed later.

RULES FOR STANDARD CFA MODELS

Meeting both necessary requirements also does not guarantee that a CFA measurement model is identified. For standard CFA models that specify unidimensional measurement—every indicator loads on just one factor and there are no measurement error correlations—there are some straightforward rules that concern minimum numbers of indicators per factor. They are summarized next:

| If a standard CFA model with a single factor has at least three indicators, the model is identified. | (Rule 6.4) |

| If a standard CFA model with ≥ 2 factors has ≥ 2 indicators per factor, the model is identified. | (Rule 6.5) |

That's it. The first heuristic just listed for single-factor models is known as the **three-indicator rule**, and the second heuristic for models with multiple constructs is the **two-indicator rule**. Recall that CFA models (and SR models, too) with factors that have only two indicators are more prone to problems in the analysis. It is better to have at least three to four indicators per factor to prevent such problems, but two indicators per factor is the minimum for identification.

Let's apply the requirements just discussed to the standard CFA models presented in Figure 6.4. The model of Figure 6.4(a) has a single factor with two indicators. This model is underidentified: With two observed variables, there are three observations but four parameters, including three variances of exogenous variables (of factor A and two measurement errors, E_1 and E_2) and one factor loading (of X_2; the other is fixed to 1.0 to scale A), so $df_M = -1$ for the model in Figure 6.4(a). The imposition of a constraint, such as one of equality, or

$$A \rightarrow X_1 = A \rightarrow X_2 = 1.0$$

may make this model estimable because df_M would be zero in the respecified one-factor, two-indicator model. For such models Kenny (1979) noted that if the correlation between the two indicators is negative, then the just-identified model that results by imposing an equality constraint on the factor loadings does not exactly reproduce the correlation. This is an example of a just-identified structural equation model that does not perfectly fit the data.

Because the single-factor model in Figure 6.4(b) has three indicators, it is identified. Specifically, it is just-identified: There are 3(4)/2 = 6 observations available to estimate the six-model parameters, including four variances (of factor A and three measurement errors) and two factor loadings ($df_M = 0$). Note that a standard, one-factor CFA model must have at least four indicators in order to be overidentified. Because each of the two factors in the model of Figure 6.4(c) has two indicators, it is identified. Specifically, it is overidentified and $df_M = 1$.

RULES FOR NONSTANDARD CFA MODELS

There is a different—and more complicated—set of rules for nonstandard CFA models that specify multidimensional measurement where some indicators load on more than a single factor or some error terms covary. Readers interested in standard CFA models

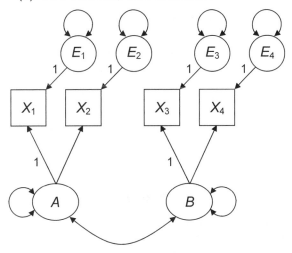

(a) Single Factor, Two Indicators   (b) Single Factor, Three Indicators

(c) Two Factors, Two Indicators

FIGURE 6.4. Identification status of three standard confirmatory factor analysis models.

only can skip this section (i.e., go to the section on SR models), but standard CFA models have more restrictive assumptions compared with nonstandard CFA models. Again, the reward of greater flexibility in hypothesis testing requires even more careful study, but you can do it.

O'Brien (1994) describes a set of rules for nonstandard measurement models where every indicator loads on a single factor but some measurement error correlations are freely estimated. These rules are applied "backwards" starting from patterns of independent (uncorrelated) pairs of error terms to prove the identification of factor loadings, then of error variances, next of factor correlations in multiple-factor models, and finally of measurement error correlations. The O'Brien rules work well for relatively simple measurement models, but they can be awkward to apply to more complex models. A different set of identification rules by Kenny, Kashy, and Bolger (1998) that may be easier to apply is listed in Table 6.1 as Rule 6.6. This rule spells out requirements that must be satisfied by each factor (Rule 6.6a), pair of factors (Rule 6.6b), and indicator (Rule 6.6c) in order to identify measurement models with error correlations.

Rule 6.6a in Table 6.1 is a requirement for a minimum number of indicators per factor, either two or three depending on the pattern of error correlations or constraints imposed on factor loadings. Rule 6.6b refers to the specification that for every pair of factors, there must be at least two indicators, one from each factor, whose error terms are not correlated. Rule 6.6c concerns the requirement for every indicator that there is at least one other indicator in the model with which it does not share an error correlation. Rule 6.6 in Table 6.1 assumes that all factor covariances are free parameters and that there are multiple indicators of every factor. Kenny et al. (1998) describe additional rules not considered here for exceptions to these assumptions.

Kenny et al. (1998) also describe identification rules for indicators in nonstandard measurement models that load on ≥ 2 factors. Let's refer to such indicators as **complex indicators**. The first requirement is listed in the top part of Table 6.2 as Rule 6.7, and it concerns sufficient requirements for identification of the multiple-factor loadings of a complex indicator. Basically, this rule requires that each factor on which a complex indicator loads has a sufficient number of indicators (i.e., each factor meets Rule 6.6a in Table 6.1). Rule 6.7 also requires that each one of every pair of such factors has an indicator that does not share an error correlation with a corresponding indicator of the other factor (see Table 6.2). If a complex indicator shares error correlations with other indicators, then the additional requirement listed as Rule 6.8 in Table 6.2 must also be

TABLE 6.1. Identification Rule 6.6 for Nonstandard Confirmatory Factor Analysis Models with Measurement Errors

For a nonstandard CFA model with measurement error correlations to be identified, all three of the conditions listed next must hold:	(Rule 6.6)
For each factor, at least one of the following must hold:	(Rule 6.6a)
1. There are at least three indicators whose errors are uncorrelated with each other.	
2. There are at least two indicators whose errors are uncorrelated and either	
a. the errors of both indicators are not correlated with the error term of a third indicator for a different factor, or	
b. an equality constraint is imposed on the loadings of the two indicators.	
For every pair of factors, there are at least two indicators, one from each factor, whose error terms are uncorrelated.	(Rule 6.6b)
For every indicator, there is at least one other indicator (not necessarily of the same factor) with which its error term is not correlated.	(Rule 6.6c)

Note. These requirements are described as Conditions B–D in Kenny, Kashy, and Bolger (1998, pp. 253–254).

TABLE 6.2. Identification Rule 6.7 for Multiple Loadings of Complex Indicators in Nonstandard Confirmatory Factor Analysis Models and Rule 6.8 for Error Correlations of Complex Indicators

Factor loadings

For every complex indicator in a nonstandard CFA model: (Rule 6.7)

In order for the *multiple factor loadings* to be identified, both of the following must hold:

1. *Each factor on which the complex indicator loads* must satisfy Rule 6.6a for a minimum number of indicators.

2. *Every pair of those factors* must satisfy Rule 6.6b that each factor has an indicator that does not have an error correlation with a corresponding indicator on the other factor of that pair.

Error correlations

In order for *error correlations* that involve complex indicators to be   (Rule 6.8)
identified, both of the following must hold:

1. Rule 6.7 is satisfied.

2. For each factor on which a complex indicator loads, there must be at least one indicator with a single loading that does not have an error correlation with the complex indicator.

Note. These requirements are described as Condition E in Kenny, Kashy, and Bolger (1998, p. 254).

satisfied, too. This rule requires that for each factor on which a complex indicator loads, there is at least one other indicator with a single loading that does not share an error correlation with the complex indicator. The requirements of Rules 6.6 and 6.7 are typically addressed by specifying that some indicators load on just a single factor.

Let's apply the identification heuristics just discussed to the nonstandard CFA models presented in Figure 6.5. To save space, I use a compact notation in the figure where latent constructs are denoted by circles, indicators by Xs, and error terms by Es. However, do not forget the variance parameter associated with each exogenous variable in Figure 6.5 that is normally represented by the ↶↷ symbol in model diagrams elsewhere in this book. The single-factor, four-indicator model in Figure 6.5(a) has two error correlations, or

$$E_{X_2} \curvearrowright E_{X_4} \quad \text{and} \quad E_{X_3} \curvearrowright E_{X_4}$$

This model is just-identified because it has no degrees of freedom ($df_M = 0$), its factor (A) has at least three indicators (X_1–X_3) whose error terms are uncorrelated (Rule 6.6a), and all other requirements of Rule 6.6 (Table 6.1) are met. The single-factor, four-indicator model in Figure 6.5(b) also has two error correlations (i.e., $df_M = 0$) but in a different pattern, or

$$E_{X_1} \curvearrowright E_{X_2} \quad \text{and} \quad E_{X_3} \curvearrowright E_{X_4}$$

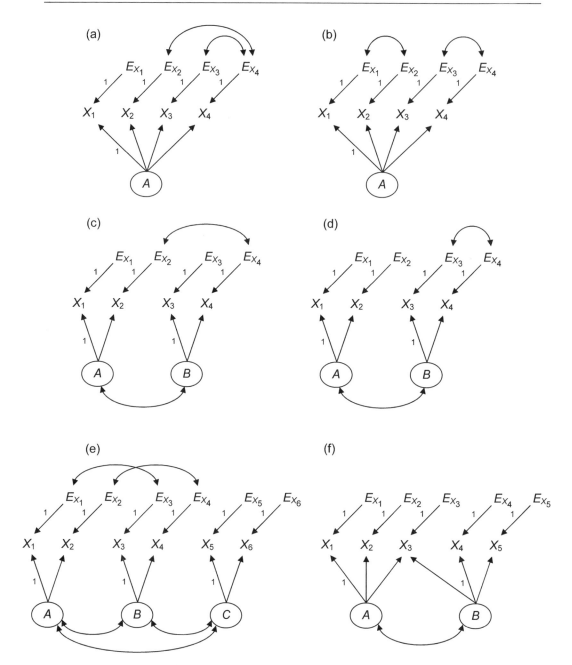

FIGURE 6.5. Identification status of nonstandard confirmatory factor analysis models.

Although this model has at least two indicators whose error terms are independent, such as X_2 and X_3, it nevertheless fails Rule 6.6a because there is no indicator of a different factor with which X_2 and X_3 do not share an error correlation. Therefore, the model in Figure 6.5(b) is not identified. However, this model would be identified if an equality constraint were imposed on the factor loadings of X_2 and X_3. That is, the specification that

$$A \rightarrow X_2 = A \rightarrow X_3$$

would be sufficient to identify the model in Figure 6.5(b) because then Rule 6.6 would be met.

The two-factor, four-indicator model of Figure 6.5(c) with a single error correlation ($E_{X_2} \smile E_{X_4}$) is just-identified because $df_M = 0$ and all three requirements for Rule 6.6 are satisfied (Table 6.1). However, the two-factor, four-indicator model in Figure 6.5(d) with a different error correlation ($E_{X_3} \smile E_{X_4}$) is not identified because it violates Rule 6.6a. Specifically, factor B in this model does not have two indicators whose error terms are independent. In general, it is easier to uniquely estimate cross-factor error correlations (e.g., Figure 6.5(c)) than within-factor error correlations (e.g., Figure 6.5(d)) when there are only two indicators per factor without imposing additional constraints. The three-factor, two-indicator model in Figure 6.5(e) with two cross-factor error correlations, or

$$E_{X_1} \smile E_{X_3} \quad \text{and} \quad E_{X_2} \smile E_{X_4}$$

is overidentified because the degrees of freedom are positive ($df_M = 4$) and Rule 6.6 is satisfied. This model also demonstrates that adding indicators—along with a third factor—allows the estimation of additional error correlations compared with the two-factor model in Figure 6.5(c). The model in Figure 6.5(f) has a complex indicator that loads on two factors, or

$$A \rightarrow X_3 \quad \text{and} \quad B \rightarrow X_3$$

Because this model meets the requirements of Rule 6.7 and has positive degrees of freedom ($df_M = 3$), it is overidentified. An exercise will ask you to add error correlations to this model with a complex indicator and then evaluate Rule 6.8 in order to determine whether the respecified models is identified.

The specification of either correlated measurement errors or of some indicators loading on multiple factors may not cause identification problems. The presence of both in the same model, though, can complicate matters. For example, it can be difficult to correctly apply the O'Brien rules or Kenny–Kashy–Bolger rules to complex models, especially models where some factors have at least five indicators. Because these requirements are sufficient, a complex nonstandard CFA model that is really identified could nevertheless fail some of these rules. Fortunately, most CFA models described in the literature do not have complex indicators, so only Rule 6.6 for error correlations in measurement models is applied most often in practice.

RULES FOR SR MODELS

This section deals with fully latent SR models in which each variable in the structural model (except disturbances) is a factor measured by multiple indicators. The identification status of partially latent SR models where at least one construct in the structural model is measured by a single indicator is considered in Chapter 10. If one understands something about the identification of structural models and measurement models, there is relatively little new to learn about SR models. This is because the evaluation of whether an SR model is identified is conducted separately for each part of the model, measurement and structural. Indeed, a theme of this evaluation is that a valid (i.e., identified) measurement model is needed before it makes sense to evaluate the structural part of an SR model.

As with CFA models, meeting the two necessary requirements does not guarantee the identification of an SR model. Additional requirements reflect the view that the analysis of an SR model is essentially a path analysis conducted with estimated variances and covariances among the factors. Thus, it must be possible for the computer to derive unique estimates of the factor variances and covariances before specific direct effects among them can be estimated. In order for the structural portion of an SR model to be identified then, its measurement portion must be identified. Bollen (1989) describes this requirement as the **two-step rule**, and the steps to evaluate it are outlined next:

In order for an SR model to be identified, both of the following must   (Rule 6.9) hold:

1. The measurement part of the model respecified as a CFA model is identified (evaluate the measurement model against Rules 6.4–6.8).

2. The structural part of the model is identified (evaluate the structural model against Rules 6.1–6.3).

The two-step rule is a sufficient condition: SR models that satisfy both parts of this rule are identified. Evaluation of the two-step rule is demonstrated next for the fully latent SR model presented in Figure 6.6(a). This model meets the necessary requirements because every latent variable is scaled and there are more observations than free parameters. Specifically, with six observed variables, there are 6(7)/2 = 21 observations available to estimate this model's 14 parameters, including nine variances of exogenous variables (of six measurement errors, one exogenous factor A, and two disturbances), three factor loadings, and two direct effects between factors ($df_M = 7$). However, we still do not know whether the model of Figure 6.6(a) is identified. To find out, we can apply the two-step

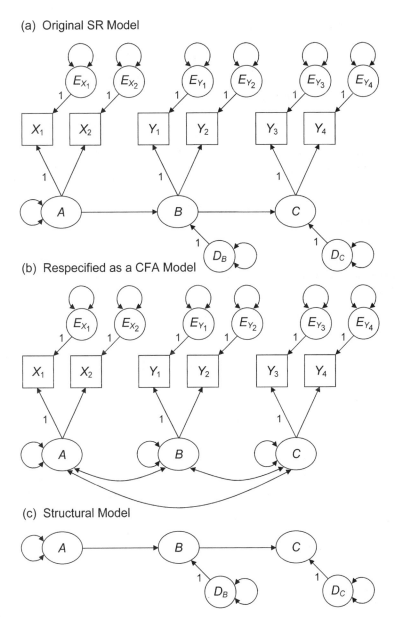

FIGURE 6.6. Evaluation of the two-step rule for identification for a fully latent structural regression (SR) model.

rule. The respecification of this SR model as a CFA measurement model is presented in Figure 6.6(b). Because this standard three-factor CFA model has at least two indicators per factor, it is identified (Rule 6.5). The first part of the two-step rule is satisfied. The structural part of the SR model is presented in Figure 6.6(c). Because the structural model is recursive, it too is identified (Rule 6.1). Because the original SR model in Figure

6.6(a) meets both parts of the sufficient two-step rule (Rule 6.9), it is identified, specifically, overidentified.

It is not always possible to determine the identification status of every fully latent SR model using the two-step identification heuristic. For example, suppose that the structural portion of an SR model is nonrecursive such that it does not have all possible disturbance correlations, nor is it block recursive. In this case, the rank condition (Rule 6.3) is not a sufficient condition for identifying the structural model. Therefore, the nonrecursive structural model is "none-of-the-above" concerning identification. Consequently, evaluation of the two-step rule cannot clearly establish whether the original SR model is identified. The same thing can happen when the measurement model of an SR model has both error correlations and complex indicators: If either the measurement or structural portions of an SR model is "none-of-the-above" such that its identification status cannot be clearly established, the two-step rule may be too strict. That is, an SR model of ambiguous identification status may fail the two-step rule but still be identified. Fortunately, many SR models described in the literature have standard measurement models and recursive structural models. In this case, identification status is clear: such SR models are identified.

A HEALTHY PERSPECTIVE ON IDENTIFICATION

Respecification of a structural equation model so that it is identified can at first seem like a shell game: Add this path, drop another, switch an error correlation and—voilà!—the model is identified or—curses!—it is not. Although one obviously needs an identified model, it is crucial to modify models in a judicious manner. That is, any change to the original specification of a model for the sake of identification should be guided by your hypotheses and theory, not by empirical ones. For example, one cannot estimate a model, find that a path coefficient is close to zero, and then eliminate the path in order to identify a model (Kenny et al., 1998). Don't lose sight of the ideas that motivated the analysis in the first place through haphazard specification.

EMPIRICAL UNDERIDENTIFICATION

Although it is *theoretically* possible (that word again) for the computer to derive a set of unique estimates for the parameters of identified models, their analysis can still be foiled by other types of problems. Data-related problems are one such difficulty. For example, extreme collinearity can result in what Kenny (1979) referred to as **empirical underidentification**. For example, if two observed variables are very highly correlated (e.g., r_{XY} = .90), then, practically speaking, they are the same variable. This reduces the effective number of observations below the value of $v (v + 1)/2$ (i.e., Rule 5.2). An effective reduction in the number of observations can also shrink the effective value of df_M, perhaps to less than zero. The good news about this kind of empirical underidentification is that it can be detected through careful data screening.

Other types of empirical underidentification can be more difficult to detect, such as when estimates of certain key paths in a nonrecursive structural model equal a very small or a very high value. Suppose that the coefficient for the path $X_2 \to Y_2$ in the nonrecursive model of Figure 6.2(b) is about zero. The virtual absence of this path alters the system matrix for the first block of endogenous variables such that the rank of the equation for Y_1 for the model in Figure 6.2(b) without the path $X_2 \to Y_2$ is zero, which violates the rank condition. You will be asked in an exercise to demonstrate this fact for Figure 6.2(b). Empirical underidentification can affect CFA and SR models, too. Suppose that the estimated factor loading for the path $A \to X_2$ in the single-factor, three-indicator model of Figure 6.4(b) is close to zero. Practically speaking, this model would resemble the one in Figure 6.4(a) in that factor A has only two indicators, which is too few for a single-factor model. A few additional examples are considered next.

The two-factor model of Figure 6.4(c) may be empirically underidentified if the estimate of the covariance (or correlation) between factors A and B is close to zero. The virtual elimination of the path $A \curvearrowright B$ from this model transforms it into two single-factor, two-indicator models, each of which is underidentified. Measurement models where all indicators load on two factors, such as the classic model for a multitrait-multimethod (MTMM) analysis where each indicator loads on both a trait factor and a method factor (Chapter 9), are especially susceptible to empirical underidentification (Kenny et al., 1998). The identification status of different types of CFA models for MTMM data is considered in Chapter 9. The measurement model in Figure 6.5(f) where indicator X_3 loads on both factors may be empirically underidentified if the absolute estimate of the factor correlation is close to 1.0. Specifically, this extreme collinearity, but now between factors instead of observed variables, can complicate the estimation of X_3's factor loadings. Other possible causes of empirical underidentification include (1) violation of the assumptions of normality or linearity when using normal theory methods (e.g., default ML estimation) and (2) specification errors (Rindskopf, 1984).

MANAGING IDENTIFICATION PROBLEMS

The best advice for avoiding identification problems was given earlier but is worth repeating: Evaluate whether your model is identified right after it is specified but before the data are collected. That is, prevention is better than cure. If you know that your model is in fact identified yet the analysis fails, the source of the problem may be empirical underidentification or a mistake in computer syntax. If a program error message indicates a failure of iterative estimation, another possible diagnosis is poor start values, or initial estimates of model parameters. How to specify better start values is discussed in Chapter 7 for structural models and Chapter 9 for measurement models.

Perhaps the most challenging problem occurs when analyzing a complex model for which no clear identification heuristic exists. This means that whether the model is actually identified is unknown. If the analysis fails in this case, it may be unclear whether the model is at fault (it is not really identified), the data are to blame (e.g., empirical underidentification), or you made a mistake (syntax error or bad start values). Ruling out a mistake does not resolve the basic ambiguity about identification. Here are some tips on how to cope:

1. A necessary but insufficient condition for the identification of a structural equation model is that an SEM computer can generate a converged solution with no evidence of technical problems such as Heywood cases, or illogical estimates (described in the next chapter). This empirical check can be applied to the actual data. Instead, you can use an SEM computer program as a *diagnostic tool* with made-up data that are anticipated to approximate actual values. This suggestion assumes that the data are not yet collected, which is when the identification question should be addressed. Care must be taken not to generate hypothetical correlations or covariances that are out of bounds (but you can check whether the matrix is positive definite; Chapter 3) or that may result in empirical underidentification. If you are unsure about a particular made-up data matrix, then others with somewhat different but still plausible values can be constructed. The model is then analyzed with the hypothetical data. If a computer program is unable to generate a proper solution, the model may not be identified. Otherwise, it may be identified, but this is not guaranteed. The solution should be subjected to other empirical checks for identification described in Chapter 9, but these checks concern only necessary requirements for identification.

2. A common beginner's mistake in SEM is to specify a complex model of ambiguous identification status and then attempt to analyze it. If the analysis fails (likely), it is not clear what caused the problem. Start instead with a simpler model that is a subset of the whole model and is also one for which the application of heuristics can prove identification. If the analysis fails, the problem is not identification. Otherwise, add parameters to the simpler model one at a time. If the analysis fails after adding a particular effect, try a different order. If these analyses also fail at the same point, then adding the corresponding parameter may cause underidentification. If no combination of adding effects to a basic identified model gets you to the target model, then think about how to respecify the original model in order to identify it and yet still respect your hypotheses.

SUMMARY

It is easy to determine whether recursive path models, standard confirmatory factor analysis models, and structural regression models with recursive structural models and standard measurement models are identified. About all that is needed is to check whether the model degrees of freedom are at least zero, every latent variable has a scale, and every factor has at least two indicators. However, the identification status of nonrecursive structural models or nonstandard measurement models is not always so clear. If a nonrecursive model does not have all possible disturbance correlations or is not block recursive, there may be no easily applied identification heuristic. There are heuristics for measurement models with either correlated errors or indicators that load on multiple factors, but these rules may not work for more complicated models with both features just mentioned. It is best to avoid analyzing a complex model of ambiguous identification status as your initial model. Instead, first analyze simpler models that you know are identified before adding free parameters. A later chapter (11) deals with identification when means are analyzed in SEM. The next chapter concerns the estimation step.

RECOMMENDED READINGS

The works listed next are all resources for dealing with potential identification problems of more complex models. Rigdon (1995) devised a visual typology for checking whether nonrecursive structural models are identified. See Kenny et al. (1998) for more detail about the identification rules for nonstandard measurement models discussed earlier. Some identification rules by O'Brien (1994) can be applied to measurement models with error correlations where some factors have five or more indicators.

Kenny, D. A., Kashy, D. A., & Bolger, N. (1998). Data analysis in social psychology. In D. Gilbert, S. Fiske, & G. Lindzey (Eds.), *The handbook of social psychology* (Vol. 1, 4th ed., pp. 233–265). Boston, MA: McGraw-Hill.

O'Brien, R. M. (1994). Identification of simple measurement models with multiple latent variables and correlated errors. *Sociological Methodology, 24*, 137–170.

Rigdon, E. E. (1995). A necessary and sufficient identification rule for structural models estimated in practice. *Multivariate Behavioral Research, 30*, 359–383.

EXERCISES

1. Write more specific versions of Rule 5.1 about model parameters for path models, CFA models, and SR models when means are not analyzed.

2. Explain why this statement is generally untrue: The specification $B \rightarrow X_3 = 1.0$ in Figure 6.4(c) assigns to factor B the same scale as that of indicator X_3.

3. Show that the factor models in Figures 6.1(a) and 6.1(b) have the same degrees of freedom.

4. Show for the nonrecursive path model in Figure 6.3 that $df_M = -1$ and also that this model fails both the order condition and the rank condition.

5. Show that the nonrecursive model in Figure 6.3 is identified when the path $X_3 \rightarrow Y_1$ is included in the model.

6. Variable X_3 of Figure 6.5(f) is a complex indicator with loadings on two factors. If the error correlation $E_{X_3} \curvearrowright E_{X_5}$ is added to this model, would the result-

ing respecified model be identified? If yes, determine whether additional error correlations involving X_3 could be added to the respecified model (i.e., the one with $E_{X_3} \leftrightarrow E_{X_5}$).

7. Suppose that the estimate of the path $X_2 \rightarrow Y_2$ in the block recursive path model of Figure 6.2(b) is close to zero. Show that the virtual absence of this path may result in empirical underidentification of the equation for at least one endogenous variable.

8. Consider the SR model in Figure 6.6(a). If the error correlations $D_B \leftrightarrow D_C$, $E_{X_1} \leftrightarrow E_{Y_1}$, and $E_{X_2} \leftrightarrow E_{Y_2}$ were all added to this model, would the resulting respecified model be identified?

APPENDIX 6.A

Evaluation of the Rank Condition

The starting point for checking the rank condition is to construct a **system matrix**, in which the endogenous variables of the structural model are listed on the left side of the matrix (rows) and all variables in the structural model (excluding disturbances) along the top (columns). In each row, a 0 or 1 appears in the columns that correspond to that row. A 1 indicates that the variable represented by that column has a direct effect on the endogenous variable represented by that row. A 1 also appears in the column that corresponds to the endogenous variable represented by that row. The remaining entries are 0's, and they indicate excluded variables. The system matrix for the model of Figure 6.2(a) with all possible disturbance correlations is presented here (**I**):

$$
\begin{array}{c}
\\
Y_1 \\
Y_2 \\
Y_3
\end{array}
\begin{array}{cccccc}
X_1 & X_2 & X_3 & Y_1 & Y_2 & Y_3 \\
\left[\begin{array}{cccccc}
1 & 0 & 0 & 1 & 0 & 1 \\
0 & 1 & 0 & 1 & 1 & 0 \\
0 & 0 & 1 & 0 & 1 & 1
\end{array}\right]
\end{array}
\qquad \textbf{(I)}
$$

"Reading" this matrix for Y_1 indicates three 1's in its row, one in the column for Y_1 itself, and the others in the columns of variables that, according to the model, directly affect it, X_1 and Y_3. Because X_2, X_3, and Y_2 are excluded from Y_1's equation, the entries in the columns for these variables are all 0's. Entries in the rows for Y_2 and Y_3 are read in a similar way.

The rank condition is evaluated using the system matrix. Like the order condition, the rank condition must be evaluated for the equation of each endogenous variable. The steps to do so for a model with all possible disturbance correlations are outlined next:

1. Begin with the first row of the system matrix (the first endogenous variable). Cross out all entries of that row. Also cross out any column in the system matrix with a 1 in this row. Use the entries that remain to form a new, reduced matrix. Row and column labels are not needed in the reduced matrix.

2. Simplify the reduced matrix further by deleting any row with entries that are all zeros. Also delete any row that is an exact duplicate of another or that can be reproduced by adding other rows together. The number of remaining rows is the rank. (Readers familiar with matrix algebra may recognize this step as the equivalent of elementary row operations to find the rank of a matrix.) For example, consider the following reduced matrix:

$$
\begin{bmatrix}
1 & 0 \\
0 & 1 \\
1 & 1
\end{bmatrix}
\qquad \textbf{(II)}
$$

The third row can be formed by adding the corresponding elements of the first and second rows, so it should be deleted. Therefore, the rank of this matrix (**II**) is 2 instead of 3. *The rank condition is met for the equation of this endogenous variable if the rank of the reduced matrix is greater than or equal to the total number of endogenous variables minus 1.*

3. Repeat steps 1 and 2 for every endogenous variable. *If the rank condition is satisfied for every endogenous variable, then the model is identified.*

Steps 1 and 2 applied to the system matrix for the model of Figure 6.2(a) with all possible disturbance correlations are outlined here (**III**). Note that we are beginning with Y_1:

(III)

$$
\begin{array}{c}
\rightarrow Y_1 \\
Y_2 \\
Y_3
\end{array}
\begin{array}{cccccc}
X_1 & X_2 & X_3 & Y_1 & Y_2 & Y_3 \\
\end{array}
\left[
\begin{array}{cccccc}
\bcancel{1} & \bcancel{0} & \bcancel{0} & \bcancel{1} & \bcancel{0} & \bcancel{1} \\
\bcancel{0} & 1 & 0 & \bcancel{1} & 1 & \bcancel{0} \\
\bcancel{0} & 0 & 1 & \bcancel{0} & 1 & \bcancel{1}
\end{array}
\right]
\rightarrow
\left[
\begin{array}{ccc}
1 & 0 & 1 \\
0 & 1 & 1
\end{array}
\right]
\rightarrow \text{Rank} = 2
$$

For step 1, all the entries in the first row of the system matrix (**III**) are crossed out. Also crossed out are three columns of the matrix with a 1 in this row (i.e., those with column headings X_1, Y_1, and Y_3). The resulting reduced matrix has two rows. Neither row has entries that are all zero or can be reproduced by adding other rows together, so the reduced matrix cannot be simplified further. This means that the rank of the equation for Y_1 is 2. This rank exactly equals the required minimum value, which is one less than the total number of endogenous variables in the whole model, or $3 - 1 = 2$. The rank condition is satisfied for Y_1.

We repeat this process for the other two endogenous variables for the model of Figure 6.2(a), Y_2 and Y_3. The steps for the remaining endogenous variables are summarized next.

Evaluation for Y_2 (**IV**):

(IV)

$$
\begin{array}{c}
Y_1 \\
\rightarrow Y_2 \\
Y_3
\end{array}
\begin{array}{cccccc}
X_1 & X_2 & X_3 & Y_1 & Y_2 & Y_3 \\
\end{array}
\left[
\begin{array}{cccccc}
1 & \bcancel{0} & 0 & \bcancel{1} & \bcancel{0} & 1 \\
\bcancel{0} & \bcancel{1} & \bcancel{0} & \bcancel{1} & \bcancel{1} & \bcancel{0} \\
0 & \bcancel{0} & 1 & \bcancel{0} & \bcancel{1} & 1
\end{array}
\right]
\rightarrow
\left[
\begin{array}{ccc}
1 & 0 & 1 \\
0 & 1 & 1
\end{array}
\right]
\rightarrow \text{Rank} = 2
$$

Evaluation for Y_3 (**V**):

(V)

$$
\begin{array}{c}
Y_1 \\
Y_2 \\
\rightarrow Y_3
\end{array}
\begin{array}{cccccc}
X_1 & X_2 & X_3 & Y_1 & Y_2 & Y_3 \\
\end{array}
\left[
\begin{array}{cccccc}
1 & 0 & \bcancel{0} & 1 & \bcancel{0} & \bcancel{1} \\
0 & 1 & \bcancel{0} & 1 & \bcancel{1} & \bcancel{0} \\
\bcancel{0} & \bcancel{0} & \bcancel{1} & \bcancel{0} & \bcancel{1} & \bcancel{1}
\end{array}
\right]
\rightarrow
\left[
\begin{array}{ccc}
1 & 0 & 1 \\
0 & 1 & 1
\end{array}
\right]
\rightarrow \text{Rank} = 2
$$

The rank of the equations for each of Y_2 and Y_3 is 2, which exactly equals the minimum required value. Because the rank condition is satisfied for all three endogenous variables of this model, we conclude that it is identified.

The rank condition is evaluated separately for each block of endogenous variables in the block recursive model of Figure 6.2(b). The steps are as follows: First, construct a system matrix for each block. For example, the system matrix for the block that contains Y_1 and Y_2 lists only these variables plus prior variables (X_1 and X_2). Variables of the second block are not included in the matrix for the first block. The system matrix for the second block lists only Y_3 and Y_4 in its rows but represents all of the variables in the whole structural model in its columns. Next, the rank condition is evaluated for the system matrix of each block. These steps are outlined next.

Evaluation for block 1 **(VI)**:

$$
\begin{array}{c}
\\
\rightarrow \quad Y_1 \\
Y_2
\end{array}
\begin{array}{cccc}
X_1 & X_2 & Y_1 & Y_2 \\
\left[\; \cancel{1} \right. & \cancel{0} & \cancel{1} & \cancel{1} \\
\left.\; \cancel{0} \right. & 1 & \cancel{1} & \cancel{1} \;]
\end{array}
\rightarrow \left[\; 1 \;\right] \rightarrow \text{Rank} = 1
\qquad \textbf{(VI)}
$$

$$
\begin{array}{c}
Y_1 \\
\rightarrow \quad Y_2
\end{array}
\begin{array}{cccc}
X_1 & X_2 & Y_1 & Y_2 \\
\left[\; 1 \right. & \cancel{0} & \cancel{1} & \cancel{1} \\
\left.\; \cancel{0} \right. & \cancel{1} & \cancel{1} & \cancel{1} \;]
\end{array}
\rightarrow \left[\; 1 \;\right] \rightarrow \text{Rank} = 1
$$

Evaluation for block 2 **(VII)**:

$$
\begin{array}{c}
\rightarrow \quad Y_3 \\
Y_4
\end{array}
\begin{array}{cccccc}
X_1 & X_2 & Y_1 & Y_2 & Y_3 & Y_4 \\
\left[\; \cancel{0} \right. & \cancel{0} & \cancel{1} & \cancel{0} & \cancel{1} & \cancel{1} \\
\left.\; 0 \right. & 0 & \cancel{0} & 1 & \cancel{1} & \cancel{1} \;]
\end{array}
\rightarrow \left[\; 0 \;\; 0 \;\; 1 \;\right] \rightarrow \text{Rank} = 1
\qquad \textbf{(VII)}
$$

$$
\begin{array}{c}
Y_3 \\
\rightarrow \quad Y_4
\end{array}
\begin{array}{cccccc}
X_1 & X_2 & Y_1 & Y_2 & Y_3 & Y_4 \\
\left[\; 0 \right. & 0 & 1 & \cancel{0} & \cancel{1} & \cancel{1} \\
\left.\; \cancel{0} \right. & \cancel{0} & \cancel{0} & \cancel{1} & \cancel{1} & \cancel{1} \;]
\end{array}
\rightarrow \left[\; 0 \;\; 0 \;\; 1 \;\right] \rightarrow \text{Rank} = 1
$$

Because the rank of the equation of every endogenous variable of each system matrix equals the number of endogenous variables minus 1 (i.e., $2 - 1$), the rank condition is met. Thus, the block recursive model of Figure 6.2(b) is identified.

7

Estimation

This chapter is organized into three main parts. Described in the first is the workhorse of SEM for the analysis, maximum likelihood (ML) estimation. It is the default method in most SEM computer tools and the most widely used method for analyses with continuous outcomes. Possible things that can go wrong in the analysis are considered and suggestions are offered about how to deal with these challenges. In the second major part of this chapter, how to interpret model parameter estimates is demonstrated through a detailed analysis of a recursive path model. Alternative estimation methods for outcomes that are not continuous are considered in the third part. The concepts and skills reviewed here will help to prepare you to learn about hypothesis testing in SEM, the subject of the next chapter.

MAXIMUM LIKELIHOOD ESTIMATION

The method of ML estimation method is the default in most SEM computer programs, and most structural equation models described in the literature are analyzed with this method. Indeed, use of an estimation method other than ML requires explicit justification (Hoyle, 2000).

Description

The term **maximum likelihood** describes the statistical principle that underlies the derivation of parameter estimates; the estimates are the ones that maximize the likelihood (the continuous generalization) that the data (the observed covariances) were drawn from this population. It is a **normal theory method** because multivariate normality is assumed for the population distributions of the endogenous variables. Only continuous variables can have normal distributions; therefore, if the endogenous variables are not continuous or if their distributions are severely non-normal, then an alternative estimation method is needed.

Most forms of ML estimation in SEM are simultaneous, which means that the estimates of model parameters are calculated all at once. Thus, ML estimation is a **full-information method**. When all statistical requirements are met and the model is correctly specified, ML estimates in large samples are asymptotically unbiased, efficient, and consistent.[1] In this sense, ML estimation has an advantage under these ideal conditions over partial-information methods that analyze only a single equation at a time. An example of the latter is **two-stage least squares** (TSLS), which was used in the late 1970s to estimate nonrecursive path models before the advent of programs such as LISREL. Nowadays, ML estimation is generally used to analyze nonrecursive models. However, the TSLS method is still relevant for SEM—see Topic Box 7.1. Implications of the difference between full- versus partial-information methods when there is specification error are considered later in this chapter.

The criterion minimized in ML estimation, or the **fit function**, is related to the discrepancy between sample covariances and those predicted by the researcher's model. The mathematics of ML estimation are complex, and it is beyond the scope of this section to describe them in detail—see Nunnally and Bernstein (1994, pp. 147–155), Ferron and Hess (2007), or Mulaik (2009, chap. 7) for more information. There are points of contact between ML estimation and more standard methods. For example, ordinary least squares (OLS) and ML estimates of coefficients in multiple regression (MR) analyses are basically identical. Estimates of error variances may differ slightly in small samples, but the two methods yield similar results in large samples.

Sample Variances

One difference between ML estimation and more standard statistical techniques concerns estimation of the population variance σ^2. In standard techniques, σ^2 is estimated in a single sample as $s^2 = SS/df$ where the numerator is the total sum of squared deviations from the mean and the denominator is the overall within-group degrees of freedom, or $N - 1$. In ML estimation, σ^2 is estimated as $S^2 = SS/N$. In small samples, S^2 is a negatively biased estimator of σ^2. In large samples, however, values of s^2 and S^2 are similar, and they are asymptotic in very large samples.

The implementations of ML estimation in some SEM computer programs, such as Amos and Mplus, calculate sample variances as S^2, not s^2. Thus, variances calculated as s^2 using a computer program for general statistical analyses, such as SPSS, may not exactly equal those calculated in an SEM computer program as S^2 for the same data. Check the documentation of your SEM computer tool to avoid possible confusion about this issue.

---

[1]A consistent estimator is one where increasing the sample size increases the probability that the estimator is close to the population parameter, and an efficient estimator has a low error variance among results from random samples.

TOPIC BOX 7.1

Two-Stage Least Squares Estimation

The method of two-stage least squares (TSLS) estimation provides a way to get around the requirement of ordinary least squares (OLS) estimation that the residuals are uncorrelated with the predictors (Chapter 2). The TSLS technique is still widely used today in many disciplines, such as economics. Many computer programs for general statistical analyses, including SAS and SPSS, have TSLS procedures. Some SEM computer tools, such as LISREL, use a special form of TSLS for latent variable models (Bollen, 1996) to calculate initial estimates of model parameters, or start values. In my experience, the TSLS-generated start values in LISREL generally perform well even for nonrecursive models.

For nonrecursive path models, TSLS is nothing more than OLS but applied in two stages. The aim of the first stage is to replace a problematic causal variable with a newly created predictor. A "problematic" causal variable has a direct effect on an outcome variable and also covaries with the disturbance of that outcome variable (i.e., a predictor is correlated with the residuals). Variables known as **instruments** or **instrumental variables** are used to create the new predictors. An instrument has (1) a direct effect on the problematic causal variable but (2) no direct effect on the outcome variable. That is, the instrument is excluded from the equation of the criterion. Note that both conditions are given by theory, not statistical analysis. An instrument can be either exogenous or endogenous. Because exogenous variables are assumed to be uncorrelated with all disturbances, exogenous variables are good candidates as instruments. In a direct feedback loop, the same variable cannot serve as the instrument for both variables in that loop. Also, one of the variables does not need an instrument if the disturbances of variables in the loop are specified as uncorrelated (Kenny, 2002).

The TSLS method works as follows. The problematic causal variable is regressed on the instrument. The predicted criterion variable in this analysis will be uncorrelated with the disturbance of the outcome variable. When similar replacements are made for all problematic causal variables, we proceed to the second stage of TSLS, which is just ordinary OLS estimation (multiple regression) conducted for each endogenous variable but using the predictors created in the first step whenever the original ones were replaced.

As an example, look back at Figure 6.2(b). This nonrecursive path model specifies two direct causes if Y_1, the variables X_1 and Y_2. From the perspective of OLS estimation, Y_2 is a problematic causal variable because it covaries with the disturbance of Y_1. This model-implied association is represented in Figure 6.2(b) by the path

$$D_2 \leftarrow\!\!\!\rightarrow D_1 \rightarrow Y_1$$

In words, the disturbance of Y_2, or D_2, covaries with the disturbance of Y_1, or D_1. Because D_2 is part of Y_2, this means that Y_2 is correlated with D_1. Note that there is no such problem with X_1, the other causal variable for Y_1. The instrument here is X_2 because it is excluded from the equation of Y_1 and has a direct effect on Y_2, the problematic causal variable (see Figure 6.2(b)). Therefore, we regress Y_2 on X_2 in a standard regression analysis. The predicted criterion variable from this first analysis, $\hat{Y}_2$, replaces Y_2 as a predictor of Y_1 in a second regression analysis where X_1 is the other predictor. The regression coefficients from the second regression analysis are taken as the estimates of the path coefficients for the direct effects of X_1 and Y_2 on Y_1. See James and Singh (1978) and Kenny (1979, pp. 83–92) for more information about TSLS estimation for path models. Bollen (1996) describes variants of TSLS estimation for latent variable models.

Iterative Estimation and Start Values

Computer implementations of ML estimation are typically iterative, which means that the computer derives an initial solution and then attempts to improve these estimates through subsequent cycles of calculations. "Improvement" means that the overall fit of the model to the data gradually improves. For most just-identified models, the fit will eventually be perfect. For overidentified models, the fit of the model to the data may be imperfect, but iterative estimation will continue until the improvements in model fit fall below a predefined minimum value. When this happens, the estimation process has converged.

Iterative estimation may converge to a solution more quickly if the procedure is given reasonably accurate **start values**, or initial estimates of the parameters. If these initial estimates are grossly inaccurate—for instance, the start value for a path coefficient is positive when the actual direct effect is negative—then iterative estimation may fail to converge, which means that a stable solution has not been reached. Iterative estimation can also fail if the covariance matrix is ill scaled (Chapter 3).

Computer programs typically issue a warning if iterative estimation is unsuccessful. When this occurs, whatever final set of estimates was derived by the computer warrants little confidence. Some SEM computer programs automatically generate their own start values. *It is important to understand, however, that computer-derived start values do not always lead to converged solutions.* Although, the computer's "guesses" about initial estimates are usually pretty good, sometimes it is necessary for you to provide better ones in order for the solution to converge, especially for more complex models. The guidelines for calculating start values for structural models presented in Appendix 7.A may be helpful. Another tactic is to increase the program's default limit on the number of iterations to a higher value, such as from 30 to 100. Allowing the computer more "tries" may lead to a converged solution.

Inadmissible Solutions and Heywood Cases

Although usually not a problem when analyzing recursive path models, it can happen in ML estimation and other iterative methods that a converged solution is **inadmissible**. This is most evident by a parameter estimate with an illogical value, such as **Heywood cases** (after H. B. Heywood; e.g., Heywood, 1931). These include negative variance estimates (e.g., an unstandardized error variance is −12.58) or estimated correlations between factors or between a factor and an indicator with absolute values > 1.0. Another indication of a problem is when the standard error of a parameter estimate is so large that no interpretation seems plausible (e.g., 999,999.99). Some causes of Heywood cases (Chen, Bollen, Paxton, Curran, & Kirby, 2001) include:

1. Specification errors;
2. Nonidentification of the model;
3. The presence of outliers that can distort the solution;
4. A combination of small sample sizes (e.g., N < 100) and only two indicators per factor;
5. Bad start values; or
6. Extremely low or high population correlations that result in empirical underidentification.

An analogy may help to give a context for Heywood cases: ML estimation (and related methods) is like a religious fanatic in that it so believes the model's specifications that it will do anything, no matter how implausible, to force the model on the data. Some SEM computer programs do not permit certain Heywood cases to appear in the solution. For example, EQS does not allow the estimate of an error variance to be less than zero; that is, it sets a lower bound of zero (an inequality constraint) that prevents a negative variance estimate. However, solutions in which one or more estimates have been constrained by the computer to prevent an illogical value should not be trusted. Instead, you should try to determine the source of the problem instead of constraining an error variance to be positive and then rerunning the analysis.

In your own analyses, always carefully inspect the whole solution, unstandardized and standardized, for any sign that it is inadmissible. Computer programs for SEM generally issue warning messages about Heywood cases or other kinds of problems with the estimates, but they are not foolproof. It can therefore happen that the solution is inadmissible but no warning was given. It is you, not the computer, who provides the ultimate quality control check for admissibility.

Scale Freeness and Scale Invariance

The ML method is generally both **scale free** and **scale invariant**. Scale free means that if a variable's scale is linearly transformed, a parameter estimated for the transformed variable can be algebraically converted back to the original metric. Scale invariant means that the value of the ML fitting function in a particular sample remains the same regardless of the scale of the observed variables (Kaplan, 2009). However, ML estimation may lose these properties if a correlation matrix is analyzed instead of a covariance matrix. That is, standard ML estimation assumes unstandardized variables, and it generally calculates standard errors for the unstandardized solution only. Thus the level of statistical significance of an unstandardized parameter estimate may not apply to the corresponding standardized estimate (Chapter 2).

Assumptions and Error Propagation

As just mentioned, default ML estimation assumes that the variables are unstandardized. It also assumes there are no missing values when a raw data file is analyzed, but there is a special form of ML estimation for incomplete data files (Chapter 3). The statistical assumptions of ML estimation include independence of the scores, multivariate normality of the endogenous variables, and independence of the exogenous variables and error terms. An additional assumption when a path model is analyzed is that the exogenous variables are measured without error, but this requirement is not specific to ML estimation.

Perhaps the most important assumption of all is that *the model is correctly specified.* This is critical because of **error propagation**. Full-information methods, including ML, tend to propagate errors throughout the model. This means that a specification error in one parameter can affect results for other parameters elsewhere in the model. Suppose that the measurement error correlation for a factor with just two indicators is really substantial but cannot be estimated due to identification (e.g., Figure 6.5(d)). This specification error may propagate to estimation of the factor loadings for this pair of indicators.[2] It is difficult to predict the direction or magnitude of this "contamination," but the more serious the specification error, the more serious may be the resulting bias in other parts of the model.

When misspecification occurs, partial-information methods may outperform ML estimation. This is because the partial-information methods may better isolate the effects of errors to misspecified parts of the model instead of allowing them to spread to other parts. Bollen, Kirby, Curran, Paxton, and Chen (2007) found in a Monte Carlo simulation study that bias in ML and various TSLS estimators for latent variable models was generally negligible in large samples when a three-factor measurement model was correctly specified. However, when model specification was incorrect, there was greater bias of the ML estimator compared with that of TSLS estimators even in large sample sizes. Based on these results, Bollen et al. (2007) suggested that researchers consider a TSLS estimator as a complement to or substitute for ML estimation when there is doubt about specification.[3]

---

[2]B. Muthén, personal communication, November 25, 2003.

[3]A drawback of partial-information methods is that there is no statistical test of overall model fit.

Interpretation of Parameter Estimates

This section concerns path models. Later chapters deal with the interpretation of parameter estimates for models with substantive latent variables. The interpretation of ML estimates for path models is straightforward:

1. Path coefficients are interpreted just as regression coefficients in MR. This is true for both the unstandardized and the standardized solution.

2. Disturbance variances in the unstandardized solution are estimated in the metric of the unexplained variance of the corresponding endogenous variable. Suppose that the observed variance of endogenous variable Y is 25.00 and that the unstandardized variance of its disturbance, D, is 15.00. We can conclude that 15.00/25.00, or .60 of the variance in total variability in Y is *unexplained*. Accordingly, 1.00 − .60 = .40 is the proportion of *explained* variance. This proportion also equals the squared multiple correlation R^2_{smc} for Y.

3. In the standardized solution, the variances of all variables (including disturbances) equal 1.0. However, some SEM computer programs, such as LISREL and Mplus, report standardized estimates for disturbances that are proportions of unexplained variance. These estimates equal $1 - R^2_{smc}$ for each endogenous variable.

DETAILED EXAMPLE

Considered next is estimation of the parameters for the recursive path model of causes and effects of positive teacher–pupil interactions introduced in Chapter 5. In the next chapter, you will learn how to evaluate the overall fit of this model (and others, too) to the data. The discussion of parameter estimation now and of model fit later is intentional. This is because too many researchers become so preoccupied with model fit that they do not pay enough attention to the meaning of the parameter estimates. Also, there is a "surprise" concerning the estimates for this example, one that could be missed by focusing too much on model fit. To not keep you in suspense, the surprise concerns suppression effects evident in the standardized solution. But you have to pay attention to the details of the computer output in order to detect such effects.

Briefly reviewed next is the work of Sava (2002), who administered measures of perceived school support, burnout, and extent of a coercive view of student discipline to 109 high school teachers. A total of 946 students of these teachers completed questionnaires about the degree of positive teacher–pupil interactions. These students also completed questionnaires about whether they viewed their school experience as positive and about their general somatic status.[4] High scores on general somatic status indicate fewer somatic complaints related to stress. Student responses were averaged in order to

---

[4]The Sava (2002) data set is actually hierarchical where students are nested under teachers, but a multilevel analysis was not conducted for this example.

generate summary scores for each teacher. Thus, the overall sample size for this analysis is $N = 109$, which is small. The path model in Figure 7.1 represents the hypothesis that teachers who suffer from burnout due to poor school support or a coercive view of discipline will have less positive interactions with students, which in turn negatively affects the school experience and somatic status of students. You should verify for this

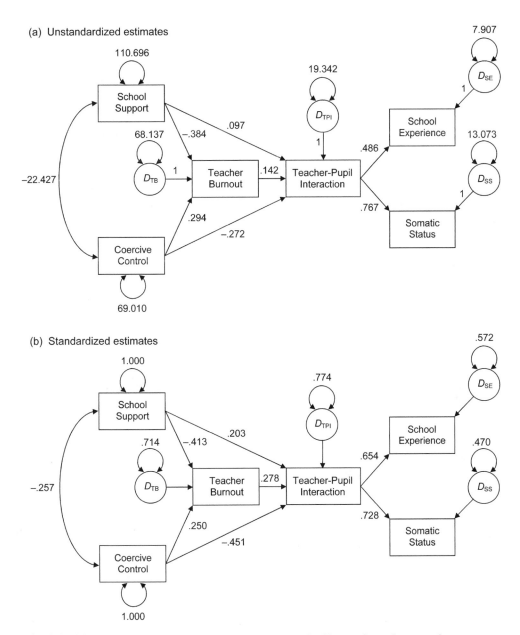

FIGURE 7.1. A recursive path model of causes and effects of teacher–pupil interactions. Standardized estimates for the disturbances are proportions of unexplained variance.

model that $df_M = 7$ (Chapter 5, Exercise 4). Because the structural model in Figure 7.1 is recursive, it is identified (Rule 6.1).

Sava (2002) screened the data for skewness and kurtosis before applying transformations to normalize scores on the teacher–pupil interactions variable. The original covariance matrix analyzed by Sava (2002) was ill scaled because the ratio of the largest variance over the smallest variance exceeded 100.0. To remedy this problem, I multiplied scores on the variable with the lowest variance (school support) by the constant 5.0, which increased its variance by a factor of 25.0. The sample correlations and rescaled standard deviations for this analysis are presented in Table 7.1. Note that the correlation between the variables teacher burnout and positive teacher–pupil interactions is .0207. This near-zero association is related to suppression effects described later in this chapter.

I used the ML method of LISREL 8.8 to fit the path model of Figure 7.1 to a covariance matrix constructed from the data in Table 7.1. You can download from this book's website (see p. 3) the EQS, LISREL, and Mplus computer files for this analysis. The analysis in LISREL converged to an admissible solution. Reported in Table 7.2 are the estimates of model parameters except for the variances and covariance of the two measured exogenous variables, school support and coercive control (Figure 7.1). The estimates of these parameters are just the sample values (Table 7.1).

Direct Effects

Let's consider first the unstandardized direct effects in Table 7.2, which are also reported in Figure 7.1(a). For example, the unstandardized direct effect of school support on teacher burnout is –.384. This means that a 1-point increase on the school support variable predicts a .384-point decrease on the burnout variable, controlling for coercive control. The estimated standard error for this direct effect is .079 (Table 7.2), so $z = -.384/.079 = 4.86$, which exceeds the critical value for two-tailed statistical significance at the .01 level, or 2.58.[5] The unstandardized path coefficient for the direct effect of coercive control on burnout is .294. Thus, a 1-point increase on coercive control predicts a .294-point increase on burnout, controlling for school support. The estimated standard error is .100, so $z = .294/.100 = 2.94$, which is also statistically significant at the .01 level. Other unstandardized path coefficients in Table 7.2 and Figure 7.1(a) are interpreted in similar ways.

Because these variables do not have the same scale, the unstandardized path coefficients for school support and coercive control cannot be directly compared. However, this is not a problem for the standardized path coefficients, which are reported in Table 7.2 and Figure 7.1(b). Note in the table that there are no standard errors for the standardized estimates, which is typical in standard ML estimation. Consequently, no informa-

---

[5]Note that test statistics for individual parameter estimates are referred to in LISREL as t statistics, but in large samples they are actually z statistics.

TABLE 7.1. Input Data (Correlations and Standard Deviations) for Analysis of a Recursive Path Model of Causes and Effects of Positive Teacher–Pupil Interactions

Variable	1	2	3	4	5	6
1. Coercive Control	1.0000					
2. Teacher Burnout	.3557	1.0000				
3. School Support	−.2566	−.4774	1.0000			
4. Teacher–Pupil Interactions	−.4046	.0207	.1864	1.0000		
5. School Experience	−.1615	.0938	.0718	.6542	1.0000	
6. Somatic Status	−.3487	−.0133	.1570	.7277	.4964	1.0000
SD	8.3072	9.7697	10.5212	5.0000	3.7178	5.2714

Note. These data are from Sava (2002); $N = 109$. Means were not reported by Sava (2002).

tion about statistical significance is associated with the standardized results in Table 7.2. The standardized coefficients for the direct effects of school support and coercive control on teacher burnout are, respectively, −.413 and .250. That is, a level of school support one full standard deviation above the mean predicts a burnout level just over .40 standard deviations below the mean, holding coercive control constant. Likewise, a level of coercive control one full standard deviation above the mean is associated with a burnout level about .25 standard deviations above the mean, controlling for school support. The absolute size of the standardized direct effect of school support on burnout is thus about 1½ times that of coercive control. Results for the other standardized direct effects in the model are interpreted in similar ways.

Inspection of the standardized path coefficients for direct effects on teacher–pupil interactions indicates suppression effects. For example, the standardized direct effect of teacher burnout on teacher–pupil interactions is .278 (Table 7.2, Figure 7.1(b)), which

TABLE 7.2. Maximum Likelihood Estimates for a Recursive Path Model of Causes and Effects of Positive Teacher-Pupil Interactions

Parameter	Unstandardized	SE	Standardized
	Direct effects		
Support → Burnout	−.384**	.079	−.413
Support → Teacher–Pupil	.097*	.046	.203
Coercive → Burnout	.294**	.100	.250
Coercive → Teacher–Pupil	−.272**	.055	−.451
Burnout → Teacher–Pupil	.142**	.052	.278
Teacher-Pupil → Experience	.486**	.055	.654
Teacher-Pupil → Somatic	.767**	.070	.728
	Disturbance variances		
Teacher Burnout	68.137**	9.359	.714
Teacher–Pupil Interactions	19.342**	2.657	.774
School Experience	7.907**	1.086	.572
Somatic Status	13.073**	1.796	.470

Note. Standardized estimates for disturbance variances are proportions of unexplained variance.
$^*p < .05$; $^{**}p < .01$.

is greater than the zero-order correlation between these two variables, or .021 at three-decimal accuracy (Table 7.1). Also, the sign of this direct effect is *positive*, which says that teachers who reported higher levels of burnout were better liked by their students, controlling for school support and coercive control. This positive direct effect seems to contradict the results of many other studies on teacher burnout, which generally indicate negative effects on teacher–pupil interactions. However, effects of other variables, such as school support, were not controlled in many of these other studies. This finding should be replicated, especially given the small sample size.

Disturbance Variances

The estimated disturbance variances reflect unexplained variability for each endogenous variable. For example, the unstandardized disturbance variance for somatic status is 13.073 (Table 7.2). The sample variance of this variable (Table 7.1) at 3-decimal accuracy is $s^2 = 5.2714^2 = 27.788$. The ratio of the disturbance variance over the observed variance is 13.073/27.788 = .470. That is, the proportion of observed variance in somatic status that is *not* explained by its presumed direct cause, teacher–pupil interactions, is .470, or 47.0%. The proportion of explained variance for somatic status is $R^2_{smc} = 1 - .470$, or .530. Thus, the model in Figure 7.1 explains 53.0% of the total variance in somatic status. The estimated disturbance variances for the other three endogenous variables are interpreted in similar ways.

Note that all the unstandardized disturbance variances in Table 7.2 differ statistically from zero at the .01 level. However, these results have basically no substantive value. This is because it is expected that error variance will not be zero, so it is silly to get excited that a disturbance variance is statistically significant. This is an example of a statistical test in SEM that is typically pointless. However, results of statistical tests for error covariances are often of interest.

Indirect Effects and the Sobel Test

Indirect effects are estimated statistically as the product of direct effects, either standardized or unstandardized, that comprise them. They are also interpreted just as path coefficients. For example, the standardized indirect effect of school support on student school experience through the mediator teacher–pupil interactions is estimated as the product of the standardized coefficients for the constituent paths, which is .203 × .654, or .133 (see Figure 7.1(b)). The rationale for this derivation is as follows: school support has a certain direct effect on teacher–pupil interactions (.203), but only part of this effect, .654 of it, is transmitted to school experience. The result .133 says that the level of positive student school experience is expected to increase by about .13 standard deviations for every increase in school support of one full standard deviation via its prior effect on teacher–pupil interactions.

The unstandardized indirect effect of school support on student school experience through teacher–pupil interactions is estimated as the product of the unstandardized coefficients for the same two paths, which is .097 × .486, or .047 (see Figure 7.1(a)). That is, school experience in its original metric is expected to increase by about .05 points for every 1-point increase on the school support variable in its original metric via its prior effect on teacher–pupil interactions. A full standard deviation on the school support variable is 10.5212 (Table 7.1). Therefore, an increase of one full standard deviation on the school support variable predicts an increase of 10.5212 × .047, or .494 points on the school experience variable in its original metric through the mediator variable of teacher–pupil interactions. The standard deviation of the school experience variable is 3.7178 (Table 7.1). A raw score change of .494 on this variable thus corresponds to .494/3.7178, or .133 standard deviations, which matches the standardized estimate of this indirect effect calculated earlier.

Coefficients for indirect effects have complex distributions, so it can be difficult to estimate standard errors for these statistics. Baron and Kenny (1986) describe some hand-calculable statistical tests for unstandardized indirect effects with a single mediator. The best known of these tests for large samples is based on an approximate standard error by Sobel (1986), which is described next. Suppose that a is the unstandardized coefficient for the path $X \rightarrow Y_1$ and that SE_a is its standard error. Let b and SE_b, respectively, represent the same things for the path $Y_1 \rightarrow Y_2$. The product ab estimates the unstandardized indirect effect of X on Y_2 through Y_1. Sobel's estimated standard error of ab is

$$SE_{ab} = \sqrt{b^2 SE_a^2 + a^2 SE_b^2} \qquad (7.1)$$

In large samples, the ratio ab/SE_{ab} is interpreted as the z test of the unstandardized indirect effect and is called the **Sobel test**. A webpage by K. Preacher automatically calculates the Sobel test after the required information is entered in graphical dialogs.[6] Exercise 2 will ask you to calculate the Sobel test for the unstandardized indirect effect of school support on school experience through teacher–pupil interactions for the model of Figure 7.1(a). However, we would not expect the results of this test to be accurate (i.e., the p value is probably wrong) because the sample size for this analysis is not large.

I am unaware of a hand-calculable test of the statistical significance of indirect effects through two or more mediators, but a rule of thumb by Cohen and Cohen (1983) seems reasonable: If all its component unstandardized path coefficients are statistically significant at the same level of α, then the whole indirect effect can be taken as statistically significant at the same level of α, too. For example, all three of the component unstandardized coefficients of the path

$$\begin{array}{ccccccc} \text{School} & & \text{Teacher} & & \text{Teacher–Pupil} & & \text{School} \\ \text{Support} & \rightarrow & \text{Burnout} & \rightarrow & \text{Interactions} & \rightarrow & \text{Experience} \end{array} \qquad (7.2)$$

[6]http://people.ku.edu/~preacher/sobel/sobel.htm

meet this requirement at the .01 level (see Table 7.2), so the whole indirect effect could be considered statistically significant at the same level.

The hypothesis of "pure" mediation between two variables, such as school support and school experience in Figure 7.1, is often tested by predicting that the direct effect between those two variables is not statistically significant. An exercise will ask you to add the path

$$\text{School Support} \rightarrow \text{School Experience}$$

to the model and then determine whether the corresponding unstandardized coefficient for this direct effect is statistically significant. If so, then the hypothesis of pure mediation would not be supported. Kenny (2008) reminds us of the points summarized next:

1. A mediational model is a causal model. For example, it is assumed in Equation 7.2 for the model of Figure 7.1 that teacher–pupil interaction (a mediator) is a cause of student school experience (the outcome) and not vice versa. If this assumption is not correct, then the results of a mediational analysis are of little value.

2. Mediation is not statistically defined. Instead, statistics such as products of direct effects can be used to evaluate a presumed mediational model.

The two points just listed also explain why researchers cannot generally test competing models with different directionalities, such as $Y_1 \rightarrow Y_2 \rightarrow Y_3$ versus $Y_2 \rightarrow Y_1 \rightarrow Y_3$, in some kind of mediational model "horse race" in order to "discover" the correct model. See Baron and Kenny (1986), Shrout and Bolger (2002), and MacKinnon, Fairchild, and Fritz (2007) for more information about mediational analysis in SEM. The analysis of mediation and moderation (i.e., interaction) when both are represented in the same path model is described in Chapter 12.

MacKinnon, Krull, and Lockwood (2000) note that within a mediational model, a suppression effect may be indicated when the direct and mediated effects of one variable on another have opposite signs. They refer to this pattern as **inconsistent mediation**, which is apparent in this analysis. For example, the standardized direct effect of coercive control on teacher–pupil interactions is negative, or –.451 (Figure 7.1(b)). However, the mediated effects of coercive control on teacher–pupil teacher interactions through teacher burnout is positive, or .070 (i.e., .250 × .278). The direct versus the mediated effect of school support on teacher–pupil interactions are also of different signs. Inconsistent mediation is contrasted with **consistent mediation**, wherein the direct and mediated effects have the same sign. See Maasen and Bakker (2001) for more information about suppression effects in SEM.

Total Effects and Effect Decomposition

Total effects are the sum of all direct and indirect effects of one variable on another. For example, the standardized total effect of school support on teacher–pupil interactions is the sum of the direct effect and its sole indirect effect through teacher burnout (Figure 7.1(b)), or

$$.203 + (-.413) (.278) = .203 - .115 = .088$$

Standardized total effects are also interpreted as path coefficients, and the value of .088 means that increasing school support by one standard deviation increases students' positive school experience by almost .10 standard deviations via all presumed direct and indirect causal links between these two variables. Unstandardized estimates of total effects are calculated in the same way but with unstandardized coefficients. For example, the unstandardized total effect of school support on teacher–pupil interactions is the sum of its direct effect and its indirect effect via teacher burnout, or

$$.097 + (-.384) (.142) = .097 - .055 = .042$$

That is, for every 1-point increase on the school support variable in its original metric, we expect about a .04-point increase on the school experience variable in its original metric via all presumed causal pathways that link these variables.

Some SEM computer programs optionally generate an **effect decomposition**, a tabular summary of estimated direct, indirect, and total effects. This is fortunate because it can be tedious to calculate all these effects by hand. The LISREL program can print both total effects and **total indirect effects**. The latter is the sum of all indirect effects of a causally prior variable on a subsequent one. Reported in Table 7.3 is the effect decomposition calculated by LISREL for direct, total indirect, and total effects of exogenous variables on endogenous variables with standard errors for the unstandardized results only. (Note that the direct effects in Table 7.3 match the corresponding ones in Table 7.2.) For example, teacher burnout is specified to have a single indirect effect on school experience (through teacher–pupil interactions; Figure 7.1). This sole indirect effect is also (1) the total indirect effect because there are no other indirect effects between burnout and school experience and (2) the total effect because there is no direct effect between these variables (see Table 7.3). In contrast, school support has no direct effects on student school experience, but it has two indirect effects (see Figure 7.1), and the unstandardized total indirect effects of school support on this endogenous variable listed in Table 7.3, or .020, is the sum of these two indirect effects. Exercise 3 will ask you to verify this fact.

Presented in Table 7.4 is the decomposition for the effects of endogenous variables on other endogenous variables. For example, teacher burnout has no direct effects on the school experience and somatic status variables (see Figure 7.1). Instead, it has a single indirect effect on each of these variables, and these sole indirect effects are also total indirect effects and total effects (Table 7.4). Note that the standard errors printed by LISREL for each unstandardized indirect effect that involve a single mediator match those within rounding error calculated using Equation 7.1 for the Sobel test.

Not all SEM computer tools print standard errors for total indirect effects or total

TABLE 7.3. Decompositions for Effects of Exogenous on Endogenous Variables for a Recursive Path Model of Causes and Effects of Positive Teacher–Pupil Interactions

Endogenous variables	Causal variables					
	School Support			Coercive Control		
	Unst.	SE	St.	Unst.	SE	St.
Teacher Burnout						
Direct	−.384**	.079	−.413	.294**	.100	.250
Total indirect	—	—	—	—	—	—
Total	−.384**	.079	−.413	.294**	.100	.250
Teacher–Pupil Interactions						
Direct	.097*	.046	.203	−.272**	.055	−.451
Total indirect	−.055*	.023	−.115	.042*	.021	.070
Total	.042	.043	.088	−.230**	.055	−.382
School Experience						
Direct	—	—	—	—	—	—
Total indirect	.020	.021	.058	−.112**	.030	−.250
Total	.020	.021	.058	−.112**	.030	−.250
Somatic Status						
Direct	—	—	—	—	—	—
Total indirect	.032	.033	.064	−.176**	.045	−.278
Total	.032	.033	.064	−.176**	.045	−.278

Note. Unst., unstandardized; St., standardized.

*$p < .05$; **$p < .01$.

TABLE 7.4. Decompositions for Effects of Endogenous on Other Endogenous Variables for a Recursive Path Model of Causes and Effects of Positive Teacher–Pupil Interactions

Endogenous variables	Causal variables					
	Teacher Burnout			Teacher–Pupil Interactions		
	Unst.	SE	St.	Unst.	SE	St.
Teacher–Pupil Interactions						
Direct	.142**	.052	.278	—	—	—
Total indirect	—	—	—	—	—	—
Total	.142**	.052	.278	—	—	—
School Experience						
Direct	—	—	—	.486**	.055	.654
Total indirect	.069**	.026	.182	—	—	—
Total	.069**	.026	.182	.486**	.055	.654
Somatic Status						
Direct	—	—	—	.767**	.070	.728
Total indirect	.109**	.041	.203	—	—	—
Total	.109**	.041	.203	.767**	.070	.728

Note. Unst., unstandardized; St., standardized.

*$p < .05$; **$p < .01$.

effects. However, some programs, such as Amos and Mplus, can use the bootstrapping method to estimate standard errors for unstandardized or standardized total indirect effects and total effects. When there is a statistically significant total effect, the direct effect, total indirect effect, or both may also be statistically significant, but this is not guaranteed.

Model-Implied (Predicted) Covariances and Correlations

The standardized total effect of one variable on another approximates the part of their observed correlation due to presumed causal relations. The sum of the standardized total effects and all other noncausal associations, such as spurious associations, represented in the model equal **model-implied correlations** that can be compared against the observed correlations. **Model-implied covariances**, or **fitted covariances**, have the same general meaning, but they concern the unstandardized solution.

All SEM computer programs that calculate model-implied correlations or covariances use matrix algebra methods (e.g., Loehlin, 2004, pp. 40–44). There is an older method for recursive structural models amenable to hand calculation known as the **tracing rule**. It is worthwhile to know about the tracing rule more for its underlying principles than for its now limited utility. The tracing rule is as follows:

A model-implied correlation is the sum of all the causal effects and   (Rule 7.1)
noncausal associations from all valid tracings between two variables
in a recursive model. A "valid" tracing means that a variable is not

    1. Entered through an arrowhead and exited by the same arrowhead, nor

    2. Entered twice in the same tracing.

Two general principles follow from the tracing rule: (1) The model-implied correlation or covariance for two variables connected by all possible paths in a just-identified portion of the structural model will typically equal the observed counterparts. (2) However, if the variables are not connected by all possible paths in an overidentified part of the model, then the predicted and observed values may differ.

As an example of the application of the tracing rule to calculate model-implied correlations with the standardized solution, look again at Figure 7.1(b) and find the variables coercive control and teacher burnout. There are two valid tracings between them. One corresponds to the presumed direct causal effect

Coercive Control → Teacher Burnout

which equals .250. The other tracing involves the unanalyzed association of coercive control with another variable, school support, that has a direct effect on teacher burnout. This tracing is

Coercive Control ↜ School Support → Teacher Burnout

The estimate for the second tracing just listed is calculated in the same way as for indirect effects: as the product of the relevant path coefficients or correlations. For the second tracing, this estimate is calculated as

$$-.257 \ (-.413) = .106$$

where $-.257$ is the sample correlation between coercive control and school support and $-.413$ is the standardized direct effect of school support on teacher burnout (see Table 7.1 and Figure 7.1(b)). The model-implied correlation between coercive control and teacher burnout thus equals

$$.250 + .106 = .356$$

which also equals the observed correlation between these two variables at three-decimal accuracy, or .356 (Table 7.1). Because the variables coercive control and teacher burnout are connected by all possible paths, it is not surprising that the structural model can perfectly reproduce their observed correlation.

Now find the variables coercive control and school experience in Figure 7.1(b). There are a total of *four* valid tracings between these two variables. These tracings include two indirect effects, one with a single mediator (teacher–pupil interactions) and the other with two mediators (teacher burnout, teacher–pupil interactions). The standardized total indirect effect across the two tracings just mentioned is –.250 (Table 7.3). This value is also the standardized total effect between coercive control and school experience. There are also two valid tracings between coercive control and school experience that involve unanalyzed associations. One is the tracing

$$\text{Coercive Control} \ \ \overset{\frown}{} \ \ \text{School Support} \rightarrow \text{Teacher–Pupil Interactions} \rightarrow \text{School Experience}$$

which is estimated as the product

$$-.257 \ (.203) \ (.654) = -.034$$

The other noncausal tracing between coercive control and school experience is

$$\text{Coercive Control} \ \ \overset{\frown}{} \ \ \text{School Support} \rightarrow \text{Teacher Burnout} \rightarrow \text{Teacher–Pupil Interactions} \rightarrow \text{School Experience}$$

which is estimated as the product

$$-.257 \ (-.413) \ (.278) \ (.654) = .019$$

Thus, the predicted correlation between coercive control and school experience is calculated as the sum of the total effect and all unanalyzed associations, or

$$-.250 - .034 + .019 = -.265$$

The sample correlation between these two variables is $-.162$ (Table 7.1), so the model-implied correlation does not perfectly reproduce the observed correlation. This is not unexpected because the structural model does not have a direct effect between coercive control and school experience (Figure 7.1). That is, this part of the model is overidentified. Use of the tracing rule is error prone even for relatively simple recursive models because it can be difficult to spot all of the valid tracings. This is a reason to appreciate that many SEM computer tools automatically calculate predicted correlations and covariances.

Residuals

The difference between a model-implied correlation and an observed (sample) correlation is a **correlation residual**. Correlation residuals are standardized **covariance residuals** or **fitted residuals**, which are differences between observed and predicted covariances. There is a rule of thumb in the SEM literature that correlation residuals with absolute values > .10 suggest that the model does not explain the corresponding sample correlation very well. Although it is difficult to say how many absolute correlation residuals greater than .10 is "too many," the more there are, the worse the explanatory power of the model for specific observed associations. This is especially true for a smaller model, or one with relatively few observed variables. There is no comparable rule of thumb about values of covariance residuals that suggest a poor explanation because covariances are affected by the scales of the original variables.

The LISREL and Mplus programs print a statistic referred to as a **standardized residual**, which is the ratio of a covariance residual over its standard error. In large samples, this ratio is interpreted as a z test of whether the population covariance residual is zero. If this test is statistically significant, then the hypothesis that the corresponding population covariance residual is zero is rejected. This test is sensitive to sample size, which means that covariance residuals close to zero could be statistically significant in a very large sample. In contrast, the interpretation of correlation residuals is not as bound to sample size. Note that the term *standardized residual* in EQS output refers to correlation residuals, not z statistics.

Reported in the top part of Table 7.5 are the correlation residuals (calculated by EQS), and presented in the bottom part of the table are the standardized residuals (z statistics, calculated by LISREL) for the path model in Figure 7.1. Remember that the standardized residuals, not the correlation residuals, indicate whether the corresponding covariance residual is statistically significant. Observe in the table that correlation residuals—and standardized residuals, too—for the variables school support, coercive control, teacher burnout, and teacher–pupil interactions are all zero. This is expected because the structural model for these variables is just-identified. There is one correlation residual with an absolute value just > .10. This value, .103—shown in boldface in the top part of Table 7.5—is for the association between coercive control and school experi-

TABLE 7.5. Correlation Residuals and Standardized Residuals for a Recursive Path Model of Causes and Effects of Positive Teacher–Pupil Interactions

Variable	1	2	3	4	5	6
			Correlation residuals			
1. Coercive Control	0					
2. Teacher Burnout	0	0				
3. School Support	0	0	0			
4. Teacher–Pupil Interactions	0	0	0	0		
5. School Experience	**.103**	.080	−.050	0	0	
6. Somatic Status	−.054	−.028	.021	0	.020	0
			Standardized Residuals			
1. Coercive Control	0					
2. Teacher Burnout	0	0				
3. School Support	0	0	0			
4. Teacher–Pupil Interactions	0	0	0	0		
5. School Experience	1.536	1.093	−.695	0	0	
6. Somatic Status	−.891	−.426	.326	0	.404	0

ence. Recall that the sample correlation between these two variables is −.162 (Table 7.1) and that the model-implied correlation calculated earlier for this association is −.265. The difference between these two correlations, or

$$-.162 - (-.265) = .103$$

(i.e., observed minus predicted) equals the correlation residual for coercive control and school experience. The corresponding standardized residual for these two variables is not statistically significant ($z = 1.536$; $p > .05$; see Table 7.5), but the power of this test is probably low due to the small sample size for this analysis.

So we have evidence that the model in Figure 7.1 does not adequately explain the observed association between coercive control and school experience. This is a critical finding because the model posits only indirect effects between these two variables, but this specification may not be correct. We also need to assess the overall fit of this model to the data in a more formal way and also to test hypotheses about an apparent misspecification. Given the small sample size for this example ($N = 109$), it is also critical to estimate statistical power. Finally, whatever model is eventually retained (if any), the possibility that there are equivalent versions of it should be considered. Chapter 8 deals with all the topics just mentioned.

BRIEF EXAMPLE WITH A START VALUE PROBLEM

This quick example concerns the analysis of a nonrecursive path model. The data for this example, summarized in Table 7.6, are from Cooperman (1996). The number of cases is

TABLE 7.6. Input Data (Correlations and Standard Deviations) for Analysis of a Nonrecursive Path Model of Mother–Child Adjustment Problems

Variable	1	2	3	4	5	6
Mother characteristics						
1. Aggression	1.00					
2. Withdrawal	.19	1.00				
3. Education	–.16	–.20	1.00			
4. Maternity Age	–.37	–.06	.36	1.00		
Child characteristics						
5. Emotional Problems	–.06	–.05	–.03	–.25	1.00	
6. Conduct Problems	.13	–.06	–.09	–.28	.41	1.00
M	.51	.47	10.87	20.57	.08	.15
SD	1.09	1.03	2.17	2.33	.28	.36

Note. These data are from Cooperman (1996); *N* = 84. Means are reported but not analyzed.

small (*N* = 84), but the purpose of this analysis is pedagogical. The sample consists of mothers participating in a longitudinal study. When these women were in elementary school, their classmates completed rating scales about aggressive or withdrawn behavior, and these cases obtained extreme scores in either area. During evaluations 10–15 years later, teachers completed rating scales about the conduct or emotional problems of the children of these women. The nonrecursive path model presented in Figure 7.2 represents the hypothesis that maternal histories of aggression or withdrawal have both direct and indirect effects on conduct and emotional problems of their children. The indirect effects are mediated by maternity age and mother's level of education, which

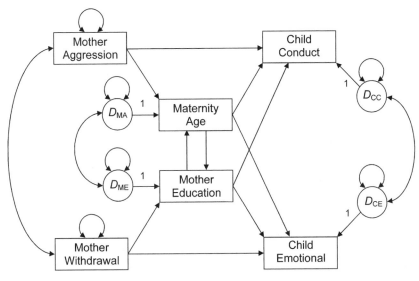

FIGURE 7.2. A nonrecursive path model of mother–child adjustment problems.

in turn are specified as the reciprocal causes of each other. For example, young women may be more likely to leave school if they are pregnant, but leaving school could be a risk factor for pregnancy.

With six observed variables in the model of Figure 7.2, there are 21 observations. The total number of free parameters is 19, including six variances of exogenous variables, three unanalyzed associations, and 10 direct effects, so $df_M = 2$. This model satisfies the order and rank conditions for the equation of every endogenous variable. (You should verify these statements.) I used the ML method of EQS 6.1 to fit the model of Figure 7.2 to the covariance matrix based on the data in Table 7.6. The program's default start values were used. These warning messages were issued after the very first iteration:

```
You have bad start values to begin with
Please provide better start values and re-run the job
```

Next, EQS recovered from this "stumble" and eventually went on to generate a converged and an admissible solution. However, at other times the analysis of a nonrecursive model may fail right away due to bad start values. The same thing can happen when analyzing an complex structural equation model of any type with many observed and latent variables.

When computer analysis is foiled by a start value problem, then it is up to you to provide better initial estimates. In the present example, I followed the suggestions in Appendix 7.A to generate start values for the reciprocal direct effects and disturbance variances for the variables maternity age and mother education in Figure 7.2. Specifically, a "typical" standardized effect size of .30 was assumed for the path from maternity age to education, and a "smaller" standardized effect size of .10 was assumed for the path from mother education to maternity age. Given the observed standard deviations for the variables mother education and maternity age—respectively, 2.17 and 2.33 (Table 7.6)—start values were calculated as follows:

Maternity Age → Mother Education:	.30 (2.17/2.33) = .28
Variance of D_{ME}:	$(1 - .10) \, 2.17^2 = .90 \, (4.71) = 4.24$
Mother Education → Maternity Age:	.10 (2.33/2.17) = .11
Variance of D_{MA}:	$(1 - .01) \, 2.33^2 = .99 \, (5.43) = 5.38$

In a second analysis with EQS, the start values just calculated were specified in program syntax. The second analysis terminated normally with no error messages, and this solution is admissible. The parameter estimates are not described here, but you can view them in the output file. Both the EQS syntax file with start value specifications and the output file for this analysis can be downloaded from this book's website (p. 3). You can also download LISREL files for the same analysis.

Some additional issues specific to the estimation of nonrecursive models are described in the chapter appendices. These issues apply whether the structural model consists of observed variables only (nonrecursive path model) or has factors (nonrecursive structural regression model). Appendix 7.B deals with effect decomposition in nonrecursive models and the assumption of equilibrium. Appendix 7.C is about the estimation of corrected R^2-type proportions of explained variance for endogenous variables involved in feedback loops.

FITTING MODELS TO CORRELATION MATRICES

Default ML estimation assumes the analysis of unstandardized variables. If the variables are standardized, ML results may be inaccurate, including estimates of standard errors and values of model fit statistics. This can happen if a model is not scale invariant, which means that its overall fit to the data depends on whether the variables are standardized or unstandardized. Whether or not a model is scale invariant is determined by a rather complex combination of its characteristics, including how the factors are scaled and the presence of equality constraints on certain parameter estimates (Cudeck, 1989). One symptom of scale invariance when a correlation matrix is analyzed with default ML estimation is the observation that some of the diagonal elements in the model-implied correlation matrix do not equal 1.0.

There is a method for correctly fitting a model to a correlation matrix instead of a covariance matrix known as **constrained estimation** or **constrained optimization** (Browne, 1982). This method involves the imposition of nonlinear constraints on certain parameter estimation to guarantee that the model is scale invariant. These constraints can be quite complicated to program manually (e.g., Steiger, 2002, p. 221), and not all SEM computer tools support nonlinear constraints (LISREL, Mplus, Mx, and TCALIS do). However, some SEM computer programs, including SEPATH and RAMONA, allow constrained estimation to be performed automatically by selecting an option. These automated methods accept as input either a raw data file or a correlation matrix. The EQS and Mplus programs can also correctly analyze correlations, but they require raw data files. There are at least three occasions for using constrained estimation:

1. A researcher is conducting a secondary SEM analysis based on a source wherein correlations are reported, but not standard deviations. The raw data are also not available.

2. There is a theoretical reason to impose equality constraints on standardized estimates, such as when the standardized direct effects of different predictors on the same outcome are presumed to be equal. When a covariance matrix is analyzed, equality constraints are imposed in the unstandardized solution only.

3. A researcher wishes to report correct tests of statistical significance for the standardized solution. This means that correct standard errors are needed for the standardized estimates, too. Note that Mplus automatically reports correct standard errors for standardized effects when the standardized solution is requested.

ALTERNATIVE ESTIMATORS

Standard ML estimation works fine for 90% or more of the structural equation models described in the literature. However, you should be aware of some alternative methods. Some of these alternatives are options when the assumption of multivariate normality is not tenable, and others are intended for noncontinuous outcome variables. In some disciplines, such as education, categorical outcomes may be analyzed as often as continuous outcomes. The methods described next are generally iterative, simultaneous, full information, and available in many SEM computer programs.

Other Normal Theory Methods for Continuous Outcomes

Two methods for endogenous variables with multivariate normal distributions include **generalized least squares** (GLS) and **unweighted least squares** (ULS). The ULS method is actually a type of OLS estimation that minimizes the sum of squared differences between sample and model-implied covariances. It can generate unbiased estimates across random samples, but it is not as efficient as ML estimation (Kaplan, 2009). A drawback of the ULS method is its requirement that all observed variables have the same scale. That is, this method is neither scale free nor scale invariant. A potential advantage is that, unlike ML, the ULS method does not require a positive-definite covariance matrix (Chapter 3). It is also robust concerning initial estimates (Wothke, 1993). This means that ULS estimation could be used to generate start values for a second analysis of the same model and data but with ML estimation.

The GLS method is a member of a larger family of methods known as **fully weighted least squares** (WLS) estimation, and some other methods in this family can be used for severely non-normal data. In contrast to ULS, the GLS estimator is both scale free and scale invariant, and under the assumption of multivariate normality, the GLS and ML methods are asymptotic. One potential advantage of GLS over ML estimation is that it requires less computation time and computer memory. However, this potential advantage is not as meaningful today, given fast processors and abundant memory in relatively inexpensive personal computers. In general, ML estimation is preferred to both ULS and GLS estimation.

Corrected Normal Theory Methods for Continuous but Non-normal Outcomes

The results of computer simulation studies generally indicate that it is best not to ignore the multivariate normality assumption of default ML estimation (e.g., Curran, West, & Finch, 1997; Olsson, Foss, Troye, & Howell, 2000). For example, when endogenous variables are continuous but have severely non-normal distributions:

1. Values of ML parameter estimates may be relatively accurate in large samples, but their estimated standard errors tend to be too low, perhaps by as much as 25–50%,

depending on the data and model. This results in rejection of the null hypothesis that the corresponding population parameter is zero more often than is correct (Type I error rate is inflated).

2. Values of statistical tests of model fit *tend* to be too high. This results in rejection of the null hypothesis that the model has perfect fit in the population more often than is correct. That is, true models tend to be rejected too often. The actual rate of this error may be as high as 50% when the expected rate assuming normal distributions is 5%, again depending on the data and model. The most widely reported model test statistic in SEM, the model chi-square χ^2_M, is described in the next chapter. Depending on the particular pattern and severity of nonnormality, the value of χ^2_M may be too small, which would favor the researcher's model. In other words, model test statistics calculated using normal theory methods when there is severe nonnormality are not trustworthy.

One option to avoid bias is to normalize the variables with transformations (Chapter 3) and then analyze the transformed data with default ML estimation. Another option for continuous but non-normal outcome variables is to use a **corrected normal theory method**. This means to analyze the original data with a normal theory method, such as ML, but use **robust standard errors** and **corrected model test statistics**. Robust standard errors are estimates of standard errors that are supposedly robust against nonnormality. The best known example of corrected model test statistics is the **Satorra–Bentler statistic** (Satorra & Bentler, 1994), which adjusts downward the value of χ^2_M from standard ML estimation by an amount that reflects the degree of kurtosis. The Satorra–Bentler statistic was originally associated with EQS but is now calculated by other SEM computer programs. Results of computer simulation studies of the Satorra–Bentler statistic are generally favorable (Chou & Bentler, 1995). Analysis of a raw data file is required for a corrected normal theory method. Of the various methods for analyzing continuous outcome variables with severely non-normal distributions described here, a corrected normal theory method may be the most straightforward to apply (Finney & DiStefano, 2006).

Normal Theory Methods with Bootstrapping for Continuous but Non-normal Outcomes

Another option for analyzing continuous but severely non-normal endogenous variables is to use a normal theory method (i.e., ML estimation) but with nonparametric bootstrapping, which assumes only that the population and sample distributions have the same shape. In a bootstrap approach, parameters, standard errors, and model test statistics are estimated with empirical sampling distributions from large numbers of generated samples (e.g., Figure 2.3). Results of a computer simulation study by Nevitt and Hancock (2001) indicate that bootstrap estimates for a measurement model were generally less biased compared with those from standard ML estimation under conditions of non-normality and for sample sizes of $N \geq 200$. For $N = 100$, however, bootstrapped estimates had relatively large standard errors, and many generated samples were unusable due to problems such as nonpositive definite covariance matrices. These problems are consistent with the caution by Yung and Bentler (1996) that a small sample size will not typically render accurate bootstrapped results.

Elliptical and Arbitrary Distribution Estimators for Continuous but Non-normal Outcomes

Another option to analyze models with continuous but non-normal endogenous variables is to use a method that does not assume multivariate normality. For example, there is a class of estimators based on **elliptical distribution theory** that requires only symmetrical distributions (Bentler & Dijkstra, 1985). These methods estimate the degree of kurtosis in raw data. If all endogenous variables have a common degree of kurtosis, positive or negative skew is allowed; otherwise, zero skew is assumed. Various elliptical distribution estimators are available in EQS.

Another option known as **arbitrary distribution function** (ADF) estimation makes *no* distributional assumptions for continuous variables (Browne, 1984). This is because it estimates the degree of both skew and kurtosis in the raw data. The calculations for the ADF estimator are complex in part because the method derives a relatively large weight matrix that is applied to the covariance residuals as part of the fit function to be minimized. The number of rows or columns in this square weight matrix equals the number of observations, or v $(v + 1)/2$ where v is the number of observed variables. For a model with many observed variables, the size of this matrix can be so large that it can be difficult for the computer to derive the inverse of this matrix. For example, if there are 15 observed variables, the dimensions of the ADF weight matrix would be 120×120, which would have a total of $120^2 = 14,400$ elements. Also, calculations in ADF estimation typically require very large sample sizes in order for the results to be reasonably accurate. Relatively simple (i.e., uninteresting) models may require sample sizes of 200–500, and thousands of cases may be required for more complex models. These requirements are impractical for many researchers. The results of some computer simulation studies indicate that ADF estimation yields overly optimistic values of fit statistics when the model is misspecified (Olsson et al., 2000).

Options for Analyzing Dichotomous or Ordered-Categorical Outcomes

Endogenous variables are not always continuous. The most obvious example is a binary or dichotomous outcome, such as relapsed–not relapsed (Chapter 2). There are also ordered-categorical (ordinal) variables with three or more levels that imply a rank order. For example, the following item has a Likert scale that indicates degree of agreement:

I am happy with my life (0 = *disagree,* 1 = *uncertain,* 2 = *agree*)

The numeric scale for this variable (0–2) can distinguish among only three levels of agreement. It would be hard to argue that the numbers assigned to the three response alternatives of this item make up a scale with equal intervals. Also, scores on variables with so few levels cannot be normally distributed. Although there is no "golden rule" concerning the minimum number of levels that is required before scores can be approximately normally distributed, a score range of at least 15 points or so may be required.[7] However, Likert scales with about 5–10 points may be favorable in terms of people's ability to reasonably discriminate between scale values (anchors). With more than 10 or so scale points for individual items, respondents may choose arbitrarily between adjacent points. Suppose that research participants are asked to rate their degree of agreement with some statement on a 25-point Likert scale. It would be difficult to think of 25 distinct verbal labels for each point along the scale that would indicate progressively increasing or decreasing levels of agreement. Even with fewer labels, participants may struggle with trying to decide what is the difference between ratings of, say, 13 versus 14 or 23 versus 24. That is, it is not practical to somehow "force" a variable with a Likert scale to become continuous by adding levels beyond 10 or so.

Results of some computer simulation studies indicate that results from standard ML estimation may be inaccurate for models with dichotomous or ordinal endogenous variables. These simulation studies generally assume a true population measurement model with continuous indicators. Within generated samples, the indicators are categorized to approximate data from noncontinuous variables. Bernstein and Teng (1989) found that when there is only a single factor in the population but the indicators have few categories, one-factor measurement models tend to be rejected too often. That is, categorization can spuriously suggest the presence of multiple factors. DiStefano (2002) found that ML parameter estimates and their standard errors were both generally too low when the data analyzed were from categorical indicators, and the degree of negative bias was higher as distributions became increasingly non-normal. The message of the studies just cited and others is that standard ML is not an appropriate method for analyzing ordered-categorical variables.

Two analytical options for ordinal outcome variables are outlined. The first involves the case where ordered-categorical outcomes are analyzed as "stand-alone" variables that are not merged or combined across a set of similar variables. This approach requires special estimators for this type of data (i.e., not ML) related to the WLS family. The second option involves analyzing parcels. A **parcel** is a total score across a set of homogeneous items each with a Likert-type scale. Parcels are generally treated as continuous variables. The score reliability of parcels (total scores) tends to be greater than that for the individual items. If the distributions of all parcels are normal, then default ML estimation could be used to analyze the data. Parcels are then typically specified as continu-

---

[7]The PRELIS program of LISREL automatically classifies a variable with less than 16 levels as ordinal, but this default can be changed.

ous indicators of underlying latent variables in a measurement model, such as in a CFA model or when analyzing a structural regression (SR) model (e.g., Figures 5.6, 5.8). But parceling is controversial. The reasons why are outlined later in this chapter.

Special WLS Methods for Ordinal Outcomes

Muthén (e.g., 1984) describes an approach to estimating models with any combination of dichotomous, ordinal, or continuous outcome variables known as **continuous/categorical variable methodology** (CVM). In CVM, bivariate associations among observed variables are estimated with polychoric correlations, which assume that a normal, continuous process underlies each observed variable (Flora & Curran, 2004). The model is then estimated with a form of WLS, and values of corrected test statistics are provided.

In the CVM approach described by Muthén and Asparouhov (2002) that is implemented in Mplus, each observed ordinal indicator is associated with an underlying **latent response variable**, which is the underlying amount of a continuous and normally distributed trait or characteristic that is required to respond in a certain category of the corresponding observed ordinal item. When the observed indicator is dichotomous, such as for items with a true–false response format, this amount, or **threshold**, is the point on the latent response variable where one answer is given (e.g., true) when the threshold is exceeded. It is also the point where the other response is given (e.g., false) when the threshold is not exceeded (Brown, 2006). Dichotomous items have a single threshold, but the number of thresholds for items with ≥ 3 response categories is the number of categories minus one. Each latent response variable is in turn represented as the continuous indicator of the underlying substantive factor that corresponds to a hypothetical construct. The data matrix analyzed in this approach is an **asymptotic correlation matrix** of the latent response variables. For dichotomous indicators, this estimated matrix will be a tetrachoric correlation matrix; for items with at least three response categories, the data matrix will be an estimated polychoric correlation matrix.

The arbitrary and elliptical estimators described earlier (e.g., ADF), which do not assume normality, are also members of the WLS family of estimators.[8] The WLS estimator can be applied to either continuous or ordinal outcomes because it does not assume a particular distributional form. In general, WLS estimation is just as computationally complex as ADF estimation, requires very large samples, and is subject to technical problems in the analysis (e.g., Finney & DiStefano, 2006, pp. 281–288), such as the failure of the computer to derive the inverse of the weight matrix. Muthén, du Toit, and Spisic (1997) describe forms of **robust WLS estimation** that deal with problems of using WLS when the sample size is not very large. These robust methods use somewhat simpler matrix calculations compared with WLS estimation.

In Mplus, two of these robust estimators are designated as **mean-adjusted weighted least squares** (WLSM) and **mean- and variance-adjusted weighted least squares**

---

[8]The GLS estimator is also a member of this family, but it assumes multivariate normality.

(WLSMV). The standard errors and parameter estimates from these two methods are the same, but WLSMV does not calculate the model degrees of freedom in the standard way, and this method may be preferred when the number of observed variables is relatively small. This method is also the default in Mplus when ordered-categorical variables are analyzed. In computer simulation studies, the WLSMV method has generally performed well except when the sample size is only about $N = 200$ or distributions on ordered-categorical variables are markedly skewed (Muthén et al., 1997). Results of computer simulation studies by Flora and Curran (2004) also indicated generally positive performance of robust WLS estimation methods in the analysis of measurement models with ordinal indicators. In contrast, these authors observed technical problems with WLS estimation when the sample size was even as large as $N = 1,000$ for larger models with about 20 indicators.

Models with ordinal outcomes are analyzed in two steps in LISREL. First, the raw data are submitted to the PRELIS program, which estimates polychoric correlations among the observed variables. These correlations and other statistical information are used to compute an **asymptotic covariance matrix**, which is then analyzed in LISREL with WLS estimation. Another option in LISREL is **diagonally weighted least squares** (DWLS) estimation, which is a mathematically simpler form of WLS estimation that may be better when the sample size is not very large. See Jöreskog (2005) for examples.

The EQS program uses a two-stage method by Lee, Poon, and Bentler (1995) for analyzing models with any combination of continuous or categorical endogenous variables. In the first stage, a special form of ML estimation is used to estimate correlations between the continuous latent variables presumed to underlie the observed variables. In the second stage, an asymptotic covariance matrix is computed, and the model is analyzed with a method that in EQS is referred to as **arbitrary generalized least squares** (AGLS) estimation, which is basically equivalent to WLS estimation (Finney & DiStefano, 2006).

Analyzing Items Parcels

Suppose that a questionnaire has 40 Likert scale items. Instead of analyzing all 40 items as "stand-alone" outcome variables, a researcher partitions the items into two nonoverlapping sets of 20 items each. The items within each set are presumed to be homogeneous; that is, they reflect a common domain. A total score is derived across the 20 items within each set, and the two resulting total scores, or parcels, are analyzed instead of the 40 items. Because the total scores are continuous and normally distributed, the researcher opts for standard ML estimation, which is easier to use than WLS estimators. This is the basic rationale of parceling. But this technique is controversial because it assumes that items within each parcel are known to measure a single construct, or are unidimensional. This knowledge may come from familiarity with the item domain or results of prior statistical analyses, such as an exploratory factor analysis.

Parceling is *not* recommended if unidimensionality cannot be assumed. Specifically, parceling should not be part of an analysis aimed at determining whether a set of items is unidimensional. This is because it is possible that parceling can mask a multidimensional factor structure in such a way that a seriously misspecified model may nevertheless fit the data reasonably well (Bandalos, 2002). There are also different ways to parcel items, including random assignment of items to parcels and groupings of items based on rational grounds (e.g., the items share similar content), and the choice can affect the results. See Bandalos and Finney (2001) and Little, Cunningham, Shahar, and Widamin (2002) for descriptions of the potential advantages and drawbacks of parceling in SEM. Williams and O'Boyle (2008) review human resource management research using parcels.

A HEALTHY PERSPECTIVE ON ESTIMATION

The availability of so many different estimation methods can sometimes seem overwhelming for newcomers to SEM. Loehlin (2004) cites the following proverb that may describe this experience: a person with one watch always knows what time it is; a person with two never does. It also doesn't help that the same general estimator may be referred to using different names in the documentation or syntax of different SEM computer tools. Actually, the situation is not so bewildering because standard ML estimation works just fine for most types of structural equation models if the data have been properly screened and distributions of continuous endogenous variables are reasonably multivariate normal. But if the normality assumption is not tenable or if you are working with outcome variables that are not continuous, you need alternative methods.

SUMMARY

The method of maximum likelihood estimation is a normal theory, full-information method that simultaneously analyzes all model equations in an iterative algorithm. General statistical assumptions include independence of the scores, independence of exogenous variables and residuals, multivariate normality, and correct specification of the model. Correct specification of the model is especially important because of error propagation, or the tendency for misspecification in one part of the model to affect estimates in other parts. Sometimes iterative estimation fails due to poor start values. When this happens, it may be necessary to specify better initial estimates in order to "help" the computer reach a converged solution. It can happen in estimation that the solution contains illogical values, such as Heywood cases, which renders the solution inadmissible. Thus, you should always carefully inspect the solution even if the computer output contains no error or warning messages. When endogenous variables are continuous but their distributions are severely non-normal, the most straightforward option is to use a corrected normal theory method that generates robust standard errors and corrected test statistics. When the endogenous variables are not continuous, then other estimation methods, including forms of robust weighted least squares, should be applied.

RECOMMENDED READINGS

Finney and DiStefano (2006) is an excellent resource for learning more about estimation options for analyzing non-normal and categorical data in SEM. Kaplan (2009, chap. 5) offers a detailed discussion of assumptions of maximum likelihood estimation and alternative estimators.

Finney, S. J., & DiStefano, C. (2006). Nonnormal and categorical data in structural equation modeling. In G. R. Hancock & R. O. Mueller (Eds.), *A second course in structural equation modeling* (pp. 269–314). Greenwich, CT: Information Age Publishing.

Kaplan, D. (2009). *Structural equation modeling: Foundations and extensions* (2nd ed.). Thousand Oaks, CA: Sage.

EXERCISES

1. Calculate R^2_{smc} for each endogenous variable in Figure 7.1 using the information in Tables 7.1 and 7.2.

2. Use the information in Table 7.2 to calculate for the model in Figure 7.1(a) the Sobel test for the unstandardized indirect effect of school support on school experience through teacher–pupil interactions.

3. Calculate for the model of Figure 7.1(a) the unstandardized total indirect effect of school support on school experience using the information in Table 7.2. Compare your result with the corresponding entry in Table 7.3.

4. Using a computer tool for SEM, analyze the model in Figure 7.1 using the data in Table 7.1 and default ML estimation. See whether your results replicate the parameter estimates listed in Table 7.2 within slight rounding error. Now rerun the analysis but add to the model the path listed next:

   School Support → School Experience

   What are values of the parameter estimates for this new path? Is this direct effect statistically significant? Also, compare the values of R^2_{smc} for the school experience variable in the models with and without the new direct effect.

5. Now analyze the model in Figure 7.1 but this time impose an equality constraint on the two direct effects for the paths listed next:

   School Support → Teacher Burnout

   Coercive Control → Teacher Burnout

   What are the values of the unstandardized direct effects? the standardized direct effects?

6. A researcher submits a covariance matrix as the input data for the analysis of

a model with a corrected normal theory method. The program ends with an error message. Why?

7. Use an SEM computer tool to fit the nonrecursive model in Figure 7.2. to the data summarized in Table 7.6. Was it necessary for you to specify start values?

8. Interpret these results: The observed correlation between a pair of endogenous variables is .41, and the estimated disturbance correlation is .38.

Start Value Suggestions for Structural Models

These recommendations concern structural models, whether those models are path models or part of a structural regression model. First, think about the expected direction and magnitude of standardized direct effects. For example, in some research areas, an absolute standardized direct effect < .10 may be considered a "smaller" effect; values around .30 a "typical" or "medium" effect; and values > .50 a "larger" effect. If the numerical values just stated do not match the qualitative interpretations for "smaller," "typical," or "larger" effects, then substitute the appropriate values (e.g., Bollen, 1989, pp. 137–138). A meta-analytic study is a good way to gauge the magnitude of "typical" versus "smaller" or "larger" effect sizes in a particular research area. Suppose that a researcher believes that the direct effect of X on Y is positive and of standardized magnitude, .30. Thus, a reasonable start value for the unstandardized coefficient for the path $X \rightarrow Y$ would be .30 (SD_Y/SD_X).

Start values for disturbance variances can be calculated in a similar way, but now think about standardized effect size in terms of the proportion of explained variance (i.e., R^2). For example, in some research areas a proportion of explained variance < .01 may indicate a "smaller" effect; values of about .10 a "typical" or "medium" effect; and values > .30 a "larger" effect. Again, the numerical values just stated can be adjusted up or down for a particular research area. Suppose that a researcher believes that the magnitude of the predictive power of all variables with direct effects on Y (including X) is "typical." This corresponds to a proportion of explained variance of about .10 and a proportion of unexplained variance to $1 - .10$, or .90. Thus, a reasonable start value for the disturbance variance would be .90 (s_Y^2).

Effect Decomposition in Nonrecursive Models and the Equilibrium Assumption

The tracing rule does not apply to nonrecursive structural models. This is because variables in feedback loops have indirect effects—and thus total effects—on *themselves*, which is apparent in effect decompositions calculated by SEM computer programs for nonrecursive models. Consider the reciprocal relation $Y_1 \rightleftarrows Y_2$. Suppose that the standardized direct effect of Y_1 on Y_2 is .40 and that the effect in the other direction is .20. An indirect effect of Y_1 on itself would be the sequence

$$Y_1 \rightarrow Y_2 \rightarrow Y_1$$

which is estimated as .40 × .20, or .08. There are additional indirect effects of Y_1 on itself through Y_2, however, because cycles of mutual influence in feedback loops are theoretically infinite. The indirect effect

$$Y_1 \rightarrow Y_2 \rightarrow Y_1 \rightarrow Y_2 \rightarrow Y_1$$

is one of these, and its estimate is .40 × .20 × .40 × .20, or .0064. Mathematically, these terms head fairly quickly to zero, but the total effect of Y_1 on itself is an estimate of all possible cycles through Y_2. Indirect and total effects of Y_2 on itself are similarly derived.

Calculation of indirect and total effects among variables in a feedback loop as just described assumes equilibrium (Chapter 5). It is important to realize, however, that there is generally no statistical way to directly evaluate whether the equilibrium assumption is tenable when the data are cross-sectional; that is, it must be argued substantively. Kaplan, Harik, and Hotchkiss (2001) note that rarely is this assumption explicitly acknowledged in the literature on applications of SEM where feedback effects are estimated with cross-sectional data. This is unfortunate because the results of a computer simulation study by Kaplan et al. (2001) indicate that violation of the equilibrium assumption can lead to severely biased estimates. They also found that the **stability index** did not accurately measure the degree of bias due to lack of equilibrium. This index is printed in the output of some SEM computer programs when a nonrecursive model is analyzed. It is based on certain mathematical properties of the matrix of coefficients for direct effects among all the endogenous variables in a structural model, not just those involved in feedback loops. These properties concern whether estimates of the direct effects would get infinitely larger over time. If so, the system is said to "explode" because it may never reach equilibrium, given the observed direct effects among the endogenous variables. The mathematics of the stability index are complex (e.g., Kaplan et al., 2001, pp. 317–322). A standard interpretation of this index is that values less than 1.0 are taken as positive evidence for equilibrium but values greater than 1.0 suggest the lack of equilibrium. However, this interpretation is not generally supported by Kaplan and colleagues' computer simulation results, which emphasize the need to evaluate equilibrium on rational grounds.

Corrected Proportions of Explained Variance for Nonrecursive Models

Several authors have noted that R_{smc}^2 calculated as one minus the ratio of the disturbance variance over the total variance may be inappropriate for endogenous variables involved in feedback loops. This is because the disturbances of such variables may be correlated with one of their presumed causes, which violates the least squares requirement that the residuals (disturbances) are uncorrelated with all predictors (causal variables). Some corrected R^2 statistics for nonrecursive models are described next:

1. The **Bentler–Raykov corrected R^2** (Bentler & Raykov, 2000) is based on a respecification that repartitions the variance of endogenous variables controlling for correlations between disturbances and causal variables. This statistic is automatically printed by EQS for nonrecursive models.

2. The LISREL program prints a **reduced-form R^2** (Jöreskog, 2000) for each endogenous variable in a structural model. In **reduced form**, the endogenous variables are regressed on the exogenous variables only. This regression also has the consequence that all direct effects of disturbances on their respective endogenous variables are removed or blocked, which also removes any contribution to all other endogenous variables (Hayduk, 2006). For recursive models, the value of the reduced-form R^2 can be substantially less than that R_{smc}^2 for the same variable.

3. Hayduk (2006) describes the **blocked-error-R^2** for variables in feedback loops or with correlated errors. It is calculating by blocking the influence of the disturbance of just the variable in question (the focal endogenous variable). An advantage of this statistic is that it equals the value of R_{smc}^2 for each endogenous variable in a recursive model. The blocked-error-R^2 is not yet automatically printed by SEM computer programs, but Hayduk (2006) describes a method for doing so using any program that reports the model-implied covariance matrix when all parameters are fixed to equal user-specified values.

Depending on the model and data, the corrected R^2s just described can be either smaller or larger than that of R_{smc}^2 for endogenous variables in feedback loops. For example, reported next are values of R_{smc}^2, the Bentler–Raykov R^2, and the reduced-form R^2 for the variables mother education and maternity age in Figure 7.2:

Endogenous variable	R_{smc}^2	BR R^2	RF R^2
Mother Education	.161	.162	.055
Maternity Age	.097	.100	.137

Note. BR, Bentler–Raykov; RF, reduced form.

The values of R^2_{smc} and the Bentler–Raykov R^2 are similar and indicate proportions of explained variance of about .16 and .10 for, respectively, mother education and maternity age. However, proportions of explained variance estimated by the reduced-form R^2 are somewhat different. Specifically, they are about .06 and .14, respectively, for the same two endogenous variables. Both sets of results just described are equally correct because they represent somewhat methods to correct for model-implied correlations between disturbances and causal variables. In written reports, always indicate the particular R^2 statistic used to estimate the proportions of explained variance for endogenous variables in nonrecursive models.

UNIVERSITY OF WOLVERHAMPTON
Harrison Learning Centre

ITEMS ISSUED:

Customer ID: WPP60509341

Title: Structural equation modeling with AMOS :
basic concepts, applications, and p
ID: 7624702587
Due: 27/11/2017 23:59

Title: Principles and practice of structural
equation modeling
ID: 7625146742
Due: 27/11/2017 23:59

Total items: 2
Total fines: £24.60
06/11/2017 16:10
Issued: 19
Overdue: 0

Thank you for using Self Service.
Please keep your receipt.

Overdue books are fined at 40p per day for
1 week loans, 10p per day for long loans.

8

Hypothesis Testing

Outlined in this chapter are methods and strategies for (1) evaluating whether a structural equation model is consistent with the sample data and (2) hypothesis-testing strategies in SEM. Two related topics are (3) statistical power analysis and (4) consideration of equivalent models or near-equivalent models that fit the same data just as well as the researcher's preferred model or nearly so. There is an emerging consensus—one expressed in a recent special issue on SEM in the journal *Personality and Individual Differences* (Vernon & Eysenck, 2007)—that standard practice about model fit evaluation has been lax. Accordingly, next I describe an even more rigorous approach to model testing compared with the one presented in the previous edition of this book. This modified approach includes the reporting of diagnostic information about specific sources of model misfit. Because the issues discussed here generalize to most SEM analyses, they warrant careful study.

EYES ON THE PRIZE

Newcomers to SEM sometimes mistakenly believe that "success" means that, at the end of the analysis, the researcher will have a model that fits the data. *However, this outcome by itself is not very impressive.* This is because any model, even one that is grossly misspecified, can be made to fit the data simply by adding free parameters (i.e., reduce df_M). If all possible free parameters are estimated ($df_M = 0$), fit will likely be perfect, but such a model would have little scientific value.

Hayduk, Cummings, Boadu, Pazderka-Robinson, and Boulianne (2007) remind us that the real goal is to *test a theory* by specifying a model that represents predictions of that theory among plausible constructs measured with the appropriate indicators. If such a model does not ultimately fit the data, then this outcome is interesting because there is value in reporting models that challenge or debunk theories. But the story is hardly over if the researcher happens to retain a model. This is because there could be equivalent or near-equivalent models that explain the same data just as well. Among plausible models with equal or near-equal fit, the researcher must explain why any one of them may actually be correct. This includes (1) directly acknowledging the existence of equivalent or near-equivalent models and (2) describing what might be done in future research to differentiate between any serious competing models. *So success in SEM is determined by whether the analysis dealt with substantive theoretical issues regardless of whether a model is retained.* In contrast, whether or not a scientifically meaningless model fits the data is irrelevant (Millsap, 2007).

STATE OF PRACTICE, STATE OF MIND

For at least 30 years the literature has carried an ongoing discussion about the best ways to test hypotheses and assess model fit. This is also an active research area, especially concerning computer simulation (Monte Carlo) studies. Discussion and research about this topic are likely to continue because there is no single, black-and-white statistical framework within which we can clearly distinguish correct from incorrect hypotheses in SEM. Nor is there ever likely to be such a thing. Part of the problem is that behavioral scientists typically study samples, not whole populations, so the problem of sampling error looms over analyses conducted with sample data. (This is not unique to SEM.) Another problem is the philosophical question of whether correct models really exist. The recognition of this possibility is based on the view that basically all statistical models are wrong to some degree; that is, they are imperfect reflections of a complex reality. Specifically, a statistical model is an approximation tool that helps researchers to structure their thinking (i.e., generate good ideas) in order to make sense of a phenomenon of interest (Humphreys, 2003). If the approximation is too coarse, then the model will be rejected. Otherwise, the failure to reject a model must not provide unjustified enthusiasm over the implied accuracy of that model; that is, a retained model is not proved (Chapter 1). MacCallum and Austin (2000) put it this way:

> With respect to model fit, researchers do not seem adequately sensitive to the fundamental reality that there is no true model . . . , that all models are wrong to some degree, even in the population, and that the best one can hope for is to identify a parsimonious, substantively meaningful model that fits observed data adequately well. At the same time, one must recognize that there may well be other models that fit the data to approximately the same degree. Given this perspective, it is clear that a finding of good fit does not imply that a model is correct or true, but only plausible. These facts must temper conclusions drawn about good-fitting models. (p. 218)

A related complication is that there is no statistical "gold standard" in SEM that automatically and objectively leads to the decision about whether to reject or retain a particular model.

Researchers typically consult various statistical measures of model–data correspondence in the analysis, but, as explained in the next section, no set of fit statistics is definitive. This means that fit statistics in SEM do not generally provide a simple yes or no answer to the question, should this model be retained? Various guidelines about how to interpret various fit statistics as providing something like a yes-or-no answer have been developed over the years, but these rules of thumb are just that. The fact that some of these interpretive guidelines probably do not apply to the whole range of structural equation models actually analyzed by researchers is becoming ever more clear. It is also true that we in the SEM community have collectively relied too much on unsubstantiated principles about what fit statistics say about our models. However, there is no disguising the fact that decisions about the viability of hypotheses and models in SEM are ultimately a matter a judgment. This judgment should have a solid basis in theory (i.e., think like a researcher) and a correct appreciation of the strengths and limitations of fit statistics. There is also no need to apologize about the role of human judgment in SEM or science in general. As Kirk (1996) and others note, a scientific decision is ultimately a qualitative judgment that is based on the researcher's domain knowledge, but it will also reflect the researcher's personal values and societal concerns. This is not "unscientific" because the evaluation of all findings in science involves some degree of subjectivity. It is better to be open about this fact, however, than to base such decisions solely on statistics that seem to offer absolute objectivity, but do no such thing. As aptly put by Huberty and Morris (1988, p. 573), "As in all statistical inference, subjective judgment cannot be avoided. Neither can reasonableness!"

Described in this chapter is what I believe is a rigorous approach to hypothesis testing that addresses problems seen in too many published reports of SEM analyses. Not all experts in SEM may agree with each and every specific detail of this approach, but most experts would likely concur that authors of SEM studies need to give their readers more information about model specification and its correspondence with the data. Specifically, I want you to be hardheaded in the way you test hypotheses by being your model's toughest critic and by holding it to higher standards than have been applied in the past. But I do not want you to be bullheaded and blindly follow the method described here as though it were the path to truth in SEM. Instead, you should use your good judgment about what makes the most sense in your research area at every step of the process at the same time you follow a rigorous method of hypothesis testing. To paraphrase Millsap (2007), this is SEM made difficult, not easy. The hard part is thinking for yourself in a lucid, disciplined way instead of hoping that fit statistics can somehow make decisions for you.

A HEALTHY PERSPECTIVE ON FIT STATISTICS

There are dozens of fit statistics described in the SEM literature, and new ones are being developed all the time. Evaluation of the statistical properties of fit statistics in computer simulation studies is also an active research topic; thus, the state of knowledge is continually changing. It is also true that SEM computer programs usually print in their output the values of many more fit statistics than are typically reported for the analysis, which presents a few problems. One problem is that different fit statistics are reported in different articles, and another is that different reviewers of the same manuscript may request statistics that they know or prefer (Maruyama, 1998). It can therefore be difficult for a researcher to decide on which particular statistics and which values to report. There is also the possibility for selective reporting of values of fit statistics. For example, a researcher keen to demonstrate acceptable model fit may report only those fit statistics with favorable values. A related problem is "fit statistic tunnel vision," a disorder apparent among practitioners of SEM who become so preoccupied with overall model fit that other crucial information, such as whether the parameter estimates actually make sense, is overlooked. Fortunately, there is a cure, and it involves close inspection of the whole computer output (Chapter 7), not just the section on fit statistics.

A more fundamental issue is the ongoing debate in the field about the merits of the two main classes of fit statistics described in the next section: model test statistics and approximate fit indexes. To anticipate some of this debate now, some methodologists argue strongly against what has become a routine—and bad—practice for researchers to basically ignore model test statistics and justify retention of their preferred model based on approximate fit indexes. Others argue that there is a role for *reasoned* use of approximate fit indexes in SEM, but not at the expense of what test statistics say about model fit. I will try to convince you that (1) there is real value in the criticisms of those who argue against the uncritical use of approximate fit indexes, and (2) we as practitioners of SEM need to "clean up our act" by taking a more skeptical, discerning approach to model testing. That is, we should walk disciplined model testing as we talk it (practice the rigor that we as scientists preach).

The main benefit of hypothesis testing in SEM is to place a reasonable limit on the extent of model–data discrepancy that can be attributed to mere sampling error. Specifically, if the degree of this discrepancy is less than that expected by chance, there is initial support for the model. This support may be later canceled by results of more specific diagnostic assessments, however, and no testing procedure ever "proves" models in SEM (Chapter 1). Discrepancies between model and data that clearly surpass the limits of chance require diagnostic investigation of model features that might need to be respecified in order to make the model consistent with the evidence.

Before any individual fit statistic is described, it is useful to keep in mind the following limitations of basically *all* fit statistics in SEM:

1. Values of fit statistics indicate only the *average* or *overall* fit of a model. That is, fit statistics collapse many discrepancies into a single measure (Steiger, 2007). It is thus possible that some parts of the model may poorly fit the data even if the value of a fit statistic seems favorable. In this case, the model may be inadequate despite the values of its fit statistics. This is why I will recommend later that researchers report more specific diagnostic information about model fit of the type that cannot be directly indicated by fit statistics alone. Tomarken and Waller (2003) discuss potential problems with models that seem to fit the data well based on values of fit statistics.

2. Because a single statistic reflects only a particular aspect of fit, a favorable value of that statistic does not by itself indicate acceptable fit. *That is, there is no such thing as a magical, single-number summary that says everything worth knowing about model fit.*

3. Unfortunately, there is little direct relation between values of fit statistics and the degree or type of misspecification (Millsap, 2007). This means that researchers can glean relatively little about just where and by how much the model departs from the data from inspecting values of fit statistics. For example, fit statistics cannot tell whether you have the correct number of factors (3, 4, etc.) in a measurement model. Other kinds of diagnostic information, such as covariance residuals and correlation residuals, speak more directly to this issue.

4. Values of fit statistics that suggest adequate fit do not also indicate that the predictive power of the model is also high as measured by statistics for individual endogenous variables such as R^2_{smc}. In fact, overall model fit and R^2_{smc} for individual outcomes are relatively independent characteristics. For example, disturbances in structural models with perfect fit can still be large (i.e., R^2_{smc}s are low), which means that the model accurately reflects the relative lack of predictive validity.

5. Fit statistics do not indicate whether the results are theoretically meaningful. For instance, the sign of some path coefficients may be unexpectedly in the opposite direction (e.g., Figure 7.1). Even if values of fit statistics seem favorable, results so anomalous require explanation.

TYPES OF FIT STATISTICS AND "GOLDEN RULES"

Described next are the two broad categories of fit statistics and the status of interpretative guidelines associated with each. Each category actually represents a different mode or contrasting way of considering model fit.

Model Test Statistics

These are the original fit statistics in SEM. A **model test statistic** is a test of whether the covariance matrix implied by the researcher's model is close enough to the sample covariance matrix that the differences might reasonably be considered as being due to sampling error. If not, then (1) the data covariances contain information that speak against the model, and (2) this outcome calls for the researcher to explain model-data discrepancies that exceed those expected by chance.

Most model test statistics are generally scaled as "badness-of-fit" statistics because the higher their values, the worse the model's correspondence with the data. This means that a statistically significant result (e.g., $p < .05$) indicates problematic model–data correspondence. That is, it is the *failure* to reject the null hypothesis (e.g., $p \geq .05$) that the model-implied covariance matrix is identical to the population covariance matrix that generated the sample covariance matrix that supports the researcher's model. This logic is "backward" from the usual **reject–support context** for statistical tests where it is the *rejection* of the null hypothesis that supports the researcher's theory. But it is perfectly consistent with an **accept–support context** where the null hypothesis represents the researcher's beliefs, or in this case where the model is consistent with the data matrix.

Steiger (2007) reminds us that accept–support tests are logically weak because lack of evidence to disprove an assertion (the null hypothesis) does not prove that the assertion is true. Low statistical power can lead to failure to reject the null hypothesis, which for an accept–support test would *favor* the researcher's model. Specifically, low power for accept–support tests means that if the researcher's model is false, then the probability of detecting this specification error is low. This explains the need to be especially concerned about the statistical power of accept–support tests in SEM. In contrast, low power works *against* the researcher's hypotheses in more conventional reject–support tests. In this case, low power means that if the researcher's hypotheses are correct, then the probability of detecting this outcome is low.

Model test statistics in SEM are usually evaluated at the conventional levels of statistical significance (α), either .05 or .01. Recall that there is nothing "magical" about either α = .05 or α = .01. These levels are actually just rules of thumb that some of us nevertheless treat as "golden rules" that somehow hold across all research areas. But just because we treat some rather arbitrary cutoff point or **threshold value**, such as $p < .05$ for test statistics, does not somehow turn a rule of thumb into a universal truth (Chapter 2). It is rare for researchers to specify α levels higher than .05. The main reason is editorial policy: Manuscripts may be rejected for publication if $\alpha > .05$. This policy would make more sense if the context for testing model fit were always reject–support where a Type I error is akin to a false positive because the evidence is incorrectly taken as supporting the researcher's hypotheses.

As noted by Steiger and Fouladi (1997), the value of α should be as low as possible in reject–support testing from the perspective of journal editors and reviewers, who may wish to guard against false claims. In accept–support testing, however, they should worry less about Type I error and more about Type II error because false claims in this context arise from *not* rejecting the null hypothesis. Insisting on low values of α in this case may facilitate publication of erroneous claims. Hayduk (1996) reminds us that is perfectly legitimate to specify a level of α higher than the conventional value of .05 when evaluating model test statistics in SEM. Higher levels of α in accept–support testing make it even more difficult to retain the null hypothesis, which works against the researcher's model. Whatever level of α is selected, it places a limit on what can be dismissed as expected random variation and what should be interpreted as evidence against the model. The outcome of the test is then the binary decision (yes or no) about whether or not to reject the null hypothesis that the researcher's model is consistent with the data within the bounds of chance. *However, the yes-or-no decision just described does not by itself determine whether to reject the model or retain it.* Other information about model–data correspondence must be considered, but a statistically significant model test statistic does provide preliminary evidence against the model. In this sense, a model test statistic is analogous to a smoke detector. When the alarm sounds, there may or may not be a fire (serious model–data discrepancy), but it is prudent to treat the alarm seriously (conduct more detailed diagnostic evaluation of fit).

Probabilities (p values) for test statistics are typically calculated assuming certain distributional characteristics of the data, such as multivariate normality in default maximum likelihood (ML) estimation. But if distributional assumptions are not tenable, then p values printed by the computer may be incorrect. If so, then p values may be too high or low, and small differences in p can make a big difference in hypothesis testing, such as $p = .03$ versus $p = .07$ when $\alpha = .05$. The p values for test statistics are also estimated in sampling distributions that assume random sampling from known populations. Random sampling is a crucial part of the **population inference model**, which concerns the validity of sample results. But most samples in SEM are not randomly selected. Instead, they are often samples of convenience, or ad hoc samples that happen to be available. A data set collected at a local hospital where cases were not selected using a chance-based method is an example of an ad hoc sample. Whether p values from test statistics apply to ad hoc samples is unknown. Lunneborg (2001) described this issue as a mismatch between statistical analysis, which assumes random sampling, and design, which rarely includes true random sampling in SEM studies.

Approximate Fit Indexes

A different mode of evaluating model fit is represented by **approximate fit indexes**. In contrast to model test statistics, (1) approximate fit indexes do not distinguish between what may be sampling error and what may be real covariance evidence against the model. (2) The outcome of an approximate fit index is not the dichotomous decision to reject or retain a null hypothesis. Instead, these indexes are intended as continuous measures of model–data correspondence. However, there is no direct relation between the degree of this correspondence and substantive problems or specification errors in the model. (Remember, there is no magic in fit statistics of any kind.) Some approximate fit indexes are scaled as badness-of-fit statistics, but most are scaled instead as goodness-of-fit statistics because the higher their values, the closer the model–data correspondence. Values of some goodness-of-fit indexes are more or less standardized so that their range is 0–1.0 where a value of 1.0 indicates the best fit.

Four categories of approximate fit indexes are described next. These categories are not mutually exclusive because some indexes can be classified under more than one category:

1. **Absolute fit indexes** are generally interpreted as proportions of the covariances in the sample data matrix explained by the model. For example, if the value of an absolute fit index is .85, then we can say that the model explains 85% of the observed covariances. These indexes are analogous to R^2 statistics except that they concern model–data matrix correspondence, not explanatory power for individual outcomes. Explaining a high proportion of the sample covariances, such as .95, does not by itself indicate the model is adequate. This is because any incorrect model can be made to explain the data

by adding parameters to the point where no degrees of freedom remain ($df_M = 0$). That is, most just-identified models will perfectly explain the observed covariances.

2. **Incremental fit indexes**—also known as **comparative fit indexes**—indicate the *relative* improvement in fit of the researcher's model compared with a statistical **baseline model**. The baseline model is typically the **independence (null) model**, which assumes zero population covariances among the observed variables. When means are not analyzed, the only parameters of the independence model are the population variances. But the assumption of zero covariances is implausible in most studies. For this reason, Miles and Shevlin (2007) noted that incremental fit indexes based on the independence model "effectively say, 'How well is my model doing, compared with the worst model that there is?' " (p. 870). Understand that incremental fit indexes do *not* measure model adequacy in any absolute sense. They indicate only the relative improvement in fit over a statistical model based on a "strawman" argument (zero covariances) that is likely to be false.

3. A **parsimony-adjusted index** includes in its formula a built-in correction ("penalty") for model complexity. This correction is related to the value of df_M. (Recall that more parsimonious models have higher degrees of freedom.) Given two models with similar fit to the same data, a parsimony-adjusted index would generally favor the simpler model. That simpler model should have adequate fit to the data. Otherwise, it makes little sense to prefer one of two failing models on the basis of parsimony, and there is nothing wrong with claiming that both models are problematic.

4. There are also **predictive fit indexes** that estimate model fit in *hypothetical* replication samples of the same size and randomly drawn from the same population as the original sample. Thus, these indexes may be seen as population based rather than sample based. There is a specific context for predictive fit indexes, but most applications of SEM do not fall under it. Predictive fit indexes may also correct for model parsimony.

There is a close connection between model test statistics and many approximate fit indexes: formulas of the latter include the value of the former. There is a similar relation in more standard analyses between test statistics and measures of effect size: many effect sizes can be expressed as functions of test statistics, and vice versa (Kline, 2004). This relation between model test statistics and approximate fit indexes means that both are based on the same distributional assumptions. If these assumptions are not tenable, however, then values of both the approximate fit index and the corresponding test statistic (and its *p* value) may be inaccurate.

A natural question about continuous approximate fit indexes concerns the range of values that indicates "acceptable" model fit. Unfortunately, there is no simple answer to this question because there is no direct correspondence between continuous values of approximate fit indexes and the seriousness or type of specification error. Most interpretive guidelines in use until recently originate from computer simulation studies conducted in the 1980s and 1990s about the behavior of approximate fit indexes under varying data and model conditions. Gerbing and Anderson (1993) review many of these early studies, and more recent examples include Hu and Bentler (1998) and Marsh, Balla, and Hau (1996). Based on these findings as well as their own simulation studies, Hu and Bentler (1999) proposed a set of thresholds for approximate fit indexes that are the most widely known and cited in the SEM literature. Whether these thresholds are really accurate—that is, should they be trusted?—is a critical question (e.g., Vernon & Eysenck, 2007).

Hu and Bentler (1999) *never* intended their rules of thumb for approximate fit indexes to be treated as anything other than just that. One reason is that it is impossible in Monte Carlo studies to evaluate the whole range of models and data analyzed in real studies. Another is that seriously misspecified models are not typically studied in computer simulations. Instead, authors of such studies tend to impose relatively minor specification errors on known models, such as a three-factor measurement model but where the factor variances are misspecified in generated samples. The case of a more serious specification error, such as when sample models have the wrong number of factors or incorrect factor–indicator correspondence, may not even be studied at all.

Despite Hu and Bentler's (1999) cautions that their suggested thresholds for approximate fit indexes should not be overgeneralized, too many researchers treat these cutoffs as "golden rules." For example, it has become common practice for researchers to claim that a model has acceptable fit based on the observation that the values of a select few approximate fit indexes fall on the "good news" (for the model) sides of their respective thresholds. This practice is especially problematic when researchers ignore significant model test statistics and decide to retain the model based on values of approximate fit indexes without looking at other statistical information about model fit. There are two problems with this practice (Barrett, 2007; Hayduk et al., 2007):

1.   Approximate fit indexes ignore (disregard) beyond-chance deviations between the model and the data. There is some arbitrariness concerning levels of statistical significance for model test statistics (e.g., α = .05 is not a golden rule), but outcomes of test statistics at least provide a relatively clear traditional demarcation between whether discrepancies with the covariance data are likely mere sampling fluctuations or whether the outcome should be taken as greater-than-chance evidence against the model. Relying on thresholds for approximate fit indexes has the consequence that they are treated as though they generate two qualitative outcomes, "acceptable" versus "unacceptable" fit (Markland, 2007). This practice is flawed because approximate fit indexes do not measure sampling error, and values of these indexes for the same model vary across samples.

2.   Relying on thresholds for approximate fit indexes to determine model adequacy would *not* be justified even if such thresholds were universal truths. The reason was stated earlier: models with apparently "acceptable" overall fit can still poorly explain the observed associations between certain pairs of variables. *This means that diagnostic assessment about fit is needed regardless of the values of approximate fit indexes and especially when test statistics indicate problems with the model.*

The results of some recent computer simulation studies cast even more doubt on the generality of thresholds for approximate fit indexes. For example, Marsh, Hau, and Wen (2004) found that the accuracy of Hu and Bentler's (1999) thresholds depends on the particular misspecified model studied in computer simulations. This was especially true for models with approximate fit index values very close to their suggested thresholds. Yuan (2005) studied properties of approximate fit indexes based on model test statistics when distributional assumptions were violated. Under these less than ideal but probably more realistic conditions, (1) expected values of approximate fit indexes had little relation to their threshold values; and (2) shapes of their distributions varied as functions of sample size, model size, and the degree of misspecification. Yuan (2005) also noted that we generally do not know the exact distributions of approximate fit indexes even for correctly specified models. Beaducel and Wittman (2005) studied the behavior of approximate fit indexes for a relatively small range of measurement models of a kind fairly typical in personality research. They found that the accuracy of thresholds was affected by the relative sizes of factor loadings and whether unidimensional or multidimensional measurement was specified. There were also relatively low intercorrelations among different approximate fit indexes calculated for the same model and data. That is, different indexes did not generally agree with each other.

Given results of the kind just summarized, Barrett (2007) suggested an outright ban on approximate fit indexes. Hayduk et al. (2007) argue that thresholds for such indexes are so untrustworthy and of such dubious utility that it is only model test statistics (and their degrees of freedom and p values) that should be reported and interpreted. These arguments have theoretical and empirical bases and cannot be blithely dismissed. Others argue that there is a place for such indexes in model testing (e.g., Mulaik, 2007, 2009), but there is general agreement that treating thresholds for approximate fit indexes as "golden rules" is no longer up to standard. Barrett (2007) also suggested that researchers pay more attention to the accuracy of predictions generated by the model as a crucial way of assessing its scientific value. True prediction studies in SEM are rare. A kind of proxy prediction analysis concerns the reporting of R^2-type statistics or effect decompositions for outcome variables. For pure measurement models of the kind estimated and analyzed in CFA, however, there are no external criteria predicted by the model, so reporting R^2s for the indicators is about the only way to address this issue.

My own view is that (1) model test statistics provide invaluable information about model–data discrepancies taking sampling error into account especially when the sample size is not large and (2) there are no grounds for ignoring evidence against the model as indicated by a statistically significant result. This is because model test statistics can provide the first detectable sign of *possible* severe specification (Hayduk et al., 2007), and approximate fit indexes can do no such thing. If the model fails a statistical test, then this result should be taken seriously. This means that the researcher should report more specific diagnostic information about the apparent sources of model–data discrepancy. In a very large sample, the magnitudes of these discrepancies could be slight but nevertheless large enough to trigger a statistically significant test result. If so, then (1) failing the statistical test may have been due more to the very large sample size than to absolute magnitudes of model–data discrepancies, and (2) it may be possible to retain the model despite a significant model test statistic. Otherwise, the model should be respecified in a theoretically meaningful way. If no such respecifications exist, then no model should be retained.

I also argue that diagnostic information about fit is needed even if a model "passes" a significance test, especially when the sample size is not very large. In this case, the power of the test may be so low that it is unlikely to detect appreciable differences between observed and predicted covariances. Finally, there is a certain set of approximate fit indexes the values of which I believe can be helpful for reviewers or other readers of an SEM study to know, *if such readers can refrain from blindly applying threshold values to these indexes*. As the author of the written summary of the analysis, you can help your readers do so by not making the same mistake yourself. At the end of the analysis, readers (and the primary researcher, too) should look to see whether model–data discrepancies are slight based on diagnostic information and be convinced that model specification is theoretically sound before tentatively concluding that model fit is adequate. But never forget that "adequate fit" (e.g., small residuals) does *not* mean "correctly specified" about models analyzed in SEM!

MODEL CHI-SQUARE

The most basic model test statistic is the product $(N - 1) F_{ML}$ where F_{ML} is the value of the statistical criterion (fit function) minimized in ML estimation and $(N - 1)$ is one less than the sample size. In large samples and assuming multivariate normality, the product $(N - 1) F_{ML}$ follows a central chi-square distribution with degrees of freedom equal to that of the researcher's model, or df_M. This statistic is referred to as the **model chi-square**, χ_M^2; it is also known as the **likelihood ratio chi-square** or **generalized likelihood ratio**. The value of χ_M^2 for a just-identified model generally equals zero, but technically it is not defined for models with no degrees of freedom. If $\chi_M^2 = 0$, the model perfectly fits the data (each observed covariance equals its counterpart implied by the model). If the fit of an overidentified model that is not correctly specified becomes increasingly worse, then the value of χ_M^2 increases, so χ_M^2 is scaled as a badness-of-fit statistic.

We continue to assume large samples and multivariate normality. For an overidentified model, χ_M^2 tests the **exact-fit hypothesis**, or the prediction that there are no discrepancies between the population covariances and those predicted by the model. For a correct model analyzed over random samples, (1) the expected value of χ_M^2 equals that of its degrees of freedom, df_M; and (2) χ_M^2 would *not* be statistically significant in 19 out 20 samples regardless of the number of cases (N) when $\alpha = .05$. That is, χ_M^2 estimates sampling error only for correct models. For such models, χ_M^2 should be as likely to have a *p* value in the .95 region as in the .05 region. This is also true for the .75 region and the .25 region, and hence striving for properly specified models is striving for models whose *p* values should ideally be considerably > .05 (Hayduk, 1996). Suppose that $\chi_M^2 = 6.50$ for a model where $df_M = 5$. The precise level of statistical significance associated with this statistic is $p = .261$.[1] Given this result, the researcher would *not* reject the exact-fit hypothesis at the .05 level.

---

[1]This result was obtained from a central chi-square probability calculator available at *http://statpages.org/pdfs.html*

Another way of looking at χ_M^2 is that it tests the difference in fit between a given overidentified model and whatever unspecified model would imply a covariance matrix that perfectly corresponds to the data covariance matrix. Suppose for an overidentified model that $\chi_M^2 > 0$ and $df_M = 5$. Adding five more free parameters to this model would make it just-identified—thereby making its covariance implications perfectly match the data covariance matrix even if that model were not correctly specified—and reduce both χ_M^2 and df_M to zero.

If χ_M^2 is not statistically significant, then the only thing that can be concluded is that the model is *consistent with* the covariance data, but whether that model is actually *correct* is unknown. The model could be seriously misspecified but one of potentially many other equivalent or nearly equivalent models that imply covariance matrices identical or similar to the observed data (Hayduk et al., 2007). This is why Markland (2007) cautioned that "even a model with a non-significant chi square test needs to have a serious health warning attached to it" (p. 853). More information about fit is needed, so passing the chi-square test is hardly the final word in model testing. This is because χ_M^2 tends to miss a single large covariance residual or a pattern of smaller but systematic residuals that indicate a problem with the model. It is also blind to whether the signs and magnitudes of the parameter estimates make sense (but you are not).

The observed value of χ_M^2 for *some* misspecified models—those that do not imply covariance matrices that closely match the one in the sample—will exceed the expected value by so much that the exact-fit hypothesis is rejected. Suppose that $\chi_M^2 = 15.30$ for a model where $df_M = 5$. For this result, $p = .009$, so the exact-fit hypothesis is rejected at the .01 level (and at $\alpha = .05$, too). Thus, the discrepancy between the observed and model-implied covariances is statistically significant, so the model fails the chi-square test. The next step is to try to diagnose the reason(s) for the failed test. How to do so is considered later.

The model chi-square test has some limitations. Some authors argue that the exact-fit hypothesis may be implausible in many applications of SEM (Miles & Shevlin, 2007; Steiger, 2007). This is because *perfection* is not the usual standard for testing statistical models. Instead, we generally expect that a model should closely approximate some phenomenon, but not perfectly reproduce it. But the model chi-square test *does* allow for imperfection up to a level within the bounds of sampling error that correspond to the level of α selected by the researcher. It is only when model–data discrepancies exceed those expected by chance (i.e., $\chi_M^2 > df_M$) that χ_M^2 begins to "penalize" the model by approaching statistical significance. The rationale for the exact-fit test assumes that there is a correct model in the population. As mentioned earlier, it is not clear whether this assumption is always justifiable in statistical modeling. Probabilities (p values) associated with χ_M^2 are estimated by the computer in sampling distributions that assume random sampling and specific distributional forms. The fact that most samples in SEM are not random was mentioned earlier, and untenable distributional assumptions mean that p values could be wrong. It is easy to reduce the value of χ_M^2 simply by adding free parameters, which makes models more complex. If parameters are added without justification, however, the resulting **overparameterized model** may have little scientific value. This is actually a misuse of the chi-square test, not an inherent flaw of it. Again, do not forget that "closer to fit" in SEM does *not* mean "closer to truth."

The observed value of χ^2_M can be affected by:

1. *Multivariate non-normality.* Depending on the particular pattern and severity of non-normality, the value of χ^2_M can be either increased so that model fit appears either *worse* than it really is or decreased so that model fit looks *better* than it really is (Hayduk et al., 2007; Yuan, Bentler, & Zhang, 2005). This is why it is so important to screen your data for severe non-normality when using a normal theory method (Chapter 3). You can also report a corrected chi-square, such as the Satorra–Bentler statistic that controls for non-normality, instead of χ^2_M (Chapter 7).

2. *Correlation size.* Bigger correlations among observed variables generally lead to higher values of χ^2_M for incorrect models. This happens because larger correlations allow greater discrepancies between observed and predicted correlations (and covariances, too).

3. *Unique variance.* Analyzing variables with high proportions of unique variance—which could be due to score unreliability—results in loss of statistical power. This property of χ^2_M could potentially "reward" the selection of measures with poor psychometrics because low power in accept–support tests favors the researcher's model. If there is low power to detect problems, but the model still fails the chi-square test, then those problems may be serious. Thus, the researcher should pay especially careful attention to χ^2_M in this case.

4. *Sample size.* For incorrect models that do not imply covariance matrices similar to the sample matrix, the value of χ^2_M tends to increase along with the sample size. In very large samples, such as N = 5,000, it can happen that the chi-square test is failed even though differences between observed and predicted covariances are slight. This result is less likely for sample sizes that are more typical in SEM, such as N = 200–300. In my experience, statistically significant values of χ^2_M for models tested in samples with only 200–300 cases often signal a problem serious enough to reject the model. In very large samples, though, it is possible that rather small model–data discrepancies can result in a statistically significant value of χ^2_M. But you won't know whether this is true without inspecting diagnostic information about model fit.

The results of some recent computer simulation studies (Cheung & Rensvold, 2002; Meade, Johnson, & Braddy, 2008) described in Chapter 9 suggest that the chi-square test is overly sensitive to sample size when testing whether the same factor structure holds across different groups, that is, whether a measurement model is invariant over samples. In contrast, the values of some approximate fit indexes were less affected by sample size in these studies. Mooijaart and Satorra (2009) remind us that the model chi-square test is generally insensitive to the presence of interaction (moderator) effects. This is because the theoretical distribution of χ^2_M may not be distorted even when there is severe interaction effect misspecification. Consequently, they cautioned against concluding that if a model with linear (main) effects only passes the chi-square test, then the underlying model must be truly linear. However, approximate fit indexes based on χ^2_M would be just as insensitive to interaction misspecification. The estimation of interaction effects in SEM is described in Chapter 12.

Due to the increasing power of χ^2_M to detect model–data discrepancies with increasing sample size, it was once common practice for researchers to (1) ignore a failed model chi-square test but then (2) refer to threshold values for approximate fit indexes in order to justify retaining the model. Many published models had statistically significant χ^2_M values (e.g., Markland, 2007), but authors tended to pay little attention to this fact. *This practice is lax and increasingly viewed as unacceptable.* One reason was mentioned: Thresholds for approximate fit indexes are not golden rules. Another reason is an emerging consensus that the chi-square test must be taken more seriously. *This means that a failed test should be treated as an indication of a possible problem, one that must be explicitly diagnosed in order to explain just why the model failed.*

One way to perform this diagnosis is to report and describe the correlation residuals, paying special attention to those with absolute values > .10 (e.g., Table 7.5). Correlation residuals are easier to interpret than covariance residuals, but, unfortunately, there is no dependable or trustworthy connection between the size of the residuals and the type or degree of model misspecification. For example, the degree of misspecification indicated by low-correlation residuals may indeed be slight but yet may be severe. One reason is that the values of residuals and other diagnostic statistics described later are themselves affected by misspecification. An analogy in medicine would be a diagnostic test for some illness that is less accurate in patients who actually have that illness. This problem in SEM is a consequence of error propagation when some parts of the model are incorrectly specified. But we do not know in advance which parts of the model are incorrect, so it can be difficult to understand exactly what the residuals are telling us.

Inspecting the *pattern* of residuals can sometimes be helpful. For example, if the residuals between variables in a structural model connected by indirect effects only are positive, this means that the model *underpredicts* their observed associations. In this case, the hypothesis of pure mediation may be cast in doubt, and a possible respecification is to add direct effects between some of these variables. Another possibility consistent with the same pattern of positive residuals is to specify a disturbance correlation. But just which type of effect to add to the model (direct effect vs. disturbance correlation) and the directionalities of direct effects (e.g., $Y_1 \rightarrow Y_3$ vs. $Y_3 \rightarrow Y_1$) are not things that the residuals can tell you. Likewise, a pattern of negative residuals suggests that the model *overpredicts* the associations between variables. In this case, respecification may involve deleting unnecessary paths between the corresponding variables. Possible respecifications in measurement models based on patterns of residuals are considered in the next chapter. Just as there is no magic in fit statistics, there is also none in diagnostic statistics, at least none that would relieve researchers from the burden of having to think long and hard about respecification.

Sometimes it happens that no theoretically justifiable respecification results in a model that generates residuals that are not large and do not indicate an obvious fit problem. If so, no model should be retained. I want to emphasize again that this is an interesting result, one with just as much scientific merit—if not even more—as retaining a structural equation model. This is because disconfirmatory evidence is necessary for science. Often the inability to support a theory points out ways that the theory may be incorrect or problems with its operationalization. This kind of result is invaluable and just as publication worthy—thesis worthy, too—as the failure to reject (retain) a model. Indeed, the latter outcome can be rather boring compared with finding a puzzle with no clear solution (at least at present). It is unexpected results that tend to motivate the biggest changes in scientific thinking, not the routine or expected. This is why there is no "shame" whatsoever in not retaining a model at the end of an SEM analysis.

Some special comment is needed for LISREL. Under ML and generalized least squares (GLS) estimation (Chapter 7), when the observed (uncorrected) covariance matrix is analyzed, LISREL prints two model chi-squares. One is the product $(N - 1) F_{ML}$ (i.e., χ_M^2), which is labeled *minimum fit function chi-square* in LISREL output and C1 in program documentation. The other chi-square is labeled *normal theory weighted least squares* (WLS) *chi-square* in output and C2 in documentation. The latter equals the product $(N - 1)$ and the value of the fit function from WLS estimation assuming multivariate normality.[2] If the normality assumption is tenable, then the values of these two test statistics are usually similar. I recommend reporting C1 instead of C2 in order to more closely match results generated by other SEM computer tools for the same model and data in "standard" analyses (i.e., ML estimation, continuous and normal endogenous variables). By default, LISREL calculates the values of approximate fit indexes based on the model chi-square using C2 (i.e., the WLS chi-square), not C1 (i.e., χ_M^2). In syntax, specification of the option "FT" in the "LISREL Output" command results in the calculation of two sets of approximate fit indexes, one based on C2 and another based on C1.

Under ML and GLS estimation and when the covariance matrix is asymptotic (i.e., it is estimated in PRELIS), the LISREL program prints two additional chi-squares. The third is labeled *Satorra–Bentler scaled chi-square* in output and C3 in documentation. The fourth statistic is labeled *chi-square corrected for non-normality* in output and C4 in documentation. The latter is $(N - 1)$ times the WLS fit function estimated under non-normality. When analyzing continuous but non-normal endogenous variables, it would make sense to report C3 (i.e., the Satorra–Bentler statistic). However, the test statistic C4 may be preferred when analyzing models with ordinal endogenous variables with a robust WLS method (Chapter 7). In such analyses, specification of the "FT" option in

---

[2]A related test statistic printed by EQS is referred to in program output as the *normal theory reweighted least squares* (RLS) *chi-square*.

the "LISREL Output" command instructs the program to print values of approximate fit indexes based on C1–C4. See Jöreskog (2004) and Schmukle and Hardt (2005) for more information about test statistics and approximate fit indexes printed by LISREL under different combinations of estimation methods and data matrices analyzed.

A brief mention of a statistic known as the **normed chi-square** (NC) is needed mainly to discourage you from ever using it. In an attempt to reduce the sensitivity of the model chi-square to sample size, some researchers in the past divided this statistic by its expected value, or NC = χ^2_M / df_M, which generally reduced the value of this ratio compared with χ^2_M. There are three problems with NC: (1) χ^2_M is sensitive to sample size only for incorrect models; (2) df_M has nothing to do with sample size; and (3) there were really never any clear-cut guidelines about maximum values of the NC that are "acceptable" (e.g., NC < 2.0?—3.0?). Because there is little statistical or logical foundation for NC, it should have no role in model fit assessment.

APPROXIMATE FIT INDEXES

Reviewed in this section are a total of four approximate fit indexes that are among the most widely reported in the SEM literature. Each describes model fit from a different perspective. These indexes are as follows.

1. Steiger–Lind root mean square error of approximation (RMSEA; Steiger, 1990), a parsimony-corrected index, with its 90% confidence interval.
2. Jöreskog–Sörbom Goodness of Fit Index (GFI; Jöreskog & Sörbom, 1982), an absolute fit index originally associated with LISREL but now also printed by other programs.
3. Bentler Comparative Fit Index (CFI; Bentler, 1990), an incremental fit index originally associated with EQS but now also printed by other programs.
4. Standardized Root Mean Square Residual (SRMR), a statistic related to the correlation residuals.

All these indexes are generally available under default ML estimation. When a different method is used, some of these indexes may not be printed by the computer. Check the documentation of your SEM computer tool for more information. There are many other approximate fit indexes in SEM, so many that they could not all be described here in any real detail. Some older indexes have problems, so it would do little good to describe them because I could not recommend their use. See Kaplan (2009, chap. 6) or Mulaik (2009, chap. 15) for more information about other fit statistics in SEM.

Before characteristics of the four indexes just listed are reviewed, we need to address some critical limitations of basically all approximate fit indexes. These limitations explain why I think it is a bad idea to rely solely on thresholds for approximate fit indexes when deciding whether or not to respecify a structural equation model:

1. Approximate fit indexes do *not* demarcate the limit between where expected levels of chance deviations between the predicted and sample covariance matrices begin and where evidence against the model begins. This is what the model chi-square test does.

2. Never ignore evidence of a potentially serious specification error indicated by a failed chi-square test by emphasizing values of approximate fit indexes that look "favorable" for your model. That is, do not hide behind approximate fit indexes when there is other evidence of a potential problem.

3. Although approximate fit indexes are continuous measures, they are not as precise as they seem for a few reasons: (a) Their values do not reliably or directly indicate the type or degree of model misspecification. For example, there are few (if any) implications for respecification if the value of a goodness-of-fit index with a range of 0–1.0 equals, say, .97 versus .91. (b) The distributions of only some approximate fit indexes are known under ideal conditions. Whether such conditions hold in real studies is doubtful. (c) Suggested thresholds for approximate fit indexes originate from computer simulation studies of a small range of models that were not grossly misspecified. Evidence that these thresholds may not generalize to actual studies was summarized earlier.

4. A healthy perspective on approximate fit indexes is to view them as providing *qualitative* or *descriptive* information about model fit. The value of this information increases when you report values of indexes that as a set assess model fit from different perspectives, such as the four indexes described next. The drawback is the potential for obfuscation, or the concealment of evidence about poor fit. This is less likely to happen if you follow a comprehensive approach to assessing model fit that includes taking the model chi-square test seriously and describing patterns of residuals.

Root Mean Square Error of Approximation

The Root Mean Square Error of Approximation (RMSEA) is scaled as a badness-of-fit index where a value of zero indicates the best fit. It is also a parsimony-adjusted index that does *not* approximate a central chi-square distribution. Instead, the RMSEA *theoretically* follows a noncentral chi-square distribution where the noncentrality parameter allows for discrepancies between model-implied and sample covariances up to the level of the expected value of χ^2_M, or df_M. Specifically, if $\chi^2_M \leq df_M$, then RMSEA = 0, but note that this result does not necessarily mean perfect fit (i.e., RMSEA = 0 does not say that $\chi^2_M = 0$). For models where $\chi^2_M > df_M$, the value of RMSEA is increasingly positive. The formula is

$$\text{RMSEA} = \sqrt{\frac{\chi^2_M - df_M}{df_M(N-1)}} \qquad (8.1)$$

The model degrees of freedom and one less than the sample size are represented in the denominator of Equation 8.1. This means that the value of the RMSEA decreases as there are more degrees of freedom (greater parsimony) or a larger sample size, keeping all else constant. However, the RMSEA does not necessarily favor models with more degrees of freedom. This is because the effect of the correction for parsimony diminishes as the sample size becomes increasingly large (Mulaik, 2009). See Mulaik (pp. 342–345) for more information about other parsimony corrections in SEM.

The population parameter estimated by the RMSEA is often designated as ε (epsilon). In computer output, the lower and upper bounds of the 90% confidence interval for ε are often printed along with the sample value of the RMSEA, the point estimate of ε. As expected, the width of this confidence interval is generally larger in smaller samples, which indicates less precision. The bounds of the confidence interval for ε may not be symmetrical around the sample value of the RMSEA, and, ideally, the lower bound equals zero. Both the lower and upper bounds are estimated assuming noncentral chi-square distributions. If these distributional assumptions do not hold, then the bounds of the confidence interval for ε may be wrong.

Some computer programs, such as LISREL and Mplus, calculate p values for the test of the one-sided hypothesis H_0: $\varepsilon_0 \leq .05$, or the **close-fit hypothesis**. This test is an accept–support test where failure to reject this null hypothesis favors the researcher's model. The value .05 in the close-fit hypothesis originates from Browne and Cudeck (1993), who suggested that RMSEA $\leq .05$ *may* indicate "good fit." *But this threshold is a rule of thumb that may not generalize across all studies, especially when distributional assumptions are in doubt.* When the lower limit of the confidence interval for ε is zero, the model chi-square test will not reject the null hypothesis that $\varepsilon_0 = 0$ at $\alpha = .05$. Otherwise, a model could *fail* the more stringent model chi-square test but *pass* the less demanding close-fit test. Hayduk, Pazderka-Robinson, Cummings, Levers, and Beres (2005) describe such models as **close-yet-failing models**. Such models should be treated as any other that fails the chi-square test. That is, passing the close-fit test does not justify ignoring a failed exact-fit test.

If the upper bound of the confidence interval for ε exceeds a value that may indicate "poor fit," then the model warrants less confidence. For example, the test of the **poor-fit hypothesis** H_0: $\varepsilon_0 \geq .10$ is a reject–support test of whether the fit of the researcher's model is just as bad or even worse than that of a model with "poor fit." The threshold of .10 in the poor-fit hypothesis is also from Browne and Cudeck (1993), who suggested that RMSEA $\geq .10$ *may* indicate a serious problem. The test of the poor-fit hypothesis can serve as a kind of reality check against the test of the close-fit hypothesis. (The tougher exact-fit test serves this purpose, too.) Suppose that RMSEA = .045 with the 90% confidence interval .009–.155. Because the lower bound of this interval (.009) is less than .05, the close-fit hypothesis is not rejected. The upper bound of the same confidence interval (.155) exceeds .10, however, so we cannot reject the poor-fit hypothesis. These two outcomes are not contradictory. Instead, we would conclude that the point-estimate RMSEA = .045 is subject to a fair amount of sampling error because it is just as consistent with the close-fit hypothesis as it is with the poor-fit hypothesis. This type of "mixed" outcome is more likely to happen in smaller samples. A larger sample may be required in order to obtain more precise results.

Some limitations of the RMSEA are as follows:

1. Interpretation of the RMSEA and the lower and upper bounds of its confidence interval depends on the assumption that this statistic follows noncentral chi-square distributions. There is evidence that casts doubt on this assumption. For example, Olsson, Foss, and Breivik (2004) found in computer simulation studies that empirical distributions from smaller models with relatively few variables and relatively small non-centrality parameters (less specification error) generally followed noncentral chi-square distributions. Otherwise, the empirical distributions did *not* typically follow noncentral chi-square distributions, including models with more specification error. These results and others (e.g., Yuan, 2005) question the generality of the thresholds for the RMSEA mentioned earlier.

2. Nevitt and Hancock (2000) evaluated in Monte Carlo studies the performance of robust forms of the RMSEA corrected for non-normality, one of which is based on the Satorra–Bentler corrected chi-square. Under conditions of data non-normality, this robust RMSEA statistic generally outperformed the uncorrected version (Equation 8.1).

3. Breivik and Olsson (2001) found in Monte Carlo studies that the RMSEA tends to impose a harsher penalty for complexity on smaller models with relatively few variables or factors. This is because smaller models may have relatively few degrees of freedom, but larger models may have more "room" for higher df_M values. Consequently, the RMSEA may favor larger models. In contrast, Breivik and Olsson (2001) found that the Goodness-of-Fit Index (GFI), was relatively insensitive to model size.

Goodness-of-Fit Index and Comparative Fit Index

The range of values for this pair of approximate fit indexes is generally 0–1.0 where 1.0 indicates the best fit. The Jöreskog–Sörbom GFI is an absolute fit index that estimates the proportion of covariances in the sample data matrix explained by the model. That is, the GFI estimates how much better the researcher's model fits compared with no model at all (Jöreskog, 2004). A general formula is

$$\text{GFI} = 1 - \frac{C_{\text{res}}}{C_{\text{tot}}} \qquad (8.2)$$

where C_{res} and C_{tot} estimate, respectively, the residual and total variability in the sample covariance matrix. The numerator in the right side of Equation 8.2 is related to the sum of the squared covariance residuals, and the denominator is related to the total sum of squares in the data matrix. Specific calculational formulas depend on the estimation method (Jöreskog, 2004).

A limitation of the GFI is that its expected values vary with sample size. For example, in computer simulation studies of CFA models by Marsh, Balla, and McDonald (1988), the mean values of the GFI tend to increase along with the number of cases. As mentioned, the GFI may be less affected by model size than the RMSEA. Values of the GFI sometimes fall outside of the range 0–1.0. Values > 1.0 can be found with just-identified models or with overidentified models where χ^2_M is close to zero, and values < 0 are most likely in small samples or when fit is very poor.

The Bentler Comparative Fit Index (CFI) is an incremental fit index that measures the relative improvement in the fit of the researcher's model over that of a baseline model, typically the independence model. For models where $\chi^2_M \leq df_M$, CFI = 1.0; otherwise, the formula is

$$\text{CFI} = 1 - \frac{\chi^2_M - df_M}{\chi^2_B - df_B} \qquad (8.3)$$

where the numerator and the denominator of the expression in the right side of Equation 8.3 estimate the chi-square noncentrality parameter for, respectively, the researcher's model and the baseline model. Note that CFI = 1.0 means only that $\chi^2_M < df_M$, not that the model has perfect fit ($\chi^2_M = 0$). The CFI is a rescaled version of the Relative Noncentrality Index (McDonald & Marsh, 1990), the values of which can fall outside the range 0–1.0. This is not true of the CFI.

All incremental fit indexes have been criticized when the baseline model is the independence model, which is almost always true. This is because the assumption of zero covariances among the observed variables is improbable in most studies. Therefore, finding that the researcher's model has better relative fit than the corresponding independence model may not be very impressive. Although it is possible to specify a different, more plausible baseline model—such as one that allows the exogenous variables only to covary—and compute by hand the value of an incremental fit index with its equation, this is rarely done in practice. Widaman and Thompson (2003) describe how to specify more plausible baseline models. Check the documentation of your SEM computer program to find out the type of baseline model it assumes when calculating the CFI.

The CFI depends on the same distributional assumptions as the RMSEA, so values of the CFI may not be accurate when these assumptions are not tenable. Hu and Bentler (1999) suggested using the CFI together with an index based on the correlations residuals described next, the SRMR. Their rationale was that the CFA seemed to be most sensitive to misspecified factor loadings, whereas the SRMR seemed most sensitive to misspecified factor covariances in CFA when testing measurement models. Their combination threshold for concluding "acceptable fit" based on these indexes was CFI ≥ .95 and SRMR ≤ .08. This combination rule was not supported in Monte Carlo studies by Fan and Sivo (2005), who suggested that the original Hu and Bentler (1999) findings about the CFI and SRMR were artifacts. Results of other computer studies also do not support the respective thresholds just listed for this pair of indexes (e.g., Yuan, 2005).

Standardized Root Mean Square Residual

The indexes described next are based on covariance residuals, differences between observed and predicted covariances. Ideally, these residuals should all be about zero for acceptable model fit. A statistic called the Root Mean Residual Square (RMR) was originally associated with LISREL but is now calculated by other SEM computer tools, too. It is a measure of the mean absolute covariance residual. Perfect model fit is indicated by RMR = 0, and increasingly higher values indicate worse fit. One problem with the RMR is that because it is computed with unstandardized variables, its range depends on the scales of the observed variables. If these scales are all different, it can be difficult to interpret a given value of the RMR.

The SRMR is based on transforming both the sample covariance matrix and the predicted covariance matrix into correlation matrices. The SRMR is thus a measure of the mean absolute correlation residual, the overall difference between the observed and predicted correlations. The Hu and Bentler (1999) threshold of SRMR ≤ .08 for acceptable fit was not a very demanding standard. This is because if the average absolute correlation residual is around .08, then many individual values could exceed this value, which would indicate poor explanatory power at the level of pairs of observed variables. It is better to actually inspect the matrix of correlation residuals and describe their pattern as part of a diagnostic assessment of fit than just to report the summary statistic SRMR.

VISUAL SUMMARIES OF FIT

It can be informative to view visual summaries of distributions of the residuals. For example, frequency distributions of the correlation residuals or covariance residuals should generally be normal in shape. A quantile-plot (Q-plot) of the standardized residuals (z statistics) ordered by their size and against their expected position in a normal curve should follow a diagonal line. Obvious departures from these patterns may indicate misspecification or violation of the multivariate normality assumption. An example is presented later in this chapter.

RECOMMENDED APPROACH TO MODEL FIT EVALUATION

The method outlined next calls on researchers to report more specific information about model fit than has been true of recent practice. The steps are as follows:

1. Always report χ^2_M—or the appropriate chi-square statistic if the estimation method is not ML—and its degrees of freedom and p value. If the model fails the exact-fit test, then explicitly note this fact and acknowledge the need to diagnose both the magnitude and possible sources of misfit. The rationale is to detect statistically significant but slight model–data discrepancies that explain the failure. This is most likely to happen in a very large sample. But even if the model passes the exact-fit test, you still need to diagnose both the magnitude and possible sources of misfit. The rationale is to detect model–data discrepancies that are not statistically significant but still great enough to cast doubt on the model. This is most likely in a small sample.

2. Report the matrix of correlation residuals, or at least describe the pattern of residuals for a large model. This includes the locations of the larger residuals and their signs. Look for patterns that may be of diagnostic value in understanding how the model may be misspecified.

3. If you report values of approximate fit indexes, then include those for the set described earlier. If possible, also report the *p* value for the close-fit hypothesis. Explicitly note whether the model fails the close-fit test. Do not try to justify retaining the model by relying solely on suggested thresholds for approximate fit indexes. This is especially so if the model failed the chi-square test and the pattern of residuals suggests a particular kind of specification error that is not trivial in magnitude.

4. If you respecify the initial model, then explain your rationale for doing so. You should also explain the role that diagnostic statistics, such as residuals or other test statistics described later, played in this respecification. That is, point out the connection between the numerical results for your initial model, relevant theory, and modifications of your original model. If you retain a respecified model that still fails the model chi-square test, then you must demonstrate that discrepancies between model and data are truly slight. Otherwise, you have failed to show that there is no appreciable ill covariance-fit evidence that speaks against the model.

5. If no model is retained, then your skills as a scholar are needed to explain the implications for the theory tested in your analysis. At the end of the day, regardless of whether or not you retained a model, the real honor comes from following to the best of your ability the process of science to its logical end. The poet Ralph Waldo Emerson put it this way: The reward of a thing well done is to have done it.

DETAILED EXAMPLE

The data set for this example was introduced in Chapter 3. Briefly, Roth et al. (1989) administered measures of exercise, hardiness—or mental toughness, also a good trait for learning about SEM— fitness, stress, and illness to 373 university students. The correlations and rescaled standard deviations among these variables are presented in Table 3.4. Presented in Figure 8.1 is one of the recursive path models tested by Roth et al. This model represents the hypothesis that the effects of exercise and hardiness on illness are purely indirect and that each effect is transmitted through a single mediator, fitness for exercise and stress for hardiness. You should verify that the model degrees of freedom are $df_M = 5$.

The model in Figure 8.1 was fitted to the covariance matrix based on the rescaled data in Table 3.4 with the ML method of EQS 6.1. You can download the EQS syntax and output files from this book's website (see p. 3) plus all LISREL and Mplus computer files for this example. The analysis in EQS converged to an admissible solution. Reported in Table 8.1 are the estimates of model parameters except for the variances and covariance of the observed exogenous variables. The latter estimates are just the sample values (Table 3.4). Briefly, the parameter estimates in Table 8.1 appear logical. For example, the

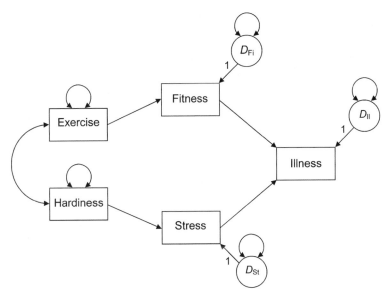

FIGURE 8.1. A recursive path model of illness factors.

direct effect of exercise on fitness is positive (the standardized path coefficient is .390), and higher levels of fitness predict lower illness levels (–.253). Proportions of explained variance (R^2_{smc}) range from .053 for the stress variable to .160 for the illness variable. You should verify this statement based on the information in Table 8.1.

Presented in column 2 of Table 8.2 are values of fit statistics for the Roth et al. path model in Figure 8.1. The model chi-square is just statistically significant at the .05 level— $\chi^2_M(5) = 11.078$, $p = .049$—so the exact-fit hypothesis is rejected. Thus, there is a need to diagnose the source(s) of this failed test. Values of approximate fit indexes for

TABLE 8.1. Maximum Likelihood Estimates for a Recursive Path Model of Illness Factors

Parameter	Unstandardized	SE	Standardized
Direct effects			
Exercise → Fitness	.216**	.026	.390
Hardiness → Stress	–.406**	.089	–.230
Fitness → Illness	–.424**	.080	–.253
Stress → Illness	.287**	.044	.311
Disturbance variances			
Fitness	1,148.260**	84.195	.848
Stress	4,251.532**	311.737	.947
Illness	3,212,567**	253.557	.840

Note. Standardized estimates for disturbance variances are proportions of unexplained variance.

**p < .01.

TABLE 8.2. Values of Fit Statistics for Two Recursive Path Models

Index	Model	
	Roth et al. model (Figure 8.1)	Sava model (Figure 7.1)
χ^2_M	11.078	3.895
df_M	5	7
p	.049	.791
RMSEA (90% CI)	.057 (.001–.103)	0 (0–.077)
$p_{\text{close-fit } H_0}$	.336	.896
GFI	.988	.989
CFI	.961	1.000
SRMR	.051	.034
χ^2_B	165.499	217.131
df_B	10	15

Note. CI, confidence interval. Probabilities for the close-fit hypothesis were computed by LISREL. All other results were computed by EQS.

the Roth et al. model present a mixed picture. The value of the RMSEA is .057, and the close-fit hypothesis is not rejected ($p = .336$) based on the value of the lower bound of the 90% confidence interval, or .001 (see Table 8.2). However, the upper bound of the RMSEA's 90% confidence interval, or .103, is large enough so that the poor-fit hypothesis cannot be rejected. The covariance matrix predicted by the model in Figure 8.1 explains about 99% of the total variability in the sample covariance matrix (GFI = .988), and the relative fit of the model is about a 96% improvement over that of the independence model fit (CFI = .961). Also reported in Table 8.2 are the values of the chi-square statistic and its degrees of freedom for the independence model.

Presented in Figure 8.2 is a Q-plot of the standardized residuals for the Roth et al. path model generated by LISREL. In a model with acceptable fit, the points in a Q-plot of the standardized residuals should fall along a diagonal line, but this is clearly not the case in the figure. Altogether, the results in Table 8.2 and the data graphic in Figure 8.2 indicate problems with the fit of the Roth et al. model. But fit statistics and visual summaries do not provide enough detail to further diagnose the apparent sources of these problems.

Presented in the top part of Table 8.3 are the correlation residuals for the Roth et al. path model. One of these residuals, −.133 for the fitness and stress variables, exceeds .10 in absolute value. Thus, the model does not explain very well the observed correlation between these two variables; specifically, the model underpredicts their association. Two other correlation residuals in Table 8.3 are close to .10 in absolute value, including .082 for the fitness and hardiness variables and −.092 for the fitness and illness variables. The standardized residuals are reported in the bottom part of Table 8.3. The test for the fitness–stress covariance residual is statistically significant ($z = 2.563$, $p < .05$). Other statistically significant z tests indicate that the model may not adequately explain

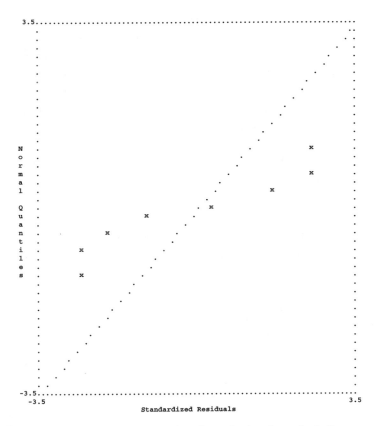

FIGURE 8.2. LISREL-generated quantile plot of standardized residuals for a recursive model of illness factors.

TABLE 8.3. Correlation Residuals and Standardized Residuals for a Recursive Path Model of Illness Factors

Variable	1	2	3	4	5
Correlation residuals					
1. Exercise	0				
2. Hardiness	0	0			
3. Fitness	0	.082	0		
4. Stress	−.057	0	−.133	0	
5. Illness	.015	−.092	−.041	.033	.020
Standardized residuals					
1. Exercise	0				
2. Hardiness	0	0			
3. Fitness	0	1.707	0		
4. Stress	−1.125	0	−2.563**	0	
5. Illness	.334	−1.944	−2.563**	2.563**	2.563**

Note. The correlation residuals were computed by EQS, and the standardized residuals were computed by LISREL.

**p < .01.

the observed variance of the illness variable or its covariances with the fitness and stress variables. These diagnostic results indicate that the fit of the path model in Figure 8.1 to the data in Table 3.4 is unacceptable.

Now look back and scan the fit statistics listed in column 3 of Table 8.2. These results are for the Sava (2002) path model of causes and effects of teacher–pupil interactions (Figure 7.1) calculated by LISREL. This model passes both the exact-fit test ($\chi^2_M(7) = 3.895$, $p = .791$) and the close-fit test ($p = .896$). Values of all approximate fit indexes seem reasonable, too. For example, RMSEA = 0 with .077 as the upper bound of its 90% confidence interval, so the poor-fit hypothesis is rejected. However, recall that this model has problems concerning its correlation residuals (Table 7.5). *Thus, I would conclude that the fit of this relatively small model is unacceptable despite what the global fit statistics say.* We will see later in this chapter that statistical power is very low for analysis of the Sava path model in a small sample ($N = 109$). For the accept–support test provided by χ^2_M, low power favors the researcher's model (i.e., we are unlikely to detect that this model is false when it is really is so).

TESTING HIERARCHICAL MODELS

This section concerns ways to test hypotheses about hierarchical models with the same data. Two models are **hierarchical** or **nested** if one is a proper subset of the other. For example, if a free parameter is dropped from model A (i.e., the parameter is replaced with a fixed value that is usually zero) to form model B, the two models are hierarchically related (model B is nested under model A).

Model Trimming and Building

Hierarchical models are compared within two main contexts: model trimming and building. In **model trimming**, the researcher typically begins the analysis with a just-identified model and simplifies it by eliminating free parameters (paths). This is done by specifying that at least one path previously estimated freely is now constrained to equal zero. The starting point for **model building** is an overidentified model to which paths are added. Typically, at least one previously fixed-to-zero path is specified as a free parameter. As a model is trimmed, its overall fit to the data usually becomes worse (χ^2_M increases). Likewise, model fit generally improves as paths are added (χ^2_M decreases). The goal of both trimming and building is to find the model with the properly specified covariance structure that fits the data *and* is theoretically justifiable (keep those eyes on the prize).

Models can be trimmed or built according to one of two different standards, theoretical or empirical. The first represents tests of specific, a priori hypotheses. Suppose that a path model contains a direct effect of X on Y_2 and an indirect effect through Y_1. If the researcher believed that the relation of X to Y_2 was entirely mediated by Y_1, then he or she could test this hypothesis by constraining the coefficient for the path $X \rightarrow Y_2$ to zero. If the fit of this constrained model is not appreciably worse than the one with

$X \rightarrow Y_2$ as a free parameter, the hypothesis about a mediated relation is supported. The main point, however, is that respecification of a model to test hierarchical versions of it is guided by the researcher's hypotheses.

This is not the case for empirically based respecification, in which free parameters are deleted or added according to statistical criteria. For example, if the sole basis for trimming paths is that their coefficients are not statistically significant, then model respecification is guided by purely empirical considerations. The distinction between theoretically or empirically based respecification has implications for interpreting the results of model trimming or building, which are considered after a model comparison test statistic is introduced.

Chi-Square Difference Test

The **chi-square difference statistic**, χ_D^2, can be used to test the statistical significance of the decrement in overall fit as free parameters are eliminated (trimming) or the improvement in fit as free parameters are added (building). As its name suggests, χ_D^2 is simply the difference between the χ_M^2 values of two hierarchical models estimated with the same data. Its degrees of freedom, df_D, equal the difference between the two respective values of df_M. The χ_D^2 statistic tests the **equal-fit hypothesis** for two hierarchical models. Specifically, smaller values of χ_D^2 lead to failure to reject the equal-fit hypothesis, but larger values lead to its rejection. In model trimming, rejection of the equal-fit hypothesis suggests that the model has been oversimplified. The same result in model building, however, supports retention of the path that was just added. Ideally, the more complex of the two models compared with χ_D^2 should fit the data reasonably well. Otherwise, it makes little sense to compare the relative fit of two nested models, neither of which adequately explains the data.

Suppose for an overidentified model that

$$\chi_M^2 (5) = 18.30, \quad p = .003$$

A direct effect is added to the model (df_M is reduced by 1), and the result is

$$\chi_M^2 (4) = 9.10, \quad p = .059$$

Given both results,

$$df_D = 5 - 4 = 1$$

$$\chi_D^2 (1) = 18.30 - 9.10 = 9.20, \quad p = .002$$

which says that the overall fit of the new model with an additional path is statistically better than that of the original model at the .01 level. In this example, the chi-square difference test is a univariate one because it concerned a single path ($df_D = 1$). When two hierarchical models that differ by two or more paths are compared ($df_D \geq 2$), the chi-square difference test is essentially a multivariate test of all added (or deleted) paths together. If $p < .05$ for χ^2_D in this case, at least one of the paths may be statistically significant at the .05 level if tested individually, but this is not guaranteed.

Note that differences between corrected (scaled) model chi-squares of two hierarchical models cannot generally be interpreted as a statistic that tests the equal-fit hypothesis. One corrected model chi-square is the Satorra–Bentler statistic, which is calculated taking account of the extent of non-normality in the data (Chapter 7). The difference between the Satorra–Bentler statistics for two hierarchical models fitted to the same data does not follow a chi-square distribution. However, the researcher can still compare the relative fits of the hierarchical models to the same data based on each model's set of fit statistics (χ^2_M, RMSEA, SRMR, etc.). If the simpler model has obviously worse correspondence with the data than the more complex model, the more complex model would be preferred. (This assumes that the fit of the more complex model is good.) Otherwise, the simpler model would be favored. Satorra and Bentler (2001) describe a way to calculate a scaled chi-square difference based on the difference between the Satorra–Bentler statistics from two hierarchical models, but this method is not yet widely implemented in SEM computer tools.

Empirical versus Theoretical Respecification

The interpretation of χ^2_D as a test statistic depends in part on whether the new model is derived empirically or theoretically. For example, if individual paths that are not statistically significant are dropped from the model, it is likely that χ^2_D will not be statistically significant. But if the deleted path is also predicted in advance to be zero, then χ^2_D is of utmost interest. If model specification is entirely driven by empirical criteria such as statistical significance, the researcher should worry—a lot, actually—about capitalization on chance. That is, a path may be statistically significant due only to chance variation, and its inclusion in the model would be akin to a Type I error. Likewise, a path that corresponds to a true nonzero causal effect may not be statistically significant in a particular sample, and its exclusion from the model would be essentially a Type II error. A sort of buffer against the problem of sample-specific results, though, is a greater role for theory in model respecification.

The issue of capitalization on chance is especially relevant when the researcher uses an "automatic modification" option available in some SEM computer tools such as LISREL. Such purely exploratory procedures drop or add paths according to empirical criteria such as statistical significance at the .05 level of a **modification index**, which is calculated for every path that is fixed to zero. A modification index is actually a univariate **Lagrange Multiplier** (LM),[3] which in this case is expressed as a

---

[3]A Lagrange Multiplier is named after the mathematician and astronomer Giuseppe Lodovico Lagrangia (1736–1813), who is known for his work in the areas of number theory and celestial mechanics. The LM statistic measures in an estimation algorithm the rate of change in the optimal value of a fit function as constraints on estimation change. A larger value means a greater potential improvement in the fit function.

chi-square statistic with a single degree of freedom, or $\chi^2(1)$. The value of an LM in the form of a modification index *estimates* the amount by which the overall model chi-square statistic, χ^2_M, would decrease if a particular fixed-to-zero parameter were freely estimated. That is, a modification index *estimates* $\chi^2_D(1)$ for adding a single path. Thus, the greater the value of a modification index, the better the predicted improvement in overall fit if that path were added to the model. Likewise, a multivariate LM estimates the effect of allowing a set of constrained-to-zero parameters to be freely estimated. Some SEM computer tools, such as Amos and EQS, allow the user to generate modification indexes for specific parameters, which lends a more a priori sense to this statistic.

Note two cautions about modification indexes. First, an SEM computer tool may print the value of a modification index for an "illegal" parameter, such as a covariance between an exogenous variable and an error term. If you actually tried to add that parameter in a subsequent run of the program, the analysis would fail. Second, modification indexes may be printed for a parameter that, if actually added to the model, would make the respecified model nonidentified. Both of these apparently anomalous results are due to the fact that modification indexes merely estimate $\chi^2_D(1)$ values. These estimates are *not* derived by the computer actually adding the parameter to the model and rerunning the analysis. Instead, the computer uses a shortcut method based on matrix algebra that "guesses" at the value of χ^2_D, given the covariance matrix and estimates for the more restricted (original) model.

The **Wald W statistic** (after the mathematician A. Wald; e.g., Wald, 1943) is a related index but one used for model trimming. A univariate Wald W statistic approximates the amount by which the overall χ^2_M statistic would *increase* if a particular freely estimated parameter were fixed to zero (trimmed). That is, a univariate Wald W statistic estimates $\chi^2_D(1)$ for dropping the same path. A value of a univariate Wald W that is not statistically significant at, say, the .05 level predicts a decrement in overall model fit that is not statistically significant at the same level. Model trimming that is entirely empirically based would thus delete paths with Wald W statistics that are not statistically significant. A multivariate Wald W statistic approximates the value of χ^2_D for trimming two or more paths from the model. Loehlin (2004) gives this good advice: *A researcher should not feel compelled to drop from the model every path that is not statistically significant*, especially when the sample size is not large. Removing such paths might also affect the solution in an important way. If there was a theoretical rationale for including the path in the first place, it would be better to leave that path in the model until replication indicates otherwise.

All of the test statistics just described are sensitive to sample size. Thus, even a trivial change in overall model fit due to adding or dropping a free parameter could be statistically significant in a very large sample. In addition to noting the statistical significance of a modification index, the researcher should also consider the absolute magnitude of the change in the coefficient for the parameter if it is allowed to be freely estimated, or the **expected parameter change**. If the expected change (i.e., from zero) is small, the statistical significance of the modification index may reflect more the sample size than it does the magnitude of the corresponding effect (see Kaplan, 2009, pp. 124–126).

Specification Searches

The results of two early computer simulation studies of **specification searches** by Mac-Callum (1986) and Silvia and MacCallum (1988) are eye opening. They took known structural equation models, imposed different types of specification errors on them, and evaluated the erroneous models using data generated from populations in which the known models were true. In MacCallum's study (1986), models were modified using empirically based methods (e.g., modification indexes). Most of the time the changes suggested by empirically based respecification were *incorrect*, which means that they typically did not recover the true model. The pattern was even more apparent for small samples (e.g., $N = 100$). It is not hard to figure out what went wrong: Purely empirical respecification chases sample-specific variation and accordingly modifies the model, but covariance patterns in one sample probably do not precisely mimic those in the population. Silvia and MacCallum (1988) followed a similar procedure except that the application of automatic modification was guided by theoretical knowledge, which improved the chances of discovering the true model. The implication of these studies is clear: learn from your data, but your data should not be your teacher (think for yourself).

A relatively new research area in SEM concerns the development of automated yet "intelligent" specification searches based on heuristics that attempt to optimize respecification compared with "dumb" specification searches (e.g., automatic model modification). These algorithms are generally based on principles of machine learning or data mining. For example, Marcoulides and Drezner (2001) describe an adaptive search algorithm based on principles of genetics and natural selection that evaluates models through successive "generations" from parent to child models. Marcoulides and Drezner (2003) describe a search algorithm that mimics the behavior of an ant colony as it collectively tries to achieve a certain goal, in this case model optimization. Intelligent specification searches are not yet widely implemented in SEM computer programs, but this may change. I am skeptical of any specification search method, "intelligent" or otherwise, that is not guided by reason. Otherwise, such methods may be little more than stepwise regression dressed in fancy clothes that give the illusion that the researcher does not have to think about respecification.

Example of Model Building

Recall that the Roth et al. recursive path model of illness factors (Figure 8.1) does not have acceptable fit to the data (Table 8.3). In EQS syntax for the analysis of this model, I requested values of modification indexes for all possible direct effects omitted from the original model, of which there are six altogether (see Figure 8.1). Listed in the middle column of Table 8.4 are the values of modification indexes for these six paths. Note in the

TABLE 8.4. Modification Indexes for a Recursive Path Model of Illness Factors

Path	Modification index	$\chi_D^2(1)$
Stress → Fitness	5.357*	5.410*
Fitness → Stress	5.096*	5.157*
Hardiness → Fitness	2.931	2.943
Hardiness → Illness	2.459	2.471
Exercise → Stress	1.273	1.275
Exercise → Illness	.577	.577

*$p < .05$.

table that (1) the modification indexes for two omitted paths, from fitness to stress and the reverse, are each statistically significant; and (2) the values of these indexes are similar, respectively, 5.357 and 5.096. This means that the addition of either path to the model would result in about the same estimated decrease in χ_M^2 for the respecified models.

Now, which respecified model just mentioned is correct (if either)? It does makes sense that level of physical fitness would affect the experience of stress: people who are in better shape may better withstand stress (Fitness → Stress). But is it not also plausible that stress could affect fitness level? For example, highly stressed people may not perform well on a fitness test (Stress → Fitness). Without theory as a guide, there is no way to select the most reasonable directionality for a direct effect between stress and fitness. Exercise 2 asks you to analyze a respecified model for this example with a direct effect between fitness and stress and then evaluate whether the respecified model has acceptable correspondence with the data. I am *not* suggesting, though, that this is the correct model.

None of the remaining modification indexes in Table 8.4 is statistically significant. They were all calculated for respecified models with no direct effect between fitness and stress, but the omission of a path between these variables could be a specification error. This is a limitation of any modification index: Specification errors elsewhere in the model could affect its accuracy. (The same is true of covariance and correlation residuals.) Listed in the third column of Table 8.4 are the $\chi_D^2(1)$ values obtained by actually adding to the model the direct effect in each row and then rerunning the analysis in EQS. These results indicate that modification indexes only estimate the corresponding $\chi_D^2(1)$ values, although that estimation for this example is close.

COMPARING NONHIERARCHICAL MODELS

Sometimes researchers compare alternative models based on the same variables measured in the same sample that are not hierarchically related. The values of χ_M^2 from two nonhierarchical models can be compared, but the difference between them cannot be interpreted as a test statistic. That is, the chi-square difference test does not apply. This is where the family of predictive fit indexes comes in handy. Recall that these statistics assess model fit in *hypothetical* replications of the same size randomly selected from the same population. Perhaps the best known predictive fit index under ML estimation is the Akaike Information Criterion (AIC). It is based on an information theory approach to data analysis that combines estimation and model selection under a single conceptual framework (Anderson, Burnham, & Thompson, 2000). It is also a parsimony-adjusted index because it may favor simpler models. Confusingly, two different formulas for the AIC are presented in the SEM literature. The first is

$$AIC_1 = \chi_M^2 + 2q \tag{8.4}$$

where q is the number of free model parameters. Equation 8.4 thus *increases* the chi-square for the researcher's model by a factor of twice the number of freely estimated parameters. The second formula is

$$AIC_2 = \chi_M^2 - 2df_M \tag{8.5}$$

which *decreases* the model chi-square by a factor of twice the model degrees of freedom. Although the two formulas are different, the key is that the relative change in the AIC is the same in both versions, and this change is a function of model complexity. Note that the relative correction for parsimony of the AIC becomes smaller and smaller as the sample size increases (Mulaik, 2009).

The AIC and related indexes are generally used in SEM to select among competing nonhierarchical models estimated with the same data. Specifically, the model with the smallest AIC value is chosen as the one most likely to replicate. This is the model with relatively better fit and fewer free parameters compared with competing models. In contrast, more complex models with comparable overall fit may be less likely to replicate due to greater capitalization on chance. An example follows. Presented in Figure 8.3 are two different path models of recovery after cardiac surgery evaluated by Romney, Jenkins, and Bynner (1992). The *psychosomatic model* of Figure 8.3(a) represents the hypothesis that patient morale dictates the effects of neurological dysfunction and diminished socioeconomic status (SES) on physical symptoms and social relationships. The *conventional medical model* of Figure 8.3(b) depicts different assumptions about causal relations among the same variables.

Reported in Table 8.5 are the correlations among the observed variables reported by Romney et al. for a sample of 469 patients. Unfortunately, Romney et al. did not report means or standard deviations, and the analysis of a correlation matrix with default ML estimation is not recommended. To deal with this problem, I used the SEPATH module of STATISTICA 9 Advanced to fit each model of Figure 8.3 to the correlation matrix in Table 8.5 using the method of constrained estimation (Chapter 7). Both analyses converged to admissible solutions.

Values of selected fit indexes for the two alternative Romney et al. path models are reported in Table 8.6. It is no surprise that the overall fit of the more complex *conven-*

(a) Psychosomatic Model

(b) Conventional Medical Model

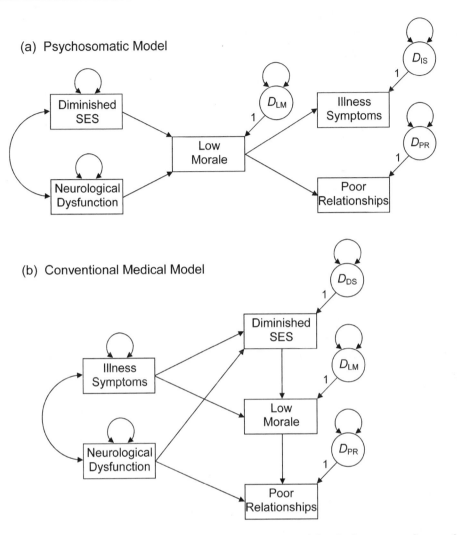

FIGURE 8.3. Alternative nonhierarchical recursive path models of adjustment after cardiac surgery.

TABLE 8.5. Input Data (Correlations) for Analysis of Nonhierarchical Recursive Path Models of Recovery after Cardiac Surgery

Variable	1	2	3	4	5
1. Low Morale	1.00				
2. Illness Symptoms	.53	1.00			
3. Neurological Dysfunction	.15	.18	1.00		
4. Poor Relationships	.52	.29	−.05	1.00	
5. Diminished SES	.30	.34	.23	.09	1.00

Note. These data are from Romney et al. (1992); $N = 469$.

TABLE 8.6. Values of Selected Fit Statistics for Two Nonhierarchical Recursive Path Models of Adjustment After Cardiac Surgery

	Model	
Index	Psychosomatic model (Figure 8.3(a))	Conventional medical model (Figure 8.3(b))
χ^2_M	40.402	3.238
df_M	5	3
p	< .001	.356
RMSEA (90% CI)	.120 (.086–.156)	.016 (0–.080)
GFI	.968	.997
CFI	.913	.999
SRMR	.065	.016

Note. CI, confidence interval.

tional medical model (df_M = 3) is better than that of the more parsimonious *psychosomatic model* (df_M = 5). But the fit advantage of the more complex model is enough to offset the penalty for having more free parameters imposed by the AIC as defined by Equation 8.4. For the more complex *conventional medical model*, AIC = 27.238, but for the *psychosomatic model*, AIC = 60.402. (Exercise 4 asks you to verify these results.) Because the former model has the lowest AIC value, it is preferred. This model also passes the chi-square test, and values of approximate fit indexes are favorable, too (Table 8.6). See Mulaik (2009, pp. 346–358) for information about other predictive fit indexes.

POWER ANALYSIS

Researchers can estimate statistical power at one of two different levels in SEM. The first concerns the power to detect an individual effect (parameter), and the best known method for estimating the power of single-*df* tests is one by Saris and Satorra (1993). Suppose that a researcher believes that the population unstandardized direct effect of *X* on *Y* is 5.0 (i.e., a 1-point increase on *X* leads to an increase on *Y* of 5 points holding constant all other causal variables). Using this and other a priori values of the parameters of the researcher's model, the researcher next generates a predicted covariance matrix under the *alternative hypothesis* (the model includes *X* → *Y*) by employing the tracing rule or methods based on matrix algebra. This model-implied covariance matrix is then specified as the input data to an SEM computer program. The model analyzed is the model under the *null hypothesis*, which does *not* include *X* → *Y* (it is fixed to zero), and the sample size specified is a planned value for the study (e.g., *N* = 400). The value of χ^2_M from this analysis approximates a noncentral chi-square statistic. Next, the researcher consults a special table for noncentral chi-square for estimating power as a function of degrees of freedom and the level of α (e.g., Loehlin, 2004, p. 263). The researcher uses *df* = 1 in these tables to obtain the estimated probability of detecting the added free parameter when testing for it.

A drawback of the method just described is that it must be repeated for every individual parameter for which an estimate of power is desired. An alternative is to use a Monte Carlo method such as the one implemented in Mplus, which estimates the proportion of generated samples where the null hypothesis that some parameter of interest equals zero is correctly rejected (Muthén & Muthén, 2002). Kaplan (1995) describes other approaches for estimating the power of tests for individual parameters in structural equation models.

An approach to power analysis at the model level by MacCallum, Browne, and Sugawara (1996) is based on the RMSEA and noncentral chi-square distributions for tests of three different null hypotheses. Two of these hypotheses include the close-fit hypothesis (H_0: $\varepsilon_0 \leq .05$) and the exact-fit hypothesis (H_0: $\varepsilon_0 = 0$). The test of each hypothesis just stated is an accept–support where low power favors the researcher's model. The third hypothesis is the **not-close-fit hypothesis**, or H_0: $\varepsilon_0 \geq .05$, which is an inversion of the close-fit hypothesis. If the upper bound of the 90% confidence interval based on the RMSEA is < .05, then the hypothesis that the model does not have close fit in the population is rejected. The test of the not-close-fit hypothesis is a reject–support test, for which low power works against the researcher's model. This is because greater power here implies a higher probability of detecting a reasonably correct model, or at least one that implies a covariance matrix that approximates the sample data matrix. The accuracy of tests for the close-fit and not-close-fit hypotheses assumes that the RMSEA actually follows a noncentral chi-square distribution.

A power analysis in the MacCallum et al. (1996) method for any of the null hypotheses just described is conducted by specifying N, α, df_M, and a suitable value of the parameter estimated by the RMSEA under the alternative hypothesis H_1, or ε_1. For example, ε_1 could be specified for the close-fit hypothesis as .08, a suggested upper threshold for reasonable approximation error. (But not a golden rule!) For the not-close-fit hypothesis, ε_1 could be specified as .01, which *may* represent the case of "good" approximate fit. A variation is to determine the minimum sample size needed to reach a target level of power, such as .80, given α, df_M, ε_1, and ε_0. The latter (ε_0) is the "terminal point" of the interval for the corresponding directional null hypothesis, which is $\varepsilon_0 = .05$ for both the close-fit and not-hypotheses.

Estimated power or sample sizes can be obtained by consulting special tables in MacCallum et al. (1996) or Hancock and Freeman (2001) for the not-close-fit hypothesis only or through use of a computer. In an appendix, MacCallum et al. (1996) give SAS/STAT syntax for power analysis based on the methods just outlined. Friendly (2009) describes a related SAS/STAT macro that carries out a MacCallum–Browne–Sugawara power analysis that can be freely downloaded over the Internet.[4] A webpage by Preacher and Coffman (2006) generates R code that conducts the same type of model-level power analysis for a given model, calculates the minimum sample size required to obtain a target level of power, estimates power for testing differences between two nested models,

---

[4]*www.math.yorku.ca/SCS/sasmac/csmpower.html*

and determines the minimum sample size needed to achieve a given level of power for a test of nested models.[5] Another option is the Power Analysis module by J. Steiger in STATISTICA 9 Advanced, which can estimate power for structural equation models over ranges of ε_1 (with ε_0 fixed to its specified value), α, df_M, and N. The ability to inspect power curves as functions of sample size and other assumptions is useful for planning a study, especially when grant applications demand power estimates. The Power Analysis module in STATISTICA also allows the researcher to specify the values of both ε_0 and ε_1. This feature is handy if there are theoretical reasons not to use the values of these parameters suggested by MacCallum et al. (1996), such as $\varepsilon_0 = .05$ and $\varepsilon_1 = .08$ for the close-fit hypothesis.

I used the Power Analysis module in STATISTICA 9 to estimate power for tests of both the close-fit hypothesis and the not-close-fit hypothesis for the Roth et al. path model of illness factors (Figure 8.1) and the Sava (2002) path model of causes and effects of teacher–pupil interactions (Figure 7.1). Also estimated for both models are the minimum sample sizes required in order to attain a level of power $\geq .80$ for each of the close-fit and not-close-fit hypotheses. The results are summarized in Table 8.7. For the Roth et al. model, the estimated power for the test of the close-fit hypothesis is .317. That is, if this model actually does *not* have close fit in the population, then the estimated probability that we can reject this incorrect model is somewhat greater than 30% for a sample size of 373 cases, given the other assumptions for this analysis (see Table 8.7). For the same model, the estimated power for the test of the not-close-fit hypothesis is .229. That is, there is only about a 23% chance of detecting a model with "good" approximate fit for the Roth et al. analysis. The minimum sample sizes required in order for power to be at least .80 for tests of the close-fit hypothesis and the not-close-fit hypothesis for the

TABLE 8.7. Power Analysis Results for Two Recursive Path Models

	Model	
Statistic	Roth et al. model (Figure 8.1)	Sava model (Figure 7.1)
N	373	109
df_M	5	7
Power		
Close-fit test[a]	.317	.153
Not-close-fit test[b]	.229	.096
Minimum N^c		
Close-fit test	1,465	1,075
Not-close-fit test	1,220	960

[a]H_0: $\varepsilon \leq .05$, $\varepsilon_1 = .08$, $\alpha = .05$.
[b]H_0: $\varepsilon \geq .05$, $\varepsilon_1 = .01$, $\alpha = .05$.
[c]Sample size rounded up to closest multiple of 5 required for power $\geq .80$.

---

[5]*http://people.ku.edu/~preacher/rmsea/rmsea.htm*

same model are, respectively, about 1,465 cases and 1,220 cases. Exercise 3 asks you to interpret the results of the power analysis in Table 8.7 for the Sava (2002) path model, but it is clear that power for this model is low, too.

The power analysis results just described reflect a general trend that power at the model level may be low when there are few model degrees of freedom even for a reasonably large sample size (e.g., $N = 373$ for the Roth et al. model of Figure 8.1). For models with only one or two degrees of freedom, sample sizes in the thousands may be required in order for model-level power to be greater than .80 (e.g., MacCallum et al., 1996, p. 144). Sample size requirements for the same level of power drop to some 300–400 cases for models when df_M is about 10. Even smaller samples may be needed for a minimum power of .80 if $df_M > 20$, but the sample size should not be less than 100 in any event. As Loehlin (2004) puts it, the results of a power analysis in SEM can be sobering. Specifically, if an analysis has a low probability of rejecting a false model, this fact should temper the researcher's enthusiasm for his or her preferred model.

Some other developments in power estimation at the model level are briefly summarized next. MacCallum and Hong (1997) extended MacCallum et al.'s (1996) work on power analysis at the model level to the GFI and AGFI fit statistics. Kim (2005) studied a total of four approximate fit indexes, including the RMSEA and CFI, in relation to power estimation and the determination of sample size requirements for minimum desired levels of power. Kim (2005) found that estimates of power and minimum sample sizes varied as a function of the choice of fit index, the number of observed variables and model degrees of freedom, and the magnitude of covariation among the variables. This result is not surprising considering that (1) different fit statistics reflect different aspects of model–data correspondence and (2) there is little direct correspondence between values of different fit statistics and degrees or types of model misspecification. As noted by Kim (2005), a value of .95 for the CFI does not necessarily indicate the same misspecification as a value of .05 for the RMSEA.

EQUIVALENT AND NEAR-EQUIVALENT MODELS

After a final model is selected from among hierarchical or nonhierarchical alternatives, **equivalent models** should be considered. Equivalent models yield the same predicted correlations or covariances but with a different configuration of paths among the same observed variables. Equivalent models also have equal values of fit statistics, including χ^2_M (and df_M) and all approximate fit indexes. For a given structural equation model, there are probably equivalent versions. Thus, it behooves the researcher to explain why his or her final model should be preferred over mathematically identical ones.

You already know that just-identified path models perfectly fit the data. By default, any variation of a just-identified path model exactly matches the data, too, and thus is an equivalent model. Equivalent versions of overidentified path models—and overidentified structural models in general—can be generated using the **Lee–Hershberger replacing rules** (Hershberger, 1994):

Within a block of variables at the beginning of the model that is just-   (Rule 8.1)
identified and with unidirectional relations to subsequent variables,
direct effects, correlated disturbances, and equality-constrained reciprocal effects (i.e., the two unstandardized direct effects are constrained
to be equal) are interchangeable. For example, $Y_1 \to Y_2$ may be
replaced by $Y_2 \to Y_1$, $D_1 \overset{\curvearrowleft}{\curvearrowright} D_2$, or $Y_1 \rightleftarrows Y_2$. If two variables are
specified as exogenous, then an unanalyzed association can be substi-
tuted, too.

At subsequent places in the model where two endogenous variables   (Rule 8.2)
have the same causes and their relations are unidirectional, all of the
following may be substituted for one another: $Y_1 \to Y_2$, $Y_2 \to Y_1$,
$D_1 \overset{\curvearrowleft}{\curvearrowright} D_2$, and the equality-constrained reciprocal effect $Y_1 \rightleftarrows Y_2$.

Note that substituting reciprocal direct effects for other types of paths would make the model nonrecursive, but it is assumed that the new model is identified (Chapter 6). Some equivalent versions may be implausible due to the nature of the variables or the time of their measurement. For example, a model that contains a direct effect from an acculturation variable to chronological age would be illogical. Also, the assessment of Y_1 before Y_2 in a longitudinal design is inconsistent with the specification $Y_2 \to Y_1$. When an equivalent model cannot be disregarded, it is up to you to provide a rationale for preferring one model over another.

Relatively simple structural models may have few equivalent versions, but more complicated ones may have hundreds or even thousands (see MacCallum, Wegener, Uchino, & Fabrigar, 1993). In general, more parsimonious structural models tend to have fewer equivalent versions. You will learn in the next chapter that measurement models can have infinitely many equivalent versions. Thus, it is unrealistic that researchers consider all possible equivalent models. As a compromise, researchers should generate at least a few substantively meaningful equivalent versions. Unfortunately, even this limited step is usually neglected. Few authors of SEM studies even acknowledge the existence of equivalent models (e.g., MacCallum & Austin, 2000). This type of confirmation bias is a pernicious problem in SEM, one that threatens the validity of most SEM studies.

Presented in Figure 8.4(a) is Romney and associates' original *conventional medical model* shown without disturbances to save space. The other three models in Figure 8.4 are generated from the original model using the Lee–Hershberger replacing rules. For example, the equivalent model of Figure 8.4(b) substitutes a direct effect for a covariance between the illness symptoms and neurological dysfunction variables. It also reverses the direct effects between diminished SES and low morale and between diminished SES and neurological dysfunction. The equivalent model of Figure 8.4(c) replaces two of three direct effects that involve diminished SES with unanalyzed associations. The equivalent model of Figure 8.4(d) replaces the unanalyzed association between illness symptoms and neurological dysfunction with an equality-constrained direct feedback loop. It also reverses the direct effects between illness symptoms and diminished

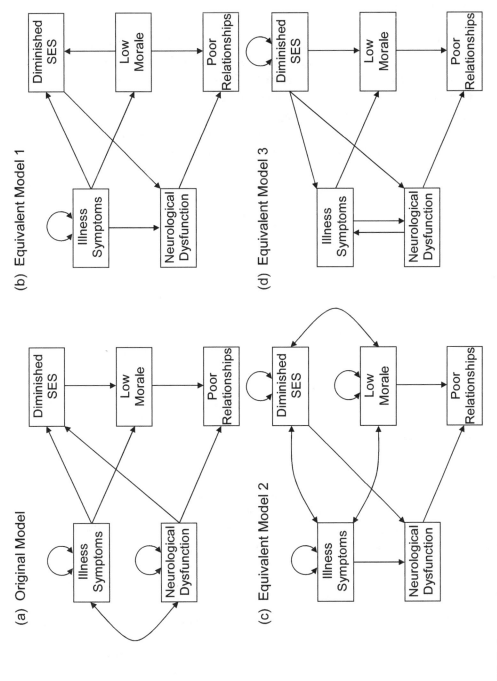

(a) Original Model

(b) Equivalent Model 1

(c) Equivalent Model 2

(d) Equivalent Model 3

FIGURE 8.4. Four equivalent path models of adjustment after cardiac surgery. Disturbances are omitted.

SES and between neurological dysfunction and diminished SES. Because the models in Figure 8.4 are equivalent, they all have the same fit to the data (i.e., $\chi_M^2(3) = 3.238$ for each model).[6] The choice among equivalent models must be based on theoretical rather than statistical grounds. Exercise 6 asks you to generate equivalent versions of the Sava (2002) path model in Figure 7.1.

In addition to equivalent models, there may also be **near-equivalent models** that do not generate the exact same predicted covariances, but nearly so. For instance, the path model in Figure 8.1 but with (1) a direct effect from fitness to stress or (2) a direct effect from stress to fitness are near-equivalent models (see Table 8.4). There is no specific rule for generating near-equivalent models. Instead, such models would be specified according to theory. In some cases, near-equivalent models may be more numerous than truly equivalent models and thus are a more serious research threat than the equivalent models.

SUMMARY

It is critical to begin the testing process with a model that represents a substantive research problem. The real goal of the analysis is not to find a model that fits the data. Instead, it is to *test a theory* and then to consider the implications for that theory of whether or not the model is consistent with the data. There is an ongoing debate in the SEM literature about optimal strategies for assessing model fit, but there is a general consensus that some routine practices are inadequate. One bad practice is ignoring a failed model chi-square test even though the sample size is not very large. Another is the claim for "good" model fit based mainly on values of approximate fit statistics that exceed—or, in some cases, fall below—suggested thresholds based on prior computer simulation studies. Instead, researchers should explicitly diagnose possible sources of misspecification by describing patterns of residuals or values of modification indexes for parameters with a basis in theory. If a model is eventually retained, then it is important also to estimate statistical power and generate at least a few plausible equivalent or near-equivalent models. If the statistical power to reject a false model is low or there are few grounds to prefer the researcher's model among equivalent versions, then little support for that model is indicated. The next chapter introduces the analysis of measurement models with the technique of confirmatory factor analysis.

RECOMMENDED READINGS

The special issue of the journal *Personality and Individual Differences* on SEM concerns the roles of test statistics and approximate fit indexes in model testing (Vernon & Eysenck, 2007). MacCallum et al. (1993) describe many examples of generating equivalent versions of models from published articles. Chapter 15 in Mulaik (2009) about model evaluation provides detail

---

[6]Applying the Lee–Hershberger replacing rules to any of the generated models in Figures 8.4(b)–8.4(d) may yield even more equivalent versions.

about additional fit statistics and strategies for hypothesis testing. Tomarken and Waller (2003) consider examples of poor explanatory power for models with apparently "good" fit based on values of fit statistics. Humphreys (2003) compares the logic of statistical modeling in the social sciences with that in the natural sciences and finds many points of contact between the two.

Humphreys, P. (2003). Mathematical modeling in the social sciences. In S. P. Turner & P. A. Roth (Eds.), *The Blackwell guide to the philosophy of the social sciences* (pp. 166–184). Malden, MA: Blackwell.

MacCallum, R. C., Wegener, D. T., Uchino, B. N., & Fabrigar, L. R. (1993). The problem of equivalent models in applications of covariance structure analysis. *Psychological Bulletin, 114*, 185–199.

Mulaik, S. A. (2009). *Linear causal modeling with structural equations*. New York: CRC Press. (Chapter 15)

Tomarken, A. J., & Waller, N. G. (2003). Potential problems with "well-fitting" models. *Journal of Abnormal Psychology, 112*, 578–598.

Vernon, P. A., & Eysenck, S. B. G. (Eds.). (2007). Structural equation modeling [Special issue]. *Personality and Individual Differences, 42*(5).

EXERCISES

1. Based on the correlation residuals in Table 7.5, how would you respecify the Sava path model in Figure 7.1 by adding one path? Fit this respecified model to the data in Table 7.1. Evaluate the fit of this revised model.

2. Respecify the Roth et al. path model in Figure 8.1 by adding a direct effect from fitness to stress. Fit this revised model to the rescaled data in Table 3.4.

3. Interpret the power analysis results in Table 8.7 for the Sava path model in Figure 7.1.

4. Calculate the AIC for both Romney et al. models in Figure 8.3.

5. Using the MacCallum et al. (1996) article on power analysis, determine the minimum samples sizes needed to attain a power level of .80 for tests of both the close-fit hypothesis and the not-close-fit hypothesis at the following values of df_M: 2, 6, 10, 14, 20, 25, 30, and 40. Comment on the results.

6. Generate two equivalent versions of the Sava path model in Figure 7.1. Prove that these models are in fact equivalent to the original model.

7. Explain why these two models are not equivalent: (a) Figure 8.1 but with the path Fitness → Stress, (b) Figure 8.1 but with the path Stress → Fitness.

8. Show calculations for the CFI based on the information presented in Table 8.2.

Measurement Models and Confirmatory Factor Analysis

This is the first of two chapters about the analysis of core latent variable models in SEM, in this case measurement models as analyzed in CFA. The multiple-indicator approach to measurement of CFA represents literally half the basic rationale of analyzing covariance structures in SEM—the analysis of structural models is the other half—so CFA is a crucial technique. It is also a primary technique for many researchers, especially those who conduct assessment-related studies. Also introduced in this chapter is multiple-sample CFA, in which a measurement model is fitted simultaneously to data from more than one group. The results provide a test of measurement invariance, or of whether a set of indicators has the same measurement properties across the groups. If you know something about CFA, then it is easier to learn about structural regression (SR) models, which have features of both path models and CFA models. The next chapter covers SR models.

NAMING AND REIFICATION FALLACIES

The specification and identification of CFA models were introduced in, respectively, Chapters 5 and 6 using model diagrams where factors were designated with letters, such as A and B (e.g., Figure 5.6). In real analyses, researchers usually assign meaningful labels to factors such as sequential processing (Figure 5.7). However, it is important to avoid two logical errors concerning factor names. The first is the **naming fallacy**: Just because a factor is named does not mean that the hypothetical construct is understood or even correctly labeled. Factors require some type of designation, though, if for no other reason than communication of the results. Although verbal labels are more "reader friendly" than more abstract symbols, such as A or ε (xi, a symbol from LISREL's matrix notation for exogenous factors), they should be viewed as conveniences and not as substitutes for critical thinking.

The second logical error to avoid is **reification**: the belief that a hypothetical construct *must* correspond to a real thing. For example, a general ability factor, often called g, is a hypothetical construct. To automatically consider g as real instead of a concept, however, is a potential error of reification. Along these lines, Gardner (1993) reminded educators not to assume that "intelligence" corresponds to a single domain that is adequately measured by IQ scores. Instead, he argued that intelligence is multifaceted and includes not only academic skills but also social, artistic, and athletic domains.

ESTIMATION OF CFA MODELS

This discussion assumes that all indicators are continuous variables. This is most likely to happen when each indicator is a *scale* that generates a total score over a set of items. A later section deals with the analysis of models where *items* are specified as indicators.

Interpretation of Estimates

Parameter estimates in CFA are interpreted as follows:

1. Factor loadings estimate the direct effects of factors on indicators and are interpreted as regression coefficients. For example, if the unstandardized factor loading is 4.0 for the direct effect $A \rightarrow X_1$, then we expect a four-point difference in indicator X_1 given a difference of 1 point on factor A. Loadings fixed to 1.0 to scale the corresponding factor remain so in the unstandardized solution and are not tested for statistical significance because they have no standard errors.

2. For indicators specified to load on a single factor, standardized factor loadings are estimated correlations between the indicator and its factor. Thus, squared standardized loadings are proportions of explained variance, or R^2_{smc}. If a standardized loading is .80, for example, the factor explains $.80^2 = .64$, or 64.0% of the variance of the indicator. Ideally, a CFA model should explain the majority of the variance ($R^2_{smc} > .50$) of each indicator.

3. For indicators specified to load on multiple factors, standardized loadings are interpreted as beta weights that control for correlated factors. Because beta weights are not correlations, one cannot generally square their values to derive proportions of explained variance.

4. The ratio of an unstandardized measurement error variance over the observed variance of the corresponding indicator equals the proportion of unexplained variance, and one minus this ratio is the proportion of explained variance. Suppose that the variance of X_1 is 25.00 and that the variance of its error term is 9.00. The proportion of unexplained variance is $9.00/25.00 = .36$, and the proportion of explained variance is $R^2_{smc} = 1 - .34 = .64$.

5. Estimates of unanalyzed associations between either a pair of factors or measurement errors are covariances in the unstandardized solution. These estimates are correlations in the standardized solution.

The estimated correlation between an indicator and a factor is a **structure coefficient**. If an indicator loads on a single factor, its standardized loading is a structure coefficient; otherwise, it is not. Graham, Guthrie, and Thompson (2003) remind us that the specification that a direct effect of a factor on an indicator is zero does *not* mean that the correlation between the two must be zero. That is, a zero pattern coefficient (factor loading) does *not* imply a zero structure coefficient. This is because the factors in CFA models are assumed to covary, which implies nonzero correlations between each indicator and all factors. However, indicators should have higher estimated correlations with the factors they are specified to measure.

Problems

Failure of iterative estimation in CFA can be caused by poor start values; suggestions for calculating start values for measurement models are presented in Appendix 9.A. Inadmissible solutions include Heywood cases such as negative variance estimates or estimated absolute correlations greater than 1.0. Results of some computer studies indicate that nonconvergence or improper solutions are more likely when there are only two indicators per factor or the sample size is less than 100–150 cases (Marsh & Hau, 1999). The authors just cited give the following suggestions for analyzing CFA models when the sample size is not large:

1. Use indicators with good psychometric characteristics that will each also have relatively high standardized factor loadings (e.g., > .70). Models with indicators that have relatively low standardized loadings are more susceptible to Heywood cases (Wothke, 1993).
2. Estimation of the model with equality constraints imposed on the unstandardized loadings of indicators of the same factor may help to generate more trustworthy solutions. This assumes that all indicators have the same metric.
3. When the indicators are items instead of continuous total scores, it may be better to analyze them in groups (parcels) rather than individually. Recall that the analysis of parcels is controversial because it requires a very strong assumption, that the items of a parcel are unidimensional (Chapter 7).

Solution inadmissibility can also occur at the parameter matrix level. Specifically, the computer estimates in CFA a factor covariance matrix and an error covariance matrix. If any element of either parameter matrix is out of bounds, then that matrix is nonpositive definite. Causes of nonpositive definite parameter matrices include the following (Wothke, 1993):

1. The data provide too little information (e.g., small sample, two indicators per factor).
2. The model is overparameterized (too many parameters).
3. The sample has outliers or severely non-normal distributions (poor data screening).
4. There is empirical underidentification concerning factor covariances (e.g., Figure 6.4).
5. The measurement model is misspecified.

Empirical Checks for Identification

It is theoretically possible for the computer to generate a converged, admissible solution for a model that is not really identified, yet print no warning message. However, that solution would not be unique. This is most likely to happen in CFA when analyzing a model with both correlated errors and complex indicators for which the application of heuristics cannot prove identification (Chapter 6). Described next are empirical checks for solution uniqueness that can be applied when analyzing any type of structural equation model, not just CFA models. These checks concern necessary but insufficient requirements. That is, if any of these checks is failed, then the solution is not unique, but passing them does not prove identification:

1. Conduct a second analysis of the same model but use different start values than in the first analysis. If estimation converges to a different solution working from different initial estimates, the original solution is not unique and the model is not identified.

2. This check applies to overidentified models only: Use the model-implied covariance matrix from the first analysis as the input data for a second analysis of the same model. If the second analysis does not generate the same solution as the first, the model is not identified.

3. Some SEM computer programs optionally print the matrix of estimated correlations among the parameter estimates. Although parameters are fixed values that do not vary randomly in the population, their estimates are considered random variables with their own distributions and covariances. Estimates of these covariances are based on the **information matrix**, which is associated with full-information methods such as ML. If the model is identified, this matrix has an inverse, which is the matrix of covariances among the parameter estimates. Correlations among the parameters are derived from this matrix. An identification problem is indicated if any of these absolute correlations is close to 1.0, which indicates linear dependency. See Bollen (1989, pp. 246–251) for additional necessary-but-insufficient empirical checks based on linear algebra methods.

DETAILED EXAMPLE

This example concerns the analysis of the measurement model for the first edition Kaufman Assessment Battery for Children (KABC-I) introduced in Chapter 5. The two-factor, eight-indicator theoretical model for this test is presented in Figure 9.1. Briefly, the first three subtests are specified to load on one factor (sequential processing) and the other five subtests on a second factor (simultaneous processing).[1] The data for this analysis are summarized in Table 9.1, which are from the test's standardization sample for 10-year-old children ($N = 200$).

Test for a Single Factor

When theory is not specific about the number of factors, this is often the first step in a series of analyses: if a single-factor model cannot be rejected, there is little point in evaluating more complex ones. Even when theory is more precise about the number of factors (e.g., two for the KABC-I), it should be determined whether the fit of a simpler, one-factor model is comparable. I submitted to Mplus 5.2 the covariance matrix based on the data in Table 9.1 for ML estimation of a single-factor CFA model. The unstandardized loading of the Hand Movements indicator was fixed to 1.0 to scale the single factor. With $v = 8$ indicators, there are 36 observations available to estimate a total of 16 free parameters, including nine variances of exogenous variables (of the single factor and eight measurement errors) and seven factor loadings, so $df_M = 20$. Estimation in Mplus converged to an admissible solution. Values of selected fit indexes for the one-factor model are listed next (Mplus does not print the GFI). The 90% confidence interval associated with the RMSEA is reported in parentheses:

$$\chi^2_M (20) = 105.427, \quad p < .001$$
$$\text{RMSEA} = .146 \ (.119\text{--}.174), \quad p_{\text{close-fit } H_0} < .001$$
$$\text{CFI} = .818; \quad \text{SRMR} = .084$$

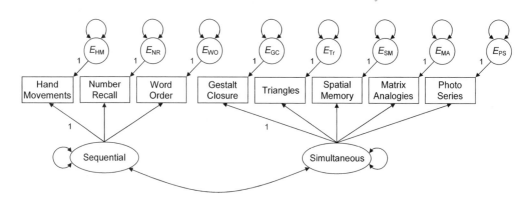

FIGURE 9.1. A confirmatory factor analysis model of the Kaufman Assessment Battery for Children, first edition.

---

[1]Keith (1985) suggested alternative names for the factors in the KABC-I's theoretical model, including "short-term memory" instead of "sequential processing" and "visual-spatial reasoning" instead of "simultaneous processing." One reason is that all three sequential tasks are immediate recall tasks, and all five simultaneous tasks involve responding to visual stimuli.

TABLE 9.1. Input Data (Correlations, Standard Deviations) for Analysis of a Two-Factor Model of the Kaufman Assessment Battery for Children

Variable	1	2	3	4	5	6	7	8
Sequential scale								
1. Hand Movements	1.00							
2. Number Recall	.39	1.00						
3. Word Order	.35	.67	1.00					
Simultaneous scale								
4. Gestalt Closure	.21	.11	.16	1.00				
5. Triangles	.32	.27	.29	.38	1.00			
6. Spatial Memory	.40	.29	.28	.30	.47	1.00		
7. Matrix Analogies	.39	.32	.30	.31	.42	.41	1.00	
8. Photo Series	.39	.29	.37	.42	.58	.51	.42	1.00
SD	3.40	2.40	2.90	2.70	2.70	4.20	2.80	3.00

Note. Input data are from Kaufman and Kaufman (1983); N = 200.

The overall fit of a one-factor model to the data in Table 9.1 is obviously poor, so it is rejected.

The test for a single factor is relevant not just for CFA models. For example, Kenny (1979) noted that such models could also be tested as part of a path analysis. The inability to reject a single-factor model in this context would mean the same thing as in CFA: the observed variables do not show discriminant validity; that is, they seem to measure only one domain. I conducted a test for single-factoredness for the five variables of the Roth et al. (1989) path model of illness factors analyzed in Chapter 8 (see Figure 8.1). A single-factor model for these variables was fitted to a covariance matrix based on the data summarized in Table 3.4 with the ML method of Mplus 5.2. Values of selected fit statistics clearly show that a single-factor model poorly explains the Roth et al. (1989) data and provide a "green light" to proceed with evaluation of a path model:

$$\chi^2_M (5) = 60.549, \quad p < .001$$
$$\text{RMSEA} = .173 \ (.135–.213), \quad p_{\text{close-fit } H_0} < .001$$
$$\text{CFI} = 644; \quad \text{SRMR} = .096$$

Two-Factor Model

There are also 36 observations available for the analysis of the two-factor model of the KABC-I in Figure 9.1. To scale the two factors, the unstandardized loadings of the Hand Movements task and the Gestalt Closure task on their respective factors were each fixed to 1.0. A total of 17 free parameters remain to be estimated, including 10 variances (of two factors and eight error terms), one factor covariance, and six factor loadings (two on the first factor, four on the second), so $df_M = 19$.

I used Mplus 5.2 to fit the two-factor model of Figure 9.1 to the data in Table 9.1

with ML estimation. You can download the Mplus syntax, data, and output files for this analysis from this book's website (see p. 3) and all EQS and LISREL computer files for the same analysis, too. The analysis in Mplus converged to an admissible solution. Presented in Table 9.2 are the parameter estimates for the two-factor model. Note in the table that unstandardized loadings of the reference variables (Hand Movements, Gestalt Closure) equal 1.0 and have no standard errors. The other six unstandardized loadings were freely estimated, and their values are all statistically significant at the .01 level. Although statistical significance of the unstandardized estimates of factor variances is indicated in the table, it is expected that these variances are not zero (i.e., there are individual differences). It would be senseless in most analyses to get worked up about the statistical significance of these terms, but results of significance tests for

TABLE 9.2. Maximum Likelihood Estimates for a Two-Factor Model of the KABC-I

Parameter	Unstandardized	SE	Standardized
	Factor loadings		
Sequential factor			
Hand Movements	1.000[a]	—	.497
Number Recall	1.147	.181	.807
Word Order	1.388	.219	.808
Simultaneous factor			
Gestalt Closure	1.000[a]	—	.503
Triangles	1.445	.227	.726
Spatial Memory	2.029	.335	.656
Matrix Analogies	1.212	.212	.588
Photo Series	1.727	.265	.782
	Measurement error variances		
Hand Movements	8.664	.938	.753
Number Recall	1.998	.414	.349
Word Order	2.902	.604	.347
Gestalt Closure	5.419	.585	.747
Triangles	3.425	.458	.472
Spatial Memory	9.998	1.202	.570
Matrix Analogies	5.104	.578	.654
Photo Series	3.483	.537	.389
	Factor variances and covariance		
Sequential	2.839	.838	1.000
Simultaneous	1.835	.530	1.000
Sequential ⌣ Simultaneous	1.271	.324	.557

Note. KABC-I, Kaufman Assessment Battery for Children, first edition. Standardized estimates for measurement errors are proportions of unexplained variance.

[a]Not tested for statistical significance. All other unstandardized estimates are statistically significant at $p < .01$.

factor covariances may be of greater interest. Note that Mplus can automatically print correct standard errors for standardized estimates, but these values are not reported in Table 9.2.

Of greater interpretive import are the standardized factor loadings in Table 9.2. Because each indicator loads on a single factor, the square of each standardized loading equals R^2_{smc} for the corresponding indicator. Some standardized loadings are so low that convergent validity seems doubtful. For example, the loadings of Hand Movements and Gestalt Closure on their respective factors are both only about .50, and $R^2_{smc} < .50$, for a total of four out of eight indicators. That is, the model in Figure 9.1 explains the minority of the observed variance for exactly half of the indicators. On the other hand, the estimated factor correlation (.557) is only moderate in size, which suggests discriminant validity.

Reported in Table 9.3 are values of structure coefficients (estimated factor-indicator correlations) for all eight indicators in the two-factor model of Figure 9.1. Coefficients presented in boldface in the table are also standardized factor loadings for indicators specified to measure either factor. For example, the Hand Movements is not specified to measure simultaneous processing (Figure 9.1). Therefore, the pattern coefficient for the Hand Movements-simultaneous processing correspondence is zero. However, the structure coefficients for the Hand Movements task are .497 and .277 (Table 9.3). The former, .497, equals the standardized loading of this indicator on the sequential processing factor (Table 9.2). The latter, .277, is the model-implied correlation between the Hand Movements task and the simultaneous processing factor. It is calculated using the tracing rule as the product of the standardized loading for the Hand Movements task and the estimated correlation between the factors, or .497 (.557) = .277. Exercise 1 asks you to derive the other structure coefficients in Table 9.3 using the tracing rule. The results in the table clearly show that the structure coefficients are not typically zero for corresponding zero pattern coefficients when the factors are substantially correlated.

TABLE 9.3. Structure Coefficients for a Two-Factor Model of the KABC-I

Indicator	Factor	
	Sequential	Simultaneous
Hand Movements	**.497**	.277
Number Recall	**.807**	.449
Word Order	**.808**	.450
Gestalt Closure	.280	**.503**
Triangles	.404	**.726**
Spatial Memory	.365	**.656**
Matrix Analogies	.328	**.588**
Photo Series	.436	**.782**

Note. KABC-I, Kaufman Assessment Battery for Children, first edition.

Tests for Multiple Factors

The chi-square reported by Mplus for the two-factor model in Figure 9.1 is $\chi^2_M (19) =$ 38.325, $p = .005$. Thus, this model fails the chi-square test, and so it is necessary to investigate the magnitude and patterns of discrepancies between model and data. We will do so momentarily, but at this point we can infer that the fit of the two-factor model is better than that of the one-factor model fitted to the same data based on their respective χ^2_M values. Now, can we compare the relative fits of these two models with the chi-square difference test? Recall that this test is only for hierarchical models (Chapter 8). Is this true of the one- and two-factor models of the KABC-I?

Yes, and here is why: the one-factor model is actually a restricted version of the two-factor model. Look again at Figure 9.1. If the correlation between the two factors is fixed to equal 1.0, then the two factors will be identical, which is the same thing as replacing both factors with just one. The results of the chi-square difference test are

$$df_{M_{1\ factor}} - df_{M_{2\ factors}} = 20 - 19 = 1$$

$$\chi^2_D (1) = \chi^2_{M_{1\ factor}} - \chi^2_{M_{2\ factors}} = 105.427 - 38.325$$

$$= 67.102, \quad p < .001$$

which says that the fit of the two-factor model is statistically better than that of the single-factor model. The meaning of this particular result is not clear at this point because the fit of the more complex two-factor model is problematic. However, the comparison just described can be generalized to models with more factors. With a four-factor model, for instance, fixing all factor correlations to 1.0 generates a single-factor model that is nested under the unrestricted model. Merging any two factors (and their indicators) in a four-factor model into a single factor results in a three-factor model that is nested under the original model, and so on.

Assessment of Model Fit

Reported in Table 9.4 are values of fit statistics and results of model-level power analyses for the two-factor model of the KABC-I (Figure 9.1). As mentioned, the model chi-square is statistically significant, so the exact-fit hypothesis is rejected. Results for the RMSEA are mixed. The lower bound of the 90% confidence interval for this statistic is .037, so the close-fit hypothesis is not rejected ($p = .171$). However, the upper bound exceeds .10, so the poor-fit hypothesis cannot be rejected. Values of the CFI and SRMR are, respectively, .959 and .072. Levels of statistical power estimated in the Power Analysis module of STATISTICA 8 Advanced for tests of the close-fit hypothesis and the not-close-fit hypothesis are both low (respectively, .440 and .302). Minimum sample sizes of over twice that of the actual size for this analysis ($N = 200$) would be needed in order for power to be at least .80 (see Table 9.4).

TABLE 9.4. Values of Fit Statistics and Power Estimates for a Two-Factor Model of the KABC-I

Fit statistics		Power estimates	
Statistic	Result	Statistic or test	Result
χ^2_M	38.325	N	200
df_M	19	df_M	19
p	.005	Power	
RMSEA (90% CI)	.071 (.038–.104)	Close-fit test[a]	.440
$p_{\text{close-fit } H_0}$	.132	Not-close-fit test[b]	.302
CFI	.959	Minimum N^c	
SRMR	.072	Close-fit test	455
		Not-close-fit test	490

Note. KABC-I, Kaufman Assessment Battery for Children, first edition; CI, confidence interval.

[a]H_0: $\varepsilon \leq .05$, $\varepsilon_1 = .08$, $\alpha = .05$.
[b]H_0: $\varepsilon \geq .05$, $\varepsilon_1 = .01$, $\alpha = .05$.
[c]Sample size rounded up to closest multiple of 5 required for power $\geq .80$.

Reported in Table 9.5 are the correlation residuals (calculated in EQS) for the two-factor model. Many of these residuals (shown in boldface in the table) exceed .10 in absolute value. Most of the larger residuals concern one of the indicators of sequential processing, Hand Movements, and most of the indicators of simultaneous processing. All of these residuals are positive, which means that the two-factor model generally underestimates correlations between Hand Movements and those specified to measure the other factor. Based on all the results described so far, the fit of the two-factor model in Figure 9.1 is unacceptable. Exercise 2 will ask you to use an SEM computer tool to derive the standardized residuals (z statistics) for this analysis.

TABLE 9.5. Correlation Residuals for a Two-Factor Model of the KABC-I

Variable	1	2	3	4	5	6	7	8
Sequential scale								
1. Hand Movements	0							
2. Number Recall	−.011	0						
3. Word Order	−.052	.018	0					
Simultaneous scale								
4. Gestalt Closure	.071	**−.116**	−.066	0				
5. Triangles	**.119**	−.057	−.037	.015	0			
6. Spatial Memory	**.218**	−.005	−.015	−.030	−.007	0		
7. Matrix Analogies	**.227**	.056	.035	.014	−.007	.024	0	
8. Photo Series	**.174**	−.061	.018	.027	.012	−.003	−.040	0

Note. KABC-I, Kaufman Assessment Battery for Children, first edition.

RESPECIFICATION OF MEASUREMENT MODELS

In the face of adversity, the protagonist of Kurt Vonnegut's novel *Slaughterhouse-Five* often remarks, "So it goes." And so it often goes in CFA that an initial model does not fit the data very well. The respecification of a CFA model is even more challenging than that of a path model because there are more possibilities for change. For example, the number of factors, their relations to the indicators, and patterns of measurement error correlations are all candidates for modification. Given so many potential variations, respecification of CFA models should be guided as much as possible by substantive considerations. Otherwise, the specification process could put the researcher in the same situation as the sailor in this adage attributed to Leonardo da Vinci: One who loves practice without theory is like a sailor who boards a ship without a rudder and compass and never knows where he or she may be cast.

Two general classes of problems can be considered in respecification. The first concerns the indicators. Sometimes the indicators fail to have substantial standardized loadings (e.g., < .20) on the factors to which they were originally assigned. One option is to specify that the indicator measures a different factor. Inspection of the correlation residuals can help to identify the other factor to which the indicator's loading may be switched. Suppose that an indicator is originally specified to measure factor A, but the correlation residuals between it and the indicators of factor B are large and positive. This would suggest that the indicator may measure factor B more than it does factor A. Note that an indicator can have relatively high loadings on its own factor but also have high residual correlations between it and the indicators of another factor. The pattern just described suggests that the indicator in question measures more than one construct (i.e., allow it to load on > 1 factor). Another possibility consistent with this same pattern is that these indicators share something that is unique to them, such as a particular method of measurement. This possibility would be represented by allowing that pair of measurement errors to covary.

The second class of problems concerns the factors. For example, the researcher may have specified the wrong number of factors. On the one hand, poor discriminant validity as evidenced by very high factor correlations may indicate that the model has too many factors. On the other hand, poor convergent validity within sets of indicators of the same factor suggests that the model may have too few factors.

A starting point for respecification often includes inspection of the correlation residuals and modification indexes. Earlier we examined the correlation residuals in Table 9.5 for the two-factor model of the KABC-I. Most of the large and positive residuals are between the Hand Movements task and tasks specified to measure the other factor. Because the standardized loading of the Hand Movements task on its original factor is at least moderate (.497; Table 9.2), it is possible that this task may measure both factors. Reported in Table 9.6 are the 10 largest modification indexes computed by Mplus for factor loadings and error covariances that are fixed to zero in the original model (Figure 9.1). Note in the table that the χ^2 (1) statistics for the paths

TABLE 9.6. Ten Largest Modification Indexes for a Two-Factor Model of the KABC-I

Path	MI
Simultaneous → Hand Movements	20.091**
$E_{WO} \curvearrowright E_{NR}$	20.042**
Simultaneous → Number Recall	7.010**
$E_{HM} \curvearrowright E_{WO}$	7.015**
$E_{HM} \curvearrowright E_{SM}$	4.847*
$E_{HM} \curvearrowright E_{MA}$	3.799
Sequential → Matrix Analogies	3.247
$E_{NR} \curvearrowright E_{PS}$	3.147
Sequential → Gestalt Closure	2.902
$E_{MA} \curvearrowright E_{PS}$	2.727

Note. KABC-I, Kaufman Assessment Battery for Children, first edition; MI, modification index; HM, Hand Movements; WO, Word Order; SM, Spatial Memory; MA, Matrix Analogies; PS, Photo Series.

*$p < .05$; **$p < .01$.

$$\text{Simultaneous} \rightarrow \text{Hand Movements} \quad \text{and} \quad E_{WO} \curvearrowright E_{NR}$$

are nearly identical (respectively, 20.091 and 20.042). Thus, either allowing Hand Movements to also load on the simultaneous processing factor or adding an error covariance between the Word Order and Number Recall tasks would reduce the value of χ^2_M by about 20 points. Among other changes suggested by the modification indexes, two have nearly the same $\chi^2 (1)$ value: allow Number Recall to also load on the sequential processing factor (7.010), or allow the errors of the Hand Movements and Word Order tasks to covary (7.015). The researcher needs a rationale for choosing among these potential respecifications. Based on my knowledge of the KABC-I (e.g., Kline, Snyder, & Castellanos, 1996) and results of other factor-analytic studies (e.g., Keith, 1985), allowing the Hand Movements task to load on both factors is plausible.

SPECIAL TOPICS AND TESTS

Different types of score reliability coefficients (test–retest, internal consistency, etc.) for individual indicators were described in Chapter 3. There are also a few different coefficients for estimating the reliability of construct (factor) measurement through all its indicators in CFA. Two of these coefficients are described in Topic Box 9.1. Values of one of these coefficients for the two-factor model of the KABC-I in Figure 9.1 are reported in the box.

For CFA models fitted to data from a single sample, the choice between analyzing factors in unstandardized versus standardized form (e.g., Figure 6.1) usually has no impact on model fit. Steiger (2002) describes an exception called **constraint interac-**

TOPIC BOX 9.1

Reliability of Construct Measurement

Raykov (1997, 2004) describes coefficients that estimate the reliability of factor (construct) measurement. This coefficient is the **factor rho coefficient**, which is a ratio of explained variance over total variance that can be expressed in terms of CFA parameters. It can also be computed for factors in SR models. For factors with no error covariances that involve their indicators (i.e., uncorrelated measurement errors), the rho coefficient is estimated in the unstandardized solution as follows:

$$\hat{\rho}_{X_i X_i} = \frac{\left(\Sigma \hat{\lambda}_i\right)^2 \hat{\phi}}{\left(\Sigma \hat{\lambda}_i\right)^2 \hat{\phi} + \Sigma \hat{\theta}_{ii}} \tag{9.1}$$

where $\Sigma \hat{\lambda}_i$ is the sum of the estimated unstandardized factor loadings among indicators of the same factor, $\hat{\phi}$ is the estimated factor variance, and $\Sigma \hat{\theta}_{ii}$ is the sum of the unstandardized error variances of those indicators. A different formula is needed for factors with indicators that share at least one error covariance:

$$\hat{\rho}_{X_i X_i} = \frac{\left(\Sigma \hat{\lambda}_i\right)^2 \hat{\phi}}{\left(\Sigma \hat{\lambda}_i\right)^2 \hat{\phi} + \Sigma \hat{\theta}_{ii} + 2\Sigma \hat{\theta}_{ij}} \tag{9.2}$$

where $\Sigma \hat{\theta}_{ij}$ is the sum of the nonzero unstandardized error covariances. Raykov (2004) describes variations of these equations for the standardized solution.

Calculation of $\hat{\rho}_{X_i X_i}$ for the sequential processing construct of the two-factor model in Figure 9.1 is demonstrated next. The errors of the three indicators of this factor are independent, so we need Equation 9.1. From Table 9.2 we obtain these numerical results: The unstandardized factor loadings are 1.000, 1.147, and 1.388. The unstandardized error variances are 8.644, 1.998, and 2.902; the estimated variance of the sequential factor is 2.839; the sum of the factor loadings is 3.535; and the sum of the error variances is 13.564. Given these totals, the estimated reliability for measurement of the sequential processing factor is

$$\hat{\rho}_{X_i X_i} = [3.535^2 \, (2.839)]/[3.535^2 \, (2.839) + 13.564] = .723$$

which is not a terrible result, but still the evidence for convergent validity among the indicators of this factor is questionable (see Table 9.2). The estimated reliability for measurement of the simultaneous processing factor by its five indicators (Figure 9.1) is somewhat higher, $\hat{\rho}_{X_i X_i} = .786$. See Hancock and Mueller (2001) for information about other factor reliability coefficients; Byrne (2006) describes factor reliability coefficients printed by EQS.

tion that can occur for CFA models where some factors have only two indicators *and* a **cross-factor equality constraint** is imposed on the loadings of indicators on different factors. In some cases the value of $\chi^2_D(1)$ for the test of the equality constraint depends on how the factors are scaled. Constraint interaction probably does not occur in most applications of CFA, but you should know something about this phenomenon in case it ever crops up in your own work. See Appendix 9.B for more information.

Some other kinds of tests with CFA models are briefly described. Whether a set of indicators is congeneric, tau-equivalent, or parallel can be tested in CFA by comparing hierarchical models with the chi-square difference test (Chapter 8). **Congeneric indicators** measure the same construct but not necessarily to the same degree. The CFA model for congenerity does not impose any constraints except that a set of indicators is specified to load on the same factor. If this model fits reasonably well, one can proceed to test the more demanding assumptions of tau equivalence and parallelism. **Tau-equivalent indicators** are congeneric and have equal true score variances. This hypothesis is tested by imposing equality constraints on the unstandardized factor loadings (i.e., they are all fixed to 1.0). If the fit of the tau equivalence model is not appreciably worse than that of the congenerity model, then additional constraints can be imposed that test for parallelism. Specifically, **parallel indicators** have equal error variances. If the fit of this model with equality-constrained residuals is not appreciably worse than that of the model for tau equivalence, the indicators may be parallel. All these models assume independent errors and must be fitted to a covariance matrix, not a correlation matrix; see Brown (2006, pp. 238–252) for examples.

It was noted earlier that fixing all factor correlations to 1.0 in a multifactor model generates a single-factor model that is nested under the original. In the factor analysis literature, the comparison with the chi-square difference test just described is referred to as the **test for redundancy**. A variation is to fix the covariances between multiple factors to zero, which provides a **test for orthogonality**. If the model has only two factors, this procedure is not necessary because the statistical test of the factor covariance in the unconstrained model provides the same information. For models with three or more factors, the test for orthogonality is akin to a multivariate test for whether all the factor covariances together differ statistically from zero. Note that each factor should have at least three indicators for the redundancy test; otherwise, the constrained model may not be identified; see Nunnally and Bernstein (1994, pp. 576–578) for examples.

Remember that estimates of equality-constrained factor loadings are equal in the unstandardized solution, but the corresponding standardized coefficients are typically unequal. This will happen when the two indicators have different variances. *Thus, it usually makes no sense to compare standardized coefficients from equality-constrained factor loadings.* If it is really necessary to constrain a pair of standardized loadings to be equal, then one option is to fit the model to a correlation matrix using the method of constrained estimation (Chapter 7).

ITEMS AS INDICATORS AND OTHER METHODS FOR ANALYZING ITEMS

There are examples of "successful" CFA analyses where the indicators are Likert scale items instead of scales with continuous total scores (e.g., Harris, 1995), but there are potential problems. One is that default ML estimation is not generally appropriate for Likert-type items, which are ordinal variables. Some special methods for ordinal indicators were described in Chapter 7, including robust WLS estimation. These special methods can be more difficult to apply than ML estimation.

Another problem is that item-level data tend to be "noisy." Specifically, people's responses to individual items may be unstable, so item reliabilities can be low. Items in exploratory factor analysis (EFA) often have relatively high secondary loadings (e.g., about .30) on factors other than the one on which they have primary loadings (e.g., > .50). Secondary loadings in EFA often account for relatively high proportions of the variance, so constraining them to zero in CFA may be too conservative. Consequently, the more restrictive CFA model may not fit the data. This is one reason the specification of a CFA model based on EFA outcomes and analyzed with the same data may lead to the rejection of the CFA model (van Prooijen & van der Kloot, 2001). That is, CFA does not generally "confirm" the results of EFA.

An alternative to analyzing items as indicators with special estimators is to analyze parcels with a normal theory method, such as ML. Recall that (1) a parcel is a total score across a set of homogeneous items and (2) parceling is controversial because it requires items that are unidimensional for each parcel. If this assumption is not tenable, then the results may be misleading (Chapter 7).

In some situations, other statistical methods for item-level analyses are better alternatives than CFA. When constructing a scale, the derivation of classical items statistics, such as item-total correlations and item difficulties (the proportion of respondents who responded correctly), with procedures in general statistical programs for analyzing scales, such as the Reliability procedure in SPSS, offers more flexibility. This is also true for EFA, which analyzes unrestricted models where each item is allowed to load on every factor. A more sophisticated alternative is the generation of **item characteristic curves** (ICC) according to **item response theory** (IRT). Briefly, the analysis of ICC yields detailed estimates about characteristics of individual items, including their difficulty, discrimination (i.e., the degree to which an item discriminates among persons in different regions on a latent variable), and susceptibility to guessing. It is also assumed in IRT that relations between items and factors as represented by the ICC are nonlinear. For example, the probability of correctly answering a particular item may be slight for low-ability examinees but increases geometrically at increasingly higher levels of ability before leveling off. In contrast, CFA assumes linear associations between indicators (items in this case) and underlying factors. The IRT method is also oriented toward the development of **tailored tests**, subsets of items that may optimally assess a particular person based on the correctness of their previous responses. If the examinee fails initial items, for instance, then the computer presents easier ones. Testing stops when more difficult items are consistently failed. See Reise, Widaman, and Pugh (1993) for a comparison of CFA and IRT for item-level analyses. Noar (2007) considers the role of SEM in test development, and Kamata and Bauer (2008) compare the specification of two-parameter IRT models and factor analysis models for dichotomous items. The use of IRT/ICC analysis as an alternative to CFA for estimating measurement invariance at the item level is considered later.

ESTIMATED FACTOR SCORES

When raw data are analyzed, it is possible to calculate factor scores for each case. Because factors are measured not directly but instead through their indicators, such scores are only estimates of the cases' relative standings on the factor. There is more than one way to calculate factor scores, however, and although scores derived using different methods tend to be highly correlated, they generally do not all yield identical rank orderings of the cases. For example, given structure coefficients, multiple regression (MR) can be used to derive estimated factor scores that are weighted combinations of the indicators and the factor. The weights derived in MR are those that lead to the closest correspondence between the underlying factor(s) and the estimated factor scores. An alternative to empirically derived weights is simply to add the scores for each case across the indicators, which weights each variable equally. The application of equal weights is called **unit weighting**. This method has the advantage of simplicity and less susceptibility to sample-specific variation, but unit weights may not be optimal ones within a particular sample. Given that there is more than one way to derive estimated factor scores, Bollen's (1989) perspective on this matter is relevant: researchers should probably refrain from making too fine a comparison on estimated factor scores.

EQUIVALENT CFA MODELS

There are two sets of principles for generating equivalent CFA models—one for models with multiple factors and another for single-factor models. As an example of the former, consider the two-factor model of self-perception of ability and achievement by Kenny (1979) presented in Figure 9.2(a) without measurement errors to save space. I used the method of constrained ML estimation in the SEPATH module of STATISTICA 9 Advanced to fit this model to the correlation matrix reported in a sample of 556 Grade 8 students that is presented in Table 9.7. Values of selected fit statistics indicate acceptable overall model fit:

$$\chi^2_M (8) = 9.256, \quad p = .321$$
$$\text{RMSEA} = .012 \ (.017–.054)$$
$$\text{GFI} = .994; \quad \text{CFI} = .999; \quad \text{SRMR} = .012$$

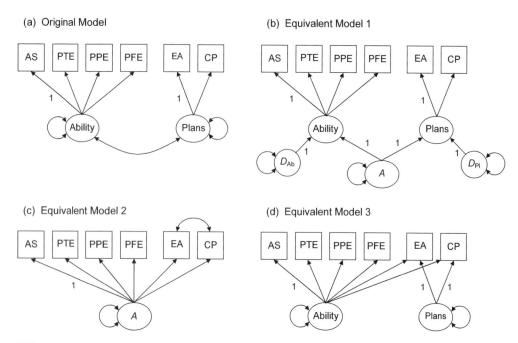

FIGURE 9.2. Four equivalent measurement models of self-perceived ability and educational plans. Measurement errors are omitted. The symbol for an unanalyzed association in (c) represents an error correlation between the corresponding pair of indicators. AS, Ability Self-Concept; PTE, Perceived Teacher Evaluation; PPE, Perceived Parental Evaluation; PFE, Perceived Friends' Evaluation; EA, Educational Aspiration; CP, College Plans.

The other three CFA models presented in Figure 9.2 are equivalent versions of the original model that yield the same values of fit statistics and predicted correlations. The equivalent model of Figure 9.2(b) is a hierarchical CFA model in which the unanalyzed association between the factors of the original model is replaced by a second-order factor (A), which has no indicators and is presumed to have direct effects on the first-order factors (ability, plans). This specification provides a specific account of *why* the two lower-order factors (which are endogenous in this model) covary. Because the second-

TABLE 9.7. Input Data (Correlations) for Analysis of Two-Factor Model of Perceived Ability and Educational Plans

Variable	1	2	3	4	5	6
1. Ability Self-Concept	1.00					
2. Perceived Parental Evaluation	.73	1.00				
3. Perceived Teacher Evaluation	.70	.68	1.00			
4. Perceived Friends' Evaluation	.58	.61	.57	1.00		
5. Education Aspiration	.46	.43	.40	.37	1.00	
6. College Plans	.56	.52	.48	.41	.71	1.00

Note. Input data are from Kenny (1979); $N = 556$.

order factor has only two indicators, it is necessary to constrain its direct effects on the first-order factors to be equal; that is:

$$A \rightarrow \text{Ability} = A \rightarrow \text{Plans} = 1.0$$

The other two equivalent versions are unique to models wherein some factors have only two indicators. The equivalent model in Figure 9.2(c) features the substitution of the plans factor with a correlation between the measurement error of its indicators. The equivalent model in Figure 9.2(d) features replacement of the correlation between the ability and plans factor with the specification that some indicators are multidimensional. Although the factors are assumed to be orthogonal in this model, all six indicators have loadings on a common factor, which explains the sample correlations just as well as the original model. Note that because the factors are specified as independent in the model of Figure 9.2(d), it is necessary to constrain the factor loadings of the educational aspiration and college plans indicators to be equal in order to identify this model.

For two reasons, the situation regarding equivalent versions of CFA models with multiple factors is even more complex than suggested by the last example. First, it is possible to apply the Lee–Hershberger replacing rules (Chapter 8) to substitute factor covariances (unanalyzed associations) with direct effects, which makes some factors endogenous. The resulting model is not a CFA model. It is an SR model, but it will fit the data equally well. For example, substitution of the factor covariance Ability ⌣⌃ Plans in the original model of Figure 9.2(a) with the direct effect Ability → Plans generates an equivalent SR model. Second, Raykov and Marcoulides (2001) show that there is actually a set of infinitely many equivalent models for standard multifactor CFA models. For each equivalent model in this set, the factor covariances are eliminated (orthogonality is specified) and replaced by one or more factors not represented in the original model with fixed unit loadings (1.0) on all indicators. These models with additional factors explain the data just as well as the original.

Equivalent versions of single-factor CFA models can be derived using Hershberger's (1994) **reversed indicator rule**, which involves the specification of one of the observed variables as a cause (formative) indicator while the rest remain as effect (reflective) indicators. Consider the hypothetical single-factor model of reading presented in Figure 9.3(a). The effect indicators represent different tasks, including word recognition, word attack, and phonics skills. An equivalent version is presented in Figure 9.3(b), and it features phonics skill as a cause of reading. Note that the factor in this equivalent model is no longer exogenous: because a casually prior variable (phonics skill) has a direct effect on it, the factor here is endogenous and thus has a disturbance. Also, the phonics skill indicator is exogenous in Figure 9.3(b). Thus, this equivalent model is actually an SR model. A total of three other equivalent models could potentially be generated, one with each of the remaining indicators specified as causes, Not all of these equivalent versions may be theoretically plausible, but at least the one with phonics skill as a cause indicator is logical (e.g., Wagner, Torgeson, & Rashotte, 1994).

The factor in Figure 9.3(b) is an example of a **multiple indicators and multiple**

(a) Original Model with Effect Indicators

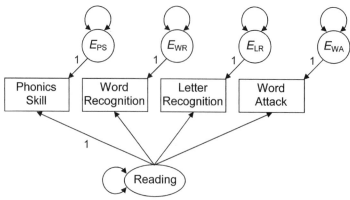

(b) Equivalent Model with a Cause Indicator

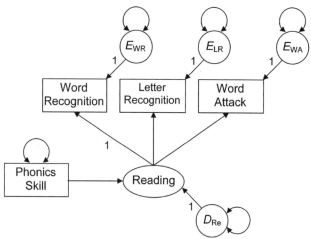

FIGURE 9.3. Application of the reversed indicator rule to generate an equivalent one-factor model of reading.

causes (MIMIC) factor. A MIMIC factor has both cause indicators and effect indicators, and they can be continuous as in the previous example or categorical. A categorical cause indicator represents group membership. We will see in Chapter 11 that a MIMIC model with a cause indicator is a special case of the SEM approach to estimating group differences on latent variables.

HIERARCHICAL CFA MODELS

It is possible to represent hypotheses about hierarchical relations among constructs through the specification of higher-order factors with presumed direct causal effects on lower-order factors. For example, the hierarchical CFA model in Figure 9.4 represents the hypotheses that (1) indicators X_1–X_3 measure verbal ability, X_4–X_6 reflect visual-spatial ability, and X_7–X_9 depend on memory ability; and (2) each of these **first-order factors** has two direct causes. One is a **second-order factor**, which represents a general ability construct (g) with no indicators. This is because second-order factors are measured indirectly through the indicators of the first-order factors. The specification of g as a common cause of the first-order factors implies that associations between the latter are spurious. The other presumed direct cause of each first-order factor is a disturbance, which represents factor variance not explained by g. Thus, the disturbances and g are exogenous, but the first-order factors are endogenous in Figure 9.4.

To identify a hierarchical CFA model, there must be at least three first-order factors. Otherwise, the direct effects of the second-order factor on the first-order factors or the disturbance variances may be underidentified. Each first-order factor should have at least two indicators. The model in Figure 9.4 satisfies both of these requirements. There are two ways to scale the second-order factor g in the figure. One way is to fix any one of g's unstandardized direct effects on a first-order factor to 1.0. This tactic corresponds to the specification

$$g \rightarrow \text{Verbal Ability} = 1.0$$

in Figure 9.4. A second option is to fix the variance of g to 1.0 (standardize it). This approach leaves all three direct effects of g on the first-order factors as free parameters.

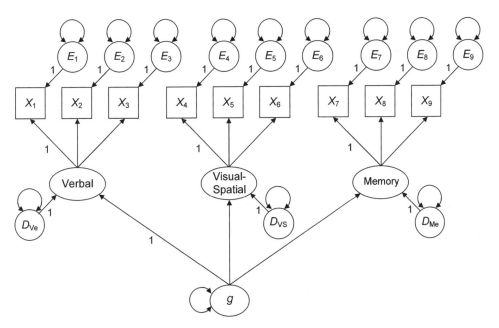

FIGURE 9.4. A hierarchical confirmatory factor analysis model of the structure of cognitive ability.

Either means of scaling g in a single-sample analysis is probably fine. In a multiple-sample analysis, however, it is typically inappropriate to standardize factors. See Neuman, Bolin, and Briggs (2000), who analyzed a hierarchical model of cognitive ability similar to that represented in Figure 9.4 for a group-administered test.

MODELS FOR MULTITRAIT–MULTIMETHOD DATA

The method of CFA can also be used to analyze data from a **multitrait–multimethod** (MTMM) study, the logic of which was first articulated by Campbell and Fiske (1959). In an MTMM study, two or more traits are measured with two or more methods. Traits are hypothetical constructs that concern cognitive abilities, personality attributes, or other stable characteristics. Methods refer to multiple test forms, occasions, methods (e.g., self-report), or informants (e.g., parents) (Marsh & Grayson, 1995). The main goals are to (1) evaluate the convergent and discriminant validity of tests that vary in their measurement method and (2) derive separate estimates of the effects of traits versus methods on the observed scores.

The earliest procedure for analyzing data from an MTMM study involved inspection of the correlation matrix for all variables. For example, convergent validity would be indicated by the observation of high correlations among variables that supposedly measure the same trait but with different methods. If correlations among variables that should measure different traits but use the same methods are relatively high, then **common method effects** are indicated. This would imply that correlations among different variables based on the same method may be relatively high even if they measure unrelated traits.

The CFA method offers a more systematic way to analyze data from an MTMM study. When first applied to the problem in the 1970s, researchers typically specified CFA models like the one presented in Figure 9.5, a **correlated trait-correlated method** (CTCM) model. Such models have separate trait and method factors that are assumed to covary, but method factors are assumed to be independent of trait factors. In the figure, indicators X_1–X_3 are based on one method, X_4–X_6 are based on another method, and X_7–X_9 are based on a third method. This model also specifies that the set of indicators (X_1, X_4, X_7) measures one trait but that each of the other two sets, (X_2, X_5, X_8) and (X_3, X_6, X_9), measures different traits. Given these specifications, relatively high loadings on trait factors would suggest convergent validity, high loadings on method factors would indicate common method effects, and moderate correlations (not too high) between the factors would indicate discriminant validity.

There are reports of "successful" analyses of CTCM models (e.g., Villar, Luengo, Gómez-Fraguela, & Romero, 2006), but others have found that such analyses tend to yield inadmissible or unstable solutions. For example, Marsh and Bailey (1991) found in computer simulation studies that illogical estimates were derived about three-quarters of the time for CTCM models. Kenny and Kashy (1992) noted part of the problem: CTCM models are not identified if the loadings on the trait or method factors are equal.

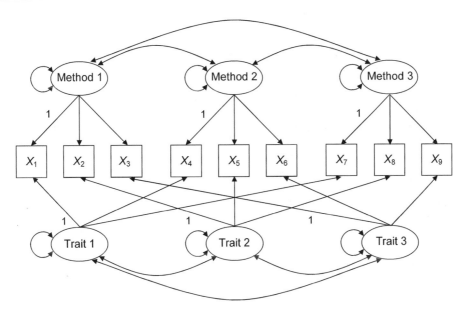

FIGURE 9.5. A correlated-trait correlated method (CTCM) model for multitrait–multimethod data. Measurement errors are omitted and assumed to be independent.

If the loadings are different but similar in value, then CTCM models may be empirically underidentified.

Some simpler alternatives to CTCM models have been proposed, including those with multiple but uncorrelated method factors, a single-method factor specified to affect all the indicators, and a model like the one in Figure 9.6, which is a **correlated uniqueness** (CU) model (Marsh & Grayson, 1995). This model has measurement error correlations among indicators based on the same method instead of separate method factors. That is, method effects are assumed to be a property of each indicator, and relatively high correlations among their residuals are taken as evidence for common method variance. Note that the similarity of methods for different traits is only one possible explanation for high measurement error correlations in CU models. Saris and Alberts (2003) evaluated alternative CFA models that could account for correlated residuals in CU models, including models that represented response biases, effects due to relative answers (when respondents compare their answers), and method effects. See Brown (2006, chap. 6) and Eid et al. (2008) for more information about MTMM analyses with CFA.

MEASUREMENT INVARIANCE AND MULTIPLE-SAMPLE CFA

Broadly defined, **measurement invariance (equivalence)** concerns whether scores from the operationalization of a construct have the same meaning under different conditions (Meade & Lautenschlager, 2004). These different conditions could involve consistency of measurement over populations, time of measurement, or methods of test administration

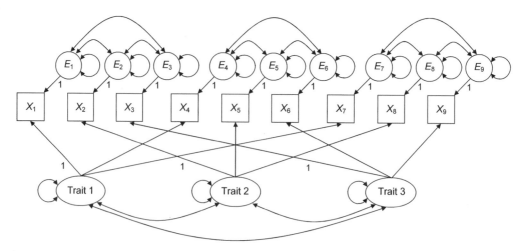

FIGURE 9.6. A correlated uniqueness (CU) model for multitrait–multimethod data.

(e.g., computer administered vs. paper-and-pencil format). Stability over time is referred to as **longitudinal measurement invariance**, and it concerns whether a set of indicators has the same factor structure across different occasions in a longitudinal design. If so, then measurement is invariant over time. Invariance over populations is related to the concept of **construct bias**, which implies that a test measures something different in one group (e.g., men) than in another (women). If not (i.e., there is no evidence for construct bias), then measurement is invariant over groups. The CFA technique is widely used to test hypotheses about measurement invariance over groups. Because the basic logic of invariance testing over groups is the same as for invariance testing over time or modes of test administration, only the former is described next. See Brown (2006, pp. 252–266) for an example of testing for longitudinal measurement invariance. See also Whitaker and McKinney (2007), who studied the invariance of job satisfaction ratings as a function of administration method (Internet vs. paper-and-pencil format) and respondent age and gender.

Testing Strategy

Hypotheses about measurement invariance over groups are tested in **multiple-sample CFA** where a measurement model is simultaneously fitted to the covariance matrices from at least two independent samples. The most basic form of measurement invariance is **configural invariance** or **equal form invariance**. It is tested by specifying the same measurement model across the groups. In this model, both the number of factors and the factor-indicator correspondence are the same, but all parameters are freely estimated within each sample. If this model does not fit the data, then measurement invariance does not hold at any level. Otherwise, the configural invariance hypothesis, H_{form}, is retained. If so, then the researcher could conclude that the same constructs are manifested in somewhat different ways in each group. These "different ways" refer to the unstandardized factor loadings, which were freely estimated in each group. This means that if factor scores were calculated, a different weighing scheme would be applied to the indicators in each group.

A stronger form of measurement invariance is **construct-level metric invariance** or **equal factor loadings**, which means that the unstandardized factor loadings of each indicator are equal across the groups. If the equal factor loadings hypothesis, or H_Λ, is retained, then the researcher could conclude that the constructs are manifested the same way in each group. This implies that if factor scores were calculated, the same weighing scheme could be applied across all groups. The hypothesis H_Λ is tested by (1) imposing cross-group equality constraints on the factor loadings and (2) comparing with the chi-square difference test two hierarchical models, one that corresponds to H_Λ and the other corresponds to H_{form}, which was estimated with no equality constraints. This assumes that H_{form} was not rejected.

If χ_D^2 for the comparison just described is not statistically significant, then the fit of the model with equality-constrained factor loadings is not appreciably worse than that of the model without these constraints. That is, H_Λ is retained. If so, the researcher can go on to test even stronger forms of measurement invariance, described momentarily. If H_Λ is rejected, though, the less strict hypothesis of **partial measurement invariance**, or H_λ, can be tested by releasing some, but not all, of the cross-group equality constraints on the unstandardized factor loadings. The goal is to locate the indicator(s) responsible for metric noninvariance at the construct level (Cheung & Rensvold, 2002). In subsequent analyses, the unstandardized loadings of these indicators are freely estimated in each sample, but the loadings of the remaining indicators are constrained to be equal across the groups. Indicators with appreciably different loadings across groups are **differential functioning indicators (items)**, and the pattern where some, but not all indicators have equal loadings in every group is **indicator-level metric invariance** (i.e., H_λ). The hypothesis of partial measurement invariance is tested by χ_D^2 for the comparison of the less restricted model represented by H_{form} with the more restricted model represented by H_λ.

One can also test additional hypotheses about even stricter forms of invariance. The hypotheses described next all generally assume that H_Λ (equal factor loadings hypothesis) was not rejected. For example, the **equivalence of construct variances and covariances** hypothesis, or $H_{\Lambda, \Phi}$, assumes that the factor variances and covariances are equal across the groups. The **equivalence of residual variances and covariances** hypothesis, or $H_{\Lambda, \Theta}$, assumes that the measurement error variance for each indicator and all corresponding error covariances (if any) are equal across the groups. Each of these hypotheses is tested by comparing with χ_D^2 the less restricted model implied by H_Λ with the more restricted model represented by $H_{\Lambda, \Phi}$ or $H_{\Lambda, \Theta}$. See Cheung and Rensvold (2002) for more information about measurement invariance hypotheses.

The testing strategy just outlined corresponds to model trimming where an initial unconstrained model (represented by H_{form}) is gradually restricted by adding constraints (e.g., next test H_Λ by constraining factor loadings to be equal across groups). It is also possible to test for measurement invariance through model building where constraints on an initially restricted model, such as one represented by $H_{\Lambda, \Theta}$ (equal loadings and error variances–covariances), are gradually released (e.g., next test H_Λ by allowing error variances–covariances to be freely estimated in each group). The goal of both approaches is the same: find the most restricted model that still fits the data and respects theory. That theory may dictate which hypothesis testing approach, model trimming or building, is best.

Cheung and Rensvold (2002) remind us that the chi-square difference test is affected by overall sample size. In invariance testing with very large samples, this means that χ^2_D could be statistically significant, even though the absolute differences in parameter estimates are of trivial magnitude. That is, the outcome of the chi-square difference test could indicate the lack of measurement invariance when the imposition of cross-group equality constraints makes relatively little difference in model fit. One way to detect this outcome is to compare the unstandardized parameter estimates across the two solutions. Another is to inspect changes in values of approximate fit indexes, but there are few guidelines for doing so in invariance testing. In two-group computer simulation analyses, Cheung and Rensvold (2002) studied the characteristics of changes in the values of 20 different approximate fit indexes when invariance constraints were added. Changes in most indexes were affected by model characteristics, including the number of factors or the number of indicators per factor. That is, model size and complexity were generally confounded with changes in approximate fit indexes. An exception is the Bentler CFI, for which Cheung and Rensvold (2002) suggested that change in CFI values less than or equal to .01 (i.e., ΔCFI $\leq$ .01) indicate that the null hypothesis of invariance should *not* be rejected. Of course, this suggested threshold is not a golden rule, nor should it be treated as such. Specifically, it is unknown whether this rule of thumb would generalize to other models or data sets not directly studied by Cheung and Rensvold (2002). A second approximate fit index that performed relatively well in Cheung and Rensvold's (2002) simulations is McDonald's (1989) **noncentrality index** (NCI).[2]

Meade, Johnson, and Braddy (2008) extended the work of Cheung and Rensvold (2002) by studying the performance of several approximate fit indexes in generated data with different levels of lack of measurement invariance, from trivial to severe. Types of lack of measurement invariance studied by Meade et al. (2008) included different factor structures (forms), factor loadings, and indicator intercepts across two groups. In very large samples studied by Meade et al. (2008), such as $n = 6,400$ per group, the χ^2_D statistic indicated lack of measurement invariance most of the time when there were just slight differences in measurement model parameters across the groups. In contrast, values of approximate fit indexes were generally less affected by group size and also by the number of factors and indicator than the chi-square difference test in large samples. The Bentler CFI was among the best performing approximate fit indexes along with the McDonald NCI. Based on their results, Meade et al. (2008) suggested that change in CFI

---

[2] NCI = exp[$-\frac{1}{2}$ ($\chi^2_M - df_M$) / N] where "exp" is the exponential function e^x and e is the natural base, approximately 2.71828. The range of the NCI is 0–1.0 where 1.0 indicates the best fit. Mulaik (2009) notes that values of the NCI tend to drop off quickly from 1.0 with small increases in lack of fit.

values less than or equal to .002 (i.e., ΔCFI $\leq$ .002) may indicate that deviations from perfect measurement invariance are functionally trivial. These authors also provide a table of values for changes in the NCI that vary depending on the number of factors and indicators (Meade et al., 2008, p. 586). Again, these suggested thresholds are not golden rules, but results by Cheung and Rensvold (2002) and Meade et al. (2008) indicate that researchers working with very large samples should look more to approximate fit indexes than statistical tests to establish measurement invariance.

Empirical Example

Sabatelli and Bartle–Haring (2003) administered to each spouse in a total of 103 married heterosexual couples three indicators of family-of-origin experiences (FOE) and two indicators of marital adjustment. The indicators of FOE are retrospective measures of the perceived quality of each spouse's relationship with his or her own father or mother and of the relationship between the parents while growing up. The marital adjustment indicators are ratings of problems and intimacy in the marital relationship. Higher scores on all variables indicate more positive reports of FOE or marital adjustment. Presented in Table 9.8 are descriptive statistics for these variables in the samples of husbands and wives. Note that means are reported in the table, but they are not analyzed here.[3]

TABLE 9.8. Input Data (Correlations, Standard Deviations) for a Two-Factor Model of Family-of-Origin Experiences and Marital Adjustment Analyzed across Samples of Husbands and Wives

Variable		1	2	3	4	5	Husbands M	SD
Marital adjustment indicators								
1. Problems		—	.658	.288	.171	.264	155.547	31.168
2. Intimacy		.740	—	.398	.295	.305	137.971	20.094
Family-of-origin experiences indicators								
3. Father		.265	.422	—	.480	.554	82.764	11.229
4. Mother		.305	.401	.791	—	.422	85.494	11.743
5. Father–Mother		.315	.351	.662	.587	—	81.003	13.220
Wives	M	161.779	138.382	86.229	86.392	85.046		
	SD	32.936	22.749	13.390	13.679	14.382		

Note. These data are from S. Bartle-Haring (personal communication, June 3, 2003); n_1 = 103 husbands (above diagonal), n_2 = 103 wives (below diagonal). Means are reported but not analyzed for the model in Figure 9.7, but means are analyzed for the model in Figure 11.5.

---

[3]It could be argued that the samples in this analysis—husbands and wives—are not really independent groups because each spousal pair is "linked" across the two samples. An alternative way to view this data set is that individuals are nested under pairs (couples); that is, the data are hierarchical and thus amenable to a multilevel analysis. This possibility is not pursued in this pedagogical example.

Scaling Factors in Multiple-Sample Analyses

The two factor, five-indicator model for this example is presented in Figure 9.7. The best way to scale the factors in a multiple-sample analysis is to select the same reference variable for each factor in each group. Here, the unstandardized loadings of the father indicator and the problems indicator were fixed to 1.0 in order to scale their respective factors in both samples. However, there are two potential complications: First, loadings fixed to 1.0 in both groups cannot be tested for statistical significance. The second complication follows from the first: because fixed loadings are excluded from tests of measurement invariance, it must be assumed a priori that the reference variables measure their factors equally well over groups. This assumption means that if the researcher decides to fix the loading of an indicator that is not metric invariant across the groups, then the subsequent results may be inaccurate. One way to address this dilemma is to reanalyze the model after fixing the loadings of other indicators to 1.0. If the unstandardized factor loadings that were originally fixed are comparable in the new analysis in which they are free parameters, then that indicator may be metric invariant. See Reise et al. (1993) for more information about factor scaling when testing for measurement invariance. Little, Slegers, and Card (2006) describe a method to scale factors in a multiple-group analysis that involves neither the arbitrary selection of a reference variable nor the standardization of factors. This method may be specially well suited to applications of CFA where group differences on factor means (i.e., the model has both a covariance structure and a mean structure) are also estimated (Chapter 11).

Invariance Testing

With five indicators in each of two samples, there are a total of 5(6)/2 × 2, or 30 observation for the analysis. Because the samples consist of married couples who share many experiences, the initial model assumed a strict form of invariance—one that corresponds

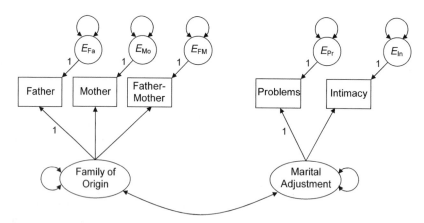

FIGURE 9.7. A measurement model of family-of-origin experiences and marital adjustment evaluated across samples of husbands and wives.

to $H_{\Lambda,\,\Phi,\,\Theta}$, or equivalence of factors loadings, factor variances–covariance, and error variances–covariances for husbands and wives. This means that cross-group equality constraints were imposed on the estimates of three factor loadings (those not already fixed to 1.0), seven variances (of two factors and five measurement errors), and one factor covariance (see Figure 9.7). There are no error covariances in the initial model, so it is assumed that all of these values are zero in both samples. Because only one estimate of each free parameter was required when equality was assumed across the samples, a total of 11 parameters require estimates across both samples, so $df_M = 30 - 11 = 19$.

I used the ML method of EQS 6.1 to simultaneously fit the model of Figure 9.7 with cross-group equality constraints to the covariance matrices for husbands and wives based on the data in Table 9.8. The program printed this warning:

```
            Do not trust this output
      Iterative process has not converged
    Maximum number of iterations was reached
 30 iterations have been completed and the program stopped
```

That is, a converged solution was not reached after 30 iterations, the default limit in EQS. In a second run with EQS, I increased its iteration limit to 100. In this second analysis, EQS generated a converged and admissible solution. Reported in Table 9.9 are values of selected fit statistics for the test of $H_{\Lambda,\,\Phi,\,\Theta}$. Because the group sizes in this analysis are not large ($n = 103$), we focus on the chi-square difference test when comparing nested models. To summarize, the initial model passes the chi-square test ($\chi_M^2(19) = 23.190$, $p = .229$), so the hypothesis of exact fit is not rejected. Values of some approximate fit indexes seem favorable (GFI = .959, CFI = .990), but the upper bound of the 90% confidence interval based on the RMSEA (.103) just exceeds .10. The result for the SRMR, .127, is not favorable (Table 9.9). Across both samples, there were a total of 16 absolute correlation residuals > .10 (9 for husbands, 7 for wives). This is a terrible result; therefore, the initial model is rejected.

TABLE 9.9. Values of Selected Fit Statistics for Hypotheses about Measurement Invariance for a Two-Factor Model of Family-of-Origin Experiences and Marital Adjustment Analyzed across Samples of Husbands and Wives

Hypothesis	χ_M^2	df_M	χ_D^2	df_D	RMSEA (90% CI)	GFI	CFI	SRMR
$H_{\Lambda,\,\Phi,\,\Theta}$	23.190^a	19	—	—	.047 (0–.103)	.959	.990	.127
$H_{\Lambda,\,\Theta}$	16.127^b	16	7.063^c	3	0 (0–.092)	.970	.999	.037
$H_{\Lambda,\,\Theta}$ except $E_{Fa} \curvearrowleft E_{Mo}$ in both groups	7.097^d	14	9.030^e	2	0 (0–.028)	.987	1.000	.026

Note. CI, confidence interval; $H_{\Lambda,\,\Phi,\,\Theta}$, equal loadings, factor variances–covariances, and measurement error variances–covariances.

$^a p = .229$; $^b p = .444$; $^c p = .070$; $^d p = .931$; $^e p = .011$.

In the next analysis, the factor variances–covariance for the model in Figure 9.7 were freely estimated in each sample (i.e., the corresponding cross-group equality constraints were dropped). This respecified model corresponds to the invariance hypothesis $H_{\Lambda, \Theta}$, which assumes equal factor loadings and measurement error variances only. This second analysis converged to an admissible solution, and values of selected fit statistics are reported in Table 9.9. The second model passes the chi-square test (χ^2_M (16) = 16.127, p = .444), and the improvement in overall fit due to dropping the equality constraint on the factor variances-covariance is almost statistically significant (χ^2_D (3) = 7.063, p = .070). The value of the SRMR is better for the second model (.037) compared with that of the original model (.127). The largest absolute correlations are −.094 for husbands and .066 for wives, both for the association between the father and mother indicators of the FOE factor. The only statistically significant modification indexes in both samples were for the error covariances between the indicators just mentioned: husbands: χ^2 (1) = 7.785, p < .01; wives: χ^2 (1) = 7.959, p < .01.

Because it is plausible that reports about quality of relationships with one's parents may have common omitted causes, the third CFA model was respecified so that the error covariances between the father and mother indicators of the FOE factor ($E_{Fa} \curvearrowright E_{Mo}$; Figure 9.7) were freely estimated in each sample. Values of selected fit statistics for this third model are reported in Table 9.9, and their values are generally favorable. For example, the improvement in overall fit compared with the second model without error covariances is statistically significant (χ^2_D (2) = 9.030, p = .011), and values of approximate fit indexes are generally good (e.g., RMSEA = 0). Furthermore, all absolute correlation residuals in both samples are < .10.

Based on these results, the third CFA model was retained as the final measurement model. To summarize, this model assumes that all factor loadings and measurement error variances are equal for husbands and wives. In contrast, the factor variances and covariance and the error covariance between the father and mother indicators were freely estimated in each sample. Overall, it seems that the five indicators represented in Figure 9.7 measure the same two factors in similar ways for both husbands and wives. You can download from the website for this book (see p. 3) the EQS syntax and output files for this analysis. Computer files for the same analysis but in LISREL and Mplus are also available for download from the site, too.

Parameter Estimates

Reported in the top part of Table 9.10 are ML parameter estimates for the final measurement model that were freely estimated in each sample. Wives may be somewhat more variable than husbands on both factors. For example, the estimated variance of the marital adjustment factor is 583.685 among wives but 452.140 among husbands. Although the estimated factor covariance is also somewhat greater for wives than for husbands (139.534 vs. 93.067, respectively), the estimated factor correlation in both samples is about .50. These correlations are consistent with discriminant validity in factor measurement because their values are not too high. Although neither error covariance between the father and mother indicators of the FOE factor is statistically significant for husbands or wives, their values have opposite signs, negative for husbands (−12.617) but positive for wives (16.351).

Reported in the bottom part of Table 9.10 are estimates for parameters of the measurement model constrained to have equal unstandardized values across the samples. Because the sizes of the groups are the same ($n = 103$), the standard errors of these estimates are also equal for husbands and wives. The pattern of standardized factor loadings is generally similar within each sample and consistent with convergent validity in factor measurement. Note in the table that, although the unstandardized factor loadings are equal for every indicator across the two samples, such as .885 for the mother indicator of the FOE factor, the corresponding standardized factor loadings are not equal. For example, the standardized loading of the mother indicator is .698 for husbands and .779 for wives (Table 9.10). This pattern is expected because EQS derives standardized estimates based on the separate variances and covariances within each group. If the groups

TABLE 9.10. Maximum Likelihood Parameter Estimates for a Two-Factor Model of Family-of-Origin Experiences and Marital Adjustment Analyzed across Samples of Husbands and Wives

Parameter	Husbands			Wives		
	Unst.	*SE*	St.	Unst.	*SE*	St.
			Unconstrained estimates			
Factor variances and covariance						
FOE	87.896	21.438	1.000	143.102	30.412	1.000
Mar Adj	452.140	105.126	1.000	583.685	146.837	1.000
FOE ⌣ Mar Adj	93.067	27.853	.467	139.534	40.774	.483
Measurement error covariance						
E_{Fa} ⌣ E_{Mo}	−12.617[a]	15.364	−.246	16.351[a]	15.634	.319
			Equality-constrained estimates			
Factor loadings						
Mar Adj → Probs	1.000[b]	—	.685	1.000[b]	—	.730
Mar Adj → Intim	.933	.146	.988	.933	.146	.991
FOE → Father	1.000[b]	—	.841	1.000[b]	—	.893
FOE → Mother	.885	.079	.698	.885	.079	.779
FOE → Fa-Mo	.897	.143	.648	.897	.143	.735
Measurement error variances						
E_{Pr}	510.199	88.407	.530	510.199	88.407	.466
E_{In}	9.687[a]	63.179	.024	9.687[a]	63.179	.019
E_{Fa}	36.249[c]	16.928	.291	36.249[c]	16.928	.202
E_{Mo}	72.411	16.533	.513	72.411	16.533	.392
E_{Fa-Mo}	97.868	16.264	.580	97.868	16.264	.459

Note. Unst., unstandardized; St., standardized; FOE, family-of-origin experiences. Standardized estimates for measurement errors are proportions of unexplained variance.

[a]$p \geq .05$; [b]Not tested for statistical significance; [c]$p < .05$; for all other unstandardized estimates, $p < .01$.

do not have the same variances and covariances (likely), then one cannot directly compare standardized estimates across the groups (Chapter 2).

Note that LISREL can optionally print up to *four* different standardized solutions in a multiple-sample analysis, including the *within-group standardized solution* and the *within-group completely standardized solution*. Both are derived from standardizing the within-group variances–covariance matrices except that only the factors are standardized in the former solution versus all variables in the latter solution. The third is LISREL's *common metric standardized solution* where the factors only are automatically scaled so that the weighted average of their covariance matrices across the samples is a correlation matrix. In contrast, all variables are so scaled in the fourth solution, the *common metric completely standardized solution*. The common metric standardized estimates may be more directly comparable across the groups than are the within-group standardized estimates, but the unstandardized estimates are still preferred for this purpose. Check the documentation of your SEM computer tool to find out how it calculates a standardized solution in a multiple-sample analysis. Raykov and Marcoulides (2000) describe a method for comparing completely standardized estimates across equal-size groups based on analyzing a correlation structure using the method of constrained estimation (Chapter 7).

Any type of structural equation model—path models, SR models, and so on—can be tested across multiple samples. The imposition of cross-group equality constraints on certain parameters allows for tests of group differences on these parameters, just as in testing for measurement invariance in CFA. In Chapter 11, I will show you how to compare two groups on latent variable means in SEM.

Alternative Methods for Item-Level Analysis of Measurement Invariance

The indicators in the empirical example just described are scales, not items. When the indicators are items instead of scales, however, IRT/ICC analysis may be a better alternative in some cases than CFA. Results of a recent computer simulation study by Meade and Lautenschlager (2004) are relevant in this regard. These authors studied the relative capabilities of CFA and IRT/ICC analysis to detect differential item functioning across groups in generated data sets for samples of three different sizes (N = 150, 500, and 1,000) and for a six-item scale that measured a single factor (i.e., unidimensional items). Neither CFA nor IRT/ICC analysis performed well in the smallest sample size, but these results were expected. In larger samples, the CFA technique was generally inadequate at detecting items with differences in discrimination parameters. The CFA methods were also generally unable to detect items with differences in difficulty parameters. In contrast, the IRT/ICC methods were generally better at detecting items with either type of differential functioning just mentioned. As noted by Meade and Lautenschlager (2004), however, the application of IRT/ICC methods to multiscale tests where different sets of items are assigned to different scales (i.e., multiple factors are measured) is problematic compared with CFA. This is because IRT/ICC methods provide no information about covariances between factors, which may be of interest in testing for measurement invariance at the scale level. Accordingly, Meade and Lautenschlager (2004) suggested that both techniques could be applied in the same analysis: IRT/ICC methods for item-level analyses within each scale, and CFA methods for scale-level analyses, both of measurement invariance. Along similar lines, Stark, Chernyshenko, and Drasgow (2006) describe and test in computer simulations a common strategy for identifying differential item functioning using either IRT/ICC of CFA.

Power in Multiple-Sample CFA

The relatively small group sizes ($n = 103$) in this example analysis limits the statistical power to detect lack of measurement invariance. In a recent computer simulation study, Meade and Bauer (2007) found that the power of tests to detect group differences in factor loadings was uniformly low (e.g., $< .40$) when the group size was 100. In contrast, power was generally high when the group size was 400, but power estimates for an intermediate group size of 200 were highly variable. This is because the power of tests for measurement invariance is affected not just by sample size but also by model and data characteristics, including the number of indicators per factor and the magnitudes of factor intercorrelations. Accordingly, Meade and Bauer's (2007) results did not indicate a single rule of thumb regarding a ratio of group size to the number of indicators that could ensure adequate power to detect the absence of measurement invariance when the group size is not large. In any event, large group sizes are typically needed in order to have reasonable statistical power when testing for measurement invariance.

SUMMARY

Many types of hypotheses about measurement can be tested with standard CFA models. For example, the evaluation of a model with multiple factors that specifies unidimensional measurement provides specific tests of both convergent and discriminant validity. Respecification of a measurement model can be challenging because many possible changes could be made to a given model. Another problem is that of equivalent measurement models. The only way to deal with both of these challenges is to rely more on substantive knowledge than on statistical considerations in model evaluation. When analyzing structural equation models across multiple samples, it is common to impose cross-group equality constraints on certain unstandardized parameter estimates. In multiple-sample analyses, cross-group equality constraints are typically imposed to test hypotheses of measurement invariance. There are degrees of measurement invariance, but a common tactic is to constrain just the unstandardized factor loadings to be equal across the groups. If the fit of the measurement model with constrained factor loadings is much worse than that of the unconstrained model, then one may conclude that the indicators measure the factors in different ways across the groups.

RECOMMENDED READINGS

The book by Brown (2006) is an excellent resource for CFA. It also includes many examples of Amos, CALIS, EQS, LISREL, and Mplus syntax for analyzing measurement models. The shorter work by Harrington (2009) is less technical and intended for social work researchers, but readers from other disciplines would be familiar with the substantive examples. The accessible presentation by Thompson (2004) deals with both EFA and CFA. Schmitt and Kuljanin (2008) describe issues in the evaluation of measurement invariance in the human resource management area.

Brown, T. A. (2006). *Confirmatory factor analysis for applied research.* New York: Guilford Press.

Harrington, D. (2009). *Confirmatory factor analysis.* New York: Oxford University Press.

Schmitt, N., & Kuljanin, G. (2008). Measurement invariance: Review of practice and limitations. *Human Resource Management Review, 18,* 210–222.

Thompson, B. (2004). *Exploratory and confirmatory factor analysis: Understanding concepts and applications.* Washington, DC: American Psychological Association.

EXERCISES

1. Reproduce the values of the structure coefficients in Table 9.3 using the tracing rule for the model in Figure 9.1 and the parameter estimates in Table 9.2.

2. Use an SEM computer tool to derive the standardized residuals for the corresponding correlation residuals in Table 9.5 for the model in Figure 9.1 and the data in Table 9.1.

3. Show the calculation of $\hat{\rho}_{X_i X_i} = .786$ for the simultaneous processing factor in Figure 9.1 with the parameter estimates in Table 9.2. (See Topic Box 9.1.)

4. Evaluate the fit of a respecified version of the model in Figure 9.1 but with a direct effect from the simultaneous processing factor to the Hand Movements task against the data in Table 9.1.

5. Derive df_M for the hierarchical CFA model in Figure 9.4.

6. Use an SEM computer tool to test the hypothesis H_{form} for the model in Figure 9.7 with the data in Table 9.8; do not include any error covariances in this analysis. Look *carefully* through the output. What did you find?

7. Why would it be incorrect to scale the factors in a multiple-sample CFA by fixing their variances to 1.0 in all samples?

Start Value Suggestions for Measurement Models

These recommendations concern measurement models, whether those models are CFA models or part of an SR model. Unstandardized variables, including the factors, are assumed. Initial estimates of factor variances should probably not exceed 90% of that of the observed (sample) variance for the corresponding reference variable. Start values for factor covariances follow the initial estimates of their variances. That is, they are the product of each factor's standard deviation (the square root of the initial estimates of their variances) and the expected correlation between them. If the indicators of the same factor have similar variances to that of the reference variable, then initial estimates of their factor loadings can also be 1.0. If the reference variable is, say, one-tenth as variable as another indicator of the same factor, the initial estimate of the other indicator's factor loading could be 10.0. Conservative start values for measurement error variances could be 90% of the observed variance of the associated indicator, which assumes that only 10% of the variance will be explained. Bentler (1995) suggests that it is probably better to overestimate the variances of exogenous variables than to underestimate them. This advice is also appropriate for Heywood cases of the type where a variance estimate is negative: in the reanalysis of the model, try a start value that is higher than that in the previous run.

Constraint Interaction in Measurement Models

Suppose that a researcher specifies a standard two-factor CFA model where the indicators of factors A are X_1 and X_2 and the indicators of factor B are X_3 and X_4. The sample covariance matrix where the order of the variables is X_1 to X_4 and $N = 200$ is as shown here:

$$\begin{bmatrix} 25.00 & & & \\ 7.20 & 9.00 & & \\ 3.20 & 2.00 & 4.00 & \\ 2.00 & 1.25 & 1.20 & 4.00 \end{bmatrix} \tag{I}$$

It is believed that the unstandardized loadings of X_2 and X_4 on their respective factors are equal. To test this hypothesis, an equality constraint is imposed on the unstandardized estimates, or

$$A \rightarrow X_2 = B \rightarrow X_4$$

and this restricted model is compared to the one without this constraint. Ideally, the value of $\chi_D^2(1)$ for this comparison should not be affected by how the factors are scaled, but this ideal is not realized for this example. If X_1 and X_3 are the reference variables for their respective unstandardized factors, then $\chi_D^2(1) = 0$. However, if instead the factor variances are fixed to 1.0 (standardized), then $\chi_D^2(1) = 14.017$ (calculated in LISREL) for the same comparison. (Try it!)

This unexpected result is an example of constraint interaction, which means that the value of the chi-square difference statistic for the test of the equality constraint depends on how the factors are scaled. It happens in this example because the imposition of the cross-factor equality constraint has the unintended consequence of making unnecessary one of the two identification constraints that scale the factors. However, removing the unnecessary identification constraint from the model with the equality constraint would result in two nonhierarchical models with equal degrees of freedom. That is, we could not conduct the chi-square difference test.

Steiger (2002) describes this test for constraint interaction: Obtain χ_M^2 for the model with the cross-factor equality constraint. If the factors are unstandardized, fix the factor loading of the reference variable to a different constant, such as 2.0. If the factors are standardized, fix the variance of one of these factors to a constant other than 1.0. Fit the model so modified to the same data. If the value of χ_M^2 for the modified model is not identical to that of the original, constraint interaction is present. If so, the choice of how to scale the factors should be based on substantive grounds. If no such grounds exist, the test results for the equality constraint may not be meaningful. See Gonzalez and Griffin (2001) for a discussion about how the estimation of standard errors in SEM is not always invariant to how the factors are scaled.

10

Structural Regression Models

Structural regression (SR) models are syntheses of path models and measurement models. They are the most general of all the core types of structural equation models considered to this point. As in path analysis, the specification of an SR model allows tests of hypotheses about effect priority. Unlike path models, though, these effects can involve latent variables because an SR model also incorporates a multiple-indicator measurement model, just as in CFA. The capability to simultaneously test hypotheses about both structural and measurement relations with a single model distinguishes SEM from other techniques. Discussed next are strategies for testing SR models. Also considered is the estimation of models where some latent variables have cause (formative) indicators instead of the more usual case where all factors have effect (reflective) indicators. The advanced techniques described in the next part of this book extend the rationale of SR models to other kinds of analyses.

ANALYZING SR MODELS

A theme common to the specification and identification of SR models (Chapters 5, 6) is that a valid measurement model is needed before it makes sense to evaluate the structural part of the model. This theme carries over to the two approaches to testing SR models described next. One is based on an earlier method by Anderson and Gerbing (1988) known as two-step modeling. A more recent method by Mulaik and Millsap (2000) is four-step modeling. Both methods generally require a fully latent SR where every variable in the structural model is a factor measured by multiple indicators. Both methods deal with the problem of how to locate the source of a specification error. An example follows.

Suppose that a researcher specified the three-factor SR model presented in Figure 10.1(a).[1] The data are collected and the researcher uses **one-step modeling** to estimate

---

[1] Only two indicators per factor are shown in Figure 10.1 to save space, but having at least three indicators per factor is better.

(a) Original SR Model

(b) Respecified as a CFA Model

(c) Structural Model

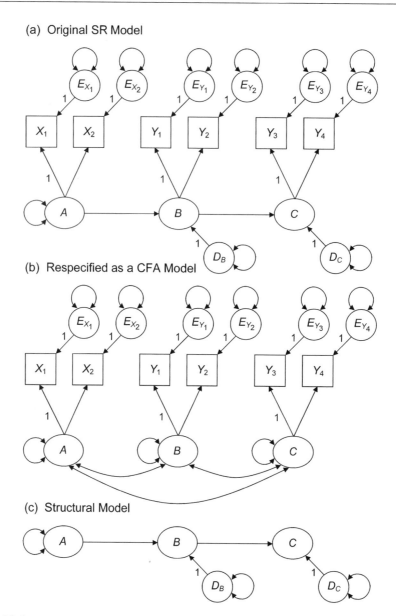

FIGURE 10.1. Two-step testing of a structural regression (SR) model.

this model, which means that the measurement and structural components of the SR model are analyzed simultaneously in a single analysis. The results indicate poor fit of the SR model. Now, where is the model misspecified? the measurement part? the structural part? or both? With one-step modeling, it is hard to precisely locate the source of poor fit. **Two-step modeling** parallels the two-step rule for the identification of SR models:

1. In the first step, an SR model is respecified as a CFA measurement model. The CFA model is then analyzed in order to determine whether it fits the data. If the fit of this CFA model is poor, then not only may the researcher's hypotheses about measurement be wrong, but also the fit of the original SR model may be even worse if its structural model is overidentified. Look again at Figure 10.1. Suppose that the fit of three-factor CFA model in Figure 10.1(b) is poor. Note that this CFA model has three paths among the factors that represent all possible unanalyzed associations (covariances, which are not directional). In contrast, the structural part of the original SR model, represented in Figure 10.1(c), has only two paths among the factors that represent direct effects. If the fit of the CFA model with three paths among the factors is poor, then the fit of the SR model with only two paths may be even worse. The first step thus involves finding an adequate measurement model. If this model is rejected, follow the suggestions in Chapter 9 about respecification of CFA models.

2. Given an acceptable measurement model, the second step is to compare the fits of the original SR model (with modifications to its measurement part, if any) and those with different structural models to one another and to the fit of the CFA model with the chi-square difference test. (This assumes that hierarchical structural models are compared.) Here is the procedure: If the structural part of an SR model is just-identified, the fits of that SR model and the CFA respecification of it are identical. These models are equivalent versions that generate the same predicted correlations and covariances. For example, if the path $A \rightarrow C$ were added to the SR model of Figure 10.1(a), then it would have just as many parameters as does the CFA measurement model of Figure 10.1(b). The SR model of Figure 10.1(a) with its overidentified structural model is thus nested under the CFA model of Figure 10.1(b). However, it may be possible to trim a just-identified portion of an SR model without appreciable deterioration in fit. Structural portions of SR models can be trimmed or built according to the same principles as in path analysis (Chapter 8).

Given an acceptable CFA measurement model, one should observe only slight changes in the factor loadings as SR models with alternative structural components are tested. If so, then the assumptions about measurement may be invariant to changes in the structural part of the SR model. But if the factor loadings change markedly when different structural models are specified, the measurement model is not invariant. This phenomenon may lead to **interpretational confounding** (Burt, 1976), which here means that the empirical definitions of the constructs (factor loadings) change depending on the structural model. It is generally easier to avoid interpretational confounding in two-step modeling than in one-step modeling.

Four-step modeling is basically an extension of the two-step method that is intended to even more precisely diagnose measurement model misspecification. In this strategy, the researcher specifies and tests a sequence of at least four hierarchical models. In order for these nested models to be identified, each factor in the original SR model should have at least four indicators. As in two-step modeling, if the fit of a model in four-step modeling with fewer constraints is poor, then a model with even more constraints should not even be considered. The steps are outlined next:

1.   The least restrictive model specified at the first step is an EFA model—one based on a principal (common) factor analysis, *not* a principal components analysis— that allows each indicator to load on every factor and where the number of factors is the same as that in the original SR model. This EFA model should be analyzed with the same method of estimation, such as maximum likelihood (ML), as used to analyze the final SR model (at the fourth step). This first step is intended to test the provisional correctness of the hypothesis regarding the number of factors, but it cannot confirm that hypothesis if model fit is adequate (Hayduk & Glaser, 2000).

2.   The second step of four-step modeling corresponds to the first step of two-step modeling: a CFA model is specified where some factor loadings (pattern coefficients) are fixed to zero. These specifications reflect the prediction that the indicator does not depend on that factor, not that the indicator is uncorrelated with that factor (i.e., the structure coefficient is not expected to equal zero). If the fit of the CFA model at the second step is acceptable, one goes on to test the original SR model. Otherwise, the measurement model should be revised.

3.   The third step involves testing the SR model with the same set of zero pattern coefficients as represented in the measurement model from the second step but where at least one unanalyzed association from the second step is respecified as a direct effect or reciprocal effect and some of the factors are specified as endogenous. That is, the CFA measurement model of the second step is respecified as an SR model.

4.   The last step involves tests of a priori hypotheses about parameters free from the outset of model testing. These tests typically involve the imposition of zero constraints, or dropping a path from the structural model. The third and fourth steps of four-step modeling are basically a more specific statement of activities that would fall under the second step of two-step modeling.

Which approach to analyzing SR models is better, two-step or four-step modeling? Both methods have their critics and defenders (e.g., Hayduk, 1996; Herting & Costner, 2000), and both capitalize on chance variation when hierarchical models are tested and respecified using the same data. The two-step method is simpler, and it does not require ≥ 4 indicators per factor. Both two-step and four-step modeling are better than one-step modeling, where there is no separation of measurement issues from structural issues. Neither method is a "gold standard" for testing SR models, but there is no such thing in SEM (Bentler, 2000). Bollen (2000) describes additional methods for testing SR models.

ESTIMATION OF SR MODELS

Discussed next are issues in the estimation of SR models.

Methods

The same estimation methods described in the previous chapters for path models and CFA models can be used with SR models. Briefly, standard ML estimation would normally be the method of choice for SR models with continuous indicators that are normally distributed. If the distributions are severely non-normal or the indicators are discrete with a small number of categories (e.g., Likert scale items as indicators), then one of the alternative methods described in Chapters 7 or 9 should be used instead.

Interpretation of Parameter Estimates and Problems

Interpretation of parameters estimates from the analysis of an SR model should not be difficult if one knows something about path analysis and CFA (and you do by now). For example, path coefficients are interpreted for SR models as regression coefficients for effects on endogenous variables from other variables presumed to directly cause them. Total effects among the factors that make up the structural model can be broken down into direct and indirect effects using the principle of effect decomposition (Chapter 7). Factor loadings are interpreted for SR models as regression coefficients for effects of factors on indicators, just as in CFA (Chapter 9).

Some SEM computer programs print estimated squared correlations (R^2_{smc}) for each endogenous variable. For SR models this includes the indicators and endogenous factors. Values of R^2_{smc} are usually computed for indicators in the unstandardized solution as one minus the ratio of the estimated measurement error variance over the sample variance of that indicator. Although variances of endogenous factors are not model parameters, they nevertheless have model-implied variances. Therefore, values of R^2_{smc} are usually calculated for endogenous factors as one minus the ratio of the estimated disturbance variance over the model-implied variance for that factor. Look out for Heywood cases, such as negative variance estimates, that suggest a problem with the data, specification, sample size, number of indicators per factor, or identification status of the model. If iterative estimation fails due to poor start values set automatically by the computer, the guidelines in Appendix 7.A can be followed for generating your own start values for the structural model or in Appendix 9.A for the measurement model.

Most SEM computer programs calculate a standardized solution for SR models by first finding the unstandardized solution with unit loading identification (ULI) constraints for endogenous factors and then transforming it to standardized form. Steiger (2002) notes that this method assumes that the ULI constraints function only to scale the endogenous variables. In other words, there is no constraint interaction. See Appendix 10.A for more information about constraint interaction in SR models.

DETAILED EXAMPLE

This example of the two-step analysis of an SR model of factors of job satisfaction was introduced in Chapter 5. Briefly reviewed, Houghton and Jinkerson (2007) measured within a sample of 263 full-time university employees three indicators each of constructive thinking, dysfunctional thinking, subjective well-being, and job satisfaction. They hypothesized that constructive thinking reduces dysfunctional thinking, which leads to an enhanced sense of well-being, which in turn results in greater job satisfaction. They also predicted that dysfunctional thinking directly affects job satisfaction. Their SR model with a standard four-factor, 12-indicator measurement model and an overidentified recursive structural model (i.e., the whole SR model is identified) is presented in Figure 5.9. We will first evaluate whether its measurement model is consistent with the data summarized in Table 10.1. All results described next are from converged, admissible solutions.

I submitted to Mplus 5.2 the correlations and standard deviations presented in Table 10.1, and Mplus converted these statistics to a sample covariance matrix. The first model I analyzed with ML estimation was a standard one-factor CFA model with 12 indicators. Values of selected fit statistics for this initial measurement model are reported in Table 10.2. It is clear that the fit of the one-factor measurement model is poor. For example,

TABLE 10.1. Input Data (Correlations, Standard Deviations) for Analysis of a Structural Regression Model of Thought Strategies and Job Satisfaction

Variable	1	2	3	4	5	6	7	8	9	10	11	12
Job satisfaction												
1. Work$_1$	1.00											
2. Work$_2$	.668	1.00										
3. Work$_3$	.635	.599	1.00									
Subjective well-being												
4. Happy	.263	.261	.164	1.00								
5. Mood$_1$	.290	.315	.247	.486	1.00							
6. Mood$_2$	.207	.245	.231	.251	.449	1.00						
Dysfunctional thinking												
7. Perform$_1$	−.206	−.182	−.195	−.309	−.266	−.142	1.00					
8. Perform$_2$	−.280	−.241	−.238	−.344	−.305	−.230	.753	1.00				
9. Approval	−.258	−.244	−.185	−.255	−.255	−.215	.554	.587	1.00			
Constructive thinking												
10. Beliefs	.080	.096	.094	−.017	.151	.141	−.074	−.111	.016	1.00		
11. Self-Talk	.061	.028	−.035	−.058	−.051	−.003	−.040	−.040	−.018	.284	1.00	
12. Imagery	.113	.174	.059	.063	.138	.044	−.119	−.073	−.084	.563	.379	1.00
SD	.939	1.017	.937	.562	.760	.524	.585	.609	.731	.711	1.124	1.001

Note. Input data are from Houghton and Jinkerson (2007); N = 263.

TABLE 10.2. Values of Selected Fit Statistics for Two-Step Testing of a Structural Regression Model of Thought Strategies and Job Satisfaction

Model	χ^2_M	df_M	χ^2_D	df_D	RMSEA (90% CI)	CFI	SRMR
Measurement model							
1-factor standard CFA	566.797[a]	54	—	—	.190 (.176–.204)	.498	.143
4-factor standard CFA	62.468[b]	48	504.329[a]	6	.034 (0–.056)	.986	.040
4-factor CFA with $E_{Ha} \smile E_{Mo_2}$	56.662[c]	47	5.806[d]	1	.028 (0–.052)	.991	.037
Structural regression model							
Just-identified structural model (6 paths)	56.662[c]	47	—		.028 (0–.052)	.991	.037
Overidentified structural model (4 paths)	60.010[e]	49	3.348[f]	2	.029 (0–.052)	.989	.043

Note. CI, confidence interval.
[a] $p < .001$; [b] $p = .078$; [c] $p = .158$; [d] $p = .016$; [e] $p = .135$; [f] $p = .188$.

this model fails the chi-square test (χ^2_M (54) = 566.797, $p < .001$), the RMSEA with its 90% confidence interval is .190 (.176–.204), and the CFI is only .498. Next, I specified the measurement portion of the Houghton–Jinkerson SR model (Figure 5.9) as a standard four-factor CFA model. Values of selected fit statistics for this four-factor CFA model are also listed in Table 10.2. The model chi-square is not statistically significant—χ^2_M (48) = 62.468, $p = .078$—so the exact-fit hypothesis is not rejected. The relative improvement in fit of the four-factor CFA model over that of the one-factor CFA model is statistically significant—χ^2_D (6) = 504.329, $p < .001$—and values of approximate fit indexes for the four-factor model are generally favorable (e.g., RMSEA = .034; CFI = .986; Table 10.2).

Close inspection of diagnostic information about the fit of the standard four-factor measurement indicated few apparent problems. For example, only two absolute correlation residuals (calculated in EQS) just exceeded .10, which is not a bad result in a larger model. There were a total of four standardized residuals (z statistics) with absolute values of about 2.00. Two of these larger residuals were for two different pairs among the three indicators of subjective well-being. One of the largest modification indexes (about 5.40) was for an error covariance between the indicators "Happy" (percent time happy) and "Mood$_2$" of this factor (see Figure 5.9).

Because it seems reasonable that shared item content across the two indicators just mentioned could be the basis for a common omitted cause, I respecified the four-factor measurement model by allowing the error covariance $E_{Ha} \smile E_{Mo_2}$ to be freely estimated in a third analysis. Reported in Table 10.2 are values of selected fit statistics for this modified measurement model. Its fit to the data is statistically better than that of the standard four-factor model with no correlated errors (χ^2_D (1) = 5.806, $p = .016$). The exact-fit hypothesis is not rejected for the respecified measurement model (χ^2_M (47) = 56.662, $p = .158$). Values of other fit statistics are generally favorable (e.g., RMSEA = .028, SRMR = .037). Finally, no absolute correlation residuals exceeded .10.

Based on the results just described, the four-factor measurement model with an error correlation presented in Figure 10.2 was retained. In contrast, Houghton and Jinkerson's (2007) final measurement model was a standard four-factor model, so my conclusion differs somewhat from theirs. Reported in Table 10.3 are estimates of factor loadings and error variances for the measurement model in Figure 10.2. Values of the standardized factor loadings for indicators of some factors are uniformly high, which suggests convergent validity. For example, the range of these loadings for the job satisfaction factor is .749–.839. A few other standardized loadings are somewhat low, such as .433 for the self-talk indicator of constructive thinking, so evidence for convergent validity is mixed. Values of R^2_{smc} for indicators range from .188 to .817. (You should verify this statement based on the information in Table 10.3.)

Estimates of factor variances and covariances and of the sole measurement error covariance for the model of Figure 10.2 are listed in Table 10.4. Two-factor covariances are not statistically significant, including one for the pair of factors about thinking styles (constructive, dysfunctional) and the other for the association between constructive thinking and subjective well-being. Estimated factor correlations range from –.480 to .466. These moderate factor intercorrelations suggest discriminant validity. The sole error covariance (–.043) is statistically significant, and the corresponding correlation

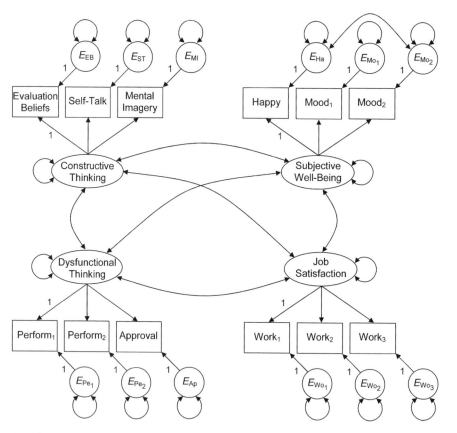

FIGURE 10.2. Measurement model for a structural regression model of thought strategies and job satisfaction.

TABLE 10.3. Maximum Likelihood Estimates of Factor Loadings and Residuals for a Measurement Model of Thought Strategies and Job Satisfaction

Indicator	Factor loadings			Measurement errors		
	Unst.	*SE*	St.	Unst.	*SE*	St.
Job satisfaction						
$Work_1$	1.000^a	—	.839	.260	.042	.297
$Work_2$	1.035	.081	.802	.368	.050	.357
$Work_3$	.891	.073	.749	.384	.044	.439
Subjective well-being						
Happy	1.000^a	—	.671	.173	.025	.550
$Mood_1$	1.490	.219	.739	.261	.044	.453
$Mood_2$	.821	.126	.591	.178	.022	.651
Dysfunctional thinking						
$Perform_1$	1.000^a	—	.830	.106	.016	.311
$Perform_2$	1.133	.080	.904	.068	.017	.183
Approval	.993	.089	.660	.300	.029	.564
Constructive thinking						
Beliefs	1.000^a	—	.648	.292	.043	.580
Self-Talk	1.056	.178	.433	1.022	.097	.812
Imagery	1.890	.331	.870	.242	.123	.242

Note. Unst., unstandardized; St., standardized. Standardized estimates for measurement errors are proportions of unexplained variance.

^{a}Not tested for statistical significance. For all other unstandardized estimates, $p < .05$.

TABLE 10.4. Maximum Likelihood Estimates of Factor Variances and Covariances and Error Covariance for a Measurement Model of Thought Strategies and Job Satisfaction

Parameter	Unstandardized	*SE*	Standardized
	Factor variances and covariances		
Job Satisfaction	.618	.081	1.000
Subjective Well-Being	.142	.031	1.000
Dysfunctional Thinking	.235	.031	1.000
Constructive Thinking	.212	.049	1.000
Constructive ⌣ Dysfunctional	$-.028^a$	.017	−.124
Constructive ⌣ Well-Being	$.024^a$	.014	.140
Constructive ⌣ Job Satisfaction	.060	.029	.165
Dysfunctional ⌣ Well-Being	−.088	.017	−.480
Dysfunctional ⌣ Job Satisfaction	−.131	.030	−.344
Well-Being ⌣ Job Satisfaction	.138	.028	.466
	Error covariance		
Happy ⌣ $Mood_2$	−.043	.018	−.243

$^a p \geq .05$. For all other unstandardized estimates, $p < .05$.

is –.243. This correlation is not large, but its presence helps to "clean up" some local fit problem in parts of the standard four-factor measurement model without this parameter.

The analyses described next concern the second step of two-step modeling—the testing of SR models with the measurement model established in the first step but with alternative versions of the structural models. The first SR model analyzed is one with a just-identified structural component. Because this SR model and the CFA measurement model in Figure 10.2 have the same number of paths among the factors (6), they are equivalent models. This fact is verified by the observation of identical values of fit statistics for the two models just mentioned (see Table 10.2). Equivalence also implies that estimates of factor loadings and measurement error variances and covariance will be identical within rounding error for the two models. Accordingly, at this point we need to consider just the parameter estimates for the structural part of the SR model, which are unique to this model.

Estimates for the just-identified structural model are presented in Figure 10.3. The direct effects in the figure depicted with dashed lines were predicted by Houghton and Jinkerson (2007) to be zero. The unstandardized path coefficient for the direct effect of constructive thinking on dysfunctional thinking (–.131) is not statistically significant, and the corresponding standardized path coefficient (–.124) indicates a relatively small effect size. It is no surprise, then, that constructive thinking explains only about 1.5% of the variance in dysfunctional thinking ($R^2_{smc} = .015$). The other two unstandardized

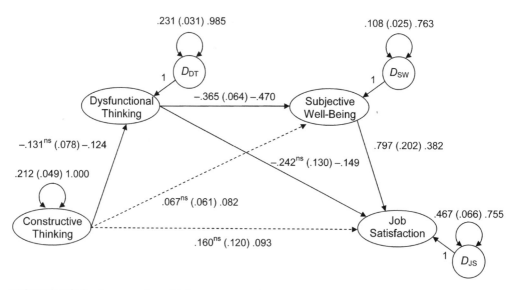

FIGURE 10.3. Structural model for a structural regression model of thought strategies and job satisfaction. Estimates are reported as unstandardized (standard error) standardized. Standardized estimates for disturbances are proportions of unexplained variance. The unstandardized estimates are all statistically significant at the .01 level except for those designated "ns," which means not significant.

path coefficients for constructive thinking, .067 and .160 for, respectively, direct effects on subjective well-being and job satisfaction, are also not statistically significant. This is consistent with predictions (Figure 10.3). Direct effects of dysfunctional thinking on subjective well-being and of subjective well-being on job satisfaction are both statistically significant and appreciable in standardized magnitude (respectively, −.470, .382). These results support the hypothesis that the effects of dysfunctional thinking strategies on job satisfaction are largely mediated through subjective well-being. Overall, about 25% of the variance in both the subjective well-being factor and job satisfaction factors is explained (the R^2_{smc} values are, respectively, .237 and .245; see Figure 10.3).

The final SR model retained by Houghton and Jinkerson (2007) had the four paths in the structural model represented with the solid lines in Figure 10.3. Values of selected fit statistics for this restricted SR model are reported in Table 10.2. The exact-fit hypothesis is not rejected for the restricted SR model (χ^2_M (49) = 60.010, p = .135), and its overall fit is not statistically worse than that of the unrestricted SR model with six direct effects (χ^2_D (2) = 3.348, p = .188). However, inspection of the correlation residuals (calculated in EQS) for the restricted SR model indicated some localized fit problems. For example, the correlation residual for the association between the "Work$_2$" indicator of job satisfaction and the "Imagery" indicator of constructive thinking is .142. Other absolute correlation residuals > .10 involved the "Beliefs" indicator of constructive thinking and both positive mood indicators of subjective well-being. Thus, dropping the two paths listed next:

Constructive Thinking → Job Satisfaction
Constructive Thinking → Subjective Well-Being

from the just-identified structural model in Figure 10.3 results in poor explanations of the observed correlations between the pairs of indicators just mentioned. This is an example of how dropping paths that are not statistically significant—here, from the structural model—can deteriorate the fit of some other parts of the model. Based on these results, I would retain the SR model with the just-identified structural model with six direct effects. You can download from this book's website (see p. 3) the Mplus syntax, data, and output files for the final four-factor measurement model (Figure 10.2) and the final SR model with six paths (Figure 10.3). Also available on the site are computer files for the same analyses in EQS and LISREL.

I used the Power Analysis procedure of STATISTICA 9 Advanced to estimate power for the final SR model with six paths in its structural model. Given N = 263, df_M = 47, and assuming α = .05 and ε_1 = .08, the power for the test of the close-fit hypothesis (H_0: $\varepsilon_0 \leq .05$) is .869. Now assuming ε_1 = .01, the power for the test of the not-close-fit hypothesis (H_0: $\varepsilon_0 \geq .05$) is .767. Thus, the probability of either rejecting a false model or detecting a correct model is quite good in this analysis, despite a sample size that is not large. This happens here because the relatively high degrees of freedom (47) for this larger model offset the negative impact of a smaller sample size on power.

EQUIVALENT SR MODELS

It is often possible to generate equivalent versions of SR models. An equivalent version of an SR model with a just-identified structural model was mentioned earlier: the measurement part of an SR model respecified as a CFA model, which assumes no causal effects among the factors, only unanalyzed associations (e.g., Table 10.2). Regardless of whether or not the structural model is just-identified, it may be possible to generate equivalent versions of it using the Lee–Hershberger replacing rules for path models (Chapter 8). For example, *any* rearrangement of the direct effects in the just-identified structural model in Figure 10.3 that respects these rules while holding the measurement model constant will result in alternative SR models that will fit the same data equally well. With the structural model held constant, it may also be possible to generate equivalent versions of the measurement model using Hershberger's reversed indicator rule, which involves reversing the direction of the causal effect between a factor and one of its indicators. That is, one indicator is specified as a cause indicator rather than as an effect indicator (Chapter 9). Given no change in the structural model, alternative SR models with equivalent measurement models would also fit the same data equally well. See Hershberger (1994) for more information and examples.

Equivalent versions of the just-identified structural model in Figure 10.3 for analysis of the Houghton and Jinkerson (2007) data include any other possible just-identified variation of this model. This includes structural models where the causal effects "flow" in the opposite direction, such as from job satisfaction to subjective well-being to dysfunctional thinking to construct thinking. Houghton and Jinkerson (2007) offered a detailed rationale of their original directionality specifications. But without such an argument, there is no way to prefer one just-identified structural model over an equivalent variation.

SINGLE INDICATORS IN PARTIALLY LATENT SR MODELS

At times a researcher has only one measure of some construct. Scores from a single indicator are unlikely to be both perfectly reliable and valid. There is an alternative to representing a single indicator in the structural part of an SR model as one would in path analysis (i.e., without a measurement error term). This alternative requires an a priori estimate of the proportion of variance in a single indicator that is due to measurement error (10%, 20%, etc.). This estimate may be based on the researcher's experience or on results of previous studies. Recall that (1) one minus a reliability coefficient, $1 - r_{XX}$, estimates the proportion of observed variance due to random error, which is only one source of measurement error (Chapter 3). (2) Specific types of reliability coefficients estimate only one kind of random error. Thus, the quantity $1 - r_{XX}$ may *underestimate* the proportion of total variance due to measurement error.

Suppose that X_1 is the only indicator of an exogenous factor A and that the researcher estimates that the 20% of X_1's variance is due to measurement error. Given this estimate, it is possible to specify an SR model like the one presented in Figure 10.4(a). Note that X_1 in the figure is specified as a single indicator *and* has an error term. The unstandardized variance of the latter is fixed to equal .20 times the observed variance, or $.2 s^2_{X_1}$. For example, if the observed variance of X_1 is 30.00, then 20% of this variance, or .2 (30.00) = 6.00, is the estimated error variance. Because factor A must be scaled, the unstandardized loading of X_1 on A is fixed to equal 1.0. With the specification of a residual term

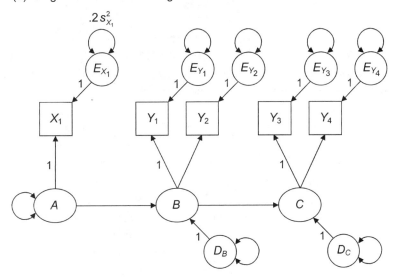

(a) Single Indicator of an Exogenous Construct

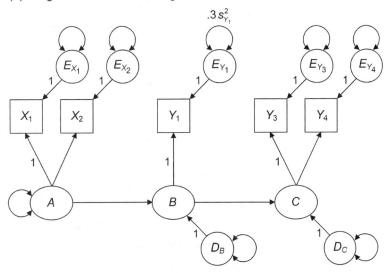

(b) Single Indicator of an Endogenous Construct

FIGURE 10.4. Two structural regression models with single indicators that correct for measurement error. It is assumed that the proportion of error variance for X_1 is .20 and for Y_1 it is .30.

for X_1, the direct effect of factor A is estimated controlling for measurement error in its single indicator.

Now look at the SR model of Figure 10.4(b), in which Y_1 is specified as the sole indicator of the endogenous factor B. The proportion of measurement error in Y_1 is estimated to be .30. Given this estimate, the variance of the error term for Y_1 is fixed to equal .30 times the observed variance of Y_1. Because Y_1 has an error term, both the disturbance variance for B and the direct effect of this factor will be estimated while controlling for measurement error in its single indicator. Three points should be noted about this method for single indicators:

1.   A common question is, why not just specify the error variance for a single indicator as a free parameter and let the computer estimate it? Such a specification may result in an identification problem (see Bollen, 1989, pp. 172–175). A safer tactic with a single indicator is to fix the value of its measurement error variance based on a prior estimate.

2.   A related question is, what if the researcher is uncertain about his or her estimate of the error variance for a single indicator? The model can be analyzed with a range of estimates, which allows the researcher to evaluate the impact of different assumptions about measurement error on the solution (i.e., conduct a sensitivity analysis).

3.   It is theoretically possible to specify a path model where every observed variable is represented as the single indicator of an underlying factor and every indicator has a measurement error term. This tactic would be akin to fitting a path model to a covariance matrix based on correlations disattenuated for unreliability (Equation 3.7). See Bedeian, Day, and Kelloway (1997) for more information.

The models in Figure 10.4 illustrate that SR models with single indicators that are identified may nevertheless fail the two-step rule for identification (Rule 6.9): when either model in the figure is respecified as a CFA measurement model, one factor (A or B) will have only one indicator, which is one less than the minimum for a standard multifactor model (Rule 6.5). Fixing the error variance of X_1 in the model of Figure 10.4(a) or Y_1 in the model of Figure 10.4(b) to a constant, however, identifies the model.

Shen and Takeuchi (2001) administered within a stratified random sample of 983 native-born Chinese Americans and immigrants of Chinese descent measures of the degree of acculturation, socioeconomic status (SES), stress, and depression. Descriptive statistics for these variables are summarized in Table 10.5. Note in the table that there is just a single indicator of depression. This data matrix is ill scaled because the ratio of the largest variance (11.834) over the smallest variance (.058) exceeds 200. Therefore, I multiplied the original variables by the constants listed in Table 10.5 in order to make their variances more homogeneous.

Presented in Figure 10.5 is the SR model analyzed by Shen and Takeuchi (2001). This model reflects the hypothesis that stress is directly affected by the degree of acculturation and that depression is directly affected by both SES and stress. Values of selected

TABLE 10.5. Input Data (Correlations and Standard Deviations) for Analysis of a Structural Regression Model of Acculturation and Mental Health Status with a Single Indicator

Variable	1	2	3	4	5	6	7	8
Acculturation								
1. Acculturation Scale	1.00							
2. Generation Status	.44	1.00						
3. Percent Life in U.S.	.69	.54	1.00					
Socioeconomic status								
4. Education	.37	.08	.24	1.00				
5. Income	.23	.05	.26	.29	1.00			
Stress								
6. Interpersonal	.12	.08	.08	.08	−.03	1.00		
7. Job	.09	.06	.04	.01	−.02	.38	1.00	
Single indicator								
8. Depression	.03	.02	−.02	−.07	−.11	.37	.46	1.00
Original s^2	.608	.168	.058	10.693	11.834	.137	.203	.102
Constant	4.00	8.00	10.00	1.00	1.00	8.00	8.00	10.00
Rescaled s^2	9.728	10.752	5.800	10.693	11.834	8.768	12.992	10.200
Rescaled SD	3.119	3.279	2.408	3.270	3.440	2.961	3.604	3.194

Note: These data are from Shen and Takeuchi (2001); $N = 983$.

fit statistics calculated by LISREL 8.8 with ML estimation for the model in Figure 10.5 are as follows:

$$\chi^2_M (16) = 59.715, \quad p < .001$$

$$\text{RMSEA} = .053\ (0.39\text{–}.068); \quad p_{\text{close-fit } H_0} = .343$$

$$\text{GFI} = .985; \quad \text{CFI} = .977; \quad \text{SRMR} = .032$$

The exact-fit hypothesis is rejected, so there is a need to understand why this test was failed. I inspected the correlation residuals (derived in EQS), and none of their absolute values are > .10. Also, the parameter estimates for the model in Figure 10.5 seemed reasonable in the converged and admissible solution. In this case, the chi-square test may be failed due more to the relatively large sample size ($N = 983$) than to appreciable discrepancies between observed and predicted correlations or covariances. This outcome indicates the need to routinely examine the residuals in every analysis.

The disturbance for the single indicator of depression in Figure 10.5 reflects both measurement error and omitted causes, which is not ideal. Assuming a score reliability of $r_{XX} = .70$, Exercise 2 will ask you to respecify the model in Figure 10.5 such that measurement error in the depression scale is estimated separately from the effects of omitted causes. Next, use an SEM computer tool to fit this respecified model to the data

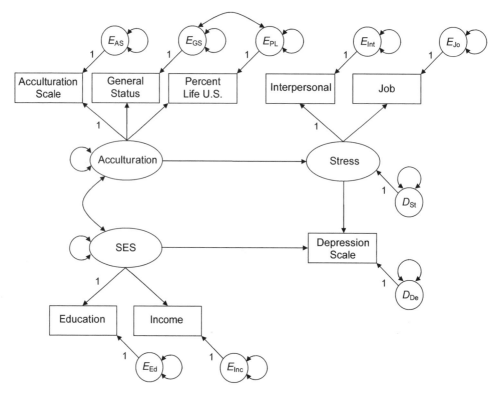

FIGURE 10.5. A structural regression model of acculturation and mental health status with a single indicator.

in Table 10.5. Look for a "surprise" among the parameter estimates. You can download the EQS and LISREL syntax and output files for the analysis just described from this book's website (p. 3).

CAUSE INDICATORS AND FORMATIVE MEASUREMENT

Observed variables in standard measurement models are represented as effect (reflective) indicators that are presumed to be caused by the underlying factors and their measurement errors. This directionality specification describes reflective measurement. This approach assumes (1) that equally reliable indicators are interchangeable, which implies that they can be substituted for one another without affecting construct definition. It also requires (2) positive intercorrelations among the indicators of the same factor. Finally, (3) factors are conceptualized in reflective measurement as unidimensional latent variables (Chapter 5).

The assumptions just listed are not suitable for some research problems, especially in areas where composites, or **index variables**, are analyzed. Recall the example from Chapter 5 of SES as a composite that is determined by measured variables such as income, education, and occupation, not the other way around. This view is consistent with a formative measurement model wherein manifest variables are specified as cause (formative) indicators (Chapter 5). The origins of formative measurement lie in the operational definition model (Diamantopoulos & Winklhofer, 2001). An older, strict form of operationalism views constructs as synonymous with the single indicator that corresponds to its definition. More contemporary forms of operationalism allow for both multiple indicators and disturbance terms for composites. The latter permits the representation of **latent composites** that are determined in part, but not entirely, by their cause indicators. Cause indicators are *not* generally interchangeable. This is because removal of a cause indicator is akin to removing a part of the underlying construct (Bollen & Lennox, 1991). Cause indicators may have *any* pattern of intercorrelations, including ones that are basically zero. This is because composites reflect the contribution of multiple dimensions, albeit with a single score for each case (i.e., composites are not unidimensional). There are many examples of the analysis of composites in economics and business research (Diamantopoulos, Riefler, & Roth, 2005).

Presented in Figure 10.6 are three "mini" measurement models that illustrate differences between reflective measurement and formative measurement. The model of Figure 10.6(a) depicts standard reflective measurement. Grace and Bollen (2008) use the term **L → M block** (latent to manifest) to describe the association between factors and their effect indicators in reflective measurement models. Measurement error in such models is represented at the indicator level by the error terms E_1–E_3 in Figure 10.6(a).[2]

A formative measurement model is represented in Figure 10.6(b). It depicts an **M → L block** (manifest to latent) because the latent composite in this model is presumed to be caused in part by its formative indicators, X_1–X_3. In Figure 10.6(b) I used a circle to represent the latent composite because, like error terms but unlike factors, a latent composite is not unidimensional. With no disturbance, the composite in Figure 10.6(b) would be just a linear combination across its cause indicators. To scale the latent composite, the unstandardized direct effect of one of its cause indicators, X_1, is fixed to 1.0. Cause indicators in formative measurement models are exogenous variables and have no error terms. This means that (1) cause indicators are free to vary and covary, which explains the presence of the symbols in Figure 10.6(b) that represent their variances and covariances (respectively, ⌢ and ⌣). Also, (2) measurement error in a formative measurement model like the one in Figure 10.6(b) is manifested in the disturbance term, D_{LC}. That is, measurement error is represented at the construct level, not at the indicator level as in reflective measurement (e.g., Figure 10.6(a)). Note that the model in Figure 10.6(b) is not identified. In order to estimate its parameters, it would be necessary to embed it in a larger model. Identification requirements of formative measurement models are considered momentarily.

---

[2]A factor can also be endogenous in a reflective measurement model, but the term L → M block still applies.

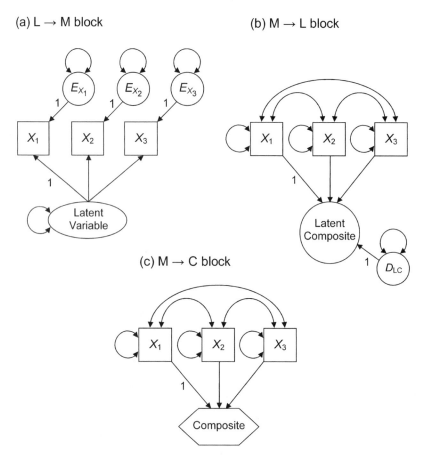

(a) L → M block

(b) M → L block

(c) M → C block

FIGURE 10.6. Directionalities of relations between indicators and a (a) latent variable, (b) latent composite, and (c) composite. M, manifest; L, latent; C, composite.

Formative measurement is also represented in Figure 10.6(c), but the composite in this model has no disturbance. Consequently, this composite is not latent, and the whole model is described as an **M → C block**, which says that the composite (C) is just a total score over the manifest variables (cause indicators). Grace and Bollen (2008) represent composites in model diagrams with hexagons, which is also used in Figure 10.6(c). This is not a standard symbol, but it does convey the fact that a composite with no disturbance is not latent. These same authors distinguish between a **fixed weights composite** where loadings (weights) are specified a priori (e.g., unit weighting) and an **unknown weights composite** where the weights are estimated with sample data. The model in Figure 10.6(c) assumes an unknown weights composite.

There is a "compromise" between specifying that the indicators of a factor are either all effect or causal. It is achieved by specifying a MIMIC (multiple indicators and multiple causes) factor with both effect and cause indicators. A MIMIC factor with a single cause indicator and the rest effect indicators is an equivalent version of a standard one-factor CFA model (Chapter 9). In other contexts, it is possible to specify MIMIC factors with ≥ 1 cause indicators along with effect indicators. There are many examples in the literature of the analysis of SR models with MIMIC factors. For example, Hershberger (1994) described a MIMIC depression factor with indicators that represented various behaviors. Some of these indicators, such as "crying" and "feeling depressed," were specified as effect indicators because they are symptoms of depression. However, another indicator, "feeling lonely," was specified as a cause indicator. This is because "feeling lonely" may cause depression rather than vice versa. Bruhn, Georgi, and Hadwich (2008) describe the analysis of a MIMIC factor of customer equity management with latent cause indicators and manifest effect indicators.

The main stumbling block to analyzing measurement models where some factors have cause indicators only and the composite is latent is identification. This is because it can be difficult to specify such a model that reflects the researcher's hypotheses and is identified. The need to scale latent composites was mentioned, but meeting this requirement is not difficult. MacCallum and Browne (1993) noted that in order for the disturbance variance of a latent composite to be identified, the latent composite must have direct effects on at least two other endogenous variables, such as endogenous factors with effect indicators. This requirement is known as the **2+ emitted paths rule**. If a factor measured with cause indicators only emits a single path, its disturbance variance will be underidentified. Another requirement for models with ≥ 2 latent composites is that if factors measured with effect indicators only have indirect effects on other such factors that are mediated by different combinations of latent composites, then some of the constituent direct effects may be underidentified.

One way to deal with the problems just mentioned is to fix the disturbance variance for the latent composite to zero, which drops the disturbance from the model and "converts" the latent composite to a weighted manifest variable (e.g., Figure 10.6(c)). However, this is not an ideal option. Recall that the disturbance of a latent composite reflects measurement error in its cause indicators. Dropping the disturbance is akin to assuming that the cause indicators are measured without error, which is unlikely. MacCallum and Browne (1993) showed that dropping from the model a weighted composite that emits a single path and converting the indirect effects of its cause indicators on other endogenous variables to direct effects result in an equivalent model. Another way to remedy identification problems is to add effect indicators for latent composites represented in the original model as measured with cause indicators only. That is, specify a MIMIC factor. For example, adding two effect indicators means that the formerly latent composite will emit at least two direct effects—see Diamantopoulos, Riefler, and Roth (2008) for examples. However, all such respecifications require a theoretical rationale.

Worland, Weeks, Janes, and Strock (1984) administered measures of the cognitive and achievement status of 158 adolescents. They also collected teacher reports about classroom adjustment and measured family SES and the degree of parental psychiatric disturbance. The correlations among these variables are reported in Table 10.6. Note that Worland and colleagues did not report standard deviations. For didactic reasons,

TABLE 10.6. Input Data (Correlations and Hypothetical Standard Deviations) for Analysis of a Model of Risk as a Latent Composite

Variable	1	2	3	4	5	6	7	8	9
Risk									
1. Parental Psychiatric	1.00								
2. Low Family SES	.42	1.00							
3. Verbal IQ	-.43	-.50	1.00						
Achievement									
4. Reading	-.39	-.43	.78	1.00					
5. Arithmetic	-.24	-.37	.69	.73	1.00				
6. Spelling	-.31	-.33	.63	.87	.72	1.00			
Classroom adjustment									
7. Motivation	-.25	-.25	.49	.53	.60	.59	1.00		
8. Harmony	-.25	-.26	.42	.42	.44	.45	.77	1.00	
9. Stability	-.16	-.18	.23	.36	.38	.38	.59	.58	1.00
SD	13.00	13.50	13.10	12.50	13.50	14.20	9.50	11.10	8.70

Note. These data are from Worland, Weeks, Janes, and Strock (1984); $N = 158$.

however, I assigned plausible standard deviations to each of the variables listed in Table 10.6. Taking this pedagogical license does not affect the overall fit of the model described next. Instead, it allows you to reproduce this analysis or test alternative models for these data with any SEM computer tool.

Suppose that the construct of *risk* is conceptualized for this example as a latent composite with cause indicators family SES, parental psychopathology, and adolescent verbal IQ. That is, high risk is indicated by any combination of low family SES, a high degree of parental psychiatric impairment, or low adolescent verbal IQ. The intercorrelations among these three variables are not all positive (see Table 10.6), but this is irrelevant for cause indicators. Presented in Figure 10.7 is an example of an identified SR model where a latent risk composite has cause indicators only. Note in the figure that the risk composite emits two direct effects onto factors each measured with effect indicators only, which satisfies the 2+ emitted paths rule. This specification identifies the disturbance variance for the risk composite. It also reflects the assumption that the association between achievement and classroom adjustment is spurious due to a common cause (risk). This assumption may not be plausible. For example, achievement probably affects classroom adjustment. Specifically, students with better scholastic skills may be better adjusted at school. But including the direct effect just mentioned— or, alternatively, the disturbance correlation $D_{Ac} \curvearrowright D_{CA}$—between these two factors in the model of Figure 10.7 would render it not identified.

I fitted the model of Figure 10.7 with a latent composite to the covariance matrix based on the data in Table 10.6 with the ML method of EQS 6.1. The syntax and output files for this analysis can be downloaded from this book's website (p. 3). The analysis converged to an admissible solution. Values of selected fit indexes are reported next:

$$\chi^2_M (22) = 75.421, \quad p < .001$$
$$\text{RMSEA} = .124 \ (.094–.155)$$
$$\text{GFI} = .915; \quad \text{CFI} = .941; \quad \text{SRMR} = .041$$

These results indicate poor overall fit of the model to the data. Inspection of the correlation residuals verifies this conclusion: several absolute residuals are close to or > .10. These high-correlation residuals generally occurred between indicators of the achievement factor and the classroom adjustment factor (Figure 10.7). Specifically, the model tends to underpredict these cross-factor correlations. This pattern is consistent with the possibility that the coefficient for the direct effect of achievement on adjustment is not zero. However, the only way to estimate this path is to respecify the model of Figure 10.7. Here are some possibilities:

1. Respecify the latent risk composite as a MIMIC factor with at least one effect indicator, such as adolescent verbal IQ.

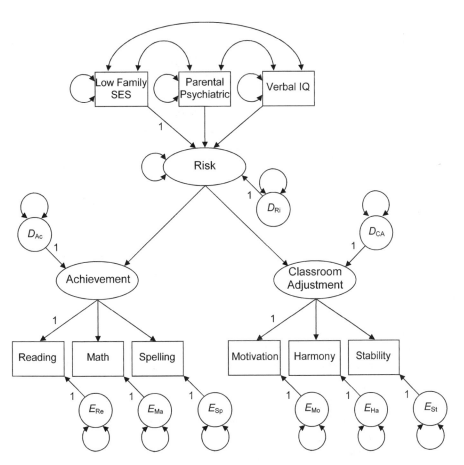

FIGURE 10.7. An identified model of risk as a latent composite.

2. Drop the disturbance D_{Ri} from the model in Figure 10.7, which would convert the latent risk composite into a weighted combination of its cause indicators. Grace (2006) argues that (a) error variance estimates for latent composites may have little theoretical significance in some contexts, and (b) the presence or absence of these error terms should not by itself drive decisions about the inclusion of composites in the model.

3. Drop the risk composite from the model in Figure 10.7 and replace it with direct effects from the three cause indicators to each of the two endogenous factors with effect indicators.

Each respecification option just described would identify the direct effect between achievement and classroom adjustment in Figure 10.7. Whether any of these options makes theoretical sense is another matter, one that in a particular study would dictate whether any of these respecifications is plausible.

Grace (2006, chap. 6) and Grace and Bollen (2008) describe many examples of the analysis of models with composites in the environmental sciences. Jarvis, MacKenzie, and Podsakoff (2003) and others advise researchers in the consumer research area— and the rest of us, too—not to automatically specify factors with effect indicators only because doing so may result in specification error, perhaps due to lack of familiarity with formative measurement models. On the other hand, the specification of formative measurement is not a panacea. For example, because cause indicators are exogenous, their variances and covariances are not explained by a formative measurement model. This makes it more difficult to assess the validity of a set of cause indicators (Bollen, 1989). The fact that error variance in formative measurement is represented at the construct level instead of at the indicator level as in reflective measurement is a related problem. Howell, Breivik, and Wilcox (2007) note that formative measurement models are more susceptible than reflective measurement models to interpretational confounding where values of indicator loadings are affected by changes in the structural model. The absence of a nominal definition of a formative factor apart from the empirical values of loadings of its indicators exacerbates this problem. For these and other reasons, Howell et al. conclude that (1) formative measurement is not an equally attractive alternative to reflective measurement and (2) researchers should try to include reflective indicators whenever other indicators are specified as cause indicators of the same construct, but see Bagozzi (2007) and Bollen (2007) for other views. See also the special issue on formative measurement in the *Journal of Business Research* (Diamantopoulos, 2008) for more information about formative measurement.

An alternative to SEM for analyzing models with both measurement and structural components is **partial least squares path modeling**, also known as **latent variable partial least squares**. In this approach, constructs are estimated as linear combinations of observed variables, or composites. Although SEM is better for testing strong hypotheses about measurement, the partial least squares approach is well suited for situations where (1) prediction is emphasized over theory testing and (2) it is difficult to meet the requirements for large samples or identification in SEM. See Topic Box 10.1 for more information.

TOPIC BOX 10.1

Partial Least Squares Path Modeling

A good starting point for outlining the logic of partial least squares path modeling (PLS-PM) is to consider the distinction between principal components analysis versus common factor analysis. Principal components analysis analyzes total variance and estimates factors as simple linear combinations (composites) of the indicators, but common factor analysis analyzes shared (common) variance only and makes an explicit distinction between indicators, underlying factors, and measurement errors (unique variances). Of these two EFA methods, it is principal components analysis that is directly analogous to PLS-PM.

The idea behind PLS-PM is based on **soft modeling**, an approach developed by H. Wold (1982) for situations in which theory about measurement is not strong, but the goal is to estimate predictive relations among latent variables. In PLS-PM, latent variables are estimated as exact linear combinations of their indicators with OLS but applied in an iterative algorithm. This method is basically an extension of the technique of canonical correlation but one that (1) explicitly distinguishes between indicators and factors and (2) permits the estimation of direct and indirect effects among factors. Similar to canonical correlation, indicators in PLS-PM are weighted in order to maximize prediction. In contrast, the goal of estimation in SEM is to minimize residual covariances, which may not directly maximize the prediction of outcome variables.

The limited-information estimation methods in PLS-PM make fewer demands of the data. For example, they do not generally assume a particular distributional form, and the estimation process is not as complex. Consequently, PLS-PM can be applied in smaller samples than SEM, and there are generally no problems concerning inadmissible solutions. This makes the analysis of complex models with many indicators easier in PLS-PM compared with SEM. It is also possible to represent in PLS-PM either reflective or formative measurement but without the strict identification requirements in SEM for estimating latent composites (Chin, 1998).

A drawback of PLS-PM is that its estimates are statistically inferior relative to those generated under full-information estimation (e.g., ML in SEM) in terms of bias and consistency, but this is less so in very large samples. Standard errors are estimated in PLS-PM using adjunct methods, including bootstrapping. There are generally no model fit statistics of the kind available in SEM. Instead, researchers evaluate models in PLS-PM by inspecting values of factor loadings, path coefficients, and R^2-type statistics for outcome variables. One could argue that PLS-PM, which generally analyzes unknown weights composites, does not really estimate substantive latent variables compared with SEM.

Until recently, the application of PLS-PM was limited by the paucity of user-

cont.

friendly software tools. However, there are now a few different computer tools for PLS-PM, some with graphical user interfaces. Presented on this book's website (p. 3) are links to other sites about graphical computer tools for PLS-PM, including PLS-Graph, SmartPLS, and Visual-PLS. These programs are either freely available over the Internet or offered without cost to academic users after registration. Temme, Kreis, and Hildebrandt (2006) describe the programs just mentioned and other computer tools for PLS-PM. They note that graphical PLS-PM computer tools rival their counterparts in SEM for ease of use, but PLS-PM programs do not yet offer the range of analytical options. For example, most PLS-PM programs analyze continuous indicators only and offer "classical" missing data techniques only. On the other hand, some programs, such as Visual-PLS and SmartPLS, can automatically estimate interactive effects of latent variables. See Vinzi, Chin, Henseler, and Wang (2009) for more information.

INVARIANCE TESTING OF SR MODELS

Just as in CFA, it is also possible to test invariance hypotheses when SR models are analyzed either over time or groups. Because SR models have both measurement and structural components, the range of invariance hypotheses that can be tested is even wider. Listed next is a series of hierarchical SR models that could be tested for invariance in a model trimming context where equality constraints are gradually added. This list is not exhaustive, and it does not cover model building where the starting point is a restricted model from which constraints are gradually released. Invariance testing across multiple samples is emphasized next, but the same logic applies to analyzing an SR model over time in a longitudinal design:

1. The least restrictive model corresponds to the configural invariance hypothesis H_{form}, which is tested by estimating the same SR model but with no cross-group equality constraints. If H_{form} is rejected, then invariance does not hold at any level, measurement or structural.

2. Next test H_Λ, the construct-level metric invariance hypothesis by imposing equality constraints on each freely estimated factor loading across the groups. If H_Λ is rejected, then evaluate the less strict hypothesis H_λ by releasing some, but not all, of the equality constraints on factor loadings. Stop if all variations of H_λ are rejected.

3. Given evidence for at least partial measurement invariance (i.e., H_Λ or H_λ is retained), then it makes sense to test for invariance of structural model parameters. For example, the hypothesis of **equal direct effects**, designated as $H_{\mathbf{B},\,\Gamma}$, is tested by imposing cross-group equality constraints on the estimates of each path coefficient. The stricter hypothesis $H_{\mathbf{B},\,\Gamma,\,\Psi}$ assumes the equality of both direct effects and disturbance

variances–covariances over groups, and the even stricter invariance hypothesis $H_{\mathbf{B}, \Gamma, \Psi, \Phi}$ also assumes equivalence of the variances and covariances of the exogenous factors. See Bollen (1989, pp. 355–365) for more information. Tests for equal direct effects can also be described as tests of moderation, that is, of interaction effects. Specifically, if magnitudes or directions of direct effects in the structural model differ appreciably across the groups, then group membership moderates these direct effects. Chapter 12 deals with the estimation of interaction effects in SEM.

REPORTING RESULTS OF SEM ANALYSES

With review of core structural equation models behind us, this is a good point to address the issue of what to report. Listed in Table 10.7 are citations for works about reporting practices, problems, and guidelines in SEM. Many of these works were cited in earlier chapters, but they are listed all together in the table. Some of these articles concern reporting practices in particular research areas (e.g., DiStefano & Hess, 2005), and others are specific to particular techniques, such as CFA (e.g., Jackson, Gillaspy, & Purc-Stephenson, 2009). Thompson's (2000) "ten commandments" of SEM, summarized in the table footnote, are also pertinent.

Presented next are recommendations for reporting SEM results organized by phases

TABLE 10.7. Citations for Works about Reporting Practices and Guidelines for Written Summaries of Results in Structural Equation Modeling

Work	Comment
Boomsma (2000)	General reporting guidelines
Breckler (1990)	Review of studies in personality and social psychology journals
DiStefano and Hess (2005)	Review of CFA studies in assessment journals
Holbert and Stephenson (2002)	Reporting practices in communication sciences
Hoyle and Panter (1995)	General reporting guidelines
Jackson, Gillaspy, and Purc-Stephenson (2009)	Review of CFA studies in psychology journals and specific reporting guidelines
MacCallum and Austin (2000)	Review of studies in psychology journals
McDonald and Ho (2002)	General reporting guidelines
Raykov, Tomer, and Nesselroade (1991)	Reporting guidelines for the psychology and aging area
Schreiber, Nora, Stage, Barlow, and King (2006)	Reporting practices in educational research
Schreiber (2008)	Reporting practices in social and administrative pharmacy
Shah and Goldstein (2006)	Reporting practices in operations management research and guidelines
Thompson (2000)	"Ten commandments" of SEM[a]

[a]No small samples; analyze covariance, not correlation matrices; simpler models are better; verify distributional assumptions; consider theoretical and practical significance, not just statistical significance; report multiple fit statistics; use two-step modeling for structural regression models; consider theoretically plausible alternative models; respecify rationally; acknowledge equivalent models.

of the analysis, from specification up through the tabulation and reporting of the results. You can refer to these recommendations as a kind of checklist for preparing or evaluating a written summary of SEM analyses. Study these suggestions carefully and use them wisely; see also Schumacker and Lomax (2004, chap. 11) for related recommendations. You already know that there are many problems concerning the reporting of SEM analyses in today's research literature. By not repeating these common mistakes, you are helping to improve the state of practice. This saying attributed to the psychologist and philosopher William James is apropos here: Act as if what you do makes a difference; it does.

Specification

• Describe the theoretical framework or body of empirical results that form the basis for specification of your model. Identify the particular research problem addressed by your model and analysis. Explain why the use of SEM is relevant for this problem.

• Give the rationale for directionality specifications. This includes both the measurement model and the structural model. For example, is standard reflective measurement appropriate for describing the directionality of factor-indicator correspondences? Or would the specification of formative measurement make more sense? For the structural model, clearly state the rationale for your hypotheses about effect priority, especially if your design is nonexperimental.

• For presumed direct effects, state their expected directions, positive or negative. Give a diagram of your initial model. Represent all error terms and unanalyzed associations in the diagram. Make sure that the diagram is consistent with your description of it in text.

• Explain the rationale for any constraints to be imposed on parameter estimation. Relate these constraints to relevant theory, previous results, or aims of your study.

• Outline any theoretically plausible alternative models. State the role of these alternative models in your plan for model testing. Describe this plan (e.g., testing nested models vs. comparing nonhierarchical models).

• In multiple-sample analyses, state the particular forms of invariance to be tested and in what sequence (i.e., model building or trimming).

Identification

• Tally the number of observations and free parameters in your initial model. State (or indicate in a diagram) how latent variables are scaled. That is, demonstrate that necessary but insufficient conditions for identification are met.

• Comment on sufficient requirements for identifying the type of structural equation model you are analyzing. For example, if the structural model is nonrecursive, is the rank condition sufficient to identify it? If the measurement model has error covariances, does their pattern satisfy the required sufficient conditions?

Data and Measures

• Clearly describe the characteristics of your sample (cases) and measures. State the psychometric properties of your measures, including evidence for score reliability and validity. Report values of reliability coefficients calculated in your sample. If this is not possible, then report the coefficients from other samples (reliability induction), but explicitly describe whether those other samples are similar to your own.

• If the sample is archival—that is, you are fitting a structural equation model within an existing data set—then mention possible specification errors due to the omission of relevant measures in this sample.

• Verify the assumption of multivariate normality in your sample when using normal theory estimators. For example, report values of the skew index and kurtosis index for all continuous outcome variables.

• Describe how data-related complications were handled. This includes the extent and strategy for dealing with missing observations, how apparent extreme collinearity was dealt with, and the use of transformations, if any, to normalize the data.

• Clearly state the type of data matrix analyzed, which is ordinarily a covariance matrix. Report this matrix—or the correlations and standard deviations—and the means in a table or an appendix. To save space, reliability coefficients and values of skew and kurtosis indexes can be reported in the same place. Give the final sample size in this summary. You should report enough summary information so that someone else could take your model diagram(s) and data matrix and reproduce your analyses and results.

• Verify that your data matrix is positive definite.

Estimation and Respecification

• State which SEM computer tool was used (and its version), and list the syntax for your final model in an appendix. If the latter is not feasible due to length limitations, then tell your readers how they can access your code (e.g., a website address).

• State the estimation method used, even if it is default ML estimation. If some other method is used, then clearly state this method and give your rationale for selecting it (e.g., some outcome variables are ordinal).

• Say whether the estimation process converged and whether the solution is admissible. Describe any complications in estimation, such as failure of iterative estimation or Heywood cases, and how these problems were handled, such as giving the computer new start values or increasing the default limit on the number of iterations.

• Always report the model chi-square and its *p* value for all models tested. If the model fails the chi-square test, then explicitly state this result.

• Never conclude that model fit is satisfactory based solely on values of fit statistics, which only indicate overall model–data correspondence. Along the same lines, do not rely on "golden rules" for approximate fit indexes to justify the retention of a particular model. This is especially true if the model chi-square test was failed.

• Describe model fit at a more molecular level by conveying diagnostic information about patterns of correlation residuals, standardized residuals, or modification indexes. For a smaller model, report the correlation residuals and standardized residuals. The point is to reassure your readers that your model has acceptable fit on both a global level and at the level of pairs of observed variables.

• When a model is respecified, explain the theoretical basis for doing so. That is, how are the changes justified? Indicate the particular statistics, such as correlation residuals, standardized residuals, or modification indexes, consulted in respecification and how the values of these statistics relate to theory.

• Clearly state the nature and number of respecifications such as, how many paths were added or dropped and which ones?

• If the final model is quite different from your initial model, reassure your readers that its respecification was not merely chasing sample-specific (chance) variation. If there is no such rationale, then the model may be overparamterized (good fit is achieved at the cost of too many parameters).

• When testing hierarchical models, report the information just described for all candidate models. Also report results of the chi-square difference test for relevant comparisons of hierarchical models.

• When testing SR models, establish that the measurement model is consistent with the data before estimating versions with alternative structural models.

Tabulation

• Report the parameter estimates for your final model (if a model is retained). This includes the unstandardized estimates, their standard errors, and the standardized estimates. In a multiple-sample analysis, describe how the standardized estimates were derived in your SEM computer tool.

• Do not indicate anything about statistical significance for the standardized parameter estimates unless you used a method, such as constrained estimation, that generates correct standard errors in the standardized solution.

• Comment on whether the signs and magnitudes of the parameter estimates make theoretical sense. Look for potential "surprises" that may indicate a suppression effect or other unexpected results.

• Report information for individual outcome variables about predictive power, such as R^2_{smc} or a corrected-R^2 for endogenous variables in a nonrecursive structural model.

• Interpret effect sizes (e.g., standardized path coefficients, R^2_{smc}) in reference to results expected in a particular research area.

Avoid Confirmation Bias

• Explicitly deal with the issue of equivalent models. Generate some plausible equivalent versions of your final model and give logical reasons why your preferred model should be favored over equivalent versions.

• It may also be possible to consider alternative models that are not equivalent but are based on the same observed variables and fitted to the same data matrix. Among alternative models that are near-covariance equivalent, give reasons why your model should be preferred.

• If a structural model was tested, do *not* make claims about verifying causality, especially if your design is nonexperimental and thus lacks design elements, such as control groups or manipulated variables, that support causal inference.

Bottom Lines and Statistical Beauty

• If no model was retained, then explain the implications for theory. For example, in what way(s) could theory be incorrect, based on your results?

• If a model is retained, then explain to your readers just what was learned as a result of your study. That is, what is the *substantive significance* of your findings? How has the state of knowledge in your area been advanced? What comes next? That is, what new questions or issues are posed?

• If your sample is not large enough to randomly split and cross-validate your analyses, then clearly state this as a limitation. If so, then replication is a necessary "what comes next" activity. Until then, restrain your enthusiasm about your model.

SUMMARY

The evaluation of a structural regression model is essentially a simultaneous path analysis and confirmatory factor analysis. Multiple-indicator assessment of constructs is represented in the measurement portion of a structural regression model, and presumed causal relations are represented in the structural part. In two-step analyses, a structural regression model is respecified as a confirmatory factor analysis model in the first step. An acceptable measurement model is required before going to the second step, which involves testing hypotheses about the structural model. The researcher should also consider equivalent versions of his or her preferred structural regression model. Equivalent versions of the structural part of a structural regression model can be generated using the same rules as for path models, and equivalent measurement models can be created according to the same principles as for CFA models. The specification of reflective measurement wherein effect indicators are specified as caused by latent variables is not appropriate in all research problems. An alternative is formative measurement where indicators are conceptualized as causes of composites. The evaluation of structural regression models represents the apex in the SEM family for the analysis of covariances. The next few chapters in Part III consider some advanced methods, starting with the analysis of means. How to avoid fooling yourself with SEM is considered in the last chapter (13), which may be the most important one in this book.

RECOMMENDED READINGS

Howell, Breivik, and Wilcox (2007) compare assumptions of standard reflective measurement with those of formative measurement. You can learn more about formative measurement in a recent special issue of the *Journal of Business Research* (Diamantopoulos, 2008). The edited volume by Vinzi, Chin, Henseler, and Wang (2009) provides in-depth coverage of the technique of PLS-PM.

Diamantopoulos, A. (Ed.). (2008). Formative indicators [Special issue]. *Journal of Business Research, 61*(12).

Howell, R. D., Breivik, E., & Wilcox, J. B. (2007). Reconsidering formative measurement. *Psychological Methods, 12,* 205–218.

Vinzi, V. E., Chin, W. W., Henseler, J., & Wang, H. (2009). (Eds.). *Handbook of partial least squares: Concepts, methods and applications in marketing and related fields.* New York: Springer.

EXERCISES

1. Calculate the rho coefficient for each factor in Figure 10.2 using the parameter estimates in Tables 10.3 and 10.4.

2. Fit the model in Figure 10.5 and to the data in Table 10.5. Now respecify this model to take direct account of measurement error in the single indicator of depression (assume $r_{XX} = .70$) and fit the respecified model to the same data. Compare estimates for direct effects on depression (from stress, SES) and also the disturbance variances for depression across the two analyses. Comment on the pattern. What is the "surprise" among other estimates?

3. Respecify the formative measurement model in Figure 10.6(b) to take direct account of measurement error at the indicator level, not the construct level.

4. Critique the model in Figure 10.5 in terms of reflective versus formative measurement.

5. Calculate a standardized effect decomposition for the structural model in Figure 10.3.

6. Show that $df_M = 47$ for the measurement model in Figure 10.2.

7. Look through the EQS or LISREL output files for the analysis of the final Houghton–Jinkerson SR model (its structural model is shown in Figure 10.3) and in particular at the sections about effect decomposition. Besides effects of factors on other factors, what else do you notice in the decomposition?

Constraint Interaction in SR Models

Recall that constraint interaction for CFA models is indicated when the value of the chi-square difference (χ_D^2) statistic for the test of the equality of the loadings of indicators for different factors depends on how the factors are scaled (Appendix 9.B). Steiger (2002) shows that the same phenomenon can happen with SR models where some factors have only two indicators and when estimates of direct effects on two or more different endogenous factors are constrained to be equal. Constraint interaction can also result in an incorrect standardized solution for an SR model if it is calculated in the way described earlier (in two steps).

The presence of constraint interaction can be detected the same way for SR and CFA models: while imposing the equality constraint, change the value of each identification constraint for the factors from 1.0 to another positive constant and rerun the analysis. If the value of the model chi square χ_M^2 changes by an amount that exceeds what is expected by rounding error, there is constraint interaction. Steiger (2002) suggests a way to deal with constraint interaction in SR models: if the analysis of standardized factors can be justified, the method of constrained estimation can be used to test hypotheses of equal standardized path coefficients and to generate correct standard errors. Constrained estimation of an SR model standardizes all factors, exogenous and endogenous.

Part III

Advanced Techniques, Avoiding Mistakes

11

Mean Structures and Latent Growth Models

The basic datum of SEM, the covariance, does not convey information about means. If only covariances are analyzed, then all observed variables are effectively mean-deviated (centered) so that substantive latent variables must have means of zero. Sometimes this loss of information is too restrictive, such as when means of repeated measures variables are expected to differ. Means are estimated in SEM by adding a mean structure to the model's basic covariance structure (i.e., its measurement or structural components). The input data for the analysis of a model with a mean structure are covariances and means (or the raw scores). The SEM approach to the analysis of means is distinguished by the capability to test hypotheses about means of substantive latent variables and the error covariance structure. The analysis of latent growth models and the multiple-sample analysis of measurement models with structured means are also considered.

LOGIC OF MEAN STRUCTURES

The technique of multiple regression (MR) provides the basic logic for analyzing covariance structures in SEM. It provides the rationale for analyzing means, too. Recall that unstandardized regression equations have both a covariance structure (B weights) and a mean structure in the form of the intercept (A) (Equation 2.1). For example, consider the scores on variables X and Y presented in Table 11.1. The unstandardized equation for predicting Y from X for these data is

$$\hat{Y} = .455\,X + 20.000$$

The regression coefficient, .455, conveys no information about the mean of either variable. The intercept, 20.000, reflects the mean of both variables and the regression coef-

TABLE 11.1. Example Bivariate Data Set

		Raw scores		Constant
Case		X	Y	△1
A		3	24	1
B		8	20	1
C		10	22	1
D		15	32	1
E		19	27	1
	M	11.000	25.000	—
	SD	6.205	4.690	—
	s^2	38.500	22.000	—

Note. $r_{XY} = .601$.

ficient, albeit with a single number. Given $M_X = 11.000$ and $M_Y = 25.000$ (Table 11.1), the intercept can be expressed according to Equation 2.5 as

$$A = 25.000 - .455 \, (11.000) = 20.000$$

Likewise, the mean of Y can be expressed as a function of the intercept, regression coefficient, and mean of X, as follows:

$$M_Y = 20.000 + .455 \, (11.000) = 25.000$$

How a computer calculates the intercept of an unstandardized regression equation provides the key to understanding the analysis of means in SEM. Look again at Table 11.1 and in particular at the column labeled △1 , which represents a constant that equals 1 for every case in this application of the McArdle–McDonald symbolism for SEM. Summarized in Table 11.2 are the results of two regression analyses with the constant. Both analyses were conducted by instructing the computer to omit from the analysis the intercept term it would otherwise automatically calculate. (This is an option in most regression modules.) In the first analysis, Y is regressed on both X and the constant. Note that the regression coefficient for X is the same as before, .455, and for the con-

TABLE 11.2. Results of Regression Analyses with a Constant for the Data in Table 11.1

Regression	Predictor(s)	Unstandardized coefficient(s)
1. Y on X and △1	X	.455
	△1	20.000
2. X on △1	△1	11.000

stant it is 20.000, which is the intercept. The second analysis in Table 11.2 concerns the regression of X on the constant. The regression coefficient in this analysis is 11.000, or the mean of X. These results illustrate two principles about mean structures:

When a criterion is regressed on a predictor and a constant, the unstandardized coefficient for the constant is the intercept.	(Rule 11.1)

When a predictor is regressed on a constant, the unstandardized coefficient is the mean of the predictor.	(Rule 11.2)

A path analytic representation of the regression analyses just described is presented in Figure 11.1. Unlike a standard path model, the one in the figure has both a covariance structure and a mean structure. The covariance structure includes the direct effects of the measured and unmeasured exogenous variables (respectively, X and D) and their variances. Estimating this covariance structure with the data in Table 11.1 using standard regression (OLS estimation) yields an unstandardized path coefficient of .455—the same as the unstandardized regression coefficient—and a disturbance variance of 14.054.[1] No information about the means is represented in this covariance structure.

The mean structure in Figure 11.1 consists of direct effects of the constant on both observed variables. Although the constant is depicted as exogenous in the figure, it is not an exogenous "variable" in the usual sense because it has no variance. The unstandardized path coefficient for the direct effect of the constant on the predictor X is 11.000, or the mean of X, just as in the corresponding regression analysis (Table 11.2). The mean of X is thus explicitly represented in the mean structure of the path model in the form of an unstandardized path coefficient.[2] Because the constant has no indirect effect on X through other variables, the unstandardized coefficient for the path $\triangle 1 \to X$ is also the total effect. The unstandardized path coefficient for the direct effect of the constant

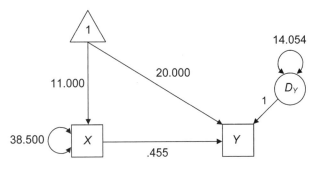

FIGURE 11.1. A path model with a mean structure.

---

[1]This error variance is calculated in OLS estimation as $(1 - r_{XY}^2)\ s_Y^2 = (1 - .601^2)\ 22.000 = 14.054$.

[2]The standardized coefficient for the path $\triangle 1 \to X$ is zero because the means of standardized variables are zero.

on the endogenous variable Y is 20.000, which is the intercept. In addition to this direct effect, the constant also has an *indirect* effect on Y through X. Using the tracing rule for this model, we obtain this result:

$$\text{Total effect of } \triangle_1 \text{ on } Y = \text{Direct effect} + \text{Indirect effect}$$
$$= 20.000 + .455 \ (11.000) = 25.000$$

which equals the mean of Y. Two additional principles about mean structures can thus be expressed in path analytic language:

The mean of an endogenous variable Y is a function of three parameters—(1) the intercept, (2) the unstandardized path coefficient(s), and (3) the mean(s) of the exogenous variable(s).	(Rule 11.3)

The model-implied (predicted) mean for an observed variable is the total effect of the constant on that variable.	(Rule 11.4)

Because the mean structure of the model in Figure 11.1 is just-identified (i.e., two observed means, two direct effects of $\triangle_1$), the predicted means for X and Y equal their observed counterparts. This fact is elaborated next.

When an SEM computer tool analyzes means, it automatically creates a constant on which variables in the model are regressed. A variable is included in the mean structure by specifying that the constant has a total effect on it. This leads to two more principles:

For exogenous variables, the unstandardized path coefficient for the direct effect of the constant is a mean.	(Rule 11.5)

For endogenous variables, though, the direct effect of the constant is an intercept but the total effect is a mean.	(Rule 11.6)

If a variable is excluded from the mean structure, the mean of that variable is assumed to be zero. Residual terms (disturbances, measurement errors) are *never* included in mean structures because their means are assumed to be zero. In fact, the mean structure may not be identified if the mean of an error term is inadvertently specified as a free parameter. Three points warrant special mention:

1. There is no standard symbol in the SEM literature for mean structures. The symbol $\triangle_1$ is used in diagrams here mainly as a pedagogical device so that you quickly recognize the presence of a mean structure and determine which variables it includes. But it is not absolutely necessary to explicitly represent mean structures in model diagrams. Some authors present just the covariance structure in a diagram and report estimates about means in accompanying tables.

2. It is theoretically possible to analyze means of observed variables in a path analysis, but this is rarely done in practice. It is more common in SEM to estimate means of latent variables (factors) represented in measurement models.

3. Special forms of maximum likelihood (ML) estimation for raw data files with missing observations, including the expectation–maximization (EM) algorithm, estimate both covariances and means. That is, they add a mean structure to the model. Depending on how these special methods are implemented in a particular SEM computer tool, it may or may not be necessary to explicitly specify a mean structure even if the original model has only a covariance structure.

IDENTIFICATION OF MEAN STRUCTURES

The two principles listed next concern identification of mean structures:

The parameters of a model with a mean structure include (1) the means of the exogenous variables, (2) the intercepts of the endogenous variables, and (3) the number of parameters in the covariance portion of the model counted in the usual way for that type of model.	(Rule 11.7)

A simple rule for counting the number of observations available to estimate the parameters of a model with both covariance and mean structures is stated next:

If v is the number of observed variables, then the number of observations equals $v(v+3)/2$ when means are analyzed.	(Rule 11.8)

The value of the expression in Rule 11.8 gives the total number of variances, nonredundant covariances, *and* means of observed variables. For instance, if there are three observed variables, then there are 3(6)/2, or nine observations, including three means, three variances, and three unique covariances (e.g., see the lower right side of Table 3.2).

In order for a mean structure to be identified, the number of its parameters cannot exceed the total number of means of the observed variables. Also, the identification status of a mean structure must be considered separately from that of the covariance structure. For example, an overidentified covariance structure will not identify an underidentified mean structure, and vice versa. If the mean structure is just-identified, it has as many free parameters as observed means; therefore (1) the model-implied means (total effects of the constant) will exactly equal the corresponding observed means; and (2) the fit of the model with just the covariance structure will be identical to that of the model with both the covariance structure and the mean structure.

For example, the mean structure of the model in Figure 11.1 has two parameters, $\triangle \to X$ and $\triangle \to Y$ (respectively, the mean of X, the intercept when regressing Y on

X). Because there are two observed means (M_X, M_Y), the mean structure here is just-identified. It was demonstrated earlier for this model that the total effect of the constant on *X* is 11.000 and on *Y* it is 25.000. Each of these predicted means equals the corresponding observed mean (Table 11.1). It is only when the mean structure is overidentified that the predicted means could differ from the observed ones. That is, one or more **mean residuals** may not equal zero. Mean residuals are calculated as the difference between observed means and model-implied (predicted) means.

ESTIMATION OF MEAN STRUCTURES

Many of the estimation methods described in earlier chapters for analyzing models with covariance structures only can be applied to models with both covariance and mean structures. This includes default ML estimation. However, incremental fit indexes, such as the Bentler CFI, may not be calculated for models with mean structures, or they may be calculated for just the covariance part of the model. When only covariances are analyzed, the baseline model is typically the independence model, which assumes zero population covariances. The independence model is more difficult to define when both covariances and means are analyzed. For example, an independence model where all covariances *and* means are fixed to zero may be very unrealistic. An alternative independence model allows for the means of the observed variables to be freely estimated (they are not assumed to be zero). Check the documentation of your SEM computer tool to determine how it defines the independence model when means are analyzed.

LATENT GROWTH MODELS

The term **latent growth model** (LGM) refers to a class of models for longitudinal data that can be analyzed in SEM or other statistical techniques, such as hierarchical linear modeling (HLM) (e.g., Raudenbush & Bryk, 2002). It may be the most common type of structural equation model with a mean structure evaluated in a single sample. The particular kind of LGM outlined below has been described by several different authors (e.g., Duncan, Duncan, Strycker, Li, & Alpert, 1999), is specified as an SR model with a mean structure, and can be analyzed with standard SEM software. The analysis of an LGM in SEM typically requires

1. A continuous dependent variable measured on at least three different occasions.

2. Scores that have the same units across time and can be said to measure the same construct at each assessment.

3. Data that are **time structured**, which means that cases are all tested at the same intervals. These intervals need not be equal. For example, a sample of children may be observed at 3, 6, 12, and 24 months of age. If some children are tested at, say, 4, 10,

15, and 30 months, their data cannot for analyzed together with those tested at other intervals. In contrast, HLM does not require time-structured data. Another advantage of HLM is that it is more flexible than the SEM approach concerning missing observations or unbalanced data (different numbers of cases are tested at different occasions). In contrast, the SEM approach offers these relative advantages: the availability of statistical indexes of whole model fit, the simultaneous analysis of multiple growth curves (e.g., multiple outcomes measured over time), and the capability to model growth curves of factors (latent variables as repeated measures outcomes).

The raw scores are *not* required to analyze an LGM. This is because such models can be analyzed with matrix summaries of the data. However, these matrix summaries must include the covariances (or correlations and standard deviations) and means of all variables, even of those that are not repeated measures variables. Willett and Sayer (1994) note that inspection of the raw scores for each case, or the **empirical growth record**, can help to determine whether it may be necessary to include curvilinear growth terms in the model. It is also possible to generate predicted growth curves for individual cases, but only when a raw data file is analyzed.

As noted by Bauer (2003), Curran (2003), and others, latent growth models analyzed in SEM are in fact multilevel (two-level) models that explicitly acknowledge the fact that scores are clustered under individuals (repeated measures). Scores from the same case are probably not independent, and this lack of independence must be taken into account in the statistical analysis. An LGM is specified differently in HLM, but HLM and SEM computer programs generate the same basic parameter estimates for the same LGM and data. This point of isomorphism between HLM and SEM is a basis for relating the two techniques (e.g., Curran, 2003), an idea that is elaborated in the next chapter.

Empirical Example

The data for this example are from Duncan and Duncan (1996), who conducted a longitudinal study of alcohol use among adolescents. A sample of 321 adolescents were surveyed annually over a 4-year period. Higher scores on the alcohol use variable indicated increasing frequencies of monthly use. The means, standard deviations, and correlations for annual reports of annual alcohol use are reported in Table 11.3. The year-to-year increases in mean levels of drinking are consistent, which suggests a positive linear trend. Also reported in the table are descriptive statistics for gender and family status. The means of these variables are, respectively, the proportion of students who are female (.573) or live with both parents (.554). These variables are analyzed later in this chapter as predictors of change.

Modeling Change

Latent growth models are often analyzed in two steps. The first concerns a change model of just the repeated measures variables. This model attempts to explain the covariances

TABLE 11.3. Input Data (Correlations, Standard Deviations, Means) for Latent Growth Models of Change in Alcohol Use over 4 Years

Variable	1	2	3	4	5	6
Alcohol use						
1. Year 1	1.000					
2. Year 2	.640	1.000				
3. Year 3	.586	.670	1.000			
4. Year 4	.454	.566	.621	1.000		
Predictors						
5. Gender	.001	.038	.118	.091	1.000	
6. Family Status	−.214	−.149	−.135	−.163	−.025	1.000
M	2.271	2.560	2.694	2.965	.573	.554
SD	1.002	.960	.912	.920	.504	.498

Note. These data are from Duncan and Duncan (1996); $N = 321$.

and means of these variables. Given an acceptable change model, the second step adds variables to the model that may predict change over time. This two-step approach makes it easier to identify potential sources of poor model fit compared with the analysis of a prediction model in a single step. There is a similar rationale for analyzing SR models in two steps (Chapter 9).

A basic model of change in alcohol use is presented in Figure 11.2. It has the following characteristics:

1.   Each annual measurement is represented as an indicator of two latent growth factors, Initial Status (IS) and Linear Change (LC). The IS factor represents the baseline level of alcohol use corrected for measurement error. Because the IS factor is analogous to the intercept in a regression equation, the unstandardized loadings on this factor are all fixed to 1 (Figure 11.2). Loadings on the LC factor are fixed to constants that correspond to times of measurement, beginning with 0 for the first measurement and ending with 3 for the last. Because these weights (0, 1, 2, 3) are positive and evenly spaced, they specify a positive linear trend. The specification that the loading of the Year 1 measurement on the LC factor equals 0 sets the initial level at this time. This means that the IS factor will be defined based on the Year 1 measurement.[3]

2.   The IS and LC factors are specified to covary. This covariance indicates the degree to which initial levels of drinking predict rates of subsequent rates of linear change. A positive covariance would indicate that adolescents with higher initial levels

---

[3]The initial level can be set to other times besides the first observation. For example, the weights (−1, 0, 1, 2) for the LC factor specify a linear trend but the initial level is now based on the second measurement. The point in time at which the initial level is set is arbitrary, but where it is set may affect estimates of factor covariances and means. It is probably simpler just to specify that the initial level corresponds to the first measurement. See Willett and Sayer (1994) for more information about where to set the initial level.

of alcohol use at Year 1 show steeper linear increases over time, and a negative covariance would indicate just the opposite.

3. The LGM of Figure 11.2 has a mean structure in which the constant has direct effects on the exogenous latent growth factors, IS and LC. This specification includes the mean of these factors as free parameters. The mean of the IS factor is the average initial level of reported alcohol use. This latent variable average is a characteristic of the whole sample. In contrast, the variance of the IS factor reflects the range of individual differences around the average initial level. Likewise, the mean of the LC factor reflects the average amount of year-to-year increase in average levels of drinking, also adjusted for measurement error. The variance of the LC factor provides information about the range of individual differences in the rate of linear annual increases in alcohol use over time.

4. The error terms of adjacent years are assumed to covary (e.g., $E_1 \smile E_2$) in Figure 11.2. Other patterns are also possible, including no error covariances (the errors are independent) or the specification of additional error covariances (e.g., $E_1 \smile E_3$). The capability to explicitly model measurement error is a potential advantage of SEM over more traditional methods for repeated measures data. For example, the analysis of variance (ANOVA) assumes that the error variances of repeated measures variables are equal and independent, which is unlikely. The technique of MANOVA (multivariate ANOVA) makes less restrictive assumptions about error variances (e.g., they can covary), but both ANOVA and MANOVA treat individual differences in growth trajectories as error variance. In contrast, one of the aims of analyzing an LGM is to model these differences.

It is no special problem to specify a linear trend if the measurement occasions are not evenly spaced. For example, Murphy, Chung, and Johnson (2002) measured levels

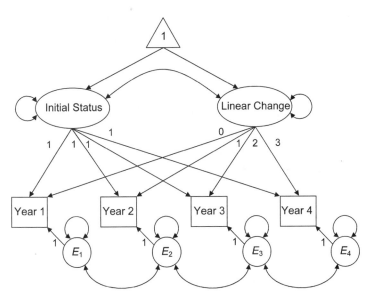

FIGURE 11.2. Latent growth model of change in level of alcohol use over 4 years.

of distress among parents at 4, 12, 24, and 60 months following the violent death of a child. Because the level of distress is expected to decline over time, the trend direction is negative. In latent growth models evaluated by Murphy et al. (2002), the loading for the initial assessment at 4 months on a linear change factor was fixed to 0 and the loading for the 12-months measurement (conducted 8 months later) was fixed to –1. Because the period of 8 months equals –1 in the slope metric, the loading of the 24-months measurement—which took place 20 months after the initial assessment—was fixed to –20/8, or –2.5. By the same logic, the loading of the 60-months measurement was fixed to –7 because it took place 56 months after the initial measurement, and –56/8 = –7. The set of loadings for the linear change factor analyzed by Murphy et al. (2002) is thus (0, –1, –2.5, –7).

It is also possible to estimate curvilinear trends in the analysis of an LGM. For example, a positive quadratic growth factor could be added to the model of Figure 11.2 by specifying that (1) loadings of the repeated measures indicators on this factor equal the square of the corresponding loadings on the LC factor (e.g., 0, 1, 4, 9); and (2) the quadratic change factor is included in the mean structure and covaries with the IS and LC factors. Improvement in model fit due to adding a quadratic growth factor to the model should be appreciable. Otherwise, the more parsimonious model with just the IS and LC factors would be preferred. It is rarely necessary to estimate curvilinear trends higher than a quadratic one for most behavioral data.

The change model of Figure 11.2 has 12 parameters. These include (1) six variances (of two factors and four measurement errors); (2) four covariances (one between the factors and three between temporally adjacent measurement errors); and (3) two factor means, or the direct effects $\boxed{1} \rightarrow$ IS and $\boxed{1} \rightarrow$ LC. With four observed variables (alcohol use over 4 years), there are 4(7)/2, or 14 observations (10 variances and unique covariances, 4 means) available to estimate the model, so $df_M = 2$. I fitted the initial change model in Figure 11.2 to the correlations, standard deviations, and means in Table 11.3 with the ML method of Mplus 5.2. The Mplus program has special syntax for latent growth models that is very compact. The analysis converged to an admissible solution. Values of selected fit statistics for the initial change model are reported in Table 11.4. Neither the exact-fit hypothesis (χ_M^2 (2) = 4.877, p = .087) nor the close-fit hypothesis (p = .266) is rejected. However, the upper bound of the 90% confidence interval based on

TABLE 11.4. Values of Selected Fit Statistics for a Latent Growth Model of Change in Level of Alcohol Use over 4 Years

Model	χ_M^2	df_M	χ_D^2	df_D	RMSEA (90% CI)	$p_{\text{close-fit } H_0}$	CFI	SRMR
Initial change model	4.877[a]	2	—	—	.067 (0–.145)	.266	.995	.019
Change model with no error covariances	8.155[b]	5	3.278[c]	3	.044 (0–.097)	.498	.994	.033
Prediction model	13.823[d]	9	—	—	.041 (0–.081)	.593	.992	.027

Note. CI, confidence interval.
[a]p = .087; [b]p = .148; [c]p = .351; [d]p = .129.

RMSEA = .067, or .145, is so high as to be consistent with the poor-fit hypothesis. Values of other approximate fit indexes seem favorable (e.g., CFI = .995), but there is a need to examine the details of the solution more closely. I inspected the parameter estimates and found that the error covariances were generally zero (range is –.063 to –.033), and none were statistically significant.

These results suggest that the initial change model is overparameterized. In a second analysis, I trimmed all three error covariances from the model with the rationale that annual measurement intervals may make these terms unnecessary. Values of selected fit statistics for the respecified change model are reported in Table 11.4. As expected, the model chi-square is larger for the respecified change model ($\chi^2_M(5)$ = 8.155) compared with that for the initial change ($\chi^2_M(2)$ = 4.877). The difference between these two model chi-squares, or $\chi^2_D(3)$ = 3.278, is not statistically significant (p = .351). However, the upper bound of the 90% confidence interval based on RMSEA = .044 for the respecified change model, or .097, is now more favorable. In addition, absolute correlation residuals (calculated in EQS) for the covariance structure of the change model are all < .06. Even though the respecified change model without error covariances departs more from perfect fit than the more complex change model with error covariances, the results for the RMSEA favor the simpler model. Based on all these results, the final model of change in reported alcohol use over 4 years is identical to the original model in Figure 11.3 except there are no measurement error correlations.

The parameter estimates for the final change model are reported in Table 11.5. The direct effects of the constant on the exogenous latent growth factors are means. The estimated mean of the IS factor is 2.291, which is close to the observed average level of alcohol use at Year 1 (2.271; see Table 11.3). The two mean values just stated are not identical because one is for an observed variable and the other is for a latent variable (IS). The estimated mean of the LC factor is .220, which indicates the average year-to-year increase in drinking. When estimating latent growth models, the statistical significance of the variances of the latent growth factors may be of substantive interest. For example, the estimated variances of the IS and LC factors are, respectively, .699 and .038, and each is statistically significant at the .01 level (Table 11.5). These results indicate that adolescents are not homogeneous in either their initial levels of drinking or the slopes of subsequent linear increases in drinking. The estimated covariance between the latent growth factors is –.080, and the corresponding estimated factor correlation is –.489. These results say that *higher* initial levels of alcohol use predict *lower* subsequent rates of linear annual increases, and vice versa. Other results reported in Table 11.5 concern measurement errors. In general, the final change model explains about 65% of the observed total standardized variance in alcohol use across the 4 years.

Means of the indicators (Year 1–4), which are endogenous, are not model parameters. However, the unstandardized total effects of the constant on the indicators are predicted means that can be compared with the observed means. For example, application of the tracing rule shows that the total effect of the constant on the first measurement of alcohol use is the sum of the indirect effects through the IS factor and through the LC factor (see Figure 11.2). Using results from Table 11.5, this total effect is calculated as follows:

TABLE 11.5. Maximum Likelihood Parameter Estimates for the Final Latent Growth Model of Change in Alcohol Use over 4 Years

Parameter	Unstandardized	SE	Standardized
	Mean structure		
Latent growth factor means			
$\triangle 1 \to IS$	2.291	.054	0
$\triangle 1 \to LC$	.220	.018	0
	Covariance structure		
Variances and covariance			
Latent growth factors			
IS	.699	.077	1.000
LC	.038	.010	1.000
IS ⌣ LC	−.080	.023	−.489
Measurement errors			
E_1	.342	.051	.328
E_2	.306	.033	.346
E_3	.273	.030	.339
E_4	.309	.046	.354

Note. $p < .01$ for all unstandardized estimates. Standardized estimates for measurement errors are proportions of unexplained variance. IS, Initial Status; LC, Linear Change.

$$
\text{Total effect of } \triangle 1 \text{ on Year 1} = \text{Indirect effect through IS} + \text{Indirect effect through LC}
$$

$$
= (\triangle 1 \to IS)(IS \to \text{Year 1}) + (\triangle 1 \to LC)(LC \to \text{Year 1})
$$

$$
= 2.291 (1) + .220 (0) = 2.291
$$

The observed mean for Year 1 is 2.271 (see Table 11.3), so the mean residual is

$$
2.271 - 2.291 = -.020
$$

that is, the predicted mean is quite close to the observed mean for Year 1. The other observed and predicted means are listed next. You should verify these results using the tracing rule:

Indicator	Observed	Predicted
Year 2	2.560	2.512
Year 3	2.694	2.732
Year 4	2.965	2.953

The final change model closely reproduces both the observed covariances and means. You can download the Mplus and EQS computer files for this analysis of the change model from this book's website (see p. 3).

Predicting Change

With an adequate model of change in hand, a model that predicts this change can now be analyzed. Predictors are added to a basic change model by (1) including them in the mean structure and (2) regressing the latent growth factors on the predictors. Consider the LGM for predicting change in alcohol use presented in Figure 11.3. The constant has direct effects on the predictors, gender and family status, which are assumed to covary. Each predictor is specified to have direct effects on both latent growth factors. This makes these factors endogenous in the prediction model, so now each has a disturbance. These disturbances are specified as correlated, which reflects the assumption that the latent growth factors share omitted causes besides gender and family status. The rest of the prediction model in Figure 11.3 is identical to the final change model analyzed earlier. The prediction model is also a MIMIC (multiple indicators and multiple causes) model because the factors have both effect and cause indicators.

With six observed variables, there are a total of 6(9)/2 = 27 observations available

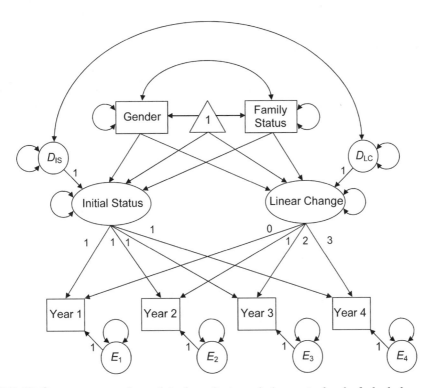

FIGURE 11.3. Latent growth model of prediction of change in level of alcohol use over 4 years.

to estimate the 16 parameters of the prediction model in Figure 11.3. These include (1) eight variances (of two observed exogenous variables, two factor disturbances, and four measurement errors); (2) two covariances (one between the predictors and another between the disturbances); (3) four direct effects on the latent growth factors (two from each predictor); and (4) four direct effects of the constant. The last four effects include the *means* of the predictors and the *intercepts* of the latent growth factors. I fitted the prediction model of Figure 11.3 with $df_M = 9$ to the data summarized in Table 10.5 with Mplus 5.2. Estimation in Mplus converged to an admissible solution, and values of selected fit statistics are reported in Table 11.4. To summarize, both the exact-fit hypothesis ($\chi_M^2 (9) = 13.823$, $p = .129$) and close-fit hypothesis ($p = .593$) are retained. The poor-fit hypothesis is rejected because the upper bound of 90% confidence for RMSEA = .041, or .081, is < .10. Values of other approximate fit indexes are reasonable (Table 11.4), and all absolute correlation residuals (calculated in EQS) are < .06. The Mplus and EQS computer files for this analysis of the prediction model in Figure 11.3 can be downloaded from this book's website (p. 3).

The ML parameter estimates for the prediction model are presented in Table 11.6. Estimates of the variances and covariance of the exogenous gender and family status variables are not reported in the table because these results are just the sample values (see Table 11.3). The results in the top part of the table concern the mean structure. The unstandardized direct effects of the constant on the exogenous predictors, gender (.573) and family status (.554), equal the observed means of each variable (Table 11.3). In contrast, unstandardized direct effects of the constant on the endogenous latent growth factors, IS (2.493) and LC (.159), are intercepts. They are intercepts because it is the total effects of the constant on IS and LC that are the estimated factor means. These means can be derived using the tracing rule as the sum of the direct effect of the constant (i.e., the intercepts) and the indirect effects through both predictors. Using results from Table 11.6, one can estimate the mean of the latent growth factors as follows where G indicates gender and F family status:

$$\text{Total effect of } \boxed{1} \text{ on IS } = (\boxed{1} \rightarrow \text{IS}) +$$
$$(\boxed{1} \rightarrow \text{G}) (\text{G} \rightarrow \text{IS}) +$$
$$(\boxed{1} \rightarrow \text{F}) (\text{F} \rightarrow \text{IS})$$

$$= 2.493 + .573 (.011) - .554 (.377)$$
$$= 2.290$$

$$\text{Total effect of } \boxed{1} \text{ on LC } = (\boxed{1} \rightarrow \text{LC}) +$$
$$(\boxed{1} \rightarrow \text{G}) (\text{G} \rightarrow \text{LC}) +$$
$$(\boxed{1} \rightarrow \text{F}) (\text{F} \rightarrow \text{LC})$$

$$= .159 + .573 (.065) + .554 (.044)$$
$$= .221$$

TABLE 11.6. Maximum Likelihood Parameter Estimates for a Latent Growth Model of Prediction of Change in Alcohol Use over 4 Years

Parameter	Unstandardized	SE	Standardized
	Mean structure		
Predictor means			
$\triangle 1 \rightarrow$ Gender	.573	.028	0
$\triangle 1 \rightarrow$ Family	.554	.028	0
Latent growth factor intercepts			
$\triangle 1 \rightarrow$ IS	2.493	.100	0
$\triangle 1 \rightarrow$ LC	.159	.034	0
	Covariance structure		
Disturbance variances and covariance			
D_{IS}	.666	.074	.950
D_{LC}	.037	.010	.961
$D_{IS} \smile D_{LC}$	−.077	.022	−.491
Direct effects			
Gender $\rightarrow$ IS	.011[a]	.105	.007
Family $\rightarrow$ IS	−.377	.106	−.244
Gender $\rightarrow$ LC	.065[a]	.035	.166
Family $\rightarrow$ LC	.044[a]	.036	.122
Measurement error variances			
E_1	.333	.050	.322
E_2	.310	.033	.349
E_3	.273	.029	.339
E_4	.312	.046	.357

Note. Standardized estimates for disturbances and measurement errors are proportions of unexplained variance. IS, Initial Status; LC, Linear Change.

[a]$p \geq .05$. For all other unstandardized estimates, $p < .01$.

These values are identical within slight rounding error to those for the final change model (see Table 11.5), and they are interpreted the same way, too.

Parameter estimates reported in the lower part of Table 11.6 concern the covariance structure of the prediction model in Figure 11.3. Standardized estimates for the disturbance variances expressed as proportions of unexplained variance indicate that the prediction model explains about $1 − .950 = .050$, or 5.0% of the variance of the IS factor, and about $1 − .961 = .039$, or 3.9% of the variance of the LC factor. The estimated disturbance correlation is negative (−.491), which says that higher initial levels of alcohol use are associated with lower rates of linear increases in alcohol use over time through their common omitted causes. This result parallels a similar one for the final change model described earlier (see Table 11.5).

The only unstandardized coefficient for a direct effect on the latent growth factors that is statistically significant is that for the direct effect of family status on the IS factor. This unstandardized coefficients equals −.377, and the corresponding standardized coefficient equals −.244. Thus, adolescents with higher scores on the family status variable have lower initial levels of alcohol use, when we adjust for measurement error and control for gender. Because this variable is coded 0 = single-parent family and 1 = two-parent family, we can say that adolescents who live with two parents have lower initial levels of drinking by .244 standard deviations compared with adolescents who live with only one parent. The unstandardized coefficient for the direct effect of gender on the LC factor, or .065, is not statistically significant. However, the standardized estimate for this path, or .166, is nearly as large in absolute value as that for the direct effect of family status on the IF factor, so here we will not ignore the former result. Because gender is coded as 0 = male and 1 = female, this result indicates that the rates of linear increase in alcohol use over time were generally greater for female than for male adolescents.

The predicted means on the alcohol use indicators for the prediction model calculated by Mplus and their observed (sample) counterparts are as follows:

Indicator	Observed	Predicted
Year 1	2.271	2.291
Year 2	2.560	2.511
Year 3	2.694	2.732
Year 4	2.965	2.953

These predicted means are very similar to the corresponding observed means. Values of the predicted means just listed can also be calculated by hand using the tracing rule, but doing so is more complicated for the prediction model of Figure 11.3 than for the final change model. This is because the total effect of the constant on each indicator in the prediction model is made up of *six* different indirect effects through the predictors (gender, family status) and both latent growth factors. Fortunately, many SEM computer programs that analyze means can automatically calculate predicted means of endogenous variables. You can download from this book's website (see p. 3) the Mplus and EQS computer files for analysis of the prediction model in Figure 11.3.

Extensions of Latent Growth Models

The basic framework for univariate growth curve modeling in a single sample just discussed can be extended in many ways. For example, the predictors in the empirical example (gender, family status) are **time-invariant predictors** in that they were measured only once. It is also possible to include **time-varying predictors** that are themselves repeated measures variables, typically measured at the same intervals as the indicators of the latent growth factors (e.g., Kaplan, 2009, chap. 8). Each predictor in the empirical example was represented as an error-free single indicator (e.g., see Figure 11.3). Given a priori estimates of error variance for observed predictors in an LGM, one could use the method described in Chapter 10 to take account of measurement error in single indicators (e.g., Figure 10.4(a)). Another way to control for measurement error is to use multiple indicators of an exogenous factor specified to predict the latent growth factors. That is, the prediction part of an LGM can be fully latent. The capability to represent latent variables as predictors in an LGM distinguishes SEM from HLM, which features no direct way to do so. It also possible to estimate in SEM indirect effects among the predictors of latent growth factors, but doing so in HLM is difficult. Even another variation that is possible in SEM is the analysis of an LGM where the repeated measures variables are all latent, each measured with multiple indicators.

It may also be possible within the limits of identification to specify that some loadings on a latent change factor as free parameters. One strategy to do so was described by Meredith and Tisak (1990) and referred to as **nonlinear curve fitting** by Kaplan (2009). In this approach for the empirical example, one would fix the loading of the Year 1 report of alcohol use on a slope factor to zero in order to estimate the intercept, fix the loading of the Year 2 report to 1 in order to scale this factor, and let the remaining two loadings be freely estimated. This tactic results in what is basically an empirical developmental function that optimally fits the slope factor to the data in a particular sample. Ratios of freely estimated loadings on the slope factor can also be formed to compare rates of development at different points in time. For instance, if the relative increases in the freely estimated loadings on the slope factor are not constant over time, the overall pattern of change may be curvilinear.

It is possible to analyze multivariate latent growth models of change across two or more domains. If these domains are measured at the same points in time, then the model reflects a **parallel growth process** (Kaplan, 2009). For example, George (2006) analyzed data from a longitudinal annual survey of students from Grade 7 to Grade 11 about their interest in science classes and attitudes about the utility of science in everyday life. George (2006) evaluated a model of **cross-domain change** in which the within-domain latent growth factors were allowed to covary across the domains. The results indicated that while students' interest in science courses steadily declines during the middle school and high school years, their views of science utility generally increase over the same time. Higher initial interest in science classes predicted a more positive attitude about science utility, and changes in one domain covaried positively with changes in the other domain. Furthermore, initial levels in each of these domains were negatively associated with change in the other domain. For example, students who in Grade 7 expressed more positive attitudes about science utility exhibited a more gradual decline in their interest in science classes from Grade 7 to 11.

Like just about any other kind of structural equation model, an LGM can be analyzed across multiple samples. For example, Benyamini, Ein-Dor, Ginzburg, and Solomon (2009) studied the impact of combat stress and posttraumatic stress symptoms on the level and growth trajectories of self-reported health among Israeli veterans of the 1982 Lebanon War who were tested at 1, 2, 3, and 20 years after the conflict. The veterans were divided into two groups, one diagnosed as exhibiting a combat stress reaction (CSR) during the war and a matched control group without this diagnosis but exposed to similar combat experiences. The CSR group showed poorer initial levels of self-reported health status. The trajectory of these veterans was positive over time (they improved), but their levels of self-reported health remained lower than that of the control group. Also, the experience of posttraumatic stress symptoms in the first few years after the war slowed the rate of subsequent improvement within the CSR group.

Bollen and Curran (2004) describe a class of models they refer to as **autoregressive latent trajectory** (ALT) models in which the indicators of latent growth factors are allowed to have direct and indirect effects on each other over time. An **autoregressive structure** is one where past values of a variable are used to predict future values of that same variable. That is, lagged (prior) variables are specified as the predictors of later measurements on the same variable. For example, the specification for the empirical example presented next

$$\text{Year 1} \rightarrow \text{Year 2} \rightarrow \text{Year 3} \rightarrow \text{Year 4}$$

illustrates an autoregressive model of one lag where the prior level of reported alcohol use has a direct effect on the current one. This model implies indirect effects, too, such as the impact of Year 1 on Year 3 through the mediator Year 2. There are many statistical techniques for analyzing autoregressive structures, including the **autoregressive integrative moving average** (ARIMA) model, which uses shifts and lags in a time series to uncover patterns, such as seasonal trends or various kinds of intervention effects. In contrast, a standard LGM does not incorporate lagged effects among the indicators. Instead, indicators are assumed to be spuriously associated due to common causes, in this case the latent growth factors (e.g., Figure 11.2). Bollen and Curran (2004) argue that this assumption is unrealistic for certain types of data. They describe an ALT model as a kind of LGM that includes direct and indirect effects among the indicators. The basic logic of an ALT model can be extended to analysis of panel data from a series of one or more repeated measures variables.

STRUCTURED MEANS IN MEASUREMENT MODELS

A standard CFA model assumes that the means of all variables are zero. However, it is possible to add a mean structure to a measurement model. An example is presented in Figure 11.4. This model's covariance structure is the measurement model of family-of-origin experiences (FOE) and marital adjustment evaluated in Chapter 9 with data collected by Sabatelli and Bartle–Haring (2003) in samples of husbands and wives. The model in Figure 11.4 also has a mean structure that includes the indicators and the factors. Based on the principles described earlier, the unstandardized path coefficients for the regression of the exogenous factors on the constant should theoretically equal the factor means. Because the indicators are endogenous, (1) the unstandardized coefficients for the direct effects of the constant on the indicators should equal the intercepts for the regressions of the indicators on the factors, and (2) the indicator means should be estimated by the total effect of the constant on each indicator.

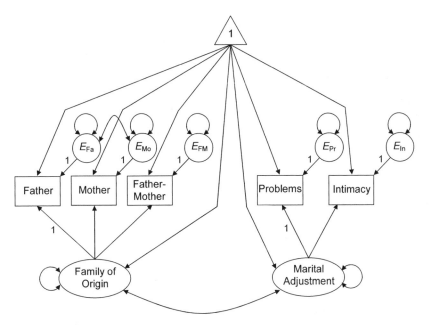

FIGURE 11.4. A measurement model of family-of-origin experiences and marital adjustment with a mean structure evaluated across samples of husbands and wives.

The model of Figure 11.4 is not identified if it was estimated with data from a single sample. This is because its mean structure would be underidentified: there are five observations (means of the five indicators), but the mean structure has seven parameters, including the means of the two factors and the intercepts of the five indicators. But if a measurement model with structured means is analyzed across multiple groups *and* constraints are imposed on certain parameter estimates, the model can be identified. A two-part strategy by Sörbom (1974) to analyze such a model is described next:

1. Fix the factor means to zero in one group, which is the same as constraining the direct effect of the constant on all factors to zero in that group. These constraints establish that group as the reference sample. The factor means are then freely estimated in all other groups, and their values are *relative* differences on the factors. Suppose that there is a treatment group and a control group. The latter is the reference sample. If the direct effect of the constant on a factor in the treatment group is –5.00, then the factor mean in the treatment group is 5 points higher than in the control group.

2. In order to reasonably estimate relative group differences on factor means, it must be assumed that the factors are defined the same way in both samples. One way to address this requirement is to scale the factors the same way by fixing the loadings of the same indicators (reference variables) to 1.0 across the groups. This tactic is recommended for multiple-sample CFA regardless of whether means are estimated (Chapter 9). Little, Slegers, and Card (2006) describe other options for scaling the factors in multiple-sample analyses of models with mean structures. The second way is to test for

measurement invariance across the groups. Specifically, there should be evidence for at least partial measurement invariance concerning the factor loadings *and* indicator intercepts. Without such evidence, there is little point in interpreting group mean differences on latent variables that are not measured the same way across the groups.

A strategy for testing measurement invariance is suggested next. First, test the equal form hypothesis, H_{form}, by freely estimating all model parameters, including those of the mean structure, in each group. If this model is rejected, then there is no basis for invariance at any level and thus none for interpreting factor mean differences. Otherwise, next test the stronger hypothesis of equal factor loadings and intercepts, $H_{\Lambda, \tau}$, by imposing cross-group equality constraints on the unstandardized estimates of each factor loading and indicator intercept. Compare this model using the chi-square difference test with the less restricted model that corresponds to H_{form}. If $H_{\Lambda, \tau}$ does not hold for a couple of indicators, then their factor loadings or intercepts can be estimated separately within each group (i.e., release the equality constraints on those parameters). This controls for unequal loadings or intercepts for regressions of the indicators on the factors across the groups. However, if none of the loadings or intercepts are equal across the groups—that is, H_{form} is the only retained invariance hypothesis—there are no grounds for interpreting factor mean contrasts.[4]

Empirical Example

In Chapter 9, we determined in a multiple-sample CFA across samples of husbands and wives that the measurement model only in Figure 11.4 is invariant concerning the unstandardized factor loadings and measurement error variances. However, it was necessary to freely estimate in each sample the factor variances and covariance and the error covariance between the mother and father indicators of the FOE factor (Tables 9.9–9.10). In this analysis, the mean structure illustrated in Figure 11.4 was added to the measurement model just described. The husbands are the reference sample, so the direct effects of the constant on both factors (the factor means) were constrained to equal zero in this group. In contrast, these two parameters were freely estimated in the sample of wives, and their unstandardized values estimate *relative* mean differences between wives and husbands on each factor. The direct effects of the constant on each indicator (the intercepts) were constrained to be equal for husbands and wives. This set of cross-group equality constraints (five in total) tests the hypothesis of equal intercepts for regressions of indicators on the factors. With five indicators in each sample, the total number of observations is 5(8)/2 × 2, or 40. The total number of free parameters is 23. This includes (1) 13 parameters constrained to be equal for husbands and wives (five indicator intercepts, five measurement error variances, and three factor loadings); (2) four parameters freely estimated within each sample (three factor variances and covari-

---

[4]A variation is to test invariance of factors loadings and intercepts over two separate steps.

ance and one error covariance) for a total of eight altogether; and (3) two factor mean differences estimated only for wives. Thus, $df_M = 40 - 23 = 17$.

The measurement model with structured means just described was simultaneously fitted using the ML method in EQS 6.1 to the covariance matrices *and* means based on the data summarized in Table 9.8 for husbands and wives. The default iteration limit of 30 in EQS was increased to 200 for this relatively complex analysis. The initial run in EQS terminated with two types of error messages. First, the program "complained" of bad start values in the initial iterations. Second, the program issued "condition codes" for three different parameters, which means that EQS was unable to calculate "proper" (admissible) estimates of these parameters without imposing inequality constraints. The problematic parameters flagged by EQS included the variance of the marital adjustment factor, the error variance of the intimacy indicator of the same factor, and the factor loading of this indicator (see Figure 11.4).

To deal with these problems, I specified in a second run with EQS start values for the parameters just mentioned. I took these values from the final measurement model for husbands and wives estimated in Chapter 9 (Table 9.10). In the second analysis with these start values, EQS issued a warning (not error) message about bad start values in the first iteration and another message about a parameter matrix that may be non-positive in the second through fourth iterations, but the program went on to generate a converged and admissible solution. You can download the EQS syntax and output files for this analysis from this book's website (p. 3). The syntax file includes specification of the start values for the second analysis. Reported next are values of selected fit statistics calculated by EQS for the covariance structure only; the 90% confidence interval based on the RMSEA is reported in parentheses:

$$\chi_M^2 (17) = 13.599, \quad p = .695$$
$$RMSEA = 0 \ (0-.033)$$
$$GFI = .986; \quad CFI = 1.000; \quad SRMR = .027$$

All absolute correlation residuals were < .10 for both the husbands and wives. The EQS program also printed a value of the RMSEA and its 90% confidence interval based on the covariances and means (i.e., the whole model of Figure 11.4), and the results are RMSEA = 0 (0–.070). We will see later in this chapter that the predicted means are similar to the observed means in both samples. Finally, none of the standardized residuals (calculated in LISREL) were statistically significant for either husbands or wives. Given all these results, the model in Figure 11.4 with equality-constrained factor loadings, indicator error variances, and intercepts was retained. You can download from this book's website (p. 3) all EQS, LISREL, and Mplus computer files for this analysis.

Reported in Table 11.7 are ML parameter estimates for the measurement model of Figure 11.4. These estimates are similar, but not identical, to those presented in Table 9.10 for the multiple-sample CFA with no mean structure. The two sets of parameter estimates are not identical because the mean structure in Figure 11.4 was estimated

TABLE 11.7. Maximum Likelihood Parameter Estimates for the Covariance Structure of a Two-Factor Model of Family-of-Origin Experiences and Marital Adjustment with Structured Means Analyzed across Samples of Husbands and Wives

Parameter	Husbands			Wives		
	Unst.	SE	St.	Unst.	SE	St.
			Unconstrained estimates			
Factor variances and covariance						
FOE	85.654	20.474	1.000	139.199	29.405	1.000
Mar Adj	459.106	106.661	1.000	595.685	149.121	1.000
FOE ⌣ Mar Adj	95.053	28.249	.479	140.477	40.883	.488
Measurement error covariance						
E_{Fa} ⌣ E_{Mo}	-8.925^a	14.293	−.161	20.781^a	14.442	.374
			Equality-constrained estimates			
Factor loadings						
Mar Adj → Probs	1.000^b	—	.688	1.000^b	—	.734
Mar Adj → Intim	.917	.142	.979	.917	.142	.984
FOE → Father	1.000^b	—	.828	1.000^b	—	.883
FOE → Mother	.859	.078	.668	.859	.078	.753
FOE → Fa-Mo	.932	.139	.663	.932	.139	.749
Measurement error variances						
E_{Pr}	510.316	89.025	.526	510.316	80.025	.461
E_{In}	16.757^a	61.705	.042	16.757^a	61.705	.032
E_{Fa}	39.421^c	15.789	.315	39.421^c	15.789	.221
E_{Mo}	78.371	15.438	.554	78.371	15.438	.433
E_{Fa-Mo}	94.944	16.096	.560	94.944	16.096	.440

Note. Unst., unstandardized; St., standardized; FOE, family-of-origin experiences. Standardized estimates for measurement errors are proportions of unexplained variance.

$^a p \geq .05$; ^{b}not tested for statistical significance; $^c p < .05$. For all other unstandardized estimates, $p < .01$.

with cross-group equality constraints imposed on the indicator intercepts. However, the results in Table 11.7 for the measurement model are so close to those in Table 9.10 that no new interpretation is needed.

Presented in the top part of Table 11.8 are the unstandardized estimates of the direct effects of the constant on the factors calculated for wives only. They are interpreted as estimated factor mean differences between husbands and wives adjusted for measurement error. The result for the FOE factor is 3.196, indicating that the mean score for wives on this factor is predicted to be about 3.2 points higher than that for husbands. That is, wives generally report more positive FOE experiences than their husbands. The estimated standard error for this factor mean difference is 1.643. In a large sample—and if we assume normality and homogeneity of variance—the ratio $3.196/1.643 = 1.95$ is interpreted as a z test of whether the estimated factor mean contrast differs statistically from zero. The positive two-tailed critical value of z at the .05 level is 1.96. Thus, the estimated mean difference between wives and husbands of about 3.2 points on the FOE factor falls just short of statistical significance at the .05 level. However, the group size for this analysis is not large ($n = 103$), and the factor variances were estimated separately for wives and husbands, so the homogeneity of variance assumption may not hold. This means that the p value for this z test may not be very accurate. The estimated mean difference on the marital adjustment factor is .665 and is not close to being statistically significant because the ratio of this difference over its standard error is $z = .665/3.275 = .203$.

Reported in the bottom part of Table 11.8 are the estimates of intercepts for regressions of the indicators on the factors when equal values are assumed for husbands and wives. Because the direct effects of the constant on both factors are constrained to zero for the husbands, the constant has no indirect effects on the indicators through the factors in this group. Thus, (1) the total effects of the constant on the indicators consist of direct effects only, and (2) these total effects are the model-implied means of the indicators for the husbands. However, the intercepts for the wives reported in Table 11.8 are not also predicted means. Because the constant has direct effects on the factors for wives, it has both direct and indirect effects on the indicators in this group. Thus, it is the *total effects* of the constant on the indicators that equal the model-implied means of the indicators for the wives. Presented in Table 11.9 are the predicted indicator means automatically calculated by EQS and also the observed means for husbands and wives.

TABLE 11.8. Maximum Likelihood Parameter Estimates for the Mean Structure of a Two-Factor Model of Family-of-Origin Experiences and Marital Adjustment with Structured Means Analyzed across Samples of Husbands and Wives

	Husbands		Wives	
Parameter	Unstandardized	SE	Unstandardized	SE
	Estimated for wives only			
Factor means				
△1 → FOE	0	—	3.196[a]	1.643
△1 → Mar Adj	0	—	.665[a]	3.275
	Equality-constrained estimates			
Indicator intercepts				
△1 → Probs	158.330	2.664	158.330	2.664
△1 → Intim	137.871	1.987	137.871	1.987
△1 → Father	83.079	1.055	83.079	1.055
△1 → Mother	84.493	1.009	84.493	1.009
△1 → Fa-Mo	81.535	1.153	81.535	1.153

Note. FOE, family-of-origin experiences. All standardized estimates are zero.
[a]$p \geq .05$. For all other unstandardized estimates, $p < .01$.

TABLE 11.9. Observed and Predicted Means for a Two-Factor Model of Family-of-Origin Experiences and Marital Adjustment with Structured Means Analyzed across Samples of Husbands and Wives

Indicator	Husbands		Wives	
	Observed	Predicted	Observed	Predicted
Marital adjustment indicators				
Problems	155.547	158.330	161.779	158.996
Intimacy	137.971	137.871	138.382	138.482
Family-of-origin experiences indicators				
Father	82.764	83.079	86.229	86.276
Mother	85.494	84.493	86.392	87.238
Father–Mother	81.003	81.535	85.046	84.514

Each predicted mean is generally similar to the corresponding observed mean in both samples.

For an example of the analysis of measurement models with means over time instead of groups, see Contrada, Boulifard, Idler, Krause, and Labouvie (2006), who estimated changes in factor means in a longitudinal study of depression among heart surgery patients.

SR Models with Structured Means

The analysis of an SR model with a mean structure over multiple groups follows the same basic rationale as for a CFA model with a mean structure. For example, factor measurement should be specified the same way in all groups. For the group selected as the reference sample, all direct effects of the constant on the factors are fixed to zero in order to identify the mean structure. A notable difference is that direct effects of the constant on endogenous factors are interpreted as relative group differences in the *intercepts* for the regression of those factors on other variables specified as direct causes, such as exogenous factors. Because of different identification requirements for an LGM, it is possible to estimate the means and intercepts of latent growth factors in a single sample. This implies that these same parameters can be estimated separately for each group when an LGM is simultaneously analyzed across multiple samples.

MIMIC MODELS AS AN ALTERNATIVE TO MULTIPLE-SAMPLE ANALYSIS

Another way to estimate group differences on latent variables is through the specification of a MIMIC model where factors with effect indicators are regressed on one or more dichotomous cause indicators that represent group membership. The total sample in this approach is not partitioned into subsamples (although subsamples are still required in the study design). Thus, there are no special identification requirements beyond the usual ones for single-sample analyses for the types of MIMIC models described next. However, the MIMIC approach described here assumes measurement invariance across the groups. Indeed, there is no way to test this assumption in the MIMIC approach to a multiple-sample analysis.

Consider the model in Figure 11.5. It is specified as a MIMIC alternative to the model of Figure 11.4, which was analyzed across separate samples of husbands and wives. The single-cause indicator in the MIMIC model of Figure 11.5 is a dichotomy that represents the spouse coded as 0 = husband and 1 = wife. This contrast variable is specified to have direct effects on an FOE factor with three effect indicators and a marital adjustment factor with two effect indicators. These are the same factors and indicators as represented in Figure 11.4, but the factors are endogenous in the MIMIC model of Figure 11.5 and thus have disturbances. These disturbances are allowed to covary, which reflects the assumption that the factors have common omitted causes besides the difference between husbands and wives. The MIMIC model of Figure 11.5 does not have a mean structure; instead, it has just a covariance structure. This implies that all means are assumed to be zero (they are not analyzed). However, the path coefficients for the

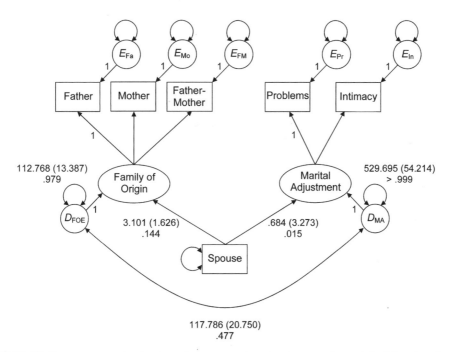

FIGURE 11.5. A MIMIC (multiple indicators and multiple causes) model of family-of-origin experiences and marital adjustment evaluated in a single sample with spouse as a cause indicator. Parameter estimates are reported as unstandardized (standard error) standardized. Standardized disturbance variances are proportions of unexplained variance.

direct effects of the spouse variable will provide information about whether the difference between husbands and wives predicts the factors.

Reported in Table 11.10 are the correlations, standard deviations, and means for the FOE indicators and marital adjustment indicators for the total sample of $N = 206$ cases (103 couples) in the Sabatelli and Bartle–Haring (2003) data set. Also reported in Table 11.10 are the correlations (specifically, point-biserial correlations, r_{pb}) between the spouse variable and each of the indicators calculated from the group means and standard deviations (Kline, 2004, p. 114). With six observed variables altogether—including five effect indicators and one cause indicator (spouse)—there are $6(7)/2 = 21$ observations.

The MIMIC model of Figure 11.5 was fitted to the covariance matrix assembled from the correlations and standard deviations in Table 11.10 with the ML method of LISREL 8.8. The factor loadings and measurement error variances were specified as fixed and equal to the corresponding values reported in Table 11.9, which assume equality of husbands and wives across these parameters. The MIMIC model of Figure 11.5 does not assume correlated errors between the father and mother indicators of the FOE factor. This is because this correlation was estimated earlier to be negative for husbands but positive for wives (Table 11.9). In the total sample, this error correlation may be about zero. With these specifications, the MIMIC model has six free parameters, including (1) three variances (of the spouse cause indicator and two-factor disturbances); (2) one covariance between the factor disturbances; and (3) the two direct effects of the dichotomous cause indicator on the factors, so $df_M = 21 - 6 = 15$.

The analysis of the MIMIC model with ML estimation in LISREL converged to an admissible solution. This occurred even though the data matrix is ill scaled (see Table 11.10)—rescale this matrix if you reproduce this analysis in a different SEM computer

TABLE 11.10. Input Data (Correlations, Standard Deviations) for Analysis of a MIMIC (Multiple Indicators and Multiple Causes) Model of Family-of-Origin Experiences and Marital Adjustment

Variables	1	2	3	4	5	6
Martial adjustment indicators						
1. Problems	1.000					
2. Intimacy	.700	1.000				
Family-of-origin experiences indicators						
3. Father	.253	.409	1.000			
4. Mother	.247	.355	.659	1.000		
5. Father–Mother	.301	.330	.622	.513	1.000	
Predictor						
6. Spouse	.097	.010	.139	.035	.145	1.000
M	158.663	138.177	84.497	85.943	83.025	.500
SD	32.064	21.463	12.357	12.748	13.813	.500

Note. These data are derived from those summarized in Table 9.8; $N = 206$. Means are reported but not analyzed.

tool and encounter a problem. Overall model fit seems adequate based on the values of selected fit indexes:

$$\chi^2_{\mathrm{M}}(15) = 14.188, \quad p = .511$$
$$\mathrm{RMSEA} = 0 \; (0\text{--}.061); \quad p_{\text{close-fit } H_0} = .890;$$
$$\mathrm{GFI} = .977; \quad \mathrm{CFI} = 1.000; \quad \mathrm{SRMR} = .032$$

Estimates for the free model parameters except for the variance of the spouse cause indicator, which is just the sample value (Table 11.10), are presented in Figure 11.5 in the proper places. The unstandardized coefficients (and standard errors) for direct effects of the spouse cause indicator on the FOE factor and on the marital adjustment factor are, respectively, 3.101 (1.626) and .684 (3.273). Because spouse is coded as 0 = husband and 1 = wife, these positive regression weights indicate higher predicted overall standings on both factors for wives than husbands. The coefficient for the direct effect of spouse on marital adjustment is not statistically significant at the .05 level because $z = .684/3.273 = .209$, $p = .835$. The standardized coefficient for this path, .015, is also quite small. The unstandardized coefficient for the direct effect of spouse on FOE experiences is nearly statistically significant because $z = 3.101/1.626 = 1.91$, $p = .057$. The standardized coefficient for this path is .144. These results obtained in the total sample for the MIMIC model are similar to those for the measurement model with structured means analyzed earlier across both samples. To summarize, wives report somewhat better FOE experiences than their husbands, but not clearly better marital adjustment. You can download all LISREL and Mplus computer files for this analysis from the book's website (p. 3). See Kano (2001) for information about the specification of MIMIC models in experimental designs where groups are compared across latent variables instead of observed variables only as in ANOVA or MANOVA.

SUMMARY

Means are estimated in SEM by regressing exogenous or endogenous variables on a constant that equals 1.0. It is usually not necessary to manually create a constant because most full-featured SEM computer programs do so automatically when means are analyzed. The parameters of a mean structure include the means of the exogenous variables and the intercepts of the endogenous variables. Means of endogenous variables are not considered model parameters, but predicted means on these variables, calculated as total effects of the constant, can be compared with the observed means. In order to be identified, the number of parameters in a mean structure cannot exceed the number of observed means. A latent growth model for longitudinal data is basically a structural regression model with a mean structure. Each repeated measures variable is specified as an indicator of at least two different factors—one representing the initial status and the other, the rate of change. These factors are usually assumed to covary, which allows for the possibility that rate of change is related to initial status. When estimating group mean differences on factors, one way to identify the mean structure is to select one sample as the reference group, constrain the factors' means or intercepts to zero in this group, but freely estimate these parameters in all other groups. The results indicate the relative difference between each of these groups and the reference sample on the factor mean or intercept. However, the hypothesis of at least partial measurement invariance of the factor loadings and indicator intercepts should be tenable in order to reasonably interpret group mean differences on factors. An alternative way to estimate group differences on latent variables is to analyze a MIMIC model with data from the total sample. The factors in the MIMIC model are regressed on at least one cause indicator that represents group membership. An advantage of this approach is that there are no special identification requirements beyond those for a single-sample analysis.

RECOMMENDED READINGS

The Duncan et al. (1999) book on latent growth curve modeling is a seminal work, and the more recent book by Bollen and Curran (2006) in this area covers newer topics and analysis techniques. Green and Thompson (2006) contrast standard techniques for analyzing multiple means, including MANOVA and discriminant analysis, with structured means modeling in SEM including the analysis of MIMIC models.

Bollen, K. A., & Curran, P. J. (2006). *Latent curve models: A structural equation perspective.* Hoboken, NJ: Wiley.

Duncan, T. E., Duncan, S. C., Strycker, L. A., Li, F., & Alpert, A. (1999). *An introduction to latent variable growth curve modeling: Concepts, issues, and applications.* Mahwah, NJ: Erlbaum.

Green, S. B., & Thompson, M. S. (2006). Structural equation modeling for conducting tests of differences in multiple means. *Psychosomatic Medicine, 68,* 706–717.

12

Interaction Effects and Multilevel SEM

This chapter introduces two advanced techniques in SEM: (1) the estimation of interaction effects of observed or latent variables and (2) multilevel SEM. Whole books have been written about these topics, so there is no way to cover both of them in great detail in a single chapter. Instead, I want to make you aware that these possibilities exist in SEM and cite enough advanced works in each area so that you can learn more through additional study. Each topic represents the expansion of SEM to other horizons, some of which may help you to evaluate an even wider range of hypotheses in the future. As the French chemist and microbiologist Louis Pasteur once said: Chance only favors invention for minds that are prepared for discoveries by patient study and persevering efforts. Keep this thought in mind as you read this chapter.

INTERACTION EFFECTS OF OBSERVED VARIABLES

Estimation of the interaction effects of continuous observed variables in SEM uses the same method as in **moderated multiple regression** (MMR). This method involves creating **product terms** that represent interaction effects. A product term is literally the product of the scores from two different variables, such as $XW = X \times W$. The same method is used to estimate curvilinear relations (trends) except that product terms in this case are created by exponentiation where the scores (base numbers) are raised to a power, such as $X^2 = X \times X$, which represents a quadratic trend. These terms are known as **power terms** or **polynomials**. Estimation of the curvilinear effects of continuous observed variables in multiple regression is not described here, but see Cohen, Cohen, West, and Aiken (2003) for more information. There is also a supplemental reading about the estimation of curvilinear effects in SEM that you can download from this book's website (see p. 3).

Consider the data in Table 12.1 where $M_W = 16.38$. The multiple correlation of predictors X and W with the criterion Y is .183. This result summarizes the linear effects

**TABLE 12.1. Data Set for an Interaction
Effect of Continuous Observed Variables**

Predictors			Criterion
X	W	XW	Y
2	10	20	5
6	12	72	9
8	13	104	11
11	10	110	11
4	24	96	11
7	19	133	10
8	18	144	7
11	25	275	5

of the predictors, but inspection of the scores in Table 12.1 indicates a more complex pattern: the relation of X to Y is linear and *positive* for cases with lower scores on W, but it is linear and *negative* for cases with higher scores on W. This conditional relation of X to Y is illustrated in the scatterplot of Figure 12.1 where cases with scores $< M_W$ are represented with closed circles and cases with scores $> M_W$ are represented with open circles. Although it is not as apparent, there is a similar change in the direction of the relation of W to Y: positive at higher levels of X, negative at lower levels. So W moderates the relation of X to Y, just as X moderates the relation of W to Y. This describes interaction, which is always symmetrical.

The product term XW in Table 12.1 represents the interaction effect just described when entered in the regression equation along with X and W as predictors.[1] The multiple correlation from this analysis is .910, much greater than the corresponding value with just X and W in the equation (.183). The unstandardized regression equation is

$$\hat{Y} = 1.768\,X + .734W - .108\,XW - 3.118 \qquad (12.1)$$

The coefficient for the product term in Equation 12.1, or –.108, estimates the interaction effect controlling for both main effects. A method to interpret this effect is briefly explained (Cohen et al., 2003). First, rearrange the unstandardized regression equation so that there is no product term. For example, the expression presented next

$$\hat{Y} = (1.768 - .108W)\,X + .734W - 3.118 \qquad (12.2)$$

is algebraically equivalent to Equation 12.1 but has no product term. The regression coefficient for X in Equation 12.2 (or 1.768 – .108W) can be seen as one that depends on the level of W.

Next, substitute in Equation 12.2 meaningful values of W and inspect the effect

---

[1]A common mistake is to omit the variables X and W when XW is entered into the equation, but XW by itself does not represent an interaction effect.

on the coefficients for X. For instance, given $M_W = 16.38$ and $SD_W = 6.02$ for the data in Table 12.1, scores on W that fall $-2, -1, 0, +1,$ and $+2$ standard deviations away from the mean are, respectively,

$$4.34, 10.36, 16.38, 22.40, \text{ and } 28.42$$

Suppose that $W = 22.40$ (i.e., $M_W + SD_W$). Plugging this value for W in Equation 12.2 generates the unstandardized regression equation presented next:

$$\hat{Y}_{W=22.40} = -.651 \, X + 13.324$$

Presented in Table 12.2 are all **simple regressions** for predicting Y from X at each of the five levels of W just defined. The slopes of these conditional equations, or **simple slopes**, progressively change from a negative slope of -1.301 for cases with scores on W two standard deviations above the mean to a positive slope of 1.299 for cases with scores on W two standard deviations below the mean. For cases with average scores on W, the simple slope is practically zero ($-.001$), so X and Y are unrelated at this level of W.

When the simple slope of a conditional regression line is divided by its standard error (Preacher, Rucker, & Hayes, 2007, p. 192), the resulting ratio is in large samples a z test of statistical significance. A related concept is that of **regions of significance**, or a range of values on W for which the conditional regression of Y on X is statistically significant. Preacher et al. (2007) refer to confidence intervals based on simple slopes as **confidence bands**, and these bands can be plotted in order to interpret interaction.

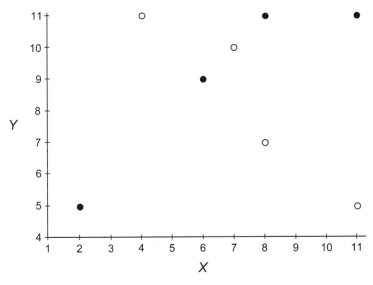

FIGURE 12.1. Scatterplot for the data set in Table 12.1 for variables X and Y. Closed dots indicate scores on W below the mean, and open dots indicate scores on W above the mean.

TABLE 12.2 Regression Equations for Predicting Y from X Conditional on the Level of W for the Data Set in Table 12.1

	W	
Level	Score	Regression equation
+2 SD	28.42	$\hat{Y} = -1.301\,X + 17.712$
+1 SD	22.40	$\hat{Y} = -.651\,X + 13.324$
Mean	16.38	$\hat{Y} = -.001\,X + 8.905$
–1 SD	10.36	$\hat{Y} = .649\,X + 4.486$
–2 SD	4.34	$\hat{Y} = 1.299\,X + .068$

Specifically, a third variable W moderates the relation between X and Y where the confidence bands do not include slopes of zero. Preacher, Curran, and Bauer (2006) describe computer tools for analyzing simple slopes, including some utilities freely available over the Internet.[2] There are also freely available scripts for SAS/STAT for visualizing interactions with three-dimensional spin plots.[3]

Standardized regression coefficients (beta weights) do not have the normal interpretation for power terms that represent interaction effects. This is because, in most cases, the product of z scores from two different variables, such as $z_X \times z_W$, does not equal the z score of the product of the corresponding unstandardized scores, or z_{XW}. As noted by Whisman and McClelland (2005), multiple regression procedures in statistical computer programs typically report beta weights for the data in Table 12.1 equivalent to the model

$$\hat{z}_Y = b_1\,z_X + b_2\,z_W + b_3\,z_{XW} \tag{12.3}$$

but the weight b_3 does not correctly estimate the standardized interaction effect. The correct standardized model would include the term "$b_3\,z_X\,z_W$," but this term does not appear in Equation 12.3. Whisman and McClelland (2005) offer this advice: It is best to avoid standardized regression coefficients in MMR, and instead one should focus on the unstandardized regression coefficients. Aiken and West (1991) describe how to obtain correct beta weights in MMR.

The method for unstandardized variables just described can be extended to estimate higher-order interactions. For example, the product term XW represents the linear × linear interaction of X and W in predicting Y. Such an interaction means that the linear relation of X to Y changes uniformly over the levels of W (e.g., Table 12.2). The product term XW^2 represents a linear × quadratic interaction, which means that the linear relation of X to Y changes faster at higher (or lower) levels of W. Estimation of this

[2]www.people.ku.edu/~preacher/interact/index.html

[3]www.ats.ucla.edu/stat/sas/faq/spplot/reg_int_cont.htm

effect would require that the terms X, W, and W^2 (i.e., the quadratic trend) are in the model along with XW^2. It is also possible to estimate three-way or higher interactions. For example, the product term XWU represents the three-way linear interaction among these variables when all lower-order effects are also included in the equation. These include terms for the linear effects (X, W, U) and all linear × linear interactions (XW, XU, WU). A three-way linear interaction means that the linear × linear interaction of X and W changes uniformly across the levels of U. Because interaction is symmetrical, the same interpretation applies to each of the other two linear × linear interactions regarding the corresponding third variable. Estimation of higher-order interactive (and curvilinear) effects requires the analysis of numerous product terms, so very large samples may be needed for adequate statistical power. See Dawson and Richter (2006) for more information about the estimation of three-way interactions in MMR.

A problem that can occur when analyzing product terms is extreme collinearity. This is because correlations between product terms and their constituent variables can be so high that the analysis can fail or the results are unstable. One way to address this problem is to mean-center the original variables before calculating product terms based on them. **Mean centering** occurs when the average of a variable is adjusted to zero (the mean is subtracted from every score), and centering tends to reduce—but not typically to eliminate—correlations between product terms and constituent variables. An alternative is to create a **residualized product term** using the technique of **residual centering** that is calculated controlling for the main effects and consequently is uncorrelated with them (Lance, 1988; Little, Bovaird, & Widaman, 2006). A residualized product term is created in two steps by first regressing the product term on all constituent main effect terms (e.g., XW scores are regressed on both X and W). The residuals from the regression analysis just described are uncorrelated with the main effects but still convey information about the interaction effect. In a second regression analysis, the criterion is regressed on X, W, and the residualized XW term created in the first analysis.

Another complication is measurement error. Score reliabilities of product terms can be lower than those of scores on the component variables. This in turn reduces both the absolute coefficient for the product term and the power of corresponding statistical tests (Jaccard & Wan, 1995). Measurement error in the outcome variable that varies across the levels of a predictor can bias the regression coefficient for product terms that involve that predictor (Baron & Kenny, 1986). One way to address these problems is to use predictor variables with excellent score reliabilities. Another is to estimate the interaction effects of latent variables in the multiple-indicator (i.e., SEM) approach described later. This method controls for score unreliability through the specification of a measurement model, just as in the technique of CFA or in the analysis of an SR model.

INTERACTION EFFECTS IN PATH MODELS

The interactive effects of observed variables are represented in path models with the appropriate product terms and all constituent variables. Consider the **moderated**

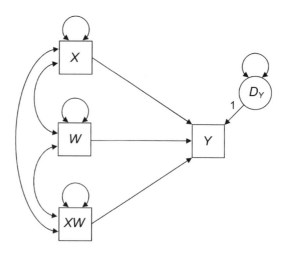

FIGURE 12.2. Path analytic representation of an interactive effect of continuous observed variables.

path analysis (MPA) model in Figure 12.2 where X, W, and the interaction XW are all specified as direct causes of Y. These three exogenous variables are specified to covary, but creation of a residualized product term would eliminate the paths $X \curvearrowleft XW$ and $W \curvearrowleft XW$ in this model. The unstandardized coefficients for the paths

$$X \to Y, W \to Y, \text{ and } XW \to Y$$

estimate, respectively, the linear effect of X, the linear effect of W, and the linear × linear interactive effect, each controlling for all other effects on Y. When means are not analyzed in MPA, there are no intercepts. However, it is still possible to analyze simple slopes, regions of significance, and confidence bands for interaction effects in MPA (Preacher et al., 2007). Keep the following points in mind:

1. Kenny (2009) reminds us that just as a mediational model is a causal model (Chapter 7), so too is a model of moderation. This means that if the basic directionality assumptions are incorrect, then the results may be of little value. For example, an interaction effect XW can be reversed if the direct effect between X and Y is reversed (i.e., Y causes X instead of the opposite).

2. Kenny (2009) gives this example of how curvilinear effects can be confounded with interactive effects. Suppose that X is income and Y is work motivation. The relation between these two variables is curvilinear such that their covariation is stronger at lower levels of X. If variable W is age, then because younger workers earn less money, the "interaction" between age and income effect could be found, such that the relation between income and motivation is stronger for younger workers. In order to avoid confusing curvilinear and interactive effects, Edwards (2009) recommends the routine inclusion of the power terms X^2 and W^2 whenever estimating coefficients for the prod-

uct term *XW*. That is, curvilinear testing cannot be disregarded when testing for interaction.

3. Edwards (2009) reminds us that although product terms such as *XW* are represented as causal variables in MPA models (e.g., Figure 12.2), they actually have no causal potency by themselves. This is because a product term does not represent a unique entity apart from its component variables. Instead, it is a mathematical construction that represents conditional or joint effects on the outcome variable (controlling for main effects) that can be examined through inspection of simple slopes, regions of significance, and confidence bands.

MEDIATION AND MODERATION TOGETHER

It is also possible to represent both mediation (indirect effects) and moderation (interactive effects) in the same structural model. Baron and Kenny (1986) described **mediated moderation**, which involves the specification that an interactive effect is mediated by at least one other variable. Consider the MPA model in Figure 12.3, which represents the hypothesis that the interaction of *X* and *W* is entirely mediated by the prior variable *M*. In the analysis of a model basically identical to that of Figure 12.3, Lance (1988) studied the relation of memory demand (*X*), complexity of social perception (*W*), and their interaction effect (*XW*) on the overall accuracy of recall of the script of a lecture (*Y*). The model also included a mediator, recollection of specific behaviors mentioned in the script (*M*), through which the interaction effect was specified to influence overall accuracy of recall. Lance's (1988) results suggested that (1) the indirect effect of the memory demand × cognitive complexity interaction was statistically significant, but (2) the direct effects of the individual component variables on overall accuracy were not

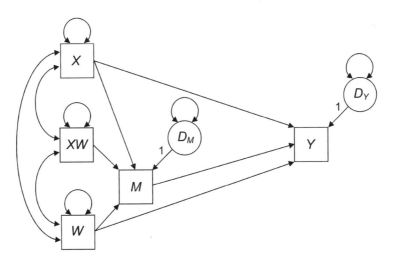

FIGURE 12.3. Path model with mediated moderation.

statistically significant. These results are consistent with "pure" mediation of the effects of memory demand, cognitive complexity, and their interaction on recall through recollection of specific behaviors.

James and Brett (1984) described **moderated mediation**, also known as a **conditional indirect effect** (Preacher et al., 2007). It is indicated when the strength of an indirect effect varies across the levels of another variable. In the multiple-sample analysis of a path model, this other variable is group membership. If the magnitude of an indirect effect differs appreciably across the groups, there is evidence for moderated mediation. If the moderator is instead a continuous variable W, then moderated mediation can be represented in a moderated path model and estimated in a single sample. There is more than one kind of moderated mediation. For example, the model in Figure 12.4(a) rep-

(a) First-stage moderation

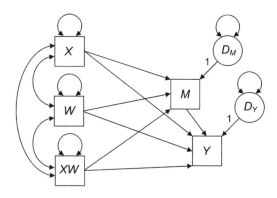

(b) Second-stage moderation

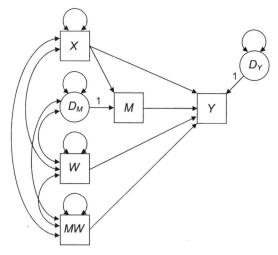

FIGURE 12.4. Two examples of moderated mediation for the indirect effect $X \rightarrow M \rightarrow Y$. (a) Path $X \rightarrow M$ depends on W. (b) Path $M \rightarrow Y$ depends on W.

resents **first-stage moderation** (Edwards & Lambert, 2007) where the first path of the indirect effect of X on Y through M, or X → M, depends on the fourth variable W. This moderation effect is represented in Figure 12.4(a) by the regression of M on X, W, and the product term XW. This model also represents the hypothesis that the first path of the indirect effect of W on Y through M, or W → M, depends on X.

The path model in Figure 12.4(b) represents **second-stage moderation** where the second path of the indirect effect of X on Y through M, or M → Y, is moderated by W. In this model, the interaction effect concerns variables W and M. The product term WM is specified to covary with the component variable W and the disturbance variance for the other component variable, M. The latter is required because mediators are always endogenous, and endogenous variables are not permitted to have unanalyzed associations with other variables in structural equation models. Regressing the outcome variable Y on X, M, W, and the product term WM estimates whether the path M → Y depends on W. Other forms of moderated mediation described by Edwards and Lambert (2007) are as follows:

1. **First- and second-stage moderation** occurs when a fourth variable W moderates both paths of the indirect effect X → M → Y. A variation is when one variable, such as W, moderates the first part of the indirect effect, or X → M, and a different variable, such as Z, moderates the second path, or M → Y.

2. Conditional indirect effects can also involve the direct effect, or the path X → Y in the examples to this point, and also the total effect of X on Y. For example, in **direct effect and first-stage moderation**, a fourth variable moderates both the direct effect between X and Y and just the first path of the indirect effect of X on Y, or X → M. In **direct effect and second-stage moderation**, an external variable moderates both the direct effect and the second path of the indirect effect, or M → Y. And in **total effect moderation**, an external variable moderates both paths of the indirect effect and also the direct effect.

Several recent works deal with the estimation of mediated moderation or moderated mediation in MPA. The approach by Preacher et al. (2007) that features the analysis of simple slopes, regions of significance, and confidence bands was mentioned earlier. Edwards and Lambert (2007) describe an approach based on effect decomposition and graphical plotting of conditional indirect effects. Fairchild and MacKinnon (2009) give equations for standard errors of mediated moderation effects and moderated mediation effects, as well as step-by-step suggestions for testing models with both kinds of effects just mentioned. Hopwood (2007) does so for applications in the area of early intervention research. For an example of the analysis of mediated moderation and moderated mediation in the same path model, see Clapp and Beck (2009). These authors, studying a sample of survivors of serious motor vehicle accidents, examined whether the indirect effects of posttraumatic stress disorder on social support through attitudes about the usefulness of social networks in coping with stress is moderated by childhood victimization and elapsed time from the accident.

INTERACTIVE EFFECTS OF LATENT VARIABLES

In the **indicant product approach** of SEM, product terms are specified as multiple indicators of latent product variables that represent curvilinear or interactive effects. We will consider only the estimation of interactive effects of latent variables, but the same basic principles apply to the estimation of curvilinear effects of latent variables. Suppose that factor A has two indicators, X_1 and X_2, and factor B has two indicators, W_1 and W_2. The reference variable for A is X_1, and the reference variable for B is X_3. Equations that specify the measurement model for these indicators are:

$$
\begin{aligned}
X_1 &= A + E_{X_1} & W_1 &= B + E_{W_1} \\
X_2 &= \lambda_{X_2} A + E_{X_2} & W_2 &= \lambda_{W_2} B + E_{W_2}
\end{aligned}
\tag{12.4}
$$

The parameters of this measurement model include the loadings of X_2 and W_2 on their respective factors ($\lambda_{X_2}, \lambda_{W_2}$), the variances of the four measurement errors, and the variances and covariance of factors A and B.

The latent product variable AB represents the interactive effect of factors A and B when they are analyzed together with A and B in the same structural model. Its indicators are the four product indicators $X_1 W_1$, $X_1 W_2$, $X_2 W_1$, and $X_2 W_2$. By taking the product of the corresponding expressions in Equation 12.4 for the nonproduct indicators, the equations of the measurement model for the product indicators are

$$
\begin{aligned}
X_1 W_1 &= AB + AE_{W_1} + BE_{X_1} + E_{X_1} E_{W_1} \\
X_1 W_2 &= \lambda_{W_2} AB + AE_{W_2} + \lambda_{W_2} BE_{X_1} + E_{X_1} E_{W_2} \\
X_2 W_1 &= \lambda_{X_2} AB + \lambda_{X_2} AE_{W_1} + BE_{X_2} + E_{X_2} E_{W_1} \\
X_2 W_2 &= \lambda_{X_2} \lambda_{W_2} AB + \lambda_{X_2} AE_{W_2} + \lambda_{W_2} BE_{X_2} + E_{X_2} E_{W_2}
\end{aligned}
\tag{12.5}
$$

These equations (12.5) show that the product indicators load on a total of *eight* additional latent product variables besides AB. For example, product indicator $X_1 W_1$ loads on latent variables AB, AE_{W_1}, BE_{X_1}, and $E_{X_1} E_{W_1}$. (The term $E_{X_1} E_{W_1}$ is the residual for $X_1 W_1$.) All the factor loadings in the model defined by Equation 12.5 are either the constant 1.0 or functions of λ_{X_2} and λ_{W_2}, the loadings of the nonproduct indicators X_2 and W_2 on their respective factors (Equation 12.4). This means that no new factor loadings need to be estimated for the product indicators.

The only other parameters of the measurement model for the product indicators are the variances and covariances of the latent product variables implied by Equation 12.5. Assuming normal distributions for all nonproduct latent variables (Equation 12.4), Kenny and Judd (1984) showed that (1) the covariances among the latent product variables and factors A and B are all zero; and (2) the variances of the latent product variables can be expressed as functions of the variances of the nonproduct latent variables as follows:

$$\sigma^2_{AB} = \sigma^2_A \, \sigma^2_B + \sigma^2_{A,B} \qquad \sigma^2_{E_{X_1} E_{W_2}} = \sigma^2_{E_{X_1}} \, \sigma^2_{E_{W_1}} \qquad (12.6)$$

$$\sigma^2_{BE_{X_1}} = \sigma^2_B \, \sigma^2_{E_{X_1}} \qquad \sigma^2_{E_{X_1} E_{W_2}} = \sigma^2_{E_{X_1}} \, \sigma^2_{E_{W_2}}$$

$$\sigma^2_{BE_{X_2}} = \sigma^2_B \, \sigma^2_{E_{X_2}} \qquad \sigma^2_{E_{X_2} E_{W_1}} = \sigma^2_{E_{X_2}} \, \sigma^2_{E_{W_1}}$$

$$\sigma^2_{AE_{W_1}} = \sigma^2_A \, \sigma^2_{E_{W_1}} \qquad \sigma^2_{E_{X_2} E_{W_2}} = \sigma^2_{E_{X_2}} \, \sigma^2_{E_{W_2}}$$

$$\sigma^2_{AE_{W_2}} = \sigma^2_A \, \sigma^2_{E_{W_2}}$$

where the term $\sigma^2_{A,B}$ represents the covariance between factors A and B. For example, the variance of the latent product variable AB equals the product of the variances for factors A and B plus their covariance. All variances of the other latent product variables are related to the variances of the nonproduct latent variables. Thus, no new variances need to be estimated, so the measurement model for the product indicators is theoretically identified.

Presented in Figure 12.5 is the whole SR model for the regression of Y on factors A, B, and their interactive effect represented by AB. The measurement models for the nonproduct indicators and the product indicators defined by, respectively, Equations 12.4 and 12.5 are also represented in the figure. Among estimates for the structural model in the figure, coefficients for the paths

$$A \rightarrow Y, B \rightarrow Y, \text{ and } AB \rightarrow Y$$

estimate, respectively, the linear effect of factor A, the linear effect of factor B, and the linear × linear interaction of these latent variables, each controlling for the other effects.

ESTIMATION WITH THE KENNY–JUDD METHOD

Kenny and Judd (1984) were among the first to describe a method for estimating structural equation models with product indicators. The **Kenny–Judd method** is generally applied to observed variables in mean-deviation form (i.e., scores on nonproduct indicators are centered before creating product indicators). It has two potential complications:

1. It requires the imposition of nonlinear constraints in order to estimate some parameters of the measurement model for the product indicators (see Equations 12.4, 12.5). Not all SEM programs support nonlinear constraints; those that do include Mplus, Mx, the TCALIS procedure of SAS/STAT, and LISREL.[4] Correctly programming all such constraints can be tedious and error prone.

---

[4]Nonlinear constraints must be specified in LISREL using its matrix-based programming language, not SIMPLIS.

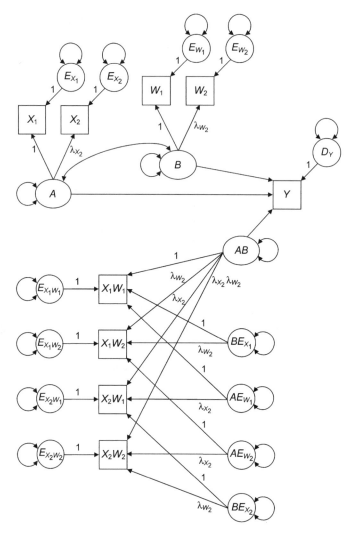

FIGURE 12.5. Model with interactive and main effects of factors A and B.

2. A product variable is not normally distributed even if each of its component variables is normally distributed. For example, the Kenny–Judd method assumes that factors A and B and the measurement errors for their nonproduct indicators in Figure 12.5 are normally distributed. But the products of these latent variables, such as AB, are not normally distributed, which violates the normality requirement of default maximum likelihood (ML) estimation. Yang–Wallentin and Jöreskog (2001) demonstrate the estimation of a model with product indicators using a corrected normal theory method that can generate robust standard errors and corrected model test statistics. Also, minimum sample sizes of 400–500 cases may be needed when estimating even relatively small models, but the need for large samples is not specific to the Kenny–Judd method per se.

Presented in Table 12.3 is a covariance matrix generated by Kenny and Judd (1984) for a hypothetical sample of 500 cases. You can download from the website for this book (see p. 3) the Mplus 5.2 syntax and data files that specify the nonlinear constraints implied by Equations 12.4 and 12.5 and fit the model in Figure 12.5 to the data in Table 12.3 using the Kenny–Judd method; the Mplus output file can be downloaded from the site, too. The Mplus syntax file is annotated with comments that explain the nonlinear constraints of this method. Because Kenny and Judd (1984) used a generalized least squares (GLS) estimator in their original analysis of these data, I specified the same estimator in this analysis with Mplus. The input data for this analysis are in matrix form, so it is not possible to use a corrected normal theory method because such methods require raw data files. You can also download from the book's website Mplus computer files for the analysis of a latent quadratic effect using the Kenny–Judd method with accompanying text that explains this supplemental example.

With a total of nine observed variables (four nonproduct indicators, four product indicators, and Y; see Figure 12.5), there are a total of 9(10)/2, or 45 observations available for this analysis. There are a total of 13 free parameters, including (1) two factor loadings (of X_2 and W_2); (2) seven variances (of A, B, E_{X_1}, E_{X_2}, E_{W_1}, E_{W_2}, and D_Y) and one covariance ($A \curvearrowright B$); and (3) three direct effects (of A, B, and AB on Y). There are no free parameters for the measurement model of the product indicators, so df_M = 45 – 13 = 32. The analysis in Mplus converged to an admissible solution. Values of selected fit statistics are reported next and generally indicate acceptable overall fit. The 90% confidence interval based on the RMSEA is reported in parentheses:

$$\chi^2_M (32) = 41.989, \quad p = .111$$

$$\text{RMSEA} = .025 \ (0\text{–}.044), \quad p_{\text{close-fit } H_0} = .988$$

$$\text{CFI} = .988; \quad \text{SRMR} = .046$$

The Mplus-generated GLS parameter estimates for the model of Figure 12.5 are very similar to those reported by Kenny and Judd (1984) in their original analysis. The main

TABLE 12.3. Input Data (Covariances) for Analysis of a Model with an Interactive Effect of Latent Variables with the Kenny–Judd Method

Variable	1	2	3	4	5	6	7	8	9
1. X_1	2.395								
2. X_2	1.254	1.542							
3. W_1	.445	.202	2.097						
4. W_2	.231	.116	1.141	1.370					
5. $X_1 W_1$	−.367	−.070	−.148	−.133	5.669				
6. $X_1 W_2$	−.301	−.041	−.130	−.117	2.868	3.076			
7. $X_2 W_1$	−.081	−.054	.038	.037	2.989	1.346	3.411		
8. $X_2 W_2$	−.047	−.045	.039	−.043	1.341	1.392	1.719	1.960	
9. Y	−.368	−.179	.402	.282	2.556	1.579	1.623	.971	2.174

Note. These data for a hypothetical sample are from Kenny and Judd (1984, p. 205); N = 500.

and interactive effects of factors A and B together explain 86.8% of the total variance in Y. The unstandardized equation for predicting Y is

$$\hat{Y} = -.169\,A + .321\,B + .699\,AB$$

This prediction equation has no intercept because means were not analyzed. However, you could use the same method described earlier to rearrange this unstandardized equation to (1) eliminate the product term and (2) generate simple regressions of, say, Y on factor B where the slope for B varies as a function of factor A. Following these steps will show that the relation between Y and B is positive for levels of A above the mean (i.e., > 0) but negative for levels of A below the mean (< 0) for the model in Figure 12.5 and the data in Table 12.3.

ALTERNATIVE ESTIMATION METHODS

When using the Kenny–Judd method to estimate latent interaction effects, Jöreskog and Yang (1996) recommend adding a mean structure to the model. (The basic Kenny–Judd method has no mean structure.) They argue that because the means of the indicators are functions of other parameters in the model, their intercepts should be added to the model in order for the results to be more accurate. They also note that a single product indicator is all that is needed for identification. In contrast, the analysis of all possible product indicators in the Kenny–Judd approach can make the model rather complicated (e.g., Figure 12.5). As a compromise between analyzing a single-product indicator and all possible product indicators, Marsh, Wen, and Hau (2006) recommend analyzing **matched-pair products** in which information from the same indicator is not repeated. For example, given indicators X_1 and X_2 of factor A and indicators W_1 and W_2 of factor B, the pair of product indicators $X_1 W_1$ and $X_2 W_2$ is a set of matched-pair indicators because no individual indicator appears twice in any product term. The pair $X_1 W_2$ and $X_2 W_1$ is the other set of matched-pair indicators for this example.

Ping (1996) describes a two-step estimation method that does not require nonlinear constraints, which means that it can be used with just about any SEM computer tool. It requires essentially the same assumptions as the Kenny–Judd method. In the first step of Ping's method, the model is analyzed without the product indicators. That is, only the linear effects of latent variables in the structural model are estimated. One records parameter estimates from this analysis and calculates the values of the parameters of the measurement model for the product indicators implied in the Kenny–Judd method. These values can be calculated either by hand or by using a set of templates for Microsoft Excel by R. Ping that can be freely downloaded over the Internet.[5] These calculated values are then specified as fixed parameters in the second step where all indicators,

---

[5]*www.wright.edu/~robert.ping/*

product and nonproduct, are analyzed together. Included in the results of the second analysis are estimates of interaction effects of latent variables.

Bollen's (1996) two-stage least squares (TSLS) method for latent variables is another estimation option. This method requires at least one product indicator of a latent product variable and a separate product indicator that is used as an instrumental variable. An advantage of this method is that it does not assume normal distributions for the indicators. Because it is not iterative, the TSLS method may also be less susceptible to technical problems in the analysis. A drawback is that because TSLS is a partial-information technique, there is no statistical test (e.g., χ_M^2) of the overall fit of the model to the data. In a simulation study, Yang–Wallentin (2001) compared standard ML estimation and Bollen's (1996) TSLS method applied to the estimation of latent interaction effects. Neither method performed especially well for sample sizes of $N < 400$, especially TSLS. For larger samples, differences in bias were generally negligible, but TSLS tended to underestimate standard errors even in large samples.

Wall and Amemiya (2001) describe the **generalized appended product indicator** (GAPI) **method** for estimating latent curvilinear or interactive effects. As in the Kenny–Judd method, products of observed variables are specified as indicators of latent product terms, but the GAPI method does not assume that any of the variables are normally distributed. Consequently, it is not assumed in the GAPI method that the latent product variables are independent. Instead, these covariances are estimated as part of the analysis. A mean structure is also added to the model. However, all other constraints of the Kenny–Judd method, including the nonlinear constraints, are imposed in the GAPI method. A disadvantage of this method is that its implementation in computer syntax can be complicated (see Marsh et al., 2006).

Marsh, Wen, and Hau (2004) describe what is basically an **unconstrained approach** to the estimation of latent interaction and quadratic effects that imposes no nonlinear constraints and also does not assume multivariate normality. It features the specification of product indicators of latent curvilinear or interaction effects, but it imposes no nonlinear constraints on estimates of the correspondence between product indicators and latent product terms. The unconstrained approach is generally easier to implement in computer syntax than the GAPI method (see Marsh et al., 2006). Results of computer simulation studies by Marsh et al. (2004) generally support this method for large samples and when normality assumptions are not met.

Klein and Moosbrugger's (2000) **latent moderated structural equations** (LMS) **method** uses a special form of ML estimation that assumes normal distributions for the nonproduct variables but takes direct account of the degree of non-normality implied by the latent product terms. This method adds a mean structure to the model, and it uses a form of the expectation–maximization (EM) algorithm (Chapter 3) in estimation. The LMS method directly analyzes raw data (there is no matrix input) from the nonproduct indicators (e.g., X_1, X_2, W_1, and W_2 in Figure 12.5) to estimate a latent interaction or curvilinear effect without creating any product indicators. Of all the methods described here, the LMS method may be the most precise because it explicitly estimates the form of nonnormality. The LMS method is computationally intensive, but Klein and Muthén (2007) describe a simpler algorithm known as **quasi-maximum likelihood** (QML) **estimation** that closely approximates results of the former. A version of the LMS/QML method is incorporated in Mplus, along with special syntax for specifying latent interaction or curvilinear effects. This syntax is very compact and much less complex than the syntax required to implement the Kenny–Judd method and some other alternative methods just described. However, most traditional SEM fit statistics, including the model chi-square (χ^2_M) and approximate fit indexes, are not available in the Mplus implementation of the LMS/QML method. Instead, the relative fit of different models is compared using the Akaike Information Criterion (AIC) (Chapter 8) or a related statistic known as the Bayesian Information Criterion (BIC) (Raftery, 1995).

Little, Bovaird, and Widaman (2006) describe an extension of the method of residualized centering for estimating the interactive or curvilinear effects of latent variables. In this approach, the researcher creates every possible product indicator and then regresses each product indicator on its own set of constituent nonproduct indicators. The residuals from the analysis represent interaction but are uncorrelated with the corresponding set of nonproduct indicators. The residualized product indicators are then specified as the indicators of a latent product factor that is uncorrelated with the corresponding nonproduct latent factors (i.e., those that represent latent linear effects only). The only other special parameterization in this approach is that error covariances are specified between pairs of residualized product indicators based on common nonproduct indicators (e.g., Little, Bovaird, & Widaman, 2006, p. 506). This method can be implemented in basically any SEM computer tool (i.e., it does not require a specific software package), and it relies on traditional fit statistics in the assessment of model–data correspondence. Based on computer simulation studies by Little, Bovaird, and Widaman (2006), their residualized product indicator method generally yielded similar parameter estimates compared with the LMS/QML method and also the Marsh et al. (2004) unconstrained method used with mean centering.

No single method for estimating curvilinear or interactive effects of latent variables has so far emerged as the "best" approach, but this is an active research area. For empirical examples, see Klein and Moosbrugger (2000), who applied the LMS method in a sample of 304 middle-aged men to estimate the latent main and interactive effects of flexibility in goal adjustment and perceived physical fitness on levels of complaining about one's mental or physical state. They found that high levels of perceived fitness neutralized the effects of goal flexibility, but effects of goal flexibility on complaining were more substantial at lower levels of perceived fitness. In a sample of 792 employees in various commercial joint ventures, Song, Droge, Hanvanich, and Calantone (2005) used the Kenny–Judd method to estimate the latent interactive effects of company technological capabilities and marketing capabilities on marketing performance (sales, profits, etc.) They analyzed their moderation model across two different groups of companies—those in areas where industry technology rapidly changes versus areas where technological developments are minor. The results suggested that the interactive effects of company technological and marketing resources on sales success depend on industry context.

RATIONALE OF MULTILEVEL ANALYSIS

The term **multilevel modeling** (MLM)—also known as **hierarchical linear modeling** and **random coefficient modeling**, among other variations—refers to a family of statistical techniques for analyzing hierarchical (nested) data where (1) scores are clustered into larger units and (2) scores within each level may not be independent. You already know that repeated measures data are hierarchical in that multiple scores are nested under the same person. Dependence among such scores is explicitly estimated in various techniques for repeated measures data. For example, the error term in repeated measures ANOVA takes account of score covariances across the levels of within-subject factors. In SEM, the capability to specify an error covariance structure for repeated measures variables, such as when analyzing a latent growth model (Chapter 11), also takes account of score dependencies.

Another situation for analyzing hierarchical data occurs in **complex sampling designs**, in which the levels of at least one higher-order variable are selected prior to sampling individual cases within each level. An example is the method of **cluster sampling**. Suppose in a study of Grade 2 scholastic skills that a total of 100 public elementary schools in a particular geographic region is randomly selected, and then every Grade 2 student in these schools is assessed. Here, students are clustered within schools. A variation is **multistage sampling** where only a portion of the students within each school are randomly selected (e.g., 10%) for inclusion in the sample. In **stratified sampling**, a population is divided into homogeneous, mutually exclusive subpopulations (strata), such as by gender or ethic categories, and then cases within each stratum are randomly selected. The resulting hierarchical data set may be representative on the variable(s) selected for stratification.

Scores clustered under a higher-level variable may not be independent. For instance, siblings are affected by their common family situation. Score dependence in complex samples means that the application of standard formulas for estimating standard errors in a single-level analysis that assume independence (e.g., Equation 2.14) may not yield correct results. Specifically, such formulas tend to *underestimate* sampling variance in complex samples. Because standard errors are the denominators of basic statistical tests (Chapter 2), underestimation tends to result in rejection of the null hypothesis too often (inflation of Type I error). This is a second motivation for MLM: the correct estimation of standard errors in a complex sampling design.

Increase of sampling error in complex samples compared with simple random sampling of individual cases with no clusters is known as the **design effect**. It is often estimated as the ratio of the variance of a statistic in a complex sample over the variance of the same statistic in a simple random sample for the same number of cases. For example, a design effect of 4.0 would mean that the variance is four times greater in a complex sampling design than if the study were based on simple random sampling. Another interpretation is that only ¼ or one-quarter as many cases would be needed in a simple random sample to measure the same statistic instead of a complex sample where the design effect is 4.0. Thus, higher estimates of the design effect indicate a lower **effective sample size** compared with a simple random sample without clusters.

The design effect is a function of the cluster size, design (sampling) weights, and degree of within-cluster score dependence. In a balanced complex sampling design, the cluster size, n_C, is a constant (e.g., 100 students are measured in each of 75 different schools). In unbalanced designs, cluster size is calculated as

$$n_C = \frac{N^2 - \sum_{g=1}^{G} n_g^2}{N(G-1)} \tag{12.7}$$

where n_g is the size of the gth cluster, G is the total number of clusters, and N is the overall sample size. **Design (sampling) weights** can be specified to adjust sample proportions of cases that belong to each cluster in order to make them conform to known population base rates. For example, if too many higher-income households were sampled in a particular geographic area, then weights could be applied to reduce the relative contribution of scores from such families. This will also increase the relative weight of scores from lower-income families. Weights can also be applied to compensate for differential response rates (missing data) over clusters; see Carle (2009) for more information.

The extent of score dependence in a complex sampling design is estimated by the **unconditional intraclass correlation**, designated here as $\hat{\rho}$. It estimates the proportion of total score variability explained by the cluster variable(s). In a between-subject design with a single cluster variable, this proportion is calculated as

$$\hat{\rho} = \frac{MS_C - MS_W}{MS_C + (df_C) MS_W} \tag{12.8}$$

where MS_C and MS_W are, respectively, the between-group (cluster) and pooled within-group mean squares from a one-way ANOVA and df_C are the between-group degrees of freedom, or one less than the number of clusters. If $\hat{\rho} = .10$, for example, then scores within the same cluster are 10% more likely to have a similar value compared with two scores selected completely at random in the population. Thus, the higher the value of $\hat{\rho}$, the more scores in a complex sample depend on the cluster variable. There is no "golden rule" concerning cutoffs for $\hat{\rho}$ above which would indicate the need for MLM. But a common rule of thumb is that $\hat{\rho} \geq .10$ may be sufficient to result in appreciable bias in standard errors if multilevel statistical techniques are not used (e.g., Bickel, 2007, chap. 3; Maas & Hox, 2005).

There is more than one way to estimate the design effect (DEFF) (Gambino, 2009). The most common way to do so in a two-level design (e.g., students within schools) is based on the formula

$$\text{DEFF} = \hat{\rho} \, (n_C - 1) + 1 \tag{12.9}$$

which indicates that the design effect is greater as either the unconditional intraclass correlation or cluster size increases. If $\hat{\rho} = 0$, then DEFF = 1.0, which means that scores at the case level are independent within the clusters. Otherwise, DEFF > 1.0, and it estimates the ratio of the actual variance of a statistic in a complex sample over that expected in a simple random sample based on the same number of cases. For example, given $n_C = 50$ cases in each of 100 clusters and $\hat{\rho} = .10$, then

$$DEFF = .10 \, (50 - 1) + 1 = 5.90$$

which says that the variance in this complex design is about six times greater than that expected in a simple random sample where $N = 5,000$. The actual size of a complex sample divided by DEFF estimates the effective sample size, taking account of score dependence and cluster size. The effective sample size in this example is 5,000/5.90, or 847.5. That is, the amount of sampling error in the complex sample is comparable to that expected in a simple random sample of about 850 cases. When estimating statistical power, the effective sample size in complex samples is used in these calculations, not the actual size (N).

A third motivation for MLM is the estimation of **contextual effects** of higher-order variables on scores of individuals in a hierarchical data set. Suppose in a study of achievement that a researcher measures gender and family income among Grade 2 students. The students attend a total of 100 different schools. The characteristics of the schools, such as size (total enrollment) and emphasis on academic excellence, are also measured. The variables just mentioned are contextual variables, or **level-2 predictors**, that could affect achievement in addition to student gender and family income, or **level-1 predictors**. It is also possible to aggregate a student-level variable up to the school level and to consider this aggregated variable as a contextual variable. For example, the proportion of students in each school who are girls is a contextual variable. In a multilevel analysis, it would be possible in this example to (1) simultaneously analyze data from two different levels, student and school; (2) correctly estimate standard errors at each level in the prediction of achievement; and (3) estimate **cross-level interactions** between individual (within) and school (between) variables on achievement. For example, if the effect of family income at the student level changes as a function of school size, then there is an interaction of a within variable and a between variable.

BASIC MULTILEVEL TECHNIQUES

There are multilevel versions of many standard statistical techniques for single-level analyses. The multilevel versions take account of design effects in complex sampling designs, and some also estimate contextual effects. For instance, **two-level regression** permits the estimation of separate regression coefficients, one for the between (cluster) level and another for the within (case) level, in a two-level data set. Results at these two different levels are not always the same. Suppose that the amount of time spent watching television (TV) and school achievement (Ach) are measured among students enrolled in four different schools. Hypothetical scatterplots for these schools are presented in Figure 12.6. Within each school, the association between TV and Ach is *negative*. That is, more time spent watching television predicts lower achievement. From the perspective of traditional SEM, the same within-group covariance structure holds across the schools.

But another aspect of the relation between TV and Ach in Figure 12.6 is apparent from a between-group perspective: There is a *positive* association between the average number of hours of television watched and the average achievement across the schools. This positive covariance is apparent if you draw a line in the figure that connects the four points that represent the group means (centroids) on both variables. The fact that the within versus between relations of TV to Ach are of different signs in this example is not contradictory. This is because the between association is estimated using group statistics (school means), but the within association is estimated using scores from individual students within the schools.

In Figure 12.6, the slopes of the within-school regression lines are identical. In a two-level data set with a more realistic number of schools, such as 100 or so, it is more likely that (1) both the slopes and the intercepts of the within regression lines will vary across schools. Furthermore, (2) part of this variability over schools may be explained by a contextual variable, such as school size. For example, the relation TV and Ach could be stronger in smaller schools but closer to zero in larger schools. It can also happen that (3) variability in slopes is related to variability in intercepts over schools. For example, a weaker versus stronger association between Ach and TV (slopes) may predict lower versus higher mean scores on both variables (intercepts). That is, the covariance between intercepts and slopes may not be zero.

All of the effects just mentioned can be estimated in a **random coefficient regression**, in which data from predictors at ≥ 2 levels can be simultaneously analyzed. In standard multiple regression (MR), slopes and intercepts are conceptualized as fixed population parameters. In contrast, slopes and intercepts in random coefficient regression can be specified as random effects that vary and covary across the population of clusters. Random coefficient regression does not estimate the slope and intercept in any

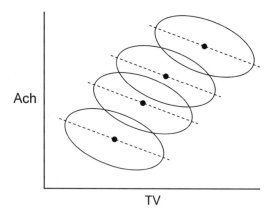

Ach

TV

FIGURE 12.6. Representation of within-school versus between-school variation in the relation between television watching (TV) and scholastic achievement (Ach).

particular sample cluster. Instead, it uses sample information to estimate the population variances and covariance of the slopes and intercepts. When a predictor, such as a contextual variable, of the random slopes or intercepts is specified, the model analyzed is referred to as a **slopes-and-intercepts-as-outcomes model**. This means that the slopes and intercepts from regression analyses at the case level (level 1) become the outcome variables in the level-2 analysis where contextual variables are the predictors. Depending on theory, it is also possible to specify that slopes only are random (**slopes-as-outcomes model**) or that intercepts only are random (**intercepts-as-outcomes model**). The complexity of the analysis increases quickly in designs with multiple level-1 or level-2 predictors or for hierarchical data sets with ≥ 3 levels (e.g., students within school within districts). This is probably why most applications of random coefficient regression in the literature concern just two levels.

The OLS method is not the typical estimation method in random coefficient regression. If the cluster sizes are all equal (a balanced design), then it may be possible to use full-information maximum likelihood (FIML) as the estimator. This requires that the number of clusters is reasonably large, say, > 75 or so, and also that the total number of cases across all clusters is large, too (Maas & Hox, 2005). In unbalanced designs, it may be necessary to use an approximate ML estimator, one that is computationally less intensive but accommodates unequal cluster sizes. An example is **restricted maximum likelihood** (REML), which is available in the Linear Mixed Models procedure of SPSS and in the MIXED procedure of SAS/STAT. Another widely used computer program for multilevel regression is Hierarchical Linear and Nonlinear Modeling (HLM) 6 (Raudenbush, Bryk, & Cheong, 2008).[6] Using the computer tools for multilevel analyses just mentioned is relatively straightforward. For example, analyses can be specified in the Linear Mixed Models procedure of SPSS with just a few clicks of the mouse cursor in graphical dialogs or by writing a few lines of syntax (see Bickel, 2007).

Some limitations of MLM are as follows (Bauer, 2003; Curran, 2003):

1.   Scores on individual- or cluster-level predictors in MLM are from observed variables that are assumed to be perfectly reliable. This is because there is no direct way in MLM to represent measurement error.

2.   There is also no direct way in MLM to represent either predictors or outcomes as latent variables (constructs) measured by multiple indicators. In other words, it is difficult to specify a measurement model as part of a multilevel analysis.

3.   Although there are methods to estimate indirect effects apart from direct effects in MLM, they can be difficult to apply in practice (see Krull & MacKinnon, 2001).

4.   There are statistical tests of individual coefficients or of variances–covariances in MLM, but there is no single inferential test of the model as a whole. Instead, the *relative* predictive power of alternative multilevel models estimated in the same sample can be evaluated (e.g., Bickel, 2007, chap. 3).

---

[6]A free student version of HLM 6 for Microsoft Windows is available at *www.ssicentral.com/hlm/student.html*

CONVERGENCE OF SEM AND MLM

The relative weaknesses of MLM correspond to the strengths of SEM. To summarize, it is straightforward in SEM to represent measurement error for either single or multiple indicators through the specification of a measurement model. Factors can be represented as either predictors or outcomes in a structural model. The estimation of direct or indirect effects in structural models is a routine part of SEM, and there are inferential tests of whether the model is consistent with the covariance data. But "unadorned" SEM has limited capabilities in areas where MLM is strong. For example, the analysis of a model across multiple samples in SEM is a kind of restricted multilevel analysis that assumes fixed population parameters for each group. Except when analyzing a particular class of latent growth model in a single-level analysis (Chapter 11), SEM does not directly take account of clustering in complex samples.

Early attempts to include more capabilities of MLM in SEM analyses were based on tricking SEM computer tools into analyzing two-level models (e.g., Duncan, Duncan, Hops, & Alpert, 1997). The trick was to exploit the capability of the software to simultaneously estimate a structural equation model across two groups. However, in this case the "groups" corresponded to two different models, a within (level-1) model and a between (level-2) model, both estimated in the same complex sample. The data matrix for the level-1 model is the pooled within-group covariance matrix based on variation of individual scores around cluster means. For the level-2 model, the data matrix is the between-group covariance matrix based on variation of cluster means around the grand means. Because older versions of most SEM computer programs had no built-in capabilities for analyzing data from complex samples, it was usually necessary to calculate these two data matrices separately using an external program, such as SPSS. The two data matrices are then submitted to the SEM computer program as external files or included as part of the syntax (command) file.

Unfortunately, the syntax required to trick older versions of SEM computer tools into analyzing even relatively simple two-level models is awkward and complicated. Stapleton (2006, p. 361) gives an example of such syntax for getting an SEM computer program to analyze a two-level regression model that corresponds to the situation depicted in Figure 12.6. Just as awkward is the use of standard SEM symbolism for model diagrams to represent a multilevel analysis. For example, the model presented in Figure 12.7(a) represents the trick just mentioned in McArdle–McDonald RAM symbolism for SEM, the system used for model diagrams in this book. Briefly, the observed variables TV and Ach are each specified as the single indicator of a within-school factor and a between-school factor. The scaling constants for the within factors equal 1, but for the between factors these constants equal the square root of the cluster size n_C. At each level (within, between) of the model in Figure 12.7(a), the Ach factor is regressed on the TV factor. These specifications tell the computer to derive separate estimates of the within- and between-group regression coefficients. If the data resembled the pattern depicted in Figure 12.6, the within coefficient would be negative but the between coefficient would be positive.

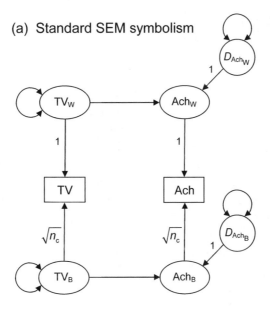

(a) Standard SEM symbolism

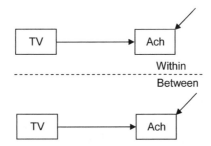

(b) Compact Mplus symbolism

FIGURE 12.7. Representation of a two-level regression model using (a) standard SEM symbolism for model diagrams and (b) compact symbolism associated with Mplus.

Bauer (2003) and Curran (2003) show that it is even more complicated to use standard SEM computer syntax to specify a slopes-and-intercepts-as-outcomes model. The model requires both a mean structure and an **individual factor loading matrix** where loadings on a slope factor are the scores from all the cases within each cluster. Not all SEM computer programs allow the specification of individual factor loading matrices, but one that does is Mx (Chapter 4). The programming becomes even more complicated if there are missing data or the cluster sizes are not all equal. Indeed, the task quickly "becomes a remarkably complex, tedious, and error-prone task" (Curran, 2003, p. 557)—that is, a data management nightmare. Representation of a slopes-and-intercepts-as-outcomes analysis with standard SEM symbolism for model diagrams is relatively complex, too.

MULTILEVEL SEM

Fortunately, more and more computer programs for SEM, including EQS, LISREL, and Mplus, feature special syntax that makes it easier to specify and analyze multilevel models in complex samples. This special syntax is more compact to use for multilevel analysis than standard SEM computer programming languages. It also allows for the full integration of SEM and MLM in a framework known as **multilevel structural equation modeling** (ML-SEM) that combines the capabilities of both families of techniques.

Because working with standard SEM model diagrams is not the best way to represent a multilevel analysis, the researcher typically conducts an ML-SEM analysis by specifying the model in syntax, not in a graphical editor. An example of special syntax in Mplus for analyzing a hypothetical slopes-and-intercepts-as-outcomes model is listed in Table 12.4. The raw data from a complex sample are contained in an external file, and the four observed variables are Ach, TV, School (attended), and Size (total enrollment). Next, the syntax in Table 12.4 specifies that TV is the within or level-1 predictor, the cluster variable is School, and the between or level-2 predictor is Size. Grand-mean centering of the TV variable is specified—centering is routine in this type of multilevel analysis (Bickel, 2007)—and the analysis type is designated as two-level with random coefficients. Syntax for the within model specifies that slopes, labeled "s" in the table, from within the regressions of Ach on TV are a random variable. Syntax for the between model specifies that the random slopes and intercepts are regressed on the school size contextual variable and that the random terms covary. See Stapleton (2006) for additional examples.

In the Mplus manual, Muthén and Muthén (1998–2010) use a special compact symbolism for diagrams of multilevel structural equation models. For example, look back at Figure 12.7(a), which is the standard diagram for tricking an SEM computer program into analyzing a two-level regression model. Presented in Figure 12.7(b) is the model

TABLE 12.4. Example of Special Mplus Syntax for a Hypothetical Slopes-and-Intercepts-as-Outcomes Model

```
TITLE: Two-level slopes-and-intercepts-as-outcomes model
       Students within schools
DATA: FILE IS "school.dat";
VARIABLE: NAMES ARE Ach TV School Size;
  WITHIN = TV; BETWEEN = Size;
  CLUSTER = School; CENTERING = GRANDMEAN (TV);
ANALYSIS: TYPE IS TWOLEVEL RANDOM;
MODEL:
  %WITHIN%
    s | Ach ON TV;
  %BETWEEN%
    Ach s ON Size;
    Ach WITH s;
OUTPUT:  SAMPSTAT;
```

for the same analysis but represented as an Mplus-type model diagram. This diagram makes it clear that the regression of Ach on TV is calculated at two different levels, within and between. It is also simpler than the standard representation in Figure 12.7(a). Residual variance is represented in Figure 12.7(b) by the lines with arrowheads oriented at 45° angles and pointing to the endogenous variables. This representation for residual variance is compact, but does not convey the fact that residual terms are ordinarily conceptualized as exogenous variables in an SEM analysis.

Another example of an Mplus-type diagram for a multilevel analysis is presented in Figure 12.8. This model corresponds to the slopes-and-intercepts-as-outcomes model specified in the syntax of Table 12.4. Random intercepts are represented in the within model of Figure 12.8 by the closed circle at the end of the path TV → Ach, and random slopes are represented by the closed circle in the middle of the same path. The random slopes are labeled "s" in the figure. Random slopes and intercepts are represented in the between model as latent variables that are regressed on school size, and the disturbances for the random terms are specified as correlated. A mean structure is implied in Figure 12.8 because intercepts are estimated, but mean structures are not explicitly depicted in Mplus-style diagrams. Curran and Bauer (2007) describe an alternative compact symbolism for diagrams of multilevel structural equation models in which mean structures are explicitly represented.

Using an SEM computer program with special syntax for multilevel analysis makes possible the basic types of ML-SEM summarized next:

1. Estimation of correct standard errors when fitting a single model to data from a complex sample. This estimation takes account of the design effect and accordingly corrects standard errors and test statistics.

2. Analysis of one model at the within level but another model at the between level. The between model could be identical to the within model (e.g., Figure 12.7(b)), but the between model could also be a different model. For example, a set of indicators may have

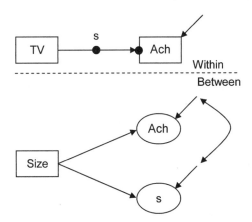

FIGURE 12.8. Representation in Mplus-type symbolism of the slopes-and-intercepts-as-outcomes model corresponding to the syntax in Table 12.4.

a three-factor structure at the within level, but at the between level the same indicators measure a single factor.

3. Analysis of a slopes-and-intercepts-as-outcomes model where random slopes and intercepts at the within level could be from either observed or latent variables that are predicted by either observed or latent variables at the between level. Structural models at either level can include indirect effects.

Two examples of ML-SEM analyses are described next. Wu (2008) administered to 333 students a series of questionnaires about life satisfaction, what respondents say they want (*amount*), and the gap between what they have and what they want (*have–want discrepancy*) in 12 different areas (social support, financial resources, etc.). Because ratings across the 12 areas are repeated measures, Wu (2008) conceptualized these areas as nested under individuals. That is, the within level concerns variation among areas for each respondent, and the between level refers to differences across people that affect their satisfaction ratings over all areas. In a **multilevel path analysis** (ML-PA), Wu (2008) tested the hypothesis that *have–want discrepancy* and *amount* have direct or indirect effects on life satisfaction. The final path model retained in Wu's (2008) analysis is presented in Figure 12.9(a) using Mplus symbolism. At the within level, *have–want discrepancy* has both direct and indirect effects on satisfaction. But at the between level, effects of *have–want discrepancy* are entirely mediated by *amount*. Wu (2008) interpreted these results as suggesting that life satisfaction involves an explicit have–want comparison, but whether its effect is entirely indirect through what people say they want depends on the level of analysis, within-person versus between-person.

Kaplan (2000, pp. 48–53) describes a **multilevel confirmatory factor analysis** (ML-CFA) in a sample of over 10,000 high school students enrolled in about 1,000 different schools. The students completed a questionnaire about their perceptions of teacher quality, negative school environment (e.g., students feel unsafe), and disruptive behavior by students. In a single-level CFA ignoring clusters (schools), Kaplan (2000) found that a three-factor model had reasonable fit to item data. The ML-CFA model analyzed by Kaplan (2000) in the same sample is presented in Figure 12.9(b) using Mplus symbolism where "It" designates "item." The within model is basically identical to the final model retained in the single-level CFA. However, the model at the between level is simpler in that all items load on a single factor. That is, variation in student ratings within schools is differentiated along three dimensions, but one general climate factor explains between-school variation. For additional examples of ML-SEM analyses, see Kaplan (2009, chap. 7), Mulaik (2009, chap. 12), and Rabe–Hesketh, Skrondal, and Zheng (2007).

There are three basic steps in analyzing a multilevel structural equation model. The first step involves calculation of the unconditional intraclass correlation $\hat{\rho}$. If $\hat{\rho} > .10$, the need for ML-SEM instead of single-level SEM is indicated. The next two steps parallel those of the two-step estimation of SR models (Chapter 10), but in ML-SEM these steps correspond to analysis of the within model only prior to simultaneous estimation of the

(a) Two-level path analysis

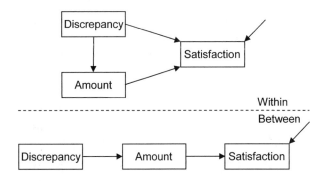

(b) Two-level confirmatory factor analysis

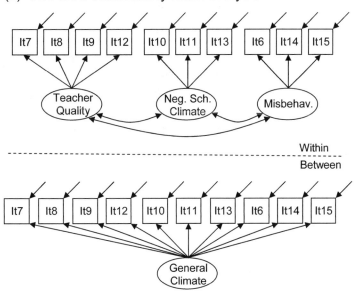

FIGURE 12.9. (a) Two-level path analysis model analyzed by Wu (2008). (b) Two-level confirmatory factor analysis model analyzed by Kaplan (2000).

within and between models. The goal is to distinguish specification error in either level, within versus between. Specifically, the within model is analyzed using the pooled-within group covariances and means, which ignores the cluster variable. Although the fit of the within model may not be satisfactory due to the omission of between-group effects, the basic parameter estimates should make sense. Finally, the between model is specified, and then both models are simultaneously fitted to the data. Stapleton (2006) describes additional possible analytic steps.

SUMMARY

In moderated path analysis, the interactive effects of observed variables are represented by product terms included in the model along with the main effect terms. Path coefficients for direct effects of the product terms estimate the corresponding interaction effects. One way to interpret an interaction between two continuous predictors is to generate the simple regressions of the outcome variable on one predictor at different levels of the other predictor. One of the first approaches to estimating interactive effects of latent variables is the Kenny–Judd method, which features all possible product indicators of latent product variables, the imposition of nonlinear constraints, and the assumption of multivariate normality. Some alternative methods do not require all possible product indicators, nonlinear constraints, or the normality assumption. Large samples are needed in all these methods regardless of the estimation method.

Researchers who know something about both SEM and multilevel modeling can test an even wider range of hypotheses compared with those who know about one technique, but not the other. The convergence of the two techniques in the form of multilevel SEM offers the capability to (1) calculate correct standard errors in hierarchical datasets; (2) analyze predictors from both the individual level and the group level (contextual effects) in the same analysis; (3) take account of unreliability when latent variables are represented as measured by multiple indicators; and (4) estimate both direct and indirect effects when structural models are analyzed. The increasing availability of SEM computer tools that directly support multilevel analyses in complex sampling designs is making it easier for researchers to actually reap these potential benefits.

RECOMMENDED READINGS

Interaction Effects

Preacher et al. (2007) describe the estimation and interpretation of conditional indirect effects in moderated path models. The edited volume by Schumaker and Marcoulides (1998) is a good resource in this area, and Marsh, Wen, and Hau (2006) describe additional estimation methods.

Marsh, H. W., Wen, Z., & Hau, K.-T. (2006). Structural equation modeling of latent interaction and quadratic effects. In G. R. Hancock & R. O. Mueller (Eds.), *Structural equation modeling: A second course* (pp. 225–265). Greenwich, CT: Information Age Publishing.

Preacher, K. J., Rucker, D. D., & Hayes, A. F. (2007). Addressing moderated mediation hypotheses: Theory, methods, and prescriptions. *Multivariate Behavioral Research, 42,* 185–227.

Schumacker, R. E., & Marcoulides, G. A. (Eds.). (1998). *Interaction and nonlinear effects in structural equation modeling.* Mahwah, NJ: Erlbaum.

Multilevel Analysis

Bickel (2007) introduces multilevel analysis by comparing it with standard multiple regression. A more advanced work for readers with strong quantitative backgrounds is Raudenbush and Bryk (2002). Stapleton (2006) offers a clear introduction to multilevel analysis in SEM.

Bickel, R. (2007). *Multilevel analysis for applied research: It's just regression!* New York: Guilford Press.

Raudenbush, S. W., & Bryk, A. S. (2002). *Hierarchical linear models* (2nd ed.). Thousand Oaks, CA: Sage.

Stapleton, L. M. (2006). Using multilevel structural equation modeling techniques with complex sample data. In G. R. Hancock and R. O. Mueller (Eds.), *Structural equation modeling: A second course* (pp. 345–383). Greenwich, CT: Information Age Publishing.

How to Fool Yourself with SEM

The family of techniques that make up SEM provide researchers with a marvelously flexible set of tools for hypothesis testing. But as with any complex set of procedures, its use must be guided by reason. Although many ways to mislead yourself with SEM were mentioned in previous chapters, they are discussed altogether here. Potential pitfalls are considered under four categories that correspond to major phases of the analysis: specification, data preparation, analysis and respecification, and interpretation. These categories are not mutually exclusive, but they correspond to the usual sequence in which researchers should address these issues. You are encouraged to use the points presented next as a checklist to guide the conduct of your own analyses. Here they are: 52 ways to take leave of your senses in SEM. This list is not exhaustive, but it contains many of the more common mistakes. I thank members of SEMNET for their comments on an earlier version of this list.

TRIPPING AT THE STARTING LINE: SPECIFICATION

Despite all the statistical machinations of SEM, specification is the most important part of the process. Occasionally, however, researchers spend the least amount of time on it. Listed here are several ways not to do your homework in this critical area:

1. *Specify the model after the data are collected rather than before.* This case concerns the specification of a model for an archival data set. Potential problems caused by placing the data cart before the theory horse are described under points that follow, but they include the realization that key variables are omitted or the model is not identified. With the data already collected, it may be too late to do anything about the identification problem. Also, adding exogenous variables in one way to remedy an identification problem for a nonrecursive structural model and adding indicators can help to identify a measurement model.

2. *Omit causes that are correlated with other variables in a structural model.* If an omitted cause is uncorrelated with causes already represented in the structural model, then estimates of direct effects are not biased because of this omission. It is rare, however, that the types of causal variables studied by behavioral scientists are independent. Depending on the pattern of correlations between an omitted variable and those in the model, estimates of causal effects can be too high or too low.

3. *Fail to include unanalyzed associations between pairs of measured exogenous variables in path models or exogenous factors in structural regression models.* Recall that these associations are represented by the symbol ↖↗ in model diagrams and reflect the fact that the model offers no explanation of *why* exogenous variables covary (and vary, too, represented by the symbol ↶↷). Because most causal variables are correlated, omitting these paths is a specification error. Even if these intercorrelations are relatively small, their omission could adversely affect the estimation of other model parameters (i.e., error propagation).

4. *Use psychometrically inadequate measures.* The analysis of variables with a lot of measurement error in the scores (e.g., unreliability) can lead to inaccurate results. The general effect of measurement error is to underestimate causal effects, but—depending on the intercorrelations—estimates can be too high. Although measurement error is taken into account in the analysis of a measurement model or structural regression model, estimates about latent variables are more precise when the indicators are psychometrically sound.

5. *Fail to give careful consideration to the question of directionality.* Directionality is a critical feature not only of structural models but also of measurement models. In structural models, specifications of direct and indirect effects are statements about the expected sequence of causality, or effect priority. Assumptions about directionality in measurement models are expressed by the specification of observed variables as either effect indicators (reflective measurement) or cause indicators (formative measurement). If solid reasons cannot be provided for the specification of directionality, then either use another type of statistical procedure (e.g., multiple regression) or test alternative models with different causal sequences. However, some alternative models may be equivalent or near-equivalent models that generate the same or very similar predicted covariances, which means that there is no way to statistically distinguish them. This is why SEM is described as being good for estimating effects when the underlying causal mechanism is known. It is also more a disconfirmatory method than a confirmatory one because SEM helps researchers to detect false models, but it basically never confirms whether a retained model is true.

6. *Specify feedback effects in structural models (e.g., $Y_1 \rightleftarrows Y_2$) as a way to mask uncertainty about directionality.* Not only do feedback relations have their own assumptions (e.g., equilibrium), but their presence also makes a structural model nonrecursive, which introduces potential problems (e.g., identification) in analyzing the model. A related mistake is to fail to rationally evaluate the equilibrium assumption for a feedback loop.

7. *Add disturbance or measurement error correlations without substantive reason.* This

is a variation on the previous point. When there is justification (e.g., repeated measurement, two indicators share a common method), specification of these types of unanalyzed associations is appropriate. Otherwise, they can be a way to improve fit simply by making a model more complex. This is especially true if the researcher initially specifies uncorrelated residuals because of the assumption of conditional independence of the indicators for a latent variable model. If the model in fact does not adequately explain the observed associations among the indicators, adding measurement error correlations without substantive reason can be a way to mask this shortcoming.

8. *Fail to include design-driven correlated residuals.* This mistake is the flip side of the one just described, and it is the failure to include theoretically justifiable correlated residuals, given measurement theory or research design. Cole, Ciesla, and Steiger (2007) remind us that the omission of such residual correlations may not in some cases harm model fit, but their omission could change the meaning of latent variables and thus lead to inaccurate results. In other disciplines such as econometrics, the specification of correlated residuals is more routine.[1] So the specification of correlated residuals should not be seen as a necessary evil. Instead, they should be included in the model when there is justification. In this sense, correlated residuals are no different from any other type of effect that could potentially be included in structural equation models.

9. *Overfit the model (i.e., forget the goal of parsimony).* Any model, even theoretically nonsensical ones, will perfectly fit the data if they are specified to be just as complex as possible (i.e., $df_M = 0$). But models just as complex as the data test no particular hypothesis. It is only more parsimonious models, in which some effects are intentionally constrained to zero ($df_M > 0$), that allow tests of specific ideas. The goal of parsimony is also important in respecification. Here one must be careful not to modify the model solely for the sake of improving fit. These comments on parsimony are not intended to dissuade you from analyzing complex models per se. This is because a phenomenon that is complex in the real world may require a relatively complex statistical model in order to reflect it basic essence. The main point is that the model should be as parsimonious as possible while respecting theory and results of prior empirical studies. Models that are complex without theoretical justification are probably so specified in order to maximize fit (i.e., it capitalizes on sample-specific variance), but such models are unlikely to replicate.

10. *Fail to have sufficient numbers of indicators of latent variables.* Measurement models with more than one factor typically require only two indicators per factor for identification. However, having only two indicators per factor may lead to problems. Such models may be more likely to be empirically underidentified than models with at least three indicators per factor. Other problems, such as nonconvergence of iterative estimation, are more likely to occur for models with only two indicators per factor, especially in small samples. It may be difficult to estimate measurement error correlations for factors with only two indicators, which can result in a specification error. Parts of the model where some factors have only two indicators are not "self-sufficient" in terms of

---

[1]W. Wothke, personal communication, November 24, 2003.

identification, which means that they have to "borrow" covariance information from other parts of the model. This may result in propagation of error from one part of the model to another. Suppose that the measurement error correlation for a factor with just two indicators is really substantial, but it cannot be estimated because of identification. This specification error may propagate to estimation of the factor loadings for this pair of indicators.[2] Two indicators per factor is the technical minimum, but at least three or four indicators per factor is a better target.

11. *Specify that indicators load on > 1 factor without a substantive reason.* The specification that an indicator depends on more than one factor may be appropriate if you really believe that it measures more than one construct. Just like measurement error correlations, though, adding factor loadings makes a measurement model less parsimonious.

12. *Specify that a set of effect indicators with low intercorrelations loads on a common factor.* The specification of effect indicators implies reflective measurement, which assumes that a set of effect indicators all measure the same underlying factor. This in turn means that their intercorrelations should all be positive and relatively high (e.g., > .50). If the assumptions of reflective measurement are not tenable, then consider the specification of formative measurement where indicators are specified as causes of composites. Of course, the specification of reflective versus formative measurement requires a theoretical basis.

13. *In a complex sampling design, assume that the within-group model and the between-group model are the same without verification.* One lesson of multilevel modeling is that different models may describe covariance patterns at different levels of analysis, within versus between. Without a basic understanding of statistical techniques for hierarchical data, including multilevel SEM, the researcher could miss this possibility.

14. *Forget that the main goal of specification is to test a theory, not a model.* The model analyzed in SEM represents predictions based on a particular body of theory or results of prior empirical studies. Outside this role, the model has no intrinsic value. That is, it provides a vehicle for testing ideas, and the real goal of SEM is to evaluate these ideas in a scientifically meaningful and valid way. Whether or not a model is retained is incidental to this purpose.

IMPROPER CARE AND FEEDING: DATA

The potential missteps presented in this section involve leaping before you look, that is, not carefully screening the data before analyzing them:

15. *Don't check the accuracy of data input or coding.* Data entry mistakes are so easy to make, whether in recording the raw data or in typing the values of a correlation or

---

[2]B. Muthén, personal communication, November 25, 2003.

covariance matrix. Even machine-based data entry is not error free (e.g., smudges on forms can "fool" an electronic scanner, software errors can result in the calculation of incorrect scores). Mistaken specification of codes in statistical programs is also common (e.g., "9" for missing data instead of "–9").

16. *Ignore whether the pattern of missing data loss is random or systematic.* This point assumes that there are more than just a few missing scores. Classical statistical methods for dealing with incomplete data, such as case deletion or single-imputation methods, generally assume that the data loss pattern is missing completely at random, which is unlikely in perhaps most data sets analyzed in the behavioral sciences. These classical techniques have little basis in statistical theory and take little advantage of structure in the data. More modern methods, including those that impute multiple scores for missing observations based on predictive theoretical distributions, generally assume that the data loss pattern is missing at random, a less strict assumption about randomness. But even these methods may generate inaccurate results if the data loss mechanism is systematic. If so, then (1) there is no "statistical fix" for the problem, and (2) you need to explicitly qualify the interpretation of the results based on the data loss pattern.

17. *Fail to examine distributional characteristics.* The most widely used estimation methods in SEM, including maximum likelihood (ML), assume multivariate normal distributions for continuous endogenous variables. Although values of parameter estimates are relatively robust against non-normality, statistical tests of individual parameters tend to be positively biased (i.e., Type I error rate is inflated). If the distributions of continuous endogenous variables are severely non-normal, then use an estimation method that does not assume normality or use corrected statistics (e.g., robust standard errors, corrected model test statistics) when normal theory methods such as ML estimation are used. If the distributions are non-normal because the indicators are discrete with a small number of categories (i.e., they are ordered-categorical variables), then use an appropriate method for this type of data, such as robust weighted least squares (WLS).

18. *Don't screen for outliers.* Even a few extreme scores in a relatively small sample can distort the results. If it is unclear whether outlier cases are from a different population, the analysis can be run with and without these cases in the sample. This strategy makes clear the effect of outliers on the results. This same strategy can be used to evaluate the effects of different methods to deal with missing data.

19. *Assume that all relations are linear.* A standard assumption in SEM is that variable relations are linear. Curvilinear or interactive relations can be represented with product terms but, in general, such terms must be created by the researcher and then included in the model. Simple visual scanning of scatterplots can detect bivariate relations that are obviously curvilinear, but there is no comparably easy visual check for interaction effects. Model test statistics, including χ_M^2, are generally insensitive to serious interaction misspecification (i.e., there is real interaction, but the model has no corresponding product terms that represent these effects).

20. *Ignore lack of independence among the scores.* This problem may arise in two contexts. First, the scores are from a repeated measures variable. The ability to specify a model for the error covariances addresses this first context. The second context refers

to hierarchical data structures in which cases are clustered within larger units, such as employees who work under the same manager. Scores within the larger unit are probably not independent. The analysis of nested data with statistical techniques that assume independence may not yield accurate results. Awareness of the possibility to incorporate multilevel modeling in an SEM analysis helps to avoid this mistake.

CHECKING CRITICAL JUDGMENT AT THE DOOR: ANALYSIS AND RESPECIFICATION

The potential pitfalls described next concern the analysis and interpretation stages. However, problems at earlier stages may make these problems more likely to happen:

21. *When identification status is uncertain, fail to conduct tests of solution uniqueness.* The identification of only some types of models can be determined by heuristics without resorting to algebraic manipulation of their equations. If it is unknown whether a model is theoretically identified but an SEM computer program yields a converged and an admissible solution, then the researcher should conduct empirical tests of the solution's uniqueness. These tests do not prove that a solution is truly unique, but if they lead to the derivation of a different solution, then the model is not identified.

22. *Fail to recognize empirical underidentification.* Estimation of models that are identified can nevertheless fail because of data-related problems, including extreme collinearity or estimates of key parameters that are close to zero or equal to each other. Modification of a model when the data are the problem may lead to a specification error.

23. *Ignore the problem of start values.* Iterative estimation may fail to converge because of poor initial estimates, which is more likely with nonrecursive structural models or measurement models where some indicators load on multiple factors and with error correlations. Although many SEM computer programs can automatically generate their own start values, these values do not always lead to converged admissible solutions, especially for complex models. When this happens, the researcher should try to generate his or her own initial estimates.

24. *Fail to check accuracy of computer syntax.* Just as with data entry, it is easy to make an error in computer syntax that misspecifies the model or data. Although SEM computer programs have become easier to use, they still cannot generally detect a mistake that is logical rather than a syntax error. A logical error does not cause the analysis to fail but instead results in an unintended specification (e.g., $Y_1 \rightarrow Y_2$ is specified when $Y_2 \rightarrow Y_1$ is intended). Carefully check to see that the model analyzed was actually the one that you intended to specify. This is where LISREL's unique capability to automatically draw the model specified in your syntax comes in handy: inspection of the computer-generated diagram gives an opportunity to verify the syntax.

25. *Fail to carefully inspect the solution for admissibility.* The presence of Heywood cases or other kinds of illogical results indicates a problem in the analysis. That is, the

solution should not be trusted. For the same reason, avoid making interpretations about otherwise sensible-looking results in an inadmissible solution.

26. *Interpret results from a nonconverged solution or one where the computer imposed a zero constraint to avoid a Heywood case.* This mistake is related to the one just described. Output from a nonconverged solution is not trustworthy. The same is true when the computer forces some estimates, such as for error variances, to be at least zero in order to avoid an illogical result, such as a negative variance estimate. Such solutions are also untrustworthy.

27. *Respecify a model based entirely on statistical criteria.* A specification search guided entirely by statistical criteria such as modification indexes is unlikely to lead to the correct model. Use your knowledge of relevant theory and research findings to inform the use of such statistics.

28. *Analyze a correlation matrix without standard deviations when it is clearly inappropriate.* These situations include the analysis of a model across independent samples with different variabilities, longitudinal data characterized by changes in variances over time, or a type of SEM that requires the analysis of means (e.g., a latent growth model), which needs the input of not only means but covariances, too.

29. *Estimate a covariance structure with a correlation matrix without using proper methods.* Standard ML estimation assumes the analysis of unstandardized variables and may yield incorrect results when a model is fitted to a correlation matrix without standard deviations. Appropriate procedures such as the method of constrained estimation should be used to analyze a correlation matrix when it is not inappropriate to do so (see the previous point).

30. *Fail to check for constraint interaction when testing for equality of loadings across different factors or of direct effects on different endogenous variables.* If the results of the chi-square difference test for the equality-constrained parameters depend on how the factors are scaled (i.e., unstandardized vs. standardized), there is constraint interaction. In this case, it makes sense to analyze the correlation matrix using the method of constrained estimation, assuming it is appropriate to analyze standardized variables.

31. *Analyze variables so highly correlated that a solution is unstable.* If very high correlations (e.g., $r > .85$) do not cause the analysis to fail or yield a nonadmissible solution, then extreme collinearity may cause the results to be statistically unstable.

32. *Estimate a complex model within a small sample.* This is a related problem. As the ratio of cases to the number of parameters is smaller, the statistical stability of the estimates becomes more doubtful. Cases-to-free parameter ratios less than 10:1 may be cause for concern, as are sample sizes < 100. These recommendations assume ML estimation. Some special methods, such as asymptotic distribution free (ADF) methods that make no distributional assumptions, may require very large samples.

33. *Report only standardized estimates.* This mistake concerns the possible fooling of others; that is, always report the unstandardized estimates in a primary analysis. Otherwise, it may be difficult to compare the results to those from later studies where either the same or a similar model is estimated in different samples. Along the same lines, do not associate information about statistical significance with standardized estimates

unless you used a method that calculates correct standard errors in the standardized solution.

34. *Set scales for latent variables inappropriately.* In multiple-sample SEM, the tactic of standardizing factors by fixing their variances to 1.0 is incorrect if groups differ in their variabilities. Fixing the loading of an indicator to 1.0 (i.e., the factor is unstandardized) is preferable, but note that (a) the same factor loading must be fixed for all groups and (b) indicators with fixed loadings are assumed to be invariant across all samples. In single-sample analyses, fixing to 1.0 the variances of factors measured over time is also inappropriate if factor variability is expected to change (see point 28).

35. *Fail to separately evaluate the measurement and structural portions of a structural regression model.* Two-step (or four-step) estimation of structural regression models can help determine whether the source of poor fit of the original model lies in the measurement component or in the structural component. These sources of poor fit are confounded in one-step estimation.

36. *Estimate relative group mean or intercept differences on latent variables without establishing at least partial measurement invariance of the indicators.* If the observed variables do not have the same basic factor structure across all groups, then it makes little sense to evaluate relative group mean differences in regression slopes or intercepts among the latent variables.

37. *Analyze parcels of items with Likert-type scales as continuous indicators without checking to see whether items in each parcel are unidimensional.* If a set of items assigned to the same parcel do not measure one common domain, then analysis of the total score across the items may not be very meaningful.

THE GARDEN PATH: INTERPRETATION

Potential mistakes described in this section concern the (mis)interpretation of the output from an SEM computer program. Some of these errors may be consequences of mistakes listed in earlier sections of this chapter:

38. *Look only at values of fit statistics; ignore other types of information about fit.* It is possible that the fit of some portion of the model is poor despite seemingly impressive values of its average correspondence to the data. Inspection of the magnitudes, directions, and pattern of correlation residuals can help to spot particular observed associations that are poorly explained by the model. A related mistake is selective reporting of fit statistics—specifically, reporting values of only those fit statistics that favor the researcher's model when results on other statistics are clearly less favorable.

39. *Ignore a failed model chi-square test.* In the past, it was common for researchers to ignore a statistically significant discrepancy between the model and the covariance data, yet justify retention of the model based on values of approximate fit indexes. This is bad practice, one that is no longer tolerable. Specifically, a failed chi-square test should result in (a) the tentative decision to reject the model and (b) the inspection of diagnos-

tic information about possible sources of model–data disagreement. Any respecification suggested by the diagnostics must be theoretically justifiable. If such respecifications result in subsequently passing the chi-square test, then diagnostic information about the fit of the respecified model is still needed. This is because a passing model can still have fit problems concerning its explanations of the observed covariances. If this diagnostic assessment indicates a problem, then the model should be rejected despite passing the chi-square test.

40. *Rely solely on suggested thresholds for approximate fit indexes to justify retaining the model.* Results of recent studies indicate that rules of thumb from the 1980s–1990s about cutoffs for approximate fit indexes that supposedly indicate "acceptable" fit are not trustworthy. This mistake is compounded when (a) the model fails the chi-square test when the sample size is not large and (b) the researcher neglects to report diagnostic information about model fit.

41. *Interpret "closer to fit" as "closer to truth."* Close model–data correspondence could reflect any of the following (not all mutually exclusive) possibilities: (a) the model accurately reflects reality; (b) the model is an equivalent or near-equivalent version of one that corresponds to reality but itself is incorrect; (c) the model fits the data in a non-representative sample but has poor fit in the population; or (d) the model has so many freely estimated parameters that it cannot have poor fit even if it is grossly misspecified. In a single study, it is usually impossible to determine which of these scenarios explains the good fit of the researcher's model. This is another way of saying that SEM is more useful for rejecting a false model than for somehow "proving" whether a given model is true (point 5).

42. *Interpret good fit as meaning that the endogenous variables are strongly predicted.* If the exogenous and mediator variables account for a small proportion of the variances of the ultimate outcome variables and a model accurately reflects this lack of predictive validity, then the overall fit of the model may be good. Fit statistics in SEM indicate whether the model can reproduce the observed covariances, not whether substantial proportions of the variance of the endogenous variables are explained.

43. *Rely solely on statistical criteria in model evaluation.* Other important considerations include model generality, parsimony, and theoretical plausibility. As noted by Robert and Pashler (2000), good statistical fit of a model indicates little about (a) theory flexibility (e.g., what it cannot explain), (b) variability of the data (e.g., whether the data can rule out what the theory explain cannot explain), and (c) the likelihood of other outcomes. These authors also suggest that a better way to evaluate a model is to determine (a) how well the theory limits outcomes (i.e., whether it can accurately predict), (b) how closely the actual outcome agrees with those limits, and (c) if plausible alternative outcomes would have been inconsistent with the theory (Sikström, 2001). That is, whether a model is statistically beautiful involves not just numbers, but ideas, too.

44. *Rely too much on statistical tests.* This entry covers several kinds of errors. One is to interpret statistical significance as evidence for effect size (especially in large samples) or for importance (i.e., substantive significance). Another is to place too much emphasis on statistical tests of individual parameters that may not be of central interest in hypoth-

esis testing (e.g., whether an error variance differs statistically from zero). A third is to forget that statistical tests of individual effects tend to result in rejection of the null hypothesis too often when non-normal data are analyzed by methods that assume normality. See point 27 for related misuses of statistical tests in SEM.

45. *Interpret the standardized solution in inappropriate ways.* This is a relatively common mistake in multiple-sample SEM—specifically, to compare standardized estimates across groups that differ in their variabilities. In general, standardized solutions are fine for comparisons within each group (e.g., the relative magnitudes of direct effects on the same endogenous variable), but only unstandardized solutions are usually appropriate for cross-group comparisons. A related error is to interpret group differences in the standardized estimates of equality-constrained parameters: the unstandardized estimates of such parameters are forced to be equal, but their unstandardized counterparts are typically unequal if the groups have different variabilities.

46. *Fail to consider equivalent or near-equivalent models.* Essentially all structural equation models have equivalent versions that generate the same predicted correlations or covariances. For latent variable models, there may be infinitely many equivalent models. There are probably also near-equivalent versions that generate almost the same covariances as those in the data matrix. Researchers must offer reasons why their models are to be preferred over some obvious equivalent or near-equivalent versions of them.

47. *Fail to consider (nonequivalent) alternative models.* When there are competing theories about the same phenomenon, it may be possible to specify alternative models that reflect them. Not all of these alternatives may be equivalent versions of one another. If the overall fits of some of these alternative models are comparable, then the researcher must explain why a particular model is to be preferred.

48. *Reify the factors.* Believe that constructs represented in your model *must* correspond to things in the real world. Perhaps they do, but do not assume it.

49. *Believe that naming a factor means that it is understood (i.e., commit the naming fallacy).* Factor names are conveniences, not explanations. For example, if a three-factor fits the data, this does not prove that the verbal labels assigned by the researcher to the factors are correct. Alternative interpretations of factors are often possible in many, if not most, factor analyses.

50. *Believe that a strong analytical method like SEM can compensate for poor study design or slipshod ideas.* No statistical procedure can make up for inherent logical or design flaws. For example, expressing poorly thought out hypotheses with a path diagram does not give them more credibility. The specification of direct and indirect effects in a structural model cannot be viewed as a replacement for an experimental or longitudinal design. As mentioned earlier, the inclusion of a measurement error term for an observed variable that is psychometrically deficient cannot somehow transform it into a good measure. Applying SEM in the absence of good design, measures, and ideas is like using a chain saw to cut butter: one will accomplish the task, but without a more substantial base, one is just as likely to make a big mess.

51. *As the researcher, fail to report enough information so that your readers can reproduce your results.* There are still too many reports in the literature where SEM was used

in which the authors do not give sufficient summary information for readers to re-create the original analyses or evaluate models not considered by the authors. At minimum, authors should generally report all relevant correlations, standard deviations, and means. Also describe the specification of the model(s) in enough detail so that a reader can reproduce the analysis.

52. *Interpret estimates of relatively large direct effects in a structural model as "proof" of causality.* As discussed earlier, it would be almost beyond belief that all of the conditions required for inference of causality from covariances have been met in a single study. In general, it is better to view structural models as being "as if" models of causality that may or may not correspond to causal sequences in the real world.

SUMMARY

So concludes this journey of discovery about SEM. As on any guided tour, you may have found some places along the way more interesting than others. Also, you may decide to revisit certain sites by using some of the related techniques in your work. Overall, I hope that reading this book has given you new ways of looking at your data and testing a broader range of hypotheses. Use SEM to address new questions or to provide new perspectives on older ones, but use it guided by your good sense and knowledge of your research area. Use it also as a means to reform methods of data analysis in the behavioral sciences by focusing more on models instead of specific effects analyzed with traditional statistical significance tests. The American politician Ivy Baker Priest once said: The world is round and the place which may seem like the end may also be the beginning. Go do yourself (and me, too) proud!

RECOMMENDED READINGS

These works all deal with the potential advantages and pitfalls of SEM. McCoach, Black, and O'Connell (2007) outline various sources of inference error in drawing conclusions from SEM analyses. Tomarken and Waller (2005) survey recent developments in SEM and describe common misunderstandings. Tu (2009) addresses the application of SEM in epidemiology and reminds us that there is no magic in SEM for inferring causality.

McCoach, D. B., Black, A. C., & O'Connell, A. A. (2007). Errors of inference in structural equation modeling. *Psychology in the Schools, 44,* 461–470.

Tomarken, A. J., & Waller, N. G. (2005). Structural equation modeling: Strengths, limitations, and misconceptions. *Annual Review of Clinical Psychology, 1,* 31–65.

Tu, Y.-K. (2009). Commentary: Is structural equation modelling a step forward for epidemiologists? *International Journal of Epidemiology, 38,* 549–551.

Suggested Answers to Exercises

CHAPTER 2

1. For the data in Table 2.1, $M_1 = 11.00$, $M_2 = 60.00$, $M_Y = 25.00$, $SD_1 = 6.2048$, $SD_2 = 14.5774$, $SD_Y = 4.6904$, $r_{Y1} = .6013$, $r_{Y2} = .7496$, and $r_{12} = .4699$, so:

$$b_1 = [.6013 - .7496\,(.4699)]/(1 - .4699^2) = .3197$$

$$B_1 = .3197\,(4.6904/6.2048) = .2417$$

$$b_2 = [.7496 - .6013\,(.4699)]/(1 - .4699^2) = .5993$$

$$B_2 = .5993\,(4.6904/14.5774) = .1928$$

$$A = 25.00 - .2417\,(11.00) - .1928\,(60.00) = 10.7711$$

$$\hat{Y} = .2417\,X_1 + .1928\,X_2 + 10.7711$$

$$R^2_{Y\cdot12} = .3197\,(.6013) + .5993\,(.7496) = .6415;\quad R_{Y\cdot12} = .8009$$

In the unstandardized solution, a 1-point difference on working memory (X_1) predicts a .24-point difference on reading achievement (Y), holding phonics skills (X_2) constant; and the expected difference on reading achievement is .19 points given a difference on phonics skills of 1 point, with working memory held constant. When scores on both working memory and phonics skills are zero, the predicted reading achievement score is 10.77. In the standardized solution, a difference of a full standard deviation on working memory predicts a difference of .32 standard deviations on reading achievement controlling for phonics skills; and a difference of a full standard deviation on phonics skills predicts a .60 standard deviation difference on reading achievement controlling for working memory. The total proportion of variance in reading achievement explained by working memory and phonics skills together is .6415, or 64.15%.

2 and 3. Unstandardized and standardized predicted scores and residuals for the data in Table 2.1 are listed next:

Case	$\hat{Y}$	$Y - \hat{Y}$	z_1	z_2	z_Y	$\hat{z}_Y$	$z - \hat{z}_Y$
A	24.0309	-.0309	-1.2893	.3430	-.2132	-.2066	-.0066
B	22.3466	-2.3466	-.4835	-.6860	-1.0660	-.5657	-.5003
C	20.9015	1.0985	-.1612	-1.3720	-.6396	-.8738	.2342
D	27.8951	4.1049	.6447	.6860	1.4924	.6172	.8752
E	29.8260	-2.8260	1.2893	1.0290	.4264	1.0289	-.6025

If you enter these scores in the data editor of a computer program for general statistical analyses, such as SPSS, you can show that the following results are correct within rounding error:

$$R_{Y \cdot 12} = r_{Y\hat{Y}}$$

$$r_{(Y-\hat{Y})1} = r_{(Y-\hat{Y})2} = r_{(z_Y - \hat{z}_Y)z_1} = r_{(z_Y - \hat{z}_Y)z_2} = 0$$

4. Applying Equation 2.4 to $R^2_{Y \cdot 12} = .6415$ for the data in Table 2.1 gives us

$$\hat{R}^2_{Y \cdot 12} = 1 - (1 - .6415)[4/(5 - 2 - 1)] = .2829$$

The shrinkage-adjusted proportion of explained variance, or .28, is substantially less than the observed proportion of explained variance, or .64, due to the small sample size ($N = 5$).

5. Given $r_{Y1} = .40$, $r_{Y2} = .50$, and $r_{12} = -.30$:

$$b_1 = [.40 - .50 \, (-.30)]/(1 - .30^2) = .6044$$

$$b_2 = [.50 - .40 \, (-.30)]/(1 - .30^2) = .6813$$

$$R_{Y \cdot 12} = [.6790 \, (.40) + .7654 \, (.50)]^{1/2} = .7632$$

There is a suppression effect because $b_1 > r_{Y1}$ and $b_2 > r_{Y2}$, specifically, reciprocal suppression.

6. Applying Equation 2.10 to $r_{XY} = .50$, $r_{XW} = .80$, and $r_{YW} = .60$ gives us

$$r_{XY \cdot W} = [.50 - .80 \, (.60)]/[(1 - .80^2) \, (1 - .60^2)]^{1/2} = 0.042$$

7. This is a variation of the local Type I error fallacy. This particular 95% confidence interval, 75.25–84.60, either contains $\mu_1 - \mu_2$ or it does not. The "95%" applies only in the long run: Of the 95% confidence intervals from all random samples, we expect 95% to contain $\mu_1 - \mu_2$, but 5% will not. Given a particular interval, such as 75.25–84.60, we do not know whether it is one of the 95% of all random intervals that contains $\mu_1 - \mu_2$ or one of the 5% that does not.

8. The answer to this question depends on the particular definitions you selected, but here is an example for one I found on Wikipedia: "In statistics, a result is called statistically significant if it is unlikely to have occurred by chance."[1] This is the odds-against-chance fallacy because p values do not estimate the likelihood that a particular result is due to chance. Under H_0, it is assumed that all results are due to chance.

---

[1]Retrieved February 4, 2009, from *http://en.wikipedia.org/wiki/Statistical_significance*

CHAPTER 3

1. First, derive the standard deviations, which are the square roots of the main diagonal entries:

$$SD_X = 42.25^{1/2} = 6.50, \; SD_Y = 148.84^{1/2} = 12.20, \text{ and } SD_W = 376.36^{1/2} = 19.40$$

Next, calculate each correlation by dividing the associated covariance by the product of the corresponding standard deviations. For example:

$$r_{XY} = 31.72/[6.50 \times 12.20] = .40$$

The entire correlation matrix in lower diagonal form is presented next:

	X	Y	W
X	1.00		
Y	.40	1.00	
W	.50	.35	1.00

2. The means are $M_X = 15.500$, $M_Y = 20.125$, and $M_W = 40.375$. Presented next are the correlations in lower diagonal form calculated for these data using each of the three options for handling missing data:

Listwise N = 6

	X	Y	W
X	1.000		
Y	.134	1.000	
W	.254	.610	1.000

Pairwise

		X	Y	W
X	r	1.000		
	N	8		
Y	r	.134	1.000	
	N	6	8	
W	r	.112	.645	1.000
	N	7	7	8

Mean Substitution N = 10

	X	Y	W
X	1.000		
Y	.048	1.000	
W	.102	.532	1.000

The results change depending on the missing data option used. For example, the correlation between Y and W ranges from .532 to .645 across the three methods.

3. Given cov_{XY} = 13.00, s_X^2 = 12.00, and s_Y^2 = 10.00. The covariance can be expressed as follows:

$$cov_{XY} = r_{XY} (12.00^{1/2}) (10.00^{1/2}) = r_{XY} (10.9545) = 13.00$$

Solving for the correlation gives us an out-of-bound value:

$$r_{XY} = 13.00/10.9545 = 1.19$$

4. The covariances and effective sample sizes derived using pairwise deletion for the data in Table 3.3 are presented next:

		X	Y	W
X	cov	86.400	−26.333	15.900
	N	6	4	5
Y	cov	−26.333	10.000	−10.667
	N	4	5	4
W	cov	15.900	−10.667	5.200
	N	5	4	6

I submitted the whole covariance matrix (without the sample sizes) to an online matrix calculator. The eigenvalues are (98.229, 7.042, −3.671) and the determinant is −2,539.702. These results indicate that the covariance matrix is nonpositive definite. The correlation matrix implied by the covariance matrix for pairwise deletion is presented next in lower diagonal form:

	X	Y	W
X	1.00		
Y	−.896	1.000	
W	.750	−1.479	1.000

5. I used SPSS to generate the normal probability plot (P–P) presented next. The departure of the data points in Figure 3.2 from a diagonal line indicates nonnormality:

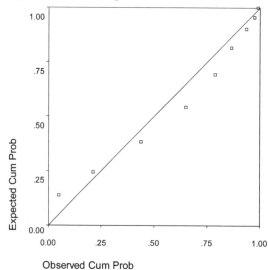

6. For the data in Figure 3.2 with the outlier removed ($N = 63$), SI = .65 and KI = $-.24$. In contrast, SI = 3.10 and KI = 15.73 when the outlier is included ($N = 64$).

7. The square root is not defined for negative numbers, and logarithms are not defined for numbers ≤ 0. Both functions treat numbers between 0 and 1.00 differently than they do numbers > 1.00. Specifically, both functions make numbers between 0 and 1.0 larger, and both make numbers greater than 1.0 smaller.

8. When the scores in Figure 3.2 are rescaled so that the lowest score is 1.0 before applying the square root transformation, SI = 1.24 and KI = 4.12. If this transformation is applied directly to the original scores in Figure 3.2, then SI = 2.31 and KI = 9.95. Thus, this transformation is not as effective if applied when the minimum score does not equal 1.0. See Osborne (2002) for additional examples.

9. The interitem correlations are presented next:

	I1	I2	I3	I4	I5
I1	1.0000				
I2	.3333	1.0000			
I3	.1491	.1491	1.0000		
I4	.3333	.3333	.1491	1.0000	
I5	.3333	.3333	.1491	.3333	1.0000

Presented next are calculations for α_C:

$$\bar{r}_{ij} = [6\ (.3333) + 4\ (.1491)]/10 = .2596$$

$$\alpha_C = [5\ (.2596)]/[1 + (5 - 1)\ .2596] = 1.2981/2.0385 = .64$$

The value of α_C reported by SPSS for these data is .63, which is within rounding error of the result just calculated by hand.

CHAPTER 5

1. Part of the association between Y_1 and Y_2 in Figure 5.3(a) is presumed to be causal, specifically, Y_1 has a direct effect on Y_2. However, there also are noncausal aspects to their relation, specifically, spurious associations due to common causes. For example, X_1 and X_2 are each represented in the model as common causes of Y_1 and Y_2. These common causes covary, so this unanalyzed association between common causes is another type of spurious association concerning Y_1 and Y_2. The relevant paths for all causal and noncausal aspects of the correlation between Y_1 and Y_2 are listed next:

Causal: $Y_1 \rightarrow Y_2$

Noncausal: $Y_1 \leftarrow X_1 \rightarrow Y_2$ $Y_1 \leftarrow X_2 \rightarrow Y_2$ $Y_1 \leftarrow X_1 \,\diagdown\!\!\diagup\, X_2 \rightarrow Y_2$

2. Yes. It is assumed in all CFA models that the substantive latent variables are causal (along

with the measurement errors) and that the indicators are the affected (outcome) variables. These assumptions concern effect priority.

3. Free parameter counts for Figures 5.3(b)–5.3(d) are as follows:

Model	Direct effects on endogenous variables		Exogenous variables		Total
			Variances	Covariances	
Figure 5.3(b)	$X_1 \rightarrow Y_1$ $X_2 \rightarrow Y_2$		X_1, X_2	$X_1 \smile X_2$	10
	$Y_1 \rightarrow Y_2$ $Y_2 \rightarrow Y_1$		D_1, D_2	$D_1 \smile D_2$	
Figure 5.3(c)	$X_1 \rightarrow Y_1$ $X_2 \rightarrow Y_1$		X_1, X_2	$X_1 \smile X_2$	10
	$X_2 \rightarrow Y_1$ $X_2 \rightarrow Y_1$		D_1, D_2	$D_1 \smile D_2$	
Figure 5.3(d)	$X_1 \rightarrow Y_1$ $X_2 \rightarrow Y_2$		X_1, X_2	$X_1 \smile X_2$	9
	$Y_1 \rightarrow Y_2$		D_1, D_2	$D_1 \smile D_2$	

4a. With six observed variables there are $p = 6(7)/2 = 21$ observations. In Figure 5.5, there are a total of seven direct effects on endogenous variables that need statistical estimates. These paths among the exogenous variables School Support and Coercive Control and among the endogenous variables Teacher Burnout, Teacher–Pupil Interactions (TPI), School Experience, and Somatic Status are listed next:

$$\text{Support} \rightarrow \text{Burnout, Coercive} \rightarrow \text{Burnout,}$$

$$\text{Support} \rightarrow \text{TPI, Coercive} \rightarrow \text{TPI, Burnout} \rightarrow \text{TPI,}$$

$$\text{TPI} \rightarrow \text{Experience, TPI} \rightarrow \text{Somatic}$$

Variances of exogenous variables ($\smile$) include two for the measured exogenous variables School Support and Coercive Control and another four for the unmeasured exogenous variables (disturbances) D_{TB}, D_{TPI}, D_{SE}, and D_{SS}, for a total of six variances. There is only one covariance between a pair of exogenous variables, or Support $\smile$ Coercive. The total number of free parameters is

$$q = 7 + 6 + 1 = 14$$

so the model degrees of freedom are calculated as follows:

$$df_M = 21 - 14 = 7$$

4b. With eight observed variables there are $p = 8(9)/2 = 36$ observations. Among the eight factor loadings in Figure 5.7, a total of two are fixed to 1 in order to scale the factors, so there are only six that require estimation. The variances and covariance of the two factors, Sequential and Simultaneous, are free parameters plus the variances of each of the eight measurement errors. The total number of free parameters is thus

$$q = 6 + 3 + 8 = 17$$

so the model degrees of freedom are

$$df_{\mathrm{M}} = 36 - 17 = 19$$

4c. With 12 observed variables there are $p = 12(13)/2 = 78$ observations. Free parameters are for the model of Figure 5.9 and are listed next in the following categories:

Direct effects on endogenous variables
Indicators (factor loadings): 2 per factor, or 8
Exogenous factors (path coefficients): 4
Total: 12

Variances and covariances of exogenous variables
Measurement error variances: 12
Factor variances: 1 (Constructive Thinking)
Disturbance variances: 3
Total: 16

There are no covariances between exogenous variables. The total number of free parameters and model degrees of freedom are:

$$q = 12 + 16 = 28$$
$$df_{\mathrm{M}} = 78 - 28 = 50$$

5. A covariate is a variable that is concomitant with another variable of primary interest and is measured for the purpose of controlling for the effects of the covariate on the outcome variable(s). In nonexperimental designs, a covariate is often a potential confounding variable that, once held constant in the analysis, may reduce the predictive power of another substantive predictor. Potential confounding variables often include demographic or background characteristics, such as level of education or amount of family income, and substantive predictors may include psychological variables. In a structural model, a covariate is typically represented as an exogenous variable with direct effects on the endogenous (outcome) variable that is assumed to covary with a substantive variable, which also has direct effects on the endogenous variable. Just as in a regression analysis, the direct effect of the substantive predictor is estimated controlling for the covariate.

6. It is possible that one model with $Y_1 \rightarrow Y_2$ and another model with $Y_2 \rightarrow Y_1$ are equivalent models with exactly the same fit to the data. Even if these two models are not equivalent, their fit to the data could be similar, in which case there is no statistical basis for preferring one model over the other. The matter is not clearer even if the fit of one model is quite better than that of the other model: This pattern of results is still affected by sampling error; that is, the same advantage for one model may not be found in a replication sample. There is also the possibility of a specification error that concerns the omission of other causes, which could bias the estimation of path coefficients for both models. Again, if you know the causal process beforehand, then you can use SEM to estimate the magnitudes of the direct effects, but SEM will not generally help you to find the model with the correct directionalities.

7. Both measurement errors and disturbances are represented as latent variables in some SEM computer tools, and their variances are typically free parameters that require a statistical estimate. Both represent residual (unexplained) variance, including that due to all omitted causes and score unreliability, too. The term *disturbance* has its roots in path analysis, and disturbances are associated with endogenous variables in structural models. In path models, all endogenous variables are observed variables, but some factors in structural regression models are endogenous, and each of the latter variables has its own disturbance. Measurement errors are associated exclusively with observed variables, specifically, with indicators in a measurement model.

8. Presented next is a basic path model shown without the symbols for disturbances (e.g., D_1 for Y_1, D_2 for Y_2) and variances of measured (X_1, X_2) or unmeasured (D_1, D_2) exogenous variables ( ). Variable X_2 is the covariate, and estimation of the effects of X_1 are corrected for its covariance with the covariate:

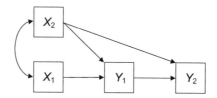

9. Sample size has nothing to do with the number of observations, the number of model parameters, df_M, or model identification. As in basically all statistical analyses, sample size in SEM affects the precision of the results in the form of standard errors (larger N, smaller standard errors, and vice versa). Large samples are generally required in SEM for acceptable precision, and some special methods may require even larger samples still. A larger sample size can also prevent some technical problems, such as iteration failure, that can occur in computer analyses.

CHAPTER 6

1. *Path models*: Parameters of path models include (a) direct effects on endogenous variables from other endogenous variables or measured exogenous variables (i.e., path coefficients); and (b) variances and covariances of measured exogenous variables and disturbances.

   CFA models: Parameters of CFA models include (a) direct effects on indicators from factors (i.e., factor loadings); and (b) variances and covariances of the factors and measurement errors.

   SR models: Parameters of SR models include (a) direct effects on endogenous variables, including factor loadings of indicators in the measurement model and direct effects on endogenous factors in the structural model; and (b) variances and covariances of exogenous variables, including measurement errors, disturbances, and exogenous factors.

2. Factor B and indicator X_3 of Figure 6.4(c) would have the same scale only if the factor explains 100% of the variance of the indicator (unlikely). Otherwise, the scale of B is related to the

scale of the *explained* variance X_3, not typically the total (observed) variance of this indicator.

3. The number of observations for both CFA models in Figure 6.1 is $6(7)/2 = 21$. The breakdown of parameters for both models is listed next. There are 13 parameters for each model, so $df_M = 8$ for both factor models:

Model	Direct effects on indicators		Exogenous variables		Total
			Variances	Covariances	
Figure 6.1(a)	$A \rightarrow X_2$	$B \rightarrow X_5$	A, B	$A \diagdown\diagup B$	13
	$A \rightarrow X_3$	$B \rightarrow X_6$	$E_1 – E_6$		
Figure 6.1(b)	$A \rightarrow X_1$	$B \rightarrow X_4$	$E_1 – E_6$	$A \diagdown\diagup B$	13
	$A \rightarrow X_2$	$B \rightarrow X_5$			
	$A \rightarrow X_3$	$B \rightarrow X_6$			

4. With four observed variables, there are $4(5)/2 = 10$ observations available to estimate the parameters of the nonrecursive path model in Figure 6.3. The parameters of this model include these five direct effects

$$X_1 \rightarrow Y_1, X_1 \rightarrow Y_2, X_2 \rightarrow Y_2, Y_1 \rightarrow Y_2, \text{ and } Y_2 \rightarrow Y_1$$

and four variances (of X_1, X_2, D_1, and D_2) and two covariances (of $X_1 \diagdown\diagup X_2$ and $D_1 \diagdown\diagup D_2$) of exogenous variables for a total of 11, so $df_M = -1$. This model fails the order condition because there are no excluded variables for Y_2 (i.e., the equation for this endogenous variable is underidentified). The same equation also fails the rank condition because the rank of the reduced system matrix for Y_2 is zero:

$$\rightarrow \quad \begin{array}{c} Y_1 \\ Y_2 \end{array} \left[\begin{array}{cccc} X_1 & X_2 & Y_1 & Y_2 \\ + & 0 & + & + \\ + & + & + & + \end{array} \right] \rightarrow \left[\quad \quad \right] \rightarrow \quad \text{Rank} = 0$$

5. After the path $X_3 \rightarrow Y_1$ and the corresponding unanalyzed associations are added to the model in Figure 6.3, there are $5(6)/2 = 15$ observations available to estimate the parameters of the respecified model, including five variances (of $X_1 – X_3$, D_1, and D_2), four covariances (of $X_1 \diagdown\diagup X_2, X_1 \diagdown\diagup X_3, X_2 \diagdown\diagup X_3$, and $D_1 \diagdown\diagup D_2$), and these six direct effects

$$X_1 \rightarrow Y_1, X_1 \rightarrow Y_2, X_2 \rightarrow Y_2, X_3 \rightarrow Y_1, Y_1 \rightarrow Y_2, \text{ and } Y_2 \rightarrow Y_1$$

for a total of 15 free parameters, so $df_M = 0$. There is at least one variable omitted from the equation of each endogenous variable (X_2 for Y_1, X_3 for Y_2), so the order condition is satisfied. Evaluation of the sufficient rank condition for the respecified model is outlined next:

Evaluation for Y_1:

$$\rightarrow \quad \begin{array}{c} Y_1 \\ Y_2 \end{array} \left[\begin{array}{ccccc} X_1 & X_2 & X_3 & Y_1 & Y_2 \\ + & 0 & + & + & + \\ + & 1 & 0 & + & + \end{array} \right] \rightarrow \left[\quad 1 \quad \right] \rightarrow \quad \text{Rank} = 1$$

Evaluation for Y_2:

$$
\begin{array}{c}
\\
\rightarrow
\end{array}
\begin{array}{c}
Y_1 \\
Y_2
\end{array}
\left[
\begin{array}{ccccc}
X_1 & X_2 & X_3 & Y_1 & Y_2 \\
+ & 0 & 1 & + & + \\
+ & + & 0 & + & +
\end{array}
\right]
\rightarrow
\left[\quad 1 \quad\right]
\rightarrow
\quad \text{Rank} = 1
$$

Because the rank of the equation for each endogenous variable equals the minimum required value, or 1, the sufficient rank condition is satisfied. Thus, the respecified model is just-identified.

6. Yes, the model in Figure 6.5(f) with complex indicator X_3 but with the error correlation $E_{X_3} \smile E_{X_5}$ is identified because this respecified model satisfies Rule 6.8 in Table 6.2. Specifically, the respecified model satisfies Rule 6.7 (and by implication Rule 6.6; see Table 6.1) and there is at least one singly loading indicator on each of factor A and B with which the complex indicator X_3 does not share an error correlation (e.g., $X_2 \leftarrow A$, $X_4 \leftarrow B$). For the second part of this question, we are now working with the respecified model presented next:

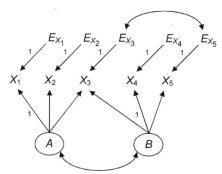

Adding the error correlation $E_{X_3} \smile E_{X_4}$ to this respecified model would result in a non-identified model that violates Rule 6.8 because there would be no indicator of B that does not share an error correlation with the complex indicator X_3. It would be possible to add either $E_{X_1} \smile E_{X_3}$ or $E_{X_2} \smile E_{X_3}$ to the respecified model (i.e., each of the resulting models would be identified), but not both. This is because the respecified model but with both error correlations just mentioned would violate Rule 6.8 in that there would be no indicator of A that shares no error correlation with X_3.

7. The virtual absence of the path $X_2 \rightarrow Y_2$ alters the system matrix for the first block of endogenous variables in Figure 6.2(b). This consequence is outlined next, starting with the matrix for the model in the figure without the path $X_2 \rightarrow Y_2$ (the rank for Y_1's equation is zero):

$$
\begin{array}{c}
\rightarrow \\
\\
\end{array}
\begin{array}{c}
Y_1 \\
Y_2
\end{array}
\left[
\begin{array}{cccc}
X_1 & X_2 & Y_1 & Y_2 \\
+ & 0 & + & + \\
0 & 0 & + & +
\end{array}
\right]
\rightarrow
\left[\quad 0 \quad\right]
\rightarrow
\quad \text{Rank} = 0
$$

8. For the SR model in Figure 6.6(a), $df_M = 7$, so it seems as though there is "room" for more effects, but let's apply the two-step rule: the measurement portion expressed as a CFA model with the error correlations $E_{X_1} \smile E_{Y_1}$, and $E_{X_2} \smile E_{Y_2}$ would be identical to the measure-

ment model in Figure 6.5(e), which is identified. The structural model after adding the disturbance correlation $D_B \nwarrow \nearrow D_C$ is presented next:

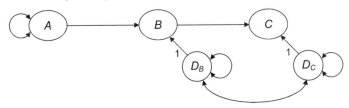

This structural model is nonrecursive with all possible disturbance correlations. The order condition is satisfied because there is one variable omitted from the equation of every endogenous variable (A for B, B for C). The sufficient rank condition is also satisfied:

Evaluation for B:

$$
\begin{array}{c}
\rightarrow \\
\end{array}
\begin{array}{c}
B \\
C
\end{array}
\begin{array}{ccc}
A & B & C \\
\end{array}
\left[\begin{array}{ccc}
\cancel{1} & \cancel{1} & 0 \\
0 & \cancel{1} & 1
\end{array} \right]
\rightarrow
\left[\begin{array}{c}
1
\end{array} \right]
\rightarrow
\quad \text{Rank} = 1
$$

Evaluation for C:

$$
\begin{array}{c}
\rightarrow \\
\end{array}
\begin{array}{c}
B \\
C
\end{array}
\begin{array}{ccc}
A & B & C \\
\end{array}
\left[\begin{array}{ccc}
1 & \cancel{1} & 0 \\
0 & \cancel{1} & \cancel{1}
\end{array} \right]
\rightarrow
\left[\begin{array}{c}
1
\end{array} \right]
\rightarrow
\quad \text{Rank} = 1
$$

Therefore, the structural part of the respecified CFA model is identified. Because both the measurement and structural models are identified, the respecified SR model is identified, too.

CHAPTER 7

1. Proportions of explained variance for the model in Figure 7.1:

Endogenous variable	R^2_{smc}
Teacher Burnout	$1 - (68.137/9.7697^2) = .286$
Teacher–Pupil Interactions	$1 - (19.342/5.0000^2) = .226$
School Experience	$1 - (7.907/3.7178^2) = .428$
Somatic Status	$1 - (13.073/5.2714^2) = .530$

2. Sobel test for the model in Figure 7.1(a) of the unstandardized indirect effect of school support on student school experience through teacher-pupil interactions:

$$
z = (.097 \times .486)/\sqrt{.486^2(.046^2) + .097^2(.055^2)} = 2.051
$$

Thus, this indirect effect is statistically significant at the .05 level but not at the .01 level. However, this result may not be accurate because the sample size is not large.

3. Unstandardized total indirect effect of school support on school experience for the model in Figure 7.1(a):

$$(.097 \times .486) + (-.384 \times .142 \times .486) = .021$$

This value matches within slight rounding error the corresponding entry in Table 7.3 for this unstandardized total indirect effect, or .020.

4. I used the student version of LISREL 8.8 to conduct this analysis and the next. For the respecified model with the direct effect from school support to school experience, $df_M = 6$. The unstandardized path coefficient for this new direct effect is $-.018$, its estimated standard error is .026, $z = -.696$, and the standardized coefficient is $-.052$. The new direct effect is not statistically significant ($z = -.696$), but power is low, and the magnitude of this new effect in standardized terms is not large. These results are consistent with the hypothesis of pure mediation. The value of the test statistic from this analysis, or $-.696$, matches within rounding that of the standardized residual for the variables school and school experience in the original model, or $-.695$ (see Table 7.3). In this case, both statistics test the effect of adding a direct effect between these two variables to the original model. In the revised model with the path from school support to school experience, $R^2_{smc} = .431$, which is only slightly greater than the corresponding statistic in the original model without this path, or $R^2_{smc} = .428$.

5. For the respecified model, $df_M = 8$ because just a single path coefficient is calculated for the two equality-constrained direct effects. In the unstandardized solution, the path coefficient for both direct effects is $-.150$. However, in the standardized solution, the coefficients for the direct effects of school support and coercive control on teacher burnout are, respectively, $-.161$ and $-.127$. Recall that equality constraints generally hold in the unstandardized solution only in default ML estimation.

6. A corrected normal theory method requires the analysis of a raw data file, not a matrix summary of the data.

7. This exercise concerned whether you could reproduce the parameter estimates in Table 7.7 for the model in Figure 7.2 and the data in Table 7.6.

8. A disturbance correlation in a path model estimates the residual (partial) correlation between a pair of endogenous variables controlling for their common measured causes. In this case, the sign of the residual correlation (.38) is positive, which indicates that shared unmeasured (omitted) causes affect these two endogenous variables in the same direction. For example, whatever omitted cause increases one endogenous variable also tends to increase the other endogenous variable, and vice versa. This makes sense because the sample correlation between this pair of endogenous variables is positive (.41). However, the residual correlation (.38) is nearly as large as the observed correlation (.41). This means that the explanatory power of the model without the disturbance correlation for this pair of endogenous variables is relatively low.

CHAPTER 8

1. The largest correlation residual in Table 7.5, or .103, is for the coercive control and school experience variables. Because the original model contains only indirect effects between these two variables, an obvious respecification is to add a direct effect from coercive control to school experience. For this revised model, EQS reported these values of the following fit statistics: $\chi^2_M (6) = 1.464, p = .962$, RMSEA = 0, GFI = .996, CFI = 1.000, and SRMR = .018. The program was unable to calculate a confidence interval based on the RMSEA, perhaps because the fit of this revised model is close to perfect. None of the correlation residuals exceed .10 in absolute value:

Variable	1	2	3	4	5	6
1. Coercive Control	0					
2. Teacher Burnout	0	0				
3. School Support	0	0	0			
4. Teacher-Pupil	0	0	0	0		
5. School Experience	0	.035	-.028	0	0	
6. Somatic Status	-.054	-.028	.021	0	.020	0

For the new path from coercive control to school experience in the revised model, the unstandardized path coefficient, standard error, z statistic, and standardized coefficient are, respectively, .055, .035, 1.568, and .123. The unstandardized path coefficient is not statistically significant, but power is low. The proportion of explained variance for the school experience variable in the revised model is $R^2_{smc} = .441$, which, as expected, is somewhat greater than the value in the original model, or $R^2_{smc} = .428$ (see Exercise 1 for Chapter 7). Based on these results for the respecified model, overall fit is acceptable, but this revised model is hardly "proved."

2. For the respecified Roth et al. path model with a direct effect from fitness to stress, EQS reported values of the following fit statistics: $\chi^2_M (4) = 5.921, p = .205$, RMSEA = .036 (0–.092), GFI = .994, CFI = .988, and SRMR = .034. None of the absolute correlation residuals exceed .10:

Variable	1	2	3	4	5
1. Exercise	0				
2. Hardiness	0	0			
3. Fitness	0	.082	0		
4. Stress	-.012	-.009	-.018	.004	
5. Illness	.029	-.095	-.006	.006	.003

3. There is only a 15.3% chance of rejecting a false model for this analysis with 109 cases, given the other assumptions stated in Table 8.7. The minimum sample size required for a minimum of power of .80 for the test of the close-fit hypothesis is about 1,075 cases. There is only a 9.6% chance of detecting a model with close approximate fit for this analysis. The minimum sample size needed for power = .80 for the test of the not-close-fit hypothesis is about 960 cases.

4. For the model in Figure 8.3(a), $df_M = 5$, which implies 10 free parameters:

$$AIC_{Fig\ 8.3(a)} = 40.402 + 2\ (10) = 60.402$$

For the model in Figure 8.3(b), $df_M = 3$, which implies 12 free parameters:

$$AIC_{Fig\ 8.3(b)} = 3.238 + 2\ (12) = 27.238$$

5. These minimum sample sizes needed for power = .80 for the test of each null hypothesis listed next are from Table 4 of MacCallum et al. (1996, p. 144):

H_0	\multicolumn{4}{c}{df_M}	\multicolumn{4}{c}{df_M}
	2	6	10	14	20	25	30	40
Close fit	3,488	1,238	782	585	435	363	314	252
Not close fit	2,382	1,069	750	598	474	411	366	307

These results make clear the reality that large samples are required for adequate statistical power when there are few model degrees of freedom.

6. Several different equivalent models could be generated from Figure 7.1, but the real test is whether a candidate equivalent model has the same values of fit statistics when fitted to the same data as the original model. Presented next are two equivalent versions of Figure 7.1. Your models may not exactly match these two models, but all equivalent versions will obtain the same values of all fit statistics (e.g., $\chi^2_M\ (7) = 3.895$, GFI = .989, etc.):

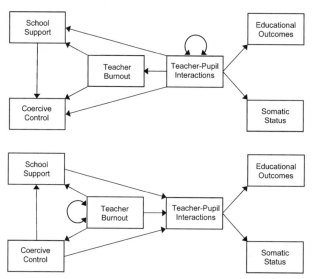

7. The two models for this problem are not equivalent because the variables fitness and stress in Figure 8.1 do not have common causes, which violates a requirement of Rule 8.2 of the Lee–Hershberger replacing rules that a direct path between two endogenous variables can be reversed if those variables have the same causes.

8. For the Roth et al. model:

$$CFI = 1 - [(11.078 - 5)]/[(165.499 - 10)] = 1 - (6.078/155.499) = .961$$

For the Sava model:

$$CFI = 1.000 \text{ because } \chi^2_M = 3.895 < df_M = 7$$

CHAPTER 9

1. Values of cross-factor structure coefficients are calculated as follows:

Indicator	Simultaneous	Indicator	Sequential
HM	.497 (.557) = .277	GC	.503 (.557) = .280
NR	.807 (.557) = .449	Tr	.726 (.557) = .404
WO	.808 (.557) = .450	SM	.656 (.557) = .365
		MA	.588 (.557) = .328
		PS	.782 (.557) = .436

2. Listed here are values of standardized residuals for this analysis computed by the student version of LISREL. Absolute values > 1.96 are statistically significant at the .05 level:

Indicator	HM	NR	WO	GC	Tr	SM	MA	PS
HM	0							
NR	−.555	0						
WO	−2.642	4.472	0					
GC	1.141	−2.237	−1.280	0				
Tr	2.141	−1.463	−.959	.438	0			
SM	3.769	−.111	−.350	−.758	−.259	0		
MA	3.791	1.166	.741	.326	−.240	.688	0	
PS	3.247	−1.816	.538	.971	.763	−.141	−1.647	0

3. Sum of unstandardized factor loadings:

$$(1.000 + 1.445 + 2.029 + 1.212 + 1.727) = 7.413$$

Sum of error variances:

$$(5.419 + 3.425 + 9.998 + 5.104 + 3.483) = 27.429$$

Estimated factor variance: 1.835

$$\hat{\rho}_{X_i X_i} = [7.413^2 (1.835)]/[7.413^2 (1.835) + 27.567] = .786$$

4. These results for the model where the Hand Movements task loads on the simultaneous processing factor are from EQS: $\chi^2_M (18) = 18.017$, $p = .454$; RMSEA = .002 with the 90% confidence interval 0–.063; CFI = .999; GFI = .977; SRMR = .035; and all absolute correlation residuals are < .10. However, the correlation residual for the Number Recall task and the Gestalt Closure task is −.098, so all problems of fit are not "cured" by this respecification.

5. The free parameters of the model in Figure 9.4 include 13 variances (of nine measurement errors, three disturbances, and g) and eight direct effects (six on indicators from first-order

factors, two on first-order factors from g) for a total of 21. With nine indicators, there are $9(10)/2 = 45$ observations, so $df_M = 45 - 21 = 24$.

6. The model in Figure 9.8 that corresponds to H_{form} is analyzed with no cross-group equality constraints, so the number of free parameters is 22 and $df_M = 30 - 22 = 8$. However, the solution is inadmissible owing to a Heywood case that involves the error variance of the intimacy indicator of the marital adjustment factor for wives, for which LISREL gives an estimate of -40.282. In EQS, the estimate for this error variance is 0, but this is because EQS automatically constrains error variances to be ≥ 0. But EQS issues a few error messages about this parameter estimates for the wives:

```
        E2,E2 VARIANCE OF PARAMETER ESTIMATE IS SET TO ZERO
*  WARNING  *  TEST RESULTS MAY NOT BE APPROPRIATE DUE TO CONDITION CODE
```

The Heywood case here is probably due to the combination of small group sizes and the presence of a factor (marital adjustment) with just two indicators.

7. Standardizing the factors assumes that the groups are equally variable on all factors. If this assumption is not correct, then the results may not be accurate.

CHAPTER 10

1. Values of the rho coefficient are using values from Tables 10.3 and 10.4 as follows:

Job Satisfaction: Loadings: $(1.000 + 1.035 + .891)^2 = 8.5615$
                    Variance: .618
                    Errors: $(.260 + .368 + .384) = 1.012$
                    $\hat{\rho}_{X_i X_i} = [8.5615\,(.618)]/[(8.5615\,(.618) + 1.012] = .839$

Well-Being: Loadings: $(1.000 + 1.490 + .821)^2 = 10.9627$
                    Variance: .142
                    Errors: $(.173 + .261 + .178) = .612$
                    Covariance: $-.043$
                    $\hat{\rho}_{X_i X_i} = [10.9627\,(.142)]/[10.9627\,(.142) + .612 + 2\,(-.043)] = .747$

Dysfunctional: Loadings: $(1.000 + 1.133 + .993)^2 = 9.7719$
                    Variance: .235
                    Errors: $(.106 + .068 + .300) = .474$
                    $\hat{\rho}_{X_i X_i} = [9.7719\,(.235)]/[9.7719\,(.235) + .474] = .829$

Constructive: Loadings: $(1.000 + 1.056 + 1.890)^2 = 15.5709$
                    Variance: .212
                    Errors: $(.292 + 1.022 + .242) = 1.556$
                    $\hat{\rho}_{X_i X_i} = [15.5709\,(.212)]/[15.5709\,(.212) + 1.5560] = .680$

2. The rescaled variance of the depression single indicator is 10.200 (Table 10.5). If

$$1 - r_{XX} = 1 - .70 = .30$$

or 30% of its variance is error, then the error variance for the depression single indicator is fixed to

$$.3 (10.200) = 3.06$$

and its loading on an underlying depression factor is fixed to 1.0. This specification is included in the LISREL and EQS syntax files for this analysis that can be downloaded from this book's website (p. 3). The overall fit of the respecified model is the same as that of the original model in Figure 10.5 (e.g., χ^2_M (16) = 59.715). Listed next are LISREL estimates of the direct effects on depression and the disturbance variance for depression outcome for the original model wherein the depression scale is represented as a single indicator but without an error term (Figure 10.5) and for the respecified model wherein the measurement error of this single indicator is directly estimated:

Parameter	Unst.	SE	St.
No error term for depression single indicator			
Stress → Depression	1.321	.114	.690
SES → Depression	−.257	.060	−.177
Variance of D_{De}	5.247	.465	.517
Error term for depression single indicator			
Stress → Depression	1.321	.114	.825
SES → Depression	−.257	.060	−.212
Variance of D_{De}	2.187	.465	.307

Note. Unst., unstandardized; St., standardized.

Because the predictors of depression in both models are factors (stress, SES) and measurement errors in their indicators are taken into account, the unstandardized regression weights are not affected by measurement error in the depression outcome. When the outcome is measured with error (i.e., the original model with no error term for the depression scale), standardized regression coefficients tend to be too small (Chapter 2). Also, the proportion of error variance is higher in the original model due to measurement error in the single indicator of depression. When this error is controlled, standardized regression coefficients are higher and the proportion of error variance is lower in the respecified model. What could be considered a "surprise" is that the estimate for the direct effect of acculturation on stress is positive in both models. Thus, participants who reported a higher degree of acculturation also reported experiencing more stress.

3. A diagram for this respecification where r_{11}, r_{22}, r_{33} are reliability coefficients and s_1^2, s_2^2, and s_3^2 are the sample variances for the indicators is presented next. This model is not identified in isolation, but it shows how to take direct account of measurement error in cause indicators:

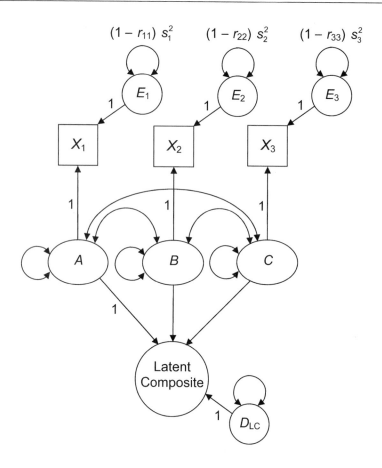

4. Socioeconomic status (SES) is represented in Figure 10.5 as a reflective construct that causes its indicators, but this specification is backward from how we usually think of SES. Along the same lines, stress is also represented in the figure as a reflective construct, but one could argue that overall stress level is affected by the experience of either work-related stress or relationship-oriented stress, not the other way around. However, because each of these factors in Figure 10.5 emits just one path, it would not be possible to respecify the model such that SES and stress each are represented as a formative construct with cause indicators only and a disturbance without changing the original structural model. But it would be possible to estimate a model where SES and stress composites each have no disturbance term and emit a single direct effect. Another alternative would be to use the technique of PLS-PM to estimate this model.

5. Standardized effect decomposition for the structural model in Figure 10.3:

		Predictor		
Outcome		Constructive	Dysfunctional	Well-Being
Dysfunctional	Direct	−.124	—	—
	Indirect	—	—	—
	Total	−.124	—	—

Well-Being	Direct	.082	−.470	—
	Indirect	−.124 (−.470) = .058	—	—
	Total	.082 + .058 = .140	−.470	—
Satisfaction	Direct	.093	−.149	.382
	Indirect	−.124 (−.149) + .082 (.382) + −.124 (−.470) (.382) = .072	−.470 (.382) = −.179	—
	Total	.165	−.329	.382

6. With 12 observed variables, there are 12(13)/2 = 78 observations for this analysis. There are a total of 31 free parameters, including 16 variances (of four factors and 12 measurement errors), seven covariances (six between each pair of the four factors and one between a pair of measurement errors), and eight factor loadings (two per factor), so $df_M = 78 - 31 = 47$.

7. Predictor (causally prior) factors have indirect effects on the indicators of outcome factors. For example, the constructive thinking factor in Figure 10.3 has indirect effects on all three indicators of the dysfunctional thinking factor, such as

$$\text{Constructive} \rightarrow \text{Dysfunctional} \rightarrow \text{Approval}$$

For example, LISREL reports that the completely standardized total effects of constructive thinking on the approval indicator of the dysfunctional thinking factor is −.082. This total effect consists of the indirect effect just listed. The standardized direct effect of constructive thinking on dysfunctional thinking is −.124, and the standardized factor loading of the approval indicator on the dysfunctional thinking factor is .660 (Table 10.3), so the whole indirect effect is estimated as −.124 (.660) = −.082.

References

Aiken, L., & West, S. (1991). *Testing interactions in multiple regression.* Hillsdale, NJ: Erlbaum.

Aiken, L. S., West, S. G., Sechrest, L., & Reno, R. R. (1990). Measurement in psychology: A survey of PhD programs in North America. *American Psychologist, 45,* 721–734.

Allison, P. D. (2001). *Missing data.* Thousand Oaks, CA: Sage.

Allison, P. D. (2003). Missing data techniques for structural equation modeling. *Journal of Abnormal Psychology, 112,* 545–557.

Anderson, D. R., Burnham, K. P., & Thompson, W. L. (2000). Null hypothesis testing: Problems, prevalence, and an alternative. *Journal of Wildlife Management, 64,* 912–923.

Anderson, J. C., & Gerbing, D. W. (1988). Structural equation modeling in practice: A review and recommended two-step approach. *Psychological Bulletin, 103,* 411–423.

Arbuckle, J. L. (1995–2009). *Amos 18.0 User's Guide.* Crawfordville, FL: Amos Development Corporation.

Arbuckle, J. L. (1996). Full information estimation in the presence of incomplete data. In G. A. Marcoulides & R. E. Schumacker (Eds.), *Advanced structural equation modeling* (pp. 243–277). Mahwah, NJ: Erlbaum.

Asparouhov, T., & Muthén, B. O. (2009). Exploratory structural equation modeling. *Structural Equation Modeling, 16,* 397–438.

Asparouhov, T., & Muthén, B. O. (2010). Bayesian analysis using Mplus. Retrieved May 15, 2010, from *www.statmodel.com/download/Bayes2.pdf*

Bagozzi, R. P. (2007). On the meaning of formative measurement and how it differs from reflective measurement: Comment on Howell, Breivik, and Wilcox (2007). *Psychological Methods, 12,* 229–237.

Bandalos, D. L. (2002). The effects of item parceling on goodness-of-fit and parameter estimate bias in structural equation modeling. *Structural Equation Modeling, 9,* 78–102.

Bandalos, D. L., & Finney, S. J. (2001). Item parceling issues in structural equation modeling. In G. A. Marcoulides & R. E. Schumacker (Eds.), *New developments and techniques in structural equation modeling* (pp. 269–296). Mahwah, NJ: Erlbaum.

Baron, R. M., & Kenny, D. A. (1986). The moderator–mediator variable distinction in social psychological research: Conceptual, strategic, and statistical considerations. *Journal of Personality and Social Psychology, 51,* 1173–1182.

Barrett, P. (2007). Structural equation modelling: Adjudging model fit. *Personality and Individual Differences, 42,* 815–824.

Bartholomew, D. J. (2002). Old and new approaches to latent variable modeling. In G. A. Marcoulides & I. Moustaki (Eds.), *Latent variable and latent structure models* (pp. 1–13). Mahwah, NJ: Erlbaum.

Bauer, D. J. (2003). Estimating multilevel linear models as structural equation models. *Journal of Educational and Behavioral Statistics, 28,* 135–167.

Beauducel, A., & Wittman, W. (2005). Simulation study on fit indices in confirmatory factor analysis based on data with slightly distorted simple structure. *Structural Equation Modeling, 12,* 41–75.

Bedeian, A. G., Day, D. V., & Kelloway, E. K. (1997). Correcting for measurement error attenuation in structural equation models: Some important reminders. *Educational and Psychological Measurement, 57,* 785–799.

Belsley, D. A., Kuh, E., & Welsch, R. E. (2004). *Regression diagnostics: Identifying influential data and sources of collinearity.* Hoboken, NJ: Wiley.

Bentler, P. M. (1980). Multivariate analysis with latent variables: Causal modeling. *Annual Review of Psychology, 31,* 419–456.

Bentler, P. M. (1990). Comparative fit indexes in structural models. *Psychological Bulletin, 107,* 238–246.

Bentler, P. M. (1995). *EQS structural equations program manual.* Encino, CA: Multivariate Software.

Bentler, P. M. (2000). Rites, wrongs, and gold in model testing. *Structural Equation Modeling, 7,* 82–91.

Bentler, P. M. (2006). *EQS 6 structural equations program manual.* Encino, CA: Multivariate Software.

Bentler, P. M., & Dijkstra, T. (1985). Efficient estimation via linearization in structural models. In P. R. Krishnaiah (Ed.), *Multivariate analysis VI* (pp. 9–42). Amsterdam: North-Holland.

Bentler, P. M., & Raykov, T. (2000). On measures of explained variance in nonrecursive structural equation models. *Journal of Applied Psychology, 85,* 125–131.

Benyamini, Y., Ein-Dor, T., Ginzburg, K., & Solomon, Z. (2009). Trajectories of self-rated health among veterans: A latent growth curve analysis of the impact of posttraumatic symptoms. *Psychosomatic Medicine, 71,* 345–352.

Bernstein, I. H., & Teng, G. (1989). Factoring items and factoring scales are different: Spurious evidence for multidimensionality due to item categorization. *Psychological Bulletin, 105,* 467–477.

Berry, W. D. (1984). *Nonrecursive causal models.* Beverly Hills, CA: Sage.

Bickel, R. (2007). *Multilevel analysis for applied research: It's just regression!* New York: Guilford Press.

Blalock, H. M. (1961). Correlation and causality: The multivariate case. *Social Forces, 39,* 246–251.

Blest, D. C. (2003). A new measure of kurtosis adjusted for skewness. *Australian & New Zealand Journal of Statistics, 45,* 175–179.

Block, J. (1995). On the relation between IQ, impulsivity, and delinquency: Remarks on the Lynam, Moffitt, and Stouthamer–Loeber (1993) interpretation. *Journal of Abnormal Psychology, 104,* 395–398.

Blunch, N. (2008). *Introduction to structural equation modelling using SPSS and AMOS.* Thousand Oaks, CA: Sage.

Bollen, K. A. (1989). *Structural equations with latent variables.* New York: Wiley.

Bollen, K. A. (1996). A limited-information estimator for LISREL models with and without heteroscedastic errors. In G. Marcoulides & R. Schumacker (Eds.), *Advanced structural equation modeling techniques* (pp. 227–241). Mahwah, NJ: Erlbaum.

Bollen, K. A. (2000). Modeling strategies: In search of the holy grail. *Structural Equation Modeling, 7,* 74–81.

Bollen, K. A. (2007). Interpretational confounding is due to misspecification, not to type of indicator: Comment on Howell, Breivik, and Wilcox (2007). *Psychological Methods, 12,* 219–228.

Bollen, K. A., & Curran, P. J. (2004). Autoregressive latent trajectory (ALT) models: A synthesis of two traditions. *Sociological Methods Research, 32,* 336–383.

Bollen, K. A., & Curran, P. J. (2006). *Latent curve models: A structural equation perspective.* Hoboken, NJ: Wiley.

Bollen, K. A., Kirby, J. B., Curran, P. J., Paxton, P. M., & Chen, F. (2007). Latent variable models under misspecification: Two-stage least squares (TSLS) and maximum likelihood (ML) estimators. *Sociological Methods and Research, 36,* 48–86.

Bollen, K. A., & Lennox, R. (1991). Conventional wisdom on measurement: A structural equation perspective. *Psychological Bulletin, 110,* 305–314.

Boomsma, A. (2000). Reporting analyses of covariance structures. *Structural Equation Modeling, 7,* 461–483.

Box, G. E. P., & Cox, D. R. (1964). An analysis of transformations. *Journal of the Royal Statistical Society,* Series B (Methodological), *26,* 211–252.

Breckler, S. J. (1990). Applications of covariance structure modeling in psychology: Cause for concern? *Psychological Bulletin, 107,* 260–273.

Breivik, E., & Olsson, U. H. (2001). Adding variables to improve fit: The effect of model size on fit assessment in LISREL. In R. Cudeck, S. Du Toit, & D. Sörbom (Eds.), *Structural equation modeling: Present and future. A Festschrift in honor of Karl Jöreskog* (pp. 169–194). Lincolnwood, IL: Scientific Software International.

Brito, C., & Pearl, J. (2003). A new identification condition for recursive models with correlated errors. *Structural Equation Modeling, 9,* 459–474.

Brown, T. A. (2006). *Confirmatory factor analysis for applied research.* New York: Guilford Press.

Browne, M. W. (1982). Covariance structures. In D. M. Hawkins (Ed.), *Topics in applied multivariate analysis* (pp. 72–141). Cambridge, UK: Cambridge University Press.

Browne, M. W. (1984). Asymptotic distribution free methods in analysis of covariance structures. *British Journal of Mathematical and Statistical Psychology, 37,* 62–83.

Browne, M. W., & Cudeck, R. (1993). Alternative ways of assessing model fit. In K. A. Bollen & J. S. Long (Eds.), *Testing structural equation models* (pp. 136–162). Newbury Park, CA: Sage.

Bruhn, M., Georgi, D., & Hadwich, K. (2008). Customer equity management as formative second-order construct. *Journal of Business Research, 61,* 1292–1301.

Burt, R. S. (1976). Interpretational confounding of unobserved variables in structural equation models. *Sociological Methods and Research, 5,* 3–52.

Burton, A., & Altman, D. G. (2004). Missing covariate data within cancer prognostic studies: A review of current reporting and proposed guidelines. *British Journal of Cancer, 91,* 4–8.

Byrne, B. M. (2006). *Structural equation modeling with EQS: Basic concepts, applications, and programming* (2nd ed.). New York: Routledge.

Byrne, B. M. (2009). *Structural equation modeling with Amos: Basic concepts, applications, and programming* (2nd ed.). New York: Routledge.

Byrne, B. M. (2010). *Structural equation modeling with Mplus: Basic concepts, applications, and programming.* New York: Routledge.

Cameron, L. C., Ittenbach, R. F., McGrew, K. S., Harrison, P., Taylor, L. R., & Hwang, Y. R. (1997). Confirmatory factor analysis of the K-ABC with gifted referrals. *Educational and Psychological Measurement, 57,* 823–840.

Campbell, D. T., & Fiske, D. W. (1959). Convergent and discriminant validation by the multitrait–multimethod matrix. *Psychological Bulletin, 56,* 81–105.

Carle, A. C. (2009). Fitting multilevel models in complex survey data with design weights: Recommendations. *Medical Research Methodology, 9*(49). Retrieved August 25, 2009, from *www.biomedcentral.com/content/pdf/1471-2288-9-49.pdf*

Chen, F., Bollen, K. A., Paxton, P., Curran, P. J., & Kirby, J. B. (2001). Improper solutions in structural equation models: Causes, consequences, and strategies. *Sociological Methods and Research, 29,* 468–508.

Chernick, M. R. (2008). *Bootstrap methods: A guide for practitioners and researchers* (2nd ed.). Hoboken, NJ: Wiley.

Cheung, G. W., & Rensvold, R. B. (2002). Evaluating goodness-of-fit indexes for testing measurement invariance. *Structural Equation Modeling, 9,* 233–255.

Chin, W. W. (1998). The partial least squares approach for structural equation modeling. In G. A. Marcoulides (Ed.), *Modern methods for business research* (pp. 295–336). Mahwah, NJ: Erlbaum.

Chou, C.-P., & Bentler, P. M. (1995). Estimates and tests in structural equation modeling. In R. H. Hoyle (Ed.), *Structural equation modeling* (pp. 37–55). Thousand Oaks, CA: Sage.

Clapp, J. D., & Beck, J. G. (2009). Understanding the relationship between PTSD and social support: The role of negative network orientation. *Behaviour Research and Therapy, 47,* 237–244.

Cohen, J. (1994). The earth is round (*p* < .05). *American Psychologist, 49,* 997–1003.

Cohen, J., & Cohen, P. (1983). *Applied multiple regression/correlation for the behavioral sciences* (2nd ed.). Hillsdale, NJ: Erlbaum.

Cohen, J., Cohen, P., West, S. G., & Aiken, L. S. (2003). *Applied multiple regression/correlation analysis for the behavioral sciences* (3rd ed.). Mahwah, NJ: Erlbaum.

Cole, D. A., Ciesla, J. A., & Steiger, J. H. (2007). The insidious effects of failing to include design-driven correlated residuals in latent-variable covariance structure analysis. *Psychological Methods, 12,* 381–398.

Cole, D. A., & Maxwell, S. E. (2003). Testing mediational models with longitudinal data: Questions and tips. *Journal of Abnormal Psychology, 112,* 558–577.

Contrada, R. J., Boulifard, D. A., Idler, E. L., Krause, T. J., & Labouvie, E. W. (2006). Course of depressive symptoms in patients undergoing heart surgery: Confirmatory analysis of the factor pattern and latent mean structure of the Center for Epidemiologic Studies Depression Scale. *Psychosomatic Medicine, 68,* 922–930.

Cooperman, J. M. (1996). *Maternal aggression and withdrawal in childhood: Continuity and intergenerational risk transmission.* Unpublished master's thesis, Concordia University, Montréal, Québec, Canada.

Cox, D. R., & Small, N. J. H. (1978). Testing multivariate normality. *Biometrika, 65,* 263–272.

Cudeck, R. (1989). Analysis of correlation matrices using covariance structure models. *Psychological Bulletin, 105,* 317–327.

Cumming, G. (2005). Understanding the average probability of replication: Comment on Killeen (2005). *Psychological Science, 16,* 1002–1004.

Curran, P. J. (2003). Have multilevel models been structural equation models all along? *Multivariate Behavioral Research, 38,* 529–569.

Curran, P. J., & Bauer, D. J. (2007). Building path diagrams for multilevel models. *Psychological Methods, 12,* 283–297.

Curran, P. J., West, S. G., & Finch, J. F. (1997). The robustness of test statistics to nonnormality and specification error in confirmatory factor analysis. *Psychological Methods, 1,* 16–29.

Dawson, J. F., & Richter, A. W. (2006). Probing three-way interactions in moderated multiple regression: Development and application of a slope difference test. *Journal of Applied Psychology, 91,* 917–926.

Diamantopoulos, A. (Ed.). (2008). Formative indicators [Special issue]. *Journal of Business Research, 61*(12).

Diamantopoulos, A., Riefler, P., & Roth, K. P. (2005). The problem of measurement model misspecification in behavioral and organizational research and some recommended solutions. *Journal of Applied Psychology, 90,* 710–730.

Diamantopoulos, A., Riefler, P., & Roth, K. P. (2008). Advancing formative measurement models. *Journal of Business Research, 61,* 1203–1218.

Diamantopoulos, A., & Siguaw, J. A. (2000). *Introducing LISREL: A guide for the uninitiated.* Thousand Oaks, CA: Sage.

Diamantopoulos, A., & Winklhofer, H. M. (2001). Index construction with formative indicators: An alternative to scale development. *Journal of Marketing Research, 38*, 269–277.

DiLalla, L. F. (2008). A structural equation modeling overview for medical researchers. *Journal of Developmental and Behavioral Pediatrics, 29*, 51–54.

DiStefano, C. (2002). The impact of categorization with confirmatory factor analysis. *Structural Equation Modeling, 9*, 327–346.

DiStefano, C., & Hess, B. (2005). Using confirmatory factor analysis for construct validation: An empirical review. *Journal of Psychoeducational Assessment, 23*, 225–241.

Duncan, O. D. (1966). Path analysis: Sociological examples. *American Journal of Sociology, 74*, 119–137.

Duncan, S. C., & Duncan, T. E. (1996). A multivariate latent growth curve analysis of adolescent substance use. *Structural Equation Modeling, 3*, 323–347.

Duncan, T. E., Duncan, S. C., Hops, H., & Alpert, A. (1997). Multi-level covariance structure analysis of intra-familial substance use. *Drug and Alcohol Dependence, 46*, 167–180.

Duncan, T. E., Duncan, S. C., Strycker, L. A., Li, F., & Alpert, A. (1999). *An introduction to latent variable growth curve modeling: Concepts, issues, and applications.* Mahwah, NJ: Erlbaum.

Dunn, W. M. (2005). A quick proof that the least squares formulas give a local minimum. *College Mathematics Journal, 36*, 64–65.

Edwards, J. R. (2009). Seven deadly myths of testing moderation in organizational research. In C. E. Lance & R. J. Vandenberg (Eds.), *Statistical and methodological myths and urban legends: Doctrine, verity and fable in the organizational and social sciences* (pp. 143–164). New York: Taylor & Francis.

Edwards, J. R., & Lambert, L. S. (2007). Methods for integrating moderation and mediation: A general analytical framework using moderated path analysis. *Psychological Methods, 12*, 1–22.

Efron, B. (1979). Bootstrap methods: Another look at the jackknife. *Annals of Statistics, 7*, 1–26.

Eid, M., Nussbeck, F. W., Geiser, C., Cole, D. A., Gollwitzer, M., & Lischetzke, T. (2008). Structural equation modeling of multitrait–multimethod data: Different models for different types of methods. *Psychological Methods, 13*, 230–253.

Enders, C. K., & Bandalos, D. L. (2001). The relative performance of full information maximum likelihood estimation for missing data in structural equation models. *Structural Equation Modeling, 8*, 430–457.

Eusebi, P. (2008). A graphical method for assessing the identification of linear structural equation models. *Structural Equation Modeling, 15*, 403–412.

Fairchild, A. J., & MacKinnon, D. P. (2009). A general model for testing mediation and moderation effects. *Prevention Science, 10*, 87–99.

Fan, X. (1997). Canonical correlation analysis and structural equation modeling: What do they have in common? *Structural Equation Modeling, 4*, 65–79.

Fan, X., & Sivo, S. A. (2005). Sensitivity of fit indexes to misspecified structural or measurement model components: Rationale of the two-index strategy revisited. *Structural Equation Modeling, 12*, 343–367.

Ferron, J. M., & Hess, M. R. (2007). Estimation in SEM: A concrete example. *Journal of Educational and Behavioral Statistics, 32*, 110–120.

Filzmoser, P. (2005). Identification of multivariate outliers: A performance study. *Austrian Journal of Statistics, 34*, 127–138.

Finney, S. J., & DiStefano, C. (2006). Nonnormal and categorical data in structural equation modeling. In G. R. Hancock & R. O. Mueller (Eds.), *A second course in structural equation modeling* (pp. 269–314). Greenwich, CT: Information Age Publishing.

Fisher, R. A. (1956). *Statistical methods and scientific inference.* Edinburgh: Oliver and Boyd.

Flora, D. B., & Curran, P. J. (2004). An empirical evaluation of alternative methods of estimation for confirmatory factor analysis with ordinal data. *Psychological Methods, 9*, 466–491.

Fox, J. (2006). Structural equation modeling with the sem package in R. *Structural Equation Modeling, 13*, 465–486.

Frederich, J., Buday, E., & Kerr, D. (2000). Statistical training in psychology: A national survey and commentary on undergraduate programs. *Teaching of Psychology, 27*, 248–257.

Frees, E. W. (2004). *Longitudinal and panel data: Analysis and applications in the social sciences.* New York: Cambridge University Press.

French, B. F., & Finch, W. H. (2008). Multigroup confirmatory factor analysis: Locating the invariant referent sets. *Structural Equation Modeling, 15*, 96–113.

Friendly, M. (2006). SAS macro programs: boxcox. Retrieved July 28, 2009, from *www.math. yorku.ca/SCS/sasmac/boxcox.html*

Friendly, M. (2009). SAS macro programs: csmpower. Retrieved November 15, 2009, from *www. math.yorku.ca/SCS/sasmac/csmpower.html*

Gambino, J. G. (2009). Design effect caveats. *American Statistician, 63*, 141–146.

Gardner, H. (1993). *Multiple intelligences: The theory in practice.* New York: Basic.

Garson, G. D. (2009). Partial correlation. Retrieved July 26, 2009, from *http://faculty.chass.ncsu. edu/garson/PA765/partialr.htm*

George, R. (2006). A cross-domain analysis of change in students' attitudes toward science and attitudes about the utility of science. *International Journal of Science Education, 28*, 571–589.

Gerbing, D. W., & Anderson, J. C. (1993). Monte Carlo evaluations of fit in structural equation models. In K. A. Bollen & J. S. Long (Eds.), *Testing structural equation models* (pp. 40–65). Newbury Park, CA: Sage.

Goldstein, H., Bonnet, G., & Rocher, T. (2007). Multilevel structural equation models for the analysis of comparative data on educational performance. *Journal of Educational and Behavioral Statistics, 32*, 252–286.

Gonzalez, R., & Griffin, D. (2001). Testing parameters in structural equation modeling: Every "one" matters. *Psychological Methods, 6*, 258–269.

Grace, J. B. (2006). *Structural equation modeling and natural systems.* New York: Cambridge University Press.

Grace, J. B. (2008). Structural equation modeling for observational studies. *Journal of Wildlife Management, 72*, 4–22.

Grace, J. B., & Bollen, K. A. (2008). Representing general theoretical concepts in structural equation models: The role of composite variables. *Environmental and Ecological Statistics, 15*, 191–213.

Graham, J. M., Guthrie, A. C., & Thompson, B. (2003). Consequences of not interpreting structure coefficients in published CFA research: A reminder. *Structural Equation Modeling, 10*, 142–153.

Green, S. B., & Thompson, M. S. (2006). Structural equation modeling for conducting tests of differences in multiple means. *Psychosomatic Medicine, 68*, 706–717.

Haller, H., & Krauss, S. (2002). Misinterpretations of significance: A problem students share with their teachers? *Methods of Psychological Research Online, 7*(1), Article 1. Retrieved August 28, 2009, from *www.dgps.de/fachgruppen/methoden/mpr-online/issue16/art1/haller.pdf*

Hancock, G. R., & Freeman, M. J. (2001). Power and sample size for the Root Mean Square Error of Approximation of not close fit in structural equation modeling. *Educational and Psychological Measurement, 61*, 741–758.

Hancock, G. R., & Mueller, R. O. (2001). Rethinking construct reliability within latent variable systems. In R. Cudeck, S. du Toit, & D. Sörbom (Eds.), *Structural equation modeling: Present and future. A Festschrift in honor of Karl Jöreskog* (pp. 195–216). Lincolnwood, IL: Scientific Software International.

Harrington, D. (2009). *Confirmatory factor analysis.* New York: Oxford University Press.

Harris, J. A. (1995). Confirmatory factor analysis of The Aggression Questionnaire. *Behaviour Research and Therapy, 33*, 991–993.

Hayduk, L., Cummings, G., Boadu, K., Pazderka-Robinson, H., & Boulianne, S. (2007). Testing! testing! one, two, three—Testing the theory in structural equation models! *Personality and Individual Differences, 42*, 841–850.

Hayduk, L. A. (1996). *LISREL issues, debates and strategies.* Baltimore, MD: Johns Hopkins University Press.

Hayduk, L. A. (2006). Blocked-error-R^2: A conceptually improved definition of the proportion of explained variance in models containing loops or correlated residuals. *Quality & Quantity, 40*, 629–649.

Hayduk, L. A., & Glaser, D. N. (2000). Jiving the four-step, waltzing around factor analysis, and other serious fun. *Structural Equation Modeling, 7*, 1–35.

Hayduk, L. A., Pazderka-Robinson, H., Cummings, G. C., Levers, M. J. D., & Beres, M. A. (2005). Structural equation model testing and the quality of natural killer cell activity measurements. *Medical Research Methodology, 5*(1). Retrieved August 18, 2009, from *www.pubmedcentral.nih.gov/picrender.fcgi?artid=546216&blobtype=pdf*

Heise, D. R. (1975). *Causal analysis.* New York: Wiley.

Hershberger, S. L. (1994). The specification of equivalent models before the collection of data. In A. von Eye & C. C. Clogg (Eds.), *Latent variables analysis* (pp. 68–105). Thousand Oaks, CA: Sage.

Herting, J. R., & Costner, H. J. (2000). Another perspective on "the proper number of factors" and the appropriate number of steps. *Structural Equation Modeling, 7*, 92–110.

Heywood, H. B. (1931). On finite sequences of real numbers. *Proceedings of the Royal Society of London, 134*, 486–501.

Holbert, R. L., & Stephenson, M. T. (2002). Structural equation modeling in the communication sciences, 1995–2000. *Human Communication Research, 28*, 531–551.

Hopwood, C. J. (2007). Moderation and mediation in structural equation modeling: Applications for early intervention research. *Journal of Early Intervention, 29*, 262–272.

Horton, N. J., & Kleinman, K. P. (2007). Much ado about nothing: A comparison of missing data methods and software to fit incomplete data regression models. *American Statistical Association, 61*, 79–90.

Houghton, J. D., & Jinkerson, D. L. (2007). Constructive thought strategies and job satisfaction: A preliminary examination. *Journal of Business Psychology, 22*, 45–53.

Howell, R. D., Breivik, E., & Wilcox, J. B. (2007). Reconsidering formative measurement. *Psychological Methods, 12*, 205–218.

Hoyle, R. H. (2000). Confirmatory factor analysis. In H. E. A. Tinsley & S. D. Brown (Eds.), *Handbook of applied multivariate statistics and mathematical modeling* (pp. 465–497). New York: Academic Press.

Hoyle, R. H., & Panter, A. T. (1995). Writing about structural equation models. In R. H. Hoyle (Ed.), *Structural equation modeling* (pp. 158–176). Thousand Oaks, CA: Sage.

Hu, L., & Bentler, P. M. (1998). Fit indices in covariance structure modeling: Sensitivity to underparameterized model misspecification. *Psychological Methods, 3*(4), 424–453.

Hu, L., & Bentler, P. M. (1999). Cutoff criteria for fit indexes in covariance structure analysis: Conventional criteria versus new alternatives. *Structural Equation Modeling, 6*, 1–55.

Hubbard, R., & Armstrong, J. S. (2006). Why we don't really know what "statistical significance" means: A major educational failure. *Journal of Marketing Education, 28*, 114–120.

Huberty, C. J., & Morris, J. D. (1988). A single contrast test procedure. *Educational and Psychological Measurement, 48*, 567–578.

Humphreys, P. (2003). Mathematical modeling in the social sciences. In S. P. Turner & P. A. Roth (Eds.), *The Blackwell guide to the philosophy of the social sciences* (pp. 166–184). Malden, MA: Blackwell Publishing.

Jaccard, J., & Wan, C. K. (1995). Measurement error in the analysis of interaction effects between continuous predictors using multiple regression: Multiple indicator and structural equation approaches. *Psychological Bulletin, 117*, 348–357.

Jackson, D. L. (2003). Revisiting sample size and number of parameter estimates: Some support for the N:q hypothesis. *Structural Equation Modeling, 10,* 128–141.

Jackson, D. L., Gillaspy, J. A., Jr., & Purc-Stephenson, R. (2009). Reporting practices in confirmatory factor analysis: An overview and some recommendations. *Psychological Methods, 14,* 6–23.

James, L. R., & Brett, J. M. (1984). Mediators, moderators, and tests for mediation. *Journal of Applied Psychology, 69,* 307–321.

James, L. R., & Singh, B. K. (1978). An introduction to the logic, assumptions, and basic analytic procedures of two-stage least squares. *Psychological Bulletin, 85,* 1104–1122.

Jarvis, C. B., MacKenzie, S. B., & Podsakoff, P. M. (2003). A critical review of construct indicators and measurement model misspecification in marketing and consumer research. *Journal of Consumer Research, 30,* 199–218.

Jöreskog, K. G. (1993). Testing structural equation models. In K. A. Bollen & J. S. Lang (Eds.), *Testing structural equation models* (pp. 294–316). Newbury Park, CA: Sage.

Jöreskog, K. G. (2000). Interpretation of R^2 revisited. Retrieved April 29, 2009, from *www.ssicentral.com/lisrel/techdocs/r2rev.pdf*

Jöreskog, K. G. (2004). On chi-squares for the independence model and fit measures in LISREL. Retrieved April 10, 2009, from *www.ssicentral.com/lisrel/techdocs/ ftb.pdf*

Jöreskog, K. G. (2005). Structural equation modeling with ordinal variables using LISREL. Retrieved June 4, 2009, from *www.ssicentral.com/lisrel/techdocs/ordinal.pdf*

Jöreskog, K. G., & Moustaki, I. (2006). Factor analysis of ordinal variables with full information maximum likelihood. Retrieved June 9, 2009, from *www.ssicentral.com/lisrel/techdocs/ orfiml.pdf*

Jöreskog, K. G., & Sörbom, D. (1982). Recent developments in structural equation modeling. *Journal of Marketing Research, 19,* 404–416.

Jöreskog, K. G., & Sörbom, D. (2006). LISREL 8.80 for Windows [Computer software]. Lincolnwood, IL: Scientific Software International.

Jöreskog, K. G., & Yang, F. (1996). Nonlinear structural equation models: The Kenny–Judd model with interaction effects. In G. A. Marcoulides & R. E. Schumacker (Eds.), *Advanced structural equation modeling* (pp. 57–88). Mahwah, NJ: Erlbaum.

Kamata, A., & Bauer, D. J. (2008). A note on the relation between factor analytic and item response models. *Structural Equation Modeling, 15,* 136–153.

Kano, Y. (2001). Structural equation modeling with experimental data. In R. Cudeck, S. du Toit, & D. Sörbom (Eds.), *Structural equation modeling: Present and future. A festschrift in honor of Karl Jöreskog* (pp. 381–402). Lincolnwood, IL: Scientific Software International.

Kaplan, D. (1995). Statistical power in structural equation modeling. In R. H. Hoyle (Ed.), *Structural equation modeling* (pp. 100–117). Thousand Oaks, CA: Sage.

Kaplan, D. (2000). *Structural equation modeling.* Thousand Oaks, CA: Sage.

Kaplan, D. (2009). *Structural equation modeling: Foundations and extensions* (2nd ed.). Thousand Oaks, CA: Sage.

Kaplan, D., Harik, P., & Hotchkiss, L. (2001) . Cross-sectional estimation of dynamic structural equation models in disequilibrium. In R. Cudeck, S. du Toit, & D. Sörbom (Eds.), *Structural equation modeling: Present and future. A festschrift in honor of Karl Jöreskog* (pp. 315–339). Lincolnwood, IL: Scientific Software International.

Kaufman, A. S., & Kaufman, N. L. (1983). *K-ABC administration and scoring manual.* Circle Pines, MN: American Guidance Service.

Keith, T. Z. (1985). Questioning the K-ABC: What does it measure? *School Psychology Review, 14,* 9–20.

Kelloway, E. K. (1998). *Using LISREL for structural equation modeling: A researcher's guide.* Thousand Oaks, CA: Sage.

Kenny, D. A. (1979). *Correlation and causality.* New York: Wiley.

Kenny, D. A. (2002). Instrumental variable estimation. Retrieved April 24, 2009, from *http:// davidakenny.net/cm/iv.htm*

Kenny, D. A. (2004). Terminology and basics of SEM. Retrieved April 1, 2009, from *http://davidakenny.net/cm/basics.htm*

Kenny, D. A. (2008). Mediation. Retrieved April 20, 2009, from *http://davidakenny.net/cm/mediate.htm*

Kenny, D. (2009). Moderator variables: Introduction. Retrieved July 13, 2009, from *davidakenny.net/cm/moderation.htm*

Kenny, D. A., & Judd, C. M. (1984). Estimating the nonlinear and interactive effects of latent variables. *Psychological Bulletin, 96,* 201–210.

Kenny, D. A., & Kashy, D. A. (1992). Analysis of the multitrait–multimethod matrix by confirmatory factor analysis. *Psychological Bulletin, 112,* 165–172.

Kenny, D. A., Kashy, D. A., & Bolger, N. (1998). Data analysis in social psychology. In D. Gilbert, S. Fiske, & G. Lindzey (Eds.), *The handbook of social psychology* (Vol. 1, 4th ed., pp. 233–265). Boston, MA: McGraw-Hill.

Killeen, P. R. (2005). An alternative to null-hypothesis significance tests. *Psychological Science, 15,* 345–353.

Kim, K. H. (2005). The relation among fit indexes, power, and sample size in structural equation modeling. *Structural Equation Modeling, 12,* 368–390.

Kirk, R. (1996). Practical significance: A concept whose time has come. *Educational and Psychological Measurement, 56,* 746–759.

Klein, A., & Moosbrugger, A. (2000). Maximum likelihood estimation of latent interaction effects with the LMS method. *Psychometrika, 65,* 457–474.

Klein, A. G., & Muthén, B. O. (2007). Quasi-maximum likelihood estimation of structural equation models with multiple interaction and quadratic effects. *Multivariate Behavioral Research, 42,* 647–673.

Kline, R. B. (2004). *Beyond significance testing: Reforming data analysis methods in behavioral research.* Washington, DC: American Psychological Association.

Kline, R. B. (2009). *Becoming a behavioral science researcher: A guide to producing research that matters.* Washington, DC: American Psychological Association.

Kline, R. B., Snyder, J., & Castellanos, M. (1996). Lessons from the Kaufman Assessment Battery for Children (K-ABC): Toward a new assessment model. *Psychological Assessment, 8,* 7–17.

Krull, J. L., & MacKinnon, D. P. (2001). Multilevel modeling of individual and group level mediated effects. *Multivariate Behavioral Research, 36,* 249–277.

Kühnel, S. (2001). The didactical power of structural equation modeling. In R. Cudeck, S. du Toit, & D. Sörbom (Eds.), *Structural equation modeling: Present and future. A Festschrift in honor of Karl Jöreskog* (pp. 79–96). Lincolnwood, IL: Scientific Software International.

Lance, C. E. (1988). Residual centering, exploratory and confirmatory moderator analysis, and decomposition of effects in path models containing interaction effects. *Applied Psychological Measurement, 12,* 163–175.

Lee, S. Y., Poon, W. Y., & Bentler, P. M. (1995). A two-stage estimation of structural equation models with continuous and polytomous variables. *British Journal of Mathematical and Statistical Psychology, 48,* 339–358.

Little, R. J. A., & Rubin, D. B. (2002). *Statistical analysis with missing data* (2nd ed.). New York: Wiley.

Little, T. D., Bovaird, J. A., & Widaman, K. F. (2006). On the merits of orthogonalizing powered and product terms: Implications for modeling interactions among latent variables. *Structural Equation Modeling, 13,* 497–519.

Little, T. D., Cunningham, W. A., Shahar, G., & Widaman, K. F. (2002). To parcel or not to parcel: Exploring the question, weighing the merits. *Structural Equation Modeling, 9,* 151–173.

Little, T. D., Lindenberger, U., & Nesselroade, J. R. (1999). On selecting indicators for multivariate measurement and modeling with latent variables: When "good" indicators are bad and "bad" indicators are good. *Psychological Methods, 4,* 192–211.

Little, T. D., Slegers, D. W., & Card, N. A. (2006). A non-arbitrary method of identifying and scaling latent variables in SEM and MACS models. *Structural Equation Modeling, 13,* 59–72.

Liu, K. (1988). Measurement error and its impact on partial correlation and multiple linear regression analyses. *American Journal of Epidemiology, 127,* 864–874.

Loehlin, J. C. (2004). *Latent variable models: An introduction to factor, path, and structural equation analysis* (4th ed.). Mahwah, NJ: Erlbaum.

Lunneborg, C. E. (2001). Random assignment of available case methods: Bootstrap standard errors and confidence intervals. *Psychological Methods, 6,* 406–412.

Lynam, D. R., Moffitt, T., & Stouthamer–Loeber, M. (1993). Explaining the relation between IQ and delinquency: Class, race, test motivation, or self-control? *Journal of Abnormal Psychology, 102,* 187–196.

Maas, C. J. M., & Hox, J. J. (2005). Sufficient sample sizes for multilevel modeling. *Methodology, 3,* 86–92.

Maasen, G. H., & Bakker, A. B. (2001). Suppressor variables in path models: Definitions and interpretations. *Sociological Methods and Research, 30,* 241–270.

MacCallum, R. C. (1986). Specification searches in covariance structure modeling. *Psychological Bulletin, 100,* 107–120.

MacCallum, R. C., & Austin, J. T. (2000). Applications of structural equation modeling in psychological research. *Annual Review of Psychology, 51,* 201–236.

MacCallum, R. C., & Browne, M. W. (1993). The use of causal indicators in covariance structure models: Some practical issues. *Psychological Bulletin, 114,* 533–541.

MacCallum, R. C., Browne, M. W., & Sugawara, H. M. (1996). Power analysis and determination of sample size for covariance structure modeling. *Psychological Methods, 1,* 130–149.

MacCallum, R. C., & Hong, S. (1997). Power analysis in covariance structure modeling using GFI and AGFI. *Multivariate Behavioral Research, 32,* 193–210.

MacCallum, R. C., Wegener, D. T., Uchino, B. N., & Fabrigar, L. R. (1993). The problem of equivalent models in applications of covariance structure analysis. *Psychological Bulletin, 114,* 185–199.

MacKinnon, D. P., Fairchild, A. J., & Fritz, M. S. (2007). Mediation analysis. *Annual Review of Psychology, 58,* 593–614.

MacKinnon, D. P., Krull, J. L., & Lockwood, C. M. (2000). Equivalence of the mediation, confounding, and suppression effect. *Prevention Science, 1,* 173–181.

Marcoulides, G. A., & Drezner, Z. (2001). Specification searches in structural equation modeling with a genetic algorithm. In G. A. Marcoulides and R. E. Schumaker (Eds.), *New developments and techniques in structural equation modeling* (pp. 247–268). Mahwah, NJ: Erlbaum.

Marcoulides, G. A., & Drezner, Z. (2003). Model specification searches using ant colony optimization algorithms. *Structural Equation Modeling, 10,* 154–164.

Mardia, K. V. (1970). Measures of multivariate skewness and kurtosis with applications. *Biometrika, 57,* 519–530.

Mardia, K. V. (1985). Mardia's test of multinormality. In S. Kotz & N. L. Johnson (Eds.), *Encyclopedia of statistical sciences* (Vol. 5, pp. 217–221). New York: Wiley.

Markland, D. (2007). The golden rule is that there are no golden rules: A commentary on Paul Barrett's recommendations for reporting model fit in structural equation modelling. *Personality and Individual Differences, 42,* 851–858.

Marsh, H. W., & Bailey, M. (1991). Confirmatory factor analysis of multitrait–multimethod data: A comparison of alternative models. *Applied Psychological Measurement, 15,* 47–70.

Marsh, H. W., Balla, J. R., & Hau, K.-T. (1996). An evaluation of incremental fit indices: A clarification of mathematical and empirical properties. In G. A. Marcoulides & R. E. Schumaker (Eds.), *Advanced structural equation modeling* (pp. 315–353). Mahwah, NJ: Erlbaum.

Marsh, H. W., Balla, J. R., & McDonald, R. P. (1988). Goodness-of-fit indices in confirmatory factor analysis: The effect of sample size. *Psychological Bulletin, 103,* 391–411.

Marsh, H. W., & Grayson, D. (1995). Latent variable models of multitrait–multimethod data. In R. H. Hoyle (Ed.), *Structural equation modeling* (pp. 177–198). Thousand Oaks, CA: Sage.

Marsh, H. W., & Hau, K.-T. (1996). Assessing goodness of fit: Is parsimony always desirable? *Journal of Experimental Education, 96,* 364–391.

Marsh, H. W., & Hau, K.-T. (1999). Confirmatory factor analysis: Strategies for small sample sizes. In R. H. Hoyle (Ed.), *Statistical strategies for small sample research* (pp. 252–284). Thousand Oaks, CA: Sage.

Marsh, H. W., Hau, K.-T., & Wen, Z. (2004). In search of golden rules: Comment on hypothesis testing approaches to setting cutoff values for fit indexes and dangers in overgeneralizing Hu and Bentler's (1999) findings. *Structural Equation Modeling, 11,* 320–341.

Marsh, H. W., Wen, Z., & Hau, K. T. (2004). Structural equation models of latent interactions: Evaluation of alternative estimation strategies and indicator construction. *Psychological Methods, 9,* 275–300.

Marsh, H. W., Wen, Z., & Hau, K. T. (2006). Structural equation modeling of latent interaction and quadratic effects. In G. R. Hancock & R. O. Mueller (Eds.), *Structural equation modeling: A second course* (pp. 225–265). Greenwich, CT: IAP.

Maruyama, G. M. (1998). *Basics of structural equation modeling.* Thousand Oaks, CA: Sage.

McArdle, J. J., & McDonald, R. P. (1984). Some algebraic properties of the Reticular Action Model for moment structures. *British Journal of Mathematical and Statistical Psychology, 37,* 234–251.

McCoach, D. B., Black, A. C., & O'Connell, A. A. (2007). Errors of inference in structural equation modeling. *Psychology in the Schools, 44,* 461–470.

McDonald, R. P. (1989). An index of goodness of fit based on noncentrality. *Journal of Classification, 6,* 97–103.

McDonald, R. P., & Ho, M.-H. R. (2002). Principles and practice in reporting structural equation analyses. *Psychological Methods, 7,* 64–82.

McDonald, R. P., & Marsh, H. W. (1990). Choosing a multivariate model: Noncentrality and goodness of fit. *Psychological Bulletin, 107,* 247–255.

McKnight, P. E., McKnight, K. M., Sidani, S., & Figueredo, A. J. (2007). *Missing data: A gentle introduction.* New York: Guilford Press.

Meade, A. W., & Bauer, D. J. (2007). Power and precision in confirmatory factor analytic tests of measurement invariance. *Structural Equation Modeling, 14,* 611–635.

Meade, A. W., Johnson, E. C., & Braddy, P. W. (2008). Power and sensitivity of alternative fit indices in tests of measurement invariance. *Journal of Applied Psychology, 93,* 568–592.

Meade, A. W., & Lautenschlager, G. J. (2004). A comparison of item response theory and confirmatory factor analytic methodologies for establishing measurement equivalence/invariance. *Organizational Research Methods, 7,* 361–388.

Meredith, W., & Tisak, J. (1990). Latent curve analysis. *Psychometrika, 55,* 107–122.

Merton, T. (1965). *The way of Chuang Tzu.* New York: New Directions.

Messick, S. (1995). Validation of inferences from persons' responses and performances as scientific inquiry into score meaning. *American Psychologist, 50,* 741–749.

Miles, J., & Shevlin, M. (2007). A time and a place for incremental fit indices. *Personality and Individual Differences, 42,* 869–874.

Millsap, R. E. (2007). Structural equation modeling made difficult. *Personality and Individual Differences, 42,* 875–881.

Mooijaart, A., & Satorra, A. (2009). On insensitivity of the chi-square model test to non-linear misspecification in structural equation models. *Psychometrika, 74,* 443–455.

Mueller, R. O. (1996). *Basic principles of structural equation modeling: An introduction to LISREL and EQS.* New York: Springer.

Mulaik, S. A. (2000). Objectivity and other metaphors of structural equation modeling. In R. Cudeck, S. du Toit, & D. Sörbom (Eds.), *Structural equation modeling: Present and future. A festschrift in honor of Karl Jöreskog* (pp. 59–78). Lincolnwood, IL: Scientific Software International.

Mulaik, S. A. (2007). There is a place for approximate fit in structural equation modelling. *Personality and Individual Differences, 42*, 883–891.

Mulaik, S. A. (2009). *Linear causal modeling with structural equations.* New York: CRC Press.

Mulaik, S. A., & Millsap, R. E. (2000). Doing the four-step right. *Structural Equation Modeling, 7*, 36–73.

Murphy, S. A., Chung, I.-J., & Johnson, L. C. (2002). Patterns of mental distress following the violent death of a child and predictors of change over time. *Research in Nursing and Health, 25*, 425–437.

Muthén, B. O. (1984). A general structural equation model with dichotomous, ordered categorical, and continuous latent variable indicators. *Psychometrika, 49*, 115–132.

Muthén, B. O. (1994). Multilevel covariance structure analysis. *Sociological Methods and Research, 22*, 376–398.

Muthén, B. O. (2001). Latent variable mixture modeling. In G. A. Marcoulides & R. E. Schumaker (Eds.), *New developments and techniques in structural equation modeling* (pp. 1–33). Mahwah, NJ: Erlbaum.

Muthén, B. O., & Asparouhov, T. (2002). Latent variable analysis with categorical outcomes: Multiple-group and growth modeling in Mplus. Retrieved June 9, 2009, from *www.statmodel.com/download/webnotes/CatMGLong.pdf*

Muthén, B. O., du Toit, S. H. C., & Spisic, D. (1997). Robust inference using weighted least squares and quadratic estimating equations in latent variable modeling with categorical and continuous outcomes. Retrieved May 2, 2009, from *www.gseis.ucla.edu/faculty/muthen/articles/Article_075.pdf*

Muthén, L. K., & Muthén, B. O. (2002). How to use a Monte Carlo study to decide on sample size and determine power. *Structural Equation Modeling, 4*, 599–620.

Muthén, L. K., & Muthén, B. O. (1998–2010). *Mplus user's guide* (6th ed.). Los Angeles: Muthén & Muthén.

Nachtigall, C., Kroehne, U., Funke, F., & Steyer, R. (2003). (Why) Should we use SEM? Pros and cons of structural equation modeling. *Methods of Psychological Research Online, 8*(2), 1–22. Retrieved March 24, 2009, from *http://aodgps.de/fachgruppen/methoden/mpr-online/issue20/art1/mpr127_11.pdf*

Neale, M. C., Boker, S. M., Xie, G., & Maes, H. H. (2003). *Mx: Statistical modeling* (6th ed.). Richmond: Virginia Commonwealth University, Virginia Institute for Psychiatric and Behavioral Genetics.

Nelson, T. D., Aylward, B. S., & Steele, R. G. (2008). Structural equation modeling in pediatric psychology: Overview and review of applications. *Journal of Pediatric Psychology, 33*, 679–687.

Neuman, G. A., Bolin, A. U., & Briggs, T. E. (2000). Identifying general factors of intelligence: A confirmatory factor analysis of the Ball Aptitude Battery. *Educational and Psychological Measurement, 60*, 697–712.

Nevitt, J., & Hancock, G. R. (2000). Improving the root mean square error of approximation for nonnormal conditions in structural equation modeling. *Journal of Experimental Education, 68*, 251–268.

Nevitt, J., & Hancock, G. R. (2001). Performance of bootstrapping approaches to model test statistics and parameter standard error estimation in structural equation modeling. *Structural Equation Modeling, 8*, 353–377.

Nevitt, J., & Hancock, G. R. (2004). Evaluating small sample approaches for model test statistics in structural equation modeling. *Multivariate Behavioral Research, 39*, 439–478.

Noar, S. M. (2007). The role of structural equation modeling in scale development. *Structural Equation Modeling, 10*, 622–647.

Nunnally, J. C., & Bernstein, I. H. (1994). *Psychometric theory* (3rd ed.). New York: McGraw-Hill.

Oakes, M. (1986). *Statistical inference: A commentary for the social and behavioral sciences.* New York: Wiley.

O'Brien, R. M. (1994). Identification of simple measurement models with multiple latent variables and correlated errors. *Sociological Methodology, 24,* 137–170.

Olsson, U. H., Foss, T., & Breivik, E. (2004). Two equivalent discrepancy functions for maximum likelihood estimation: Do their test statistics follow a non-central chi-square distribution under model misspecification? *Sociological Methods and Research, 32,* 453–500.

Olsson, U. H., Foss, T., Troye, S. V., & Howell, R. D. (2000). The performance of ML, GLS, and WLS estimation in structural equation modeling under conditions of misspecification and non-normality. *Structural Equation Modeling, 7,* 557–595.

Osborne, J. (2002). Notes on the use of data transformations. *Practical Assessment, Research & Evaluation, 8*(6). Retrieved February 23, 2009, from *http://PAREonline.net/ getvn.asp?v=8&n=6*

Pearl, J. (2000). *Causality: Models, reasoning, and inference.* New York: Cambridge University Press.

Pedhazur, E. J., & Schmelkin, L. P. (1991). *Measurement, design, and analysis: An integrated approach.* Hillsdale, NJ: Erlbaum.

Peng, C.Y. J., Harwell, M., Liou, S.M., & Ehman, L. H. (2007). Advances in missing data methods and implications for educational research. In S. S. Sawilowsky (Ed.), *Real data analysis* (pp. 31–78). Charlotte, NC: Information Age Publishing.

Peng, C.-Y. J, Lee, K. L., & Ingersoll, G. M. (2002). An introduction to logistic regression analysis and reporting. *Journal of Educational Research, 96*(1), 3–14.

Peters, C. L. O., & Enders, C. (2002). A primer for the estimation of structural equation models in the presence of missing data. *Journal of Targeting, Measurement and Analysis for Marketing, 11,* 81–95.

Ping, R. A. (1996). Interaction and quadratic effect estimation: A two-step technique using structural equation analysis. *Psychological Bulletin, 119,* 166–175.

Preacher, K. J., & Coffman, D. L. (2006). Computing power and minimum sample size for RMSEA. Retrieved November 15, 2009, from *http://people.ku.edu/~preacher/rmsea/rmsea.htm*

Preacher, K. J., Curran, P. J., & Bauer, D. J. (2006). Computational tools for probing interaction effects in multiple linear regression, multilevel modeling, and latent curve analysis. *Journal of Educational and Behavioral Statistics, 31,* 437–448.

Preacher, K. J., Rucker, D. D., & Hayes, A. F. (2007). Addressing moderated mediation hypotheses: Theory, methods, and prescriptions. *Multivariate Behavioral Research, 42,* 185–227.

Provalis Research. (1995–2004). SimStat for Windows (Version 2.5.5) [Computer software]. Montréal, Québec, Canada: Author.

Rabe-Hesketh, S., Skrondal, A., & Zheng, X. (2007). Multilevel structural equation modeling. In S.-Y. Lee (Ed.), *Handbook of computing and statistics with applications: Vol. 1. Handbook of latent variable and related models* (pp. 209–227). Amsterdam: Elsevier.

Raftery, A. E. (1995). Bayesian model selection in social research. *Sociological Methodology, 25,* 111–163.

Raudenbush, S. W., & Bryk, A. S. (2002). *Hierarchical linear models* (2nd ed.). Thousand Oaks, CA: Sage.

Raudenbush, S. W., Bryk, A. S., & Cheong, Y. F. (2008). HLM 6.06 for Windows [computer software]. Lincolnwood, IL: Scientific Software International.

Raykov, T. (1997). Estimation of composite reliability for congeneric measures. *Applied Psychological Measurement, 21,* 173–184.

Raykov, T. (2004). Behavioral scale reliability and measurement invariance evaluation using latent variable modeling. *Behavior Therapy, 35,* 299–331.

Raykov, T., & Marcoulides, G. A. (2000). *A first course in structural equation modeling.* Mahwah, NJ: Erlbaum.

Raykov, T., & Marcoulides, G. A. (2001). Can there be infinitely many models equivalent to a given covariance structure? *Structural Equation Modeling, 8,* 142–149.

Raykov, T., Tomer, A., & Nesselroade, J. R. (1991). Reporting structural equation modeling results in *Psychology and Aging*: Some proposed guidelines. *Psychology and Aging, 6,* 499–503.

Reise, S. P., Widaman, K. F., & Pugh, R. H. (1993). Confirmatory factor analysis and item response theory: Two approaches for exploring measurement invariance. *Psychological Bulletin, 114,* 552–566.

Rigdon, E. E. (1995). A necessary and sufficient identification rule for structural models estimated in practice. *Multivariate Behavioral Research, 30,* 359–383.

Rindskopf, D. (1984). Structural equation models: Empirical identification, Heywood cases, and related problems. *Sociological Methods and Research, 13,* 109–119.

Robert, S., & Pashler, H. (2000). How persuasive is a good fit? A comment on theory testing in psychology. *Psychological Review, 107,* 358–367.

Robinson, D. H., Levin, J. R., Thomas, G. D., Pituch, K. A., & Vaughn S. (2007). The incidence of "causal" statements in teaching-and-learning research journals. *American Educational Research Journal, 44,* 400–413.

Rodgers, J. L. (1999). The bootstrap, the jackknife, and the randomization test: A sampling taxonomy. *Multivariate Behavioral Research, 34,* 441–456.

Rogosa, D. R. (1988). *Ballad of the casual modeler.* Retrieved July 25, 2009, from *www.stanford.edu/ class/ed260/ballad*

Romney, D. M., Jenkins, C. D., & Bynner, J. M. (1992). A structural analysis of health-related quality of life dimensions. *Human Relations, 45,* 165–176.

Rosenberg, J. F. (1998). Kant and the problem of simultaneous causation. *International Journal of Philosophical Studies, 6,* 167–188.

Roth, D. L., Wiebe, D. J., Fillingim, R. B., & Shay, K. A. (1989). Life events, fitness, hardiness, and health: A simultaneous analysis of proposed stress-resistance effects. *Journal of Personality and Social Psychology, 57,* 136–142.

Roth, P. L. (1994). Missing data: A conceptual review for applied psychologists. *Personnel Psychology, 47,* 537–560.

Sabatelli, R. M., & Bartle–Haring, S. (2003). Family-of-origin experiences and adjustment in married couples. *Journal of Marriage and Family, 65,* 159–169.

Sagan, C. (1996). *The demon-haunted world: Science as a candle in the dark.* New York: Random House.

Saris, W. E., & Alberts, C. (2003). Different explanations for correlated disturbance terms in MTMM studies. *Structural Equation Modeling, 10,* 193–213.

Saris, W. E., & Satorra, A. (1993). Power evaluations in structural equation models. In K. A. Bollen & J. S. Long (Eds.), *Testing structural equation models* (pp. 181–204). Newbury Park, CA: Sage.

Satorra, A., & Bentler, P. M. (1994). Corrections to test statistics and standard errors on covariance structure analysis. In A. von Eye & C. C. Clogg (Eds.), *Latent variables analysis* (pp. 399–419). Thousand Oaks, CA: Sage.

Satorra, A., & Bentler, P. M. (2001). A scaled difference chi-square test statistic for moment structure analysis. *Psychometrika, 66,* 507–512.

Sava, F. A. (2002). Causes and effects of teacher conflict-inducing attitudes towards pupils: A path analysis model. *Teaching and Teacher Education, 18,* 1007–1021.

Schmidt, F. L., & Hunter, J. E. (1997). Eight common but false objections to the discontinuation of significance testing in the analysis of research data. In L. L. Harlow, S. A. Mulaik, & J. H. Steiger (Eds.), *What if there were no significance tests?* (pp. 37–64). Mahwah, NJ: Erlbaum.

Schmitt, N., & Kuljanin, G. (2008). Measurement invariance: Review of practice and limitations. *Human Resource Management Review, 18,* 210–222.

Schmukle, S. C., & Hardt, J. (2005). A cautionary note on incremental fit indices reported by LISREL. *Methodology, 1,* 81–85.

Schreiber, J. B. (2008). Core reporting practices in structural equation modeling. *Research in Social and Administrative Pharmacy, 4,* 83–97.

Schreiber, J. B., Nora, A., Stage, F. K., Barlow, E. A., & King, J. (2006). Reporting structural equation modeling and confirmatory factor analysis results: A review. *Journal of Educational Research, 99,* 323–337.

Schumacker, R. E., & Lomax, R. G. (2004). *A beginner's guide to structural equation modeling* (2nd ed.). Mahwah, NJ: Erlbaum.

Schumacker, R. E., & Marcoulides, G. A. (Eds.). (1998). *Interaction and nonlinear effects in structural equation modeling.* Mahwah, NJ: Erlbaum.

Shah, R., & Goldstein, S. M. (2006). Use of structural equation modeling in operations management research: Looking back and forward. *Journal of Operations Management, 24,* 148–169.

Shen, B.-J., & Takeuchi, D. T. (2001). A structural model of acculturation and mental health status among Chinese Americans. *American Journal of Community Psychology, 29,* 387–418.

Shieh, G. (2006). Suppression situations in multiple linear regression. *Educational and Psychological Measurement, 66,* 435–447.

Shrout, P. E., & Bolger, N. (2002). Mediation in experimental and nonexperimental studies: New procedures and recommendations. *Psychological Methods, 7,* 422–445.

Sikström, S. (2001). Forgetting curves: Implications for connectionist models. *Cognitive Psychology, 45,* 95–152.

Silvia, E. S. M., & MacCallum, R. C. (1988). Some factors affecting the success of specification searches in covariance structure modeling. *Multivariate Behavioral Research, 23,* 297–326.

Skrondal, A., & Rabe-Hesketh, S. (2004). *Generalized latent variable modeling: Multilevel, longitudinal, and structural equation models.* Boca Raton, FL: Chapman & Hall/CRC.

Sobel, M. E. (1986). Some new results on indirect effects and their standard errors in covariance structure models. In N. B. Tuma (Ed.), *Sociological methodology* (pp. 159–186). San Francisco: Jossey-Bass.

Song, M., Droge, C., Hanvanich, S., & Calantone, R. (2005). Marketing and technology resource complementarity: An analysis of their interaction effect in two environmental contexts. *Strategic Management Journal, 26,* 259–276.

Sörbom, D. (1974). A general method for studying differences in factor means and structure between groups. *British Journal of Mathematical and Statistical Psychology, 27,* 229–239.

Spearman, C. (1904). General intelligence, objectively determined and measured. *American Journal of Psychology, 15,* 201–293.

Sribney, B. (1998). Problems with stepwise regression. Retrieved January 23, 2009, from *www.stata.com/support/faqs/stat/stepwise.html*

Stapleton, L. M. (2006). Using multilevel structural equation modeling techniques with complex sample data. In G. R. Hancock & R. O. Mueller (Eds.), *Structural equation modeling: A second course* (pp. 345–383). Greenwich, CT: Information Age Publishing.

Stark, S., Chernyshenko, O. S., & Drasgow, F. (2006). Detecting differential item functioning with confirmatory factor analysis and item response theory: Toward a unified strategy. *Journal of Applied Psychology, 91*(6), 1292–1306.

StatSoft, Inc. (2009). STATISTICA 9 [Computer software]. Tulsa, OK: Author.

Steele, J. D. (2009). Structural equation modelling (SEM) for fMRI using Matlab. Retrieved July 30, 2009, from *www.dundee.ac.uk/cmdn/staff/douglas_steele/structural_equation_modelling*

Steiger, J. H. (1990). Structural model evaluation and modification: An interval estimation approach. *Multivariate Behavioral Research, 25,* 173–180.

Steiger, J. H. (2001). Driving fast in reverse: The relationship between software development, theory, and education in structural equation modeling. *Journal of the American Statistical Association, 96,* 331–338.

Steiger, J. H. (2002). When constraints interact: A caution about reference variables, identification constraints, and scale dependencies in structural equation modeling. *Psychological Methods, 7,* 210–227.

Steiger, J. H. (2007). Understanding the limitations of global fit assessment in structural equation modeling. *Personality and Individual Differences, 42,* 893–898.

Steiger, J. H., & Fouladi, R. T. (1997). Noncentrality interval estimation and the evaluation of statistical models. In L. L. Harlow, S. A. Mulaik, & J. H. Steiger (Eds.), *What if there were no significance tests?* (pp. 221–257). Mahwah, NJ: Erlbaum.

Systat Software, Inc. (2009). SYSTAT (Version 13.0) [Computer software]. Chicago: Author.

Temme, D., Kreis, D., & Hildebrandt, L. (2006). PLS path modeling—A software review (SFB 649 Discussion Paper 2006-084). Berlin: Sonderforschungsbereich 649: Ökonomisches Risiko. Retrieved June 20, 2009, from *http://edoc.hu-berlin.de/series/sfb-649-papers/2006-84/PDF/84.pdf*

The MathWorks (2010). MATLAB (Version 7.10, Release 2010a) [Computer software]. Natick, MA: Author.

Thompson, B. (1992). Two and one-half decades of leadership in measurement and evaluation. *Journal of Counseling and Development, 70,* 434–438.

Thompson, B. (1995). Stepwise regression and stepwise discriminant analysis need not apply here: A guidelines editorial. *Educational and Psychological Measurement, 55,* 525–534.

Thompson, B. (2000). Ten commandments of structural equation modeling. In L. G. Grimm & P. R. Yarnold (Eds.), *Reading and understanding more multivariate statistics* (pp. 261–283). Washington, DC: American Psychological Association.

Thompson, B. (Ed.). (2003). *Score reliability.* Thousand Oaks, CA: Sage.

Thompson, B. (2004). *Exploratory and confirmatory factor analysis: Understanding concepts and applications.* Washington, DC: American Psychological Association.

Thompson, B., & Vacha-Haase, T. (2000). Psychometrics is datametrics: The test is not reliable. *Education and Psychological Measurement, 60,* 174–195.

Thorndike, R. M., & Thorndike-Christ, T. M. (2010). *Measurement and evaluation in psychology and education* (8th ed.). Boston, MA: Pearson Education.

Tomarken, A. J., & Waller, N. G. (2003). Potential problems with "well-fitting" models. *Journal of Abnormal Psychology, 112,* 578–598.

Tomarken, A. J., & Waller, N. G. (2005). Structural equation modeling: Strengths, limitations, and misconceptions. *Annual Review of Clinical Psychology, 1,* 31–65.

Tu, Y.-K. (2009). Commentary: Is structural equation modelling a step forward for epidemiologists? *International Journal of Epidemiology, 38,* 549–551.

Vacha-Haase, T., Ness, C., Nilsson, J., & Reetz, D. (1999). Practices regarding reporting of reliability coefficients: A review of three journals. *Journal of Experimental Education, 67,* 335–341.

van Prooijen, J.-W., & van der Kloot, W. A. (2001). Confirmatory analysis of exploratively obtained factor structures. *Educational and Psychological Measurement, 61,* 777–792.

Vernon, P. A., & Eysenck, S. B. G. (Eds.). (2007). Structural equation modeling [Special issue]. *Personality and Individual Differences, 42*(5).

Villar, P., Luengo, M. Á., Gómez-Fraguela, J. A., & Romero, E. (2006). Assessment of the validity of parenting constructs using the multitrait–multimethod model. *European Journal of Psychological Assessment, 22,* 59–68.

Vinzi, V. E., Chin, W. W., Henseler, J., & Wang, H. (Eds.). (2009). *Handbook of partial least squares: Concepts, methods and applications in marketing and related fields.* New York: Springer.

Vriens, M., & Melton, E. (2002). Managing missing data. *Marketing Research, 14,* 12–17.

Wagner, R. K., Torgeson, J. K., & Rashotte, C. A. (1994). Development of reading-related phonological processing abilities: New evidence of a bidirectional causality from a latent variable longitudinal study. *Developmental Psychology, 30,* 73–87.

Wald, A. (1943). Tests of statistical hypotheses concerning several parameters when the number of observations is large. *Transactions of the American Mathematical Society, 54,* 426–482.

Wall, M. M., & Amemiya, Y. (2001). Generalized appended product indicator procedure for nonlinear structural equation analysis. *Journal of Educational and Behavioral Statistics, 26,* 1–29.

West, S. G. (2001). New approaches to missing data in psychological research [Special section]. *Psychological Methods, 6*(4).

Wherry, R. J. (1931). A new formula for predicting the shrinkage of the coefficient of multiple correlation. *Annals of Mathematical Statistics, 2,* 440–451.

Whisman, M. A., & McClelland, G. H. (2005). Designing, testing, and interpreting interactions and moderator effects in family research. *Journal of Family Psychology, 19,* 111–120.

Whitaker, B. G., & McKinney, J. L. (2007). Assessing the measurement invariance of latent job satisfaction ratings across survey administration modes for respondent subgroups: A MIMIC modeling approach. *Behavior Research Methods, 39,* 502–509.

Widaman, K. F., & Thompson, J. S. (2003). On specifying the null model for incremental fit indexes in structural equation modeling. *Psychological Methods, 8,* 16–37.

Wiggins, R. D., & Sacker, A. (2002). Strategies for handling missing data in SEM: A user's perspective. In G. A. Marcoulides & I. Moustaki (Eds.), *Latent variable and latent structure models* (pp. 105–120). Mahwah, NJ: Erlbaum.

Wilkinson, L., & the Task Force on Statistical Inference. (1999). Statistical methods in psychology journals: Guidelines and explanations. *American Psychologist, 54,* 594–604.

Willett, J. B., & Sayer, A. G. (1994). Using covariance structure analysis to detect correlates and predictors of individual change over time. *Psychological Bulletin, 116,* 363–381.

Williams, L. J., & O'Boyle, E. H. (2008). Measurement models for linking latent variables and indicators: A review of human resource management research using parcels. *Human Resource Management Review, 18,* 233–242.

Wold, H. (1982). Soft modeling: The basic design and some extensions. In K. G. Jöreskog & H. Wold (Eds.), *Systems under indirect observation: Causality, structure, prediction* (Vol. 2, pp. 1–54). Amsterdam: North-Holland.

Wolfle, L. M. (2003). The introduction of path analysis to the social sciences, and some emergent themes: An annotated bibliography. *Structural Equation Modeling, 10,* 1–34.

Worland, J., Weeks, G. G., Janes, C. L., & Strock, B. D. (1984). Intelligence, classroom behavior, and academic achievement in children at high and low risk for psychopathology: A structural equation analysis. *Journal of Abnormal Child Psychology, 12,* 437–454.

Wothke, W. (1993). Nonpositive definite matrices in structural equation modeling. In K. A. Bollen & J. S. Long (Eds.), *Testing structural equation models* (pp. 256–293). Newbury Park, CA: Sage.

Wright, R. E. (1995). Logistic regression. In L. G. Grimm & P. R. Yarnold (Eds.), *Reading and understanding multivariate statistics* (pp. 217–244). Washington, DC: American Psychological Association.

Wright, S. (1918). On the nature of size factors. *Genetics, 3,* 367–374.

Wu, C. H. (2008). The role of perceived discrepancy in satisfaction evaluation. *Social Indicators Research, 88,* 423–436.

Yang-Wallentin, F. (2001). Comparisons of the ML and TSLS estimators for the Kenny–Judd model. In R. Cudeck, S. du Toit, and D. Sörbom (Eds.), *Structural equation modeling: Present and future: A Festschrift in honor of Karl Jöreskog* (pp. 425–442). Lincolnwood, IL: Scientific Software International.

Yang-Wallentin, F., & Jöreskog, K. G. (2001). Robust standard errors and chi-squares for interaction models. In G. A. Marcoulides & R. Schumacker (Eds.), *New developments and techniques in structural equation modeling* (pp. 159–171). Mahwah, NJ: Erlbaum.

Yeo, I., & Johnson, R. (2000). A new family of power transformations to improve normality or symmetry. *Biometrika, 87,* 954–959.

Yin, P., & Fan, X. (2001). Estimating R-squared shrinkage in multiple regression: A comparison of different analytical methods. *Journal of Experimental Education, 69,* 203–224.

Yuan, K.-H. (2005). Fit indices versus test statistics. *Multivariate Behavioral Research, 40,* 115–148.

Yuan, K.-H., Bentler, P. M., & Zhang, W. (2005). The effect of skewness and kurtosis on mean and covariance structure analysis: The univariate case and its multivariate implication. *Sociological Methods and Research, 34,* 240–258.

Yung, Y.-F., & Bentler, P. M. (1996). Bootstrapping techniques in analysis of mean and covariance structures. In G. A. Marcoulides and R. E. Schumacker (Eds.), *Advanced structural equation modeling* (pp. 195–226). Mahwah, NJ: Erlbaum.

Zumbo, B. D., & Koh, K. H. (2005). Manifestation of differences in item-level characteristics in scale-level measurement invariance tests of multi-group confirmatory factor analyses. *Journal of Modern Applied Statistical Methods, 4,* 275–282.

Author Index

Subject Index

Italic page numbers refer to figures.

About the Author

Rex B. Kline, PhD, is Professor of Psychology at Concordia University in Montréal, Quebec, Canada. Since earning a doctorate in clinical psychology, he has conducted research on the psychometric evaluation of cognitive abilities, child clinical assessment, structural equation modeling, training of behavioral science researchers, and usability engineering in computer science. Dr. Kline has published five books, six chapters, and more than 40 articles in research journals.